Market-Based Management

Strategies for Growing Customer Value and Profitability

W9-BMN-395

FIFTH EDITION

Market-Based Management

Strategies for Growing Customer Value and Profitability

Roger J. Best

Emeritus Professor of Marketing
University of Oregon

PEARSON
Prentice
Hall

Upper Saddle River, New Jersey 07458

Library of Congress Cataloging-in-Publication Data

Best, Roger J.
    Market-based management : strategies for growing customer value and profitability/
Roger J. Best.—5th ed.
        p. cm.
    Includes bibliographical references.
    ISBN-13: 978-0-13-233653-6 (pbk. : alk. paper)
    1. Marketing—Management. I. Title.

HF5415.13.B46 2009
658.8—dc22   2008004557

Editorial Director: Sally Yagan
Executive Editor: Melissa Sabella
Product Development Manager: Ashley Santora
Editorial Project Manager: Melissa Pellerano
Marketing Manager: Anne Fahlgren
Marketing Assistant: Susan Osterlitz
Permissions Project Manager: Charles Morris
Permissions Specialist: Kathy Weisbrod
Senior Managing Editor: Judy Leale
Production Project Manager: Debbie Ryan
Senior Operations Supervisor: Arnold Vila
Operations Specialist: Michelle Klein
Art Director: Jayne Conte
Cover Designer: Margaret Kenselaar
Cover Image: Leon Zemitsky/Stock Illustration Source/Images.Com.
Composition: Laserwords
Full-Service Project Management: BookMasters, Inc.
Printer/Binder: Edwards Brothers
Typeface: 10.5/12 Times

Credits and acknowledgments borrowed from other sources and reproduced, with permission, in this textbook appear on page 489.

Copyright © 2009, 2005, 2004, 2000, 1997 Pearson Education, Inc., Upper Saddle River, New Jersey, 07458.
Pearson Prentice Hall. All rights reserved. Printed in the United States of America. This publication is protected by Copyright and permission should be obtained from the publisher prior to any prohibited reproduction, storage in a retrieval system, or transmission in any form or by any means, electronic, mechanical, photocopying, recording, or likewise. For information regarding permission(s), write to: Rights and Permissions Department.

Pearson Prentice Hall™ is a trademark of Pearson Education, Inc.
Pearson® is a registered trademark of Pearson plc
Prentice Hall® is a registered trademark of Pearson Education, Inc.
Pearson Education Ltd., London

Pearson Education Singapore, Pte. Ltd
Pearson Education Canada, Inc.
Pearson Education–Japan
Pearson Education Australia PTY, Limited
Pearson Education North Asia, Ltd., Hong Kong

Pearson Educación de Mexico, S.A. de C.V.
Pearson Education Malaysia, Pte. Ltd.
Pearson Education Upper Saddle River, New Jersey

PEARSON
Prentice
Hall

10 9 8 7 6 5 4
ISBN-13: 978-0-13-233653-6
ISBN-10: 0-13-233653-7

To Robin, Oliver, Mary, Mike and Mitchell

BRIEF CONTENTS

Preface xx
About the Author xxvi
Acknowledgments xxvii

PART I ■ Market Orientation and Performance 3

Chapter 1   Customer Focus and Managing Customer Loyalty 5
Chapter 2   Marketing Performance and Marketing Profitability 35

PART II ■ Market Analysis 67

Chapter 3   Market Potential, Market Demand, and Market Share 69
Chapter 4   The Customer Experience and Value Creation 101
Chapter 5   Market Segmentation and Segmentation Strategies 139
Chapter 6   Competitor Analysis and Source of Advantage 175

PART III ■ Marketing Mix Strategies 207

Chapter 7   Product Positioning, Branding, and Product Line Strategies 209
Chapter 8   Value-Based Pricing and Pricing Strategies 243
Chapter 9   Marketing Channels and Channel Mapping 279
Chapter 10   Marketing Communications and Customer Response 307

PART IV ■ Strategic Marketing 335

Chapter 11   Portfolio Analysis and Strategic Market Planning 337
Chapter 12   Offensive Strategies 365
Chapter 13   Defensive Strategies 385

PART V ■ Marketing Plans and Performance 409

Chapter 14   Building a Marketing Plan 411
Chapter 15   Performance Metrics and Strategy Implementation 447
Chapter 16   Market-Based Management and Financial Performance 469

Credits 489
Glossary 490
Index 499

CONTENTS

Preface xx
About the Author xxvi
Acknowledgments xxvii

PART I ■ MARKET ORIENTATION AND PERFORMANCE 3

CHAPTER 1 CUSTOMER FOCUS AND MANAGING CUSTOMER LOYALTY 5

Customer Focus and Profitability 6

How to "Underwhelm" Customers and Shareholders 6
Customer Focus and Customer Satisfaction 7
Customer Satisfaction: A Key Marketing Performance Metric 8
A Wide-Angle View of Customer Satisfaction 9
De-Averaging Customer Satisfaction and Customer Profitability 10
Profit Impact of Customer Dissatisfaction 13

Profit Impact of Customer Retention 14

Customer Satisfaction and Customer Retention 15
Estimating Customer Retention 16
Customer Retention and Customer Life Expectancy 16
The Lifetime Value of a Customer 17
Net Promoter Score 19

Customer Loyalty and Managing Customer Loyalty 21

Measuring Customer Loyalty 21
Managing Customer Loyalty 22
Top Performers 22
High Potentials 23
New Opportunities 24
Nonprofits 24

Customer Focus 26

Customer Focus and Marketing Knowledge 26
Customer-Focused Behaviors and Practices 27
Marketing Performance 28
Marketing Profitability 28

Summary 29
Market-Based Strategic Thinking 30
Marketing Performance Tools 31
Notes 32
Appendix 1.1 Present Value Table 33

CHAPTER 2   MARKETING PERFORMANCE AND MARKETING PROFITABILITY 35

Marketing Performance Versus Financial Performance 36
Measuring and Tracking Marketing Performance 37

A Market-Based Strategy 38

Marketing Performance Metrics 39

Internal Versus External Performance Metrics 40
Process Versus Result Marketing Metrics 41

Profit Impact of Marketing Performance Metrics 42

Marketing Profitability and Profits 42
Marketing Profitability and Performance Metrics 44
Marketing Profitability and Product Lines 46
Managing Marketing Profitability—A Product Focus 47
Managing Marketing Profitability—A Customer Focus 49

Profit Impact of Marketing Strategies 51

Market Growth Strategy 52
Market Share Strategy 53
Customer Revenue Strategy 54
Cost Reduction Strategy 54
Advertising Strategy 55
Channel Strategy 55

Benchmarking Marketing Profitability 56

Marketing Return on Sales 57
Marketing Return on Investment 58
Profit Impact of Marketing Profitability Metrics 59
Managing Marketing Performance and Marketing Profitability 60

Summary 61
Market-Based Strategic Thinking 62

Marketing Performance Tools 63
Notes 64

PART II ■ MARKET ANALYSIS 67

CHAPTER 3   MARKET POTENTIAL, MARKET DEMAND, AND MARKET SHARE 69

Market Definition—What Business Are We In? 70
Broad Market Vision 72

Market Potential 73

Market Development Index 77
Untapped Market Potential 77
Market Potential and Market Growth 79

Managing Market Growth 80
Accelerating Market Growth 81
Customer Adoption Forces 82
Product Adoption Forces 83

Product-Market Versus Product Life Cycle 84
Product Life-Cycle Demand and Profits 85
Market Demand and Prices 86
Product Life-Cycle Margins and Marketing Expenses 88
Product Life Cycle and Marketing Profitability 89
Share Performance Metrics 91
Market Share Index 94
Share Potential and Market Share Management 94
Market Share Potential 95
Share Development Index 96

Summary 97
Market-Based Strategic Thinking 98
Marketing Performance Tools 99
Notes 99

CHAPTER 4   THE CUSTOMER EXPERIENCE AND VALUE CREATION 101

The Total Customer Experience 102
Empathic Design 102
Hypothetical Videos: Current Versus Desired Customer Experience 103

The Customer Experience of Lead Users 104
Reverse Innovation—Invent to Order 106
Managing Customer Touch Points 107

Mass Collaboration 108

Prosumers—Customers as Co-Inventors 110
Partners—Engaging Professionals 110
Suppliers—Leveraging Supplier Participation 110
Employees—An Under-Leveraged Opportunity 111

Life-Cycle Cost and Customer Value 111

Price Paid 113
Acquisition Costs 113
Usage Costs 114
Ownership Costs 115
Maintenance Costs 115
Disposal Costs 116

Price-Performance and Value Creation 117

Relative Performance 117
Relative Price 118
Customer Value 119
Value Mapping 120

Perceived Benefits and Value Creation 120

Product Benefits 120
Service Benefits 121
Company or Brand Benefits 122
Overall Customer Benefits 123
Cost of Purchase Index 123
Customer Value Index 124

Emotion Benefits and Value Creation 126

Emotional Benefits and Psychological Value 126
Brand Personality and Value Creation 127

Transaction Cost and Value Creation 128

Space Value 128
Transaction Value 129
Value Creation Across the Supply Chain 129

Identifying Value Drivers 130

Customer Preferences 131
Customer Value 132

Summary 133
Market-Based Strategic Thinking 135

Marketing Performance Tools 136
Notes 137
Appendix 4.1 Trade-Off Analysis Computations 138

CHAPTER 5   MARKET SEGMENTATION AND SEGMENTATION STRATEGIES 139

Needs-Based Market Segmentation 140
Customer Needs 143
Forces That Shape Consumer Market Needs 143
Demographic Influences 144
Lifestyle Influences 144
Usage Behaviors 144
Forces That Shape Business Market Needs 144
Firm Demographics 145
Business Culture 145
Usage Behaviors 146

Needs-Based Market Segmentation 146
The Demographic Trap 147
Needs-Based Market Segments 148
Segment Identification 149
Segment Attractiveness 150
Segment Profitability 151
Segment Positioning 154
Segment Strategy Acid Test 155
Segment Marketing Mix Strategy 156

Segmentation Strategies 157
Mass-Market Strategy 157
Large-Segment Strategy 157
Adjacent-Segment Strategy 158
Multi-Segment Strategies 159
Small-Segment Strategy 161
Niche-Segment Strategies 161
Sub-Segment Strategies 161

Customer Relationship Marketing 163
Customer Value Versus Company Value 164
Database Marketing 165
Mass Personalization 166
Mass Customization 166
Customer Relationship Management 167

Summary 169
Market-Based Strategic Thinking 170

Marketing Performance Tools 171
Notes 172

CHAPTER 6   COMPETITOR ANALYSIS AND SOURCES OF ADVANTAGE 175

Sources of Competitive Advantage 177
Cost Advantage 177

Variable Cost Advantage 178
Marketing Cost Advantage 180
Operating Cost Advantage 180

Differentiation Advantage 181

Product Advantage 181
Service Advantage 182
Reputation Advantage 183

Marketing Advantage 183

Market Share Advantage 184
Product Line Advantage 185
Channel Advantage 186

Knowledge as a Source of Advantage 187
Competitor Intelligence 189

Benchmark Competitors 189
Competitor Analysis 191
Obtaining Competitor Intelligence 191
A Sample Competitor Analysis 193
Competitive Benchmarking 194

Industry Analysis 196

Barriers to Entry 196
Barriers to Exit 197
Customer Buying Power 197
Supplier Selling Power 197
Product Substitutes 197
Competitive Rivalry 198
The Prisoner's Dilemma 199

Sustainable Advantage 199

Summary 200
Market-Based Strategic Thinking 201
Marketing Performance Tools 202
Notes 202
Appendix 6.1 Estimating an Experience Curve Coefficient and the Percent
    Experience Curve 204

PART III ■ MARKETING MIX STRATEGIES 207

CHAPTER 7   PRODUCT POSITIONING, BRANDING, AND PRODUCT LINE STRATEGIES 209

Product Positioning 210

Product Positioning and Market Share 212
Product Positioning Strategies 213

Production Positioning and Differentiation 215

Product Differentiation 215
Service Differentiation 218
Brand Differentiation 219
Low Cost of Purchase 220

Branding and Brand Management Strategies 221

Brand Identity 221
Brand Encoding 221
Brand Name Development 225
Creating a New Brand Name 226

Brand Equity 227

Brand Assets 227
Brand Liabilities 229
Brand Equity 229

Brand and Product Line Strategies 231

Product Line Development 232
Umbrella and Flanker Brands 232
Product Line Extensions 234
Bundling and Unbundling Strategies 236
Product Line Substitution Effects 238
Product Line Scale Effects 238

Summary 239
Market-Based Strategic Thinking 240
Marketing Performance Tools 241
Notes 242

CHAPTER 8   VALUE-BASED PRICING AND PRICING STRATEGIES 243

Value-Based Pricing 244

Value-in-Use Pricing 244
Perceived-Value Pricing 246
Performance-Based Pricing 248

Price-Margin Management 252

Pocket-Price Bandwidth 253

Product Life-Cycle Pricing Strategies 255

Skim Pricing 255
Single-Segment Pricing 256
Penetration Pricing 257
Low-Cost-Leader Pricing 258
Multi-Segment Pricing 258
Plus-One Pricing 259
Reduced-Focused Pricing 260
Harvest Pricing 260

Pricing and Profitability 262

Price Elasticity and Profitability 264

Inelastic Price Management 264
Elastic Price Management 266

Prince and Break-Even Analysis 268

Price and Break-Even Volume 269
Price and Break-Even Market Share 269

Product Line Pricing 270

Pricing Substitute Products 270
Pricing Complementary Products 271

Summary 273
Market-Based Strategic Thinking 275
Marketing Performance Tools 276
Notes 277

CHAPTER 9   MARKETING CHANNELS AND CHANNEL MAPPING 279

Channel Mapping 280

Marketing Channel Performance 283

Customer Reach 284
Operating Efficiency 285
Service Quality 286

Alternative Marketing Channels 287

Direct Channels 288
Indirect Channels 289
Mixed Channels 289
B2C Channels 289

B2B Channels 290
B2B and B2C Marketing Channels 292

Marketing Channels That Improve Customer Value 292

Product Benefits 293
Service Benefits 293
Brand Image 295
Company Benefits 295
Improving Cost Efficiency 297

Marketing Channels and Competitive Advantage 299

Sales Force Advantage 299
Sales Productivity 299
Distribution Advantage 300

Profit Impact of Alternative Marketing Channels 301

Summary 303
Market-Based Strategic Thinking 304
Marketing Performance Tools 304
Notes 305

CHAPTER 10   MARKETING COMMUNICATIONS AND CUSTOMER RESPONSE 307

Building Advertising Awareness 311

Customer Response Index 313

Strategies to Increase Customer Response 314

Building Customer Awareness and Comprehension 317

Media Selection and Customer Awareness 317
Message Frequency and Customer Awareness 317
Ad Copy and Customer Response 320

Message Reinforcement 321

Message Reinforcement and Pulsing 321
Heavy-Up Message Frequency 322

Stimulating Customer Action 322

Pull Versus Push Communications Strategies 322

Pull Communications and Customer Response 324

Advertising Elasticity 324
Advertising Carryover Effects 325
Direct Marketing Promotions 327
Promotional Price Elasticity 328

Push Communications and Customer Response 329

Trade Promotions and Customer Response 329
Market Infrastructure and Push Communications 330

Summary 331
Market-Based Strategic Thinking 331
Marketing Performance Tools 332
Notes 333

PART IV ■ STRATEGIC MARKETING 335

CHAPTER 11   PORTFOLIO ANALYSIS AND STRAGETIC MARKET PLANNING 337

Strategic Market Planning 338
Product Life Cycle/Market Share Portfolio 344

GE/McKinsey Portfolio Analysis 345

Competitive Position 348
Portfolio Analysis and Strategic Market Plans 350

Offensive Portfolio Strategy 352
Defensive Portfolio Strategy 354

Portfolio Diversification 355

Two Levels of Diversification 355

Marketing Mix Strategy and Performance Plan 357

Marketing Mix Strategy 357
Performance Plan 358

Summary 361
Market-Based Strategic Thinking 362
Marketing Performance Tools 363
Notes 364

CHAPTER 12   OFFENSIVE STRATEGIES 365

Strategic Market Plans 366
Offensive Strategic Market Plans 367
Offensive Core Strategy I: Invest to Grow Sales 369

Offensive Strategy IA: Grow Market Share 369
Offensive Strategy IB: Grow Revenue per Customer 370
Offensive Strategy IC: Enter New Market Segments 371
Offensive Strategy ID: Expand Market Demand 372

Offensive Core Strategy II: Improve Competitive Position 374

Offensive Strategy IIA: Improve Customer Loyalty and Retention 375
Offensive Strategy IIB: Improve Differentiation Advantage 375
Offensive Strategy IIC: Lower Costs/Improve Marketing Productivity 376
Offensive Strategy IID: Build Marketing Advantage 376

Offensive Core Strategy III: Enter New Markets 377

Offensive Strategy IIIA: Enter Related New Markets 377
Offensive Strategy IIIB: Enter Unrelated New Markets 378
Offensive Strategy IIIC: Enter New Emerging Markets 379
Offensive Strategy IIID: Develop New Markets 380

Choosing Offensive Strategic Market Plans 381

Summary 382
Market-Based Strategic Thinking 382
Marketing Performance Tools 383
Notes 384

CHAPTER 13 DEFENSIVE STRATEGIES 385

Defensive Strategic Market Plans 386
Defensive Core Strategy I: Protect Position 389

Defensive Strategy IA: Protect Market Share 389
Defensive Strategy IB: Build Customer Retention 395

Defensive Core Strategy II: Optimize Position 395

Defensive Strategy IIA: Maximize Net Marketing Contribution 396
Defensive Strategy IIB: Reduce Market Focus 399

Defensive Core Strategy III: Monetize, Harvest, or Divest 400

Defensive Strategy IIIA: Manage for Cash Flow 400
Defensive Strategy IIIB: Harvest or Divest for Cash Flow 400

Selecting a Defensive Strategy 403

Summary 404
Market-Based Strategic Thinking 405
Marketing Performance Tools 406
Notes 406

PART V ■ MARKETING PLANS AND PERFORMANCE 409

CHAPTER 14 BUILDING A MARKETING PLAN 411

Creativity Versus Structure 412
Benefits of Building a Market Plan 413

Identifying Opportunities 413
Leveraging Core Capabilities 414
Focused Market Strategy 414
Resource Allocation 414
Building a Performance Roadmap 414

Building a Marketing Plan 415
Part I: Situation Analysis—Where Are We Now? 415

Step 1: Current Situation 417
Step 2: SWOT Analysis 426

Part II: Marketing Strategy—Where Do We Want to Go? 427

Step 3: Strategic Market Plan 427
Step 4: Marketing Mix Strategy 429

Part III: Performance Plan—What Is the Expected Impact? 434

Step 5: Develop a Revenue Plan and Marketing Budget 435
Step 6: Develop a Profit Plan 438
Step 7: Performance Review 443

Summary 444
Market-Based Strategic Thinking 445
Marketing Performance Tools 446
Notes 446

CHAPTER 15 PERFORMANCE METRICS AND STRATEGY IMPLEMENTATION 447

Marketing Performance Metrics 449
Process Versus Result Metrics 451

Process Marketing Performance Metrics 451
Result Marketing Performance Metrics 452

Successful Strategy Implementation 453
Managing Successful Strategy Implementation 454

Owning the Strategic Market Plan 455
Supporting the Strategic Market Plan 457
Adapting the Market Plan 459
Assessing the Implementation of a Market Plan 460

Variance Analysis 461

Summary 465
Market-Based Strategic Thinking 466
Marketing Performance Tools 467
Notes 467

CHAPTER 16 MARKET-BASED MANAGEMENT AND FINANCIAL PERFORMANCE 469

How to Overwhelm Customers and Shareholders 471

Customer Satisfaction and Profitability 472

How Market Strategies Affect Profitability 474

Customer Volume 474
Margin per Customer 475
Gross Profit 477
Net Marketing Contribution 477
Net Profit (Before Taxes) 477

How Market Strategies Affect Assets 478

Investment in Accounts Receivable 478
Investment in Inventory 479
Investment in Fixed Assets 480

Return Measures of Profitability 480

Measures of Shareholder Value 482

Market-Based Management 484

Summary 486
Market-Based Strategic Thinking 487
Marketing Performance Tools 487
Notes 488

Credits 489
Glossary 490
Index 499

PREFACE

■ Gains in marketing knowledge without
application are missed learning
opportunities.
— *Dr. Roger J. Best*

Based on positive feedback from students, professors, and those working in the field of marketing, I was encouraged to continue to build on this philosophy with this fifth edition of *Market-Based Management*. The strength of the book retains its focus on performance orientation and the processes and tools for building marketing strategies that deliver superior levels of customer satisfaction, value, and profitability. The differentiating feature of this book is its focus on marketing performance and marketing profitability and the role marketing strategies play in building the profits of a business. The best way to accomplish this is with market-driven strategies that attract, satisfy, and retain target customers with a value that is superior to competing products or services.

The fifth edition builds on this theme in several ways. A special effort was made to include more coverage of ways to understand the Total Customer Experience, Customer Loyalty, Customer Value, Marketing Profitability, Marketing Performance Metrics, Market Share Management, Branding and Product Line Strategies and, perhaps even more important, the addition of Marketing Performance Tools at the end of each chapter. These online Marketing Performance Tools have been enhanced and expanded to allow users of *Market-Based Management* the opportunity to apply their marketing knowledge and develop further marketing insights with the use of these tools. The fifth edition Web site will allow users to save their data as well as compare before/after changes in data on the same screen. For instructors, Marketing Performance Tools can be used to create additional assignments.

Market-based management is intuitively easy but deceptively difficult. The reason marketing students and marketing professionals like this book is because it is readable and it presents the tools and processes needed to actually build a market-driven strategy. The concepts, by themselves, are important and are the backbone of market-based management. However, they are of limited value if they cannot be applied in a way that delivers superior customer value and profitability. Those in marketing need to take a greater level of responsibility for managing profits and the external performance metrics of a business. This is an important benefit of this book. It is my hope that this book will help you in your understanding of, commitment to, and practice of market-based management.

Roger J. Best
Emeritus Professor of Marketing
University of Oregon

MODIFICATIONS, ADDITIONS, AND IMPROVEMENTS

Part I: Market Orientation And Marketing Performance

Chapter 1: Customer Focus and Managing Customer Loyalty (new title)

- Figure 1-9 (new)—presents how to estimate customer retention.
- Net Promoter Score—This section and Figure 1-3 are new and explain how to measure customer promotion—customer recommendation of products to others.
- Managing Customer Loyalty (Figure 1-15) is revised and a much simpler method of managing customer loyalty and profitability.
- **Marketing Performance Tools** (revised online interactive tools)—(1) Customer Satisfaction, (2) Customer Retention, (3) Customer Lifetime Value, and (4) Managing Customer Loyalty.

Chapter 2: Marketing Performance and Marketing Profitability

- Figure 2-1 (new) provides overview of the need for marketing performance metrics and marketing profitability.
- Figure 2-13 (new) Marketing Profitability Portfolio illustrates how to present products in portfolio with Marketing ROS and Marketing ROI as axes.
- Figure 2-20 (new) presents an overview of how market-based management contributes to marketing performance and marketing profitability and indirectly to the overall financial performance of a business and company.
- **Marketing Performance Tool**s (new online interactive tools)—(1) Product Focused Marketing Profitability, (2) Customer Focused Marketing Profitability, (3) Marketing Profitability Metrics, and (4) Benchmarking Marketing Profitability Metrics.

Part II: Market Analysis

Chapter 3: Market Potential, Market Demand, and Market Share

- Figures 3-1 and 3-2 are new and help illustrate how product-markets grow and evolve in terms of products and market structure.
- Estimating Market Potential is explained with several examples and the steps outlined in Figure 3-5.
- Managing Growth Potential and Figure 3-20 are revised to better explain and illustrate this important concept.
- **Marketing Performance Tools** (new online interactive tools)—(1) Market Potential vs. Market Demand Index, (2) Forecasting Sales. (3) Managing Market Share, and (4) Product Lifecycle Profits.

Chapter 4: The Customer Experience and Value Creation
(new title)

- A stronger emphasis is placed on the "Total Customer Experience" as a path to understanding opportunities for Value Creation.
- Reverse Innovation -Invent to Order (Figure 4-7), Managing Customer Touch Points, and Mass Collaboration (Figure 4-8) are new topics added to this chapter. Mass collaboration is especially important addition build around the use of the internet in building collaborative relationships with pro-sumers, professionals, suppliers, and employees in creating higher value-added customer solutions.
- **Marketing Performance Tools** (new online interactive tools)—(1) Economic Value Analysis, (2) Customer Value Analysis, and (3) Transaction Value Analysis.

Chapter 5: Market Segmentation and Segmentation Strategies
(new title)

- The first part of this chapter has need revised to strengthen the importance of "Needs-Based Segmentation."
- Conjoint measurement (Figure 5-4 and 5-5) are used early in the chapter to illustrate how customers trade-off price with different performance attributes and levels of performance for each attribute. This trade-off based on needs and price is at the heart of needs-based segmentation.
- **Marketing Performance Tools** (new online interactive tools)—(1) Needs-Based Segmentation—Feature Preference, (2) Needs-Based Segmentation—Price/Feature Trade-Off, (3) Segment Profitability, and (4) Segment Acid Test.

Chapter 6: Competitor Analysis and Sources of Advantage

- Chapter opens with three major sources of competitive advantage (cost, differentiation and marketing) and explains how each relates to customer value and profitability.
- Figures 6-5 was added to help readers estimate the cost position of a product or business.
- Figures 6-8, 6-9, 6-10, and 6-11 are all new and go into greater depth in demonstrating product, service, brand, and market share sources of advantage and their impact on profits.
- **Marketing Performance Tools** (new online interactive tools) include—(1) Cost Advantage, (2) Differentiation Advantage, (3) Marketing Advantage, and (4) Industry Analysis.

Part III: Marketing Mix Strategies

Chapter 7: Product Position, Branding, and Product Line Strategies

- Factors that make strong brands more profitable (Figure 7-1) and presentation of five assets even strong brand has.
- Seven brand name strategies has been revised and simplified.

- **Marketing Performance Tools** (new online interactive tools) include—(1) Estimating Brand Equity, (2) Profit Impact of Product Line Substitute, and (3) Profit Impact of Product Line Changes.

Chapter 8: Value Pricing and Pricing Strategies (new title)

- Stronger chapter emphasis on value pricing and how it differs from cost-based pricing (Figures 8-1 and 8-2).
- Value Price strategies are explicitly demonstrated in Figures 8-4 to 8-9 with respect to trade-offs between price, value, and profits.
- New section on Price-Margin Management (new Figures 8-10 and 8-11). Pocket price and pocket price bandwidth are new concepts introduced in this revised chapter.
- Profit impact of Price-Volume strategies is revised as presented in Figures 8-19, 20, and 21.
- **Marketing Performance Tools** (new online interactive tools) include— 1) Value In-Use Pricing, (2) Perceived Value Pricing, (3) Performance-Based Pricing, (4) Price-Volume Profit Pricing, and (5) Product Line Pricing.

Chapter 9: Marketing Channels and Channel Mapping (new title)

- The process of channel mapping (new) is introduced (Figure 9-1) and its application demonstrated with channel map pocket price (Figure 9-2) and channel map profitability (Figure 9-3).
- Special section on e-marketing channels is created and demonstrated in Figures 9-6 to 9-8.
- **Marketing Performance Tools** (new online interactive tools) include—(1) Channel Mapping and Pocket Price, (2) Marketing Channel Profits, and (3) Alternative Channel Profitability.

Chapter 10: Marketing Communications and Customer Response

- Figure 10-2 illustrates a new approach to selecting a communications strategy based on communications objective and customer response (new). Pure brand communications, brand interaction and pure promotion communications are explained and demonstrated with advertisements in Figures 10-1, 10-3, 10-4, 10-5, and 10-6.
- Figure 17 (new) was added to help better understand how to estimate the profit impact of communications effort and the advertising elasticity needed to achieve an incremental profit.
- **Marketing Performance Tools** (new online interactive tools) include—(1) Marketing Communications and Customer Response, (2) Estimating Advertising Elasticity, and (3) Estimating Advertising Carryover Sales Effects.

Part IV: Strategic Marketing

Chapter 11: Portfolio Analysis and Strategic Market Planning
(new title)

- A stronger emphasis is placed on portfolio analysis as a basis for strategic market planning (Figure 11-1).
- Product life cycle and competitive position are used as starting point in building a portfolio of products or markets. Figures 11-3, 11-6, and 11-7 are new. This portfolio analysis is then extended into a more complex model represented by the GE/McKinsey model.
- **Marketing Performance Tools** (new online interactive tools) include—(1) Product Lifecycle Portfolio, (2) Market Development—Share Development Portfolio, and (3) GE/McKinsey Portfolio Analysis.

Chapter 12: Offensive Strategies

- Opens with example of Starbuck's various offensive strategies and how they contributed to Starbuck's sales growth from 2004 to 2006. Figure 12-1 is new.
- **Marketing Performance Tools** (new online interactive tools) include—Offensive Strategies (1) Core Strategy I—Growing in Existing Markets, (2) Core Strategy II—Improving Margins, and (3) Core Strategy III—Diversified Growth.

Chapter 13: Defensive Strategies

- Figure 13-1 and 13-2 (new) start the chapter with an example of how defensive strategies applied across a product line could increases profits by more than five-fold with modest reductions in market share and sales with modest price increases but significant gains in margins.
- **Marketing Performance Tools** (new online interactive tools) include—Defensive Strategies (1) Core Strategy I—Protect Position, (2) Core Strategy II—Optimize Position, and (3) Monetize Position.

Part V: Marketing Plans And Performance

Chapter 14: Building a Marketing Plan

- MBM (book) marketing plan sales and marketing profitability is compared to actual Stericycle sales and marketing profits for every three years from 1995 to 2006 along with an estimate of sales and marketing profits for 2008 (new Figure 14-1).
- The process of building a marketing plan is clearly partitioned into three phases—Situation Analysis, Marketing Strategy and Performance Plan. This is illustrated with new figures also (Figure 14-3 and 14-4).
- The sample plan is brought into the chapter with the sample plan pages presented for each of the three distinct parts of the marketing plan.

- The Stericycle Sample Plan is revised and all pages of the sample (figures) are new.
- **Marketing Performance Tools** (new online interactive tools) include—(1) Small Quantity Customer Segment, (2) Large Quantity Generator Segment, and (3) Market Share Strategies.

Chapter 15: Performance Metrics and Strategy Implementation

- The Marketing Performance Scorecard (new) is introduced and demonstrated in Figure 15-1 (new).
- Figure 15-2 (new) summarizes all of the Marketing Performance Metrics presented throughout the book and each is referenced to the chapter each was presented and explained.
- **Marketing Performance Tools** (new online interactive tools) include—(1) Variance Analysis—Market Demand and Market Share, (2) Variance Analysis—Revenue and Cost per Customer, and (3) Variance Analysis—Marketing Expenses.

Chapter 16: Market-Based Management and Financial Performance

- Marketing ROS and Marketing ROI are added to overall financial performance (new) as demonstrated in Figures 16-1 and 16-10 (all new).
- Marketing investment and marketing profitability is extended to show how it impacts profits and earnings per share. Net marketing contribution per share is a new concept introduced in this chapter and demonstrated in Figures 16-2, 16-7, and 16-12 (all new figures)
- Stericycle financial performance is revised and linked to the Stericycle Marketing Plan (see new Figures 16-9, 16-10, and 16-11)
- **Marketing Performance Tools** (new online interactive tools) include—(1) Market Demand and Market Share, (2) Percent Margin and Marketing Expenses, and (3) Asset Management and Invested Capital.

INSTRUCTIONAL SUPPORT

Various teaching supplements are available to accompany this textbook. They consist of the following:

- Instructor's Manual
- Test Item File and TestGen software
- PowerPoint Set
- Web site with student resources

You may access all these materials at www.prenhall.com/best.

ABOUT THE AUTHOR

Roger J. Best is an Emeritus Professor of Marketing at the University of Oregon. He earned a Bachelor of Science in Electrical Engineering from California State Polytechnic University and, following graduation, joined the General Electric Company where he worked in engineering, product management, and marketing. While at GE, he received a patent and completed his M.B.A. at California State University, Hayward. He and went on to obtain a Ph.D. in Business from the University of Oregon while continuing to work with GE in corporate consulting and marketing education. He taught at the University of Arizona from 1975 to 1980 and University of Oregon until 2000.

Over the past 30 years, he has published more than 50 articles and won numerous teaching awards. He is the co-author of *Consumer Behavior* (10 ed.). In 1998, he received the American Marketing Association Distinguished Teaching in Marketing Award. In 1988, the Academy of Marketing Science voted an article on marketing productivity by Del Hawkins, Roger Best, and Charles Lillis as the Outstanding Article of the Year. Dr. Best developed the Marketing Excellence Survey, an assessment tool used to benchmark the marketing knowledge of marketing managers, and MarkPlan, a software program for building performance-driven marketing plans. Both of these products are now owned and operated by the Corporate Executive Board.

Dr. Best has also worked extensively with a variety of companies in marketing consulting and executive education. These companies include 3M, General Electric, Dow Chemical, Dow Corning, DuPont, Eastman Kodak, Hewlett-Packard, Lucas Industries, Tektronix, ESCO, Pacific Western Pipe, James Hardie Industries, and many others. Dr. Best has also taught many executive management education programs at INSEAD Fontainebleau, France.

ACKNOWLEDGMENTS

A book such as this is an assimilation of knowledge from many sources. It is an integration of perspectives intended for a particular audience. An author's added value is in the focus, integration, and presentation, but the basic knowledge is derived from many sources. I would like to acknowledge specific individuals whose knowledge contributed to my understanding of marketing and shaped many of the ideas presented in this fifth edition of *Market-Based Management*. These individuals include Stewart Bither, George Day, Del Hawkins, Jean-Claude Larreche, and Charles Lillis.

Second, I would like to acknowledge the valuable feedback I received from the following reviewers for the fifth edition. Their thoughtful reviews and suggestions for improvement are appreciated and greatly enhanced this edition.

- Sunder Narayanan, *New York University*
- Steven E. Permut, *University of Arizona*
- Mike Parent, *Utah State University*
- Sue Umashankar, *University of Arizona*
- Erika Matulich, *University of Tampa*
- John "Andy" Wood, *West Virginia University*
- Glenn Christensen, *Brigham Young University*

Finally, I would like to thank marketing managers from 3M, Dow Chemical, and Hewlett-Packard for their comments and encouragement. Their real-world perspective and feedback help me continue to pursue a more applied approach in presenting *Market-Based Management*. Also, the fifth edition would not have been possible without the tremendous support and assistance of Robert Lofft. His participation and contributions were critical to every aspect of this edition and are greatly appreciated. Finally, my wife, Robin, deserves a great deal of credit for enduring my ups and downs in the writing of this fifth edition.

Market-Based Management

Strategies for Growing
Customer Value and Profitability

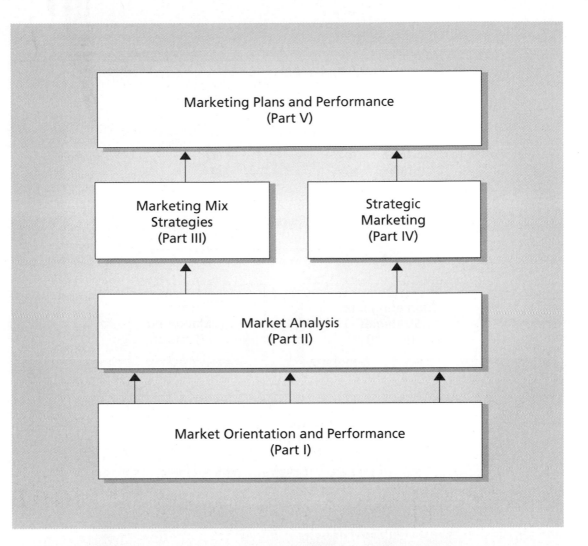

This model represents both the logic of market-based management and the organization of this book. Market Orientation and Marketing Performance (Part I) are the bedrock of market-based management and foster a Market Analysis (Part II) built around customer needs, market trends, and competition.

A commitment to a market orientation and ongoing market analysis allows the development of focused Marketing Mix Strategies (Part III) and Strategic Marketing (Part IV). Marketing Plans and Performance (Part V) are the culmination of this process.

Successful implementation of this process is designed to create and deliver higher levels of customer value that enhance customer satisfaction and contribute to higher levels of profitability.

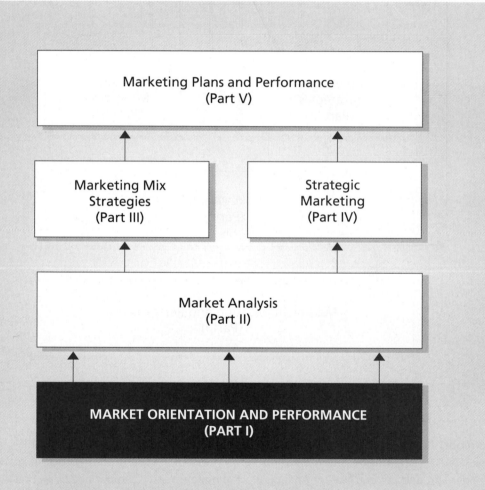

Market Orientation and Performance

■ Marketing isn't somebody's responsibility; marketing is everybody's responsibility.
— *Jack Welch, CEO, 1981–2001*
General Electric Co.

A market-based business has a strong market orientation that all functions and employees of the organization reflect. While the marketing personnel have the primary responsibility for creating marketing excellence, in a market-based business all members of the organization are market oriented. All members are sensitive to customers' needs, are aware of competitors' moves, and work well across the organization's structure toward a timely market-based customer solution. What's the payoff? Market-based businesses with a strong market orientation are more profitable.

Part I demonstrates the connectivity that exists among market orientation, customer satisfaction, profitability, and market-based management. Chapter 1 examines the fundamental components of a market orientation and how each is related to customer satisfaction and retention. From this perspective, we will calculate the profit impact of a lifetime customer, as well as the high cost of customer dissatisfaction. We will see that a strong market orientation is primarily intended to improve a business's chances for long-run survival, but marketing efforts to improve customer satisfaction and retention can also increase short-run profits.

A strong market orientation cannot be created by mere proclamation. To attain a strong market orientation, a business needs to adopt a market-based management philosophy. The organization restructures itself around markets rather than products or factories, and it develops an employee culture responsive to customers and changing market conditions. Market-based management also requires a business to use marketing performance metrics to measure profits at the market level and to track a variety of other market-related performance indicators. These topics and their relation to marketing strategies and profitable growth are discussed in Chapter 2.

CHAPTER 1

Customer Focus and Managing Customer Loyalty

■ Satisfied is not good enough. *Completely* satisfied—that's a big deal. A completely satisfied customer is at least three times more likely to return than one who's just satisfied.
— *Andrew Taylor, CEO*
Enterprise Rent-A-Car[1]

Enterprise Rent-A-Car, a company with 6,500 offices and 600,000 vehicles, is committed to having "*completely* satisfied" customers. Every month, Enterprise interviews a sampling of customers from each of its rental offices to determine the level of customer satisfaction. Company promotions go to those managers whose offices have above-average levels of customer satisfaction. If during a customer interview an employee is mentioned by name, the next morning that employee receives a copy of the customer's comments. If a customer mentions that the vehicle was dirty or expresses any other dissatisfaction, the comment goes to the manager of the office where the customer rented it. Enterprise trains its new personnel not only in its procedures for renting vehicles to the public, but in the company's philosophy of customer focus. All employees learn what's important to customers and what's important in terms of being a good team member.

In today's globally competitive world, customers expect more, have more choices, and are less brand loyal. Sears, Kodak, and General Motors are examples of companies that at one time seemed invincible in terms of their market domination. In each case, however, these companies have had to restructure (reengineer) their organizations to address changing customer needs and emerging competitive forces. In the long run, the survival of every business is at risk. Although companies such as Dell, Microsoft, and Wal-Mart were business heroes of the 1990s, there is no guarantee these same companies will continue to dominate over the next decade. The only constant is *change*.

■ Customers will continue to *change* in needs, demographics, lifestyle, and consumption behavior.
■ Competitors will continue to *change* as new technologies emerge and barriers to foreign competition shift.
■ The environment in which businesses operate will continue to *change* as economic, political, social, and technological forces shift.

The companies that *survive* and *grow* will be the ones that *understand change* and are leading, and often creating, change. Others, slow to comprehend change, will follow with reactive strategies, while still others will disappear, unaware that change was even occurring.

CUSTOMER FOCUS AND PROFITABILITY

A sports reporter once asked Wayne Gretzky what made him a great hockey player. Gretzky's response was, "I skate to where the puck is going, not to where it is." Gretzky's approach to hockey demonstrates his instinct for change. As a player, he was able to position himself as change was occurring in such a way that he could either score a goal or assist in scoring a goal. Businesses that sense the direction of change and lead in bringing it about will prosper and grow. Those who first become aware of change from reading about it in *The Wall Street Journal* are hopelessly behind the pace of the game and can only "skate" in an attempt to catch up.

Businesses that are able to skate to where the puck is going have a strong market orientation. They are constantly in tune with customers' needs, competitors' strategies, changes in the business climate, and emerging technologies, and they seek ways to continuously improve the solutions they bring to target customers. This process enables them to move with—and often lead—change.

The major benefit of a strong customer focus is long-run survival. Western cultures have long been criticized for their extremely short-term perspective. A business with a short-term perspective usually lacks a strong customer focus and a commitment to building long-term customer relationships as a primary management goal. Managers are often judged on last quarter's results and not on their efforts to ensure the long-run survival of the business. Likewise, shareholders can be more interested in immediate earnings than in long-run success.

Although the long-run benefits of a strong customer focus are crucial to business survival and a nation's economic health, the purpose of this chapter is to demonstrate both the short- and long-run benefits of a strong customer focus. Businesses with a strong customer focus not only outperform their competition over the long term by consistently delivering higher levels of customer satisfaction, but they also realize higher profits in the short run. A customer-focused business creates greater customer value and manages customer loyalty as a way to create greater shareholder value.

How to "Underwhelm" Customers and Shareholders

Perhaps the best way to understand the marketing logic that links customer focus to shareholder value is to examine the sequence of events that evolves when a business has little or no customer focus. A business with a weak customer focus "underwhelms" both customers and shareholders. It has only a superficial understanding of customer needs and the competition.

Moving clockwise from the top in Figure 1-1, we can see that little or no customer focus translates into an unfocused value proposition and minimal customer satisfaction.[2] The result is a low level of customer loyalty because customers are easily attracted to competitors. Marketing efforts designed to restrain customer switching are expensive, as are efforts to acquire new customers to replace lost customers. Low levels of customer loyalty and higher marketing costs contribute to disappointing profits. In response, short-term sales tactics and accounting maneuvers are used to bolster short-run financial results. But investors and Wall Street analysts are able to see through these facades, and shareholder value generally stagnates. Perhaps worse, as shown by the example in

FIGURE 1-1 "UNDERWHELMING" CUSTOMERS AND SHAREHOLDERS

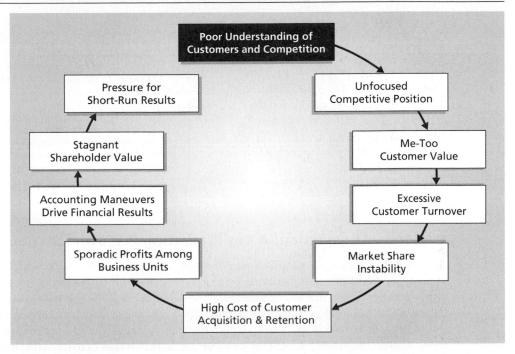

Figure 1-1, managers are now under even greater pressure to produce short-run profits, diminishing their time and motivation to understand customer needs and unravel competitors' strategies. The result is a continuation of the vicious circle of poor performance displayed in Figure 1-1.

Customer Focus and Customer Satisfaction

In contrast to the situation presented in Figure 1-1, a business with a strong customer focus stays in close contact with customers in an effort to deliver a high level of customer satisfaction and build customer loyalty. Marketing strategies in these businesses are centered on customer needs and other sources of customer satisfaction. The strength of a business's customer focus also depends on how well it understands key competitors and evolving competitive forces. This aspect of customer focus enables a business to track its relative competitiveness in pricing, product quality, product availability, service quality, and customer satisfaction.

A strong customer focus and higher levels of customer satisfaction lead primarily to a high level of customer loyalty.[3] Keeping good customers is the first priority of market-based managers. As shown in Figure 1-2, a business with a strong customer focus is well positioned to develop and implement strategies that deliver high levels of customer satisfaction and loyalty. In turn, customer satisfaction and loyalty drive customer profitability. We will see that very satisfied, loyal customers are the ones who shape the profitability of a business.

FIGURE 1-2 CUSTOMER FOCUS, CUSTOMER SATISFACTION, AND PROFITABILITY

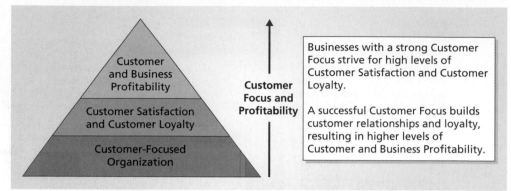

Customer Satisfaction: A Key Marketing Performance Metric

A market-based business uses a variety of marketing performance metrics to measure its performance and progress, and one essential performance metric is customer satisfaction. Although many marketing strategies are effective in attracting new customers, the business that completely satisfies customers is the business that will keep them. While this statement is sometimes seen as perhaps true but nevertheless inconsequential by those who do not wholly accept the concepts of market-based management, we will discover in this chapter that a business can in fact create a tremendous leverage by growing profits from a base of "very satisfied" customers and proactively managing dissatisfied customers.

One of the many ways to measure customer satisfaction is to compute a customer satisfaction index (CSI) based on customers' ratings of their overall satisfaction. A CSI is derived from a six-point scale that ranges from "very dissatisfied" to "very satisfied." As shown, each level of customer satisfaction is given a rating that ranges from zero for "very dissatisfied" customers to 100 for "very satisfied" customers.

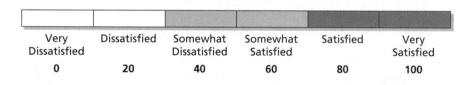

To determine a CSI for a given sampling of customers, a business simply computes the average of the customers' satisfaction ratings.

Let's assume an interview with 100 Hewlett-Packard (HP) printer customers produced a CSI of 72. By itself, an average customer satisfaction level of 72 does not tell us much and is not likely to attract management's attention. Is a CSI of 72 a good level of performance? That depends on the CSI obtained in earlier measurements, the target objective of the current measurement, and the CSI given to a leading competitor. Let's say HP's CSI of 72 is an improvement over earlier measurements and that the CSI of a leading competitor is 62.

FIGURE 1-3 CUSTOMER SATISFACTION—A WIDE-ANGLE VIEW

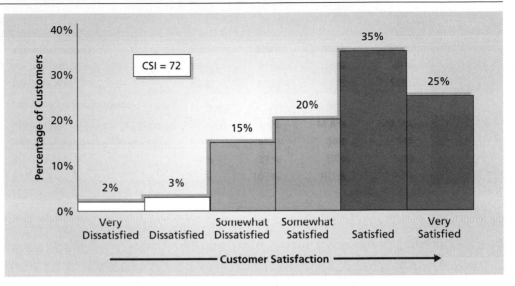

Those numbers could easily lead HP to be pleased with its level of performance among printer customers and perhaps become complacent in its pursuit of customer satisfaction with its printers. Additionally, because efforts to increase customer satisfaction take money, some may argue that the incremental benefit is not sufficient to justify the cost. That argument, however, would not have any merit for HP or any other business where customer satisfaction is a top corporate performance metric and priority. To really understand customer satisfaction and to leverage its profit potential, we need to expand our view of it.

A Wide-Angle View of Customer Satisfaction

A customer satisfaction index of 72 (where 100 is the maximum) may be seen as acceptable, and even very good. However, managing to the average masks a true understanding of customer satisfaction and opportunities for increased profits.[4] If we expand our view of customer satisfaction by including the percentage for each category on our customer satisfaction scale, a more meaningful set of insights emerges. As illustrated in Figure 1-3, the CSI of 72 was derived from 80 percent who reported varying degrees of satisfaction and 20 percent who reported varying degrees of dissatisfaction. The 20 percent who were "somewhat satisfied" are certainly vulnerable to competitor moves, but it is the 20 percent with varying degrees of dissatisfaction who are serious candidates for exit as customers. Management's immediate concern should be these customers.

The reason customer satisfaction is a valuable marketing performance metric is its ability to forecast future revenues and profits. This metric deserves high regard because:

> Customer satisfaction is a forward-looking indicator of business success that measures how well customers will respond to the company in the future. Other measures of market performance, such as sales and market share, are backward-looking measures of success. They tell how well the firm has done in the past, but not how well it will do in the future.[5]

FIGURE 1-4 CUSTOMER SATISFACTION AND PROFITABILITY

Customer Satisfaction	Customer Percent	CSI Score	Customer Sales	Percent Margin	Gross Profit	Retention Cost	Customer Profit
Very Satisfied	25%	100	$1,200	60%	$720	$100	$620
Satisfied	35%	80	$800	50%	$400	$100	$300
Somewhat Satisfied	20%	60	$300	40%	$120	$100	$20
Somewhat Dissatisfied	15%	40	$80	40%	$32	$100	−$68
Dissatisfied	3%	20	$60	40%	$24	$100	−$76
Very Dissatisfied	2%	0	$50	40%	$20	$100	−$80
Weighted Average		72	$655	48.5%	$350	$100	$250

A business may have produced excellent financial results but was nevertheless disappointing customers. In markets where customers cannot switch to alternatives quickly, a high percentage of dissatisfied customers would signal a coming exodus from a business and the resulting decline in sales and profitability. As a key indicator of operating performance, customer satisfaction considers realities not addressed in "backward-looking measures of success."

For many businesses, quarterly measures of customer satisfaction are an effective way to project future performance. If customer satisfaction declines, this early-warning sign gives management time to take preventive action before real damage is done. Of course, if a business does not track customer satisfaction, it remains oblivious of any decline and foregoes the opportunity to correct the situation before sales and profits also decline.

De-Averaging Customer Satisfaction and Customer Profitability

De-averaging the CSI to a wide-angle view of customer satisfaction allows managers to see more completely the opportunities for improvement. De-averaging, however, is even more important in understanding customer profitability.[6] As shown in Figure 1-4, the average customer revenue in our example is $655. Notably, "very satisfied" customers spend an average of $1,200 per year—almost two times the average.

Even more impressive is the role that "very satisfied" customers play in profitability.[7] Whereas the average annual customer profitability is $250, "very satisfied" customers produce $620. "Very satisfied" customers not only buy more, but they also buy higher-margin products and services, as Figure 1-4 illustrates.

Dissatisfied customers, in contrast, buy in smaller amounts and often buy low-margin or promotional products. In this example, after considering the cost of marketing, these customers lose the company money. "Somewhat satisfied" customers are profitable but are well below the average customer profitability, which is largely determined by the profit impact of "very satisfied" customers. De-averaging customer satisfaction demonstrates the importance of "very satisfied" customers to the overall profits of a business. When we chart customer profitability against customer satisfaction, as in Figure 1-5, we can clearly see that it is the "very satisfied" customers who drive profitability.

**FIGURE 1-5 DE-AVERAGING CUSTOMER SATISFACTION
AND CUSTOMER PROFITABILITY**

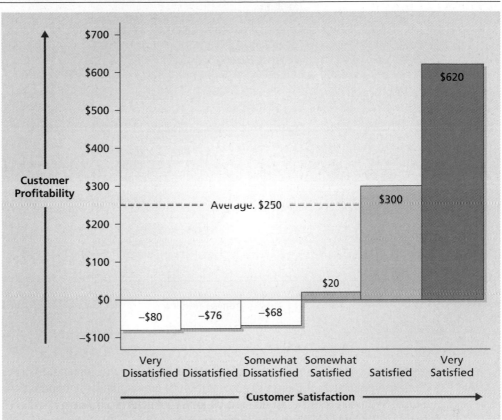

Yet, despite their less significant role in profitability, a market-based management business gives its dissatisfied customers as much attention as its "very satisfied" customers. When a dissatisfied customer leaves, a business suffers several economic consequences that lower profits. But mainly because it costs much more to attract a new customer than to retain a customer, a market-based management business knows it cannot neglect its dissatisfied customers.

Dissatisfied customers usually do not complain, but they do walk and they do talk. Studies have found that a surprisingly small percentage of dissatisfied customers complain to a business.[8] In Figure 1-6, of the 54,000 dissatisfied customers who do not complain, 42,120—or 78 percent—will exit. Exiting customers directly erode market position, and they make it more difficult to attract new customers as they will each tell 8 to 10 others of their dissatisfaction.

Figure 1-6 illustrates the importance of a focus on dissatisfied customers who do not complain. The business in this case has 200,000 customers, 70 percent satisfied and 30 percent dissatisfied. Each year the business loses nearly 50,000 customers who must be replaced to maintain the customer base of 200,000. Of the 140,000 satisfied customers, the business loses only 7,000. The other 43,000 lost customers are dissatisfied customers,

FIGURE 1-6 CUSTOMER SATISFACTION, COMPLAINT BEHAVIOR, AND CUSTOMER RETENTION

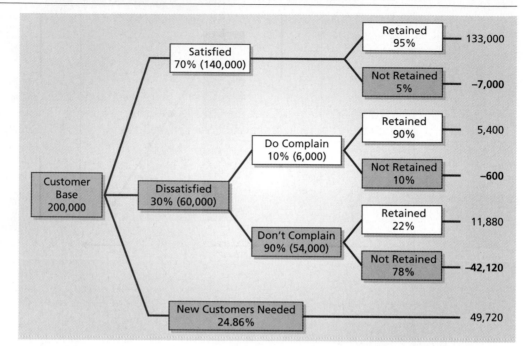

most of whom do not complain. In this example, 10 percent of the 60,000 dissatisfied customers complain and, of these, 90 percent (5,400) are retained. By contrast, of the 54,000 dissatisfied customers who do not complain (90 percent of all dissatisfied customers), 22 percent are retained (11,800) and 78 percent are lost (42,120). A quick calculation tells us that the dissatisfied customers who do not complain represent an astonishing 85 percent of the customers lost by the business each year.

It gets worse. Many dissatisfied customers become "customer terrorists"; they vent their dissatisfaction by telling others about it. Because each dissatisfied customer tells 8 to 10 others, the 42,120 dissatisfied customers will communicate their dissatisfaction to approximately a quarter-million individuals. Although not everyone who hears an unfavorable report would be a potential customer, this level of negative word-of-mouth communication makes new-customer attraction much more difficult and expensive.[9]

To prevent a poor reputation from developing by word of mouth, some businesses encourage dissatisfied customers to complain. One example is Domino's Pizza, which instituted a program that simply asks its dissatisfied customers to complain.[10] The company's efforts have resulted in obtaining complaints from 20 percent of its dissatisfied customers. For those who complain, Domino's can resolve 80 percent of the problems within 24 hours. When complaints can be resolved quickly, 95 percent of the complaining customers are retained. For dissatisfied customers whose complaints cannot be resolved within 24 hours, the retention rate falls to 46 percent.

While it may seem odd at first, the job of a market-based management team includes not only tracking customer satisfaction but also encouraging dissatisfied customers to complain. Only by learning the details of a customer complaint can a business take corrective action.

Profit Impact of Customer Dissatisfaction

MBNA America is a Delaware-based credit card company that in the early 1990s became frustrated with customer dissatisfaction and defection. All 300 employees were brought together in an effort to understand the problem and develop methods of delivering greater levels of customer satisfaction with the intent of keeping each and every customer. At the time, MBNA America had a 90 percent customer retention rate. After several years of dedicating itself to improved customer satisfaction and retention, the company raised customer retention to 95 percent. That may seem like a small difference, but the impact on profit was a 16-fold increase, and the company's industry ranking went from 38th to 4th.[11] The marketing efforts to satisfy and retain customers paid off to a far greater extent than we might have first expected from only a 5 percent increase in customer retention. As we see in Figure 1-6, most dissatisfied customers do not complain. They just walk away and tell others. To hold market share in a mature market, a business must replace its lost customers.

Let's use the customer retention tree in Figure 1-6 to take a closer look at the enormous profit impact of customer dissatisfaction. In this example, the business is in a mature market with 200,000 customers. Each year, the business loses about 50,000 customers and, to hold a customer base of 200,000, it must replace those customers with about 50,000 new customers. As shown, the business is operating at a 70 percent level of customer satisfaction, and we can see that its overall customer retention rate is about 75 percent. But of the 30 percent of customers who are dissatisfied (60,000 customers), the retention rate is only 29 percent (17,280 customers). It bears repeating that most of the lost customers come from the ranks of those dissatisfied customers who do not complain.

The customer profitability profile in Figure 1-7 reflects the information in Figure 1-6. It shows the average annual revenue, margin, and marketing expense per customer for retained customers, lost customers, and new customers. The retained customers are the profit driver of this business, producing 80 percent of the sales revenue and 89 percent of the gross profit.

FIGURE 1-7 PROFITABILITY AT 75 PERCENT CUSTOMER RETENTION

Customer Performance	Retained Customers	Lost Customers	New Customers	Overall Performance
Number of Customers	150,000	−50,000	50,000	200,000
Revenue per Customer	$800	$200	$400	$675
Sales Revenue (millions)	$120	$10	$20	$150
Percent Margin	50%	25%	25%	43.8%
Margin per Customer	$400	$50	$100	$295
Gross Profit (millions)	$60.0	$2.5	$5.0	$67.5
Marketing Expense per Customer	$60	$60	$300	
Marketing Expenses (millions)	$9.00	$3.00	$15.00	$27.0
Net Marketing Contribution (millions)	$51.00	−$0.50	−$10.00	$40.5
Operating Expenses (millions)				$33.0
Net Profit Before Taxes (millions)				$7.5
Return on Sales				5.0%

FIGURE 1-8 PROFITABILITY AT 80 PERCENT CUSTOMER RETENTION

Customer Performance	Retained Customers	Lost Customers	New Customers	Overall Performance
Number of Customers	160,000	–40,000	40,000	200,000
Revenue per Customer	$800	$200	$400	$675
Sales Revenue (millions)	$128	$8	$16	$152
Percent Margin	50%	25%	25%	43.8%
Margin per Customer	$400	$50	$100	$295
Gross Profit (millions)	$64.0	$2.0	$4.0	$70.0
Marketing Expense per Customer	$65	$65	$300	
Marketing Expenses (millions)	$10.40	$2.60	$12.00	$25.0
Net Marketing Contribution (millions)	$53.60	–$0.60	–$8.00	$45.0
Operating Expenses (millions)				$33.0
Net Profit Before Taxes (millions)				$12.0
Return on Sales				**7.9%**

Because most lost customers were first dissatisfied customers and were likely reducing their purchases before leaving, and also because they were not with the business for the full year, the annual revenue per lost customer is much lower than the revenue per retained customer. However, dissatisfied customers who are retained also result in relatively low revenue per customer because of the additional costs of the efforts to keep them. These efforts often involve price concessions, adjustments to inventory or terms of sale, greater customer service, and more work for the sales force. The net result of losing dissatisfied customers in this example is a *negative* net marketing contribution of $500,000 per year. The net marketing contribution shown in Figure 1-7 is the total revenue received from customers less the variable costs of producing that revenue and less the direct marketing expenses needed to serve this level of customer volume. Net marketing contribution is discussed in detail in Chapter 2.

New customers are also less profitable. Advertising and sales promotion dollars must be spent to generate sales leads and produce trial purchases. These expenses raise the marketing costs associated with attracting, qualifying, and serving new customers. New customers also generally buy less because they are in the evaluation stage and not yet fully committed to the business or its products. Their fewer and smaller purchases lower both the annual revenue and margin produced by each new customer. The result in this example is that the business actually loses $10 million in net marketing contribution each year in its efforts to replace lost customers, as shown in Figure 1-7.

PROFIT IMPACT OF CUSTOMER RETENTION

For the business situation presented in Figure 1-7, overall sales revenues of $150 million produced a net profit of $7.5 million, for a 5 percent return on sales. But what would be the profit impact of improved customer retention? Let's assume that the company decides to dedicate $1 million to reducing the number of dissatisfied customers, with the goal of retaining 80 percent of all customers each year. The additional $1 million increases the marketing expense from $60 per customer in Figure 1-7 to $65 per customer in Figure 1-8. The marketing logic and profit impact of this strategy can be summarized as follows:

> If the business can retain 80 percent of its customers each year instead of 75 percent, the business will reduce the cost associated with customer dissatisfaction and exit and will not have to spend as much on marketing efforts to attract new customers. Also, because retained customers produce a higher annual revenue and margin per customer than do lost or new customers, the total profits of the business should increase.

The $1 million spent on customer retention efforts would produce only a slight increase in sales revenues, as shown in Figure 1-8. The business, however, would see a tremendous improvement in marketing efficiency and profitability. Because retained customers are more profitable than new customers, the gross profit derived from retained customers would increase from $67.5 million to $70 million. Although the overall marketing expenses would be higher because of the $1 million added to the marketing budget to achieve 80 percent customer retention, the result would be a $4.5 million improvement in net marketing contribution derived from retained customers.

More importantly, the net loss of managing dissatisfied customers who exit and the net loss associated with attracting new customers would be reduced by a total of $2.5 million. The cumulative impact of increased customer satisfaction and retention is an increase in net profit before taxes from $7.5 million to $12 million. This incremental gain in net profit results from a larger number of retained customers, the reduced cost of serving dissatisfied customers, and the reduced expenses associated with acquiring new customers to maintain the same customer base. The gain represents a 60 percent increase in net profit before taxes, with essentially no change in market share or sales revenue.

We can readily see the immense potential for increased profit and cash flow when a company places a high priority on customer satisfaction and retention. Every additional customer who is retained increases net profit. Inefficient costs associated with serving dissatisfied customers and the costs of acquiring new customers to replace them are reduced. There is a tremendous financial leverage in satisfying and retaining customers.

Customer Satisfaction and Customer Retention

The relationship between customer satisfaction and customer retention is intuitively easy to discern. Different competitive conditions, however, modify this relationship.[12] For example, in less competitive markets, customers are more easily retained even with poor levels of customer satisfaction because substitutes are few or switching costs are high. In markets where relatively few choices are available—such as phone service, water, electricity, and hospital care—customers stay even when dissatisfied. Businesses with no or limited competition have high levels of customer retention despite any low level of customer satisfaction.

In highly competitive markets, however, even high levels of customer satisfaction may not ensure against customer defection. Grocery store, restaurant, and bank customers can switch quickly if not completely satisfied. Although the time between purchases is longer, customers who periodically buy personal computers, automobiles, appliances, and electronic equipment can also easily move to another brand. In these and

FIGURE 1-9 ESTIMATING CUSTOMER RETENTION

How likely are you to buy this product or brand again on your next purchase?

Definitely Will Not Repurchase	Will Not Repurchase	Probably Will Not Repurchase	Probably Will Repurchase	Plan to Repurchase	Definitely Will Repurchase

Intention to Repurchase	Percent	Probability
Definitely Will Repurchase	25%	1.00
Plan to Repurchase	35%	0.80
Probably Will Repurchase	20%	0.60
Probably Will Not Repurchase	15%	0.40
Will Not Repurchase	3%	0.20
Definitely Will Not Repurchase	2%	0.00
Total:	100%	0.72

Customer Retention	72%

similar markets, customer retention is much more difficult, and a much higher level of customer satisfaction is needed to ensure a high percentage of retained customers.

Estimating Customer Retention

Banks, wholesale suppliers, and other businesses that engage in recorded customer transactions can figure their customer retention rates fairly easily. Most businesses, however, are one step removed from end-user customers and cannot determine their customer retention rates based on records. To estimate their retention rates, these businesses can use a customer survey as outlined in Figure 1-9.

Customer Retention and Customer Life Expectancy

Customer satisfaction and retention are important linkages to a market-based strategy and to profitability. The ultimate objective of any marketing strategy should be to attract, satisfy, and retain target customers. If a business can accomplish this objective with a competitive advantage in attractive markets, it will produce above-average profits.

The customer as a critical component in the profitability equation is completely overlooked in financial analyses and annual reports. Customers are a marketing asset that businesses have yet to quantify in their accounting systems, even though the business that can attract, satisfy, and keep customers over their lifetimes of purchases is in a powerful position to deliver superior levels of profitability. Businesses that lack a market orientation see customers as individual purchase transactions. A market-based management business

FIGURE 1-10 CUSTOMER LIFE EXPECTANCY AND CUSTOMER RETENTION

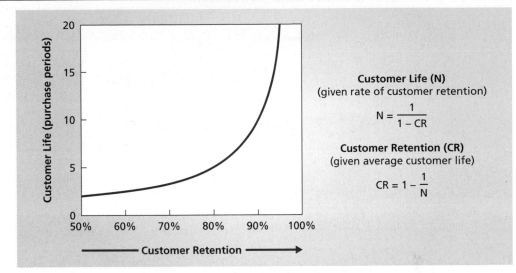

sees them as lifetime partners. *The New York Times,* as an example, tracks its customer retention and the retention rates of competing newspapers by length of subscription.[13] Among mature subscribers—those subscribing longer than 24 months—*The New York Times* has a retention rate of 94 percent. Its closest competitor has an 80 percent retention rate.

The higher a business's customer retention rate, the greater the profit impact. In the short run, we showed this to be true on the basis of increased profits from retained customers, reduced losses from defecting customers, and the subsequent lower cost of attracting new customers to maintain the customer base. But higher levels of customer retention also have a long-term positive impact on profits because a higher rate of retention lengthens the average life of customers, increasing their lifetime value.

A business that has a 50 percent customer retention rate has a fifty-fifty chance of retaining any one customer from one year to the next. This fact translates into an average customer life of 2 years, as shown in Figure 1-10. The average life expectancy of a customer is equal to one divided by the figure arrived at by subtracting the rate of customer retention from one. As customer retention increases, the customer's life expectancy increases. More importantly, customer life expectancy increases exponentially with customer retention.

As an example, the average rate of customer retention among health care providers is 80 percent.[14] This level of retention produces an average customer life of 5 years. If a health care provider could increase its customer retention rate to 90 percent, the increase would produce an average customer life of 10 years. We can see, then, that as a business moves to higher levels of customer retention, the life expectancy of a customer grows dramatically.

The Lifetime Value of a Customer

The Cadillac Division of General Motors estimates each of its customers will spend approximately $350,000 over a lifetime on automotive purchases and maintenance. If Cadillac loses a customer early, it loses upwards of $250,000 in future cash flow. To

FIGURE 1-11 LIFETIME VALUE OF A CUSTOMER

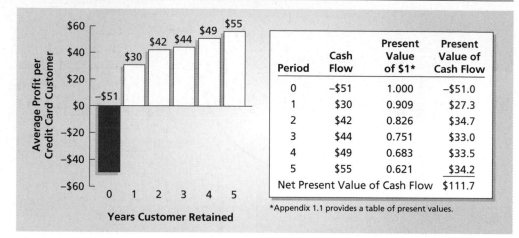

Period	Cash Flow	Present Value of $1*	Present Value of Cash Flow
0	–$51	1.000	–$51.0
1	$30	0.909	$27.3
2	$42	0.826	$34.7
3	$44	0.751	$33.0
4	$49	0.683	$33.5
5	$55	0.621	$34.2
Net Present Value of Cash Flow			$111.7

*Appendix 1.1 provides a table of present values.

replace that lost customer, Cadillac would need to attract a new customer, which is an expensive process. The cost of marketing efforts to ensure customer satisfaction is small, then, in comparison with the current and future benefits of customer purchases, as well as the cost of replacing customers who become dissatisfied and leave. In general, it costs five times more to replace than to keep a customer.

Figure 1-11 illustrates the average profit per credit card customer generated over a 5-year period. Acquiring and setting up accounts for new credit card customers nets an annual loss of $51 per customer. Newly acquired credit card customers are also slow to use their cards; new customers produce an average profit of $30 the first year, $42 the second year, and $44 the third year. By year 5, the average profit obtained from a credit card customer is $55. The value of a credit card customer, then, grows fairly significantly over time. Of course, if a credit card company loses a customer in year 5 because of dissatisfaction, the company incurs the cost of replacing the customer. The cost in the first year following customer exit is a considerable $106, which consists of the $55 in lost profit from the exiting customer and the $51 loss associated with attracting a replacement customer.

In this example, the average customer life is 5 years. Working backward, we can estimate customer retention to be 80 percent, as shown here:

$$\text{Customer Retention} = 1 - \frac{1}{N} = 1 - \frac{1}{5} = 0.80 \text{ (or } 80\%)$$

To estimate the lifetime value of a customer at this rate of retention, we need to compute the net present value of the customer cash flow shown in Figure 1-11. The $51 cost in acquiring this customer is immediately gone. Because it takes a year to achieve the initial $30 in profit, its present value is less than an immediate $30 profit. In this example, the business has a discount rate of 10 percent. Therefore, the present value of $1 received after 1 year is $0.909 (the rate at which $1 is discounted for 1 year at 10 percent). Accordingly, $30 to be received 1 year later is presently worth $27.30 ($30 × 0.909).

FIGURE 1-12 NET PRESENT VALUE OF ONLINE CUSTOMERS

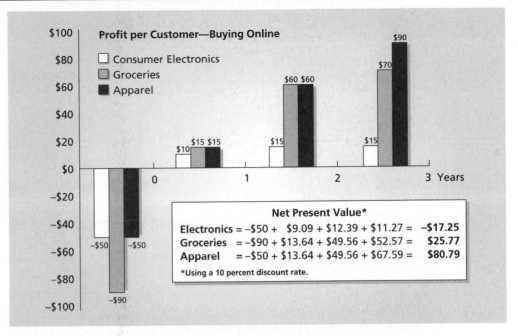

The discounting is performed for each year's receipts, and the values are totaled to arrive at the net present value of this cash flow. When each year's cash flow is properly discounted, the sum of these cash flows is equal to $111.70, the amount this customer is worth in today's dollars. If the customer life expectancy were only 3 years, the customer value (net present value) would be considerably smaller. The higher the rate of customer retention, the longer the average customer life expectancy and the greater the customer value.

To better understand this concept, let's look at the customer value (net present value) over a 3-year period for online shoppers for consumer electronics, groceries, and apparel,[15] as illustrated in Figure 1-12. The cost of acquiring an online grocery customer is almost twice the cost of acquiring an online consumer electronics or apparel customer. After 3 years, the average online grocery customer has a positive net present value of $25.77, while the online consumer electronics customer has a negative net present value of $17.25. The average online apparel customer is the most profitable, with a net present value of $80.79 after the 3 years.

Net Promoter Score

Because of their link to profitability, customer satisfaction and retention are important customer metrics. Another key determinant of customer loyalty is customer conviction. We can measure the psychological commitment a customer has to a brand or business by considering a variety of factors, but a customer's recommendation of a brand or business to others stands as the best sign of customer conviction. When customers recommend a product or service, they undoubtedly have the utmost confidence in its value.

FIGURE 1-13 NET PROMOTER SCORE

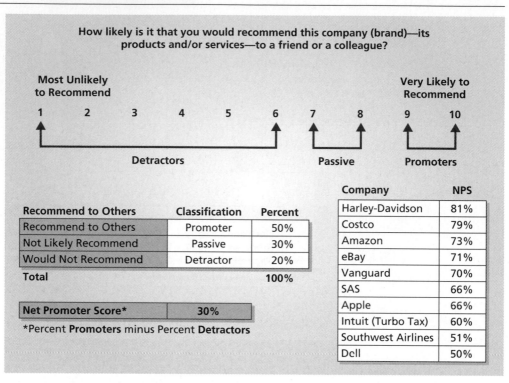

How likely is it that you would recommend this company (brand)—its products and/or services—to a friend or a colleague?

Most Unlikely to Recommend   Very Likely to Recommend

1   2   3   4   5   6   7   8   9   10

Detractors   Passive   Promoters

Recommend to Others	Classification	Percent
Recommend to Others	Promoter	50%
Not Likely Recommend	Passive	30%
Would Not Recommend	Detractor	20%
Total		100%

Net Promoter Score*	30%

*Percent **Promoters** minus Percent **Detractors**

Company	NPS
Harley-Davidson	81%
Costco	79%
Amazon	73%
eBay	71%
Vanguard	70%
SAS	66%
Apple	66%
Intuit (Turbo Tax)	60%
Southwest Airlines	51%
Dell	50%

Enterprise Rent-A-Car, Southwest Airlines, Costco, Apple, FedEx, and many other companies build strategies that encourage customers to share their product conviction with others. A study by Bain and Company revealed only 22 percent of the world's major firms achieved a sustainable sales growth of 5 percent over the 10-year period from 1994 to 2004.[16] One path to sales growth and higher profits is to have customers promote a company's product to potential customers. After many years of researching customer retention and loyalty, Fred Reichheld devised a simple formula for computing a "net promoter score."

Net Promoter Score = Promoters − Detractors

Promoters: Percentage of customers who would promote the brand or product.
Detractors: Percentage who would not recommend the brand or product.

Using the scale in Figure 1-13, a company can sample customers to determine the percentages for "Promoters," "Passive," and "Detractors," and then compute the net promoter score. The figure also lists several companies with outstanding net promoter scores, each company benefiting from a "customer advantage" that contributes to sales growth and profits. With a high percentage of customers promoting their products, these companies enjoy superior levels of marketing productivity (marketing profits per dollar of marketing investment).

CUSTOMER LOYALTY AND MANAGING CUSTOMER LOYALTY

Any measurement of customer loyalty should include the elements of customer satisfaction and customer retention, as well as customer recommendation to potential customers. Each of these customer metrics—satisfaction, retention, and recommendation—has a known relationship with profitability. It only makes sense to combine all three into one measure of customer loyalty.

Measuring Customer Loyalty

Using findings on customer satisfaction, customer retention, and customer recommendation, a company can determine its overall customer loyalty score (CLS) by first computing a separate loyalty score for the customers at each of the six levels of customer satisfaction. We can use the following formula to figure the scores for each category:

$$\text{CLS} = \text{Customer Satisfaction} \times \text{Customer Retention} \times \text{Customer Recommendation}$$

The loyalty scores for each level of satisfaction are then weighted by the percentage of customers at that level. The total of the weighted scores is the business's overall customer loyalty score, as shown in Figure 1-14.

The CLS is a more accurate indicator of a business's overall customer commitment level than is the customer retention rate by itself. A business with a weak customer satisfaction index may still have a high customer retention rate when switching costs are high or no attractive alternatives exist. For example, multiplying the CSI for a business's "somewhat satisfied" customers (CSI of 60) by a 90 percent retention rate for that group yields a seemingly acceptable index of 54 for those customers. But if the business were to ask its "somewhat satisfied" customers, "Would you recommend our product to others?" and only 10 percent reply that they would, a completely different picture emerges. A low level of customer recommendation signals a low level of customer loyalty. When the customer recommendation rate of 10 percent is taken into account for the "somewhat satisfied" customers, the CLS for that group drops from 54 to 5.4:

$$\text{CLS} = 60 \times .90 \times .10 = \textbf{5.4}$$

FIGURE 1-14 CUSTOMER LOYALTY SCORE

Customer Satisfaction Level	Percent of Customers	CSI	Customer Retention	Would Recommend	Loyalty Score	Weighted Loyalty Score
Customer Loyalty Score: 42.1						
Very Satisfied	25%	100	95%	95%	90.3	22.6
Satisfied	35%	80	95%	70%	53.2	18.6
Somewhat Satisfied	20%	60	75%	10%	4.5	0.9
Somewhat Dissatisfied	15%	40	20%	0%	0	0
Dissatisfied	3%	20	0%	0%	0	0
Very Dissatisfied	2%	0	0%	0%	0	0
	100%	72	75%	50%		42.1

The low CLS for this group of customers would contribute to a low overall CLS, which would be a red flag for the management of any business managing customer loyalty. Clearly, retained customers unwilling to recommend the company's product to others are "captive customers." The customers would exit if an opportunity were to emerge. The customer retention rate by itself, then, can be a false indicator of accomplishment, as a business's customer loyalty may actually be quite low.

We can see in Figure 1-14 how customer loyalty varies for the sampling of HP printer customers we have been tracking. As we would expect, the "very satisfied" customers have a high rate of planned repurchase and a high rate of recommendation. This yields a CLS of 90 for "very satisfied" customers. The "satisfied" customers are less loyal, with a CLS of 53. The "somewhat satisfied" customers are much less loyal due to a lower rate of planned repurchase and a lower rate of recommendation, but they still have some measure of loyalty (CLS = 5). The three levels of dissatisfied customers all have a CLS equal to zero based on zero or very low levels of planned repurchase and recommendation.

When we weight the loyalty score for each category of customers by the relative size of that group and then total the weighted scores, we arrive at the business's overall CLS of 42.1.

$$\textbf{Overall CLS} = 25\% \times 90.3 + 35\% \times 53.2 + 20\% \times 4.5 + 15\% \times 0 + 3\% \times 0 + 2\% \times 0 = \textbf{42.1}$$

The overall CLS provides a benchmark from which a company can judge its customer loyalty and track changes in response to improvement efforts.

Managing Customer Loyalty

Because customer satisfaction and retention have a positive impact on profitability, a business will always have customers it wants to keep. But it can also have customers it should abandon.[17] Likewise, in attracting new customers, there are those the business should pursue and those it should avoid. Attracting the right customers is part of a process called customer relationship marketing, which Chapter 5 discusses.

We can facilitate the effective management of customer relationships with regard to retention by classifying customers on the basis of customer loyalty and profitability.[18] Not all customers are the same. Some may be loyal and profitable, some profitable but not loyal, some loyal but not profitable, and some neither loyal nor profitable. These four major customer classifications are shown in Figure 1-15. One goal of customer relationship marketing is to manage the four customer types in an effort to obtain higher levels of loyalty and profitability.[19]

Top Performers

"Top performers" are the "golden nuggets" or "crown jewels" of any business. With their above-average loyalty and customer profitability, they account for most of a business's profits. Top performers are likely to have customer loyalty scores above 70 and as high as 90. They come in two varieties:[20]

- **Advocates**—"Advocates" buy nearly everything a business has to sell and purchase regularly. They do the business's marketing for it by extolling its products to others and thereby generating new customers. Advocates are a business's unpaid sales force.

FIGURE 1-15 MANAGING CUSTOMER LOYALTY

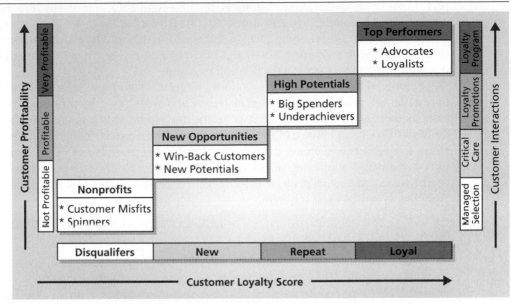

- **Loyalists**—"Loyalists," although less ardent than advocates, would nevertheless and with little prompting recommend a business's products to others. They have a high level of dedication to a particular business, prefer to buy from that business over any other, and are very profitable customers.

One of the primary objectives of customer relationship marketing is to develop sustainable, long-term, one-on-one relationships with top performers through loyalty programs tailored to deliver superior levels of customer satisfaction. For many businesses, top performers comprise 30 to 36 percent of the businesses' customer portfolios.[21]

High Potentials

"High potentials" are the "rough-cut diamonds" of a business's customer portfolio. They are repeat customers with a high profit potential but are not loyal customers. Two types of high potentials often make up 15 to 20 percent of a business's customer portfolio:

- **Big Spenders**—Repeat customers who buy at above-average levels and frequently purchase products for others are a business's "big spenders." They are highly profitable customers who continue to buy from one business, but they also buy from competitors. The are "satisfied" or "very satisfied" customers with an excellent retention rate, but they are less likely than top performers to recommend only one business's product.
- **Underachievers**—Customers who buy often but make relatively small purchases are "underachievers." Their potential with respect to both profit and loyalty is unfulfilled. A loyalty promotion program targeted at underachievers can lead to an increase in their average purchase amount.

High potentials are often mismanaged, with opportunities for upgrading them to top performers overlooked. These customers, because competitors can easily lure them away, are at risk of becoming lost customers. An effective effort to build loyalty among high potentials is vital for retaining them and the profits they produce. An objective of customer relationship marketing is to invest in strengthening their loyalty through offerings designed to increase their satisfaction and retention.

Figure 1-15 cites "loyalty promotions" targeted at the product needs of high potentials as an effective form of customer interaction with this group. Loyalty promotions have as their goal improved customer relationships that will produce a higher level of customer loyalty and profitability. One company, PearlParadise.com, offers special sales to underachievers to increase the customer loyalty and profitability of this group of customers.[22] Instead of offering sales to the general public, PearlParadise.com has grown its profits from underachievers by e-mailing them messages with a link that takes them to a Web site with offers just for them.

New Opportunities

"New opportunities" are the "new discoveries," the "unpolished gems," of a business's customer portfolio. They are first-time or returning customers who are not yet loyal or profitable. With respect to customer interactions, they require "critical care." They have expectations that need to be carefully managed in an effort to nurture them to a higher level of loyalty. They could represent 15 to 20 percent of a business's customer portfolio. The two types of new opportunities in Figure 1-15 are:

- **Win-Back Customers**—Many high potentials and top performers who switched to a competitor, often because they were mismanaged, will for various reasons return to a business. These "win-back customers" already know the business's products and services and are likely to resume their former purchasing patterns. As Figure 1-16 shows, in 5 years the "second lifetime value" of a win-back customer has a net present value almost three times higher than the average lifetime value of an entirely new customer.
- **New Potentials**—"New potentials" fit the business's profile for target customers. They possess many of the same traits that loyal customers have. The challenge is "critical care," as illustrated in Figure 1-15. How they are managed as new customers will determine how their purchasing patterns and customer loyalty will develop. For them, positive customer experiences are essential in building customer satisfaction and retention.

Nonprofits

"Nonprofits" are the result of mismanaged customer selection. They are unprofitable and unlikely ever to be loyal. Nonprofits are a drain on a business's profits because the cost of acquiring them can never be recouped. They can be 30 to 35 percent of a business's customer portfolio. A business with a strong and well-managed customer focus can significantly reduce its percentage of nonprofits with improved customer selection management, as illustrated in Figure 1-15. The two types of nonprofits are:

- **Misfits**—These may be wonderful people and great customers, but for some other business. The offerings of the business simply do not match these customers' needs. While

FIGURE 1-16 LIFETIME VALUE OF WIN-BACK CUSTOMERS

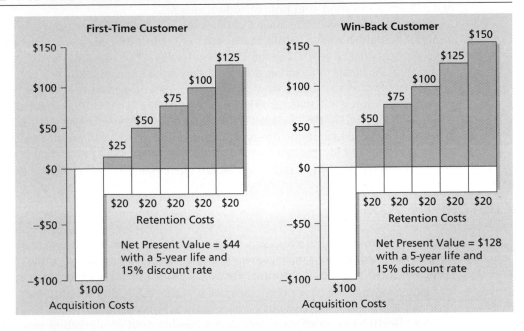

they were initially attracted to this business and its value proposition, they will never be satisfied.[23] They are unlikely to be retained no matter how hard the business tries. The best thing, and the hardest, is to help them leave as a customer.

■ **Spinners**—These customers buy one time and then exit. Typically, they buy because a product is being offered at an attractive price or with another promotional incentive. Telephone companies, for instance, are known for their incentives, and for their spinners. AT&T found that 1.7 million of its customers switched carriers an average of three times a year.[24] Improved customer selection management, with better targeting of promotions, would keep the ranks of a business's spinners to a minimum.

We know a business can do better if it avoids attracting nonprofits. By being aware of the general characteristics of its previous nonprofits, a business can market more selectively to its target customers. Dr. Charles Lillis, former CEO of MediaOne, has said:

> I will know when our businesses have done a good job of market segmentation when they can tell me to whom we should not sell.

Understanding the differences between target and nontarget customers is a fundamental aspect of customer relationship marketing. A profile that identifies those who are not target customers is just as valuable as a profile that identifies those who are target customers. A customer-acquisition process that profiles nonprofits and avoids them will lower the total cost of attracting new customers and improve a business's customer retention rate. In contrast, unrestrained customer acquisition will attract many who will be neither loyal nor profitable, resulting in a negative rather than positive impact on profit due to the cost of customer acquisition with little offsetting income.

Every business loses customers at one time or another. Some were profitable customers whom the business would like to win back. Most of them were mismanaged customers who switched to a competitor due to dissatisfaction. Lost customers would also include any the business abandoned because they were unprofitable.

Managing customer interactions is an intrinsic part of managing customer loyalty and profitability. Successful customer relationship marketing involves managing all customer relationships based on the customer's level of loyalty and profit potential. An effective program starts with identifying the target customers a business can acquire and retain, and it includes strategies for managing new customers and abandoning unprofitable ones. Each customer relationship has an impact on overall retention levels and profitability.

CUSTOMER FOCUS

A key part of marketing success and building profits is a strong customer focus. It is at the heart of market-based management and any successful marketing strategy. We have already learned a lot about customer focus, its profit impact, and the customer metrics that gauge satisfaction, retention, customer lifetime value, the net promoter score, and customer loyalty. But we have not yet succinctly defined customer focus.

An effective customer focus relies on a combination of marketing attitudes, practices, and market-based metrics, as expressed in this definition:

> Customer focus is a perspective that passionately maintains a customer orientation (marketing attitude) across the organization and motivates customer-oriented practices and behaviors (market-based management), using marketing performance metrics to measure the effectiveness of this perspective with regard to customer satisfaction, retention, the net promoter score, and customer loyalty.

Customer Focus and Marketing Knowledge

An understanding of the attitudes, practices, and performance metrics associated with a customer-oriented perspective, as well as an awareness of the importance of building a market-based management culture, will be new marketing knowledge for some. For others, it will be knowledge they already possess but do not use. In either instance, a business's customer focus will grow when this marketing knowledge is put into practice.

Figure 1-17 demonstrates the relationship between customer focus and marketing knowledge based on our studies involving 50,000 managers around the world.[25] The strength of the managers' customer focus is correlated to their level of marketing knowledge. Managers with a higher level of marketing knowledge had a stronger customer focus, while managers with a lower level of marketing knowledge had a weaker customer focus. Our studies found the same to be true for "competitor orientation" and "working across job functions": managers with a higher level of marketing knowledge had a better understanding of their competitors, and a better understanding of the importance of organization-wide cooperation in meeting customer needs.

The relationship between marketing knowledge and marketing education is also demonstrated in Figure 1-17. While our studies indicated that marketing experience by itself was the source of the marketing knowledge of some managers, we found that formal education

FIGURE 1-17 CUSTOMER FOCUS AND MARKETING KNOWLEDGE

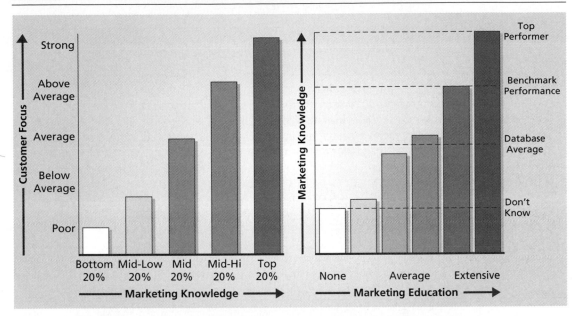

was a far greater and more consistent contributor. Overwhelmingly, the more marketing education managers had, the higher their marketing knowledge scores were on our surveys. By contrast, our studies found that those reporting no formal marketing education had as a group the same marketing knowledge as someone who would flip a coin to determine responses to true-false questions. We refer to this level of marketing knowledge as the "don't know" level.

As a group, those managers who reported having an intermediate level of formal marketing education produced a score on our survey's marketing knowledge section close to the average of all 50,000 participating managers—the overall "database average." Those with extensive marketing education did much better, producing an average score equal to the average score of the top 20 percent of managers in the database.

Customer-Focused Behaviors and Practices

Marketing knowledge and marketing attitudes are the fundamental drivers of market-based management. In Figure 1-18, we see that marketing knowledge drives marketing attitudes, and that both marketing knowledge and marketing attitudes lead to behaviors, strategies, and practices that improve profitability. Businesses committed to market-based management naturally exhibit a strong customer focus. Figure 1-19 presents many of the customer-oriented behaviors and practices of these businesses.

Each of the behaviors and practices in Figure 1-19 contributes to the realization of an effective customer focus. Leadership, organization, training, and some level of investment are required to bring about full acceptance of these behaviors and practices across the business. The extent to which a business lives by them determines its performance and the profit benefits that a strong customer focus can produce. The actual behaviors and practices of a truly customer-focused business are the qualities that distinguish it from a business promulgating a corporate mantra consisting only of words.

FIGURE 1-18 MARKET-BASED MANAGEMENT

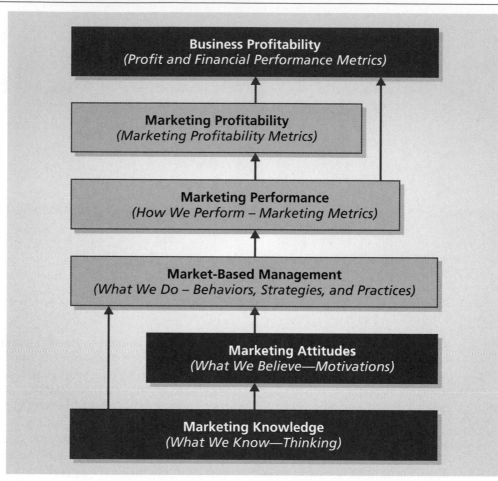

Marketing Performance

The market-based management behaviors and practices outlined in Figure 1-19 also create a market-measurement culture in which a business uses a wide variety of marketing performance metrics to measure external conditions related to the business's marketing performance and profitability.[26] In this chapter, we have seen that the customer metrics that measure satisfaction, retention, and loyalty are indicators of a business's health in much the same way that financial metrics are. Management's decisions in response to the information these metrics provide can significantly increase profits.

Marketing Profitability

We have also learned in this chapter that the longer the customer life, the more profitable the customer is. Categorizing customers with respect to their levels of loyalty and then managing each category to improve customer lifetime value leads to improved marketing profitability. All of the metrics presented in this chapter have either a direct or indirect

FIGURE 1-19 MARKET-BASED MANAGEMENT AND CUSTOMER FOCUS

VOICE OF THE CUSTOMER

- **Customer Experience**—Every customer interaction is seen as an opportunity to better understand the total customer experience and how to improve it with the business's products or services.
- **Customer Solutions**—The business strives to understand customer needs and to recognize that customers are different and require different customer solutions. We build solutions, not sell products.
- **Customer Complaints**—The business seeks comments from dissatisfied customers and addresses their complaints in an effort to retain them as customers.

CUSTOMER PERFORMANCE

- **Customer Metrics**—Customer performance metrics such as satisfaction, retention, and loyalty are reported regularly with the same importance as financial performance metrics.
- **Customer Profile**—All managers and key employees understand our target-customer profile with respect to demographics and customer needs. Just as importantly, they know the attributes of non-target customers.
- **Customer Intelligence**—In continuously gathering customer information, managers encourage employees to provide customer insights, sharing the information across the organization.

CUSTOMER-FOCUSED LEADERSHIP

- **Management Leadership**—The business's managers at all levels are passionate about customers and regularly visit with them to better understand their needs.
- **Employee Training**—New employees receive training on customer focus and the role employees play in creating satisfying customer experiences. All employees are routinely shown tapes related to customer focus to maintain their awareness.
- **Customer Involvement**—Customer feedback, good and bad, is shared across the organization. Employees are coached on how their job impacts the customer and provided information as to how customers use the company's products and the frustrations and problems they encounter.

impact on marketing profitability. For example, the lifetime value of a customer has a direct impact on customer profitability while changes in customer satisfaction lead indirectly to changes in marketing profitability.

Chapter 2 discusses how businesses can use two other marketing profitability metrics measure its marketing profitability and create two marketing profitability metrics: marketing ROS (return on sales) and marketing ROI (return on investment).

We are beginning to see the great extent to which market-based management is performance driven, with the overall effectiveness of the behaviors and practices associated with market-based management measured by marketing profitability, as Figure 1-18 indicates. The chapters ahead will take us from this beginning point to a full understanding of market-based management and how it improves profitability.

■ Summary

A business's effectiveness in developing market-based strategies that deliver high levels of customer satisfaction depends on the strength of its customer focus. A few years ago, many managers considered that statement to be a nice academic philosophy but without any application for a company in business to make a profit. Today, however, the evidence shows that businesses with higher levels of customer satisfaction are more profitable.

They are more profitable because they retain a higher percentage of their customers, resulting in less time and money spent in attracting new customers to replace lost customers. These businesses also have less rework, and therefore less expense, caused by poor product or service quality.

Customer profitability rests upon customer loyalty. A business may have a high retention rate, but retained customers who are not loyal will eventually leave for a competing alternative. The net promoter score enables a business to determine whether its retained customers might be "captive customers." When customers are retained but would not recommend a business's product, they have no true loyalty, and the business, unless it nurtures these customers, has no chance of keeping them for very long. The managers of market-based management businesses, however, can see the positive impact on profits that long-term customers have, and they engage in customer relationship marketing to improve customer loyalty. Because not all new, retained, and returning customers are the same in terms of loyalty and purchasing patterns, a market-based management business categorizes its customers and manages each group with programs and offerings tailor-designed for improving the group's retention and profitability. The more effectively a business manages customer relationships, the greater its customer loyalty and profitability.

For a business to have an effective customer orientation, a high level of marketing knowledge among its managers is essential. The more marketing knowledge a business's managers have, the stronger the business's customer focus. And, overwhelmingly, the more marketing education managers have, the greater their marketing knowledge. Marketing knowledge drives the attitudes, behaviors, and practices that build a strong customer focus, resulting in greater customer loyalty and profitability. One of these practices is the use of customer metrics, which indirectly drive profitability, to track customer satisfaction, retention, and loyalty.

■ Market-Based Strategic Thinking

1 How would a business with a strong customer focus differ from one with a weak market orientation?

2 How does a strong customer focus impact profitability and shareholder value?

3 Why are "very satisfied" customers critical to the overall profits of a business?

4 Why are customer satisfaction and customer retention important drivers of profitability?

5 Why are average measures of customer satisfaction misleading indicators of market-based performance?

6 How does the mix of customers who are satisfied, neutral, and dissatisfied affect a business's net profit?

7 Using the diagram in Figure 1-6, determine how customer retention would change if the business increased its percentage of satisfied customers from 70 to 80 percent.

8 Why do high levels of customer dissatisfaction make attracting new customers more difficult?

9 How do high levels of customer dissatisfaction increase the cost of marketing and hence decrease net profit?

10 Why are satisfied customers crucial to a business's net profit?

11 Why does a high net promoter score contribute to customer loyalty, sales growth, and profitability?

12 How does customer selection affect customer loyalty and profitability?

13 Why is customer recommendation of a brand or company an important element of customer loyalty?

14 How could a business have a high customer retention rate but a low customer loyalty score?

15 Why would marketing knowledge influence customer focus?

16 How would marketing knowledge influence market-based management and the use of marketing performance metrics such as customer satisfaction, customer retention, the net promoter score, and customer loyalty?

Marketing Performance Tools

Four **Marketing Performance Tools** are accessible online for a better understanding of the profit impact of customer focus and managing customer loyalty. For each of these applied-learning tools, three questions are presented to give insight into the power and value of the tools. To access them, go to *www.rogerjbest.com.*

1.1 Customer Satisfaction—Figure 1-4 is operationalized as a marketing performance tool with the following questions:

- How would average customer sales and average customer profit change if the business had 10 percent "very satisfied" customers, 35 percent "satisfied" customers, and 55 percent "somewhat satisfied" customers?

- How would the average customer sales and average customer profit change if this business were able to improve customer satisfaction to 35 percent "very satisfied," 35 percent "satisfied," and 30 percent "somewhat satisfied"?

- Would this level of customer satisfaction be worth the effort if the cost of retention increased from $100 to $150 per customer?

1.2 Customer Retention—Figure 1-6 is operationalized as a marketing performance tool with the following questions:

- How would customer retention change if the percentage of all dissatisfied customers decreased to 15 percent and the percentage of all satisfied customers increased to 85 percent?

- Using the original data, how would customer retention change if the percentage who complained increased from 10 to 50 percent?

- How would customer retention change if both changes posed above took place?

1.3 Lifetime Customer Value—Figure 1-11 is operationalized as a marketing performance tool with the following questions:

- How does the lifetime value of the average customer change when the customer life is reduced from 5 to 4 years?

- How does the lifetime value change when the customer life is extended from 5 to 6 years and in year 6 the net cash flow is $60?

- How does the lifetime value change when customer retention increases from 80 to 87.5 percent, assuming the net cash flow increases by $5 per year for each additional year of customer life?

1.4 Managing Customer Loyalty—Figure 1-14 is operationalized as a marketing performance tool with the following questions:

- How would the following improvements in customer satisfaction change the customer loyalty score: 30 percent "very satisfied," 35 percent "satisfied," 25 percent "somewhat satisfied," and 10 percent "somewhat dissatisfied"?

- How would an improvement in customer retention from .70 to .90 among all levels of satisfied customers impact overall retention and the customer loyalty score?

- What would be the impact on customer loyalty?

Notes

1. "Enterprise Asks What Customers Thinking and Acts," *USA Today*, May 22, 2006.
2. Bradley Gale, "Tracking Competitive Position Drives Shareholder Value," *Global Management* (1992): 367–71.
3. Frederick F. Reichheld and W. Earl Sasser, Jr., "Zero Defections: Quality Comes to Services," *Harvard Business Review* (September–October 1990): 106–111; and Frederick F. Reichheld, "Loyalty-Based Management," *Harvard Business Review* (March–April 1993): 64–73.
4. Patrick Byrne, "Only 10% of Companies Satisfy Customers," *Transportation and Distribution* (December 1993); and Tom Eck, "Are Customers Happy? Don't Assume," *Positive Impact* (July l992): 3.
5. Steven Schnaars, *Marketing Strategy* (New York: Free Press, 1998): 186–205.
6. Larry Seldon and Geoffrey Colvin, *Angel Customers and Demon Customers* (New York: Portfolio, 2003): 45–59.
7. Peter Doyle, *Value-Based Marketing* (Hoboken, NJ: Wiley, 2000): 8–85.
8. TARP, "Consumer Complaint Handling in America: An Update Study," White House Office of Consumer Affairs, Washington, DC, 1986; TARP, "Consumer Complaint Handling in America, Final Report," U.S. Office of Consumer Affairs, Washington, D.C., 1979; and Kathy Rhoades, "The Importance of Customer Complaints," *Protect Yourself* (January 1988): 15–18.
9. A. M. McGahan and Pankaj Ghemawat, "Competition to Retain Customers," *Marketing Science* 13 (Spring 1994): 165–176; and Mark H. McCormack, "One Disappointed Customer Is One Too Many," *Positive Impact* 4 (September 1993): 7–8.
10. T. Lucia, "Domino's Theory—Only Service Succeeds," *Positive Impact* 3 (February 1992): 6–7.
11. Reichheld and Sasser, "Zero Defections: Quality Comes to Services," 106–111; and Reichheld, "Loyalty-Based Management," 64–73.
12. Thomas Jones and W. Earl Sasser, Jr., "Why Satisfied Customers Defect," *Harvard Business Review* (November–December 1995): 88–89.
13. Frederick F. Reichheld and Phil Schefter, "E-Loyalty: Your Secret Weapon on the Web," *Harvard Business Review* (July–August 2000): 105–113.
14. Roberta Clarke, "Addressing Voluntary Disenrollment," *CDR Healthcare Resources* (1997): 10–12.
15. Michael Johnson and Anders Gustafsson, *Improving Customer Satisfaction, Loyalty, and Profit* (New York: Jossey-Bass, 2000).
16. Frederick Reichheld, *The Ultimate Question* (Boston, Massachusetts: Harvard Business School Press, 2006).
17. Paul Nunes and Brian Johnson, "Are Some Customers More Equal than Others?" *Harvard Business Review* (November 2001): 37–50.
18. Shaun Smith and Joel Wheeler, *Managing the Customer Experience* (Upper Saddle River, NJ: Prentice Hall, 2002).
19. Melinda Nykamp, *The Customer Differential* (AMACOM, 2001); and S. Gupta and D. Lehmann, "Customers as Assets," *Journal of International Marketing* (2003).
20. Werner Reinartz and V. Kumar, "The Mismanagement of Customer Loyalty," *Harvard Business Review* (July 2002): 86–94.
21. Reinartz and Kumar, "On the Profitability of Long-Life Customers in a Noncontractual Setting: An Empirical Investigation and Implications for Marketing," *Journal of Marketing* (October 2000): 17–35.
22. Melissa Campanelli, "Happy Returns," *Entrepreneur* (January 2004): 39; and Jill Griffin and Michael Lowenstein, *Customer Winback* (New York: Jossey-Bass, 2001).
23. Ravi Dhar and Rashi Glazer, "Hedging Customers," *Harvard Business Review* (May 2003): 86–92.
24. Steve Schriver, "Customer Loyalty—Going, Going....," *American Demographics* (September 1997): 20–23.
25. Roger Best, "Determining the Marketing IQ of Your Management Team," in *Drive Marketing Excellence* (New York: Institute for International Research, 1994); and Best, *Marketing Excellence Survey, www.mesurvey.com*, 2007.
26. S. Singh, *Market Orientation, Corporate Culture and Business Performance* (Burlington, Vermont: Ashgate, 2004); John C. Narver and Stanley F. Slater, "The Effect of a Market Orientation on Business Profitability," *Journal of Marketing* 54 (October 1990): 20–35; and Stanley F. Slater and John C. Narver, "Does Competitive Environment Moderate the Market Orientation-Performance Relationship," *Journal of Marketing* 58 (January 1994): 46–55.

Present Value Table

Period (N)	DR = 8%	DR = 9%	DR = 10%	DR = 11%	DR = 12%	DR = 13%	DR = 14%	DR = 15%
0	1.000	1.000	1.000	1.000	1.000	1.000	1.000	1.000
1	0.926	0.917	0.909	0.901	0.893	0.885	0.887	0.870
2	0.857	0.842	0.826	0.812	0.797	0.783	0.769	0.756
3	0.794	0.772	0.751	0.731	0.712	0.693	0.675	0.658
4	0.735	0.708	0.683	0.659	0.636	0.613	0.592	0.572
5	0.681	0.650	0.621	0.593	0.567	0.543	0.519	0.497
6	0.630	0.596	0.564	0.535	0.507	0.480	0.456	0.432
7	0.583	0.547	0.513	0.482	0.452	0.425	0.400	0.376
8	0.540	0.502	0.467	0.434	0.404	0.376	0.351	0.327
9	0.500	0.460	0.424	0.391	0.361	0.333	0.308	0.284
10	0.463	0.422	0.386	0.352	0.322	0.295	0.270	0.247
11	0.429	0.388	0.350	0.317	0.287	0.261	0.237	0.215
12	0.397	0.356	0.319	0.286	0.257	0.231	0.208	0.187
13	0.368	0.326	0.290	0.258	0.229	0.204	0.182	0.163
14	0.340	0.299	0.263	0.232	0.205	0.181	0.160	0.141
15	0.315	0.275	0.239	0.209	0.183	0.160	0.140	0.123
16	0.292	0.252	0.218	0.188	0.163	0.141	0.123	0.107
17	0.270	0.231	0.198	0.170	0.146	0.125	0.108	0.093
18	0.250	0.212	0.180	0.153	0.130	0.111	0.095	0.081
19	0.232	0.194	0.164	0.138	0.116	0.098	0.083	0.070
20	0.215	0.178	0.149	0.124	0.104	0.087	0.073	0.061

Present Value Formula: $PV = \dfrac{1}{(1+DR)^N}$

PV = Preset Value of $1.00
N = Number of periods before the $1.00 will be received
DR = Discount Rate (cost of borrowing or desired rate of return)

Example I: N = 5 periods and the Discount Rate (DR) = 10%

$$PV = \frac{1}{(1+0.1)^5} = \frac{1}{1.611} = 0.621\,(\$1.00 \text{ received in 5 years is worth } \$0.621 \text{ today})$$

Example II: N = 2.33 periods and the Discount Rate (DR) = 10%

$$PV = \frac{1}{(1+0.1)^{2.33}} = \frac{1}{1.249} = 0.801\,(\$1.00 \text{ received in 2.33 years is worth } \$0.801 \text{ today})$$

Marketing Performance and Marketing Profitability

■ The reason for marketing's low level of credibility is its lack of disciplined financial-return measures for assessing the value of its contribution to the enterprise.[1]

Two studies in recent years confirm the statement above. The first was a survey of CEOs that showed the number-one concern CEOs had with marketing was its failure to provide measures of its contributions to financial performance.[2] Many CEOs also reported a low regard for marketing at the senior and other levels of management, which may also be due to marketing's failure to demonstrate its role in contributing to profits.

The second study was based on an assessment of the marketing knowledge of over 50,000 marketing managers from *Fortune* 500 companies.[3] Of the four areas of marketing knowledge measured by this study, the managers' poorest performance was in marketing profitability. Their average score was only slightly above the "don't know" level, almost equivalent to having flipped a coin to answer the true-false questions presented.

The results of these two studies, summarized in Figure 2-1, clearly indicate marketing managers and marketing professionals must do more to show the positive impact marketing has on profits. They need to provide credible measures of marketing profitability and marketing's contributions to a business's overall financial performance.

FIGURE 2-1 THE NEED FOR MARKETING PERFORMANCE AND MARKETING PROFITABILITY METRICS

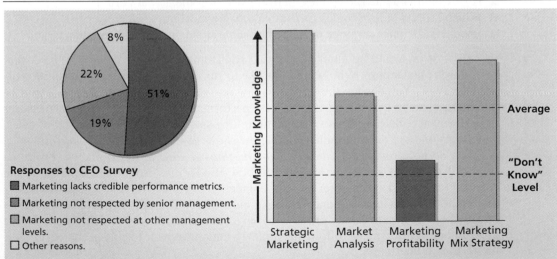

Responses to CEO Survey

■ Marketing lacks credible performance metrics.
■ Marketing not respected by senior management.
□ Marketing not respected at other management levels.
□ Other reasons.

FIGURE 2-2 BIOTRONICS' 3-YEAR FINANCIAL PERFORMANCE

BioTronics' Performance (millions)	Base Year	Year 1	Year 2	Year 3
Sales Revenues	$254	$293	$337	$390
Cost of Goods Sold	$183	$210	$225	$270
Gross Profit	$71	$83	$112	$120
Marketing and Sales Expenses	$30	$35	$40	$45
Other Operating Expenses	$25	$27	$29	$31
Net Profit (before taxes)	$16	$21	$43	$44
Financial Metrics				
Return on Sales (Net Profit/Sales)	6.1%	7.2%	12.8%	11.3%
Asset Turnover (Sales/Assets)	1.20	1.25	1.33	1.38
Return on Assets (Net Profit/Assets)	7.4%	9.0%	17.0%	15.6%

MARKETING PERFORMANCE VERSUS FINANCIAL PERFORMANCE

BioTronics is a $390 million business that manufactures high-tech specialty electronics equipment for the biotech industry. A few years ago, a new management team was put in place after several years of disappointing performance. The new management team reorganized the business and designed programs to lower unit costs, control overhead expenses, and facilitate better management of assets. In addition, the new management team implemented an extensive sales training program that improved the productivity of the sales force from $5 million to $7.5 million per salesperson.

The results were sensational! In 3 years, the new management team increased sales by $136 million and, more importantly, almost tripled net profit before taxes. As shown in Figure 2-2, BioTronics' return on sales grew from 6.1 to 11.3 percent, and its return on assets more than doubled, from 7.4 to 15.6 percent. On the basis of the information in the table:

- How would you rate BioTronics' performance over the 3-year period?
- Which aspects of BioTronics' performance were most impressive?
- Should BioTronics continue to follow the same strategy it used during this period?

Most of us would be quick to say that BioTronics' performance over the 3-year period was outstanding. Who would not like to run a business with that level of profitable growth? Yet, despite the impressive increases in sales and profits, we could be making a mistake by judging BioTronics' performance solely on *financial* measures of performance. Sales revenues, net profit, return on sales, assets as a percent of sales, and return on assets are certainly reliable measures of internal financial performance, but they do not provide an *external or market-based view* of performance. From the financial measures alone, we cannot tell how BioTronics performed relative to the external benchmarks of market growth, competitive pricing, relative product and service quality, and satisfying and retaining customers. The strategy BioTronics used during the 3-year period may or may not have been the best way to achieve profitable growth, and continuing to follow that strategy may or may not achieve the best possible results in the future.

FIGURE 2-3 BIOTRONICS' 3-YEAR MARKETING PERFORMANCE METRICS

Marketing Performance Metrics	Base Year	Year 1	Year 2	Year 3
Market Metrics				
Market Growth (% dollars)	20.5%	22.1%	21.5%	20.8%
BioTronics' Sales Growth	18.3%	15.4%	15.0%	15.7%
Market Share	21.2%	20.0%	18.9%	18.1%
Customer Metrics				
Customer Satisfaction Index	78	73	68	64
Customer Retention (%)	77%	75%	69%	65%
Net Promoter Score	43.0%	39.0%	35.0%	33.0%
Competitiveness Metrics				
Relative Service Quality	19	17	15	11
Relative Product Performance	0	–3	–7	–9
Relative Customer Value	28	25	16	8

In actuality, we can show that BioTronics, as remarkable as its growth seems, should have increased its profits by another $37 million, profits that in effect the corporation and its shareholders lost. BioTronics' hidden, less impressive performance comes to light when marketing performance metrics are applied. Had BioTronics used these marketing performance metrics to help guide its strategic thinking, rather than relying on financial metrics alone, the corporation's profits would have been—and should have been—reflective not only of a company in the rapidly growing biotech market, but of a company that was growing its share of this growing market.

MEASURING AND TRACKING MARKETING PERFORMANCE

To complement its internal financial performance, a business needs a parallel set of external marketing metrics to track its market-based performance.[4] Although these external measures of performance may lack some of the elegance associated with financial accounting, collectively they provide a more strategic view of a business's performance.

Figure 2-3, with its set of marketing performance metrics, paints a picture of BioTronics' 3-year performance much different than the one portrayed by the financial measures shown in Figure 2-2. We can readily see three significant deficiencies. First, the corporation's sales, while showing impressive growth, increased at a rate less than the growth rate for the biotech market. BioTronics actually lost share during the 3-year period. Second, product and service performance each diminished relative to competition. These declines do not necessarily mean that BioTronics' product and service quality actually diminished. Competitors may have simply moved ahead in delivering superior product and service performance. The competition's more rapid progress could have caused BioTronics to lose ground in these two areas, relative to its competitors, leading to a reduction in customer value. Third, customer satisfaction declined, probably due in part to the diminished product and service quality, resulting in a decrease in the customer retention rate.

FIGURE 2-4 MARKET-BASED STRATEGY TO HOLD MARKET SHARE

BioTronics' Performance (millions)	Base Year	Year 1	Year 2	Year 3
Market Demand	$1,200	$1,465	$1,780	$2,150
Market Share	21.2%	21.2%	21.2%	21.2%
Sales Revenues	$254	$310	$377	$455
Cost of Goods Sold	$183	$222	$252	$315
Gross Profit	$71	$88	$125	$140
Marketing and Sales Expenses	$30	$35	$40	$46
Other Operating Expenses	$25	$27	$29	$31
Net Profit (before taxes)	$16	$26	$56	$63
Financial Metrics				
Return on Sales	6.1%	8.5%	15.0%	13.8%
Asset Turnover	1.20	1.25	1.33	1.38
Return on Assets	7.4%	10.6%	19.9%	19.1%
Lost Profits*	$0	–$5	–$13	–$19

*Net Profit in Figure 2-2 minus Net Profit in Figure 2-4.

Instead of the highly favorable impression that the financial metrics presented, we now have a much different opinion of BioTronics' 3-year performance. The corporation's management and shareholders, however, undoubtedly remain unaware of the serious erosion in BioTronics' overall 3-year performance, a performance marked by increased profits, true, but also by customer defection, a decline in market share, and greatly diminished customer value. From the financial metrics, BioTronics' management and shareholders know they made money, but, without the marketing metrics, they don't know how much they really lost and will continue to lose.

A Market-Based Strategy

What would have been the impact of a strategy by BioTronics to hold market share? To hold its base-year 21 percent share in the growing biotech market, the corporation's marketing activities and its product research and development efforts should have kept pace with market demand and competitors. Had BioTronics adequately invested in marketing and R&D to maintain its 21 percent market share, very possibly it would have achieved the results shown in Figure 2-4.

Although the market-based strategy to hold share would have delivered approximately the same return on assets as the internally driven strategy, it would have produced an additional $37 million in net profit (before taxes). This is the $37 million that the corporation essentially gave up in bottom-line cash. Further, BioTronics' "lost" income will be greater over the next 3-year period even if halts the erosion of its market share and market growth completely subsides. If BioTronics' market share continues to erode and the biotech market continues to grow, the "lost profits" over the three years could easily amount to $100 million.

FIGURE 2-5 FINANCIAL VERSUS MARKETING PERFORMANCE METRICS

FINANCIAL METRICS	Performance	MARKETING METRICS	Performance
PROFIT METRICS		**MARKET METRICS**	
• Return on Sales	6.1%	• Market Growth (% dollars)	20.5%
• Return on Assets	7.4%	• BioTronics' Sales Growth	16.2%
• Return on Capital	10.5%	• Market Share	20.3%
COST METRICS		**CUSTOMER METRICS**	
• Cost of Goods Sold (% sales)	72%	• Customer Satisfaction	78
• Marketing & Sales Expenses (% sales)	11.8%	• Customer Retention (%)	77%
• Overhead Expense (% sales)	10%	• Net Promoter Score	43%
ASSET MANAGEMENT METRICS		**COMPETITIVENESS METRICS**	
• Asset Turnover	1.2	• Relative Product Performance	19
• Accounts Receivable (days)	75	• Relative Service Quality	0
• Inventory (days)	60	• Relative Customer Value	28

The BioTronics story underscores the importance of marketing performance metrics. They are the foundation of market-based management. The financial systems of most businesses are set up to track revenues, costs, factory overhead, accounts receivable, operating expenses, and profits, but they usually overlook the fact that a business's customers are its most important asset and the one significant source of positive cash flow. Not attracting new customers during a period of market growth simply means a business will have to work harder and spend more to regain its previous market share. It will need at a sizeable expense to quickly attract a large number of new customers.

MARKETING PERFORMANCE METRICS

Most business have excellent financial performance metrics that report important ratios for profits, costs, and assets, as shown in Figure 2-5. These metrics help the business understand its profitability. These internal, financial performance metrics, however, do not provide any insight into how the business or a product is performing in the market. The marketing performance metrics[5] shown in Figure 2-5 are external metrics, many of which are leading indicators of future financial performance. For example, if customers' intentions to repurchase are declining, customer retention and profitability can be expected to decline.

Marketing performance metrics are at the heart of market-based management because they tell us how a product or business is performing in the market.[6]

Metrics should be necessary (i.e., a company cannot do without them), precise, consistent, and sufficient (i.e., comprehensive) for review purposes.[7]

They are important for two reasons. First, they provide measures of marketing performance, such as customer satisfaction, retention, and loyalty. Second, marketing performance metrics are correlated with profitability. Although they do not directly affect present profitability, they are a barometer of future financial performance. If customer retention is declining, for example, a business will need to attract more new customers to hold market share. Because it is more expensive to acquire new customers than to serve retained customers, profits can be expected to decline even if market share doesn't.

Marketing performance metrics fall into four classes, three of which are presented in Figure 2-5:

1. **Market Metrics**—Market metrics measure a market with respect to current performance and profit impact. For example, a product or business's relative market share is a market metric that assesses a business's market share relative to the business's three top competitors. As shown in Figure 2-6, the higher a business's relative market share, the higher its profits. This metric is discussed in Chapters 6 and 15. Other market metrics are presented in Chapters 3, 6, and 15.
2. **Customer Metrics**—Customer metrics gauge a business or product in terms of its performance with customers. In Chapter 1, we learned about several customer metrics, and others are discussed in Chapters 3, 9, and 15. We already know how they indirectly impact profitability. As shown in Figure 2-6, for example, a business that increases its customer retention rate can expect to improve its profits.
3. **Competitiveness Metrics**—These marketing performance metrics index a business or product against benchmark competitors with respect to product performance, service quality, brand image, cost of purchase, and customer value. For example, Figure 2-6 shows that relative service quality has a positive relationship with profitability. This and other competitiveness metrics are presented in Chapters 4, 6, and 15.

A bit later in this chapter we will discuss the fourth category of marketing performance metrics, called marketing profitability metrics, and Chapter 15 summarizes all the marketing performance metrics with respect to (1) how they are calculated, (2) how they impact profitability, and (3) how they can be used to improve both marketing performance and profitability. With the help of marketing performance tools at the end of each chapter, you will learn to use the marketing performance metrics in building a customized marketing performance scorecard.

Internal Versus External Performance Metrics

To be successful, a business needs both internal and external performance metrics. As presented in Figure 2-5, internal measures are essential for tracking unit costs, expenses, asset utilization, employee and capital productivity, and overall financial profitability. Market-based performance metrics, in contrast, provide a view of a business's external market-based performance. Although CPA firms have done an excellent job in developing procedures for internal measures of performance, the next frontier for either CPA firms or market research firms will be the development of standardized external measures of a business's market-based performance. With the benefit of both sets of metrics available to them, managers, financial analysts, and shareholders will be in a much better position to evaluate a business's marketing effectiveness and overall financial performance.

FIGURE 2-6 MARKETING PERFORMANCE METRICS—PROFIT IMPACT

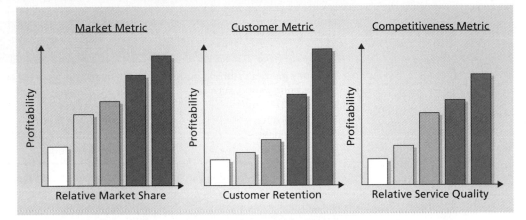

Process Versus Result Marketing Metrics

The primary purpose of marketing metrics is to maintain an ongoing measure of marketing performance and profitability.[8] The results of those metrics that serve as predictors of financial performance are then used in developing a strategy to improve performance. Not all marketing metrics forecast financial performance. There are *process marketing metrics* and *result marketing metrics*,[9] as presented in Figure 2-7. Both are important, but process marketing metrics are especially important because they are indicators of future financial performance. Result marketing metrics correspond more closely to past financial performance, for a fiscal period just ended.

> Results measures tell us where we stand in efforts to achieve goals, but not how we got there or what to do differently.[10]

Product awareness, intentions to purchase, product trial, and customer satisfaction and dissatisfaction, along with customer perceptions of relative product quality, service quality, and customer value, all serve as process marketing metrics. Significant changes in these metrics, positive or negative, generally precede actual changes in customer purchasing behavior. As a result, these process measures of customer thinking and attitude are key indicators of future purchasing behavior and, hence, of future revenue and profit.

A business's customers, for example, can be satisfied but still perceive the value they derive from the business's product, relative to competing alternatives, as steadily diminishing. The business may not have done anything to dissatisfy customers; instead, competitors may have simply improved in delivering customer value by adding benefits without major price increases. The business's customers then perceive the value derived from the business's product as having diminished, and this change in perception inclines customers to buy the competitors' products. With an early warning signal, a market-based business can take corrective action before customers switch. Without process marketing metrics, problems may go undetected until declines in financial performance make it clear, too late, that something went wrong.

Some of the external result marketing metrics are relative market share, market share, customer retention, and revenue per customer, as shown in Figure 2-7. Result marketing

FIGURE 2-7 INTERNAL AND EXTERNAL METRICS AS PROCESS AND RESULT METRICS

Measurement Perspective	Time Perspective	
	PROCESS Metrics	**RESULT Metrics**
INTERNAL Company Metrics	Company metrics occurring during an operating period, such as: ■ Product Defects ■ Late Deliveries ■ Late Payments ■ Inventory Turnover	Company metrics reported at the end of an operating period, such as: ■ Sales Revenues ■ Percent Gross Profit ■ Net Profit Before Tax ■ Return on Assets
EXTERNAL Marketing Metrics	Marketing metrics occurring during an operating period, such as: ■ Customer Awareness ■ Customer Satisfaction ■ Perceived Performance ■ Intent to Repurchase	Marketing metrics reported at the end of an operating period, such as: ■ Relative Market Share ■ Market Share ■ Customer Retention ■ Revenue per Customer

metrics are generally applied at the end of a financial performance period, and each provides a different set of performance diagnostics and insights.

Let's assume sales revenues are increasing ahead of forecast and profits are higher than expected. Most businesses would be pleased with this performance. But if result marketing metrics show the business is losing share in a growing market and a poor customer retention rate is masked by new customer growth, management would have cause for concern. Without result marketing metrics, management has only the limited insights of an internal perspective on end-result performance.

PROFIT IMPACT OF MARKETING PERFORMANCE METRICS

In Figure 2-6, each of the three marketing performance metrics presented correlates with profitability. Most marketing performance metrics do in fact measure underlying forces that drive profit up or down. But only in the most committed market-based management companies do senior managers fully understand the relationship between marketing performance metrics and profitability, giving marketing metrics the same high regard as financial metrics. A business's return on sales tells senior managers how they are doing in producing net profit as a percent of sales, but tracking customer retention reveals how they could improve their return on sales. Each of the marketing performance metrics carries the profitability gene, and a business highly committed to measuring and tracking marketing performance will be rewarded with higher levels of profitability.

Marketing Profitability and Profits

Devising marketing performance metrics that relate to profitability is a significant step forward in addressing the concerns presented in Figure 2-1. The concerns are more fully

FIGURE 2-8 SANTA FE SPORTSWEAR—PROFITS AND MARKETING PROFITABILITY

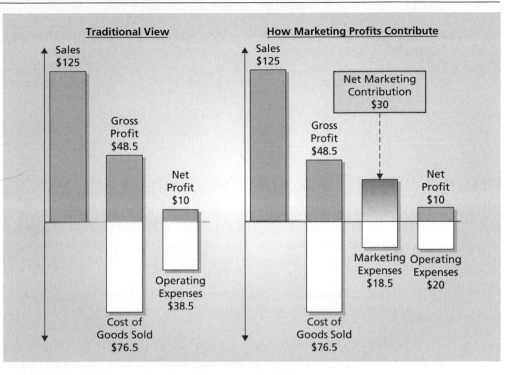

addressed if the metrics include one that specifically measures marketing profitability. Such a measure must operate within the boundaries of reported financial information, and it must clearly demonstrate the contribution that a marketing strategy and the investment in it make to the profit of a business. A marketing profitability metric needs to be strategic. It must be related to the marketing strategy in a way that the marketing profitability of an overall strategy or a particular marketing tactic can be determined and reported with the same credibility as the results of a financial profitability metric.

Let's start with a very basic and traditional view of a business's accounting profit and work toward a measure of its marketing profits.[11] Figure 2-8 and the following calculations show the net profit for Santa Fe Sportswear, a company that manufactures and markets a narrow line of specialty clothing through high-end retail clothing boutiques. To figure the net profit, we can simply deduct the cost of the goods sold and the business's operating expenses from the sales revenue.

> **Net Profit** (before taxes) = Sales Revenue − Cost of Goods Sold − Operating Expenses
> **$10 million** (before taxes) = $125 million − $76.5 million − $38.5 million

We can also figure net profit before taxes by using gross profit as a percent of sales. From sales of $125 million, we deduct the $76.5 million in cost of goods sold to arrive at a gross profit of $48.5 million. This gross profit represents 38.8 percent of the sales revenue. We then multiply sales revenue by the percentage of gross profit and deduct operating expenses. Many businesses prefer this approach since the actual dollar amount for the cost of goods sold changes with sales, but the cost of goods sold as a percentage of gross profit remains relatively constant unless there is a major change in cost or strategy.

Net Profit (before taxes) = Sales Revenues × Percent Gross Profit − Operating Expenses
$10 million (before taxes) = $125 million × 38.8 percent − $38.5 million

By simply separating marketing expenses from the other operating expenses, we can obtain a measure of marketing's contribution to profit.[12] Marketing expenses are all the expenses associated with developing and executing marketing strategies. Figure 2-9 shows these expenses as the costs for marketing administration, sales and service, and advertising. Marketing expenses do not include research and development costs and other operating and corporate overhead expenses.

Knowing the marketing expenses allows us to figure the net marketing contribution (NMC) shown in Figure 2-8. Santa Fe Sportswear's NMC, or marketing profit, was $30 million. The NMC is derived from sales of $125 million and a gross profit of 38.8 percent. The gross profit ($48.5 million) is the amount the marketing strategies produced before deducting marketing expenses. After deducting the $18.5 million in marketing expenses, we have a net marketing contribution to profits of $30 million.

Net Marketing Contribution = Sales Revenues × Percent Gross Profit − Marketing Expenses
$30 million (before taxes) = $125 million × 38.8 percent − $18.5 million

The NMC of $30 million is the only source of positive profit. From it, all other expenses are deducted. For Santa Fe Sportswear, the $30 million produced in marketing profits paid for $20 million in other operating expenses to produce $10 million in net profit before taxes, as shown here.

Net Profit (before taxes) = Net Marketing Contribution − Operating Expenses
$10 million (before taxes) = $30 million − $20 million

Marketing Profitability and Performance Metrics

As with financial performance metrics, we need to convert the overall measure of marketing profitability to standardized ratios that allow for comparing the results of different sales levels. Two marketing profitability metrics that serve this function are marketing ROS (return on sales) and marketing ROI (return on investment).

Marketing ROS computes marketing profitability (NMC) as a percent of sales. For Santa Fe Sportswear, we can figure the marketing ROS in two ways:

Marketing ROS = Net Marketing Contribution / Sales × 100%
        = $30 million / $125 million × 100%
        = **24%**

Marketing ROS = Gross Profit (% of Sales) − Marketing Expenses (% of Sales)
        = 38.8% − 14.8%
        = **24%**

FIGURE 2-9 DEFINITIONS OF MARKETING EXPENSES AND OTHER COSTS

COST OF GOODS SOLD—The cost of producing the volume sold	
Variable Cost	Includes materials, labor, packaging, and all other costs that vary with each unit produced.
Manufacturing Overhead	These are fixed costs associated with equipment, facilities, manpower, and other manufacturing expenses that are in place but do not vary with each unit sold.
MARKETING EXPENSES*—The cost of the marketing strategy for the volume sold	
Marketing Administration	These include marketing management, marketing professionals, and other marketing staff as well as purchased expenses such as market research.
Sales & Service Expenses	These include all sales, support, and customer service expenses needed to execute a market strategy.
Advertising Expenses	These include all advertising, promotions, tradeshow, product, literature, and Web site costs needed to implement the communications of a marketing strategy.
OTHER EXPENSES—The nonproduction/nonmarketing cost of running the business	
Research & Development	Expenses asssociated with developing new products and reengineering existing products.
Corporate Overhead	Overhead (nonproduct) expenses associated with corporate management, staff, legal counsel, corporate advertising, professional services, and the corporation's board of directors.

*Most businesses report Sales, General, and Administrative (SG&A) expenses of which marketing and sales expenses are a large portion.

Marketing ROI computes marketing profitability (NMC) as a percent of expenses. We divide the profit produced by the investment, which is the cost of the marketing effort that produced the marketing profit.[13] As with marketing ROS, we can figure marketing ROI in two ways:

$$\textbf{Marketing ROI} = \text{Net Marketing Contribution / Marketing Expenses} \times 100\%$$
$$= \$30 \text{ million} / \$18.5 \text{ million} \times 100\%$$
$$= \textbf{162\%}$$

$$\textbf{Marketing ROI} = \text{Marketing ROS / Marketing Expenses (\% of sales)}$$
$$= 24\% / 14.8\%$$
$$= \textbf{162\%}$$

As Figure 2-10 shows, these two marketing profitability metrics, along with the actual net marketing contribution, provide marketing managers a way to demonstrate marketing's contribution to profit within the financial framework of the business and

FIGURE 2-10 MARKETING PROFITABILITY METRICS

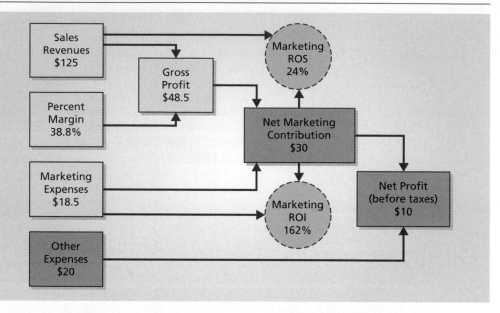

therefore in a way familiar to senior management. Let's next examine how NMC, marketing ROS, and marketing ROI might be used in a business discussion of profits.

Marketing Profitability and Product Lines

Santa Fe Sportswear has five product lines contributing to the corporation's total sales of $125 million. Overall, the corporation is profitable, but two product lines have not performed well. In response, the senior management team has scheduled a meeting to review product line profitability. In preparation for the meeting, the finance manager has prepared a product line profitability summary, presented as the first part of Figure 2-11, and plans to make the following argument:

> We are wasting resources on the casual shorts and knitted sweaters product lines. One makes no money and the other loses money. I recommend we drop both product lines and focus our efforts on the profitable product lines.

Would this be a good decision? How can the marketing manager present a different interpretation of the profit performance of the casual shorts and knitted sweaters product lines?

Using net marketing contribution as a measure of profitability, the marketing manager could present the same information as the finance manager, but with marketing expenses separated from other expenses. The marketing manager could show the marketing profitability for each product line, as in the second part of Figure 2-11.

Let's look more closely at the marketing profitability for just the casual shorts line. If this product were dropped, what impact would the decision have on profit? While the line's overall profit before taxes is a minus $1 million, this line is producing a marketing profit of plus $1 million. The marketing profit does not cover the $2 million in unrelated operating expenses, but the casual shorts line does make a contribution to profit of $1 million. To fully understand marketing profitability and how marketing strategies impact it, we need to examine more closely the marketing elements that impact marketing profitability. To do this, we need to systematically break down the elements of profitability and market strategy and examine how they interact.[14]

$$\begin{aligned}
\text{Net Profit} \atop \text{Before Taxes} \ &= \text{Sum of Net Marketing Contributions for All Products} - \text{Operating Expenses} \\
&= (\text{NMC } 1 + \text{NMC } 2 + \text{NMC } 3 + \text{NMC } 4 + \text{NMC } 5) - \text{Operating Expenses} \\
&= (\$15.5 \text{ million} + \$6 \text{ million} + \$5.5 \text{ million} + \$1\text{million} + \$2 \text{ million}) - \$20 \text{ million} \\
&= \textbf{\$10 million}
\end{aligned}$$

Perhaps the best way to understand how the marketing profit from casual shorts contributes to corporate profit is to compute overall net profit without the casual shorts product line. As shown in the following equation, the overall marketing profit drops by $1 million but the operating expenses remain at $20 million. This results in lowering net profit before taxes from $10 million to $9 million. Even worse, if both the casual shorts and the knitted sweaters product lines were eliminated, net profit before taxes would fall to $7 million.

$$\begin{aligned}
\text{Net Profit} \atop \text{Before Taxes} \ &= (\text{NMC } 1 + \text{NMC } 2 + \text{NMC } 3 + \text{NMC } 4 + \text{NMC } 5) - \text{Operating Expenses} \\
&= (\$15.5 \text{ million} + \$6 \text{ million} + \$5.5 \text{ million} + \$0 + \$2 \text{ million}) - \$20 \text{ million} \\
&= \textbf{\$9 million}
\end{aligned}$$

Managing Marketing Profitability—A Product Focus

Net marketing contribution viewed from a financial perspective is important because senior management and finance managers can in this way understand marketing's contribution to corporate profit. But to fully manage marketing profitability, we need to expand the definition of NMC to include other factors that a marketing manager must consider in building a profitable marketing strategy. Besides the financial perspective of NMC, we also need a *strategic* perspective.

The first step is to break down sales into more meaningful marketing variables. As shown in the following equation, NMC can be separated into its component variables. Each of these marketing variables has strategic importance in shaping the profit impact of a marketing strategy.[15]

$$\begin{aligned}
\text{Net Marketing} \atop \text{Contribution} \ &= \frac{\text{Sales}}{\text{Revenues}} \times \frac{\text{Percent}}{\text{Margin}} - \frac{\text{Marketing}}{\text{Expenses}} \\[6pt]
& \underbrace{\frac{\text{Market}}{\text{Demand}} \times \frac{\text{Market}}{\text{Share}} \times \frac{\text{Average}}{\text{Selling Price}} \times \frac{\text{Channel}}{\text{Discount}}}
\end{aligned}$$

Market Demand (units)—The size (number of units purchased per year) in the served market.

Market Share (%)—The business's market share of the served market.

FIGURE 2-11 SANTA FE SPORTSWEAR—PRODUCT LINE MARKETING PROFITABILITY

FINANCE MANAGER'S PRESENTATION OF PRODUCT LINE PROFITABILITY

Santa Fe Sportswear Performance (millions)	Khaki Pants	Wind Breakers	Classic Polo	Casual Shorts	Knitted Sweaters	Company Total
Sales Revenues	$60.0	$25.0	$15.0	$10.0	$15.0	$125.0
Cost of Goods Sold	$37.5	$16.0	$7.5	$8.0	$11.0	$80.0
Gross Profit	$22.5	$9.0	$7.5	$2.0	$4.0	$45.0
Operating Expenses	$17.0	$7.0	$4.0	$3.0	$4.0	$35.0
Net Profit (before taxes)	$5.5	$2.0	$3.5	–$1.0	$0.0	$10.0

MARKETING MANAGER'S PRESENTATION OF PRODUCT LINE PROFITABILITY

Santa Fe Sportswear Performance (millions)	Khaki Pants	Wind Breakers	Classic Polo	Casual Shorts	Knitted Sweaters	Company Total
Sales Revenues	$60.0	$25.0	$15.0	$10.0	$15.0	$125.0
Percent Margin	40.0%	40.0%	50.0%	25.0%	30.0%	38.8%
Gross Profit	$24.0	$10.0	$7.5	$2.5	$4.5	$48.5
Marketing Expenses	$8.5	$4.0	$2.0	$1.5	$2.5	$18.5
Net Marketing Contribution	$15.5	$6.0	$5.5	$1.0	$2.0	$30.0
Operating Expenses	$10.0	$4.0	$2.0	$2.0	$2.0	$20.0
Net Profit (before taxes)	$5.5	$2.0	$3.5	–$1.0	$0.0	$10.0

Average Selling Price ($ per unit)—The price paid by end customers who will use the product.

Channel Discount (1–CD%)—One minus the percent channel discount is the percent of the market sales that the company will obtain after compensating channel intermediaries for channel services, such as sales, distribution, and customer service.

Percent Margin (%)—Gross profit as a percentage. It is also equal to (price – unit cost)/price.

Marketing Expenses ($)—The investment in marketing to produce a 12.5 percent market share and a net marketing contribution of $15.5 million.

Perhaps the best way to understand a strategic view of marketing profitability is to apply it to the Santa Fe Sportswear khaki pants product line. As shown in the following equation, net sales of $60 million for the khaki pants line is the result of a certain market demand (12 million units), the market share (12.5%), the average selling price ($80), and the channel discount (50%). With an average margin of 40 percent, the product line produced a gross profit of $24 million, as shown in Figure 2-12. By deducting from this gross profit the cost of the marketing effort ($8.5 million), we arrive at a net marketing contribution of $15.5 million.

FIGURE 2-12 MANAGING MARKETING PROFITABILITY

Santa Fe Sportswear Performance (millions)	Khaki Pants	Wind Breakers	Classic Polo	Casual Shorts	Knitted Sweaters	Company Total
Market Demand (million)	12.0	10.0	16.7	20.0	6.7	65.3
Market Share	12.5%	5.0%	3.0%	2.0%	3.0%	5.3%
Unit Volume Sold	1.5	0.5	0.5	0.4	0.2	3.1
Average Selling Price	$80.00	$100.00	$60.00	$50.00	$150.00	$80.65
Channel Discount	50%	50%	50%	50%	50%	50%
Net Selling Price	$40.00	$50.00	$30.00	$25.00	$75.00	$40.32
Sales Revenues	$60.0	$25.0	$15.0	$10.0	$15.0	$125.0
Cost per Unit	$24.00	$30.00	$15.00	$18.75	$10.50	$24.68
Percent Margin	40.0%	40.0%	50.0%	25.0%	30.0%	38.8%
Gross Profit	$24.0	$10.0	$7.5	$2.5	$4.5	$48.5
Marketing Expenses	$8.5	$4.0	$2.0	$1.5	$2.5	$18.5
Net Marketing Contribution	$15.5	$6.0	$5.5	$1.0	$2.0	$30.0
Operating Expenses	$10.0	$4.0	$2.0	$2.0	$2.0	$20.0
Net Profit (before taxes)	$5.5	$2.0	$3.5	–$1.0	$0.0	$10.0
Marketing Profitability Metrics						
Marketing ROS	25.8%	24.0%	36.7%	10.0%	13.3%	24.0%
Marketing ROI	182%	150%	275%	67%	80%	162%

$$\frac{\text{NMC}}{\text{Khaki Pants}} = \frac{\text{Market}}{\text{Demand}} \times \frac{\text{Market}}{\text{Share}} \times \frac{\text{Average}}{\text{Selling Price}} \times \frac{\text{Channel}}{\text{Discount}} \times \frac{\text{Percent}}{\text{Margin}} - \frac{\text{Marketing}}{\text{Expenses}}$$

$$= \underbrace{\$12\text{ million} \times 12.5\% \times \$80 \times (1-50\%)}_{\substack{\$60\text{ million}\\ \text{Net Sales}}} \times 40\% - \$8.5\text{ million}$$

$$= \$60\text{ million} \times 0.4 - \$8.5\text{ million}$$

$$= \textbf{\$15.5 million}$$

The marketing ROS for khaki pants is 25.8 percent, and the marketing ROI is 182 percent, both above the product-line averages for marketing ROS (24 percent) and marketing ROI (162 percent). As the numbers in Figure 2-12 show and the diagram in Figure 2-13 illustrates, the khaki pants product line is the second-best line with respect to these two marketing profitability metrics. The best is the classic polo line, which produces a marketing ROS of 36.7 percent and a marketing ROI of 275 percent. The casual shorts line produces the lowest results when these two marketing profitability metrics are applied.

Managing Marketing Profitability—A Customer Focus

The accounting systems of most businesses are built around production. Revenues and costs are associated with a product or service. Costs not directly related to production are allocated to the product or service using agreed-upon accounting rules that have nothing to do with satisfying customers or making money. To develop market strategies

FIGURE 2-13 PRODUCT LINE–MARKETING PROFITABILITY PORTFOLIO

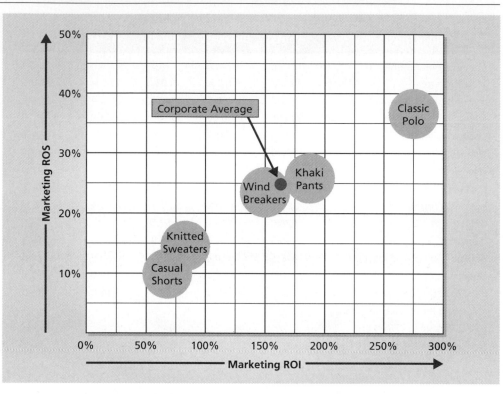

that satisfy customers and grow profits, we need an alternate accounting system, one that will better serve the marketing function in managing marketing profitability. This system will be a more meaningful method for tracking a business's revenues, variable costs, fixed expenses, and net profit.

While it is convenient to report performance by product, for several reasons we should also track performance by markets and customers. It is the customer who, when buying a product or service, produces cash flow for a business. Regardless of the appeal level of a business's products or services, the number of potential customers in any given market is finite. The objective of a marketing strategy should be to attract, satisfy, and retain target customers in a way that grows the profits of the business.

By using customers and the market segments they belong to as the accounting units, we can acquire a more insightful understanding of market-based profitability and ways to grow it. But let's first see what a market-based profitability statement would look like.

In Figure 2-14, we have rebuilt the performance of Santa Fe Sportswear around the three markets served. We notice at once that the product-based and market-based accounting approaches produce the same total revenue, gross profit, net marketing contribution, and net profit. Each approach, however, presents its own insights for market-based managers. Both approaches are important and meaningful. The product-focused accounting statement represented by Figure 2-12 helps us understand product unit volume, product

FIGURE 2-14 CUSTOMER-FOCUSED MARKETING PROFITABILITY

Santa Fe Sportswear Performance	Traditional Buyer	Fashion Buyer	Trend Setter	Company Total
Market Demand (customers)	7,000,000	5,890,000	8,000,000	20,890,000
Market Share	9.0%	3.5%	6.0%	6.3%
Customer Volume	630,000	206,150	480,000	1,316,150
Average Revenue per Customer	$180.00	$360.00	$130.00	$189.96
Channel Discount	50%	50%	50%	50%
Net Revenue per Customer	$90.00	$180.00	$65.00	$94.98
Sales Revenues	$56.7	$37.1	$31.2	$125.0
Cost of Goods per Customer	$54.00	$115.38	$39.00	$58.14
Percent Margin	40.0%	35.9%	40.0%	38.8%
Gross Profit	$22.7	$13.3	$12.5	$48.5
Marketing Expenses	$7.0	$6.5	$5.0	$18.5
Net Marketing Contribution	$15.7	$6.8	$7.5	$30.0
Operating Expenses	$8.0	$6.5	$5.5	$20.0
Net Profit (before taxes)	$7.7	$0.3	$2.0	$10.0
Marketing Profitability Metrics				
Marketing ROS	27.7%	18.4%	24.0%	24.0%
Marketing ROI	224%	105%	150%	162%

price, and product unit margin. The customer-focused accounting statement represented by Figure 2-14 helps us understand customer demand, customer share, customer volume, revenue per customer, and variable cost per customer. With the customer-focused approach, we readily see that all three market segments produced a positive net profit, but in the product-focused statement two product lines—casual shorts and knitted sweaters—did not produce a positive net profit. But because each of the three marketing segments in Figure 2-14 has a positive NMC, eliminating any product would result in a lower net profit for its market segment and lower overall profits for Santa Fe Sportswear.

PROFIT IMPACT OF MARKETING STRATEGIES

Recognizing the product or customer as a unit of analysis, we can evaluate different aspects of net marketing contribution in order to gain more insight into the development of marketing strategies designed to grow profitability.[16] As shown in Figure 2-14, each element of the NMC equation offers the potential to create a marketing strategy that will improve profit. The NMC of any proposed strategy must exceed the current NMC in order to increase a business's net profit, a fact that limits the number of fundamental marketing strategies a business can use.

Consider Santa Fe Sportswear's performance among traditional buyers, as presented in Figure 2-14. Traditional buyers produced an NMC of $15.7 million, derived from net sales of $56.7 million, a 40 percent margin, and $7 million in marketing expenses. Sales revenues were a result of a market demand of 7 million customers, a 9 percent market share, an average revenue per customer of $180, and a 50 percent channel discount.

$$
\begin{aligned}
\underset{\substack{\text{Traditional} \\ \text{Buyer}}}{\text{NMC}} &= \underbrace{\underset{\text{Customers}}{\text{7 million}} \times \underset{\text{Share}}{9\%} \times \underset{\text{per Customer}}{\$180} \times \underset{\text{Discount}}{50\%}}_{\substack{\$56.7 \text{ million} \\ \text{Net Sales}}} \times \underset{\text{Margin}}{40\%} - \underset{\text{Marketing Expenses}}{\$7 \text{ million}} \\[2mm]
&= \$56.7 \text{ million} \times 0.4 - \$7 \text{ million} \\
&= \mathbf{\$15.7 \ million}
\end{aligned}
$$

A marketing strategy to grow the marketing profitability of traditional buyers could address market demand, market share, revenue per customer, channel discounts, the variable costs affecting margin, marketing expenses, or any combination of these factors.

We are now ready to discuss the market-based strategies suggested in Figure 2-15 and assess how selected strategies in each area might affect the profits of Santa Fe Sportswear.

Market Growth Strategy

In many markets, a significant part of the challenge is bringing more customers into the market. We can safely assume, for example, that a major reason for the growth during recent years in the profitability of businesses that offer portable music players, cellular telephones, and personal computers has been a strategy by these businesses to increase the number of potential customers by growing market demand. In many other markets as well, marketing strategies to hold or grow share while attracting new customers to the market offer one way to grow net profit. Profits will grow, as we have seen, only if the NMC produced by the proposed marketing strategy exceeds the current NMC.

For example, the Santa Fe Sportswear's traditional-buyer marketing manager believes market demand could be grown from 7 to 8 million customers with a $1 million increase in marketing expenses. If this growth in demand could be achieved, and Santa Fe Sportswear could maintain a 9 percent share among traditional buyers, the number of these buyers would grow to 720,000, an increase of 90,000 customers. But would this strategy improve the marketing profitability for the traditional-buyer segment and increase the business's overall profitability?

From the following calculations we can see that this would indeed be a worthwhile marketing strategy. NMC would increase by $2.2 million, from $15.7 to $17.9 million. The gain of 90,000 new customers, with their additional contribution, would more than justify the additional $1 million in marketing expenses required to achieve this growth.

FIGURE 2-15 MARKETING STRATEGIES AND MARKETING PROFITABILITY

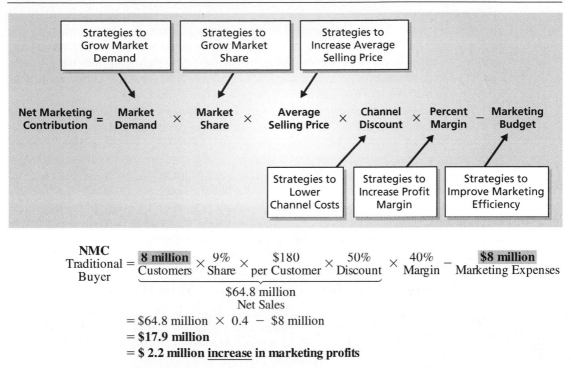

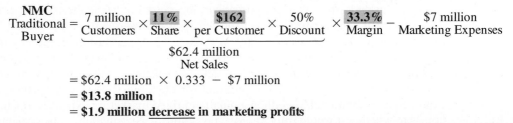

In some instances, a business may induce a lower NMC in the short run in order to build demand and future profits. However, the discounted cash flow projected by the long-term strategy has to exceed that of the current strategy for this approach to be viable.

Market Share Strategy

Perhaps the most common marketing strategy for increasing revenue and profit is market penetration. For any served market, managers develop a strategy to grow the business's share of its served market. The same rules apply: A market penetration strategy is likely to cost money, margin, or both, and the NMC of the penetration strategy needs to exceed the current NMC for the business to improve profitability. For example, in the traditional-buyer segment, Santa Fe Sportswear might consider a strategy to increase its market share from 9 to 11 percent by lowering prices 10 percent. As the calculations show, the additional 2 percent in market share would fall far short of offsetting the lower margin—the margin falls from 40 to 33.3 percent—that would result from the 10 percent price reduction. The outcome would be a $1.9 million decrease in NMC, from $15.7 million to $13.8 million.

Customer Revenue Strategy

In a mature market with a strong share position, a business may find it unprofitable to grow market demand or market share. The business's customers, however, remain its best strategic asset, and an examination of customer needs might identify new products and services to better serve those needs and grow revenues. In evaluating the overall profit impact of such a marketing strategy, a business would project the required increase in the average cost per unit and the higher price that could be attained.

A business would also need to consider the likelihood of greater marketing expenses. Additional advertising dollars would be necessary to make existing customers aware of new products or services, or of improvements in existing products and services. Managers must examine all aspects of a strategy to increase price per unit to ensure that the strategy leads to an increase in net marketing contribution.

To illustrate the profit impact of a strategy to build revenue per customer, suppose that in the traditional-buyer segment customers generally were not fully aware of the high quality of the product line. With more effective advertising, the average revenue per customer could be increased from $180 to $200. While this raises the margin from 40 to 46 percent, an additional $3 million in marketing expenses would be needed to communicate product quality and design. As shown, this market strategy would produce an incremental gain of $3.3 million in NMC when compared with the current NMC of $15.7 million.

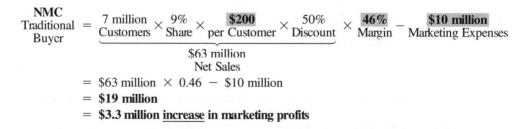

$$
\begin{aligned}
\text{NMC}\\
\text{Traditional} &= \underbrace{\frac{7\text{ million}}{\text{Customers}} \times \frac{9\%}{\text{Share}} \times \frac{\$200}{\text{per Customer}} \times \frac{50\%}{\text{Discount}}}_{\substack{\$63\text{ million}\\\text{Net Sales}}} \times \frac{46\%}{\text{Margin}} - \frac{\$10\text{ million}}{\text{Marketing Expenses}}\\
\text{Buyer}
\end{aligned}
$$

$= \$63\text{ million} \times 0.46 - \$10\text{ million}$

$= \$19\text{ million}$

$= \$3.3\text{ million }\underline{\text{increase}}\text{ in marketing profits}$

Cost Reduction Strategy

Another way to grow net profit is by lowering the variable cost per unit. Perhaps transportation costs and sales commissions could be lowered with a new distribution strategy for a given market or market segment. This strategy would lower the variable cost per unit and increase margin per unit, but the business would need to be certain the new distribution strategy will not adversely impact the level of customer satisfaction. If customer satisfaction declines, so will customer retention—and in the long run, net profit will erode even though the business achieves a lower variable cost and higher margin per unit. A successful marketing strategy must hold or increase customer satisfaction while growing net profit through increases in NMC.

Continuing with Santa Fe Sportswear, the marketing manager for the traditional-buyer segment is evaluating a new order-entry and billing system that would lower the variable cost of serving customers by an average of $9 per customer, thereby increasing margin from 40 to 45 percent. The marketing manager believes the new system would significantly improve the accuracy and detail of customer bills, and it would make the ordering process easier and more pleasant for customers. This new system, however, would cost an additional $1 million annually in fixed marketing expenses, raising a question as to whether it would truly improve profitability. By calculating the projected NMC, we find that the new order-entry and billing system would increase the net marketing contribution by $1.8 million. Putting the system in place makes good sense financially and very probably in terms of customer satisfaction as well.

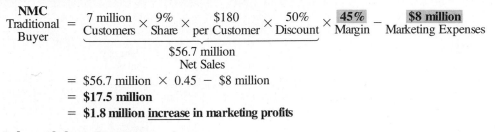

$$
\begin{aligned}
\text{NMC Traditional Buyer} &= \underbrace{\underset{\text{Customers}}{7\text{ million}} \times \underset{\text{Share}}{9\%} \times \underset{\text{per Customer}}{\$180} \times \underset{\text{Discount}}{50\%}}_{\substack{\$56.7\text{ million} \\ \text{Net Sales}}} \times \underset{\text{Margin}}{45\%} - \underset{\text{Marketing Expenses}}{\$8\text{ million}}
\end{aligned}
$$

= $56.7 million × 0.45 − $8 million

= **$17.5 million**

= **$1.8 million increase in marketing profits**

Advertising Strategy

A business could also improve the profitability of its marketing efforts by using advertising to grow market share. For the example we will use, the business's proposed strategy calls for an additional $2 million in marketing expenses solely for advertising to increase market share from 9 to 10 percent. In this case, we will use the marketing profitability equation to solve for the market share needed to produce the current level of marketing profit (an NMC of $15.7 million).

As shown in the following equation, the strategy would require a 9.8 percent market share to pay for the increase in marketing expenses just to maintain the same level of marketing profit. Even achieving the goal of a 10 percent market share would provide very little incremental profit. This strategy would lower marketing profit if the market share achieved is less than 9.8 percent. The risk of not obtaining the full 10 percent share outweighs the small profit that would result.

$$
\underset{\substack{\$15.7\text{ million} \\ \text{NMC} \\ \text{Traditional} \\ \text{Buyer}}}{} = \underset{\text{Customers}}{7\text{ million}} \times \underset{\text{(MS\%)}}{\text{Market Share}} \times \underset{\text{Customer}}{\substack{\$180 \\ \text{per}}} \times \underset{\text{Discount}}{50\%} \times \underset{\text{Margin}}{40\%} - \underset{\text{Marketing Expenses}}{\$9\text{ million}}
$$

$15.7 million = **MS%** × $252 million − $9 million

MS% = ($15.7 million + $9 million) / $252 million

= **9.8% Market Share**

With this market share, the business makes the same marketing profit of $15.7 million

Channel Strategy

Still another way to improve the profitability of a marketing strategy is to bypass the channel and thereby eliminate most of the channel cost. In Figure 2-16, the current strategy for the traditional buyer produces market sales of $113.5 million. Half of these sales dollars are offset by the current indirect channel strategy, leaving $56.75 million in net sales. This results in a gross profit of $22.7 (40% margin). Deducting the marketing expenses of $7 million produces a net marketing contribution of $15.7 million.

An alternate channel strategy could make use of the Internet as the point of purchase. This direct channel strategy could propose lowering the average selling price from $180 to $120, with the business shipping directly to customers. The channel cost in this case would drop to 10 percent of sales. Although prices are reduced by 33 percent, eliminating most of the indirect channel discount of 50 percent allows the business to improve net sales from $57.75 million to $68 million. The gross profit increases due to

FIGURE 2-16 MARKETING PROFITABILITY—CHANNEL STRATEGIES

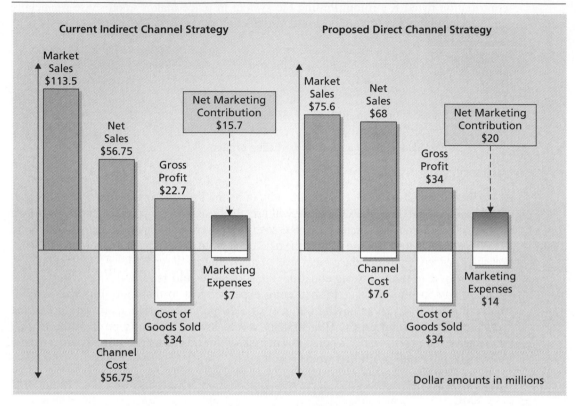

both higher net sales and higher percent margins (40% to 50%). Marketing expenses, however, will need to double to more aggressively advertise the price reductions and the online purchasing venue. If successfully implemented, this channel strategy would be more profitable than the current indirect channel strategy, as shown in the following equation. Perhaps an even better strategy would be to separate the traditional buyer segment into two groups based on preferred point of purchase and price, and then use two channels to serve this market segment.

$$
\begin{array}{c}
\text{NMC} \\
\text{Traditional} \\
\text{Buyer}
\end{array}
=
\underbrace{
\frac{7 \text{ million}}{\text{Customers}} \times \frac{9\%}{\text{Share}} \times \frac{\$120}{\text{per Customer}} \times \frac{90\%}{\text{Discount}}
}_{\substack{\$68.0 \text{ million} \\ \text{Net Sales}}}
\times \frac{50\%}{\text{Margin}} - \frac{\$14 \text{ million}}{\text{Marketing Expenses}}
$$

$$= \$68.0 \text{ million} \times 0.5 - \$14 \text{ million}$$

$$= \textbf{\$20 million}$$

$$= \textbf{\$4.3 million } \underline{\textbf{increase}} \textbf{ in marketing profits}$$

BENCHMARKING MARKETING PROFITABILITY

Although the net marketing contribution allows us to measure the profit impact of a marketing strategy, a comparison of NMCs of competing businesses would enable a business to better understand its marketing efficiency in producing marketing profits. The following

FIGURE 2-17 BENCHMARKING MARKETING PROFITABILITY

Performance (millions)	Rossignol	Salomon	K2	Head	Average
Sales Revenues	$556	$807	$582	$388	$584
Percent Margin	64%	41%	30%	40%	44%
Gross Profit	$356	$331	$175	$155	$257
Marketing Performance					
Marketing Expenses (% sales)	19.9%	19.8%	14.8%	28.5%	19.9%
Net Marketing Contribution	$245	$171	$88	$45	$141
Marketing ROS	44%	21%	15%	12%	24%
Marketing ROI	222%	107%	103%	40%	121%
Financial Performance					
Return on Sales	11.3%	4.8%	2.7%	−0.7%	5.0%
Return on Equity	61.7%	30.3%	6.9%	−1.1%	24.0%
Return on Invested Capital	28.5%	12.3%	5.2%	−0.8%	11.0%

SG&A (Sales General, and Administrative) expenses were used to estimate marketing expenses as businesses rarely report marketing expenses separately in their financial statements.

shows one year's marketing profits produced by Rossignol, a major manufacturer of sports equipment.

$$\begin{array}{l} \text{Net Marketing} \\ \text{Contribution} \\ \text{Rossignol} \end{array} = \frac{\text{Sales}}{\text{Revenues}} \times \begin{array}{l}\text{Percent}\\\text{Gross}\\\text{Profit}\end{array} - \begin{array}{l}\text{Marketing}\\\text{Expenses}\end{array}$$

$$= \$556 \text{ million} \times 64\% - \$110.6 \text{ million}$$

$$= \textbf{\$245 million}$$

$$\textbf{Marketing ROS} = \textbf{44\%}$$

$$\textbf{Marketing ROI} = \textbf{222\%}$$

While Rossignol can compare this performance with another year and report the results of having applied marketing profitability metrics by product line, a more strategic insight could be gained by comparing the business's performance with that of competitors.

Marketing Return on Sales

The first marketing profitability metric we will benchmark is marketing return on sales. This marketing profitability metric, as we saw earlier, is the difference between percent margin and percent of sales spent on marketing. Rossignol's marketing ROS of 44.1 percent is derived from a gross margin of 64 percent and marketing expenses of 19.9 percent.

What level of marketing ROS indicates good performance? Let's also examine the marketing ROS of three competitors. Figure 2-17 shows the sales, gross profit, and marketing profitability for Rossignol and its three major competitors in the sports equipment market. The following shows the marketing ROS of each and how it was determined.

Rossignol, although not the leader in sales, produced the best marketing ROS at 44.1 percent. Its marketing ROS was due to a very high profit margin and an average

Competitor	Marketing ROS	=	% Gross Margin	−	%Marketing Expenses
Rossignol	**44.1%**	=	64%	−	19.9%
Salomon	**21.2%**	=	41%	−	19.8%
K2	**15.2%**	=	30%	−	14.8%
Head	**11.5%**	=	40%	−	28.5%

level of marketing expenses as a percent of sales. Salomon had the second-best market-ing ROS, based on a 41 percent profit margin and an average level of marketing expenses as a percent of sales. Head had approximately the same percent profit margin as K2 but incurred much higher marketing expenses as a percent of sales (28.5%), resulting in only an 11.5 percent marketing ROS. K2 had the lowest profit margin (30%) and lowest marketing expenses as a percent of sales (14.8%). The net result was a mar-keting ROS of 15.2 percent, just slightly lower than Salomon's.

When we compare the marketing profits of these four competitors, we readily see that overall profitability corresponds with marketing ROS. In each case, the higher the market-ing ROS, the better the financial performance as measured by the three financial perfor-mance metrics shown in Figure 2-17. Benchmarking marketing ROS enables a business to judge its marketing profitability relative to other businesses in the same industry.

Marketing Return on Investment

Another marketing profitability metric we want to consider is marketing ROI. Again, we saw earlier that this metric can be computed for a business or product by dividing the net marketing contribution by the marketing expenses. It can also be computed by dividing the marketing ROS by marketing expenses as a percent of sales, as shown here for each of the four competitors in the sports equipment market.

Competitor	Marketing ROI	=	Marketing ROS	÷	%Marketing Expenses
Rossignol	**222%**	=	44.1%	÷	19.9%
Salomon	**107%**	=	21.2%	÷	19.8%
K2	**103%**	=	15.2%	÷	14.8%
Head	**40%**	=	11.5%	÷	28.5%

Rossignol had the highest marketing ROS, and it also produced the highest marketing ROI, more than double that of Salomon and K2. Head, with a low marketing ROS and high marketing expenses as a percent of sales, produced a marketing ROI well below the average of 121 percent shown in Figure 2-17. When we compare the marketing ROI of the four competitors, we see that marketing ROI, like marketing ROS, corresponds with over-all profitability as measured by the three financial performance metrics in Figure 2-17.

Figure 2-18 uses both marketing ROS and marketing ROI to illustrate the marketing profitability of each competitor. This benchmark portfolio of marketing profitability graphically presents the four competitors' marketing profitability relative to each other. A diagram similar to this, showing the return on invested capital for any business's major competitors, would give management a clear understanding that higher levels of market-ing profitability contribute to higher levels of financial performance.

FIGURE 2-18 BENCHMARKING MARKETING PROFITABILITY METRICS

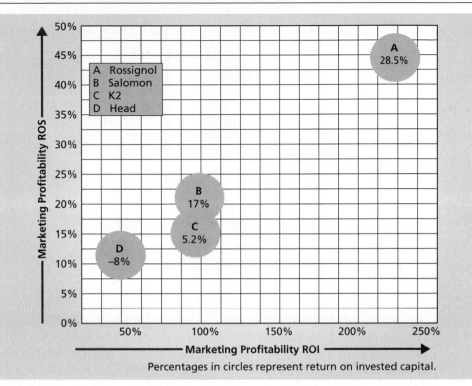

Profit Impact of Marketing Profitability Metrics

The bar charts in Figure 2-19 for a sampling of major companies further validate the profit impact of marketing ROS and marketing ROI. For most companies in this sampling, marketing and sales expenses were not available, so the charts use sales, general, and administrative (SG&A) expenses, of which marketing and sales expenses are the majority. Using these data, the bottom third of the companies in marketing ROS achieved less than a 10 percent ROS and earned an average pre-tax return on investment (ROI) of less than 5 percent. The middle third in marketing ROS had an average pre-tax ROI of roughly 17 percent. However, the top third in marketing ROS, those companies with a marketing ROS greater than 25 percent, produced an average pre-tax ROI of 30 percent.

The pre-tax ROI also varied with different levels of marketing ROI. The bottom third in marketing ROI (less than 100%) had an ROI less than 5 percent, while the top third (greater than 250%) had an ROI of 30 percent.

A market-based business engages in three distinguishing practices:

1. It tracks market-based measures of marketing performance;
2. It measures marketing profits by product, market, or both; and
3. It organizes around markets rather than products.

Without an external set of market-based performance metrics, a business will never know its market performance. For BioTronics, reliance solely on traditional measures

FIGURE 2-19 FINANCIAL PERFORMANCE AND MARKETING PROFITABILITY METRICS

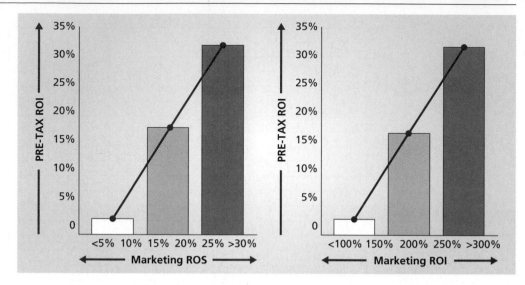

of internal performance cost the business and its shareholders $37 million in net profit. For any business desiring the benefits of operating as a market-based business, the development of a key set of external marketing metrics is essential. These marketing performance metrics include *process* marketing metrics, which typically precede financial performance measurement, and *result* marketing metrics, which are more likely to coincide with financial performance measurements.

Managing Marketing Performance and Marketing Profitability

Marketing managers play a strategic role in shaping the overall profit of a company. This role, however, extends beyond sales, distribution, and advertising. Marketing managers also must be able to demonstrate the contributions that marketing makes to a business's financial performance.

Figure 2-20 illustrates the way in which a market-based business makes marketing metrics central to its decision-making and planning. A market-based business thinks and behaves in terms of marketing performance because its managers know that success rests upon marketing performance. Internal financial metrics are valuable in that they track what has happened, but by themselves they provide a limited view of the reasons for a particular level of profit performance. The key to understanding the underlying forces contributing to financial performance, and the key to superior financial performance, are the marketing performance metrics we have been discussing, as well as others we will examine in later chapters.

No matter how well marketing managers may do in delivering high levels of marketing performance, senior management and finance managers will want tangible proof of

FIGURE 2-20 PROFIT IMPACT OF MARKETING PERFORMANCE AND MARKETING PROFITABILITY

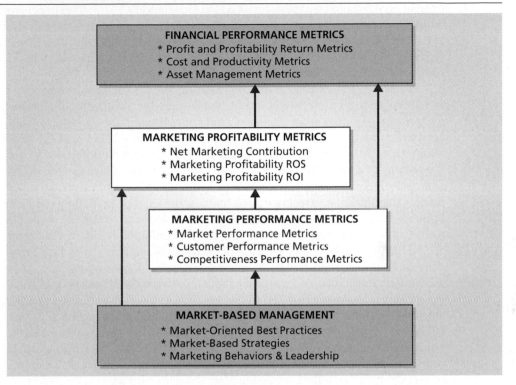

marketing's contributions to overall profit. In response, net marketing contribution offers a financially derived performance metric. As illustrated in Figure 2-20, marketing profitability metrics have a direct linkage to company profit. It is pretty simple: The more money a marketing strategy produces, the more money there is for other expenses and profits.

To operationally expand net marketing contribution as a corporate metric, we presented marketing ROS and marketing ROI. These two marketing profitability metrics allow management to evaluate the effectiveness of various market strategies and to compare marketing efficiency across products and markets. They also enable a business to benchmark its marketing productivity against competitors and top performers it would like to emulate.

■ Summary

A market-based business engages in three distinguishing practices:

1. It tracks market-based measures of marketing performance;
2. It measures marketing profits by product, market, or both; and
3. It organizes around markets rather than products.

Without an external set of market-based performance metrics, a business will never know its marketing performance. For BioTronics, reliance solely on traditional measures of internal performance cost the business and its shareholders $37 million in net profit. For any business desiring the benefits of operating as a market-based business, the development of a key set of external market metrics is essential. These metrics include process metrics, which typically precede financial performance measurement, and result metrics, which are likely to coincide with financial performance measurement.

To develop and implement marketing strategies that will increase customer satisfaction and grow profit, a business must be able to measure the profitability of a proposed marketing decision. To determine whether a marketing decision would be profitable, managers need to be aware of the revenues that result from serving a target market of customers and all the costs associated with serving that market. A common problem that arises in most accounting systems is the need to allocate overhead costs, which has the potential for distorting profitability. As a result, managers without the benefit of marketing performance metrics may make incorrect decisions that lead to reduced profitability. To grow profit, a business needs to grow its net marketing contribution, with overhead costs allocated after the NMC has been computed so that market-level profitability can be clearly observed.

Marketing strategies for growing net marketing contribution include growing market demand, increasing market share, lowering variable cost, improving marketing efficiency, and lowering channel costs. Two marketing profitability metrics address the efficiency of marketing strategies. Marketing ROS (NMC divided by sales) helps in evaluating the effectiveness of a marketing strategy with respect to marketing profits and sales revenue. This metric can also be used to compare the financial performance of various businesses even when they have significantly different sales levels. Marketing ROI (NMC divided by marketing expenses) allows us to evaluate the productivity of a marketing strategy with respect to marketing profits and marketing investment. Both marketing profitability metrics are closely correlated with financial performance as measured by a business's return on invested capital.

■ Market-Based Strategic Thinking

1 Why are measures of marketing performance critical to achieving profitable growth?

2 How do marketing measures of performance differ from internal measures of performance?

3 Why does a business need both internal (financial) measures of performance and external (marketing) measures of performance?

4 What roles do measures of marketing performance play in achieving profitable growth?

5 Why are performance metrics important?

6 What is the fundamental difference between a marketing performance metric and a financial performance metric?

7 Why are process metrics an important part of a successful marketing strategy? What is the relationship between process metrics and result metrics?

8 What are some of the fundamental differences between product-based accounting and customer-based accounting?

9 How does the net marketing contribution enable a business to better understand the profit impact of a marketing strategy?

10 What is the difference between a variable cost and a fixed expense?

11 Why is the cost of goods sold considered a variable expense? Why could we consider fixed marketing expenses as actually being "semi-variable" expenses?

12 How can treatment of operating expenses distort interpretations of profitability?

13 How would you go about assessing the profit impact of a specific marketing strategy?

14 Under what conditions would you expect operating expenses to change with changes in marketing strategies?

15 What fundamental marketing strategies can a business pursue to grow marketing profits?

16 Explain how any given marketing strategy might affect different components of the net marketing contribution.

17 Why would a business want to measure its profitability by market segment?

18 How does a marketing profitability metric such as marketing ROS help in comparing the marketing profits of two competitors?

19 What does a marketing ROS of 20 percent mean?

20 What does it mean when a competitor with approximately the same sales has a marketing ROI half as large?

21 Using Figures 2-17 and 2-18, explain how marketing ROS and marketing ROI relate to financial performance.

Marketing Performance Tools

The **Marketing Performance Tools** described here may be accessed online at *www.rogerjbest.com*. These applied-learning exercises will give you an in-depth understanding of the profit impact of marketing profitability and managing marketing profitability.

2.1 Product-Focused Marketing Profitability (Figure 2-12)

■ Evaluate the profit impact of eliminating the casual shorts and knitted sweaters product lines.

■ What would be the profit impact of increasing share from 2 to 3 percent for the casual shorts product line if marketing expenses were doubled ($1.5 million to $3 million)?

■ Would a better strategy be to increase price for the casual shorts line and give up a 0.5 percent in market share (market share would decline from 2 to 1.5 percent)?

2.2 Market-Focused Marketing Profitability (Figure 2-14)

■ Evaluate the profit impact of exiting the fashion segment.

■ In the fashion segment, how much market share would the business have to obtain to keep the same level of marketing profit if the business doubled marketing expenses in that segment?

■ What would be the profit impact in the trend-setter segment of a strategy to use a lower-cost indirect channel (40% channel discount) if this strategy meant that the average selling price for a customer transaction would decrease from $130 to $99?

2.3 Marketing Profitability and Marketing Profitability Metrics (Figure 2-10)

■ For a company of interest, obtain the required input from a company annual report. Evaluate the company's marketing profitability and how it contributes to net profit before taxes.

- How would marketing profit and net profit change if sales increased by 25 percent?
- Evaluate the profit impact of a strategy in which the percent margin is increased by 5 points and marketing expenses are increased by 2 percentage points.

2.4 Benchmarking Marketing Profitability Metrics (Figures 2-17 and 2-18)

- For a company of interest, go online and obtain for that company the data needed to complete Figure 2-17. How would you evaluate the company's marketing profitability and financial performance? You will probably need to use SG&A (sales, general, and administrative) expenses for marketing expenses, as companies rarely report marketing expenses separately in their financial statements.
- Next, collect the same data for a major competitor and input the data in Figure 2-17. How does the first company compare with this competitor in terms of marketing profitability metrics and financial performance?
- Add two more major competitors to Figure 2-17 and evaluate the first company's marketing profitability metrics and financial performance with respect to the three major competitors.

Notes

1. P. Hyde, E. Landry, and A. Tipping, "Making the Perfect Marketer," *Strategy + Business* (Winter 2004).
2. Hyde, Landry, and Tipping, "Making the Perfect Marketer."
3. Roger Best, *Marketing Excellence Survey,* www.MESurvey.com.
4. Bradley Gale, "Tracking Competitive Position Drives Shareholder Value," *Global Management* (1992): 367–371.
5. Tim Ambler, Flora Kokkinaki, and Stefano Puntoni, "Assessing Marketing Performance: Reasons for Metrics Selection," *Journal of Marketing Management* (2004), 475–498.
6. Paul Farris, Neil Bendle, Phillip Pfeifer, and David Reibstein, *Marketing Metrics* (Wharton School Publishing, 2007).
7. Tim Ambler, *Marketing and the Bottom Line: New Metrics of Corporate Wealth* (Prentice Hall, 2000).
8. Robert Kaplan and David Norton, "The Balanced Scorecard—Measures That Drive Performance," *Harvard Business Review* (January–February 1992): 71–79; and Robert Eccles, "The Performance Measurement Manifesto," *Harvard Business Review* (January–February 1991): 131–137.
9. George Cressman, "Choosing the Right Metric," *Drive Marketing Excellence* (November 1994), New York: Institute for International Research.
10. Christopher Meyer, "How the Right Measures Help Teams Excel," *Harvard Business Review* (May–June 1994): 95–103.
11. Yuxin Chen, James Hess, Ronald Wilcox, and Z. John Zhang, "Accounting Profits Versus Marketing Profits: A Relevant Metric for Category Management," *Marketing Science*, 18, no. 3 (1999): 208–229.
12. John Shank and Vijay Govindarajan, "The Perils of Cost Allocation Based on Production Volumes," *Accounting Horizons* 4 (1988): 71–79; and John Shank and Vijay Govindarajan, "Making Strategy Explicit in Cost Analysis: A Case Study," *Sloan Marketing Review* (Spring 1988): 15–30.
13. Delbert Hawkins, Roger Best, and Charles Lillis, "The Nature of Measurement of Marketing Productivity in Consumer Durables," *Journal of the Academy of Marketing Science* (1987).
14. John Shank and Vijay Govindarajan, *Strategic Cost Analysis* (New York: Irwin, 1989): 99–112.
15. Michael Morris and Gene Morris, *Market-Oriented Pricing* (New York: NTC Business Books, 1990): 99–100; and Don Schultz, "Spreadsheet Approach to Measuring ROI for MCI," *Marketing News* 28 (February 1994): 12.
16. William Christopher, "Marketing Achievement Reporting: A Profitability Approach," *Industrial Marketing Management* (New York: Elsevier North Holland, Inc. 1977): 149–162; Patrick Dunne and Harry Wolk, "Marketing Cost Analysis: A Modularized Contribution," *Journal of Marketing* (July 1977): 83–94; Stanley Shapiro and V. H. Kirpalard, *Marketing Effectiveness: Insights from Accounting and Finance* (Needham Heights, MA: Allyn and Bacon, 1984): 377–424; and Jean-Claude Larreche and Hubert Gatignon, MARKSTRAT (New York: Scientific Press, 1990): 22–23.

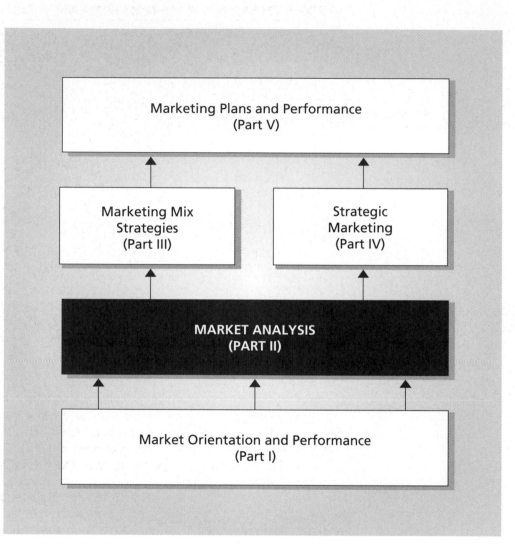

PART II

Market Analysis

■ Marketing is a $450 billion industry, and we are making decisions with less data and discipline than we apply to $100,000 decisions in other aspects of our business.*

Market analysis is an essential input to the development of market-based management strategies that deliver superior levels of customer satisfaction and profitability. The continuous pursuit of customer needs, ongoing monitoring of competitors' moves and capabilities, and tracking market-based performance are the core competencies of a market-focused business.

Part II consists of four chapters that consider the fundamental inputs of market analysis: market demand, customer analysis, market segmentation, and competitor analysis. The first of these chapters, Chapter 3, examines market definition, market potential, market demand, and market growth opportunities. Markets, however, do not buy products. *Customers* buy products. Chapter 4 focuses on customer analysis and the discovery of benefits that provide superior customer value.

Because customers in any market differ in many ways, rarely can one marketing strategy adequately serve all their needs. Chapter 5 addresses needs-based market segmentation and the development of segment strategies. Finally, Chapter 6 focuses on competitor analysis, competitive position, and sources of competitive advantage.

*Statement by the chief marketing officer at Procter & Gamble, *Marketing Metrics* (Wharton School Publishing, 2007): XV.

CHAPTER 3

Market Potential, Market Demand, and Market Share

■ The tipping point in a product-market occurs when consumption behavior shifts from virtually unnoticed to epidemic-like proportions.[1]

I n his book, *Tipping Point*, Malcolm Gladwell describes how product-market adoption of innovations suddenly increases once demand reaches a tipping point. Every product-market once had an emerging market demand that remained unattractive until the tipping point occurred. When black-and-white

TV sets came on the market in the 1940s, for example, purchases stayed below the tipping point until prices declined. Once market demand reached the tipping point, it then grew exponentially, as illustrated in Figure 3-1.

With the introduction of color TV in the 1960s, the market for color sets grew gradually

FIGURE 3-1 PRODUCT-MARKET DEMAND AND PRODUCT LIFE-CYCLE DEMAND

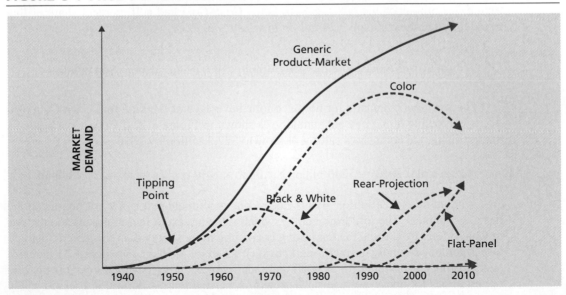

until reaching its tipping point in the 1970s. The price was higher, but the benefits were greater. Demand for black-and-white sets then began a slow decline. In the 1980s, rear-projection sets offered new benefits and emerged as a relatively high-priced complement to color TV.

The demand for digital flat-panel sets began slowly but quickly accelerated once it reached its tipping point. As prices come down on those sets, demand for conventional color TVs is dropping, as happened with black-and-white sets.

From this example, we can see the importance of understanding that every market has a generic product-market demand, as well as a variety of product-technology life cycles that underlie the overall market demand.

MARKET DEFINITION—WHAT BUSINESS ARE WE IN?

Perhaps the greatest threat to a business's survival, and a major cause of missed market opportunities, is a narrow focus on existing product-markets. Businesses that do not look at the broader picture of customers, market demand, and forces that shape unserved market demand expose themselves to this risk.[2] Theodore Levitt's perspective on marketing myopia applies today as much as it did when he first wrote on the subject some 50 years ago:

> A myopic vision of the potential markets a business might serve translates into a narrow product-focused market definition.[3]

Marketing leaders with a broad market vision see the world differently. Their view of market demand goes beyond existing products and customers and enables them to recognize untapped or emerging market opportunities that others overlook. With their unrestricted market vision, their businesses can move quickly to control their own destinies.[4]

A market definition is essential for any business in order to understand and measure market demand, market potential, and market share. A global company like Coca-Cola, for example, has a broad market definition that encompasses the worldwide $240 billion market for non-alcoholic beverages. In 2006, Coca-Cola had a 10 percent share of that market, giving the company $24 billion in sales revenue.

Coca-Cola Sales (2006) = $240 billion $\times$ 10% market share = **$24 billion**

The worldwide demand for non-alcoholic beverages of the kind that Coca-Cola produces is growing at 3.2 percent annually, as shown in Figure 3-2. If Coca-Cola holds its market share, the company's sales will grow to $27.2 billion by 2010.

Coca-Cola (2010) = $240 billion $\times 1.032^4 \times$ 10% market share = **$27.2 billion**

A broad market definition allows Coca-Cola to compete in a variety of non-alcoholic beverage markets. The soft drink market, which is the largest of these markets and the one in which Coca-Cola is the market leader, is growing more slowly than the generic market, just 2 percent annually. Growth markets such as sports drinks, growing at 23 percent; energy drinks, growing at 31 percent; and other non-alcoholic beverage markets provide opportunities for above-average sales growth. A narrow market definition focused solely

FIGURE 3-2 BEVERAGE MARKET GROWTH AND PRODUCT-MARKET STRUCTURE

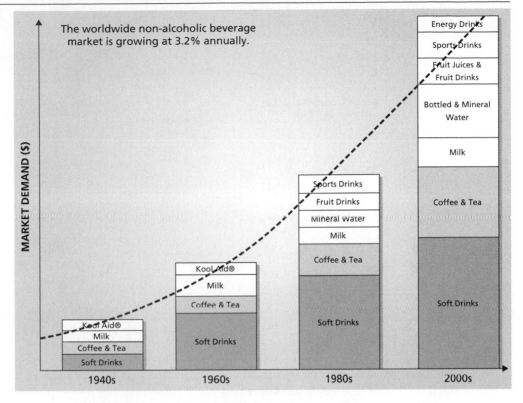

on the soft drink market would have greatly reduced Coca-Cola's potential for future sales growth and increased profits.

But a narrow market definition, one adopted by design, is not always a limitation. Red Bull, the fast-growing energy drink company, has an 80 percent share of a $3.4 billion market that is growing at 31 percent annually. The company recognizes it is but part of the much larger non-alcoholic beverage market, but its market definition at this time is focused on energy drinks, with a strategy to hold its high share in a market that has passed its tipping point and entered a stage of hypergrowth.

From one perspective, Red Bull has a 1.1 percent share of the $240 billion worldwide non-alcoholic beverage market.

Red Bull Sales (2006) = $240 billion $\times$ 1.1% market share = **$2.7 billion**

From a market-based management perspective, Red Bull has an 80 percent market share of the $3.4 billion energy drink market.

Red Bull Sales (2006) = $3.4 billion $\times$ 80% market share = **$2.7 billion**

With the energy drink market projected to grow at 31 percent annually, Red Bull's sales will increase by nearly 300 percent over a 4-year period if the company remains

FIGURE 3-3 BEVERAGE MARKET AND MARKET DEFINITION

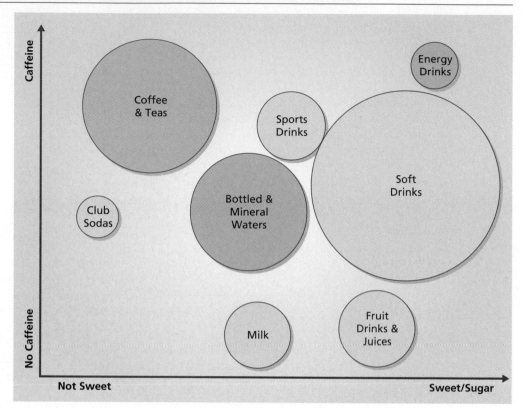

focused on its market definition and invests the necessary marketing resources to hold its 80 percent market share.

$$\textbf{Red Bull Sales } (2010) = \$3.4 \text{ billion} \times 1.31^4 \times 80\% \text{ market share} = \textbf{\$8 billion}$$

While growth of this size would be an otherwise reasonable strategic objective, the energy drink market has not gone unnoticed by the big beverage companies. Coca-Cola, Pepsi, and Anheuser-Busch are among those companies that have entered the energy drink market with brands such as KMX, Full Throttle, Adrenaline Rush, and South Beach. Holding an 80 percent share of the energy drink market could prove challenging for Red Bull; yet, faced with similar competition, Gatorade has been successful in maintaining an 80 percent share of the sports drink market.

Broad Market Vision

Figure 3-3 shows the kinds of products that make up the non-alcoholic beverage market as it is today. Forty years ago, several of these products were not being marketed to any real extent, and some that were being marketed had not yet reached their tipping points. The newer products, it is interesting to note, emerged and quickly gained a significant share of the market as the result of strategies implemented by relatively small, new businesses.

The big beverage companies, almost without exception, were late in entering the product-markets of bottled water, sports drinks, fruit drinks, iced coffee, and energy drinks. Their tardiness serves as an excellent example of how short-term vision, with its limited view of a market, can overlook a chance to grow profits. Such opportunities can be missed especially when a company is doing well. Focused on their existing products, and with the worldwide market for those products rapidly expanding, the big beverage companies did not see the potential that alternative beverages held until the companies noticed the prosperity of the market's newly arrived businesses.

Developing a broad vision of a market is the first step in understanding market demand.[5] A market vision limited to a particular product focus will only maintain the status quo. A business with a narrow market focus does not see beyond the *articulated needs* of served customers.[6] A market definition encompassing only the articulated needs of current customers will result in unfulfilled market potential as the business's served market moves left to right and becomes a greater part of the *unserved* market ignored by the narrow market definition. The inclination of many managers is to define their markets based on the customers they presently serve, which limits the managers' perceptions and strategies. As a result, their businesses do not grow beyond the narrow view of the articulated needs of served customers, leaving a vast untapped market opportunity.

A broad market vision enables a business to better serve the needs of its customers. But a broad market vision goes even further than this, enabling a business to see completely *unserved needs* that no one is addressing. For Fred Smith, founder of FedEx, a broad market vision saw unserved customer needs that led him to conceive of a business that would provide overnight deliveries around the world, an idea many bankers and industry experts said would never work. For Phil Knight, founder of Nike, a broad market vision led to a transformation of the athletic footwear and sports apparel markets. And for Bill Gates, cofounder of Microsoft, a broad market vision foresaw millions of people using computers in their daily lives, revolutionizing the way they work, communicate, learn, and recreate.

A strategic market definition includes all potential substitute products. The likelihood that consumers will substitute one product in a certain market for another product in a different market is affected by the distance, in terms of their similarities, between the markets.[7] The closer one market is to another, the greater the possibility that consumers will substitute products. A strategic market definition, because it enables managers to see a broad set of customer needs, leads to the discovery of new market opportunities. As a business assesses the possibility of entering new markets, a wide range of market-based strategies will emerge.

A broad market definition, then, provides a market-based business three key benefits:

- It reveals new opportunities in light of a broader set of customer needs;
- It enables management to recognize potential substitutes and competitive threats; and
- It provides management with a thorough understanding of fundamental customer needs.

MARKET POTENTIAL

Once a served market definition has been established,[8] a business is in a better position to understand several important aspects of market potential. The first, and most crucial, is the size of the market demand: How many customers make up the maximum potential for

FIGURE 3-4 MARKET DEMAND AND MARKET POTENTIAL—PERSONAL COMPUTER

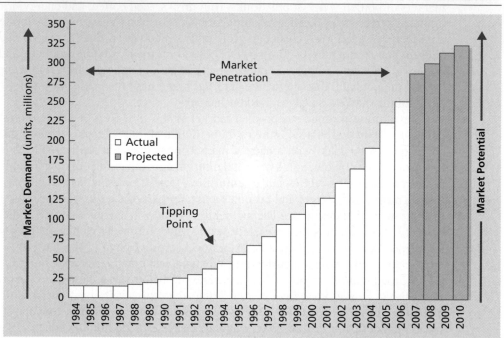

the served market definition?[9] This assessment of market demand includes a determination of the maximum unit and dollar potential if all potential consuming units entered the market.

At any point in time, a business has an *existing* pool of current and prospective customers who make up current market demand and a *potential* pool of prospective customers who provide the opportunity to grow market demand. But because for every product and service a fixed number of customers buy at a certain rate of purchase, any product or service will have a certain level of market demand, and this demand over time is finite.

For example, the personal computer market emerged in the early 1980s but did not reach a tipping point until the early 1990s, as illustrated in Figure 3-4. From then on, growth accelerated quickly as products improved and prices declined. However, within the realm of any one technology the market demand has an upper limit, a ceiling that cannot be exceeded without a change in technology or in the way the product is used. This is the market potential—the maximum number of units that can be consumed by the world population, or other defined market, at any point in time.

Knowing the maximum number of units that can be consumed by the defined market is of great strategic importance to a business: Once a market reaches its full potential, or saturates, new customers will be hard to find. For the personal computer market, the full market potential is currently estimated at 350 million units per year, as shown in Figure 3-4. By 2010, the market will be approaching its market potential, with an estimated market demand for that year of 325 million units. But this could change as the result of unusually large price declines, radically new computer technology, or other unpredictable developments.

FIGURE 3-5 ESTIMATING MARKET POTENTIAL—PERSONAL COMPUTER

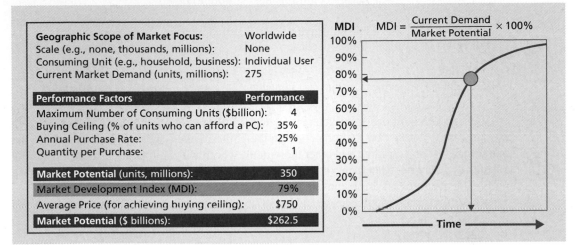

Geographic Scope of Market Focus:	Worldwide
Scale (e.g., none, thousands, millions):	None
Consuming Unit (e.g., household, business):	Individual User
Current Market Demand (units, millions):	275

Performance Factors	Performance
Maximum Number of Consuming Units ($billion):	4
Buying Ceiling (% of units who can afford a PC):	35%
Annual Purchase Rate:	25%
Quantity per Purchase:	1

Market Potential (units, millions):	350
Market Development Index (MDI):	79%
Average Price (for achieving buying ceiling):	$750
Market Potential ($ billions):	$262.5

$$\text{MDI} = \frac{\text{Current Demand}}{\text{Market Potential}} \times 100\%$$

Published information on the market potential for any given market is difficult or impossible to find. But by using "facts, logic, and assumptions,"[10] we can arrive at a reasonable estimate of a market's potential. We should use no more than 10 years as the time horizon, because a market's potential can change significantly over time, for better or worse, in response to such influences as technological advances, changes in customer behavior, and regional or worldwide economic conditions.

Figure 3-5 presents a systematic approach for estimating market potential. The first step is to define the geographical boundaries and the consuming units. The consuming units could be defined in terms of individuals, families, households, businesses, or other purchasing entities. For the personal computer, the market is worldwide, and individuals are its consuming units. The world's population is 6 billion, but we can logically estimate that 2 billion are not old enough, lack the ancillary requirements, or are otherwise incapable of using a computer, which now sets the maximum number of consuming units at 4 billion. This number is further reduced by the fact that only a relatively small percentage of the world's population can afford a computer, even at the estimated price of $750 for 2010. This price estimate is based on a long-running market trend of price declines of about 7 percent annually. Using economic data on the populations of the world's nations, we now further reduce the maximum number of consuming units by 65 percent, to 1.4 billion. For the personal computer industry, then, 1.4 billion is the estimate for the worldwide number of personal computer users when the market saturates.

Market Potential = 4 billion potential × 35% buying ceiling = **1.4 billion users**

If we assume one personal computer per user, and that users replace their computers on average every 4 years, the number of units sold per year at full market potential would be 350 million. At the estimated price of $750 per unit, the annual sales at full market potential would be $262.5 billion, barring any unpredictable major developments. These calculations are embodied in the following formula for figuring a market's annual sales when it reaches its potential:

$$\frac{\text{Market}}{\text{Potential (\$)}} = \frac{\text{Maximum}}{\text{Buying Units}} \times \frac{\text{Buying}}{\text{Ceiling}} \times \frac{\text{Purchase}}{\text{Rate}} \times \frac{\text{Purchase}}{\text{Quantity}} \times \frac{\text{Average Selling}}{\text{Price or Transaction}}$$

$$\frac{\text{Market}}{\text{Potential (\$)}} = \frac{\text{4 billion}}{\text{people}} \times \frac{35\%}{\text{ceiling}} \times \frac{\text{25\% re-buy}}{\text{annually}} \times \frac{\text{1 PC per}}{\text{user}} \times \frac{\$750 \text{ per}}{\text{purchase}} = \frac{\textbf{\$262.5 billion}}{\textbf{annually}}$$

For the U.S. soft drink market, retail sales at full market potential can be estimated in the same way. Of the 300 million people in the United States, we would exclude from the market very young children and other individuals whom we could not consider as potential consumers, leaving 80 percent of the population as the maximum number of consuming units. The average soft drink consumer buys 365 soft drinks a year. At an average price of $1 per drink, annual retail sales would be $87.6 billion if all potential consumers entered the market.

$$\frac{\text{Market}}{\text{Potential (\$)}} = \frac{\text{300 million}}{\text{people}} \times \frac{80\%}{\text{ceiling}} \times \frac{\text{365 units}}{\text{annually}} \times \frac{\$1 \text{ per}}{\text{unit}} = \frac{\textbf{\$87.6 billion}}{\textbf{annually}}$$

For flat-panel TVs, lets assume the number of households in the United States will grow to 120 million in 10 years. If we further assume 80 percent of the households would buy a flat-panel TV at an average selling price of $500, and each household would buy one TV every 5 years, the market potential would be an estimated $9.6 billion annually. If the average price were to fall to $400, and the consuming units grew to 90 percent of the households, the market potential would drop to $8.6 billion.

$$\frac{\text{Market}}{\text{Potential (\$)}} = \frac{\text{120 million}}{\text{households}} \times \frac{80\%}{\text{ceiling}} \times \frac{\text{20\% re-buy}}{\text{annually}} \times \frac{\text{1 unit per}}{\text{household}} \times \frac{\$500 \text{ per}}{\text{unit}} = \frac{\textbf{\$9.6 billion}}{\textbf{annually}}$$

In estimating the U.S. market potential for golf carts, as another example, we would similarly rely on "facts, logic, and assumptions." First, we would research various sources to find the information we need. Let's suppose we learn that the United States has 17,000 golf courses, that 5 percent of them do not have golf carts, that the other 95 percent have an average of 100 golf carts, that golf courses typically replace their fleets every three years, and that the cost of a new cart is $2,500. In this mature market, we can assume the selling price will stay about same over the next 10 years.

$$\frac{\text{Market}}{\text{Potential (\$)}} = \frac{\text{17,000 golf}}{\text{courses}} \times \frac{95\%}{\text{ceiling}} \times \frac{\text{33.3\% buy}}{\text{annually}} \times \frac{\text{100 carts}}{\text{per course}} \times \frac{\$2,500}{\text{per cart}} = \frac{\textbf{\$1.3 billion}}{\textbf{annually}}$$

Because the golf cart market matured sometime ago, the present market demand is close to the market potential. However, if a significant number of new courses are built, market potential would increase. With golf's popularity continuing to grow, many new courses are a strong likelihood. Additionally, because an ever-increasing number of courses are requiring their golfers to use golf carts in order to increase the daily number of rounds that can be played, the average fleet size will probably increase.

FIGURE 3-6 MARKET DEVELOPMENT AND MARKET POTENTIAL

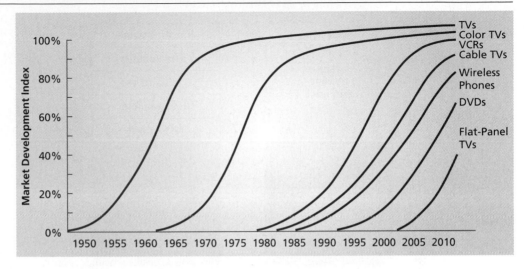

MARKET DEVELOPMENT INDEX

Figure 3-6 illustrates the market development of several well-known product-markets. Each had a well-defined tipping point, followed by periods of rapid growth and eventually a leveling-off period as the market approaches its market potential. As shown earlier in Figure 3-4, the personal computer market is now approaching its full market development. To help us understand the evolution of a market and to measure a market's potential for future growth, we can use a calculation called the market development index. This index is simply a ratio of current market demand to market potential.

$$\text{Market Development Index}_{\text{Personal Computers}} = \frac{\text{Current Market Demand}}{\text{Market Potential}} \times 100\%$$

$$= \frac{275 \text{ million}}{350 \text{ million}} \times 100\% = \mathbf{79\%}$$

A market development index (MDI) of less than 33 percent, for example, would suggest considerable growth potential for a product's market. When the MDI is between 33 and 67 percent, further development of the market is based on addressing benefit deficiencies and reducing prices. As the MDI rises above 67 percent, the potential for growth remains, but the task will be more difficult because the business now faces the potent forces that impede full market development.

Untapped Market Potential

With a carefully arrived-at estimate of market potential, even mature businesses may discover they have considerable untapped market potential, as illustrated in Figure 3-7. Many new markets and most global markets, because large numbers of potential customers

FIGURE 3-7 FACTORS LIMITING FULL MARKET DEVELOPMENT

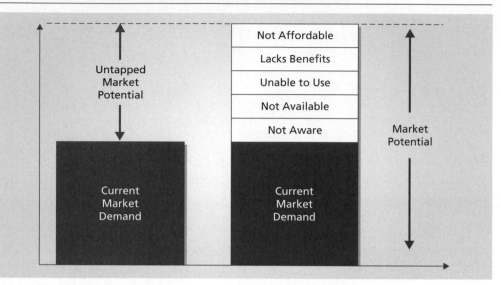

have not yet entered them, are well below their market potentials. Figure 3-7 lists five major forces that tend to restrict a market or product from realizing its market potential.

Awareness
Consumer awareness means not just *product awareness,* but also a *complete comprehension of benefits*. Even potential customers who are aware of a product will not recognize its potential value to them if they do not fully see its benefits. For the personal computer, most potential customers in the worldwide market are aware of the product, but many do not know all the benefits personal computers offer. Because the product is complex and experiential, its most compelling benefits are appreciated only after a period of use.

Availability
The second force that influences market demand is *availability*. For mature markets, product unavailability generally is not a significant factor in restricting market demand. But even in mature markets, market demand is hampered if products are in short supply, difficulties arise in distribution, or support services are inadequate. When the personal computer market was in its early stages, many individuals and businesses who saw the benefits of PCs were reluctant to buy because they did not have access to information technology support services.

Ability to Use
The ability of potential consumers to use a product is another force contributing to market expansion. People in many parts of the world could benefit from the use of a computer, but if they do not have electricity, they cannot use one. Further, the ability to use a computer requires a certain level of education. In response to this need, Apple Computer, Microsoft, and other businesses in the information technology sector have funded educational programs that, besides benefiting students and their communities, should contribute to the development of the personal computer market.

Benefits

To reach its market potential, a product's benefits must appeal to consumers. For some consumers, the benefits of a given product may not be compelling enough for them to enter the market. The benefit proposition is simply deficient—too weak to stimulate purchase regardless of the strength of the other forces influencing a decision to buy. Because consumers have varied lifestyles and preferences, a product may be unable to accommodate all the needs and desired benefits in its market. In these cases, a practical limit is placed on market potential. But a practical limit can also restrict a market from reaching its maximum potential. Computer companies, for example, could have easily excluded older people from the potential PC market in the belief that older people would see no benefit in owning a computer. But with e-mail, online banking, and online shopping now commonplace, and with the vast number of other services and resources made possible by the Internet, older people have become an important source of new customers for the personal computer companies. Had the companies set a practical limit on their potential markets by excluding the older population, they would have unnecessarily limited the market potential for their products.

Affordability

Many of the products some people take for granted are not affordable for others. Although the benefits are known and attractive, the product may be too expensive for many potential customers. As we have seen, a product-focused business never looks beyond its current customer market, and its senior managers never challenge their engineers and production managers to produce lower-cost versions of the business's products. The largest portion of new-customer purchases in the PC market is now in the under $1,000 price segment. The introduction of the $100 computer, though small and limited in capabilities, will surely greatly expand the market potential of PCs to many who cannot afford more expensive PCs.

Market Potential and Market Growth

Recognizing that every market has some upper limit—its market potential—marketing managers naturally want to know how fast their markets will grow to their potential. For marketing managers, any catalyst that might spur market growth holds great intrigue.

Figure 3-6 presents growth curves for television products, cable service, and wireless phones. The upper limit in each case represents the market potential for each product-market. The rate at which customers enter a market is a market-specific phenomenon based on product attractiveness, customer characteristics, and marketing efforts.[11] However, the early pattern established by the rate of customer entry into a market offers enough information to project the market growth rate accurately in most cases.[12]

Three fundamental forces affect the rate of market growth and hence the shape of the market growth curve:

1. **Market Potential:** The maximum number of customers the market could attract, given a specific definition for the served market.
2. **Market Penetration:** The number of customers who have entered a market at a certain point in time.
3. **Rate of Entry:** The percentage of potential customers who enter the market during a given period.

FIGURE 3-8 CUSTOMER ENTRY AND MARKET DEVELOPMENT

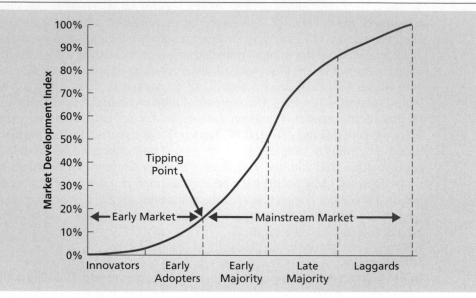

These three elements define the parameters of a market's customer attraction and growth. They can vary greatly from one product-market to another. Some markets, we know, grow much faster and reach their potential much sooner than others. But why? What makes some product-markets grow quickly, and others grow slowly? The next section addresses this question and provides marketing strategies for accelerating market growth.

MANAGING MARKET GROWTH

For eventual success in a new market, a business's first need is new customers. For many products, finding those customers isn't easy. The risks associated with being an early buyer of a new product or service make most potential customers highly reluctant. New products are usually priced higher at first, customers may not know how to make them work, and early versions often quickly give way to much-improved versions. Some new products also encounter societal or cultural resistance because they represent too much of a change. They are just *too* different for most people. Emerging markets, then, are relatively small. They consist of *innovators* and *early adopters*, as shown in Figure 3-8. Customers who make up the *early market* possess more knowledge, are less price sensitive, more benefit driven, and less dependent on what others do or think than most people. These *lead customers* are critical. If they cannot be attracted, satisfied, and retained, the market is likely to die. The mainstream market will not buy if the lead customers haven't. The first job in developing a new product-market is to identify the lead customers and penetrate this early market.

For a new market to move from the *early market* to the *mainstream market* requires the development of *complete solutions*.[13] Although customers in the early market are generally more willing to struggle with a new product until it performs as desired, those in the mainstream market are not so patient with less-than-complete solutions; they want a 100 percent solution.

To successfully reach the mainstream market, a business must carefully identify its target customers and focus on the delivery of a complete solution as viewed by those target customers. The complete solution must be one that has all the necessary features, functions, and supporting products and services.[14]

One more challenge awaits a business seeking to project a product into the mainstream market. Figure 3-8 identifies five groups of customers based on their entry points to a market. Each group of customers represents a stage in the development of the market, and at each stage the benefits customers regard as the complete solution can be different.[15] Success in the mainstream market is dependent to a great extent on the experience of lead users—the innovators and early adopters—and their influence on potential mainstream customers. But success also requires adjustments to attract the potential mainstream customers. The more quickly a business addresses the complete solution needed for mainstream customers, the more quickly the market will grow. A look at the five customer groups will help us gain a better understanding of the kinds of adjustments that might be necessary.

1. **Innovators** (2.5%)—As the first to buy a new product or service, these customers see genuine value in it and are willing to pay a premium price, despite any deficiencies in ease of use, support services, and the features set.
2. **Early Adopters** (13.5%)—Because they are well informed, these customers are aware of the innovators' experience and satisfaction with a new product or service. They are attracted to the product's benefits and are willing to pay a premium price even though the product or service lacks the refinements that will come later.
3. **Early Majority** (34%)—A product has penetrated the mass market when the early majority of customers has adopted it. The price is affordable, the product useable, and the feature set attractive. Until these product attributes are met, the market's development will be delayed. The early majority customers are quality conscious, fairly well informed, and somewhat price sensitive.
4. **Late Majority** (34%)—The customers in the late majority are skeptics. They wait to see if the product or service will really deliver meaningful benefits. These customers are more price sensitive than early majority customers and often not as well informed about new products, but they do notice the new products being used around them. Lower prices, increased availability, advertising, observing the use of the product by others, and hearing the experiences of others all contribute to the late majority's entry to the market.
5. **Laggards** (16%)—As the name implies, these are the last customers to adopt a new product or service. They are often price constrained, do not see the need for the new product, or both. Promotions and lower prices bring these customers into the market.

Accelerating Market Growth

Developing and delivering a complete solution requires more than improving the product and making its price affordable to the mainstream market. The rate at which the mainstream market adopts a new product also depends on customer characteristics, product

FIGURE 3-9 CUSTOMER AND PRODUCT FORCES THAT SHAPE MARKET GROWTH

Customer Forces	Relative Importance	Customer Rating	Description of Customer Tipping Point
Need	30%	8	There is a strong, recognized need for this product or service.
Risk	10%	9	There is little or no economic, social, or performance risk.
Buying	20%	3	This product may be purchased without the approval of others.
Observation	20%	6	This product is easily observed in use.
Trial	20%	3	This product is easy to try before purchase.
Total	100%	5.7	Overall score on scale from 0 to 10.

Product Forces	Relative Importance	Customer Rating	Description of Customer Tipping Point
Advantage	30%	9	Meaningful advantage over other products.
Affordable	20%	3	Price is affordable.
Ease of Use	15%	6	Product is easy to install, use, and service.
Performance	20%	6	There is little risk product will not perform as expected.
Available	15%	8	The product is available where customers prefer to buy.
Total	100%	6.6	Overall score on scale from 0 to 10.

positioning, and market influences. Given adequate product awareness and availability, a number of forces can act to accelerate or slow customer attraction and the rate of market growth.[16] As shown in Figure 3-9, there are five customer adoption forces and five product adoption forces affecting new product-market penetration.

Customer Adoption Forces

Customer adoption forces affect the rate at which customers enter a market. First, customers must *feel a need* for the product. The strength of that felt need can vary, however. When the felt need for a product is low, customer attraction will be slow. For years, many potential customers simply did not feel a strong need to have a microwave oven, slowing the rate at which customers entered this product-market. Additionally, many people saw a safety *risk* with the product, and this perception also slowed market growth. Customer perceptions of risk, the second of the five customer adoption forces, are not limited to safety risks. Customers might also envision risks associated with the loss of money or loss of status.

The third customer adoption force is the *buying decision*. If the decision to buy a product or service can be made without the agreement or input of several people, market growth will develop more rapidly. An individual decision maker can act quickly, without first needing the approval of others. Conversely, when decisions to purchase a product are likely to be group decisions, such as those by a married couple, an organization's governing board, or the managers or owners of a business, the rate of customer entry into a market is slowed.

The fourth influence on the growth of a product's market demand is the extent to which the use of the product by current customers is *observed* by potential customers.

The demand for products easily observed, such as televisions and fashionable sunglasses, grows faster than for products less observable, such as household cleaners and insurance programs.

Trialability is the fifth factor affecting market growth. Products that can be tried at the point of purchase or offered on a trial basis will penetrate their markets more quickly than products that customers cannot try before buying. The easier it is to try or sample a product before buying, the faster the rate of market penetration.

To help project a new product's rate of market penetration, we can measure the strength of the customer forces. As shown in the top portion of Figure 3-9, we first estimate the relative importance of each customer force and then assign each force a customer rating on a scale from 0 to 10, where 10 indicates the strongest possible appeal for a potential customer. We then multiply the relative importance rating for each force by its customer rating, totaling the results to give us the overall score. Naturally, the higher the overall score, the more rapid the market penetration. In our example, the customer adoption forces are moderately favorable with an overall score of 5.7. This score for customer forces will contribute to a slightly above-average rate of market penetration, but five product adoption forces also have a say in this matter.

Product Adoption Forces

The strength of a product's positioning—its relative benefits—has a major effect on the rate of market growth. The stronger the benefits *advantage* and the more *affordable* the price, the greater the customer value created by the product and the faster the rate of customer market entry.

Unfortunately, many businesses never go beyond creating a strong benefits package and setting an affordable price. These businesses fail to examine their products' *ease of use, performance*, and *availability* as perceived by potential customers.

If a product is incompatible with the normal routines of potential customers, or if the potential customers think it would be difficult to use, they will be reluctant to purchase it. The microwave oven when first introduced was expensive, but it had very attractive benefits. Some potential customers, as mentioned earlier, shied away from the product because they didn't feel the need for it or because they perceived risks associated with its use. Other potential customers were deterred by the price of early models. But undoubtedly a significant percentage of potential mainstream customers delayed buying a microwave because they didn't know how to use one. For many high-tech products, the relative advantages are enormous, but the perceived difficulty in using the products can discourage purchases.

Similarly, consumer doubts about the *performance* of a product will hurt market penetration. A perception that microwaved food is not as appetizing as conventionally cooked food is probably still keeping some consumers from entering the market.

The fifth and last product force is *availability*. Not only must the product itself be available to consumers at their preferred points of purchase, but any necessary support or maintenance services must also be readily accessible. A lack of after-sales customer service can kill product adoption. Because new products often present new challenges for customers, inadequate after-sales customer support can doom a new product by bad word-of-mouth reports.

FIGURE 3-10 CUSTOMER AND PRODUCT FORCES DRIVING MARKET GROWTH

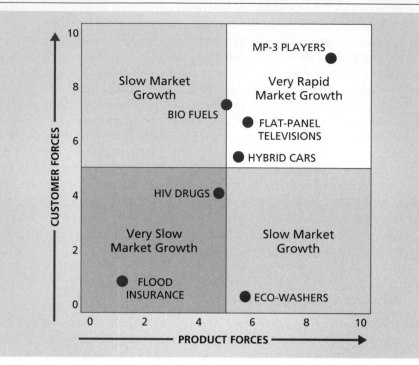

As with the overall score for customer forces, the higher the overall score for product forces, the more rapid the market penetration. In the bottom portion of Figure 3-9, the overall score for product forces is 6.6. This favorable score means the current strength of the product forces, while not exceptional, is nevertheless favorable for market penetration.

Figure 3-10 shows how overall scores for customer forces and product forces affect market growth. Products or services with weak overall scores for both customer forces and product forces, such as flood insurance and HIV drugs, encounter very slow market growth. A relatively high overall score for customer forces but a relatively low score for product forces, such as for bio-fuels, leads to a somewhat faster market growth, but still slow. Similarly, moderately strong product forces but very weak customer forces, such as for eco-washers, produces a faster but still slow growth. The best results naturally occur when both the customer forces and the product forces are strong overall, as with flat-panel TVs, hybrid cars, and MP-3 players. Then we have very rapid market growth. The conclusion is obvious: The best way to grow a market quickly is to ensure that both the overall customer forces and the overall product forces are strong.

PRODUCT-MARKET VERSUS PRODUCT LIFE CYCLE

Every market has a generic product-market life cycle. The generic life cycle encompasses many product life cycles, as illustrated for the different Intel microprocessors in Figure 3-11. The generic market demand plotted on this graph is for the product life

FIGURE 3-11 GENERIC PRODUCT-MARKET LIFE CYCLE VERSUS PRODUCT LIFE CYCLE

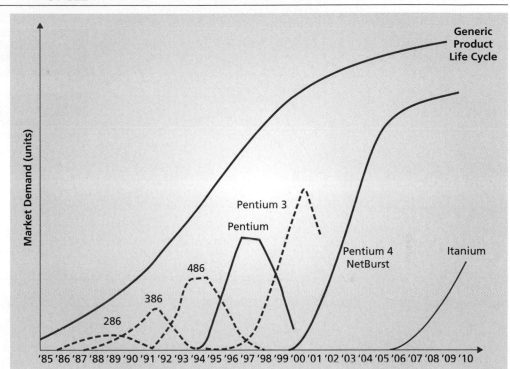

cycle of a product-market category—in this case, Intel microprocessors. By no means is a generic product-market life cycle the same as the product life cycle for a specific product. As the personal computer market has grown, along with the demand for faster and larger memories, Intel has gone through entire product life cycles for several products, as the graph illustrates. In most cases, the newer products accelerated the decline of the existing products.

In Figure 3-12, we can clearly see the introductory and growth stages of a product life cycle. As the market demand approaches the market potential, growth slows. Eventually the market becomes a mature market with little or no growth. The product has now entered a critical phase in its life cycle. Whereas the volume during the product's introductory and growth stages was derived from both market demand and market share, gains in volume can now be achieved only with gains in market share. When a market fully matures, declining volumes are inevitable.

Product Life-Cycle Demand and Profits

With the realization that a business's volume depends on market demand and market share, any business would want to increase both demand and share by implementing an effective marketing and sales program. In the early stages of a product life cycle, as Figure 3-12 shows, marketing and sales expenses are greater than gross profit because

FIGURE 3-12 PRODUCT LIFE CYCLE, DEMAND, AND PROFITS

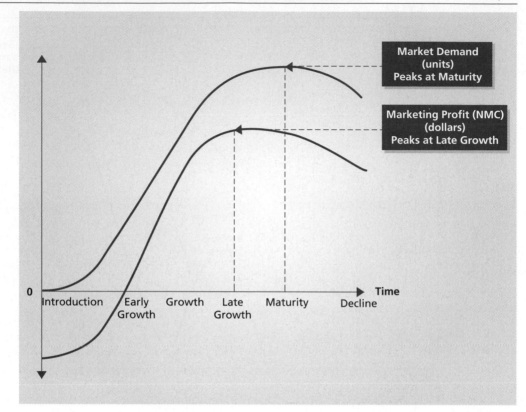

volumes are small, resulting in a negative net marketing contribution (NMC). As the product moves into the growth stage, it reaches a break-even NMC, with gross profit equaling marketing and sales expenses. Beyond that point, the annual NMCs grow and eventually peak in the late growth stage of the product life cycle. As the market matures, the combination of flat market demand, lower margins, and high marketing and sales expenses results in lower NMCs. In the decline stage of the life cycle, marketing profits continue to fall with decreases in market demand, despite any efforts to milk the product for profits by reducing marketing and sales expenses.

Market Demand and Prices

One of the reasons demand grows as a product moves from introduction through early adoption and into the growth and late growth stages is an ongoing decline in the average selling price of a product. Figure 3-13 shows the average selling prices for six consumer electronics products. In most cases, prices decline rapidly in the early stages of the product life cycle, as illustrated for VCRs, cellphones, and DVD players. As products move into their growth phases, prices decline at a more linear rate. Declining prices allow more customers to enter the market, increasing both market demand and sales revenues.

FIGURE 3-13 AVERAGE SELLING PRICE OF CONSUMER ELECTRONICS PRODUCTS

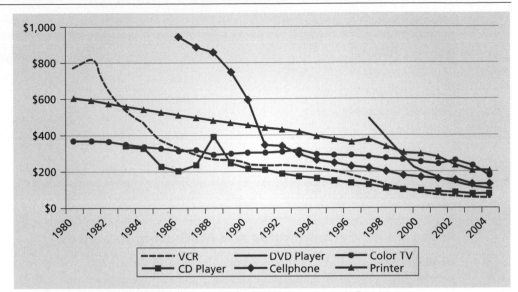

Recognizing that volumes grow and prices decline in the growth stages of the product life cycle, we can estimate future market demand and the market development index (MDI) by projecting the assumed market growth rate over a 3-year planning period. In Figure 3-14, market demand in the base year is 12 million units. The market potential is estimated at 20 million units, giving us an MDI of 60 percent. This means the market is just over the halfway point in its life cycle. If we assume the market will grow at the rate of 10 percent annually for the next 3 years, we can project market demand to reach 16 million in 3 years. At this point, the market will be at 80 percent of full development.

One of the important benefits of estimating market potential is the ceiling it places on market demand. Too often, a business that has enjoyed years of growth will project continued growth beyond the market potential. This could occur only if the MDI were greater than 100 percent, which would require market demand to be greater than market potential, something that could happen only if the market potential has been underestimated. In the example in Figure 3-14, the actual growth rate is likely to be lower than the stated 10 percent as the market approaches an MDI of 80 percent in 3 years. As indicated by Figure 3-15, market growth and sales-revenue growth rates typically begin to level off as the MDI nears 80 percent. If the market growth is indeed still 10 percent annually, then the market potential has probably been underestimated and should be re-estimated.

The business in Figure 3-14 has a 10 percent market share in the base year, and management's strategy is to hold this market share. If the strategy succeeds, unit sales will grow from 1.2 million to 1.6 million units. With an average selling price of $500 in the base year, the result is sales revenues of $600 million. Assuming the average selling price will decrease $25 annually, by year 3 it will be $425. In a market growing 10 percent annually, the combination of holding a 10 percent market share and reducing prices allows sales revenues to grow from $600 million in the base year to $679 in year 3. Any changes in market growth, market share, or price would naturally alter the estimated sales revenues for any given year.

FIGURE 3-14 ESTIMATING PRODUCT LIFE-CYCLE DEMAND AND SALES

Market Potential: 20 Million Units				
	Base Year	**Year 1**	**Year 2**	**Year 3**
Market Growth	10%	10%	10%	10%
Market Demand (millions)	12.0	13.2	14.5	16.0
Market Development Index	60	66	73	80
Market Share	10%	10%	10%	10%
Volume Sold (millions)	1.2	1.32	1.5	1.6
Average Selling Price	$500	$475	$450	$425
Sales Revenues (millions)	**$600**	**$627**	**$653**	**$679**

Product Life-Cycle Margins and Marketing Expenses

In addition to growth in volume sold and declines in the average selling price over the product life cycle, important changes occur in the average cost per unit sold and the marketing expenses needed to support market growth. As shown in Figure 3-16, prices tend to decrease at a rate faster than decreases in unit costs. In turn, margins per unit tend to decline over the product life cycle.

Figure 3-16 also shows that marketing expenses increase over the introductory and early growth phases of the product life cycle. These marketing expenses are essential in creating product awareness and communicating product benefits to potential customers. Marketing expenses as a percentage of sales tend to level off as a product approaches the maturity stage of its product life cycle, and they decrease during the decline stage.

FIGURE 3-15 ESTIMATING GROWTH FOR MARKET DEMAND AND SALES

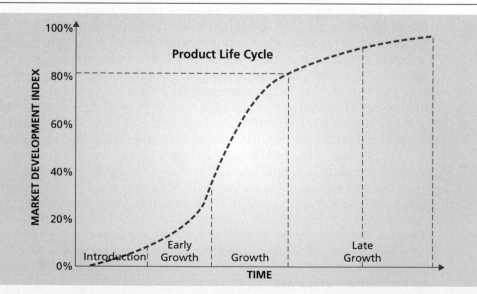

FIGURE 3-16 LIFE-CYCLE DEMAND, MARGINS, AND MARKETING EXPENSES

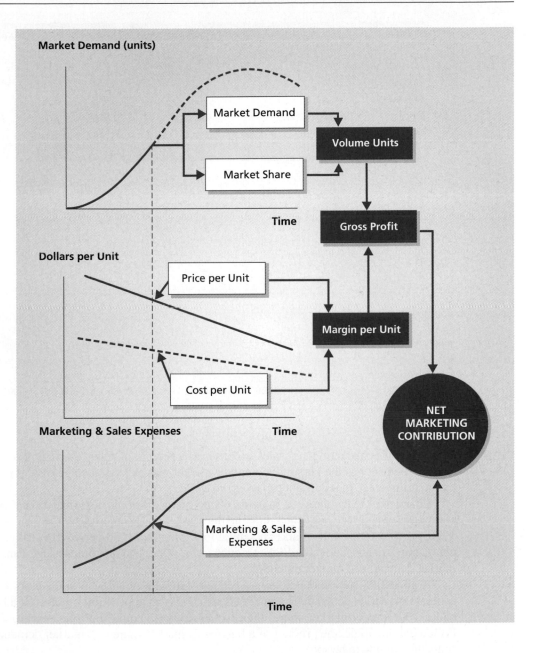

Product Life Cycle and Marketing Profitability

Figure 3-17 illustrates how profits can vary over the product life cycle. For the personal computer, we can see continued growth beyond the life cycle's late growth stage in both sales revenues and market demand in units. However, slower growth in volume and declining prices will contribute to lower margins and industry gross profit. Even with

FIGURE 3-17 PERSONAL COMPUTER LIFE-CYCLE MARKETING PROFITABILITY

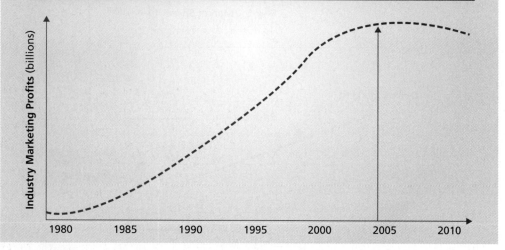

Industry Market Performance	1990	1995	2000	2005	2010
Market Demand (millions)	24	58	130	225	325
Average Selling Price	$2,970	$2,690	$1,950	$1,550	$1,300
Industry Sales (billions)	$71	$156	$254	$349	$423
Average Margin (%)	45%	30%	22%	18%	15%
Industry Gross Profit (billions)	$32	$47	$56	$63	$63
Marketing & Sales Expenses (% sales)	18%	16%	12%	8%	6%
Marketing Profits (billions)	$19	$22	$25	$35	$38

efforts to lower marketing and sales expenses as a percent of sales, marketing profits will decline modestly as the personal computer market moves from a stage of late growth to the maturity stage of its product-market life cycle.

Changes in technology, worldwide economic conditions, customer use of personal computers, and price could each redefine the market potential, as discussed earlier. In the 1950s, IBM estimated the market potential for computers at 50 per year, a striking example of how changes in technology, product form, price, and customer usage can reshape market demand and market potential.

A good first step in developing a reliable estimate of sales is to develop a reliable estimate of market demand. The market demand sets an upper limit on sales. If a business had a 100 percent market share, then its sales would equal the total market demand. Following this logic, the product of a business's market share and market demand represents the volume to be sold.

Volume Sold (units) = Market Demand (units) × Market Share

Dell Inc., for example, sold 14.5 million PCs in 2000, based on Dell's 11.2 percent share of a market demand of 130 million PCs. Over the next 5 years, the market grew to

225 million units, while Dell grew its market share to 15 percent. The combination of market growth and Dell's share growth produced sales of 33.8 million units in 2005.

Dell PC Unit Sales (2000) = 130 million units $\times$ 11.2% = **14.6 million units**
Dell PC Unit Sales (2005) = 225 million units $\times$ 15% = **33.8 million units**

Dell's future sales will depend on the same two factors: market demand and market share. By accurately projecting demand and share, Dell obtains a reliable sales projection for use in planning cost effectively for production.

Dell PC Unit Sales (2010) = 325 million units $\times$ 15% = **48.8 million units**

Share Performance Metrics

But how does Dell hold or grow a 15 percent market share from 2005 to 2010? Projecting a business's future market share can involve complex mathematical propositions, but a reasonable estimate is easily arrived at by using simple marketing logic. We begin by developing an understanding of *how market share is achieved.*

Figure 3-18 shows a process for estimating a *market share index* based on a set of sequential market share metrics. Each step along the *share development path* indicates how the customer response to a strategy influences market share.[17] Because many other factors also affect market share, the market share index derived from the customer responses is simply an indicator of the level that market share *should* reach, given certain expected levels of market performance.

Each of the five effects on market share presented in Figure 3-18 is derived from one of the five basic kinds of marketing strategies. As a group, we call these five sets of strategies the "marketing mix." This marketing mix consists of a business's marketing strategies with respect to "promotion, product, price, place, and service."

- **Promotion** strategies create awareness of a product and its benefits.
- **Product** positioning strategies promote product attractiveness and preferences based on product benefits.
- **Price** strategies stimulate purchases by offering attractive customer value.
- **Place** strategies ensure product availability and customer service at points of purchase.
- **Service** strategies enhance customer satisfaction and retention.

The share development path traces these five market share effects, measuring the favorable customer response for each set of strategies. The path ends at a particular level of indexed market penetration—the market share index—which is the product of the five rates of favorable customer response to the five elements of the marketing mix.

Market Share Index = Promotion $\times$ Product $\times$ Price $\times$ Place $\times$ Service
= .7 $\times$ .5 $\times$ .6 $\times$ .7 $\times$ .7
= **10.3%**

Perhaps the most important point the market share development path illustrates is that the market share index results from an interaction among all share effects. One poorly performing set of strategies significantly lowers the index. For instance, if the percentage of customers with a favorable service experience were to fall from 70 to 50 percent, the market

FIGURE 3-18 MARKET SHARE METRICS AND SHARE DEVELOPMENT PATH

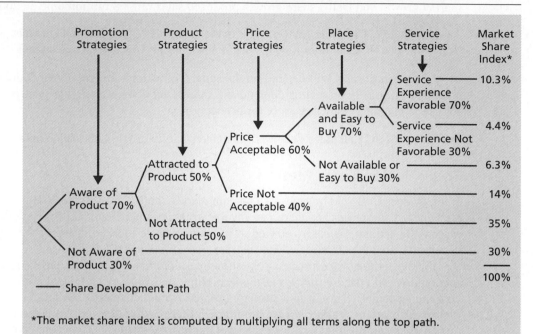

*The market share index is computed by multiplying all terms along the top path.

share index would fall from 10.3 to 7.4 percent, a 28 percent drop. Similarly, increases in the rates of favorable customer response can significantly raise market share potential. Figure 3-19 shows how increases of just 10 and 15 percent in the effect rates would jump the market share index to 24.5 percent, an increase of 238 percent. In managing market share, a business must develop successful strategies for every element of the marketing mix.

Product Awareness

The first share effect on the share development path is product *awareness*: the percentage of the market who are aware of the product. For mature products like Coca-Cola soft drinks, Kodak film, or Ford cars, product awareness is not an issue because virtually all target market customers already know about the products. Low product awareness is more commonly a problem in emerging markets, particularly for new businesses.

But even a large, long-established business can encounter awareness problems. In the early 1980s, Hewlett-Packard began to consider whether it might offer computers and printers for the consumer market. HP was already a familiar name in the office machine sector, so the company thought awareness would not be an issue. HP learned otherwise when a survey of U.S. households revealed that less than 10 percent had any awareness of the company.

Awareness is a particular problem for businesses that serve industrial and commercial markets. They must rely mostly on advertising in trade journals, exhibiting at trade shows, and sales calls to communicate their product positioning and to generate awareness. Consumer goods manufacturers, in contrast, can use a variety of broadcast and print media, as well as in-store merchandising techniques, to build awareness of their products. But whether the business manufactures capital equipment or consumer goods, the first

FIGURE 3-19 CURRENT VERSUS POTENTIAL MARKET SHARE INDEX

Share Performance Metric	Customer Response	Potential Response	Performance Gap*
Product Awareness	70%	80%	−10.0%
Product Attractiveness	50%	60%	−10.0%
Price Affordable	60%	75%	−15.0%
Product Availability	70%	80%	−10.0%
Service Experience	70%	85%	−15.0%
Market Share Index	10.3%	24.5%	−14.2%

*Performance Gap = Customer Response − Potential Response

challenge in expanding market share is to create a high level of product awareness among the business's target customers.

For a product in a very mature market, awareness may already be at the highest level reasonably possible. When this is the case, using another share metric in place of the awareness metric, such as a metric that would measure interest in the product, would be preferable in figuring the market share index.

Product Attractiveness

We know by now that making target customers aware of a product is not enough. The product must also be *attractive* to them. Target customers must have favorable attitudes and an interest in the product and the benefits it offers. If most potential target customers are indifferent or negative, the share development path encounters a major obstruction that dramatically reduces the market share index. A business has little chance of gaining market share from unimpressed potential customers. In the example presented in Figure 3-18, 70 percent of the target customers are aware of the product, but only 50 percent find the product benefits attractive. As a result, a business's share potential is significantly limited.

Price Acceptable

While a product may offer attractive benefits, its price must still be at an *acceptable* level for customers to have a genuine intent to purchase. When intentions to buy are generally lacking, possibly the price is too high. Even when prices are acceptable, customers are not always able to buy immediately, quite often because of inconveniences or drawbacks associated with switching from a competitor's product. Learning the reasons why interested customers have low intentions to buy could uncover a creative marketing solution that would help grow share.

In the share development path presented in Figure 3-18, 60 percent of the target customers who are aware of the product and are attracted to it also find the price acceptable. The 40 percent of the potential customers for whom the price is not acceptable result in a 14 percent reduction of the market share index. To increase the percentage of those who find the price acceptable, a business could offer incentives. A sales promotion program that provides trial usage can be an effective marketing tool for countering price barriers. Once potential customers have tried a product, they can more fully appreciate its benefits.

Buy-back programs, rebates, price promotions, and customer financing are other possible customer solutions when attractiveness is high but intentions to buy are low.

Product Availability

The fourth factor in building market share is product *availability*. If a high percentage of interested customers like a product but cannot find it at their preferred points of purchase, the business's potential for gaining market share is severely diminished. As shown in Figure 3-18, diminished product availability results in a 6.3 percent reduction in potential market share. If the business in this example could increase its product's availability to interested customers from 70 to 80 percent, it would increase its market share index from 10.3 to 11.8 percent.

Service Experience

While the share development path shown in Figure 3-18 takes a potential customer to the point of purchasing a product, a bad *service experience* can negate the entire marketing effort. Most banks and supermarkets have high awareness among potential customers, offer basically the same products at comparable prices, and have convenient locations. For these and similar businesses, it is the quality of customer service that most influences customer purchase. As shown in Figure 3-18, only 70 percent of the potential customers who could buy this product had a positive service experience. Increasing this market metric to 85 percent would improve the company's market share index from 10.3 percent to 12.5 percent.

Market Share Index

The market share index that a business computes by using the share development path in Figure 3-18 will rarely correspond with the business's actual market share. Although a business's actual market share may be higher or lower, the market share index serves as a diagnostic approximation based on market share performance metrics that contribute to a certain level of market share. The index also provides three more important benefits:

- It helps identify the major causes of lost market share opportunity.
- It provides a mechanism for assessing market share change when improvement efforts are directed to an area of poor performance.
- It enables a business to estimate a reasonable potential for its market share, given the levels of performance for each set of strategies along the share development path.

Share Potential and Market Share Management

Figure 3-19 shows the marketing performance gaps between *actual* customer response and *desired* customer response along the share development path. For each step on the path, the performance gap indicates the extent of lost market share due to the lower customer response rates on the path, as opposed to the desired response rates. On the basis of the performance gaps in Figure 3-19, a business could estimate the share and revenue loss due to the lower-than-expected performance levels of its strategies.

Assume that the business represented in Figures 3-18 and 3-19 serves a $500 million market and has an actual market share of 8 percent. If the business can improve product awareness from 70 to 80 percent, it would increase its market share index from 10.3 to 11.8 percent.

$$\begin{array}{c}\textbf{Market Share}\\\textbf{Index}\end{array} = \begin{array}{c}\text{Product}\\\text{Awareness}\\80\%\end{array} \times \begin{array}{c}\text{Product}\\\text{Preference}\\50\%\end{array} \times \begin{array}{c}\text{Price}\\\text{Acceptable}\\60\%\end{array} \times \begin{array}{c}\text{Product}\\\text{Availability}\\70\%\end{array} \times \begin{array}{c}\text{Service}\\\text{Experience}\\70\%\end{array}$$

$$= \textbf{11.8\%}$$

The increase in the estimated market share index is 1.5 percentage points. In a $500 million market, a share of 10.3 percent would result in $51.5 million in sales. A share of 11.8 percent would yield $59 million. The $7.5 increase represents a 14.6 percent improvement in sales revenue. We cannot say that this level of improvement will actually take place, because many other factors affect actual market share. But it is safe to say that some level of improvement may be expected.

But instead of spending more on advertising to create product awareness, the management of the business has decided to implement a channel strategy to improve product availability from 70 to 85 percent. Management sees this move as raising the market share index to 12.5 percent.

$$\begin{array}{c}\textbf{Market Share}\\\textbf{Index}\end{array} = \begin{array}{c}\text{Product}\\\text{Awareness}\\70\%\end{array} \times \begin{array}{c}\text{Product}\\\text{Preference}\\50\%\end{array} \times \begin{array}{c}\text{Price}\\\text{Acceptable}\\60\%\end{array} \times \begin{array}{c}\text{Product}\\\text{Availability}\\85\%\end{array} \times \begin{array}{c}\text{Service}\\\text{Experience}\\70\%\end{array}$$

$$= \textbf{12.5\%}$$

The improvement of 2.2 percentage points in the market share index represents a 21.3 percent increase in the index. With an actual market share of 8 percent, and assuming a similar increase there, management can estimate actual share to improve to 9.7 percent. However, because of the many other influences on actual market share, management knows a proportional impact won't necessarily follow. Nevertheless, management can certainly expect a fairly significant increase in actual market share as the result of improved product availability.

Market Share Potential

Establishing a *desired level of response* at each step along the share development path provides a basis for estimating a business's market share potential. Using Figure 3-19, we can compute a market share index on the basis of the desired rate of favorable customer responses, as shown here:

Market Share Index (Potential) $= 80\% \times 60\% \times 75\% \times 80\% \times 85\% = \textbf{24.5\%}$

A business that establishes a desired level of performance at each step along the share development path and then implements strategies to reach those performance levels should achieve a market share index considerably greater than its current index. Using this process, a business can assess its actual market share relative to its market share potential, and it can determine the level of growth it could achieve with market share gains.

FIGURE 3-20 MANAGING A BUSINESS'S GROWTH POTENTIAL

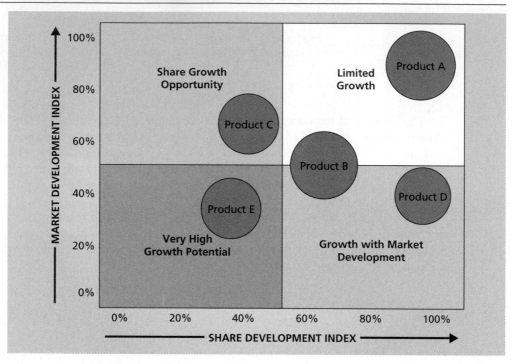

Share Development Index

Having determined its market share potential, a business is now in the position to assess its opportunity for market share development. In our example, the business's current market share is 8 percent, but it should be 10.3 percent based on the business's market share index. Obviously, some secondary factors are keeping the actual market share at only 8 percent. We further estimated that the business's market share index potential would be 24.5 percent if the business could achieve the desired level of positive customer response along the share development path. A ratio of the market share index to the market share index potential provides a share development index (SDI).

$$\textbf{Share Development Index} = \frac{\text{Market Share Index}}{\text{Share Index Potential}} \times 100 = \frac{10.3\%}{24.5\%} \times 100 = \textbf{42}$$

The SDI of 42 means the business is achieving only 42 percent of its potential market share performance. If the business can deliver a marketing strategy that will be effective in achieving the desired customer response rate at each step along the share development path, the market share index will then equal the market share index potential, resulting in an SDI of 100.

By combining the market development index (MDI) with the SDI, we can create a valuable planning matrix that will reveal opportunities for growth. In Figure 3-20, the vertical axis is the scale for the MDI, the degree to which the overall market for a product has been developed. The horizontal axis is the scale for the SDI, the level of market share development the business has achieved. Combining the two indexes to create this matrix provides a way for a business to evaluate the growth opportunities for its product. In developing marketing strategies that will contribute to profitable growth, the matrix will indicate whether a business should concentrate on market development or share development or both, depending on its situation.

For example, we know the business we have been discussing has an SDI of 42, but we don't know the MDI for the market it serves. We do know the current demand in this market produces industry-wide sales of $500 million. By researching facts and using logic and assumptions, we learn the market potential—the level of demand if all potential customers enter the market—is $800 million. The ratio of current demand to maximum demand multiplied by 100 percent gives us the MDI, which is 63 percent. The combined SDI and MDI places this business in the quadrant marked "Share Growth Opportunity," meaning that further growth for this business could best be achieved with a share development strategy.

■ Summary

A critical first step in formulating a marketing strategy is to determine the size of the market. A business with a narrow product focus will see only the products it sells in its current market. By adopting a broad, strategic view of its market, a business will see more possibilities for developing its market, and it will become aware of substitute products and of adjacent markets that might serve as new opportunities for growth.

A broad view of a business's defined market enables the business to determine the maximum potential of its market. The market development index indicates the extent to which a market has reached its maximum demand. In some instances, the market may be well below its maximum demand potential. In an underdeveloped market, it is important to determine the sources of lost market demand: What are the factors that keep customers from entering the market? We learned that the strength of five customer adoption forces and five product adoption forces determine the rate of market growth. Market demand over time is an important aspect of market planning and strategy development. In many of today's markets, market demand is made up of both new customers and existing customers making replacement purchases. Based on the rate at which new customers come into the market, the time it takes for all potential customers to enter the market, and the rate of product replacement, market demand can be projected over time. The rate at which a market approaches its full potential is a function of target customer characteristics, product positioning, and marketing effort. Each of these factors can be influenced by the marketing strategies developed by a business and its competitors.

Market demand typically grows slowly at first, with the product attracting only innovators and early adopters, together known as lead users. During this introductory stage of the product life cycle, before it enters the mainstream market, marketing expenses exceed the gross profit, resulting in a negative net marketing contribution. With successful strategies, the product emerges from this stage, and growth in volume rapidly accelerates. During this stage of the product life cycle, prices and margins decline, and marketing expenses increase. But the much greater volumes result in net marketing contributions that increase throughout the growth phase of the product life cycle. As growth slows, net marketing contributions peak and then begin a slow decline as the product life cycle enters a maturity stage. The market saturates, leaving little or no room for further market development.

The demand for a business's products is also based on the share of market it can extract from a given level of market demand. Market share is simply the proportion of sales a business can obtain from the total market demand at any given time, but a business needs to evaluate its share performance to avoid overlooking deficiencies in the share development path. Five marketing mix factors—promotion, product, price, place, and service—are used to create an index of market share response. The market share index helps a business understand its share potential.

Combining the market development index with a share development index can reveal opportunities to increase sales revenues. For a given market, depending on the market's potential for development, a business can determine its best opportunities for sales growth, depending on its potential to develop share.

■ Market Based Strategic Thinking

1 How does a product-focused market definition differ from a strategic market definition?

2 What are some of the benefits of a strategic market definition?

3 Why is market vision an important element of market demand?

4 Why is it important to establish the maximum potential for market demand?

5 How would you estimate the worldwide market potential for toothbrushes?

6 What would be your estimate of the market development index for toothbrushes?

7 What forces would restrict today's market demand for disposable diapers from reaching the maximum market demand?

8 What factors help accelerate market growth? How can a business affect these factors to accelerate market growth?

9 How does a market development index help a business in its market planning?

10 How do customer adoption forces accelerate or impede market penetration?

11 How do product adoption forces accelerate or impede market penetration?

12 How could a business accelerate the rate of market penetration?

13 Why is it important to view market demand in terms of both replacement and new purchases?

14 Why do volumes, prices, and margins vary over the product life cycle?

15 In Figure 3-12, why is the net marketing contribution negative in the introductory stage of the product life cycle?

16 Why does the net marketing contribution peak during the late growth stage of the product life cycle?

17 What performance factors underlie market share performance?

18 How would a business use an index of its current and potential market share?

19 What are the advantages of computing a market share index?

20 Why might a business's actual market share be different from its market share index for a given target market?

21 How could a matrix combining the MDI and SDI be used to develop international market strategies?

Marketing Performance Tools

Four **Marketing Performance Tools** related to the content of Chapter 3 may be accessed online at *www.rogerjbest.com*. The tools described here are interactive applied-learning exercises designed to improve your understanding of market development, market demand, share management, and the product life cycle as it relates to profits.

3.1 Market Potential and Market Development Indexes (Figure 3-5)
- How would the market potential and market development indexes change if each person had an average of 1.25 personal computers, that is, every fourth person had two personal computers?
- Estimate the worldwide market potential for soft drinks. Make any assumptions you believe are reasonable.

3.2 Forecasting Sales (Figure 3-14)
- How do sales and the market development index change when sales growth is adjusted downward to 5 percent annually?
- What would be the sales impact if the business could hold prices at $500

per unit over the 3-year planning period but lost 0.5 share points each year?

3.3 Market Share Management (Figures 3-18 and 3-19)
- How much would the market share index and share development index change if product attractiveness could be improved from 50 to 60 percent with more effective advertising?
- How much would the market share index and market share development index change if product availability could be improved from 70 to 80 percent?

3.4 Product Life-Cycle Profits (Figure 3-17)
- How would product life-cycle profit change if the market grew at a slower rate between 2005 and 2010 such that in 2010 market demand would be 275 million units?
- What would be the impact on product life-cycle profits be if the average selling price dropped to $1,000 by 2010 and percent margins dropped to 13 percent?

Notes

1. Malcolm Gladwell, *Tipping Point* (New York: Lisle, Brown and Company, 2000).
2. Noel Tichy and Stratford Sherman, *Control Your Destiny or Someone Else Will* (New York: Harper Business, 1993); and Richard Ott, "The Prerequisite of Demand Creation," in *Creating Demand* (Burr Ridge, IL: Business One Irwin, 1992): 3–10.
3. Theodore Levitt, "Marketing Myopia," *Harvard Business Review* (July–August 1960): 45–56.
4. Jerry Porras and James Collins, "Successful Habits of Visionary Companies," *Built to Last* (New York: Harper Collins, 1994); and Burt Nanus, *Visionary Leadership* (San Francisco: Jossey-Bass, 1992).
5. Philip Kotler and Fernando Trias de Bes, *Lateral Marketing* (New York: Wiley, 2003).
6. Gary Hamel and C. K. Prahalad, *Competing for the Future* (Cambridge, MA: Harvard Business School Press, 1994): 103.
7. R. E. Bucklin and V. Srinivasan, "Determining Interbrand Substitutability Through Survey Measurement of Consumer Preference Structures," *Journal of Marketing Research* (February 1991): 58–71; "Car Makers Use Image Map as Tool to Position Products," *The Wall Street Journal* (March 22, 1984): 33; and "Mapping the Dessert Category," *Marketing News* (May 14, 1982): 3.
8. Derek Abell and John Hanunond, *Strategic Market Planning* (Upper Saddle River, NJ: Prentice Hall, 1979): 185–186.
9. Philip Kotler, *Marketing Management,* 7th ed. (Upper Saddle River, NJ: Prentice Hall, 1991): 240–260.

10. J. Pfeffer and R.Sutton, "Why Managing by Facts Works," *Strategy+Business* (Spring 2006).

11. Roger Calantorte, Anthony di Benedetto, and Sriraman Bhoovaraghavan, "Examining the Relationship Between the Degree of Innovation and New Product Success," *Journal of Business Research* 30 (June 1994): 143–148; and Fareena Sultan, John Farley, and Donald Lehmann, "A Meta-Analysis of Applications of Diffusion Models," *Journal of Marketing Research* (February 1990): 70–77.

12. Frank Bass, Trichy Krishonan, and Dipak Jain, "Why the Bass Model Fits Without Decision Variables," *Marketing Science* 13 (Summer 1994): 203–223.

13. Geoffrey Moore, *Inside the Tornado* (New York: Harper Collins, 1985): 11–26.

14. William Davidson, *Marketing High Technology* (New York: Free Press, 1986).

15. John Naisbitt, *Global Paradox: The Bigger the World Economy, the More Powerful Its Smallest Players* (New York: Morrow, 1994).

16. Delbert Hawkins, Roger Best, and Kenneth Coney, *Consumer Behavior—Implications for Marketing Strategy*, 8th ed. (New York: Irwin, 2001): 250–251.

17. Doug Schaffer, "Competing Based on the Customer's Hierarchy of Needs," *National Productivity Review* (Summer 1995).

CHAPTER 4

The Customer Experience and Value Creation

■ Only 8 percent of customers describe their experience as superior, yet 80 percent of companies believe the experience they provide is indeed superior.[1]

The observation above, based on a survey of 362 companies by Bain & Company, tells us that few companies make much of an effort to know the total customer experience. While many companies do measure customer satisfaction, this marketing performance metric does not identify *the reasons why* customers are satisfied or dissatisfied.

Because satisfaction is a composite of the total customer experience—the good aspects of the experience minus the bad ones—a business that knows how it performs in every aspect of the customer experience then understands the reasons behind its customer satisfaction index.

Some companies believe adding more features to a product improves the customer experience. With experienced customers, the opposite can be true.[2] For them, extra features are often a nuisance. For this reason, Lexus will not add a feature to its automobiles unless the company is certain the new feature will enhance the driving experience. Figure 4-1 illustrates the Lexus approach to improving the customer experience by looking beyond Its product to its customers. With the knowledge Lexus gains from its customers, the company can then introduce new product and service benefits that will truly add to the customer experience.

FIGURE 4-1 LEXUS CUSTOMER EXPERIENCE AND CUSTOMER VALUE

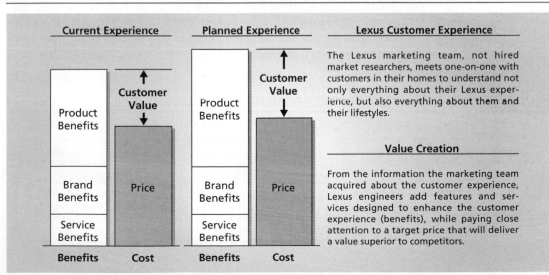

Lexus Customer Experience

The Lexus marketing team, not hired market researchers, meets one-on-one with customers in their homes to understand not only everything about their Lexus experience, but also everything about them and their lifestyles.

Value Creation

From the information the marketing team acquired about the customer experience, Lexus engineers add features and services designed to enhance the customer experience (benefits), while paying close attention to a target price that will deliver a value superior to competitors.

THE TOTAL CUSTOMER EXPERIENCE

To discover new customer benefits, the Lexus marketing team knows it must have a good awareness of its customers' lifestyles and demographics, as well as the features customers like or dislike. The Lexus team wants to know all it can about the total customer experience.

The total customer experience is much more than the interactions a customer has with a company. The customer experience, as shown in Figure 4-2, includes the purchase experience with respect to information, evaluation, order placement, and payment.[3] During the purchase experience, most touch points are proactive. The usage experience, being at a greater distance, is harder to observe, but it is during this stage that the true value of a product becomes apparent. Yet few businesses have a good knowledge of their customers' user experience. The last stage of the customer experience is the replacement stage. As customers consider replacing or upgrading their products, a business has the opportunity for a few more touch points. For some businesses, this stage includes product disposal. It's another opportunity for customer interaction, especially if disposal is difficult and a barrier to repurchasing.

A customer's level of satisfaction depends on all three stages in Figure 4-2. These separate stages are the framework a business can use in identifying areas of satisfaction and dissatisfaction. Once a business knows its weaknesses at any stage, it then sees ways it can improve its product and service benefits.

Empathic Design

An effective way to develop an improved recognition of customer desires and needs is to become the customer.[4] Customers' statements of their preferences are important but, when asked, customers often do not mention the frustrations they encountered in the purchase and use of a product. For this reason, Honda's effort to improve customer value includes observation of customers' actual experiences. To better understand the difficulties people have in loading their car trunks, for instance, Honda sent a crew to supermarket parking lots to videotape people loading their groceries. The videos showed most people arranged their bags to keep them from falling over. Some first placed their bags so they leaned against the rear-end wall of the compartment well, but these people then found they couldn't close their trunk doors. The videos gave Honda engineers a way to put themselves "in the customers' shoes." By seeing and feeling users' experiences, the engineers could then envision better trunk designs.

FIGURE 4-2 THE TOTAL CUSTOMER EXPERIENCE

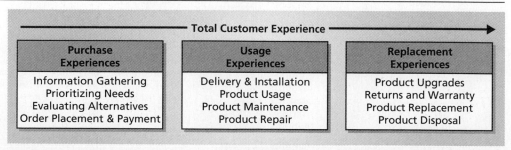

Videotaping customer product use is one form of the *empathic design*. It is an observational approach to understanding customer needs and discovering the problems customers commonly encounter in acquiring, using, and disposing of a product. Intuit, the maker of the personal finance software Quicken, has a Follow-Me-Home program. Product developers obtain permission from first-time buyers to observe their initial experience with the software in their own homes. In this way, Intuit's product developers see the other software applications on the customer's system and whether those applications are compatible with Quicken. From their in-home observations, Intuit product developers learned that many small business owners used Quicken to keep their accounting books. That discovery led to a new product line called QuickBooks.

Empathic design gives a business the opportunity to learn more about the customer's usage experience, as depicted in the center box of Figure 4-2. But by itself, empathic design does not provide full insight into the total customer experience.

Hypothetical Videos: Current Versus Desired Customer Experience

Although actual observation is preferred, observing customers in many consumer, business, and industrial markets isn't possible. As an alternative, a business could create two "hypothetical videos" of the customer experience.[5] Video 1 would be a scripted sequence of scenes that describe a typical customer's experiences with respect to the acquisition, installation, use, maintenance, and disposal of the product. In creating its hypothetical video, the business pays particularly close attention to those parts of each scene that, from the customer's perspective, hold the greatest satisfaction, as well as to those parts that present problems and frustrations. Video 1 is not product specific; it is a narrative of the process a customer goes through in acquiring and using the current solution for the customer's needs.

In "making" hypothetical Video 2, the business would re-describe the scenes of Video 1 as though the product's desired features were already a reality. It is this video that provides the opportunity for a business to discover new ways to improve and communicate customer value.

To fully understand this approach to using the customer experience for adding product benefits and improving customer value, let's examine how Weyerhaeuser Corporation, a leading wood products company, applied it to the use of particleboard by furniture makers. The initial prompt for creating hypothetical Video 1 occurred when a Weyerhaeuser marketing team visited a large furniture maker to learn more about the product benefits the furniture maker looked for when purchasing particleboard. The furniture maker was clear that it mainly wanted consistent high quality and a low price. Weyerhaeuser presented a compelling case for the high quality of its product, but the customer, who also wanted that low price, was not swayed. The Weyerhaeuser representatives could not improve customer value because they could not compete on price against a competitor that had a considerable cost advantage.

This is where most businesses would have stopped in their analyses of customer needs. Weyerhaeuser, however, put together a multifunctional team to revisit the furniture maker to gain a better understanding of the processes the manufacturer employed in purchasing, inventorying, modifying, and using particleboard in making furniture. This time, Weyerhaeuser sought to understand how the furniture maker used particleboard, not just the furniture maker's product-specific purchase criteria.

FIGURE 4-3 CURRENT CUSTOMER EXPERIENCE

Customer Use Process	Customer Frustration	Cost to Customer
Cut the particleboard	Saw blades wear out quickly from excess grit	Production downtime and saw blade sharpening and replacement
Build furniture	Need to use thicker pieces	Lamination process to glue pieces
Produce finished product	Desired finish not achieved	Requires sanding for desired finish

By focusing on the actual *use* of a product, not just on the product, Weyerhaeuser discovered two major shortcomings in the particleboard then available to furniture makers. One was the grit present in the particleboard. A high level of grit, Weyerhaeuser's hypothetical video would show, requires more production downtime for sharpening saw blades, as well as more expense due to shorter blade life. Heavy grit also often resulted in an unsatisfactory surface, requiring that pieces be sanded for the desired smoothness.

The second shortcoming of the particleboard was that it was only available in sheets that were too thin for many applications. The furniture maker Weyerhaeuser visited often had to laminate pieces of particleboard to obtain the thickness needed for some furniture. Figure 4-3 summarizes the customer's current use, frustrations, and associated costs as uncovered during the customer visit to create the hypothetical Video 1.

With these insights into customer use, Weyerhaeuser responded with hypothetical Video 2, a sequence of scenes where the furniture maker has the benefit of a less gritty, thicker particleboard. In the video, the reduced grit lessens blade wear and eliminates the sanding, and the increased thickness eliminates the laminating. The result of using the new product, although more costly to purchase, is an overall substantial savings for the customer. Figure 4-4 indicates how the product benefits would translate into meaningful customer value, and Figure 4-5 represents one way that Weyerhaeuser communicated this customer value.

The Customer Experience of Lead Users

Not all customers use products the same way. Some are new users who lack experience with the product, and others are occasional users with somewhat limited experience. Observing or querying these customers for sources of dissatisfaction usually results in minimal insight. Many products, however, have *lead users*—highly knowledgeable and skilled users who extend the boundaries of a product's application to achieve a more complete customer solution.

FIGURE 4-4 DESIRED CUSTOMER EXPERIENCE

Customer Process	Ideal Solution	Benefit to Customer
Cut the particleboard to size	Saw blades last longer	Less production downtime and lower saw blade expense
Build furniture	Buy thicker pieces	Eliminate lamination process
Produce finished product	Smoother finish	Less sanding required for finish

FIGURE 4-5 TRANSFORMING BAD CUSTOMER EXPERIENCES INTO CUSTOMER VALUE

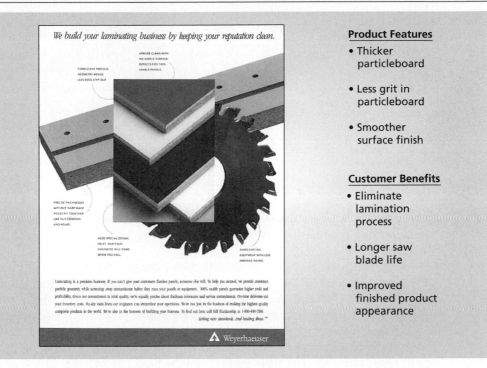

Product Features

- Thicker particleboard

- Less grit in particleboard

- Smoother surface finish

Customer Benefits

- Eliminate lamination process

- Longer saw blade life

- Improved finished product appearance

Studying the experience of lead users provides insights for improving a product by adding new features or modifying it in other ways. A good understanding of lead users' needs and desired solutions can result in major, incremental improvements in product benefits and customer value. Lead users of cellular phones, as an example, devised ways to extend the capabilities of the phones beyond their intended application by using them to access the Internet—a technology that is spawning many new products and companies.

Figure 4-6 shows the four steps in developing new customer solutions with the help of a product's lead users.[6] Identifying these users is step one. Discovering how they use the product to solve their own problems, step two, opens the door to insights on how a product may be adapted for a more complete customer solution. At step three, a business

FIGURE 4-6 LEVERAGING LEAD USER CUSTOMER EXPERIENCE

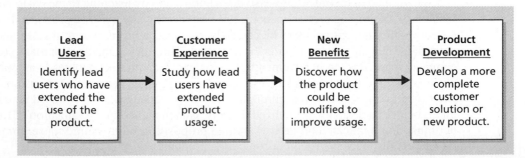

Lead Users	Customer Experience	New Benefits	Product Development
Identify lead users who have extended the use of the product.	Study how lead users have extended product usage.	Discover how the product could be modified to improve usage.	Develop a more complete customer solution or new product.

FIGURE 4-7 REVERSE INNOVATION—INVENT TO ORDER

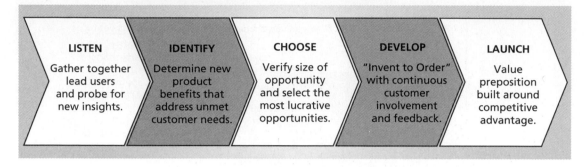

considers developing value-added features, functions, and services. Step four involves reengineering products or developing new ones that offer the more complete customer solutions.

In applying this process, 3M identified lead users in the transport of museum pieces. The need to protect valuable, highly fragile items during transport had led museum personnel to devise several innovative solutions. After learning how these lead users had adapted conventional packaging materials for museum pieces, 3M developed a new line of off-the-shelf material for packaging fragile items.[7] Further, 3M found that developing new products by researching and refining lead user applications of existing products produces eight times more revenue than generating new products by other analyses of customer needs.[8]

Reverse Innovation—Invent to Order

Companies seeking discontinuous innovations need more than incremental product improvements that come from lead user analysis. However, the investment required for large-scale innovations is expensive, typically in the billions of dollars, and these innovations often result in dead ends or intriguing products that nobody wants. Dow Chemical uses "reverse innovation" to improve its odds of success in developing disruptive innovations by starting with the customer. The company's approach is to learn *what customers want but cannot get from existing products.* If the company can make what the customers want and find enough other customers with the same need, Dow will go to the lab with a prescription it calls "invent to order."[9]

As outlined in Figure 4-7, reverse innovation starts by listening to the customer experience and identifying product benefits not provided by any existing products. Each proposed product benefit needs to be carefully analyzed with respect to market and profit potential. Then an "invent to order" is specified. Throughout the development process, a company maintains the involvement of customers. As a product evolves from concept to physical form, it typically undergoes many design changes in response to customer feedback. The first Lexus car went through 1,000 design changes, mostly based on customer input, before its design was finalized. Finally, launch and commercialization of the product must communicate and deliver a value proposition built around these unique customer benefits, ones not found in competing products.

FIGURE 4-8 CUSTOMER TOUCH POINTS

Customer Touch Points	Customer Problems and Interaction Opportunities to Improve the Customer Experience and Build Customer Value
Order Planning	Customers do not recognize the business's solution as relevant
Order Development	Insufficient or incomplete information for meaningful evaluation
Order Evaluation	Customers encounter difficulties/frustrations in placing orders
Order Placement	Difficulties in placing order with your business
Order Entry	Order recorded or priced incorrectly
Order Processing	Order in process but customer not aware of order status and delivery
Order Delivery	Product delivered late or damaged; wrong product delivered
Customer Invoice	Bill has errors, no one to contact, and calls lead to voice mail hell
After-Sale Services	Problems after purchase with no one to call; calls not returned
Product Usage	Inadequate Instructions; no hotline offered
Product Problems	Product does not work and must be returned at customer's expense
Returns and Claims	Customer has to fight to get warranty claim resolved

Dow pioneered reverse innovation in 1991 when its plastics business was performing poorly. By 2004, with an intense customer focus, Dow plastics had achieved four times the volume and three times the sales. More recently, the company used reverse innovation to address an unmet need in the apparel industry, successfully launching XLA, a product with more stretch, less shrinkage, better wrinkle resistance, and more texture than competing products.

Managing Customer Touch Points

During a customer's process of buying and using a product, a business has several opportunities to impact a customer's experience. The business can respond either proactively by anticipating possible problems and then reaching out to and helping the customer at the various touch points, or it can respond reactively, letting the customer make the first contact. A business could, for instance, take a close look at its customer ordering process from the customer's viewpoint, with the objective of uncovering any potential problems or sources of frustration in the purchasing process. This day-in-the-life-of-a-customer approach might be described as "stapling yourself to an order"[10] in an effort to discover the touch points where a business can improve the customer experience.

The customer experience outlined in Figure 4-8 involves tracking the customer order process from the early stages of order planning to the resolution of claims whenever after-purchase problems arise. Each step of the ordering cycle has the potential for causing customers problems or frustrations. The earlier any problems or frustrations occur, the less likely a customer is to buy from that business. Problems or frustrations that emerge later in the process hurt the chances of repurchase, lowering the customer retention rate.

A business could begin its assessment of its ordering process by asking, "What are the worst things we could do to a customer at each stage of the customer order cycle?" On the basis of the level of customer frustration that these actions or omissions would create, and the frequency with which they could occur, a market-based business would identify and implement preventive measures and look for other ways to add customer value by improving the purchasing process. A market-based business with a strong customer focus can use its order cycle to create important sources of customer value that the business's product-focused competitors will never see.

Weyerhaeuser's, Intuit's, Honda's, and 3M's efforts to create additional customer benefits went beyond product-focused thinking. They each engaged in an analysis of the customer experience and the problems customers encountered. With a better knowledge of customer usage, these businesses were able to engineer customer solutions for needs that were poorly met by the then-available products.[11] Had Weyerhaeuser focused on product features, paying little attention to customer needs, the business would not have discovered a profitable customer solution. If Intuit had focused on selling as many copies of its Quicken software as it could, without the knowledge gained from home visits that its customers were extending the program's application, the business would never have developed QuickBooks.

All customers have problems that require solutions. Whereas product-focused businesses are *providers of products*, market-based businesses are *providers of solutions*.[12] To be a provider of customer solutions requires a broad view of customers' underlying problems, a view that transcends products or services to include a comprehensive understanding of customer usage and needs. Such a perspective leads to otherwise unseen opportunities for improving customer value. Any business that concentrates on offering customer solutions has the high ground when it comes to recognizing, developing, and adding meaningful and profitable product benefits.

MASS COLLABORATION

Businesses that value the opinions of their customers and employees have in the past relied on the suggestion box to obtain ideas for improving products and processes. But suddenly the suggestion box has become old fashioned. Its replacement is the Internet, a much more efficient and far-reaching means for businesses to tap into the knowledge and experience of consumers, professionals, suppliers, and employees. Web sites created by Wikipedia give large groups of individuals around the world the ability to share their ideas and to comment on the proposals of others. The result has been a major new development in the area of product improvement known as *mass collaboration*, a concept skillfully laid out in B. D. Tapscott and A. D. Williams's book, *Wikinomics: How Mass Collaboration Changes Everything*.[13]

Wiki Web sites can take many different forms and involve different kinds of collaborators, but in all cases the main purpose is to create an avenue for dialogue that lets a business draw upon the expertise of a large group. With mass collaboration, a business essentially outsources its research and development effort to people all over the globe, any one of whom could make the discovery, find the solution, or propose the idea the business is looking for. Mass collaboration gives businesses a dramatically new approach to value creation, and quickly it has become almost a necessity. In the words of A. G. Lafley, CEO of Procter & Gamble:

> No company today, no matter how large or how global, can innovate fast enough or big enough by itself. Collaboration—externally with consumers and customers, suppliers, and business partners, and internally across business and organizational boundaries—is critical. Wikinomics represents the next historic step—the art and science of mass collaboration where companies open up to the world.

FIGURE 4-9 MASS COLLABORATION AND VALUE CREATION

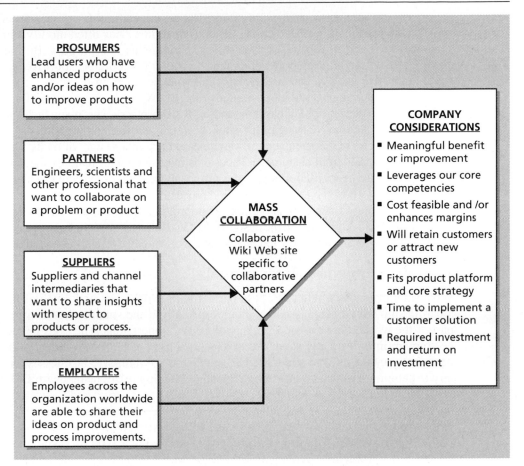

Procter & Gamble is one of the many companies using mass collaboration to develop improved products. An example aired by National Public Radio illustrates the process. In the example, P&G has its own scientists working in research and development but, with the goal of quickly finding a molecule that will remove red wine and similar stains from fabric, the company decided to use mass collaboration, offering a cash award to the first scientist anywhere in the world who produces an effective and safe molecule. The reasoning behind the decision makes sense: Would the discovery of the new molecule more likely come from the relatively few scientists working for P&G or from the hundreds of thousands of scientists worldwide? With mass collaboration, P&G gains access to expertise and creativity far beyond its own domain, and it likely finds a solution more quickly and with a smaller investment.

A business could seek the collaborative input of a unique group of individuals, such as scientists in a specific field, or it could look to a broad spectrum of individuals, such as all current and prospective users of a particular product. The four groups businesses most frequently involve in mass collaboration are prosumers, partnerships with professionals or specialists, suppliers, and employees, as outlined in Figure 4-9.

Prosumers—Customers as Co-Inventors

Prosumers are product-consumer inventors. The customers in this unique subset of consumers take product usage beyond its intended capability. They often modify a product in some way so it performs better or even serves an altogether new purpose. Businesses that engage prosumers in product development through mass collaboration frequently discover innovative ways to increase the customer value of their products.

For example, among automobile enthusiasts, BMW enjoys a reputation for reliability and high-quality design. BMW has thousands of R&D professionals, many dedicated to specific aspects of automotive design. But when it came time to rethink the company's telemetric features, such as GPS navigation, BMW released a digital design kit on its Web site and asked for proposals from customers. Thousands responded with features they envisioned, and BMW's engineers used many of the proposals in developing value-added benefits. Figure 4-9 shows how the mass collaboration process leads to possible solutions.

Apple also used mass collaboration for improving the iPod, and LEGO involved its target customers—children—in the design of LEGO Robots. As might be expected, LEGO's collaborative Web site also attracted many engineers who offered some good ideas, too.

Partners—Engaging Professionals

What small business wouldn't want to partner with BMW? But how likely is it that such a partnership would actually come about, especially if the small business is in a remote part of the world, far removed from any of BMW's operations. The odds of such a partnership are infinitesimally small. Or at least they used to be. BMW now hosts a virtual design agency on its Web site that gives small and medium-size businesses an opportunity to submit ideas that could very well lead to ongoing relationships with BMW.

Consider a Canadian gold mine, which over a 50-year period had seemingly depleted one of its properties of its available gold. Like any large mining company, this company employed its own geologists, and for years they had worked on the possibility of extracting the "unavailable" gold from the property. Then, using a Wiki Web site, the company presented its problem to geologists around the world. This worldwide audience of professionals reviewed the property's geology and the company's activities to date, and they also reviewed the recommendations and comments of one another. From this group of geologists came new ideas that resulted in an extraction that equaled the entire amount of gold mined from the site during the previous 50 years.

Eli Lilly and IBM serve as other examples of companies that use mass collaboration. Eli Lilly's Wiki site allows scientists around the world to participate in developing cures and preventions for diseases. IBM estimates its collaboration with open source communities saves the company almost $1 billion annually over the cost of maintaining an in-house operation that would produce the same results.

As Figure 4-9 illustrates, businesses must dedicate resources to filtering and aggregating partner contributions. The reward is that mass collaborations with outside professionals and specialists lead to product enhancements in less time and at a lower cost than the conventional closed approach.

Suppliers—Leveraging Supplier Participation

In the world of mass collaborations, suppliers must also have the opportunity to share their ideas on product and process improvement. Using the old approach, a company would develop the design specifications for a product and the suppliers would use those specifications in preparing their bids—a process that greatly limited the use of suppliers' creativity. With mass collaboration, suppliers become part of the design process.

Boeing's sleek, fuel-efficient 787, for example, is the result of a collaborative effort among some 100 suppliers in six countries. Boeing structured this truly collaborative design effort as a horizontal network of partners who worked together to produce a product with an exceptionally high level of performance. By targeting suppliers as its collaborators, Boeing gained access to the best ideas and capabilities in the worldwide aircraft industry.

Channel intermediaries are another group that businesses frequently involve. An intermediary who sees customers daily develops a good knowledge of their likes and dislikes, as well as a keen awareness of their needs. For businesses with indirect sales channels, the collaboration of intermediaries can rapidly lead to products with greater customer value.

Employees—An Under-Leveraged Opportunity

A business's frontline employees are perhaps in the best position to see possibilities for improvements to products and processes. These employees, however, can rarely break through the firewall surrounding those who are in positions to evaluate the ideas and take steps to adopt new product benefits and processes. By encouraging employee participation through mass collaboration, a business overcomes the invisible barrier between the front line and the front office.

At a large company, the employees are also often consumers of the company's products. Many Procter & Gamble employees, for instance, undoubtedly use the company's products in their daily lives. Why wouldn't management want to hear from them about how the products might be improved?

On the product floor, it could be that a maintenance supervisor has found a way to extend the life of an expensive piece of equipment. With an effective way to share that information with other maintenance managers, the business would realize a tremendous cost savings. Mass collaboration of this type provides yet another source of value creation for businesses and customers.

LIFE-CYCLE COST AND CUSTOMER VALUE

Customers are willing to pay more for products and services that have an economic value, or, more plainly, for products and services that save them money. To determine a product's economic value, we first determine its *life-cycle cost*, which is the overall cost of purchasing, owning, and disposing of a product.

Life-Cycle Cost = Price Paid + Acquiring Cost + Ownership Cost + Disposal Cost

To arrive at a product's economic value, we then compare our product's life-cycle cost with that of the competing product currently used by the customer. The difference in the two products' life-cycle costs is our product's economic value. Because customer value is essentially a product's total benefits minus the cost of acquiring those benefits, a product with economic value, despite its higher price, typically has more customer value than a competitor's similar product. Delivering *economic value* requires that the customer achieve a *net economic gain* during the product's life cycle.

Economic Value = Competing Product's Life-Cycle Cost − Our Product's Life-Cycle Cost

FIGURE 4-10 LIFE-CYCLE COST AND ECONOMIC VALUE

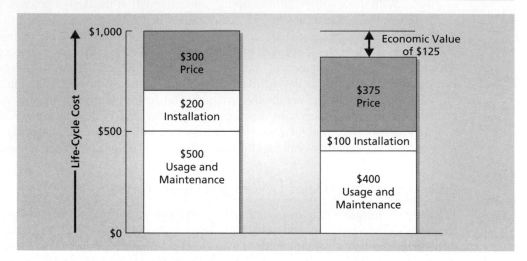

We saw how Weyerhaeuser developed a product with economic value for furniture makers. Weyerhaeuser's conventional product, even though it was of high quality, could not compete on cost among furniture makers, but the new product—in essence a specialty product—can now do so. Even though Weyerhaeuser's new product costs more than competitors' products, its economic value is greater. The money furniture makers save by using the Weyerhaeuser product, instead of a competitor's less expensive product, more than offsets the higher purchase price. Weyerhaeuser first went looking for an unmet customer solution. The company then provided the solution and gained a competitive edge.

In Figure 4-10, the total life-cycle cost of the customer's current product in use, a telecommunications switch, is $1,000. This cost is derived from a $300 price per unit, a $200 installation cost, and a $500 usage and maintenance cost. A competing product with a lower life-cycle cost would offer $125 in economic value, even though it would be priced higher, since the other costs contributing to the life-cycle cost are much lower.[14]

Economic Value = $1,000 Life-Cycle Cost (Switch A) − $875 Life-Cycle Cost (Switch B)
= **$125**

In this case, everybody wins. The customer saves $125 per switch and the manufacturer receives a price $75 higher than a competing product. Both the customer and the manufacturer will be more profitable as a result.[15]

Figure 4-11 outlines the six primary costs that make up the life-cycle cost. The purchase price for a product or service stands out as the most obvious of these costs, and it is the one that businesses most commonly use in communicating economic value to their customers. Customers have no difficulty understanding that a product of the same quality as a competitor's but with a lower price offers more economic value. But the other sources of value creation can, from a customer's perspective, be even more important. The economic value of a product benefit that would eliminate a time-consuming step, for instance, would be seen immediately by affected customers as ultimately saving much more money than would a lower price. It is by spending a day in the life of a customer

FIGURE 4-11 SOURCES OF ECONOMIC BENEFIT AND VALUE CREATION

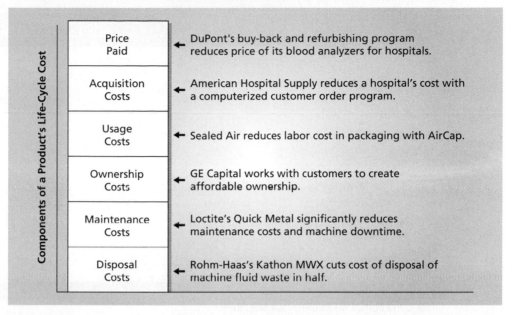

that marketers can discover the value-creation opportunities that may be present in any of the six component costs of the life-cycle cost.

Price Paid

Quite often, the price or payment terms destroy customer value. A product may offer an excellent customer solution, but its price can be too high relative to the benefits provided. For example, DuPont found that for its more expensive blood analyzers, large hospitals could justify the higher price in light of the overall benefits. Small hospitals, however, had lower volumes of blood chemistry work—not enough to justify purchasing the more sophisticated and more costly blood analyzers.

DuPont ran into another problem when it rolled out a still more advanced blood analyzer. The company met resistance from the large hospitals, which said they could not justify the expense because their present blood analyzers were adequate and still fairly new. This situation led to a strategy in which DuPont offered to buy back the large hospitals' blood analyzers when the hospitals purchased new analyzers. DuPont then refurbished the analyzers it bought back and resold them to small hospitals. In this way, the company created a combination of benefits affordable for both large and small hospitals.

Acquisition Costs

American Hospital Supply found that half of every dollar spent by hospitals on pharmaceuticals, chemicals, and equipment went to the purchasing process and inventory of these products. Acquisition costs, as shown in Figure 4-11, are a part of the total life-cycle cost. By placing computers in hospitals to streamline order entry, logistics, and inventory procedures, the company gave its products economic value by making them less expensive for

FIGURE 4-12 ECONOMIC VALUE ANALYSIS

Life-Cycle Cost Components	Specific Cost	Company AirCap	Competitor Cardboard	Cost Difference
Price Paid	Direct Purchase	$1.05	$0.80	$0.25
Discounts/Rebates (negative number)				
Delivery	Shipping Cost	$2.40	$2.60	−$0.20
Installation				
Shipping Materials	Shipping Carton	$0.55	$0.55	$0.00
Inventory (Holding Cost)				
Financing Cost (Loan Interest)				
Owning Cost (Insurance)				
Usage Cost (Cost of Use)	Labor per Shipment	$0.13	$0.83	−$0.70
Maintenance Cost				
Replacement Cost				
Disposal Cost				
Resale Value (negative number)				
Life-Cycle Cost		**$4.13**	**$4.78**	**−$0.65**
Life-Cycle Period for Product Is: 1 Shipment				

hospitals to order, track, and inventory. As a result, American Hospital Supply won a large share of the market for its products.

Usage Costs

A product that will eliminate or significantly reduce costs that customers presently incur has a substantial economic value. For many businesses, this is the source of their products' economic value. By reducing the manufacturing costs of furniture makers and thereby giving its product economic value, Weyerhaeuser was able to deliver superior customer value with its new particleboard, even at a higher price. The same is true for the telecommunications switch in Figure 4-10. The customer's current switch had a total cost (life-cycle cost) of $1,000. The purchase price was only $300, but installation and start-up costs took an additional $200, and usage and other after-sale costs came to $500. The new switch offered customers a solution that would cut start-up costs in half and reduce the usage cost by $100. As Figure 4-10 shows, this solution created an economic value of $200. However, the product had to be priced in a way that created improved customer value and an increase in profit. In response, the manufacturer set a price of $375, compared to the $300 price for the existing customer solution. The price was $75 higher, but it created a customer solution that added $125 per switch to the customer's bottom line.

Figures 4-12 and 4-13 present another example of creating economic value by reducing usage costs. The lower freight and labor costs made possible by a packaging material more than offsets its higher price. For each carton a manufacturer ships to a customer, Sealed Air's AirCap packaging material costs the manufacturer 25 cents more to buy than a competing product, but AirCap produces an economic value of 65 cents with each carton

FIGURE 4-13 COMMUNICATING ECONOMIC VALUE

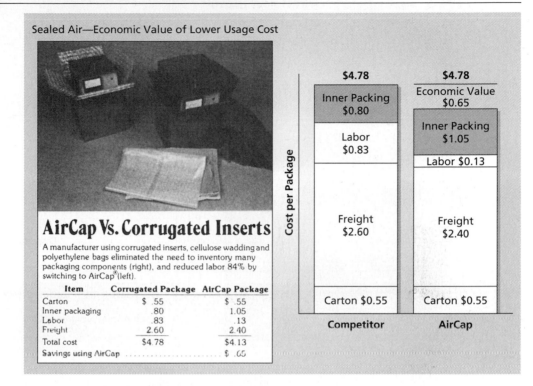

Sealed Air—Economic Value of Lower Usage Cost

AirCap Vs. Corrugated Inserts

A manufacturer using corrugated inserts, cellulose wadding and polyethylene bags eliminated the need to inventory many packaging components (right), and reduced labor 84% by switching to AirCap®(left).

Item	Corrugated Package	AirCap Package
Carton	$ .55	$ .55
Inner packaging	.80	1.05
Labor	.83	.13
Freight	2.60	2.40
Total cost	$4.78	$4.13
Savings using AirCap		$ .65

Competitor — $4.78: Inner Packing $0.80, Labor $0.83, Freight $2.60, Carton $0.55

AirCap — $4.78: Economic Value $0.65, Inner Packing $1.05, Labor $0.13, Freight $2.40, Carton $0.55

the manufacturer ships. This means that, compared to the lower-priced competitor's product, using the AirCap material saves the manufacturer 65 cents per shipment.

Ownership Costs

Products with high ownership costs are typically expensive items that buyers finance and insure. The interest and premiums account for the high ownership costs. General Electric many years ago developed GE Capital to create affordable ownership with GE financing. GE Capital became highly successful and is today a large business, serving both GE and non-GE customers. A business that can make owning its product less expensive than owning a competitor's similar product gives its product economic value. The purchase price of the product might be more, but the total cost to the customer (life-cycle cost) is less because ownership costs are lower.

Maintenance Costs

Maintenance and repair is another area where economic value can be added to a product. Products with good performance records or those with all-inclusive warranties may cost more to buy but will have a lower total cost. To guarantee lower maintenance costs, many products come with a manufacturer's warranty and maintenance contract. Electronic document processing equipment, for example, can be expensive to repair. In response to this risk, Xerox has created a customer satisfaction program that guarantees product performance for an extended period.

FIGURE 4-14 LOWER DISPOSAL COST AS A SOURCE OF ECONOMIC VALUE

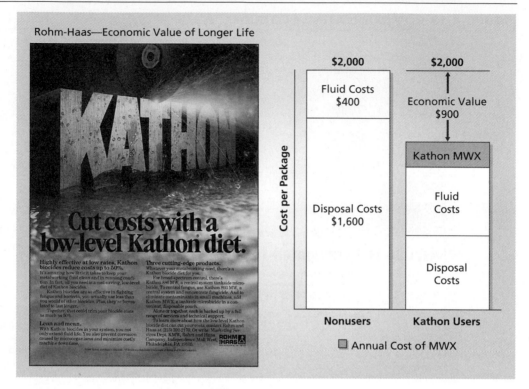

Additionally, any product that can reduce a customer's maintenance and repair costs has economic value for the customer. Loctite's Quick Metal, one of the examples in Figure 4-11, can be applied to worn or cracked machine parts to avoid an extended shutdown. Quick Metal's value proposition, *"Keep the machinery running until the new part arrives,"* tells customers how Quick Metal can create a major savings (economic value) for them.

Disposal Costs

Another source of potential economic value lies in the disposal costs of a product. By reducing or eliminating a customer's disposal cost, a business creates economic value in the product. FP International (FPI), a manufacturer of styrene packaging materials, picks up waste styrene packaging from its customers and then sells the recycled packaging back to its customers at a premium price. Because FPI lowers the total cost of the product by solving its customers' problem of disposing of the waste packaging, the company can charge a higher price and remain competitive.

Figure 4-14 describes another example. Kathon MWX is a product that creates economic value for machine shop owners by extending the life of metalworking machine fluids. The longer life of the fluids reduces their disposal cost over time. In Figure 4-15, we have a third example in competing vehicle models made by Ford and Honda. We can see that Ford offers a lower price paid for two of the three competing models, but the total cost of purchase (life-cycle cost) for all three Ford models is higher. A little research reveals that Honda's lower life-cycle cost is largely due to a lower rate of

FIGURE 4-15 LIFE-CYCLE COST AND ECONOMIC VALUE

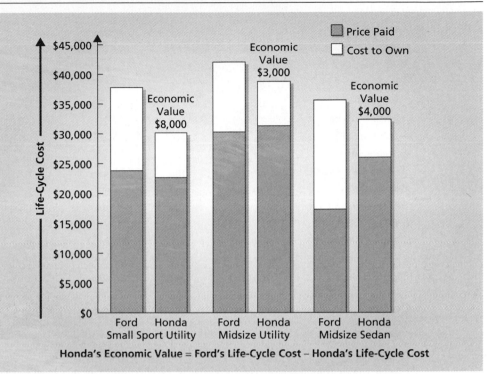

Honda's Economic Value = Ford's Life-Cycle Cost – Honda's Life-Cycle Cost

depreciation.[16] Honda has created economic value in its vehicles by giving them higher resale value or, in other words, by reducing their cost of disposal.

PRICE-PERFORMANCE AND VALUE CREATION

While economic value provides a powerful basis for creating a cost-based customer value, some aspects of product performance are more difficult to quantify in the total cost of purchase. Performance can also include product features and functions that do not save money but enhance usage and, in that way, create customer value. A car can have cost-based value for its owner in its fuel economy, maintenance requirements, and resale value. A car can also offer customer value with comfort and safety features. Although these latter forms of customer value are difficult to quantify with respect to the total cost of owning a car, they can be evaluated with respect to performance. *Consumer Reports,* which rates the performance of a great many products and their features, can be of help in evaluating the relative performance of competing products.

Relative Performance

The overall performance ratings for 15 toasters based on *Consumer Reports'* evaluations of eight product features appear in Figure 4-16.[17] On a scale from 0 to 100, the overall performance of the toasters ranged from a low of 55 to a high of 88, with an average performance of 69. We can create a relative measure of performance by dividing the overall rating of each

FIGURE 4-16 RELATIVE PERFORMANCE, RELATIVE PRICE, AND CUSTOMER VALUE

Name and Model of Toaster	Overall Performance	Relative Performance	Toaster Price	Relative Price	Customer Value
1 Cuisinart CPT-60	88	128	$70	215	-87
2 Sunbeam	82	119	28	86	34
3 KitchenAid	81	117	77	237	-120
4 Black & Decker	77	112	25	77	35
5 Cuisinart CPT-30	75	109	40	123	-14
6 Breadman	74	107	35	108	-1
7 Proctor-Silex 22475	72	104	15	46	58
8 Krups	70	101	32	98	3
9 Oster	65	94	45	138	-44
10 Toastmaster B1021	63	91	16	49	42
11 Proctor-Silex 22415	60	87	35	108	-21
12 Toastmaster B1035	58	84	21	65	19
13 Betty Crocker	58	84	25	77	7
14 Proctor-Silex 22208	57	83	11	34	49
15 Rival	55	80	13	40	40
Average	69	100	$32.50	100	0

toaster by the overall average. This measure of product performance will help us more readily assess performance around a benchmark average of 100, as in the following formula.

$$\text{Relative Performance} = \frac{\text{Product's Performance Rating}}{\text{Average Performance Rating}} \times 100$$

$$\text{Relative Performance} = \frac{82}{69} \times 100 = \mathbf{119}$$

When each toaster's *Consumer Reports* rating is divided by the average of all ratings (69) and multiplied by 100, we have a measure of relative performance in which the average performance is rated at 100. Now we can readily assess performance as it varies from a low of 80 to a high of 128. Sunbeam, for example, has a relative performance of 119, which means Sunbeam's overall performance is 19 percent better than the average of the 15 toasters evaluated.

Relative Price

To acquire Sunbeam's above-average relative performance requires paying a certain amount of money. The price is reported as $28, but it is difficult to infer the attractiveness of this price in absolute dollars. A measure of relative price is also important in understanding value creation. For the 15 toasters evaluated, the overall average price was $32.50. When the average price is used as a performance benchmark, Sunbeam's relative price is 86.

$$\text{Relative Price} = \frac{\text{Product Price}}{\text{Average Price}} \times 100 = \frac{\$28}{\$32.50} \times 100 = \mathbf{86}$$

FIGURE 4-17 PRICE-PERFORMANCE VALUE MAP

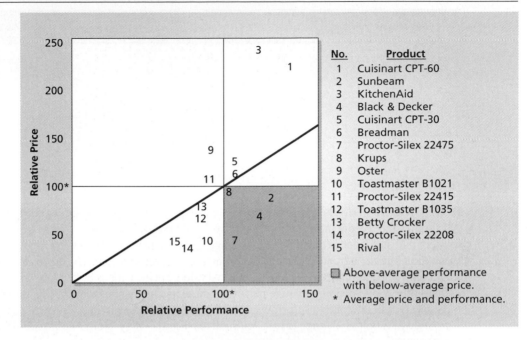

A relative price of 86 means Sunbeam's toaster is 14 percent lower than the average price of the 15 toasters. As Figure 4-16 shows, the relative prices of the toasters ranged from a low of 34 to a high of 237. A customer buying at the lowest price would pay a price 66 percent below the average price, and at the high end a customer would pay 137 percent more than the average price. The Sunbeam relative price, although attractive, does not have the lowest relative price.

Customer Value

With measures of relative performance and relative price, we can determine whether products are above or below average in performance and price. To infer customer value, we compute the difference in these two relative measures, as shown here for Sunbeam.

$$\textbf{Customer Value} = \text{Relative Performance} - \text{Relative Price} - 119 - 86 - \textbf{33}$$

In this example, Sunbeam has a positive customer value of 33. A customer value of zero would mean that the relative performance was offset by the relative price. This offset could occur for a product with above- or below-average performance. The Breadman toaster, for example, has an above-average relative performance (107) that is more than offset by an above-average relative price (108). The net difference is a customer value of –1.

Using this measure of customer value, we can assess the value of different combinations of performance and price. As Figure 4-16 shows, the customer value for these 15 toasters ranges from a low of –120 to a high of 58. To better understand this range of customer values, let's examine these results a little more.

FIGURE 4-18 PRODUCT BENEFITS INDEX

Customer-Determined Product Benefits	Relative Importance	Business Rating	Competitor			Relative Advantage
			A	B	C	
Machine Uptime	40	8	7	5	6	27
Print Speed	30	9	8	5	5	20
Image Quality	20	7	7	7	6	0
Ease of Use	10	4	6	7	6	−10
	100					37

Relative Product Benefits: 100 + 37 = 137

Value Mapping

Plotting relative performance versus relative price gives us a value map, as in Figure 4-17. All the toasters below the diagonal line have positive customer values. Four of these nine toasters that stand out as having above-average performance have below-average prices. For these four brands, attractive pricing has created customer value. Price-sensitive customers might well find alternative 7 the most attractive value, because it has both a low relative price and slightly above-average relative performance. A performance-oriented customer would most likely find alternative 2 the most attractive value, because it offers above-average performance at a below-average price. Alternatives 1 and 3 may seem overpriced relative to performance.

PERCEIVED BENEFITS AND VALUE CREATION

Economic value, relative performance, and relative price are excellent indicators of customer value, and value mapping is an effective way to infer customer value in competing products. But value mapping does not take into consideration a brand's reputation and the general perceptions of its product benefits. In evaluating products for their customer value, we often need to go beyond economic and price-performance measures to include customer *perceptions* of a brand, for these perceptions impact customer value. This section examines the ways we can use customer perceptions of a broad range of benefits and costs to infer customer value in a business's products or services.

Product Benefits

Value creation is logically affected by perceptions of product benefits. These perceived benefits cannot be plotted as obvious, tangible, and objectively rated economic and performance benefits; yet it is customer perceptions that drive purchase behavior. We therefore need a method for measuring customer perceptions of product benefits, and we need a way to determine the relative value derived from customer perceptions when compared with a competitive benchmark.[18]

Figure 4-18 shows four product benefits customers look for in commercial copiers. Each benefit is weighted with respect to its relative importance. "Machine uptime" is weighted twice as important as "image quality," four times as important as "ease of use," and so on. To determine the degree to which a relative advantage is created in delivering

FIGURE 4-19 SERVICE BENEFITS INDEX

Customer-Determined Service Benefits	Relative Importance	Business Rating	Competitor A	B	C	Relative Advantage
Repair Time	60	5	7	6	5	−20
Response Time to Problems	30	5	5	6	2	10
Quality of Service	10	7	7	6	8	0
	100					−10

Relative Service Benefits: 100 − 10 = 90

these product benefits, a business evaluates each customer benefit relative to competing products. In this case, three competitors are used to benchmark each benefit's perceived performance and overall relative advantage.

The benefit ratings shown for the business and the three competitors are based on a scale that ranges from 0 (disastrous) to 10 points (outstanding). If a business's product benefit outperforms a competitor by more than one point, it receives all of the relative importance points allocated to that product benefit. As an example, for "machine uptime" the business is rated only one point above competitor A, but the business is more than one point above the other two competitors. The business has no perceived advantage over competitor A, and so the business receives zero relative importance points with respect to that competitor. But because the business is perceived as better than competitors B and C by more than one point in both cases, it receives from each of the two competitors the 40 relative importance points allocated for "machine uptime." When the three perceived performance impacts are averaged, we obtain an overall relative advantage score of 27 for machine uptime.

$$\frac{\text{Relative Advantage}}{\text{Machine Uptime}} = \frac{0 + 40 + 40}{3} = \mathbf{27}$$

For "print speed," the business also outperformed two of the competitors by more than one point. The business therefore received two-thirds of the relative importance points allocated for "print speed." For "image quality," the business had no perceived relative advantage, and, with respect to "ease of use," the business was rated more than one point below each of the three competitors. The 10 relative importance points allocated for "ease of use" were therefore awarded to each of the three competitors—a total of −30 points from the business's perspective—which made the business's relative advantage score for this product benefit −10 (−30 divided by 3).

When the relative advantage scores for all four product benefits are totaled, the result is the business's overall relative advantage, which in this case is 37. The score of 37 means that, on the basis of perceived ratings of product benefits relative to the competition, the business produces 37 percent greater benefits. When this overall relative advantage is added to a base index of 100, a relative product benefits index of 137 is produced.

Service Benefits

For many markets or segments, product differentiation is minimal because competitors have been able to emulate the best features of each other's products. Whenever product features

FIGURE 4-20 COMPANY OR BRAND BENEFITS INDEX

Customer-Determined Company Benefits	Relative Importance	Business Rating	Competitor A	B	C	Relative Advantage
Customer Commitment	60	8	7	6	4	40
Reputation for Quality	40	9	8	9	8	0
	100					40
Relative Company Benefits: 100 + 40 = 140						

are basically identical from competitor to competitor, service quality becomes a crucial source of differentiation and competitive advantage.[19] To measure a business's perceived service benefits, we can use the same approach we used for perceived product benefits.

Figure 4-19 provides a measure of perceived service benefits for the same business evaluated in Figure 4-18. With respect to repair time, the business is about equal to two of its benchmark competitors and slightly below one of them. But this position detracts from the business's overall perceived service benefits because 60 percent of all relative importance points are allocated to repair time. For response time to problems, the business roughly matches competitors A and B, and it outperforms competitor C. The net result is a slight advantage. Because the average competitor performance with respect to response time is already somewhat weaker than the business's performance, the business has an excellent opportunity to move ahead in this service benefit. The business's current relative advantage score for response time to problems is figured as follows:

$$\text{Response Time to Problems} = \frac{0 + 0 + 30}{3} = 10$$

With respect to quality of service, the business failed to capture any relative advantage. Overall, the business produced a service benefits index of 90, which means the business is 10 percent less attractive than its competitors in delivering service benefits to customers.

Company or Brand Benefits

A third source of perceived customer benefits is the reputation that the name of a company or brand has with the public. Whether a company such as Nordstrom or Hewlett-Packard or a brand such as Lexus and Perrier, the name itself can be a benefit for many customers. The Nordstrom name is practically a byword for customer service, an added benefit that goes beyond actual customer service, and many HP customers value that company's reputation for innovation, a benefit that is neither product nor service specific. The names Lexus and Perrier convey an element of status, which many customers find appealing.

To measure a business's perceived benefit from its company or brand reputation, we follow the same method that was used for measuring perceived product and service benefits. The benefits for the business in Figure 4-20 were driven by two factors: customer commitment and reputation for quality. In this case, the business leads two of the three benchmark competitors in customer commitment but has no relative advantage in reputation for quality. The net result of these customer perceptions is an overall index of 140 with respect to relative company benefits.

FIGURE 4-21 OVERALL BENEFITS INDEX

Customer-Determined Overall Benefits	Relative Importance	Relative Advantage	Overall Benefits
Product Benefits	0.60	137	82
Service Benefits	0.30	90	27
Company Benefits	0.10	140	14
	1.00		123
	Overall Relative Benefits = 123		

Overall Customer Benefits

To arrive at an overall measure of perceived customer benefits, we need a way to combine the three sources of customer-perceived benefits. Combining perceived product benefits, perceived service benefits, and perceived company or brand reputation benefits requires weighing the relative importance of each group. In Figure 4-21, most weight is given to product benefits (0.60), less weight to service benefits (0.30), and the least weight to company benefits (0.10). When these relative importance ratings are weighted by the respective relative benefits indexes, an overall index of perceived benefits can be obtained. In this case, the overall perceived benefits score of 123 means that the business is 23 percent ahead of its competition in delivering perceived customer benefits.

But has the business created a superior customer value? We still don't know. The level of perceived customer value cannot be determined until we also determine the perceived cost of acquiring these benefits.

Cost of Purchase Index

In determining the overall level of value created for customers, we must first determine the perceived relative cost of purchase, a process similar to computing perceived relative benefits. We begin by identifying the components of the purchase cost that a typical customer would consider in a decision to buy, and then assigning each component relative importance points on a percentage basis.

Figure 4-22 lists four sources of cost that copier customers would likely consider in arriving at the total cost of purchase. The purchase price logically has the most relative

FIGURE 4-22 COST OF PURCHASE INDEX

Customer Cost of Purchase Componet	Relative Importance	Business Rating	Competitors' Ratings			Relative Advantage
			A	B	C	
Purchase Price	40	7	8	5	5	27
Service and Repair	30	5	6	7	6	−10
Toner	20	5	8	7	5	−14
Paper	10	6	6	5	5	0
	100					3
	Relative Cost of Purchase = 100 + 3 = 103					

importance, and 40 points are allocated to it. Three other costs—for service and repairs, toner, and paper—are also component costs of the perceived total cost of purchase.

In figuring the cost of purchase index, the *higher* the rating for each cost component, the *higher* the cost with respect to that component. The rating scale, then, is the opposite of the scale used for determining the indexes for product, service, and company or brand benefits. Accordingly, the *higher* the business's relative advantage score for each cost component, the *weaker* its competitive position.

In this example, the business's purchase price is rated at 7, about equal to competitor A's rating of 8. Because the difference in the two ratings is not more than one point, the business does not lose the 40 relative importance points. But because the business is rated more than one point higher than both competitors B and C, the business is assigned 40 points from each of them. The business's high relative advantage score of 27 for purchase price, figured as follows, indicates the business charges a premium price for its product and, as a result, has a weak competitive position with regard to the cost of purchase component.

$$\frac{\textbf{Relative Advantage}}{\text{Purchase Price}} = \frac{0 + 40 + 40}{3} = \textbf{27}$$

For the cost of toner, which has a relative importance of 20, the company is rated more than one point lower than both competitors A and B and equal to competitor C. The relative advantage score for this cost component, –14, means the toner for the business's copier is less expensive for customers than the average cost of toner for the competitors' copiers. More than half of the 27 relative advantage points charged to the business because of its high purchase price are offset by the customers' lower toner costs.

$$\frac{\textbf{Relative Advantage}}{\text{Cost of Toner}} = \frac{-20 + -20 + 0}{3} = \textbf{-14}$$

Similarly, we can compute the business's relative advantage with respect to service and repair costs and paper costs. The overall relative advantage score—the sum of the relative advantage scores for each cost component—is 3, which results in a relative cost of purchase index of 103. The index of 103 means the total cost of purchase for the business's copier is 3 percent less attractive to customers than is the average total cost of purchase for competing copiers.

Customer Value Index

Once customers' perceptions of overall benefits and total cost of purchase have been determined, a business can evaluate the level of value it creates for its customers.[20] Figure 4-23 shows the customer value created by the copier company. Each area of perceived benefit is plotted in the first bar on the graph using the relative advantage scores in Figure 4-21. The total of the scores is the overall benefits index. For the cost of purchase index, which is computed differently than the benefits index, the bar shows the overall relative cost of purchase, with the index equaling the sum of the scores for each cost area plus 100, as presented in Figure 4-22.

FIGURE 4-23 CUSTOMER VALUE AND VALUE MAP

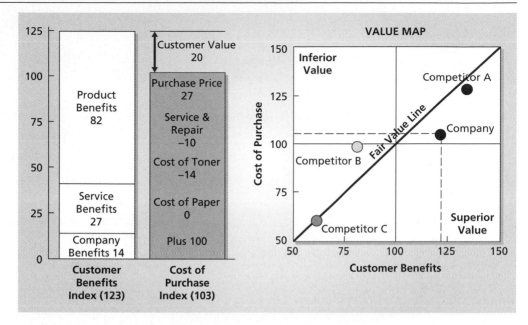

The individual cost areas are not plotted because, as we saw, their relative advantage scores inversely reflect competitive advantage—the higher the score, the lower the advantage.

The difference between the benefits index (123) and the cost of purchase index (103) creates a customer value index of 20. This means the business has created superior customer value while commanding a price premium. If the business wanted to further improve its perceived customer value without lowering price, it could address its weaknesses in ease of use and repair time. To the degree that these two areas could be improved, the business would improve the value it creates for customers and still maintain a price premium.

While the correlation is not perfect, businesses or products with higher customer value indexes have been shown to produce higher levels of profitability than businesses with lower customer value indexes. Businesses along the fair value line typically produce average levels of profitability, while businesses in the superior value region are more profitable. Perhaps as important, businesses in the inferior value region—those with a negative customer value index—have been shown to be lower in profitability.

Figure 4-24 presents the relationship between customer value and profitability as a way to infer the profit potential of a business's customer value. Because many other factors can affect actual measures of return, Figure 4-24 is only a guideline for assessing profit impact. As shown, the company in which we are interested, with a customer value index of 20, should produce a higher profit than competitor C, which has a customer value index of –21.

FIGURE 4-24 CUSTOMER VALUE AND PROFIT IMPACT

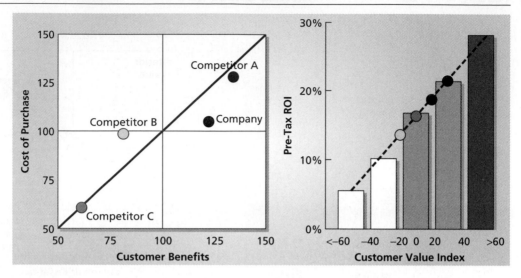

EMOTIONAL BENEFITS AND VALUE CREATION

So far, we have looked at customer benefits that we might describe as *rational* benefits. The rational appeal of an automobile, for instance, includes price, gas economy, maintenance cost, safety features, and resale value. Less tangible rational benefits include the quality of repair service, friendliness of service personnel, and the manufacturer's reputation. Certain products also offer *emotional* benefits tied to the customer's personal psychological needs. The same can be true in many business-to-business purchases in which emotional benefits might be tied to security, reputation, or friendship. To be thorough in our examination of customer benefits and value creation, we need to consider sources of emotional customer benefits and the ways they contribute to customer value.

Emotional Benefits and Psychological Value

We know that every individual has both physical and psychological needs. Physical needs such as food, shelter, sleep, and safety naturally receive our priority. Once those necessities are met, we can devote more attention to our psychological needs, such as close relationships, affiliation, recognition, respect, enjoyment, and self-fulfillment. Because many products have, in a sense, "personalities" that serve our psychological needs, we can say they have emotional benefits. The psychological needs of customers frequently draw them to the products with the types of brand personalities that would satisfy those needs.[21]

Customers' Psychological Needs → Brand Personality → **Emotional Benefits**

An individual with a need to be seen as rugged and self-sufficient might be attracted to a Chevy pick-up advertised as durable, powerful, and "like a rock." On the other hand, individuals with a need for status, recognition, and respect would likely be more attracted to a Mercedes. Products that project a "brand personality," then, can create customer value by delivering emotional benefits.

FIGURE 4-25 BRAND PERSONALITY AND PERSONALITY TRAITS

Brand Personality	Personality Trait	Not at All Descriptive				Extremely Descriptive
Sincerity	Down to earth	—	—	—	—	—
	Honest	—	—	—	—	—
	Wholesome	—	—	—	—	—
	Cheerful	—	—	—	—	—
Excitement	Daring	—	—	—	—	—
	Spirited	—	—	—	—	—
	Imaginative	—	—	—	—	—
	Up-to-date	—	—	—	—	—
Competence	Reliable	—	—	—	—	—
	Intelligent	—	—	—	—	—
	Successful	—	—	—	—	—
Sophistication	Upper class	—	—	—	—	—
	Charming	—	—	—	—	—
Ruggedness	Outdoorsy	—	—	—	—	—
	Tough	—	—	—	—	—

Brand Personality and Value Creation

Figure 4-25 lists five dominant brand personalities that a comprehensive study of human personality and brand personality identified.[22] As you look over the five dominant brand personalities and their related personality traits, ask yourself which of the five would best describe the following brands and companies: Nike, Betty Crocker, Timberland, Lexus, and Hewlett-Packard.

Most people would align Nike with excitement. Nike has finely honed its brand personality to exemplify daring, spiritedness, imagination, and being on the leading edge (up-to-date) in both fashion and technology. Betty Crocker imparts on us a wholesome, honest, down-to-earth image characteristic of sincerity. Timberland footwear has a brand personality that projects ruggedness, Lexus evokes sophistication, and HP elicits an image of competence characterized by intelligence, success, and reliability. In a market or segment where two or more brands meet a consumer's rational needs—those related to price, product, and service benefits—the consumer will be drawn to the brand with the personality that most fully corresponds to the consumer's emotional needs.

Let's suppose Nike had used UCLA's famous coach John Wooden instead of Chicago Bulls' star Michael Jordan to endorse Nike Air basketball shoes, later named Air Jordan. The personality of the Nike brand of basketball shoes would today be quite different, and the emotional benefits created by the product would be considerably less for the product's target customers.

Products do have personalities. The development of those personalities, of course, is largely a function of advertising that, to help accomplish its objective, often identifies products with well-known, real-life personalities. Consumers in turn derive a measure of satisfaction or enjoyment, or have other psychological needs met, by using products that project a particular image or set of personal attributes. To the degree that a business delivers

FIGURE 4-26 INTERMEDIARY'S TRANSACTION VALUE AND VALUE CREATION

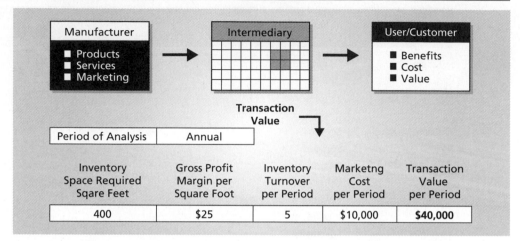

Inventory Space Required Sqare Feet	Gross Profit Margin per Square Foot	Inventory Turnover per Period	Marketng Cost per Period	Transaction Value per Period
400	$25	5	$10,000	**$40,000**

such emotional benefits in its product, it will contribute to the overall value customers derive from purchasing and using that product.

TRANSACTION COST AND VALUE CREATION

A customer buying a refrigerator is interested in such product features as size, color, storage configuration, freezer capacity, and operating efficiency. The customer also wants to know the costs and benefits associated with the price paid, the terms of payment, the return policy, the warranty, and delivery. In contrast, a channel intermediary is not so much interested in end-user customer benefits as in the value created by the sales transaction. Whether a Kool-Aid stand or Wal-Mart, the channel intermediary's basic purpose is to connect producers with consumers. To open this channel, intermediaries must invest in space to store and display products, marketing resources to promote products, and people to handle customer transactions. Value for the channel intermediary is derived from a combination of (1) profitable use of space, (2) inventory turnover, and (3) the marketing expenses needed to promote the merchandise held in that space.

Space Value

Figure 4-26 illustrates a channel intermediary with 5,000 square feet of space. Each square in the chart's center box represents 100 square feet, and the 400 square feet represented by the four shaded squares is the space the intermediary—The Home Depot, for example—has allocated to the sale of major appliances. The first step in managing value in this situation is to determine the value the intermediary can obtain from the 400 square feet of appliances. Let's assume for major appliances the average margin per square foot is $25. The space is then worth $10,000 annually if every year customers buy the entire inventory.

$$\text{Space Value} = \text{Margin per Square Foot} \times \text{Square Footage of Inventory}$$
$$= \$25 \text{ per Square Foot} \times 400 \text{ Square Feet}$$
$$= \mathbf{\$10,000}$$

If the channel intermediary were to place merchandise with a $30 margin per square foot in the same space, the space would have a value of $12,000. All things being equal, the alternative at $30 per square foot would produce a much better space value. Overall value to the intermediary, however, also depends on the rate at which the inventory sells—or the rate of inventory turnover—and the associated marketing expenses. It may be that the merchandise with a higher margin per square foot does not sell as fast as lower-margin appliances, or perhaps the higher-margin items require more marketing expenses to attract and serve customers. In figuring the transaction value, we must take into account all these factors.

Transaction Value

In converting the $10,000 profit potential for the intermediary's major appliance space to gross profit, we must know the rate of inventory turnover. The intermediary's major appliance inventory in Figure 4-26 is sold five times every year, and so the 400 square feet of space allocated to major appliances produces $50,000 in annual gross profit. To generate this level of sales transactions, the intermediary invests heavily in marketing, spending $10,000 annually on advertising, in-store displays, sales training, and promotions. The net result is a transaction value of $40,000.

$$\text{Transaction Value} = \text{Space Value} \times \text{Inventory Turnover} - \text{Marketing Expenses}$$
$$= \$10,000 \times 5 \text{ Turnovers per Year} - \$10,000$$
$$= \$50,000 - \$10,000$$
$$= \mathbf{\$40,000}$$

A channel intermediary's transaction value, then, will vary depending on margins, use of space, inventory turnover, and marketing expenses. Each of these factors can be affected by the manufacturer's product, market demand, margins, and marketing policies.

The Home Depot, for example, wanted to sell major appliances but did not want to carry a large inventory of many sizes and colors. Carrying an inventory of this nature is expensive in terms of retail floor space, warehouse space, and financing costs. To create an attractive transaction value, GE offered to hold the inventory and assume responsibility for delivering the appliances to customers from GE warehouses. GE's plan meant The Home Depot needed to carry only a few floor models for display, with customers making their color and size selections at computer kiosks that GE placed in The Home Depot's stores. The result for The Home Depot was less space allocated to major appliances, less investment in inventory, no delivery expenses, and reduced marketing expenses at the point of sale. Each of these factors improved the transaction value for The Home Depot, with a sizable improvement overall, and GE benefited by gaining access to the millions of consumers who shop at The Home Depot.

Value Creation Across the Supply Chain

In many markets, the supply chain involves more than one intermediary. For most building products the supply chain includes a channel intermediary, builder, and owner. As Figure 4-27 shows, each of these is a customer with distinct needs and unique ways of determining customer value.

Silent Floor is a building product that creates different types of customer value across the supply chain. The product is a partially assembled flooring system that does not squeak or bounce when walked on. In focus-group interviews, homeowners indicated

FIGURE 4-27 CUSTOMER VALUE ACROSS THE SUPPLY CHAIN

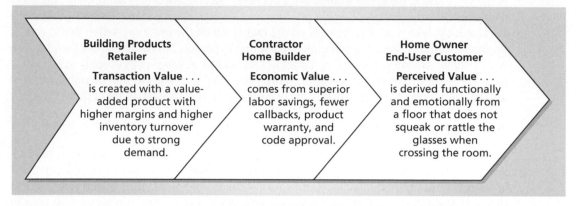

they would pay more for a floor that didn't squeak or bounce. In developing a product that would meet these criteria, the manufacturer also had to address the needs of other customers in the value chain, as identified in Figure 4-27.

The value drivers that influenced retailers and builders were less focused on the product itself and more on the process of selling and using it. For building product retailers, transaction value was derived from margin per square foot, inventory requirements, inventory turnover, and marketing expenses. Value for contractors and home builders was in the economic value created from lower installation costs, fewer callbacks for rework, a manufacturer's warranty that limited liability, and a code-approved product that accelerated the completion process. Silent Floor created an attractive customer value for each of these different types of customers in the supply chain.

IDENTIFYING VALUE DRIVERS

We have seen that a business can create customer value in several ways, but determining exactly which aspects of customer value are the key value drivers can be challenging for any business. Asking customers directly is one approach, but businesses have found that customers cite a very wide range of benefits. From a customer's perspective, anything or everything can be important. We can more accurately determine the benefits that customers value by asking them to make choices among products that have different benefits and different prices. By examining how customers make trade-offs when choosing among various combinations of price and benefits, we can create a set of preference curves using *conjoint analysis*.[23]

For the Silent Floor product, nine hypothetical flooring systems were proposed from four dimensions of potential value, as presented in Figure 4-28.[24] Each of the nine flooring options offered different combinations of different levels of labor savings, warranty life, price, and callback frequency. Home builders were asked to assume the role of buyers of flooring and to rank the nine Silent Floor systems according to their preferences. Figure 4-28 includes the results of the builders' rankings, and Figure 4-29 presents the preference curves based on a conjoint analysis of the rankings.

FIGURE 4-28 ALTERNATIVE FLOORING SYSTEMS

Flooring System A	Flooring System B	Flooring System C
Labor Savings..............None	Labor Savings..............None	Labor Savings..............None
Product Warranty.......5 years	Product Warranty.......10 years	Product Warranty.......None
Delivered Price...........Competitive	Delivered Price...........+20%	Delivered Price...........+40%
Customer Callbacks....None	Customer Callbacks....Frequent	Customer Callbacks....Some
Customer Ranking: 5	**Customer Ranking: 6**	**Customer Ranking: 8**

Flooring System D	Flooring System E	Flooring System F
Labor Savings..............20%	Labor Savings..............20%	Labor Savings..............20%
Product Warranty.......10 years	Product Warranty.......10 years	Product Warranty.......5 years
Delivered Price...........Competitive	Delivered Price...........+20%	Delivered Price...........+40%
Customer Callbacks....Some	Customer Callbacks....None	Customer Callbacks....Frequent
Customer Ranking: 1	**Customer Ranking: 7**	**Customer Ranking: 9**

Flooring System G	Flooring System H	Flooring System I
Labor Savings..............40%	Labor Savings..............40%	Labor Savings..............40%
Product Warranty.......None	Product Warranty.......5 years	Product Warranty.......10 years
Delivered Price...........Competitive	Delivered Price...........+20%	Delivered Price...........+40%
Customer Callbacks....Frequent	Customer Callbacks....Some	Customer Callbacks....None
Customer Ranking: 3	**Customer Ranking: 2**	**Customer Ranking: 4**

Builder's Preference Ranking: D, H, G, I, A, B, E, C, F
Conjoint analysis used in this ranking to create the preferences curves.
(See Appendix 4.1 for details)

Customer Preferences

In the Silent Floor example, the preference curves represent the value that home builders placed on different levels of the four attributes of the flooring. The higher the number on the value axis (.00 to 1.00) for each of the three levels of an attribute, the more important that level of the attribute was for the builder.[25]

We can see, for example, that the builders considered a 40 percent labor savings (1.00) as considerably more important than a 20 percent labor savings (0.33). The larger the range from low score to high score on an attribute's preference curve, the more important that attribute was to the builders when they ranked the nine options. The low-to-high ranges for warranty life and callback frequency are both 0.58, which means these two attributes were equally important to the builders. But these two ranges are not as large as those for the more important attributes of price (a maximum range of 1.00) and labor savings (a range of .83)

The percentage next to the attribute's name above each of the four preference curves in Figure 4-29 represents the relative importance that attribute had for the builders. We can calculate the relative importance percentage by dividing an attribute's low-to-high range by the sum of all four ranges. Price, the most important factor for the builders, accounted for 34 percent of the overall influence on the builders' rankings. Labor savings

FIGURE 4-29 PREFERENCE CURVES FOR FLOORING SYSTEM ATTRIBUTES

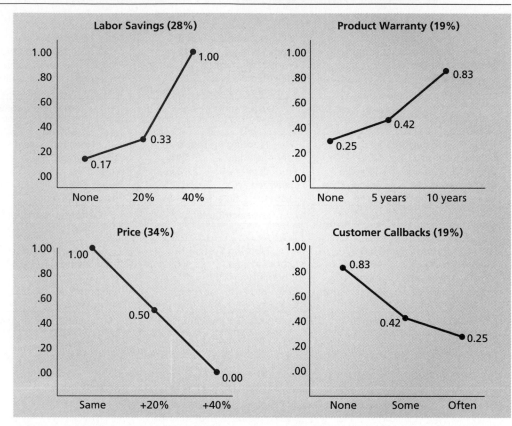

Note: To estimate the importance of each preference curve, the low to high score is summed for each of the preference curves (2.99) and then each low to high range is divided by this sum. When each is expressed as a percent, it represents the importance that performance feature had on the ranking of alternatives.

was the second-most important attribute, with 28 percent of the overall influence. Warranty life and callback frequency each accounted for 19 percent of the influence.

Customer Value

To determine the value driver of any flooring system, we need to create a *customer value index* (CVI) for a specific flooring system, which we will call the "conventional flooring system." This system offers a competitive price but no labor savings and no warranty, and it entails frequent callbacks. The CVI for the conventional flooring system is derived from the performance features and price of the system, and the extent to which the home builders valued the performance features and price as scored on the performance curves in Figure 4-29. For the conventional flooring system, price is clearly the value driver (1.00) because it makes up 60 percent of the total CVI of 1.67.

Customer Value Index = Labor Savings + Warranty + Price + Callbacks

CVI of Conventional Flooring System = None (.17) + None (.25) + Competitive (1.0) + Often (.25)

= **1.67**

FIGURE 4-30 CUSTOMER PREFERENCES AND CUSTOMER VALUE

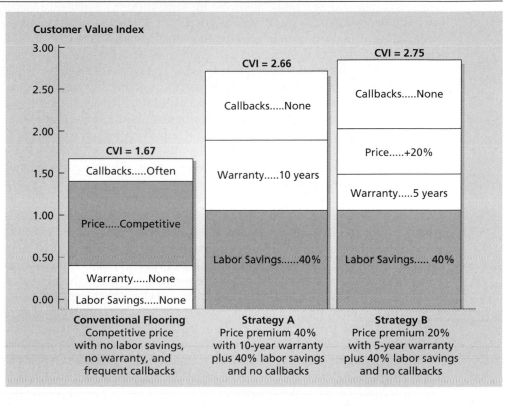

Another flooring system, one that offers a 40 percent labor savings and no customer callbacks, could be positioned in two ways. Strategy A in Figure 4-30 has the full labor savings and customer callback benefits, along with a 10-year warranty and a price 40 percent higher than the current conventional flooring system. This combination produces a customer value index of 2.66, 59 percent higher than the customer value index produced by a conventional flooring system. Home builders, then, would find Strategy A more attractive than the conventional system. The value driver for this strategy is the labor savings (1.00 of 2.66) because it is the largest contributor to the overall customer value index.

Strategy B provides the same labor savings and customer callback performance as Strategy A, but it is priced only 20 percent higher than the conventional flooring system and offers just a 5-year warranty. The customer value index for this combination of performance features and price is 2.75, 65 percent higher in value than the conventional flooring system. The value driver for Strategy B is also labor savings. Strategies A and B are both superior to the conventional flooring system in terms of customer value, but Strategy A is likely to be more profitable with its much higher price premium.

■ Summary

A strong customer focus and an ongoing commitment to understanding customers' needs and the problems customers encounter are at the core of any market-based strategy. Too often, businesses oversimplify the analysis of customer needs by narrowly focusing on specific product features and price. Although this assessment is important, it is more important for a business to look beyond current product features and price to see the customer experience in its totality. Knowing the total customer experience—encompassing the customer's acquisition, use, and disposal of a product—enables a business to add meaningful customer value to its product. Empathic design, a day in the life of a customer, lead user analysis, and management of customer touch points are all practical ways for managers to see customers' needs and respond with new product and service benefits that will add to customer value and raise the business's customer satisfaction index.

With the advent of mass collaboration, market-based management businesses have a new, highly effective tool for engaging prosumers, partnership groups, suppliers, and employees in developing product benefits and improving manufacturing and other internal processes to create greater customer value. Wikinomics can save a business research and development costs while enabling it to develop an effective customer solution more quickly than a closed, in-house effort.

End-user customers are interested in product benefits, service benefits, brand image (emotional benefits), and the cost of purchase. In contrast, the channel intermediaries who sell manufacturers' products to end users assess customer value in terms of a product's transaction value. Transaction value is the economic value derived from marketing a product based on the margin it produces per square foot of space, inventory turnover, and the marketing expenses associated with promoting the product. Any one of these components can be modified to improve an intermediary's transaction value. When we look across the entire supply chain, we may find that different members of the supply chain have different ways of inferring customer value. Creating value for these different intermediaries is an additional challenge for those manufacturers who rely on others to reach and serve end-user customers.

We examined three kinds of benefits—economic benefits, perceived benefits, and emotional benefits—and the way customers derive value from these benefits. Economic benefits result in measurable differences in savings for the customer and a stronger competitive financial position for the business. A lower price is an obvious source of economic value, but other sources of economic benefit can be created. Savings from lower acquisition costs, usage, ownership, maintenance, and disposal costs offer ways to lower the total cost of purchase, thereby creating more customer value.

But not all benefits can be quantified into an economic value expressed in dollar savings. Customer benefits derived from a product's appearance, exceptional service, or reputation are more difficult to put a dollar value on. Likewise, customer perceptions of performance have a strong influence on product preference and purchase behavior. By measuring customer perceptions of product benefits, service benefits, and brand benefits relative to competition, we are able to develop an overall index of total benefits derived from a business's product. By also measuring perception of price and nonprice costs of purchase relative to competition, we can develop an overall index of the total cost of purchase. The difference between total perceived benefits and cost provides a measure of perceived customer value. The larger the customer value, the greater is the potential to attract, satisfy, and retain customers.

A third area of customer benefit and customer value creation is emotional benefits. Products that serve an underlying psychological need, personality type, or the personal values of customers have emotional benefits that enhance customer value. Understanding these aspects of a target market is essential in positioning a product and enhancing its perceived value. Products, like people, have personalities, and the more a business can position its product with respect to the target customer's emotional needs, the greater will be the product's customer value.

Finally, trade-off analysis was introduced to help us quantify the value created by different combinations of price and product positioning. The customer trade-off process enables us to uncover the degree to which different aspects of a product are driving customer preferences. This analysis in turn enables a business to index the value it creates relative to key competitors and to evaluate the impact alternative positioning strategies would have on customer preference and relative value. Overall, customer analysis and value creation are important inputs in developing marketing strategies designed to yield high levels of customer satisfaction.

■ Market-Based Strategic Thinking

1 What is the advantage to understanding the customer's total experience with a product?

2 Why is it more valuable for the Lexus managers themselves to interview customers in attempting to understand a customer's total experience? Managers are busy people. Wouldn't it be more cost effective to use a market research firm?

3 How does empathic design help a business discover customer problems and new opportunities for value creation?

4 What is the purpose of spending a day in the life of a customer?

5 Why is understanding a lead user's total customer experience potentially more valuable than spending the same amount of time with an average customer? Why would this approach likely result in better product improvements than those that engineers with the company might design?

6 How can a business improve the customer experience by managing customer touch points?

7 How would a business that manufactures and sells hardwood flooring through building supply stores make the best use of mass collaboration in improving product benefits?

8 What is the difference between product features and product benefits?

9 Why should the scenes in each of the two hypothetical videotapes of a day in the life of a customer go beyond the product or service and focus on the customer's use of the product or service?

10 What is economic value for the customer?

11 What are the ways a business could create a more attractive economic value?

12 Why is it important to measure perceived benefits and perceived costs?

13 In what ways can a business improve the perceived value of its product?

14 How should customer preference and purchase behavior change as perceived value increases or decreases?

15 Why are emotional benefits important?

16 How do psychological motives help shape emotional benefits and customer perceptions of value?

17 How does the personality of a spokesperson used in advertising help shape the emotional benefits of the product?

18 Using Figure 4-25, discuss the brand personalities of Kodak, Mountain Dew, and Prudential Insurance, and how these brand personalities were created.

19 What is transaction value?

20 Explain how a convenience store could estimate its transaction value in selling Coca-Cola products.
21 How could Coca-Cola improve the convenience store owner's transaction value?
22 What is trade-off analysis? How does it help us understand customer preferences?
23 How could a business determine if customers would prefer a proposed new service?

Marketing Performance Tools

The three **Marketing Performance Tools** described here may be accessed online at *www.rogerjbest.com*. These applied-learning exercises will add to your understanding of economic value, customer value, and transaction value.

4.1 Economic Value Analysis (Figure 4-12)
- If Sealed Air priced its AirCap product equal to the competing product, how would the economic value change? Why shouldn't Sealed Air do this since it creates more economic value for the customer?
- What price would Sealed Air charge for its AirCap product to produce a zero economic value? This would make more money for Sealed Air, but why would this be an unwise move?
- Evaluate the impact of adding a breakage cost of 10 cents per shipment for cardboard and 1 cent per shipment for AirCap. How much more could Sealed Air charge per foot and maintain a customer economic value of 65 cents per shipment?

4.2 Customer Value Analysis (Figures 4-18 to 4-24)
- How would the company's customer value change if it raised its repair time rating from 5 to 7? How would this impact the competitors' customer values?
- What would be the value impact of improving the ease-of-use product benefit from 4 to 6? Would this improve customer value more than addressing the repair time benefit problem in the previous question?
- Assuming the company made both changes, how would the company's customer value index change? Why could this make the company more profitable?

4.3 Transaction Value Analysis (Figure 4-26)
- How would an intermediary's transaction value change with a new supplier that offered $20 per square foot in margin with no marketing expenses? Should the intermediary switch to the new supplier?
- What would be the value impact of a marketing strategy that increased inventory turnover from 5 to 6 but required a 50 percent increase in marketing expenses?
- What would be the profit impact of increasing the inventory space from 400 to 600 square feet and doubling the marketing expenses? Should the channel intermediary do this?

Notes

1. Christopher Meyer and Andre Schwager, "Understanding Customer Experience," *Harvard Business Review* (February 2007): 118.
2. Barry Schwartz, "More Isn't Always Better," *Harvard Business Review* (June 2006).
3. James Womack and Daniel Jones, "Lean Consumption," *Harvard Business Review* (March 2005).
4. Dorothy Leonard and Jeffrey Rayport, "Spark Innovation through Empathic Design," *Harvard Business Review* (November–December 1997).
5. Michael Lanning, *Delivering Profitable Value* (Reading, MA: Perseus Books, 1998): 228–253.
6. Eric von Hippel, "Lead Users: An Important Source of Novel Product Concepts," *Management Science* 32, no. 7 (July 1986): 791–805.
7. Craig Henderson, "Finding, Examining Lead Users Push 3M to Leading Edge of Innovation," in *Practice Case Study Series*, American Productivity & Quality Center, 2000.
8. Gary Lillien, Pamela Morrison, Mary Sonnack, and Eric von Hippel. "Performance Assessment of the Lead User Idea Generation Process for New Product Development," working paper, ISBM No. 4-2001, The Pennsylvania State University.
9. Rocky Kneten and David Rudes, "Inventing to Order" *Business Week* (July 5, 2004): 84–85.
10. Benson Shapiro, V. Kasturi Rangan, and John Sviokla, "Staple Yourself to an Order," *Harvard Business Review* (July–August 1992): 113–122.
11. Robert Yeager, "Customers Don't Buy Technologies; They Buy Solutions: Here's How Five Advanced Technology Marketers Saw the Light and Avoided Becoming High-Tech Commodities," *Business Marketing* (November 1985): 61–76.
12. Michael Hammer, *The Agenda,* (New York: Crown Business, 2001).
13. B. D. Tapscott and A. D. Williams, *Wikinomics: How Mass Collaboration Changes Everything* (New York: The Penguin Group, 2006).
14. John Forbis and Nitin Mehta, "Value-Based Strategies for Industrial Products," *Business Horizons* (May 1981): 32–42.
15. Gerald Smith and Thomas Nagle, "A Question of Value," *Marketing Management* (July–August 2005), 39–43.
16. David Kiley, "On Cars, Big Rebates Aren't Always Big Savings," *USA Today* (August 5, 2003); also visit www.edmunds.com for other total cost-of-purchase comparisons.
17. "Ratings and Recommendation: Toasters and Toaster-Oven/Broilers," *Consumer Reports* (August 1998): 42–43.
18. Gerald Smith and Thomas Nagle, "Measuring the Unmeasurables," *Marketing Management* (May–June 2005):39 12–13.
19. Morris Holbrook, "The Nature of Customer Value: An Axiology of Services in the Consumption Experience," in *Service Quality: New Directions in Theory and Practice*, Roland Rust and Richard Oliver, ed. (London: Sage Publications, 1991): 21–71.
20. Bradley Gale, *Managing Customer Value* (New York: Free Press, 1994).
21. Delbert Hawkins, Roger Best, and Kenneth Coney, "The Changing American Society: Values and Demographics," in *Consumer Behavior: Implications for Marketing Strategy*, 6th ed. (New York: Irwin, 1995): 66–88.
22. Jennifer Aaker, "Dimensions of Brand Personality," *Journal of Marketing Research* (August 1997): 347–356.
23. Donald Tull and Delbert Hawkins, *Marketing Research: Measurement and Method*, 6th ed. (New York: Macmillan, 1993): 406–418; and M. Agarwal and P. Green, "Adaptive Conjoint Analysis Versus Self-Explicated Models," *International Journal of Research* (June 1991): 141–146.
24. John Morton and Hugh Devine, "How to Diagnose What Buyers Really Want," *Business Marketing* (October 1985): 70–83.
25. J. Axelrod and N. Frendberg, "Conjoint Analysis," *Marketing Research* (June 1990): 28–35; P. Green and V. Srinivasan, "Conjoint Analysis in Marketing Research," *Journal of Marketing* (October 1990): 3–19; D. Wittink and P. Cattin, "Commercial Use of Conjoint Analysis," *Journal of Marketing* (July 1989): 19–96; and A. Page and H. Rosenbaum, "Redesigning Product Lines with Conjoint Analysis," *Journal of Product Management* (1987): 120–137.

Trade-Off Analysis Computations

Step 1. Determine individual scores for each attribute (factor/level) by summing the scores for that attribute.

Labor Savings	Price		
	Same	+20%	+40%
None	Some 5 years (A) 5	Often 10 years (B) 6	None None (C) 8 = 19
20%	None 10 years (D) 1	Some None (E) 7	Often 5 years (F) 9 = 17
40%	Often None (G) 3	None 5 years (H) 2	Some 10 years (I) 4 = 9
	= 9	= 15	= 21

Product Warranty

None	= 8 + 7 + 3	= 18
5 years	= 5 + 9 + 2	= 16
10 years	= 6 + 1 + 4	= 11

Customer Callbacks

None	= 8 + 1 + 2	= 11
Some	= 5 + 7 + 4	= 16
Often	= 6 + 9 + 3	= 18

Step 2. Rank attributes and summed attribute scores from lowest to highest. (X's below)

	X	Y
+40% Labor Savings	9	1.00
Same Price	9	1.00
10 Years Product Warranty	11	0.83
No Callbacks	11	0.83
Price +20%	15	0.50
5 Years Product Warranty	16	0.42
Some Callbacks	16	0.42
+20% Labor Savings	17	0.33
No Product Warranty	18	0.25
Often Callbacks	18	0.25
No Labor Savings	19	0.17
Price + 40%	21	0.00

Step 3. Determine the maximum score, minimum score, and difference between the maximum and minimum scores.

Step 4. Rescale the raw scores, (X's) using the following Normalization Formula:

Normalization Formula:

$$Y = \frac{X_{max} - X}{X_{max} - X_{min}}$$

$$Y = \frac{21 - X}{21 - 9}$$

$$Y = \frac{21 - X}{12}$$

Now, all scores will vary between zero and one, depending on their overall attractiveness to this customer segment.

CHAPTER 5

Market Segmentation and Segmentation Strategies

■ Many companies forget that solving customer problems requires a deep knowledge of who their target customers are and what they need.[1]

In segmenting a market, perhaps the biggest mistake marketers can make is starting at the wrong place.[2] Market segmentation does not start with how old target customers are, where they live, if they like sports, or how many children they have. It starts with the benefits customers are seeking in solving a particular customer problem. Because different customers seek different solutions for the same problem, our first challenge is to identify and understand the various customer needs that drive product consideration.

Once we have grouped customers into *needs-based segments*, we can then ask, "What

are the demographics, usage behaviors, and psychographics that distinguish one group of customers from another?" Knowing the factors that differentiate one segment from another helps us to identify the segments. Figure 5-1 shows how we might divide the market for home siding into two segments—a cost-sensitive segment and a quality-conscious segment—based on needs.

Needs-based segmentation provides the basic guidelines for positioning strategies and marketing communications. With the market properly segmented, we can now develop a value proposition that will attract new customers and retain existing ones.

FIGURE 5-1 NEEDS-BASED MARKET SEGMENTATION

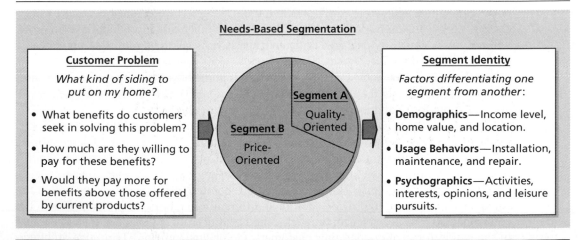

FIGURE 5-2 MASS-MARKET STRATEGY VERSUS SEGMENT STRATEGY

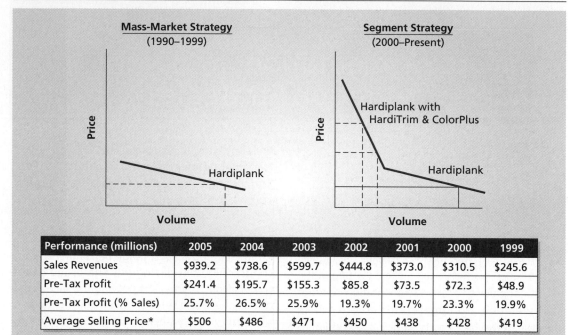

Performance (millions)	2005	2004	2003	2002	2001	2000	1999
Sales Revenues	$939.2	$738.6	$599.7	$444.8	$373.0	$310.5	$245.6
Pre-Tax Profit	$241.4	$195.7	$155.3	$85.8	$73.5	$72.3	$48.9
Pre-Tax Profit (% Sales)	25.7%	26.5%	25.9%	19.3%	19.7%	23.3%	19.9%
Average Selling Price*	$506	$486	$471	$450	$438	$428	$419

*Price per thousand square feet

NEEDS-BASED MARKET SEGMENTATION

James Hardie is a leading manufacturer of home siding. The U.S. annual demand for siding is 12.5 billion square feet, and James Hardie's product, known as Hardiplank, has a 12 percent share of the market. Hardiplank is a fiber-cement siding used in new construction and for re-siding existing structures.

While cultivating the market for fiber-cement siding in the 1990s, James Hardie relied on a mass-marketing strategy. The company at first assumed its product would need to be price competitive with wood, vinyl, and aluminum siding. The combined benefits of fiber-cement siding, however, are greater than those of any other siding product. It is fireproof, will not rot, is not easily damaged or dented, and is resistant to bug infestations. Because of the product's durability, James Hardie provides a 50-year warranty. Although builders are cost sensitive, they know that quality-conscious home buyers will pay more for houses built with products that have a high customer value. Quality-conscious home owners will also pay more for a superior product when re-siding their homes.

This knowledge led James Hardie to divide the siding market into two broad segments. Roughly 30 percent of the market fell into a quality segment and 70 percent into a price segment, as illustrated in Figure 5-1. In addition to the normal product benefits fiber-cement siding offers, the quality segment wanted an exceptional appearance. In response to this need, James Hardie created a pre-painted fiber-cement siding with a finished appearance and, to provide additional differentiation, branded it "ColorPlus." The company also introduced a trim product, called "HardiTrim," to enhance the appearance of the siding for quality-conscious customers. ColorPlus and HardiTrim give architects

FIGURE 5-3 NEEDS-BASED MARKET SEGMENTATION—FEATURES VERSUS PRICE

Fiber-Cement Siding Product Features	Level 1	Level 2	Level 3
Finish Trim	None	Basic	Full Trim
Cost per Square Foot	$0	$0.35	$1.00
Paint Finish	Unpainted	Primed	Color
Cost per Square Foot	$0	$0.25	$0.75

Price (square foot)		The lowest total price is $1.00 per square foot – base cost of $1.00 per square foot with no finish trim and unpainted. The highest price per square foot would be $2.75.
Base Cost	$1.00	
Finish Trim	$0.00	
Paint Finish	$0.00	
Total Price	**$1.00**	

Segment A - Quality Segment		Segment B - Price Segment	
Base Cost	$1.00	Base Cost	$1.00
Finish Trim	$0.78	Finish Trim	$0.15
Paint Finish	$0.58	Paint Finish	$0.12
Average Price	**$2.36**	**Average Price**	**$1.27**

and home builders the opportunity to enhance the appearance of a home. James Hardie sold these value-added products at higher prices and higher margins.

The price segment consisted primarily of builders of tract homes, manufactured homes, and multiunit housing. For builders, a key need was keeping the cost of materials low so the purchase price of their houses or multiunit dwellings could be kept within an acceptable range for potential buyers. To better serve the price segment, James Hardie modified the product to make it easier and faster to install. Figure 5-2 shows that this multi-product segmentation strategy allowed the company to grow its average price per thousand square feet from $419 in 1999 to $506 in 2005, while increasing sales almost fourfold from $245.6 million to $939.2 million. The bottom line: This segmentation strategy allowed James Hardie to grow pre-tax profits almost fivefold, from $48.9 million in 1999 to $241.4 million in 2005.

The features and performance level that customers want in a product are at the heart of needs-based market segmentation, and so is price. We might want all the benefits of an expensive car or a dream vacation, but these desires would be unrealistic if we could not afford the cost. Price is a key component in needs-based market segmentation, and often it is the factor that shapes a particular segment.

One approach to discovering which benefits customers want and are willing to pay for is to present them the product or service at a base price and allow them to select the features and performance levels they prefer in light of the costs. Let's look at fiber-cement siding as an example. In Figure 5-3, the base price of $1 per square foot is the lowest price available to customers. At this price, the customer would not receive the trim product, and the siding would not be primed or painted. Many in segment A, the quality segment, would be willing to pay extra for the full trim ($1 per square foot) and the color

FIGURE 5-4 CUSTOMER PREFERENCES FOR FEATURES VERSUS PRICE

Laptop Computer

Product Features	Level 1	Level 2	Level 3
Processor Speed (Hz)	X	1.5X	
Cost	$0	$200	
Memory (MB)	X	2X	4X
Cost	−$50	$0	$50
Hard Drive (GB)	X	2X	3X
Cost	−$50	$0	$50
Media Drive	CD-ROM	DVD	DVD+RW
Cost	−$50	$0	$100
Operating System	Basic	Pro	
Cost	$0	$50	
Carrying Case	None	Nylon	Leather
Cost	−$50	$0	$50
Warranty	90 Days	1 Year	3 Years
Cost	$0	$25	$50

Price	Total
Base Price	$1,000
Added Cost	$0
Total Price	**$1,000**

Lowest Purchase Price

Customer Perferences	Price Paid
Base Price	$1,000
Processor Speed (Hz)	$0
Memory (MB)	−$50
Hard Drive (GB)	−$50
Media Drive	−$50
Operating System	$0
Carrying Case	−$50
Warranty	$0
Total Price	**$800**

Highest Purchase Price

Customer Perferences	Price Paid
Base Price	$1,000
Processor Speed (Hz)	$200
Memory (MB)	$50
Hard Drive (GB)	$50
Media Drive	$100
Operating System	$50
Carrying Case	$50
Warranty	$50
Total Price	**$1,550**

finish (75 cents per square foot). But because not all segment A customers would buy finish trim or a paint finish, the *average* amount per customer that the business receives for each of these two features is then their purchase price. In all, the customers in segment A would pay an average of about $2.36 per square foot to obtain what they want.

In segment B, the price segment, most customers would purchase just the unfinished siding at the base price of $1 per square foot, but some would also buy a basic or full trim finish, or primed or color painted siding, or various combinations. Segment B customers would spend an average of $1.27 per square foot. Of course, the customers buying at the base price would have to paint the siding themselves and add their own trim.

Let's consider another example more familiar to us, the purchase of a laptop computer. Figure 5-4 lists a laptop computer with a base price of $1,000. This price cannot be adjusted upward or downward should the customer want more or fewer features, or a different performance level. But, to understand customer needs, including price, we need to let customers select the features and performance levels they prefer in view of the price they want to pay. As we see in Figure 5-4, a price-sensitive customer with a lesser need for performance could buy this laptop at $800. If the number of customers who buy below the $1,000 price is significant, then the computer company would want to have a separate market segment consisting of cost-sensitive target customers.

FIGURE 5-5 FORCES THAT SHAPE DIFFERENCES IN CONSUMER NEEDS

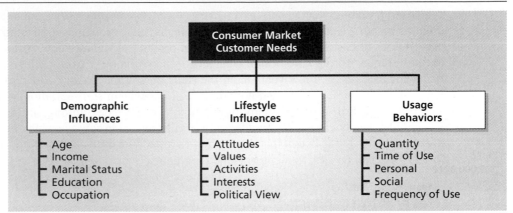

At the other extreme, customers who buy all of the extended features pay $1,550. The needs of these customers are different, and they are willing to pay more to obtain the high performance a maximally configured laptop offers. Again, if the number of customers buying at costs well over $1,000 is significant, a market segment for potential customers who want extra features and high performance would be in order.

There are 324 combinations of product features and price. The purpose of needs-based segmentation is to offer product benefits that satisfy the needs, including price, of different sets of target customers. Or, with a multi-product segment strategy, various products are designed for the needs of different segments, each of which has target customers who differ meaningfully in the product benefits they desire and can afford.

CUSTOMER NEEDS

Understanding customer needs is the first step in successful market segmentation. A business with a strong market orientation seeks to understand the needs of its target customers and then develops strategies to attract, satisfy, and retain them. Because potential customers will rarely have all the same needs, a business with a strong market orientation will divide its served market into segments. A segment may be concisely defined as follows:

> A market segment is a specific group of customers with similar needs, purchasing behaviors, and identifying characteristics.[3]

Both consumers and businesses have market needs, but the factors influencing their needs differ in important ways. Understanding why customers have different needs is helpful in determining how to divide a market into useful needs-based market segments.

Forces That Shape Consumer Market Needs

Consumers differ in a great many ways. Obviously people have different preferences in automobiles, toothpaste, and entertainment. Not so obvious are the factors that influence those preferences. Although many factors contribute to these differences,[4] three primary forces shape the needs of consumers, as summarized in Figure 5-5.

Demographic Influences

Needs and preferences often shift as a person moves *demographically* from one life situation to another. Changes in income, occupation, and educational level all contribute to a changing set of customer needs for a variety of products. Consider how customer needs and preferences for an automobile change as a person moves from college student to management trainee. A few years later, the same person may marry and start a family, and changes in marital status and household will once again shift automobile needs and preferences. Because of the many demographic differences among individuals and households, we should expect a wide array of differences in what consumers need, can afford, and buy. To the extent that demographics reflect the needs and preferences of customers, they can be used to identify market segments.

Lifestyle Influences

Demographics are not alone in shaping customer needs and market demand. *Lifestyle forces* created by differences in values, attitudes, and interests also contribute to differences in customer needs. Two consumers who are demographically the same may differ significantly in their attitudes and value orientations. A consumer with strong environmental values is likely to prefer a different car than a demographically identical person whose values are focused on fun, enjoyment, and personal gratification. Differences in lifestyle, including different values, attitudes, and interests, are forces that create different needs and product preferences among customers. To the extent that lifestyle attributes reflect the needs and buying preferences of customers, they can be used to identify market segments.

Usage Behaviors

A third major force in shaping customer needs is *usage behavior*. How the product is used, when it is used, and how much it is used are all forces that determine customer needs for a great many products. A family with two children under age 10 will have a different set of usage behaviors for an automobile than a family with two children over age 16. In addition, if parents are buying a first car for their child as a graduation gift, their needs are likely to be different from those who are buying a car for the family or for business. To the extent that usage behaviors reflect the needs and buying preferences of customers, they can be used to identify market segments. Figure 5-6 presents a list of characteristics commonly used in consumer markets to identify segments.

Forces That Shape Business Market Needs

Quite often, discussions of market segmentation are limited to consumer markets, and as a result managers in business-to-business, industrial, high-tech, and commercial markets are left to extrapolate how segmentation might apply to their markets. Much like consumer markets, business-to-business markets are influenced by firm demographics, lifestyle (business culture), and usage behaviors. Figure 5-7 shows the three fundamental forces that shape customer needs in business-to-business markets, along with the factors that contribute to these forces.

FIGURE 5-6 CONSUMER MARKET—SEGMENT IDENTIFICATION

Consumer Segment Profile	SEGMENTS				
Consumer Demographics	A	B	C	D	E
Age					
Income					
Working Status					
Marital Status					
Children					
Education					
Occupation					
Home Ownership					

Consumer Lifestyles	A	B	C	D	E
Enjoy Reading					
Prefer Outdoor Sports					
Like Music					
Watch TV (> 4 hours per day)					
Dine Out (> 3 nights per week)					
Travel					

Usage Behaviors	A	B	C	D	E
Purchase Frequency					
Purchase Quantity					
Time of Use					
Use Situation					
Preferred Point of Purchase					

Firm Demographics

In consumer markets, one of the key forces is demographics. In business-to-business markets, we use the term *firm demographics*. Differences in the size of a commercial or industrial customer with respect to both employees and sales are likely to contribute to differences in customer needs. Industries can also be identified by the Standard Industrial Classification (SIC) code. These industry differences often correspond to different product applications and different needs for products. Additionally, the newness of a business, number of locations, and financial stability are also important firm demographics that may play a role in shaping customer needs in non-consumer, business-to-business markets.

Business Culture

Just as consumer markets have lifestyles, commercial markets have *cultures* (styles) that can have a profound impact on customer needs. Two commercial customers that are similar in firm demographics may have very different needs due to major differences in their

FIGURE 5-7 FORCES THAT SHAPE DIFFERENCES IN B2B CUSTOMER NEEDS

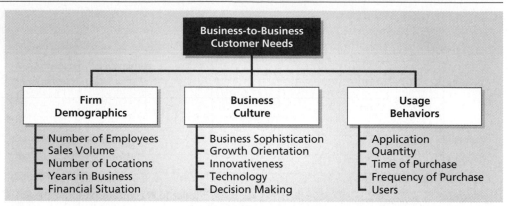

corporate style or culture. A firm with a strong technological base and growth orientation is going to have a different set of needs than a commodity business with no aspirations for growth. Other differences in attitudes with respect to innovation, risk, and centralized versus decentralized decision making can also shape customer needs.

Usage Behaviors

Finally, as in consumer markets, usage behavior often has a significant role in shaping the needs of commercial customers. How much a business buys, how often it purchases, who uses the product, and how it is used all influence the specific needs a business-to-business customer will have in selecting one vendor or product over another. Commercial customers are interested not merely in the products they are buying but also in the support, service, and integrity of the supplier companies.

As with consumer segments, business segments are created based on product and price needs unique to each segment. However, to make the segments actionable we need to identify each segment based on a different combination of firm demographics, business culture (style), and usage behaviors. In an effort to identify needs-based segments in business markets, we can modify Figure 5-6 using the forces that shape business needs as presented in Figure 5-7.

For example, the several million small businesses in the United States can be divided into many narrow segments, but they broadly fall into just two core segments: *growth-oriented entrepreneurs* and *cost-focused sustainers*. As shown in Figure 5-8, the businesses in each segment have different needs, firm demographics, and purchase behaviors. Growth-oriented entrepreneurs are better educated, more sophisticated, better organized, and have a passion to grow their businesses. By contrast, cost-focused sustainers are more centered on maintaining the status quo at the lowest cost. The small businesses in this core segment also tend to be less sophisticated in their operations, have a lower level of formal education at the leadership level, and are less likely to have a working financial plan. To sell successfully to businesses in either segment requires a strategy that recognizes the unique needs and behaviors of each segment.

NEEDS-BASED MARKET SEGMENTATION

Understanding customer needs is a basic tenet of market-based management. Although demographics, lifestyle, and usage behaviors help shape customer needs, they are not

FIGURE 5-8 MARKET SEGMENTATION OF THE SMALL-BUSINESS MARKET

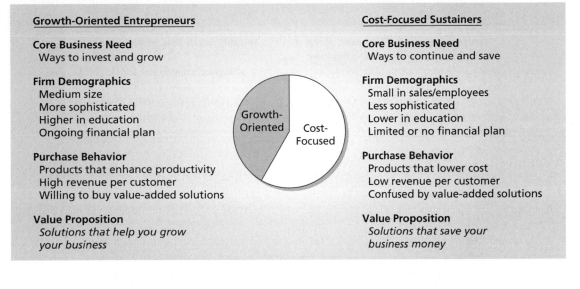

Growth-Oriented Entrepreneurs

Core Business Need
 Ways to invest and grow

Firm Demographics
 Medium size
 More sophisticated
 Higher in education
 Ongoing financial plan

Purchase Behavior
 Products that enhance productivity
 High revenue per customer
 Willing to buy value-added solutions

Value Proposition
 Solutions that help you grow
 your business

Cost-Focused Sustainers

Core Business Need
 Ways to continue and save

Firm Demographics
 Small in sales/employees
 Less sophisticated
 Lower in education
 Limited or no financial plan

Purchase Behavior
 Products that lower cost
 Low revenue per customer
 Confused by value-added solutions

Value Proposition
 Solutions that save your
 business money

always the best ways to identify groups of similar customers. Too many variables and too many meaningless combinations exist. Instead, the market segmentation process should start with customer needs as described here:

> First, group customers with like needs and then discover which of the many demographics, lifestyle forces, and usage behaviors make them distinct from customers with different needs.

In this way, we can let customer needs drive the market-segmentation process and let the unique combination of external forces that shaped them follow. This approach reduces the possibility of an artificial segmentation of the market based on a combination of demographics and usage behaviors that are *not* key forces in shaping customer needs. But before we proceed with the process of needs-based segmentation, let's first examine the demographic trap.

The Demographic Trap

Marketers new to market segmentation will often fall into the *demographic trap*. Given the strong role demographics, lifestyle, and usage play in shaping customer needs, it seems logical to segment a market on the basis of these differences. For example, in the consumer financial services market, we could segment the market on the basis of differences in income, education, and age, as well as differences in amount invested, frequency of transactions, and type of investments purchased. If we created three meaningful categories for each of these six variables, we would have over 700 possible market segments!

$$\text{Number of Segments} = (3 \text{ categories per variable})^6 = \textbf{729}$$

This is too many segments to consider if we are to develop a meaningful marketing strategy for each customer group, and a good portion of these 729 segments would not have much relevance to customer needs. It may be convenient to group customers into

FIGURE 5-9 NEEDS-BASED SEGMENTATION PROCESS

Steps in Segmentation Process	Description
1. Needs-Based Segmentation	Group customers into segments based on similar needs and benefits sought by customer in solving a particular consumption problem.
2. Segment Identification	For each needs based segment, determine which demographics, lifestyles, and usage behaviors make the segment distinct and identifiable (actionable).
3. Segment Attractiveness	Using predetermined segment attractiveness criteria, determine the overall attractiveness of each segment.
4. Segment Profitability	Determine segment profitability (net marketing contribution).
5. Segment Positioning	For each segment, create a "value proposition" and product-price positioning strategy based on that segment's unique customer needs and characteristics.
6. Segment Strategy "Acid Test"	Create "segment storyboards" to test the attractiveness of each segment's positioning strategy.
7. Marketing Mix Strategy	Expand segment positioning strategy to include all aspects of the marketing mix: product, price, promotion, place, and service.

demographic, lifestyle, or usage categories, but the demographics selected may or may not affect customer needs. Although markets are heterogeneous, and people differ from one another by demographics, personal attitudes, and life circumstances, demographic segmentation seldom provides much guidance for product development or message strategies.[5] It makes more sense to start the market-segmentation process with customer needs and then group customers on the basis of similar needs.

Needs-Based Market Segments

To illustrate the importance of needs-based segmentation, consider again how we might segment the market for investment services. Relevant demographics that might be considered to cause differences in needs could include income, assets, age, occupation, marital status, and education. Relevant use behaviors might include experience with investments, size of investment portfolio, portfolio diversification, and amount of average transaction. We could legitimately argue that each of these demographic factors is an important force in shaping customer needs, but attempting to segment this market on the basis of all of these differences would be a hopeless task. Instead, the first step in the market segmentation process outlined in Figure 5-9 is to determine customers' investment needs and the benefits they hope to derive from their investment decisions. A study of female investors' needs, for example, might produce three *needs-based segments*:[6]

- **Segment A:** Investors who seek investments that outperform inflation with minimum tax consequences.
- **Segment B:** Investors who seek investments that provide appreciation with limited risk.
- **Segment C:** Investors who seek investments that produce high levels of current income with minimal risk.

FIGURE 5-10 SEGMENT IDENTIFICATION—FEMALE INVESTOR MARKET SEGMENTS

Core Need: Segment Profile:	Growth Without Taxes Segment A	Appreciation with Minimal Risk Segment B	Income with Minimal Risk Segment C
Demographics			
Age	35–45	35–55	55–75
Income > $50,000	86%	3%	63%
Working	100%	43%	17%
Professional	83%	9%	13%
Married	56%	13%	35%
Youngest Child < 5	24%	83%	5%
College Educated	78%	23%	17%
Lifestyle			
Investment Attitude	Confident	Concerned	Conservative
Interests	Sports/Reading	Family	Leisure
Entertainment	Concerts	Movies	Television
Key Value	Individualistic	Cooperative	Traditional
Usage Behaviors			
Experience	Some/Extensive	None/Limited	Limited/Moderate
Risk Preference	Moderate/High	Low	Low/Moderate
Net Worth	Growing	Fixed	Fixed

It would not take much for a financial adviser to figure out which type of investments would best suit each segment of investors. But on the basis of needs alone, we do not know who these customers are. The main benefit of needs-based market segmentation is that the segments are based on specific customer needs. The main disadvantage is that we cannot identify in advance the individual customers who would fall into each segment. We need to determine the observable demographics and behaviors that differentiate one segment from another in order to make a needs-based segmentation actionable.

Segment Identification

After dividing a market into needs-based segments, step 2 in the segmentation process is segment identification. For a segmentation scheme to be actionable, it must characterize segments by demographics or other measurable variables for purposes of targeting and positioning.[7] For each needs-based segment, we must determine the demographics, lifestyles, and usage behaviors that make one segment meaningfully different from another. The key descriptive factors that make segment A distinct from the other segments are career orientation, occupation, college education, and above-average income, as shown in Figure 5-10. Women in this segment are also more likely to be self-confident and individualistic, and to have interests outside the home. On the basis of these characteristics, this segment is labeled the *career woman* segment. With accurate delineation of segment needs and identification, we can begin to visualize a self-confident career woman who has discretionary income to invest but wants her investments to grow at a rate greater than inflation without the burden of additional taxes.

FIGURE 5-11 FORCES THAT SHAPE SEGMENT ATTRACTIVENESS

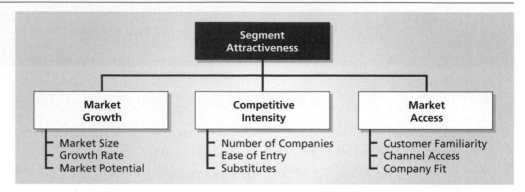

Although segment B is in the same general age category as segment A, customers in segment B have lower incomes, are more likely to have young children, and are less likely to be married. They have less experience with investments and are more likely to be apprehensive of investment decisions. This is the *single parent* segment, given both the unique family situation and lifestyle orientation that characterize it.

Segment C is called the *mature woman* segment because of age, conservative outlook, and wealth level that define its makeup. These investors look for investments that can deliver a good return, in the form of current income, with limited risk. We see, then, that all three segments have unique needs and identities that enable us to accomplish the first two steps in the needs-based segmentation process outlined in Figure 5-9.

Segment Attractiveness

What makes one segment attractive and another unattractive? Although every business might answer this question somewhat differently according to its industry perspective, when we step back and look more broadly at the factors that make a market attractive, we find few differences. Common to most assessments of segment attractiveness would be measurements of *market growth*, *competitive intensity*, and *market access*.

Market Growth

As Figure 5-11 shows, in assessing market growth we consider the present size of the segment, its rate of growth, and its market potential. Large, growing segments with the potential for long-term future growth are naturally more attractive than small, static segments with no indications of future growth. Market size, growth rate, and growth potential all influence a business's prospect for improved performance. A first step in assessing segment attractiveness is to determine the extent to which these key market forces contribute to the attractiveness of the segment.

Competitive Intensity

The number of competitors, the number of substitutes, and the level of competitive rivalry affect the attractiveness of a segment. Even if a segment is attractive because of favorable market-growth forces, intense rivalry among the segment's competitors could more than offset the favorable forces and make the segment unattractive. Many competitors and relatively easy market entry also diminish the attractiveness of a segment because these conditions make it more difficult to achieve market share and margin objectives. In addition, in a segment with many substitute products and limited product differentiation, margins will be further compressed. An attractive segment is one with relatively few competitors, little price competition, very few substitutes, and high barriers to competitor entry.

Market Access

To be attractive, a segment has to be accessible. The first requirement is access to channels that reach target segment customers. Without customer familiarity and channel access, there is little opportunity for success. Accessing a market also requires that the core capabilities of a business fit well with the needs of its target segment. The better the match between customer needs and a business's sources of advantage, the easier it is to access markets. Without sufficient marketing resources, market access is seriously impeded. Segment attractiveness is greatly enhanced when a business has cost-effective access to customers, and the business's capabilities are a good fit for its customer needs.

The importance of market segmentation and segment attractiveness is highlighted in Figure 5-12. The health insurance company in this example attempted to sell to all willing buyers without first segmenting the market. However, a later segmentation based on the insurance needs of target customers revealed that the business's greatest market penetration was in the smallest and least profitable segment, segment I. Given the relative attractiveness of the other two segments, which had more revenue per customer and fewer claims problems, the health insurance carrier revised its marketing efforts around segments II and III. A key benefit of market segmentation is identifying segments that should *not* be pursued. The quote in Chapter 1 by Chuck Lillis, CEO of MediaOne Group, bears repeating: "I will know when our businesses are doing a good job of market segmentation when they can articulate to whom we should *not* sell." In making this statement during a marketing training session, Mr. Lillis in effect was saying that businesses that do not segment their markets generally sell to everyone, and in doing so they may hurt profits without even knowing it.

Segment Profitability

Although the market attractiveness of a segment may be acceptable, a business may elect not to pursue that segment if it does not offer the desired level of profit potential. In assessing segment profitability, a business estimates the net marketing contribution expected at a certain level of segment market penetration.

For example, the market for silicon sealants can be divided into three segments based on customer needs and product-market uses, as illustrated in Figure 5-13. Although the silicon-based product is the same in each market segment, the segment strategies are customized around different customer needs for (1) product amount, (2) product package, (3) product applicator, (4) engineering support, (5) technical service, (6) availability, and (7) price.

The *engineered solutions segment,* the smallest of the three segments, buys 100 million pounds per year. The manufacturer has captured a 20 percent market share with a segment strategy designed for engineering applications. This segment is served with easy-to-use smaller containers of the product, a special product applicator, and technical service in the form of a one-on-one relationship between the company and the customer. Based on this level of product customization and service, a price of $10 per pound is obtained in this segment of the market. At this price, margins are 60 percent and marketing expenses are 20 percent of sales. As shown here, this segment strategy yields a net

FIGURE 5-12 MARKET SEGMENTATION OF THE HEALTH INSURANCE MARKET

Health Insurance Market Segment	Have and Will Not Drop	Do Not Have but Intend to Add	Plan to Drop to Cut Cost	Do Not Have and Would Not Add
Segment I: Insurance Minimizers				
Life Insurance				
Accidental Death				
Prescription Drugs				
Long-Term Disability				
Second Opinion of Surgery				
Separate Coverage for Accidents				
Segment II: Basic Buyers				
Life Insurance				
Accidental Death				
Prescription Drugs				
Long-Term Disability				
Second Opinion of Surgery				
Separate Coverage for Accidents				
Segment III: Premium Buyers				
Life Insurance				
Accidental Death				
Prescription Drugs				
Long-Term Disability				
Second Opinion of Surgery				
Separate Coverage for Accidents				

▧ Denotes segment average

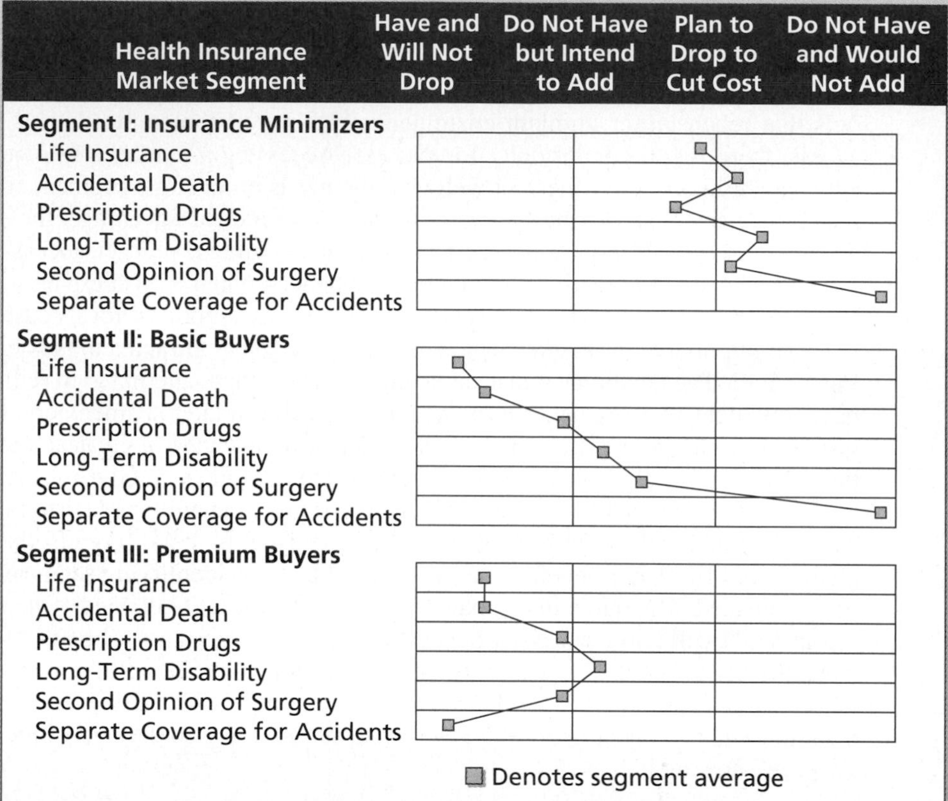

Segment	Size	Revenue per Customer*	Claims Problems*	Company Share
Insurance Minimizers	30%	100	100	40%
Basic Buyers	34%	163	71	27%
Premium Buyers	36%	181	66	19%

*Indexes set equal to 100 for Insurance Minimizers.

marketing contribution of $80 million, a marketing ROS of 40 percent, and a marketing ROI of 200 percent.

$$\begin{array}{l}\text{Net}\\ \textbf{Marketing}\\ \textbf{Contribution}\end{array} = \begin{array}{l}\text{Segment}\\ \text{Demand}\end{array} \times \begin{array}{l}\text{Segment}\\ \text{Share}\end{array} \times \begin{array}{l}\text{Price per}\\ \text{Unit}\end{array} \times \begin{array}{l}\text{Percent}\\ \text{Margin}\end{array} - \begin{array}{l}\text{Marketing}\\ \text{Expenses}\end{array}$$

$$= 100 \text{ million} \times .20 \times \$10 \times .6 - \$40 \text{ million}$$
$$= \$120 \text{ million} - \$40 \text{ million}$$
$$= \textbf{\$80 million}$$

Marketing ROS = ($80 million / $200 million) × 100% = **40%**
Marketing ROI = ($80 million / $40 million) × 100% = **200%**

FIGURE 5-13 SEGMENT MARKETING PROFITABILITY

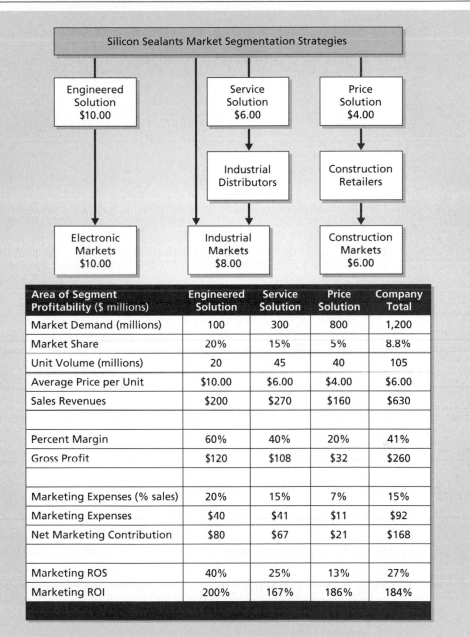

Area of Segment Profitability ($ millions)	Engineered Solution	Service Solution	Price Solution	Company Total
Market Demand (millions)	100	300	800	1,200
Market Share	20%	15%	5%	8.8%
Unit Volume (millions)	20	45	40	105
Average Price per Unit	$10.00	$6.00	$4.00	$6.00
Sales Revenues	$200	$270	$160	$630
Percent Margin	60%	40%	20%	41%
Gross Profit	$120	$108	$32	$260
Marketing Expenses (% sales)	20%	15%	7%	15%
Marketing Expenses	$40	$41	$11	$92
Net Marketing Contribution	$80	$67	$21	$168
Marketing ROS	40%	25%	13%	27%
Marketing ROI	200%	167%	186%	184%

The *service solutions segment* strategy, which serves the industrial segment, is differentiated based on package size, applicator, and direct sales and support. To enhance the strategy, industrial distributors are used to provide local availability and delivery. In this segment, the net price is $6 per pound and the margin is 40 percent of the selling price. Marketing expenses in the service solution segment are 15 percent of sales. As shown in Figure 5-13, this yields a marketing ROS of 25 percent and a marketing ROI of 167 percent.

FIGURE 5-14 SEGMENT STORYBOARDS FOR ACID TEST OF SEGMENT STRATEGIES

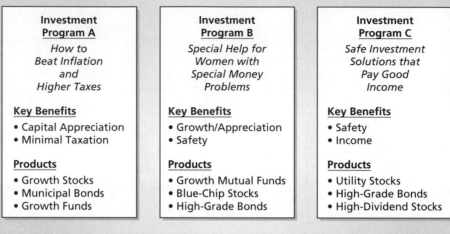

Potential customers are instructed to examine each "segment storyboard" and select the one that best fits their investment needs. The degree to which target segment customers select the storyboard designed for them determines the degree to which the segment positioning strategy would be judged to be working.

The *price segment* is served with a large-size package sold indirectly through construction retailers with no end-user sales or support. The net price in this segment is $4 per pound, with a margin of 20 percent of sales. The marketing expenses are 7 percent of sales. This yields a net marketing contribution of $21 million. The price segment's marketing ROS is 13 percent, and the marketing ROI is 186 percent. Although the segment strategies vary considerably across these three segments based on customer needs, each segment strategy is profitable and contributes to the overall marketing profit of $168 million.

Segment Positioning

Each target segment presents its own set of marketing challenges. A business needs to develop a customized *value proposition* for each positioning strategy that delivers value to target customers in each segment.[8] A value proposition includes all the key elements of the situation and the benefits the target customer is looking for in this purchase. For the female investor market described in Figure 5-10, segment A included middle-aged professional women who were seeking investments that would have above-average growth with minimal tax consequences. The value proposition for this segment might be: "*How to beat inflation and taxes with thoughtful investment planning.*" Ideally, the value proposition for a segment should capture the key benefits sought by the target customer. As a result, the value propositions for segment B and segment C would be radically different from segment A because of the radically different needs, benefits, and purchase behaviors of these segments.

To develop a segment positioning strategy for each of the three segments, let's return to Figure 5-10 as a guide. Because the three segments differ in primary needs, demographics, lifestyle, and purchase behaviors, it is important to use all this information in developing a customized positioning strategy for each segment.

Figure 5-14 presents a storyboard for each of the three segments. Shortly we will take a closer look at storyboards, but, briefly stated, they are a tool marketing managers use to assess the merits of a proposed marketing communication and the strategy behind the communication. Each of the three storyboards in this example outlines a value proposition and positioning strategy designed to meet its segment's unique needs. Product differences based on segment needs are relatively easy to determine. This is the first sign of an effective segmentation effort. If a business can readily link customer needs to specific product features and benefits, then it is on the right track to a successful segment strategy. If this linkage is difficult or arbitrary, target customers will be less likely to recognize a segment strategy as being unique. Because pricing is less important in the investment market than in, for example, the retail market, it is not a key part of the segment positioning strategy for any of the three segments. Had a segment emerged as price sensitive, then pricing would have been critical to both the value proposition and the segment positioning strategy.

Promotion is essential in delivering the value proposition and in communicating to potential customers the type of person for whom the proposition has greatest meaning. Both the ad copy and the media selected for advertising communications will impact customer response. For segment A, the ad copy would portray a career woman in a business setting; media could include *Business Week* and *The Wall Street Journal*. Segment B requires a different approach because the family plays a larger role, as does limited experience in financial planning. The promotion strategy for segment C also has to be carefully customized to the needs, lifestyle, and usage behavior of mature female investors. To reach customers in any of these segments, a business must again be sensitive to the needs and lifestyle of the target customer. For the career woman segment, lunchtime seminars at or near the workplace could be used to more effectively deliver the value proposition and product portfolio that would best serve this segment's needs and desired benefits. Similarly, morning or evening seminars at local schools could be used to reach the single parent segment. A meeting room at a hotel could be the site for a seminar designed for the mature woman segment. Interestingly, seminars targeted at the mature segment are sometimes offered aboard cruise ships, with participants able to write off a portion of their trip expenses.

Segment Strategy Acid Test

To test our understanding of segment needs and our ability to translate that understanding into a value proposition, the next step in the segmentation process is the "acid test" of our strategy.[9] To conduct the acid test, we will use the storyboards in Figure 5-14. In creating these storyboards, we wanted each to delineate a different value proposition and segment positioning strategy. Our next step is to recruit a group of female investors and use a set of questions to determine for our information which of our three segments each of them falls into. We then ask them to critique each segment's storyboard before selecting the one that most appeals to them. Our marketing strategy holds promise for success if most of the potential customers in each target segment select the storyboard created for them. The higher the percentage of correct classifications, the more likely the segment strategy will succeed. Of course, if a majority of target customers indicate that none of the segment storyboards fits their needs, then we have failed on all accounts to translate segment needs into a meaningful value proposition and segment positioning strategy.

A telecommunications business that used this acid test learned that five segments found the storyboards created for them attractive, although the participants had suggestions on how to improve them, while one segment failed to find any of the segment storyboards attractive. The business had to do more research, probing deeper into the overall needs of customers in the segment that failed to find an attractive storyboard. After additional customer research,

FIGURE 5-15 DUPONT SEGMENT VALUE PROPOSITIONS AND POSITION STRATEGIES

Commercial Fishing

Value Proposition: *This boat hull of Kevlar saves fuel, gets there faster, and can carry more fish.*

Aircraft Design

Value Proposition: *Our L-1011 is 807 pounds lighter because of Kevlar 49.*

and a second time through the acid test, the business was able to develop storyboards attractive enough for all segments of target customers, and it then moved forward in the segmentation process.

Another example of using the segment strategy acid test involved a bank that wanted to be certain of its segment strategies. One segment of the bank's customers rejected the storyboard designed for them because it did not include the cost of a new service. A revised value proposition included both the benefits and the cost of the service. In all cases, an important part of the acid test is to ask customers for ways in which the value proposition can be modified to better fit their needs, usage behavior, and lifestyle.

Segment Marketing Mix Strategy

Customer research, the storyboard process, and a careful assessment of a proposed strategy won't guarantee success. Despite the best preparations, failure is a certainty when a segment strategy is poorly executed. To be successful, the strategy next needs to be expanded to include all elements of the marketing mix. The segment positioning strategy may include both product and price, but a complete marketing mix strategy needs to include promotion (communications), place (sales and distribution), and service strategies.[10] If target-segment customers are not adequately aware of the segment value proposition or cannot acquire the product at preferred points of purchase, the segment strategy will fail. For example, in Figure 5-15 we can see how DuPont developed different advertisements to execute a

FIGURE 5-16 MARKET SEGMENTATION STRATEGIES

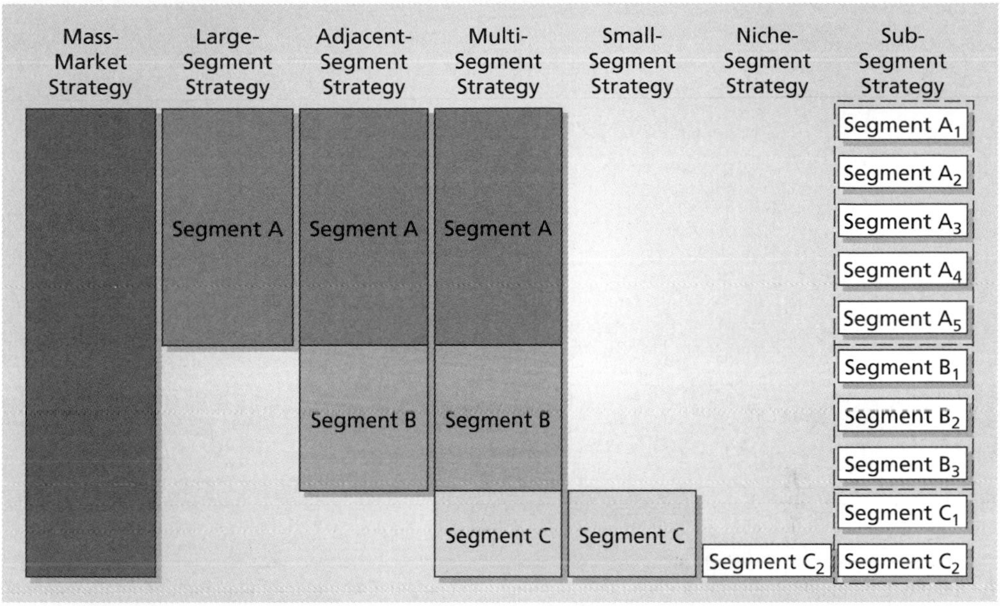

Mass-Market Strategy	Large-Segment Strategy	Adjacent-Segment Strategy	Multi-Segment Strategy	Small-Segment Strategy	Niche-Segment Strategy	Sub-Segment Strategy
						Segment A$_1$
						Segment A$_2$
	Segment A	Segment A	Segment A			Segment A$_3$
						Segment A$_4$
						Segment A$_5$
						Segment B$_1$
		Segment B	Segment B			Segment B$_2$
						Segment B$_3$
						Segment C$_1$
			Segment C	Segment C		Segment C$_2$
					Segment C$_2$	

multi-segment strategy for Kevlar. Note the attention to distinct segment value propositions and the product positioning differences that are unique to each target segment.[11] A generic ad highlighting product features would not have had the impact that each segment-specific ad has.

SEGMENTATION STRATEGIES

On the basis of segment attractiveness, profit potential, and available resources, there are several segment strategies a business can pursue. As Figure 5-16 shows, segment strategies can range from a *mass-market* strategy, with no segment focus, to *sub-segment strategies*, with numerous niche segments within segments.

Mass-Market Strategy

When differences in customer needs are small or demographics are not distinctive, a business may elect to use a mass-market strategy. This strategy presents a generic value proposition built around the core customer need and the business's generic positioning strategy. Wal-Mart, for example, pursues a mass-market strategy built around a low-cost value proposition that has worked effectively for over 30 years. Coca-Cola, Caterpillar, Sony, Marlboro, Phillips, Toyota, Volvo, and Kodak are some of the many well-recognized global brands that use a global marketing strategy, while sometimes modifying their products and marketing communications to meet customer needs in different international markets.

Large-Segment Strategy

When a market is segmented and marketing resources are limited, a business could elect to pursue a large-segment strategy. As illustrated in Figure 5-16, a mass-market strategy could

FIGURE 5-17 TOYOTA'S ADJACENT-SEGMENT STRATEGY

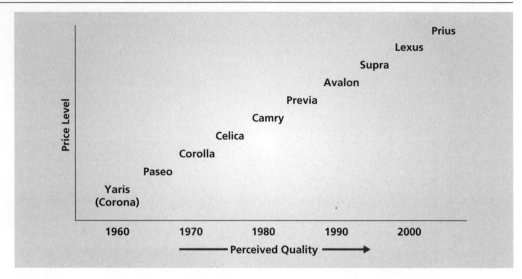

divide a market into three core segments. A large-segment strategy would focus on segment A, because it is the largest, representing 50 percent of the market. Unlike a mass-market strategy, a large-segment strategy addresses one set of core customer needs. A large-segment strategy, then, engages the benefits of market segmentation while also providing a relatively large market demand. Chevy's truck strategy is a large-segment strategy. Because market demand is somewhat limited and a large segment exists, this strategy provides a cost-effective way to reach a large number of target customers.

Adjacent-Segment Strategy

Businesses quite often find themselves in situations where they have pursued a single-segment focus but have reached the point of full market penetration. When this is the case, an adjacent-segment strategy offers an attractive opportunity for market growth. Whenever resources are limited, a closely related attractive segment is tackled first. With profits derived from this segment, the next most attractive adjacent segment is addressed.

In Figure 5-16, segment B is profiled as being most similar to segment A. When a business has reached full penetration in segment A with a large segment strategy, it may pursue new growth by entering segment B, an adjacent segment with respect to product and price needs. An example of this segmentation strategy is Toyota's adjacent-segment strategy in the U.S. car market. Toyota entered the U.S. market with the Corona at the low-price end of the market (today the Yaris serves this segment). As Toyota penetrated this segment, it moved to an adjacent segment in terms of price and quality by adding the Paseo, as shown in Figure 5-17. In the late 1980s, higher priced products were developed for the quality-conscious segments. Next came entry into the luxury-car segment with Lexus, an adjacent segment for the Supra and Avalon, and most recently the new hybrid segment in which Toyota is a pioneer. Over a 40-year period, Toyota has effectively used

FIGURE 5-18 SEGMENTATION OF GASOLINE CUSTOMER MARKET

Segment	Size (%)	Core Customer Needs	Use Behavior	Key Demographics
Road Warriors	16	Premium Products and Quality Service	Drive 25,000 to 50,000 miles a year, buy premium gas, drinks, and sandwiches.	Higher Income, middle-aged men.
Generation F3	27	Fast Fuel, Fast Service, and Fast Food	Constantly on the go; drive a lot, snack heavily, and want fuel and food fast.	Upwardly mobile men and women, half under 25.
True Blues	16	Branded Products and Reliable Service	Brand and station loyal; buy premium gas, pay cash.	Men and women with moderate to high income.
Home Bodies	21	Convenience	Use whatever gasoline is conveniently located.	Usually housewives who shuttle children during day.
Price Shoppers	20	Low Price	Neither brand nor station loyal.	Usually on tight budget.

an adjacent-segment strategy and today enjoys a strong position in nearly all segments of the automotive market.

Multi-Segment Strategies

Market segmentation opens the door to multiple market-based strategies and greater marketing efficiency. For decades, gas stations operated on the fundamental belief that gasoline purchases were made primarily on the basis of price, and it was this belief that guided their marketing strategy. However, a study of gas station–customer needs uncovered five distinct segments, only one of which could be described as price shoppers.[12] The top three segments illustrated in Figure 5-18 were more concerned with quality, service, and the availability of other products, such as coffee, soft drinks, sandwiches, and snack foods. In addition, each of the top three segments in the figure (Road Warriors, Generation F3, and True Blues) produced more revenue per customer than Home Bodies (convenience buyers) and Price Shoppers. These three target segments, which make up 59 percent of gas station customers, produce more revenue per customer because they buy more gas, premium products, and food and beverages. In addition, the average margin per customer in each of these segments is also higher than in the other two groups because the products they buy often have higher margins. By focusing on these three segments, a gas retailer could implement a series of marketing strategies to better serve the needs of these target segments and, if successful, grow revenues and profits.

An even more challenging multi-segment marketing strategy was one developed by an electrical equipment manufacturer. Some 7,000 entities make up the electrical power generation and distribution market in the United States. A segmentation study of this market produced 12 distinct needs-based segments that differed in customer needs, firm

FIGURE 5-19 MULTI-SEGMENT STRATEGY FOR POWER GENERATION MARKET

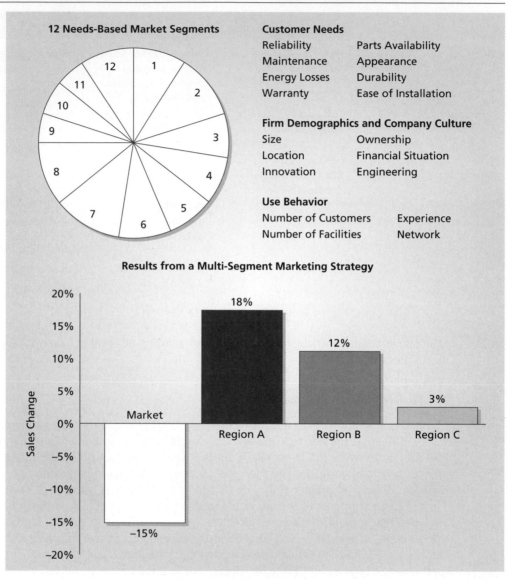

demographics, and usage behavior,[13] as shown in Figure 5-19. At one extreme was a segment that included big, publicly owned utilities that had large engineering and maintenance staffs, and at the other extreme were small co-ops that produced electricity for rural areas. One segment actually included businesses that produced electricity for their own consumption and sold excess power to the local utilities. The Los Angeles Performing Arts Center is a customer in this segment. The electrical equipment manufacturer found all identified segments attractive and already had sales to customers in each of them. The only difference was that, before the segmentation study, the business used a mass-market strategy and treated all customers roughly the same. On the basis of the unique needs of each segment, 12 separate marketing programs were designed. Designing them required 12 different segment product-positioning and marketing approaches in order to build a strong value proposition for each segment.

The year the multi-segment strategy was implemented, the overall market experienced a decline of 15 percent in sales. In addition, one regional vice president had elected not to participate in the implementation of the multi-segment marketing strategy. Despite the market's overall decline, regions A and B had significant sales increases, and region C, the control group, had a nominal increase, as shown in Figure 5-19. The business as a whole achieved a sales growth of more than 10 percent in a year that saw the market decline by 15 percent in sales volume. It is also important to note that this increase was achieved with essentially no change in marketing budget—simply a clearer market focus and a better allocation of marketing resources.

Small-Segment Strategy

Although a market may offer opportunities in several segments, a business with limited resources and certain capabilities may elect to compete in only the smallest segment. The smallest segment, as represented by segment C in Figure 5-16, is often ignored by large competitors, who may use mass-market or large-segment strategies. Even businesses with a multi-segment strategy may not be able to compete effectively with a business that has a singular-focus small-segment strategy. For example, Mercedes for many years used a small-segment strategy focused on the luxury car market. Having built a certain prestige in this market, Mercedes was reluctant to move into lower price-quality adjacent segments. However, because of the growing attractiveness of adjacent segments, Mercedes now pursues a dual-segment strategy.

Niche-Segment Strategies

Dividing a market into *homogeneous segments*—groups of customers with like needs—is never a perfect process. Even when customers in a given segment share common needs, there are still differences in demographics or usage behaviors that cannot be fully addressed by a strategy designed for that segment. This situation provides an opportunity for another business to carve out a niche within the segment, using a highly refined marketing effort directed at this overlooked small group of target customers.

Consider the case of Sub-Zero refrigerators.[14] This business, with less than a 2 percent share of the U.S. refrigerator market, competes with industry giants who have large economies of scale and marketing resources. Sub-Zero, though, holds 70 percent of the "super-premium" segment, a niche segment within the refrigerator market. Sub-Zero specializes in very expensive built-in refrigerators that start at $3,500. Target customers claim, "To own a Sub-Zero refrigerator is to have something special." It is hard to outperform niche competitors such as Sub-Zero because all their marketing resources are focused on the specific needs of a certain type of customer. Sub-Zero stays completely focused on a *niche market* that consists only of high-end customers who are seeking a super-premium refrigerator. For Sub-Zero, a needs-based market strategy is customized to the specific needs, lifestyle, and usage behavior of its niche customer.

Sub-Segment Strategies

Whether a market is divided into 2 segments or as many as 12, as in Figure 5-19, further customer differences can always be identified. We might ask, then, "How many segments

FIGURE 5-20 CORE AND SUB-SEGMENTS IN THE FIBER-CEMENT SIDING MARKET

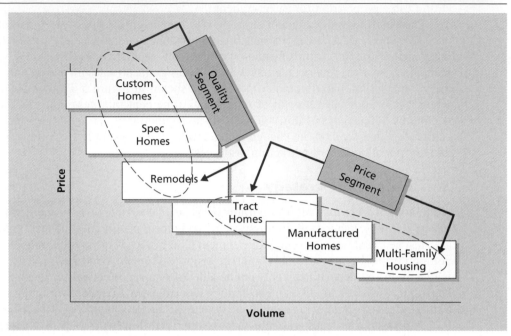

are enough?" A better question is: "Are there meaningful differences in customer needs within segments that are not being met with the current segmentation?"

If the answer to the second question is yes, then further needs-based segmentation is warranted. If the answer is no, and core needs are met, then no further needs-based segmentation is required. Yet it is still possible that sub-segments within a core segment could be addressed with more precise marketing strategies to better serve customer needs in those sub-segments.

Figure 5-16 shows a market divided into three needs-based core segments: A, B, and C. Within each core segment are sub-segments that could be served with more customized marketing programs based on differences in product use or demographics. In this illustration, the segment strategy for segment A could be further customized to the use situation experienced for each of the five sub-segments (A1, A2, A3, A4, and A5). Each one represents an opportunity to refine the core segment marketing strategy, tailoring it to the individual needs of the target customers in those sub-segments.

For example, in Figure 5-20 we have expanded the two needs-based core segments of the fiber-cement home siding market presented in Figure 5-1 to include sub-segments within each core segment. In the quality segment, the custom-home buyers and spec-home builders generally have greater need for high-quality appearance. Because architects and custom-home builders are important members of this sub-segment, a sub-segment strategy could be developed to better serve their application needs. James Hardie developed the ColorPlus and HardiTrim products to better serve the needs of these sub-segment customers. Also within the same quality segment are remodels done by both builders and home owners who want a quality appearance but have slightly different needs. Sub-segment strategies could be developed to better serve the unique needs of this remodel sub-segment.

The price segment is also divided into three sub-segments. Although driven primarily by price and installation costs, these sub-segment customers differ in the problems they encounter in using fiber-cement siding in tract homes, manufactured homes, and in the construction of multi-family housing units. Appropriate sub-segment strategies could be developed to meet the needs of each of these smaller customer groups. Any sub-segment that does not warrant a specific marketing strategy is served with the core strategy for the price segment.

The addition of sub-segment customization allows a business to add value to its product and build customer loyalty. But there is a trade-off between the cost of extending extra benefits to sub-segments of a core segment and the incremental financial benefit to the company. In some instances, the improvement in customer profitability and loyalty may be so slight that a sub-segment strategy cannot be justified. When this is the case, the sub-segment customers may be served with the core-segment strategy created for that segment's needs and use behaviors. As the profit potential for any given sub-segment increases, it becomes more advantageous for a business to reach these sub-segment customers with personalized marketing communications.

CUSTOMER RELATIONSHIP MARKETING

Many businesses work hard to acquire new customers, but this is where the effort to promote good customer relations often stops. By contrast, customer relationship marketing is more focused on what happens after a customer is acquired, with the intent of building a long-term customer relationship that benefits both the customer and the company. Consider how Wells Fargo looks at individual customer relationships:

> Much of the time, the opening of a new customer account is simply an opportunity to lose money. Most single-account households are unprofitable. We have to build a relationship to make a profit. If we can build a relationship, then we can keep customers through relationship building—not pushing products. They will reward us by buying more, buying profitably, and keeping more of their money with us.[15]

As the potential for greater company value and customer value increases to higher levels, the opportunity exists to extend a business's market segmentation to individual customers. As shown in Figure 5-21, customer relationship marketing has different strategies based on different levels of value (benefits minus cost) for the company and its customers.

Before we discuss these different individualized marketing strategies, we need to understand the difference between customer relationship marketing and customer relationship management.

- *Customer relationship marketing* includes a range of one-on-one relationship marketing programs based on the level of company and customer value, as illustrated in Figure 5-21.
- *Customer relationship management* is a high-level customer relationship marketing program that attempts to build one-on-one relationships with certain customers when both company and customer value are high enough to warrant this level of marketing effort.

FIGURE 5-21 CUSTOMER RELATIONSHIP MARKETING STRATEGIES

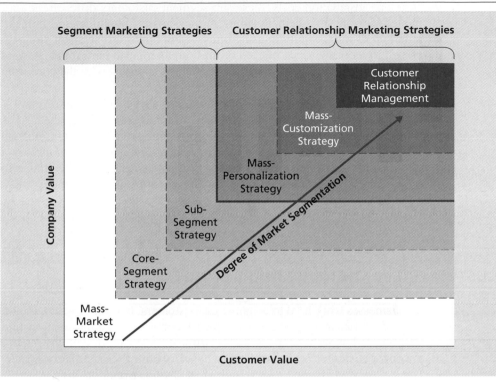

Customer Value Versus Company Value

Before going any further, we should define company value and how it differs from customer value in building a one-on-one customer relationship. Customers achieve greater customer value when the overall perceived benefits derived from products, services, and brand exceed by a meaningful margin the cost of obtaining these benefits (see "Customer Value Index" in Chapter 4). Customer relationship marketing attempts to create additional customer value through personalized communications, extra services, customized products, and special price offerings. Of course, these added customer benefits come at some cost to the customer. When the customer perceives the overall benefits exceeding the overall costs by a meaningful margin, there is an attractive level of customer value in the one-on-one customer relationship.

Companies view value in more economic terms. As we saw in Chapter 1, higher levels of repeat purchase extended over longer periods of time create a higher lifetime customer value. As customer loyalty grows and customer retention increases, the lifetime value of the customer relationship also increases. Highly satisfied loyal customers have been shown to be more profitable. They typically buy more and often buy premium-priced products and services. The combination of higher customer profitability and higher customer loyalty creates a higher lifetime customer value based on the discounted cash flow over the life of the customer (see "The Lifetime Value of a Customer" in Chapter 1).

Figure 5-21 indicates that as customer value and company value grow to the benefit of both, a business may engage in higher levels of customer relationship marketing. Within any given segment or sub-segment, not all customers will have the potential for high levels of company value and customer value. For example, perhaps only 10 percent of all the builders and architects in the custom-home sub-segment of the fiber-cement siding quality-market segment will offer the right combination of company value and customer value to warrant a customer relationship management program. The other 90 percent of the custom-home sub-segment could be served with a mass-personalization strategy, as shown in Figure 5-21.

Customer relationship marketing requires a higher level of marketing effort and expense, which must be warranted. When both customer value and company value are favorable, a business can justify a one-on-one customer relationship marketing program. It is also possible that customers can migrate in customer loyalty and profitability and thereby receive different customer relationship marketing programs over time. A mass-personalization customer program or a mass-customization customer program could increase the purchases and profitability of some customers to a point where a customer relationship management program of individualized customer services would be developed for those customers to further build their loyalty. Before discussing the three customer relationship marketing approaches in Figure 5-21, we need to examine the role of database marketing.

Database Marketing

At the core of customer relationship marketing is *database marketing.*[16] In customer relationship marketing, each customer is treated as unique, and the goal is to build a more personal relationship between the business and the customer. The only differences in the three basic kinds of customer relationship marketing programs are the level of company effort and the level of customer benefit. To determine how much effort a customer deserves, a business must have enough data to know each customer's individual needs, buying behavior, and individual product preferences.

Advances in database marketing technologies have lured many businesses down a side road where technology is seen as the solution instead of as a tool for implementing the solution. Without a solid commitment to serving individual customer needs, these businesses can fall into a *technology trap*. Many millions of dollars have been wasted developing technological solutions without first strategizing a customer relationship marketing program.

The amount of customer data required depends on the customer relationship marketing strategy to be used. Some customers may be targeted with a *mass-personalization* program that relies on personalized communications. Others may be served with a *mass-customization* strategy based on their buying behavior and individual needs for product and service customization. Still others, based on high levels of customer value and company value, may be good candidates for an individualized *customer relationship management* program.

It could be that certain customers across segments are excellent candidates for different types of customer relationship marketing programs. For example, referring to Figure 5-20, it is possible that certain contractors in the tract-home building sub-segment would be best served with a mass-personalization strategy while others warrant a customer relationship management program. The overall goal of customer relationship marketing is to serve customer needs as much as possible, subject to the cost of serving these needs (extra marketing expenses) in light of the results (customer loyalty and long-term customer profitability). The rest of this chapter discusses the three customer relationship marketing programs that comprise the field of database marketing.

Mass Personalization

The first level of customer relationship marketing is a *mass-personalization strategy* that recognizes individual customers by name, needs, and buying behavior. A business's database marketing system, then, must be able to track individual customers and their buying history, segment needs, and segment value proposition. This information is then used to develop personalized marketing communications for target customers.

American Express is a good example of a company that has had success with a mass-personalization strategy. The company has a core market segment labeled "Zero Spenders."[17] Zero Spenders are customers who hold an American Express Card and pay the annual fee but rarely or never use their cards. These customers are marginally profitable and the most likely to defect. But not all customers in this segment are the same. Some are not using the card because they can't afford much discretionary spending, while others are using cash or a competitor's card. To identify these sub-segments, American Express developed a mass-personalization promotional program for this core segment in the hope of attracting the high-potential sub-segment customers. High-potential customers attracted to these promotions self-select to participate in them, which enables American Express to identify this sub-segment for future promotions in an effort to build card usage and customer loyalty.

Another example is the United Airlines Frequent Flyer Mileage Plus program. This mass-personalization program allows customers to extend their involvement with United Airlines by joining the Frequent Flyer Program, which in turn allows United to establish personalized communications and mileage awards based on the level of each customer's travel. Customers who travel more are given more customer benefits. Frequent flyers can migrate to United Premium, Executive Premium, and 100K customer status. At each level, customer personalization increases with respect to mileage bonuses, ticket class upgrades, and personalized services provided, including exclusive 800-numbers for faster customer reservations and problem solving.

With Mileage Plus, United Airlines is striving to build customer retention and customer profitability with mass-personalization programs that add value for its frequent flyers. The goal is to personalize customer interaction with the company, extending different levels of benefits to target customers based on the potential for growing customer loyalty and customer profitability. As United expands these marketing efforts to include extra services or modified product offerings in building one-on-one marketing relationships, the company is moving closer to a mass-customization program.

Mass Customization

Although market segmentation and sub-segmentation recognize that customers value a product's benefits differently, some customers within a segment are willing to pay more for extra benefits.[18] It is difficult, however, to offer customers in the same segment different product-price configurations. Mass customization allows for this because the marketing mix is customized to the level of individual customer product preferences, extended services, and prices. Mass customization allows each customer to build a custom product to meet that customer's specific needs, personal constraints, and price considerations.

For example, Sun Microsystems allows for individual customer price customization and product configuration of its computer network solutions.[19] At Sun, the mass-customization strategy treats every customer as a separate market segment in that individual customers are able to build the mix of products they prefer, with the functions and service features that work best for their needs, considering the price they want to pay. With mass customization, customers build the product around their needs and the company delivers it to their specifications. This marketing strategy can only be done effectively when the incremental value is greater for the customers and for the company. Ford, for example, expects mass customization to significantly reduce the $10 billion it spends on promotional pricing each year. Efforts like discount financing and cash-back programs have historically been offered to all customers on a broad range of models over a specific period of time. Mass customization allows Ford to finely target the price promotions for specific models and the customers who would most likely respond to a certain type of price promotion.[20]

Perhaps the most successful example of mass customization is Dell Inc. On Dell's Web site, customers can choose from a variety of options to create their own computer configurations, which are then built to order and shipped within a short time.

Figure 5-22 illustrates how mass customization can be applied to the purchase of a notebook computer. Customers start with a base model and can then choose to customize it with options that fit their needs and budget. A great many different configurations are possible for a notebook computer, and this process lets potential customers weigh the costs and benefits of each before selecting the one best suited for their personal situations.

The use of mass customization essentially allows customers to become their own individual market segments. This is good for the customer as well as the business, because even the same customer, as we have seen, may have different needs over time. A number of companies are launching programs of mass customization, giving some validity to the word "customer." Products ranging from a Lexus to a Barbie doll can now be individualized to suit a buyer's unique tastes. The whole point of mass customization is to let customers "build their products" according to their individual needs and price sensitivity. Mass customization combines the advantages of a niche-segment strategy with the breadth of opportunity available with multi-segment marketing strategies.

Customer Relationship Management

When the potential exists for high levels of both customer value and company value, a customer relationship management (CRM) program can be justified. Although needs-based market segmentation strives to build programs around target customers' needs in an effort to satisfy and retain customers, the ultimate goal of customer relationship management is to build one-on-one customized relationships between a business and individual customers.[21]

The first step in building a successful customer relationship management program is to identify the level of company value and the level of customer value for each customer. This requires a complete understanding of individual customer needs, product preferences, buying behaviors, customer loyalty, and customer profitability. A database marketing program

FIGURE 5-22 MASS CUSTOMIZATION FOR ONLINE PURCHASE OF A NOTEBOOK COMPUTER

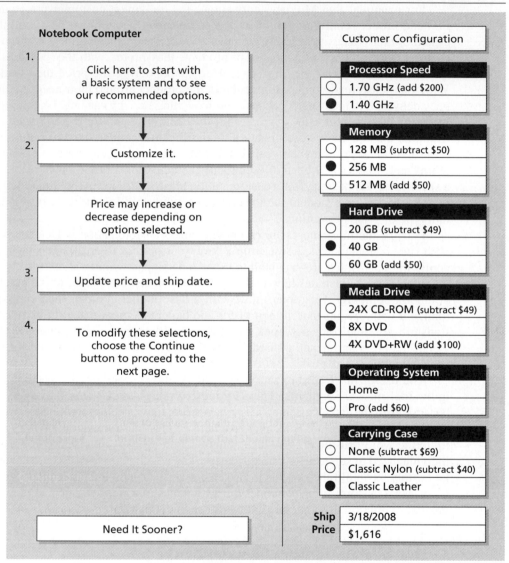

is an essential tool in developing this understanding, but customer relationship management is much more than just technology. Successful CRM actually develops and maintains one-on-one relationships with key customers.[22] Outlined here are four steps critical to the success of any customer relationship management program.

Step I: Qualify current customers for customer relationship management based on attractive levels of potential customer value and company value.

Step II: Understand individual customer needs, product preferences, and use behaviors.

Step III: Create individualized customer solutions based on individual customer needs and establish one-on-one customer touch points in building and sustaining this relationship.

Step IV: Track customer experiences and all aspects of customer satisfaction to ensure that high levels of customer satisfaction and customer loyalty are achieved.

To better understand this process, let's examine how Marriott uses customer relationship management to serve its top performers and high-potential customers. Marriott has a segment it calls the "business traveler." The business traveler customer has unique needs and travel patterns that require a customized customer solution. In Step I, certain business travelers were identified as potentially profitable and loyal customers. Step II involved building a Marriott customer database of target customer profiles based on past customer requests and preferences that were stored when customers called to make reservations. Based on individual customer needs, tee times are scheduled, dinner reservations arranged, and recreation itineraries are created (Step III). With this individualized customer relationship solution in place, Marriott carries out Step IV by maintaining individual contact with customers to measure all aspects of their customer experience. This level of customer interaction facilitates the process of building customer loyalty and tracking customer performance.

For Marriott, high customer-satisfaction scores have translated into higher levels of repeat business and customer loyalty. Marriott has learned that customers who participate in its Personal Planning Service (a one-on-one marketing program) produce significantly higher customer-satisfaction scores and spend an average of $100 per day *more* on services beyond the room rate. The program has not only improved customer loyalty among business travelers who spend more on supplementary services, but it has also resulted in an occupancy rate 10 percentage points higher than the industry average.

An important concept in customer relationship management is *customer touch points*. Every interaction with a customer or a potential customer is a *touch point*. Customer touch points include in-store interactions, Web sites, voice mail systems, direct-mail advertising, mass e-mail messages, order desks, return counters, and service calls. Indirect customer touch points are less obvious but sometimes even more important in turning potential customers into actual customers. These are often informational contacts, such as news articles and word-of-mouth advertising, yet they are powerful forces in shaping the beliefs and attitudes of potential customers toward the business and its products and services.

At every point of contact—before, during, and after a sale—a business's communications affect its relationships with customers and potential customers. The way a business manages each customer relationship from the first touch point determines the long-run profit potential of that customer.

■ Summary

At the heart of market-based management is a skillfully executed market-segmentation effort. Market segmentation is the core of a market-based strategy because it is built around unique customer needs, different lifestyles, and different usage behaviors. To the extent that a business understands differences in its customer's needs, lifestyles, and product usage, it can translate them into actionable segment strategies.

The segmentation process we examined with the most detail emphasized the identification of needs-based segments. Although it may be easy to create segments based of differences in demographics or behavior, doing so can lead to a marketing strategy that does not deliver a needs-based customer solution. Demographics shape customer needs, and demographics also serve as a measurable way to identify needs-based market segments, but not always. The first step is to identify segments based on needs. Then needs-based segments must be demographically identified so that actionable strategies can be created for each segment.

These first two steps are critical. The next steps in the segmentation process require that we index overall segment attractiveness and estimate segment profit potential to select target segments. A value proposition and marketing mix strategy must be developed for each target segment selected. To ensure that we have accurately translated target customer needs and identity characteristics into our positioning strategy (value proposition and marketing mix), the segment "acid test" is applied. The test enables a business to determine whether a segment's target customers are adequately attracted to the segment value proposition and the segment strategy designed for them. On the basis of customer feedback, a revised strategy can be developed and implemented.

In some instances, resources may be limited and only a single segment or niche (subsegment) within a segment may be pursued. In other instances, a business may have the resources and capabilities to implement a multi-segment strategy. But the more segments a business has, the more difficulty it encounters in maintaining a distinct marketing strategy for each. With the use of database marketing, a business can actually take either a single-segment strategy or a multi-segment strategy one step further with mass-personalization and mass-customization strategies. The first lets a business personalize its marketing communications to target customers, using a refined value proposition. The second essentially lets customers custom design the product for their individual needs. An effective mass-customization program enables a multi-segment business to obtain the advantages of a niche marketer; it can serve not only its larger segments, but also sub-segments and even additional sub-segments, or niches, within those sub-segments.

A logical extension of mass customization is customer relationship management. The ultimate goal of customer relationship management is an ongoing individual relationship between a business and its most profitable individual customers. Because not all customers can be served by CRM, we first determine the levels of customer value and company value for each customer. Once customers for a CRM program are identified, customized solutions can be built through individual customer touch points in an effort to increase the loyalty and profitability of these customers.

■ Market-Based Strategic Thinking

1 How did market segmentation help James Hardie in its marketing strategy?
2 Why should customer needs be the driving force in segmenting a market?
3 What kind of problems can occur if a business segments a market on the basis of demographics or usage?
4 How are customer needs shaped and what role do these forces play in the segmentation process?
5 What happens when a business is able to segment a market on the basis of needs but unable to demographically or behaviorally identify the segments?

6 How do firm demographics help shape business-to-business customer needs?

7 What forces shape market attractiveness and how should they be measured in order to develop an overall index of market attractiveness?

8 What criteria should be used in determining the segments a business should pursue?

9 What is a segment value proposition? Why is it a crucial part of the segmentation process?

10 How would you develop a value proposition for a retail gasoline business's target customers?

11 What is a segment marketing mix strategy? How did the marketing mix strategy differ for each of the three segments of the female investor services market?

12 What is the segment strategy "acid test"? What are the advantages of applying the test?

13 How did DuPont create an effective multi-segment strategy for Kevlar?

14 What is an adjacent-segment strategy? Why would a business pursue an adjacent-segment strategy when several other segments are also attractive and offer good profit potential?

15 When would a business pursue a single-segment marketing strategy?

16 Why is a niche strategy often difficult for competitors to outperform?

17 What is mass customization? How could a business using a mass-customization strategy match the effectiveness of smaller niche competitors?

18 What is customer relationship marketing? How should it improve customer satisfaction and retention?

19 Why is market segmentation a critical first step in building a customer relationship marketing program?

20 What are customer touch points and what role do they play in customer relationship management?

Marketing Performance Tools

The five **Marketing Performance Tools** described here may be accessed online at *www.rogerjbest.com.* The instructions are for the online examples, not the book's related figures cited after the captions for the first four tools. These applied-learning exercises will add to your understanding of segmentation strategies.

5.1 Needs-Based Segmentation (Figure 5-4)
■ Using the laptop product-price configuration provided, create a needs-based segment for laptop users who have home businesses and work on their laptops 4 to 6 hours a day, including while on out-of-town business trips.

■ Next, using the laptop product-price configuration provided, create a needs-based segment for a consumer with a limited budget who wants to buy a laptop for school assignments, e-mail communications, and entertainment.

■ How are these needs-based segments different?

5.2 Segmentation Identification (Figure 5-6)
■ For the home business segment, edit the consumer profile characteristics

and indicate which consumer demographics, lifestyle, and usage behaviors would make this type of potential customer identifiable.

■ For the other segment, edit the consumer profile characteristics and indicate which consumer demographics, lifestyle, and usage behaviors would make this type of potential customer identifiable.

■ What are the most important characteristics that differentiate one segment from the other? How would this help you develop a marketing communications strategy?

5.3 Segment Profitability (Figure 5-13)

■ For the price segment, what would be the profit impact of a 10 percent decrease in price if market share could be increased from 2 to 3 percent?

■ For the quality segment, what would be the profit impact of a strategy to increase the marketing budget from 10 percent of sales to 15 percent of sales in an effort to increase market share from 2 to 3 percent?

5.4 The Acid Test for Segment Strategies (Figure 5-14)

■ For the price segment, create a storyboard similar to the ones presented in Figure 5-14. If possible, add a picture from a magazine that represents the customer identity of this segment.

■ Do the same for the quality segment.

■ Create a third storyboard with no segment identity, average product features, and a mid-range price.

■ Now ask some people you know to evaluate the three storyboards and to select the one that most appeals to them. In each case, ask why the selected storyboard appealed to the person. Based on your knowledge of these "potential customers" and the segment in which each would fall, did the storyboards accurately capture the product-price needs of your "potential customers"?

5.5 Customer Relationship Marketing

■ How would the customer profitability and lifetime value change for the mass-personalization program if the customer retention dropped from 67 to 60 percent?

■ At what level of percent margin would the mass-customization program no longer produce a positive customer profit?

■ At what level of revenue per customer would the customer relationship management program not produce a positive lifetime value?

Notes

1. Ranjay Gulati, "Silo Busting: How to Execute on the Promise of Customer Focus," *Harvard Business Review* (May 2007): 98–108.
2. Daniel Yankelovich and David Meer, "Rediscovering Market Segmentation, *Harvard Business Review* (February 2006): 131
3. Wendell Smith, "Product Differentiation and Market Segmentation as Alternative Marketing Strategies," *Marketing Management* (Winter 1995): 63–65.
4. Delbert Hawkins, Roger Best, and Kenneth Coney, *Consumer Behavior: Implications for Marketing Strategy*, 6th ed. (New York: Irwin, 1995): 4–25.
5. Marshall Greenberg and Susan McDonald Schwartz, "Successful Needs/Benefits Segmentation: A User's Guide," *Journal of Consumer Marketing* (Summer 1989): 29–36.
6. "Merrill Lynch Campaign Targeted at Women Stresses Investment Options," *Marketing News* (November 30, 1979): 11.
7. Sachin Gupta and Pradeep Chintagunta, "On Using Demographic Variables to Determine Segment Membership in Logit Mixture Models," *Journal of Marketing Research* (February 1994): 128.
8. Michael Lanning, *Delivering Profitable Value* (Reading, MA: Perseus Books, 1998): 39–88.
9. William Band, "Customer-Accelerated Change," *Marketing Management* (Winter 1995): 19–33.
10. P. Dickson and J. Ginter, "Market Segmentation, Product Differentiation, and Marketing Strategy," *Journal of Marketing* (April 1987): 1–10.
11. G. Coles and J. Culley, "Not All Prospects Are Created Equal," *Business Marketing* (May 1986): 52–59.

12. Allanna Sullivan, "Mobil Bets Drivers Pick Cappuccino Over Parties," *The Wall Street Journal* (January 30, 1995): B1.
13. Dennis Gensch, "Targeting the Switchable Industrial Customer," *Marketing Science* (Winter 1984): 41–54.
14. J. Levine, "Cool!" *Forbes* (April 1996): 98.
15. Melinda Nykamp, *The Customer Differential* (New York: AMACOM, 2001): 11.
16. Stan Rapp and Tom Collins, *MaxiMarketing* (New York: McGraw-Hill, 1987); Jonathan Berry, "Database Marketing—A Potent New Tool for Selling," *Business Week* (September 5, 1995): 56; and Robert Buzzell and Rajendra Sisoda, "Information Technology and Marketing," in *Companion Encyclopedia of Marketing*, Michael Baker, ed. (Los Angeles: Rutledge, 1995).
17. Louise O'Brien and Charles Jones, "Do Rewards Really Create Loyalty," *Harvard Business Review* (May–June, 1995): 75–82.
18. James Gilmore and Joseph Pine II, "The Four Faces of Mass Customization," *Harvard Business Review* (January–February 1997): 91–103.
19. Scott McNealy, "Welcome to the Bazaar," *Harvard Business Review* (March 2001): 18–19.
20. Walter Baker, Mike Marn, and Craig Zawada, "Price Smarter on the Net," *Harvard Business Review* (February 2001): 122–127.
21. Don Peppers and Martha Rogers, *The One-On-One Future: Building Relationships One Customer at a Time* (New York: Doubleday, 1997).
22. Don Peppers and Martha Rogers, *One to One B2B: Customer Development Strategies for the Business to Business World* (New York: Doubleday, 2001).

CHAPTER 6

Competitor Analysis and Sources of Advantage

■ A competitive advantage enables a business to create a superior value for customers and superior profits for itself.

Businesses with a *cost advantage* are able to create superior customer value with products that have average customer benefits and below-average cost. Businesses with a meaningful *differentiation advantage* are likewise able to create superior customer value with above-average benefits, even at above-average prices. Figure 6-1 illustrates how either low customer cost or high customer benefits can create customer value, and how customer value can be mapped. Businesses with either of these two sources of competitive advantage find it easier to attract and retain customers. It is important to keep in mind, however, that the two sources of customer value attract two kinds of customers. The first group

FIGURE 6-1 COMPETITIVE ADVANTAGE AND CUSTOMER VALUE

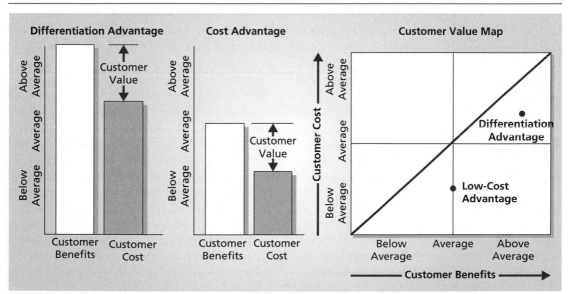

FIGURE 6-2 COMPETITIVE ADVANTAGE, CUSTOMER VALUE, AND PROFITABILITY

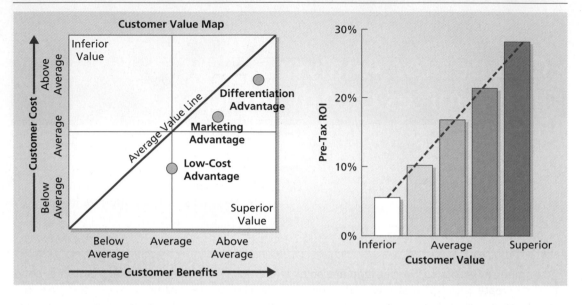

consists of price-sensitive customers attracted by a lower purchase price, and the second group consists of quality-conscious customers attracted by superior benefits despite a premium price. In either case, the superior customer value results in superior profits. As Figure 6-2 illustrates, businesses with above-average customer value produce higher levels of pre-tax return on investment. Businesses with an average customer value, where costs equal benefits, produce average pre-tax profits. The businesses in this second group need to spend more to acquire customers and have more difficulty keeping customers because their value propositions are merely average. The net result is average profits.

Businesses with a negative customer value, where costs exceed benefits, produce an inferior value and have difficulties attracting customers and even more difficulties keeping them. These businesses have been shown to produce lower profits and tend to lose market share, which has an additional adverse impact on profitability.

Either a cost advantage or a differentiation advantage improves a business's competitiveness. A third source of competitive advantage takes the form of a *marketing advantage*. Businesses that can create a superior customer value with high

levels of market share and brand awareness, along with broad product lines and highly effective distribution systems, have a marketing advantage. Businesses with a marketing advantage, as illustrated in Figure 6-2, are the market share leaders. In many instances, a business will have a market share two or three times higher than its closest competitor. Its market presence creates high brand awareness and brand recognition, making it easier to attract customers. While such a business does not offer lower cost or greater benefits, it does create customer value with high brand credibility, a broad product line offering a variety of choices, and excellent product distribution that lowers customers' transaction costs and possibly reduces purchase risk. As Figure 6-2 shows, businesses with a marketing advantage typically have prices at or slightly above average prices. The combination of high share (high volume) and slightly higher prices (higher margins) contributes to above-average profits.

To achieve above-average profits, a business has to develop some source of competitive advantage that provides target customers superior customer value. The first part of this chapter takes a closer look at each source of competitive advantage.

FIGURE 6-3 SOURCES OF COMPETITIVE ADVANTAGE

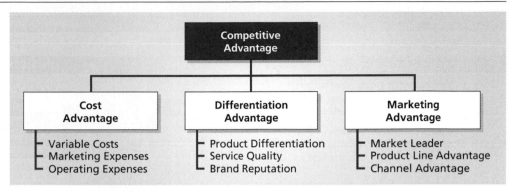

SOURCES OF COMPETITIVE ADVANTAGE

As a business begins to more fully grasp its position relative to key competitors, it gains more insight into potential sources of competitive advantage. For a source of relative advantage to be a competitive advantage requires (1) that the area of relative advantage be meaningful to target customers, and (2) that the relative advantage be sustainable (not easily copied by competitors). Wal-Mart, for example, has developed a cost advantage that has enabled it to attract and satisfy target customers by offering lower prices. Hewlett-Packard has built a differentiation advantage with product innovation and quality, and Nordstrom has built a differentiation advantage with service quality. Both companies attract and satisfy customers with differentially superior products or services. Nike, on the other hand, has developed a marketing advantage with creative and aggressive marketing efforts and with retailing that attracts and satisfies target customers. In each case, the business developed a source of competitive advantage that is meaningful to target customers. This source of competitive advantage becomes an area that managers work on each day in order to sustain their business's level of competitive advantage.

The three primary sources of competitive advantage, as described in the chapter's introductory text and listed in Figure 6-3, may be summarized in this way:

■ **Cost Advantage:** A significantly lower cost position from which to create lower prices while still achieving desirable profit margins.
■ **Differentiation Advantage:** A meaningful differentiation that creates desired customer benefits at a level superior to those of competitors.
■ **Marketing Advantage:** A market position and marketing effort that dominates the competition in brand recognition, product line, and channels of distribution.

COST ADVANTAGE

As demonstrated in Figure 6-4, a cost advantage relative to competition contributes to higher levels of profitability. A business can achieve three different types of cost advantage, as listed in Figure 6-3. It can achieve a lower variable cost per unit sold, a lower

FIGURE 6-4 COST ADVANTAGE AND PROFITABILITY

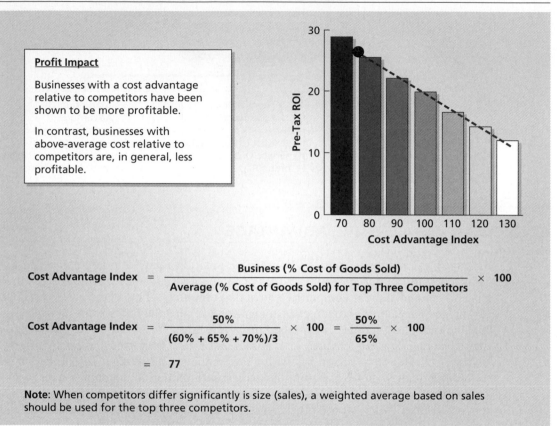

Profit Impact

Businesses with a cost advantage relative to competitors have been shown to be more profitable.

In contrast, businesses with above-average cost relative to competitors are, in general, less profitable.

$$\text{Cost Advantage Index} = \frac{\text{Business (\% Cost of Goods Sold)}}{\text{Average (\% Cost of Goods Sold) for Top Three Competitors}} \times 100$$

$$\text{Cost Advantage Index} = \frac{50\%}{(60\% + 65\% + 70\%)/3} \times 100 = \frac{50\%}{65\%} \times 100$$

$$= 77$$

Note: When competitors differ significantly is size (sales), a weighted average based on sales should be used for the top three competitors.

level of marketing expenses, or a lower level of operating and overhead expense. Each type of cost advantage can be achieved in several ways.

Variable Cost Advantage

Businesses with a lower unit cost are able to achieve the same (or better) margins at lower prices than competing businesses. Unit or variable costs include manufacturing costs and costs associated with distribution, such as discounts, sales commissions, transportation, and other transaction costs.

But how does a business achieve a variable cost advantage? Volume is a key factor. Businesses with a substantial market share advantage (volume) can generally achieve a lower unit cost.[1] As volume increases, the cost per unit generally decreases. For example, as demonstrated in Figure 6-5, the cost of cellular phone service decreases at the rate of 20 percent every time the volume of customers in a geographic market doubles. When a cellular business doubles its customer base from 400,000 to 800,000, the unit cost decreases by 20 percent. In this case, the business that attains the largest customer penetration (volume) achieves the lowest unit cost.

FIGURE 6-5 UNIT COST AND EXPERIENCE CURVE

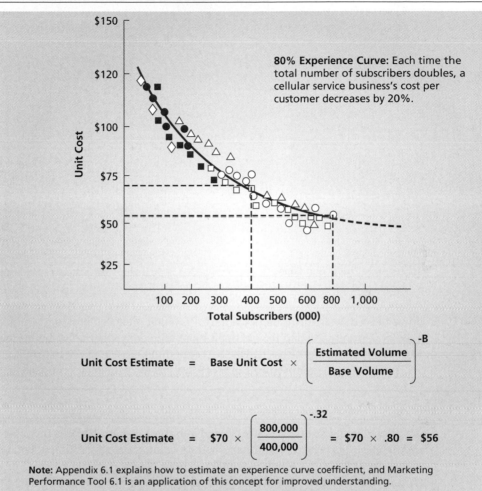

80% Experience Curve: Each time the total number of subscribers doubles, a cellular service business's cost per customer decreases by 20%.

$$\text{Unit Cost Estimate} \ = \ \text{Base Unit Cost} \times \left(\frac{\text{Estimated Volume}}{\text{Base Volume}} \right)^{-B}$$

$$\text{Unit Cost Estimate} \ = \ \$70 \times \left(\frac{800{,}000}{400{,}000} \right)^{-.32} = \$70 \times .80 = \$56$$

Note: Appendix 6.1 explains how to estimate an experience curve coefficient, and Marketing Performance Tool 6.1 is an application of this concept for improved understanding.

A larger production volume allows for production and purchasing economies that lower the unit cost of a product, thereby creating a *scale effect*. With volume purchases, Wal-Mart has been able to negotiate a lower cost of goods. The same scale effect would occur for a manufacturer who doubles production capacity. As Honda has increased its production capacity, there has been some reduction in unit cost due to a scale effect for a certain component product, as illustrated in Figure 6-6.

Likewise, when a business adds products to its product line that have similar manufacturing processes, and which are made of the same purchased materials as its other products, the business is able to lower the average unit cost of all products. This is a *scope effect*. For Honda, the cost of ignition switches is lower because the same ignition switch components are used in cars, motorcycles, lawn mowers, all-terrain vehicles, snowblowers, snowmobiles, jet skis, and generators. Honda's extension of its product line has provided a cost advantage across products due to the increased volume, and hence the reduced cost, of the common component parts.

Finally, as a business builds more of the same product, there is a greater opportunity for *learning effects*. These non-scale, non-scope effects contribute to lower costs through process

FIGURE 6-6 IGNITION SWITCH COST ADVANTAGE DUE TO SCALE AND SCOPE EFFECTS

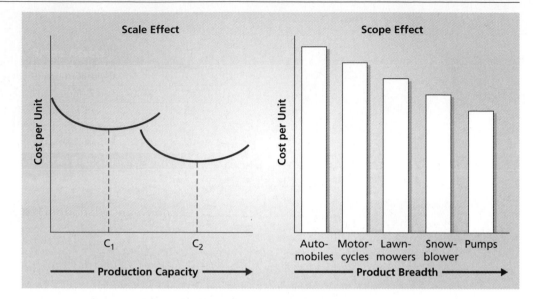

improvements that are the result of learning. Each unit produced provides additional learning and the opportunity to build the next unit more efficiently. Naturally, the business with the most production experience has had the best opportunity to learn from experience. This learning normally leads to improvements in processes that result in a lower cost per unit.

Marketing Cost Advantage

Quite often, businesses fail to look beyond variable costs for sources of a cost advantage. Many of these businesses could benefit from marketing cost efficiencies derived from product line extensions, which is another way to gain a cost advantage. For example, it takes a certain number of salespeople to adequately cover a target market. As the sales force is given more products to sell to the same customers, a *marketing cost scope effect* is created. As illustrated in Figure 6-7, Procter & Gamble's sales force expense per pound of detergent sold should decrease as more brands of detergent are added to its product line. A competitor with far fewer brands would need to have the same sales call frequency to adequately serve retailers and, therefore, would experience a higher cost per pound sold because it has fewer brands to sell.

Another area of marketing cost advantage is derived from the advertising cost efficiency of a brand extension strategy. Campbell's Soup, as an example, is the banner brand for a vast line of soups. Each time an individual soup is advertised, it is reinforcing top-of-the-mind awareness of Campbell's Soup and other soups in the product line. In this way, the scope effect created by additional soups lowers the advertising dollars spent per ounce of soup sold.

Operating Cost Advantage

Although an operating cost advantage is generally outside the control or influence of the marketing function, lower operating expenses relative to competitors contribute to a

FIGURE 6-7 PRODUCT SCOPE AND MARKETING COST ADVANTAGE

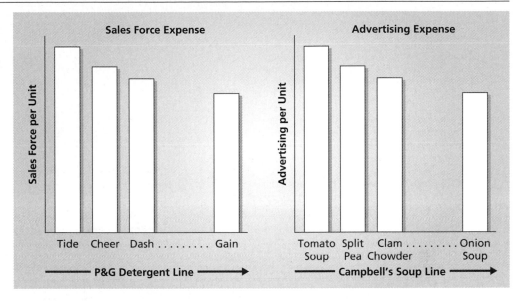

low-cost advantage. Wal-Mart achieves an operating-expense-to-sales ratio of less than 20 percent of sales, while many of its competitors' operating expenses are well over 20 percent. This difference gives Wal-Mart another source of cost advantage from which to create greater customer value with lower prices, and greater shareholder value with lower operating expenses.

Similarly, McDonald's has been able to cut construction costs of new restaurants by 50 percent since 1990 by using standardized building designs. Because the building is an asset that needs to be depreciated, this source of operating expense is drastically lower than it would be if each building had a unique design. A standardized building design, along with rapid store expansion, has contributed to McDonald's earnings and shareholder value.

DIFFERENTIATION ADVANTAGE

Every business must manage its costs, but not every business can have a cost advantage. To achieve above-average profits, a business needs some source of competitive advantage. A differentiation advantage with respect to product, service, or brand reputation is a potential source of competitive advantage, as we have seen. But like every source of competitive advantage, a differentiation advantage has to be meaningful to target customers as well as sustainable (not easily duplicated by competitors).

Product Advantage

A business can build a differentiation advantage around any of a product's many aspects. A product's durability, reliability, performance, features, appearance, and conformance to a specific application all have the potential of being a differentiation advantage.[2] ESCO Corporation, for example, is a manufacturer of earthmoving equipment

FIGURE 6-8 PRODUCT DIFFERENTIATION ADVANTAGE AND PROFITABILITY

Profit Impact

Businesses with a product advantage that outperforms competitors in delivering superior product benefits have been shown to be more profitable.

In contrast, as in this example, an inferior competitive position with respect to product benefits sought by target customers has been correlated with poorer financial performance.

Intel, Microsoft, and Apple have each built a product advantage in the markets they serve.

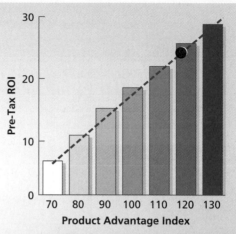

Product Benefits (Voice of the Customer)	Rel. Imp.	Our Bus.	Competitors			Product Advantage
			A	B	C	
Reliable Performance	50	8.3	7.5	5.4	6.7	17
Ease of Use	30	5.6	5.1	7.7	4.9	−10
Product Life	20	7.6	5.2	5.2	6.1	13
	100					20

Product Advantage Index = 100 + 20 = 120

parts used in very demanding mining and construction applications. The company has developed a differentiation advantage in the wear life of its products due to proprietary steel chemistry and product design. The end result is that its products last longer and are less likely to break than are the products of its competitors. Both of these customer benefits save the customer money even when the products are sold at a higher price. Overall, businesses with a relative advantage in product quality produce higher levels of profitability, as illustrated in Figure 6-8.

Service Advantage

A business can achieve a differentiation service advantage in the same way it can achieve a differentiation product advantage.[3] The same baseline conditions are required. First, the service advantage has to be meaningful and important to target customers, and second, it has to be sustainable. FedEx tracks its performance on 10 service quality indicators (each weighed by the customer pain a failure creates). This service quality index is carefully monitored each day to help FedEx maintain a service quality advantage. As its service quality index improves, customer satisfaction improves and the overall cost per package decreases. By tracking its service performance each day, FedEx is able to create greater overall customer satisfaction with fewer errors, lower costs, and greater profits for shareholders. As Figure 6-9 shows, businesses with a service advantage produce higher levels of profitability.

FIGURE 6-9 SERVICE DIFFERENTIATION ADVANTAGE AND PROFITABILITY

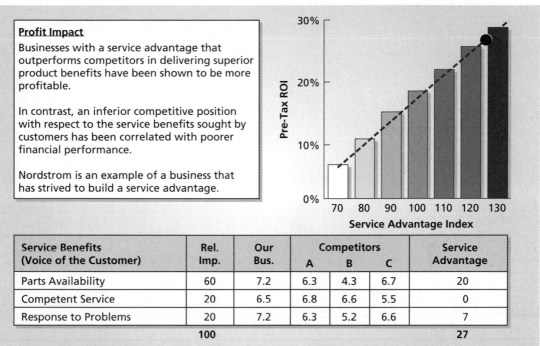

Profit Impact

Businesses with a service advantage that outperforms competitors in delivering superior product benefits have been shown to be more profitable.

In contrast, an inferior competitive position with respect to the service benefits sought by customers has been correlated with poorer financial performance.

Nordstrom is an example of a business that has strived to build a service advantage.

Service Benefits (Voice of the Customer)	Rel. Imp.	Our Bus.	Competitors			Service Advantage
			A	B	C	
Parts Availability	60	7.2	6.3	4.3	6.7	20
Competent Service	20	6.5	6.8	6.6	5.5	0
Response to Problems	20	7.2	6.3	5.2	6.6	7
	100					**27**

Service Advantage Index = 100 + 27 = 127

Reputation Advantage

Another source of differentiation competitive advantage is brand reputation. Although competing watchmakers may match the quality of a Rolex watch, they cannot easily match Rolex's brand reputation advantage. Brands such as Chanel, Nikon, and Perrier also have built reputations that provide a source of competitive advantage in their ability to attract target customers. For these companies, the stature of their brand names add a dimension of appeal that is an important customer benefit for many less price-sensitive, more image-conscious consumers.

A brand reputation advantage can be measured in the same way as a product or service advantage. Businesses with an advantage in brand reputation can both attract customers and obtain a price premium. As Figure 6-10 shows, the reputation of a consumer product or service can have a greater impact on price premiums than a product advantage. Even in business-to-business markets, an advantage in brand or company reputation helps to support price and, hence, margins.

MARKETING ADVANTAGE

A business that dominates markets with a relative advantage in sales coverage, distribution, or marketing communications can control (and often block) market access. A marketing advantage can be a business's best source of competitive advantage. Whether

FIGURE 6-10 BRAND ADVANTAGE AND PROFITABILITY

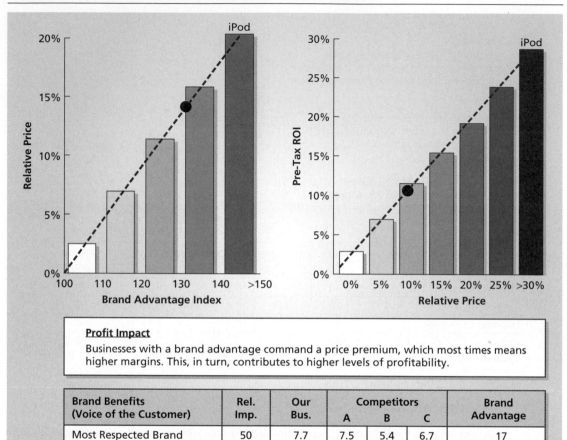

Profit Impact

Businesses with a brand advantage command a price premium, which most times means higher margins. This, in turn, contributes to higher levels of profitability.

Brand Benefits (Voice of the Customer)	Rel. Imp.	Our Bus.	Competitors			Brand Advantage
			A	B	C	
Most Respected Brand	50	7.7	7.5	5.4	6.7	17
Known for Quality	50	7.5	6.7	6.6	3.5	17
	100					34

Brand Advantage Index = 100 + 34 = 134

through sales, distribution, or marketing communications, Eastman Kodak, Procter & Gamble, Campbell's Soup, and many other companies have developed solid competitive advantages as a result of their marketing expertise.

Market Share Advantage

Market leaders often do not pose a strong differentiation or cost advantage. Their competitive advantage is derived from market dominance. As Figure 6-11 shows, the more dominant the share leader is with respect to market share when compared to its top three competitors, the greater the profits. Market leaders have well-known, trusted brands; many variations in their product lines; and very effective distribution systems.

Nike has high-quality products at attractive prices. But the main thing that makes Nike a tough competitor is the level of market awareness and identity it has developed with creative

FIGURE 6-11 MARKET SHARE ADVANTAGE AND PROFITABILITY

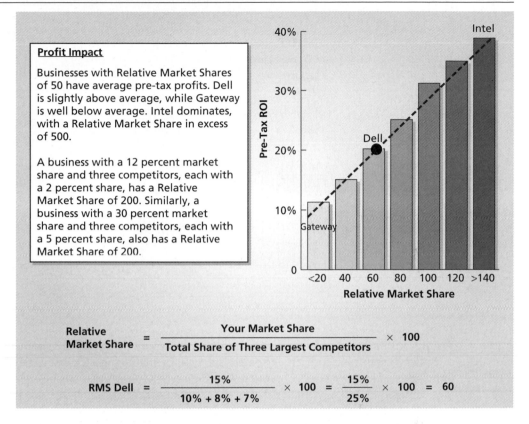

Profit Impact

Businesses with Relative Market Shares of 50 have average pre-tax profits. Dell is slightly above average, while Gateway is well below average. Intel dominates, with a Relative Market Share in excess of 500.

A business with a 12 percent market share and three competitors, each with a 2 percent share, has a Relative Market Share of 200. Similarly, a business with a 30 percent market share and three competitors, each with a 5 percent share, also has a Relative Market Share of 200.

$$\text{Relative Market Share} = \frac{\text{Your Market Share}}{\text{Total Share of Three Largest Competitors}} \times 100$$

$$\text{RMS Dell} = \frac{15\%}{10\% + 8\% + 7\%} \times 100 = \frac{15\%}{25\%} \times 100 = 60$$

ad copy, pervasive promotion of the Nike swoosh, careful selection of product spokespersons, and heavy advertising. This level of competitive advantage makes it difficult for competitors, even those who might in fact have a better product or lower prices with comparable quality. Nike's name, logo recognition, and top-of-the-mind awareness make it easier for Nike to attract customers for its existing products, launch line extensions, or introduce entirely new product lines under the Nike name and logo.

This type of competitive advantage, like all others, is relevant only when the communications created are meaningful and important to target customers. To obtain and sustain a marketing communications advantage takes more than advertising dollars. It goes right to the core of market-based management. Who are our customers? What do they want? And how do we communicate our product in a way that best serves their needs?

Product Line Advantage

The more products a business has to sell, the more ways it has to attract and satisfy customers. A broad line of products creates more selling opportunities for the sales force and channel partners. A business with a narrow line of products has to be more focused in order to be cost effective in its marketing efforts.

FIGURE 6-12 PRODUCT LINE ADVANTAGE AND PROFITABILITY

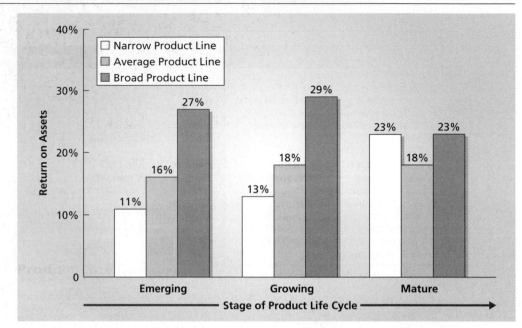

Because a broad product line gives a business more prospective customers and the potential to sell more to each customer, this type of marketing efficiency translates into more sales and higher levels of profitability. Figure 6-12 shows that businesses with broad product lines are more profitable during the emerging and growing stages of a product life cycle than are businesses with narrow product lines. It is particularly important, then, to expand a business's product line during these stages of the product life cycle.

Quite often, a company will want to expand from one market segment into an adjacent segment in order to grow sales and profits. Product line expansion requires considerable product differentiation and careful positioning because the same company is now going to ask for a different price for a different combination of product, service, and brand benefits. Toyota sequentially expanded its product line from a low product-price segment in the 1960s to the point where Toyota today offers a full line of automobiles, each with a different product-price position and a unique brand-name identity, as illustrated in the next chapter's Figure 7-17.

In the beer market, Anheuser-Busch's product line strategy utilizes separate brand names for each of the several positioning strategies it has pursued, also as shown in Figure 7-17. Each brand has a distinct product-price position that is attractive to different types of customers or different use situations. In recent years, Anheuser-Busch has expanded its product line to the microbrew segment with the introduction of Michelob Hefeweizen, added Kirin to create an import brand position, and developed Michelob Ultra to create a product position with a low-carbohydrate beer.

Channel Advantage

Markets in which distribution is required for market access have a limited number of distributors, whether retailers in consumer markets or dealers in business-to-business markets.

FIGURE 6-13 CHANNEL ADVANTAGE AND PROFITABILITY

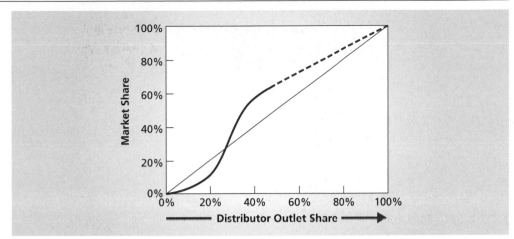

Further, the number of top-notch distributors is even fewer. A business that can dominate these distributors can control channels in a given market and, to some degree, control market access. This is a source of competitive advantage independent of a cost or differentiation advantage.

Figure 6-13 shows the relationship between distributor share and market share. As a business is able to dominate the channels to market, it is able to achieve a larger relative market share, and a larger relative share in turn corresponds with greater profitability.[4]

KNOWLEDGE AS A SOURCE OF ADVANTAGE

More than 2,500 years ago (510 B.C.), the Chinese general Sun Tzu wrote a military manual called *The Art of War.*[5] Sun Tzu concluded that the out-and-out destruction of an enemy resulted in greater *losses* than *gains*. He believed deception, restraint, and minimalism were the best ways to defeat an enemy. Though it seems paradoxical, the major premise in *The Art of War* is neutralizing and subjugating a competitor into following, without fighting the competitor. Today, *The Art of War* is among the world's most widely read books, and its principles of competition are studied in many major corporations.[6]

In his manual, Sun Tzu presents competitive strategy as the process of developing a *knowledge advantage* and then attacking *obliquely,* almost unnoticeably, in a way that eventually causes your competitor to follow you. With a less confrontational approach, Sun Tzu believed better results could be achieved without significant losses. Focused on a knowledge advantage, he built competitive strategies based on superior knowledge of both the terrain (customers) and the enemy (competitors).

In any competitive environment, knowledge is the principal source of competitive advantage. In business, attracting customers is the mission a business seeks to accomplish, and the competitors are the forces it is fighting to achieve its mission. Without adequate knowledge of both customers and competitors, a business is severely handicapped in developing strategies to gain customers and grow market share. A knowledge

FIGURE 6-14 COMPETITIVE STRATEGY BASED ON A KNOWLEDGE ADVANTAGE

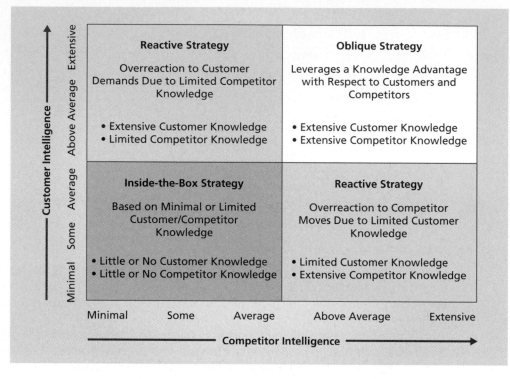

advantage is necessary to develop a successful oblique strategy. Partial knowledge may seem an advantage, but it often results in *reactive strategies,* as presented in Figure 6-14. A business with excellent customer knowledge but limited competitor knowledge will likely overreact to customer demands. Similarly, having excellent competitor knowledge without adequate customer knowledge will likely result in an overreaction to competitors' moves.

As Figure 6-14 shows, businesses that lack both customer knowledge and competitor knowledge are working with an *inside-the-box strategy* as they make competitive moves from an internal perspective with no real market knowledge. These businesses can only make blind attempts at success, usually in the end losing more ground than they hoped to gain. Other businesses with partial intelligence on customers or competitors are likely to employ reactive strategies, which is the normal response to customer or competitor pressures when a business sees only one aspect of the marketplace. An oblique strategy requires superior customer intelligence and superior competitor intelligence.

With a knowledge advantage, a market-based strategy can be devised to achieve desired gains without sustaining excessive losses. Following Sun Tzu's general approach, market-based strategies that leverage a knowledge advantage with respect to both customers and competitors can be implemented with a nonconfrontational approach that minimizes losses. We have labeled this an oblique strategy because it seeks to gain a competitive advantage without direct confrontation. A competitive strategy with limited or partial customer and competitor knowledge could be more easily drawn into a frontal attack strategy—a direct attack on a competitor's position.

COMPETITOR INTELLIGENCE

Selecting competitive environments that favor profit potential is a key aspect of the industry analysis a business conducts when considering entry into new markets. But no matter how attractive a new market may be in light of the competition, it has been shown that developing a strong competitive position is still critical.[7] To understand the degree to which a business has a position of competitive advantage, we need to engage in a detailed analysis of competitors. An important question is, "Which competitors should a business analyze?" We want to maintain a broad market definition to include all meaningful competing substitutes, while recognizing that most businesses would find it impractical to analyze every competitor.[8] We therefore need a mechanism to help us identify a relevant competitor set as a way of prioritizing the competitors to analyze and benchmark.

Benchmark Competitors

Many ways exist to identify a business's top competitors. Perhaps the best is to have customers evaluate the degree to which they consider competitors as interchangeable substitutes. The more similar two competitors are from a customer perspective, the more likely customers are to switch from one to the other. Conversely, the more dissimilar customers perceive any two competitors, the less likely it is that customers will switch from one to the other. Businesses can survey a sampling of their customers, asking them to rate each competitor on the basis of how far that competitor is from their ideal product or supplier. From these customer perceptions, we can create a *perceptual map* that will give us a better understanding of the competitive position of the business and help us identify the key competitors to benchmark.

Perceptual mapping is a technique used to capture customer perceptions of competing products or services.[9] Without specifying criteria for evaluating competing products, customers are simply asked to rate the degree to which they perceive two competing products to be different from one another. Each product is matched one-on-one with every competing product, so that customers evaluate the differences between only two competing products at a time, as with the luxury cars in Figure 6-15. In this figure, Volvo, Mercedes, BMW, Lincoln, Honda, and Buick are competing substitutes. As shown, Volvo and BMW were rated very close in *perceived* similarity, whereas Lincoln and Honda were rated as very dissimilar.

By also asking customers to rate each car with respect to how close it is to their ideal car, we can gain a better understanding of competitive position and key competitors. In the example in Figure 6-15, the customer ratings relative to the ideal car produced two different segments. Two different sets of customer needs and product preferences were operating in this sample market. The ideal car for segment A is almost equidistant from the Honda, Buick, BMW, and Volvo. These four competitors would be the most likely choices for customers in segment A. If we were on the marketing team for Buick, we would then view Honda, Volvo, and BMW as our key competitors in serving segment A, even though Mercedes and Lincoln are equally close to Buick. However, if we were more interested in serving segment B, then Lincoln and Mercedes would be the competitors to benchmark.

A business can use a variety of multidimensional scaling programs to create a perceptual map,[10] such as the one at the bottom of Figure 6-15. In this example, inter-brand differentiation is graphed in two dimensions.[11] In most applications, over 90 percent of competitor differentiation can be captured in two dimensions. With a perceptual map of its competition, a business can easily discern two things: (1) which competitors it will compete against in a

FIGURE 6-15 CUSTOMER PERCEPTIONS OF INTER-BRAND DIFFERENTIATION

Competing Alternatives	◄——— Degree of Perceived Differentiation ———►

Competing Alternatives	Very Similar									Very Different
Mercedes—Volvo	0	1	2	3	4	5	⑥	7	8	9	10
Mercedes—Lincoln	0	1	②	3	4	5	6	7	8	9	10
Mercedes—Honda	0	1	2	3	4	5	6	7	8	⑨	10
Mercedes—Buick	0	1	2	3	4	5	⑥	7	8	9	10
Mercedes—BMW	0	1	2	③	4	5	6	7	8	9	10
Mercedes—Ideal A	0	1	2	3	4	5	⑥	7	8	9	10
Mercedes—Ideal B	0	1	②	3	4	5	6	7	8	9	10
Volvo—Lincoln	0	1	2	3	4	5	6	⑦	8	9	10
Volvo—BMW	0	1	2	③	4	5	6	7	8	9	10
Volvo—Buick	0	1	2	3	④	5	6	7	8	9	10
Volvo—Honda	0	1	2	3	4	⑤	6	7	8	9	10
Volvo—Ideal A	0	1	②	3	4	5	6	7	8	9	10
Volvo—Ideal B	0	1	2	3	4	⑤	6	7	8	9	10
Lincoln—Honda	0	1	2	3	4	5	6	7	8	9	⑩
Lincoln—BMW	0	1	2	3	④	5	6	7	8	9	10
Lincoln—Buick	0	1	2	3	4	5	⑥	7	8	9	10
Lincoln—Ideal A	0	1	2	3	4	5	6	7	⑧	9	10
Lincoln—Ideal B	0	1	②	3	4	5	6	7	8	9	10
BMW—Honda	0	1	2	3	4	5	6	7	⑧	9	10
BMW—Buick	0	1	2	3	4	⑤	6	7	8	9	10
BMW—Ideal A	0	1	2	3	4	⑤	6	7	8	9	10
BMW—Ideal B	0	1	2	③	4	5	6	7	8	9	10
Buick—Honda	0	1	2	3	4	⑤	6	7	8	9	10
Buick—Ideal A	0	1	②	3	4	5	6	7	8	9	10
Buick—Ideal B	0	1	2	3	④	5	6	7	8	9	10
Honda—Ideal A	0	1	2	3	④	5	6	7	8	9	10
Honda—Ideal B	0	1	2	3	4	5	6	7	8	⑨	10

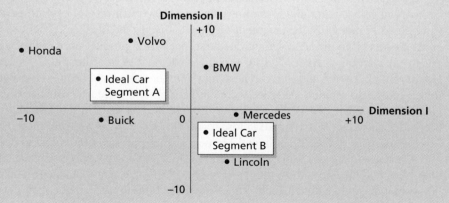

Perceptual Map

FIGURE 6-16 KNOWING WHEN A COMPETITOR IS IN TROUBLE

Behaviors exhibited by a competitor *under pressure to improve profits/cash flow*:

- Laying off employees and closing plants or sales offices
- Across the board price increases without market justification
- Reducing advertising and not attending trade shows
- Cutting investment in research and development
- Increasing the average days in accounts payable
- Taking on more debt/increasing debt-to-equity ratio
- Tightening the terms of sale and payment conditions
- Not recruiting new people as employees retire; shrinking workforce
- Pay sales people to collect unpaid bills

Behaviors exhibited by a competitor that *lacks marketing leadership/market focus*:

- Frequent changes in advertising message; changes ad agencies often
- Lower-than-average sales per salesperson
- Higher-than-average marketing expenses as a percent of sales
- Frequent new-product failures
- Hollow/vague value proposition
- Uses cost-based pricing/does not understand the value of its products
- Frequently cutting prices to increase volume
- Frequent changes in senior management/marketing management

particular market segment, and (2) its competitive position relative to these competitors in attracting and satisfying customers in this segment. However, to improve or maintain a position relative to competitors and the customers' ideal car, a business must also know on what basis target customers are differentiating competing products.

Competitor Analysis

Once a business has identified which competitors it should benchmark, the business then engages in a more detailed analysis of them. A detailed competitor analysis is a difficult undertaking, something most businesses are inclined to do only periodically. However, a market-based business, because of its strong market orientation, is gathering competitor intelligence all the time and, as a result, has continuously evolving competitor profiles from which to evaluate its own competitiveness and competitive advantages.[12]

Obtaining Competitor Intelligence

A great deal of competitive intelligence is public and readily available from dealers, the trade press, the business press, industry consultants, trade shows, financial reports, industry reports, the general press, government documents, and customers.[13] But unless a business has created a market-based culture in which everyone in the organization is an information gatherer, sources of competitive intelligence that are more valuable but also more difficult to find will slip by unnoticed.

Figure 6-16 presents a list of competitor behaviors that signal when a competitor is in trouble or lacks marketing leadership. This type of competitor intelligence is readily available

FIGURE 6-17 COMPETITOR INFORMATION SEARCH

Outlined here are the questions posed and the sources of information from which competitive intelligence was gathered in 1 hour by a research expert.

1. How big is the circuit board market served by Merix, and what is its current market share?

The *Market Share Reporter* gives market size and share of hundreds of sectors in the economy, but Merix did not appear. *Predicast* provides market sizes and reference to *SMT Trends* (a trade journal) that reports the market share statistics of the top 10 circuit board producers, but not Merix. However, the *Corp Tech Dictionary of Technology Companies* turned out to be the mother lode. It gives Merix's SIC (standard industrial classification) and lists other companies in that sector. From this information, an estimate of market size and share was computed.

2. Merix has been dependent on a few large customers. Is it adding to its customer base?

A search of a local newspaper uncovered an article "Merix Wants More Customers." It quotes the company as saying 70 percent of revenues come from its top five customers. Merix's most recent annual report also states that 69.3 percent of revenues come from four customers. In addition, the SEC Edgar Web site reports not much progress has been made in adding new customers to Merix's customer base.

3. Develop a biographical profile of Merix's CEO and her approach to business.

Standard & Poor's *Register of Directors and Executives* provides a short bio on the CEO, Debi Coleman, and her e-mail address. The *Biography and Genealogy Master Index, Dun & Bradstreet Reference Book of Corporate Management, Who's Who*, and *Who's Who of American Women* provide no details. However, *Who's Who in Finance and Industry* provides a detailed résumé.

4. Will Merix have a booth at any upcoming trade shows? If so, where and when?

Trade Shows Worldwide and the current editions of *Trade Show and Exhibits Schedule* and *Trade Show Week Data Book* provide the answers needed.

5. Merix hired a new chief operating officer. What biographical information is available?

Predicast reported that a chief operating officer was hired, and *Business Wire* press releases provided a bio on the new COO.

Other sources considered but not used included *Business News Bank* (a CD-ROM database), *Business Index* (another CD-ROM database), *Value Line*, and *Red Chip Review*. Had time permitted, the *Manufacturers Register* (every state has one) and trade magazines would have been used.

through published articles, financial reports, and information that salespeople could observe in customer visits or while talking with distributors. In each case, the competitive behavior opens the door to marketing strategies that could be implemented at a time when it would be difficult for the competitor to respond. If a competitor is investing less in research and development, for example, it would be an excellent time for a business to accelerate new-product introductions. If a competitor is changing ads and ad agencies often, that is a good time for a business to further promote its own value proposition to customers.

In today's expanding information age, ever more information on markets and competitors is becoming available. As an illustration of just how much competitor intelligence can be gathered, consider the success of the reference librarian at Multnomah County Library in Portland, Oregon. He was challenged to see how much competitor intelligence he could find in 1 hour. Five questions were posed with respect to Merix Corporation, a small circuit board manufacturer. Outlined in Figure 6-17 is a summary of

FIGURE 6-18 COMPETITOR ANALYSIS OF ROSSIGNOL VERSUS BENCHMARK COMPETITORS

Performance (millions)	Rossignol	Salomon	K2	Head	Advantage
Relative Market Share	31	53	33	20	Salomon
Sales Revenue	$558	$807	$582	$388	Salomon
Percent Margin (%)	64	41	30	40	Rossignol
Gross Profit	$357	$331	$175	$155	Rossignol
Marketing Performance					
Marketing & Sales (% Sales)*	19.9	19.8	14.8	26.5	K2
Net Marketing Contribution	$259	$172	$88	$52	Rossignol
Marketing ROS (%)	46	21	15	13	Rossignol
Marketing ROI (%)	364	263	341	126	Rossignol
Financial Performance					
Return on Sales (%)	11.3	4.8	2.7	−0.7	Rossignol
Return on Equity (%)	61.7	30.3	6.9	−1.1	Rossignol
Return on Invested Capital (%)	28.5	12.3	5.2	−0.8	Rossignol

*Based on sales, general, and administrative expenses reported.

the competitive information and sources used to answer the questions posed. As shown, all five questions were adequately answered in 1 hour by a skilled person.[14]

A Sample Competitor Analysis

Rossignol is tied for second place behind Salomon, the leader in the recreation snow sports equipment market. Although this market has many competitors, it is important that Rossignol understand its strengths and weaknesses relative to its three largest competitors: Salomon, K2, and Head. Using publicly available information, Rossignol can create a competitor analysis that benchmarks its performance against these three competitors.

Figure 6-18 shows 11 performance metrics for Rossignol, Salomon, K2, and Head. Salomon has a higher market share and sales but slightly lower gross profit. However, Rossignol has a margin advantage based on percent of sales. Relative to K2, Rossignol has more that twice the percent margin. Although K2 has the lowest cost of marketing as a percent of sales, Rossignol outperforms K2 and the other competitors in all three marketing profitability metrics. Rossignol also outperforms these three competitors in three financial performance metrics.

The level of detail included in a competitor analysis can vary considerably. In the example shown in Figure 6-19, the competitor analysis is broken down into two categories: market-based performance and operating performance. Each area is further broken down into more specific performance metrics that are applied for the business and a benchmark competitor. In this example, the business has almost one-third of the market share of the benchmark competitor. This competitive gap corresponds closely with similar

FIGURE 6-19 COMPETITOR ANALYSIS FOR AN INDUSTRIAL BUSINESS

Dimension of Competitiveness	Business Performance	Competitor Performance	Performance Gap*
Market-Based Performance			
Market Share (%)	6	17	11 behind
Relative Price	115	100	15 higher
Relative Product Quality	115	105	10 better
Relative Service Quality	93	113	20 worse
Number of Distributors	87	261	174 fewer
Sales Force (number)	36	60	24 fewer
Advertising & Promotion (% of sales)	2.0	2.0	0 equal
Sales, General, and Administrative (% of sales)	16.0	17.0	1.0 lower
Operating Performance			
Cost of Goods Sold (% of sales)	48.0	50.8	2.8 lower
Direct Materials (% of sales)	26.0	17.6	8.4 higher
Overhead (% of sales)	12.0	10.0	2.0 higher
Return on Assets (%)	17.1	19.5	2.4 lower
Return on Sales (%)	7.4	11.1	3.7 lower
Asset Turnover	2.3	1.6	0.7 higher
Accounts Receivable (days)	46	38	8 higher
Sales per Employee	$1.5 mil	$2.1 mil	0.6 lower

*Performance Gap = Business Performance − Competitor Performance

competitive gaps in number of distributors, number of distributor locations, and sales force coverage. To close its share gap, the business undoubtedly needs to address adverse competitive gaps in distribution and sales coverage.

Overall, the business is behind its benchmark competitor in most aspects of market-based performance. The competitive gaps shown help create performance targets and management incentives to close those gaps. This, of course, is a key input into the development of a successful market-based strategy. From an internal perspective, this business is also poorly positioned in almost all areas of operating performance. Higher overhead costs and accounts receivable and lower return on sales per employee contribute to lower profitability and productivity. Each of these gaps may be difficult to close, and competitors are not likely to cooperate by sharing information on the methods they use for achieving better performance. To successfully close important competitive gaps, a business may then need to go outside its industry to find better competitive practices.

Competitive Benchmarking

By going outside its industry to benchmark a business known to be superior in a particular business process, a business almost always gains insight into its own operations.

FIGURE 6-20 COMPETITIVE BENCHMARKING—XEROX BILLING ERRORS

Competitive Benchmarking	Xerox: Billing Errors
1. Identify a key area of competitive weakness.	1. Xerox found billing errors were more frequent than those of competitors.
2. Identify a benchmark company.	2. Xerox looked at Citicorp, AT&T, and American Express.
3. Track the benchmark company's process advantage.	3. With the cooperation of American Express, Xerox developed new systems to reduce billing errors.

General Mills' experience in this regard is a good example. The company uses the same production lines to make a variety of related food products. For instance, the same production line used for scalloped potatoes is used for au gratin potatoes. Making the necessary equipment changes between production runs once took as long as 12 hours. General Mills had made extensive efforts to reduce downtime during production changeovers, but those efforts brought only small, incremental improvements. The company then decided to benchmark a NASCAR pit team's process for changing equipment when a race car comes off the track for servicing. A better exemplar of preparedness, precision, and quickness would have been hard to find. What General Mills learned enabled it to implement a new process that reduced changeover time to as little as 20 minutes.

Competitive benchmarking is a process developed initially at Xerox to improve its competitive position relative to key competitors. The idea is for a business to identify a key area of competitive weakness, such as billing errors in Figure 6-20, and then benchmark a business or other entity outside its industry that is recognized as a world-class performer in this area.[15] In this way, a business can hope to gain access to the underlying processes that produce this best practice and develop a system that, when successfully implemented, has the potential of being better than that of its key competitors.

The first step in competitive benchmarking is to identify a key area of competitive weakness that affects customer satisfaction or profitability or both. For Xerox, a large number of billing errors was an annoying competitive weakness. It was a source of considerable customer frustration, and it hurt overall perceptions of performance and customer satisfaction. The second step was to identify several companies that would be recognized as among the best in the world in this area of performance. Xerox identified Citicorp, American Express, and AT&T. After talking with these companies, Xerox selected American Express and gained its cooperation in order to study its billing systems, which had a significantly lower error rate and many more transactions.

Once inside American Express, Xerox could observe the systems and processes that led to a more error-free billing system. This knowledge was used to develop several programs for making Xerox more competitive in this key area of competitive weakness. Performance benchmarks were set in an effort to work toward decreasing billing errors. It took time, but Xerox reached its goal and turned a competitive weakness into a competitive strength. Xerox had a similar success story in competitive benchmarking of order cycle time (the time it takes to deliver the product after the customer places the order), using L.L.Bean as the benchmark company.

FIGURE 6-21 INDUSTRY ANALYSIS—INDUSTRY FORCES AND PROFIT POTENTIAL

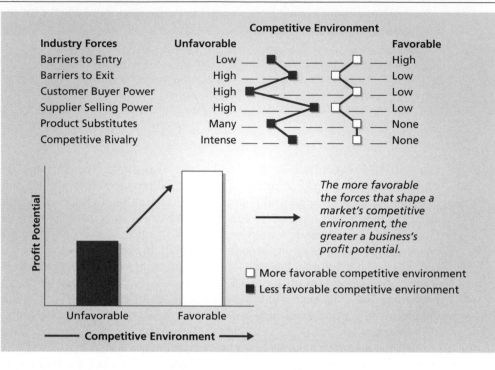

INDUSTRY ANALYSIS

In preparing an industry analysis, a business first determines the attractiveness of the competitive environment. In an unattractive market, a business can encounter low profitability even when its competitive position is relatively strong.[16] Choosing the right markets (industries) in which to compete is a crucial step in market analysis and strategy development.

Figure 6-21 lists the industry forces that shape the attractiveness of a competitive environment. Each of these industry forces can be evaluated along a continuum from unfavorable to favorable. As the sum of these forces favors a more attractive competitive environment, the potential for profit is greater. A new business with a favorable set of industry forces has a far better chance of succeeding than a business in a market with low entry barriers, high exit barriers, high levels of customer and supplier power, many substitutes, and intense rivalry among competitors.

Barriers to Entry

Market entry can be blocked in many ways. International markets are often blocked by political barriers. These barriers reduce competition and enhance profit potential for protected competitors. Technology or low-cost manufacturing can also create entry barriers. Businesses with a superior technological or cost advantage have built competitor entry barriers of their own. Another entry barrier might be the substantial resources it would take for a new business to succeed in a given market. A market that necessitates high start-up and operating costs for a business considering entry to that market helps preserve the market for the businesses already in it. An example is the pharmaceutical industry: Heavy investments in R&D, costs related to patents and federal approval, high advertising expenses, and the large sales forces needed for calling on physicians deter competitor entry and contribute to the attractiveness of the competitive environment.

Barriers to Exit

The competitive environment is also enhanced when weak competitors can easily exit a market. Legal barriers, specialized assets, or the strategic importance of a business often prevent businesses from exiting markets when they should. A pharmaceutical company that is losing money on a particular prescription drug may want to exit the market for that drug, but legal, political, or social forces could create an environment in which market exit would be difficult.

Likewise, a business that has invested in specialized assets (capital or people or both) may find it difficult to exit a market because these assets are not easily sold or transferred to another business application. Businesses that have specialized in nuclear fuel reprocessing, for instance, would find market exit difficult because of their specialized assets. Finally, a business that is dependent on products that are strategically important to its image or ability to market other products may not exit a market even though it is producing less-than-desired levels of profitability.

Customer Buying Power

When relatively few customers buy in large quantities and can easily switch suppliers, the customers' strong buying power diminishes market attractiveness. Large, concentrated groups of customers possess a buying power that enables them to negotiate lower prices or better terms and conditions of sale. Likewise, when customers can easily switch from one supplier to another, they force increased competition, which can lower prices as well as raise the cost of serving customers. In addition, when the purchased product or service is of limited importance to the customer, supplier dependence is much lower.

For the pharmaceutical industry, customer buying power is relatively low. Patents protect many well-known prescription drugs well into the future, and customers who benefit from these drugs usually have few, if any, alternatives. As a result, the pharmaceutical industry has relatively low customer buying power, which enhances the competitive environment and profit potential.[17]

Supplier Selling Power

The flip side of customer buying power is supplier selling power. If a business is a large purchaser of a commodity product (less important to the buyer) and is in an industry where switching costs are low, supplier power is generally low. For a business, this is a favorable market condition, one that strengthens industry attractiveness and profit potential. Because businesses in the pharmaceutical industry purchase supplies in large volumes and have fairly low switching costs, supplier seller power is relatively weak, contributing to the overall attractiveness of the industry.

Product Substitutes

The more substitute products available to customers, the easier it is for them to switch. Ease of switching intensifies competition and lowers profit potential and industry

FIGURE 6-22 PERFORMANCE IMPACT OF PRICE RIVALRY AND THE PRISONER'S DILEMMA

Business's Marketing Strategy	Competitor's Marketing Strategy	
	Hold Price	Cut Price 5%
Hold Price	Market Share = 10%	Market Share = 8%
	Volume = 1 million units	Volume = 800,000 units
	Price = $100 per unit	Price = $100 per unit
	Margin = $40 per unit	Margin = $40 per unit
	Total Contribution = $40 million	Total Contribution = $32 million
Cut Price 5%	Market Share = 12%	Market Share = 10%
	Volume = 1.2 million units	Volume = 1 million units
	Price = $95 per unit	Price = $95 per unit
	Margin = $35 per unit	Margin = $35 per unit
	Total Contribution = $42 million	Total Contribution = $35 million

attractiveness. In the soft drink industry, product substitutes are numerous, making premium pricing impossible. With the market definition broadened to include mineral water, fruit drinks, juice drinks, energy drinks, and coffee drinks, this level of choice places enormous pressure on competitors serving these markets. A business with a broad market definition, as presented in Chapter 3, recognizes the impact of substitutes in evaluating industry attractiveness. Stiff competition is the rule in industries with many substitutes, as in the automotive and beverage industries, but competitors have little to fear from one another in those industries where substitutes are few, as in the petroleum and pharmaceutical industries.

Competitive Rivalry

The more competitors an industry has, the lower will be the differentiation among those competitors, and low differentiation leads to stepped-up competitive rivalry. An excess capacity within an industry can also cause competitors to intensify their moves against one another. The greater the excess capacity, the more intense the moves will likely be. Intense competitive rivalry invariably leads to lower prices and margins, as well as higher marketing expenses, in the battle to attract and retain customers. The net effect is an unattractive industry, one in which the profit potential is relatively low.

The personal computer industry has a much higher level of competitive rivalry today than during the 1980s and early 1990s. The industry since then has attracted many competitors with considerable capacity. In addition, product differentiation has become minimal. Add to these factors the slowdown in the growth of the PC market, and we have the perfect conditions for fierce competitive rivalry. By contrast, the pharmaceutical industry has relatively few competitors, product differentiation is high and very often protected by patents, and the market for pharmaceuticals keeps growing. As a result, competitive rivalry in this industry is relatively low.

The Prisoner's Dilemma

Intense competitive rivalry can evolve into what is known as *the prisoner's dilemma.*[18] In such situations, downward price moves by one competitor force "follower moves" by other competitors in order to minimize lost profits. Actually, all competitors would be better off if none cut prices to begin with.

Consider the example presented in Figure 6-22. The current situation has both the business and its competitor holding price, which yields a total contribution (margin per unit multiplied by unit volume) of $40 million for the business. If the competitor cuts price by 5 percent and the business holds price, the business will lose two share points and $8 million in total contribution. Of course, if the business were to lead with a price cut against its competitor who did not follow, the business could gain two share points and $2 million in total contribution. The worst outcome of the prisoner's dilemma, from an industry-wide perspective, occurs when the competitor cuts price and the business matches the cut. Although the loss to the business's contribution is $3 million less than if it had held price, the competitor's profits also fall, resulting in severely diminished profits for the industry as a whole. Yet, if the business does not match its competitor's cut, its own profits will fall more.

SUSTAINABLE ADVANTAGE

The successes of Anixter, Dell, and Google are impressive. But even for these businesses, maintaining a competitive advantage is difficult because the competitive environment is always changing. To stay ahead, these companies must continuously update their customer and competitor knowledge and monitor their level of competitive advantage. Think about General Motors, NBC, or Sears: It was not so long ago that the competitive position of each of these market leaders changed dramatically. For General Motors, it was foreign competition that eroded its competitive position—first with lower prices and then with higher levels of product quality. For NBC, CBS, and ABC, it was first ESPN, CNN, Fox, and then a multitude of cable networks and the Internet. For Sears and other large retailers of consumer goods, it was Wal-Mart, Target, and Costco.

In each case, the market leader once held a strong, almost impenetrable competitive position. In each case, when new competitive forces emerged, the competitive position of the market leader seriously eroded. It is important to recognize that in each example, the market leader had not lowered quality, raised prices, or cut back on marketing efforts. On the contrary, each had made intense efforts to improve products, reduce prices, and expand marketing efforts to retain customers. But in each case, the competitive forces brought to bear on its market first challenged, and then eroded, the market leader's competitive position.

Figure 6-23 outlines the three main factors affecting competitive position that we have been discussing. In summary, the first is the level of competitive advantage that a business has. A cost, differentiation, or marketing advantage, or any combination of them, strengthens a business's competitive position and contributes to profitable performance. A market-based management business continuously analyzes its sources of advantage relative to competitors. The process alerts the business to any gains in competitor strengths, and it leads to the discovery of new sources of competitive advantage.

FIGURE 6-23 COMPETITIVE FORCES THAT SHAPE COMPETITIVE POSITION AND PROFITABILITY

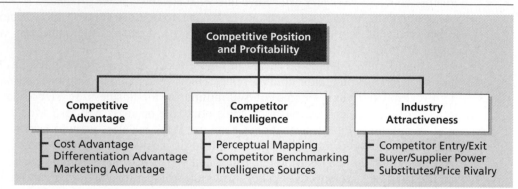

Second, within an industry or market, a market-based management business is always gathering intelligence on its competitors. External market measures of relative product quality, service quality, customer satisfaction, brand awareness, and market share are crucial market metrics that benchmark the strength of a business's position relative to competitors. Internal metrics, such as unit cost, order cycle time, delivery costs, accounts receivable, and sales per employee, are equally important in benchmarking and managing competitiveness. A business with an operations or process weakness also needs to benchmark world-class performance outside its industry to convert the weakness to an advantage. Perceptual mapping, competitor benchmarking (within the business's market), competitive benchmarking (outside the business's market), and skillful researching of information sources all promote a strong competitive position and superior financial performance.

The third set of forces in Figure 6-23 is related to the characteristics of the industry in which the business operates or is considering entry. As part of its market analysis, a market-based management business includes an industry analysis to determine the extent to which industry forces are favorable or unfavorable to a strong competitive position. We would expect a business in an industry where entry is difficult and exit easy, where buyers and suppliers have little power, where product substitutes are few, and where pricing is steady to have a very respectable performance record.

■ Summary

Competitor analyses are an important aspect of formulating a marketing strategy and strengthening a business's market orientation. A high level of marketing knowledge with respect to competitors is a source of a competitive advantage in the same way that a good knowledge of customers is. With a knowledge advantage, a business can pursue an oblique, indirect strategy that forces competitors to follow. An oblique strategy is more profitable than a direct frontal attack, which requires greater resources and may or may not result in a market share gain.

There are three primary dimensions to competitor analysis: assessing the sources of a business's competitive advantage, engaging in competitor intelligence, and assessing industry attractiveness. A market-based management business includes this last assessment in its market analysis. Industry forces such as competitor entry and exit, number of substitutes, buyer and supplier power, and competitive rivalry all affect profit potential. When the collective sum of these forces is favorable, the profit potential is greater.

Conducting a competitor analysis helps a business understand its competitive position in a given market. A complete competitor profile, including information obtained by intelligence gathering, enables a business to see its key strengths and weaknesses.

Businesses frequently overlook fundamental weaknesses that affect their competitive positions. A competitor gap analysis is intended to expose any major weaknesses. Often, a competitor gap analysis will reveal an operational or process weakness that needs to be examined in depth for ways to strengthen it. The business then goes outside its market to observe the highly effective practices of a non-competing business. This process, called *competitive* benchmarking (as opposed to *competitor* benchmarking) gives a business insights to the steps it must take to correct the weakness and gain a competitive advantage.

■ Market-Based Strategic Thinking

1 How would a market leader in an emerging market use a low-cost advantage to build customer value and above-average profits?

2 What is Apple's iPod's primary source of competitive advantage? How does this source of competitive advantage help build a superior customer value for iPod and above-average profits for Apple?

3 How would Nokia use a marketing advantage to build customer value and profitability in the cellphone market?

4 How would a marketing knowledge advantage be a source of competitive advantage in the cellphone market for a company like Nokia?

5 What areas of relative advantage does Wal-Mart use to drive its competitive position? How should Target and Sears drive their competitive positions?

6 Why are businesses with a relative advantage in market share, unit cost, or product quality more profitable than businesses that have no advantage in any of those areas?

7 Identify for each area of differentiation advantage a business that has a competitive advantage in that area. Explain how each business's source of differentiation advantage helps the business attract and satisfy target customers.

8 Identify businesses that have developed different types of marketing advantage, and explain for each how this advantage affects profitability.

9 How could a business with a niche market strategy develop a marketing advantage as a source of competitive advantage?

10 How has the Internet affected competitor intelligence gathering? What traditional sources of competitor intelligence would most likely be available on the Internet?

11 What is the benefit of a competitor gap analysis? How would the results be used in strategy development?

12 What is the main difference between competitor benchmarking and competitive benchmarking? When should a business engage in competitive benchmarking, and what are its benefits?

13 Cost and differentiation are well-known sources of competitive advantage, but why is a marketing advantage also a potential source of competitive advantage?

14 What are the various ways a business can achieve a cost advantage?

15 Why do share leaders often have a cost advantage?

16 How could the industry forces for a regional phone company be different from the industry forces for a regional bank?

17 How will the industry change as competitors enter the regional phone market? How will profit potential be affected?

18 What impact would Procter & Gamble's "everyday-low-price" strategy have on competitive rivalry and the prisoner's dilemma?

Marketing Performance Tools

The four **Marketing Performance Tools** described below may be accessed online at *www.rogerjbest.com*. These applied-learning exercises will add to your understanding of competitor analysis and sources of competitive advantage.

6.1 Cost Advantage

■ Estimate the experience curve coefficient for a cost curve with an initial unit cost of $100, an initial cumulative volume of 50,000 units, a current unit cost of $70, and a cumulative volume of 300,000 units.

■ What is the estimated unit cost when the business hits a cumulative volume of 1 million units?

■ What cost advantage will the business have at a cumulative volume of 1 million units if we assume the business's closest competitor is on the same experience curve with a cumulative volume of 500,000 units?

6.2 Differentiation Advantage

■ Create three product attributes for an MP3 player and indicate the relative importance of each, with the sum of the relative values equaling 100.

■ Use Apple's iPod as the company product and specify three competing MP3 players. Then rate each product attribute

of Apple's iPod and each attribute of the three competing products on a scale that ranges from 0 (disastrous) to 10 (outstanding), where 5 is average.

■ What is Apple's product advantage index and what does it imply with respect to customer value and profitability?

6.3 Marketing Advantage

■ How would the market share advantage change for the company that increased its market share from 20 to 23 percent while competitors each lost one share point? How would this impact profitability?

■ This same company is in a growing market and is willing to invest in expanding its product line from an average position to a broad product line position. How would this impact its marketing advantage and profitability?

■ How would the company's market share and profits change if it went from a 25 percent distributor outlet share to a 30 percent distributor outlet share?

6.4 Industry Analysis (Figure 6-21)

■ Rate the industry attractiveness for the iPhone and personal computer.

■ How does the overall industry attractiveness differ for each?

■ Which industry is likely to be more profitable?

Notes

1. William Boulding and Richard Staelin, "A Look on the Cost Side: Market Share and the Competitive Environment," *Marketing Science* (Spring 1993): 144–166.
2. David Garvin, "Competing on the Eight Dimensions of Quality," *Harvard Business Review* (November–December 1987): 101–109.
3. Bradley Gale, *Managing Customer Value* (New York: Free Press, 1994): 309.
4. Robert Buzzell and Bradley Gale, *The PIMS Principles: Linking Strategy to Performance* (New York: Free Press, 1987).
5. Sun Tzu, *The Art of War*, A Reader's Companion (New York: Spark Publishing, 2003).
6. Gary Gagliardi, *The Art of War Plus the Art of Marketing,* 2nd ed. (Seattle: Clearbridge Publishing, 2002).
7. George Day and Prakash Nedungadi, "Managerial Representations of Competitive Advantage," *Journal of Marketing* (April 1994): 31–44; Richard Rumelt, "How Much Does Industry Matter?" *Strategic Management Journal* (March 1991): 67–86; and Ralf Boscheck, "Competitive Advantage: Superior Offer or Unfair Dominance," *California Management Review* (Fall 1994): 132–151.
8. Joseph Porac and Howard Thomas, "Taxonomic Mental Models of Competitor Definition," *Academy of Management Review* 15 (1990): 224–240.
9. Hugh Devine Jr. and John Morton, "How Does the Market Really See Your Product?" *Business Marketing* (July 1984): 70–79.
10. Donald Tull and Delbert Hawkins, *Marketing Research: Measurement and Method,* 6th ed. (New York: Macmillan, 1993): 431.
11. Glen Urban and Steven Star, *Advanced Marketing Strategy* (Upper Saddle River, NJ: Prentice Hall, 1991): 144.
12. Stanley Slater and John Narver, "Does Competitive Environment Moderate the Market Orientation–Performance Relationship?" *Journal of Marketing* (January 1994): 46–55; and John Narver and Stanley Slater, "The Effect of Market Orientation on Business Profitability," *Journal of Marketing* (October 1990): 20–35.
13. Leonard Fuld, *The New Competitive Intelligence—The Complete Resource for Finding, Analyzing, and Using Information about Your Competitors* (New York: John Wiley & Sons, 1995).
14. "Intelligence," *Oregon Business* (May 1988): 28–32.
15. Robert Camp, *Benchmarking—The Search for Industry Best Practices That Lead to Superior Performance* (Milwaukee, WI: Quality Press, 1989); Kathleen Leibfried and C. McNair, *Benchmarking: A Tool for Continuous Improvement* (New York: Free Press, 1992); Jeremy Main, "How to Steal the Best Ideas Around," *Fortune* (October 9, 1992): 102–106; Gregory Watson, *Strategic Benchmarking* (New York: Wiley, 1993); and Gregory Watson, *Benchmarking for Competitive Advantage* (Portland, OR: Productivity Press, 1993).
16. Michael Porter, *Competitive Strategy* (New York: Free Press, 1980): Chapter 1.
17. Anita McGahan, "Industry Structure and Competitive Advantage," *Harvard Business Review* (November–December 1994): 115–124.
18. Sharon Oster, "Understanding Rivalry: Game Theory," in *Modern Competitive Analysis,* 2nd ed. (Kinderhook, NY: Oxford 1994): 237–251.

Estimating an Experience Curve Coefficient and the Percent Experience Curve

Variables	Symbol	Example
Unit Cost at Time 1	UC1	$100
Unit Cost at Time 2	UC2	$80
Cumulative Volume at Time 1	CV1	40,000
Cumulative Volume at Time 2	CV2	120,000

Estimating the Experience Curve Coefficient (B)

$$B = \frac{\ln(UC2 / UC1)}{\ln(CV2 / CV1)} = \frac{\ln(80 / 100)}{\ln(120{,}000 / 40{,}000)} = \frac{-0.223}{1.10}$$

$$B = -0.203$$

Percent Experience Curve $= (2)^B \times 100\% = (2)^{-.203} \times 100\% = 87\%$

Forecasting Unit Cost

$$\text{Unit Cost (at 600,000)} = \$100 \times (600{,}000 / 40{,}000)^{-.203} = 0.577103$$
$$= \$100 \times .577$$
$$= \$57.70$$

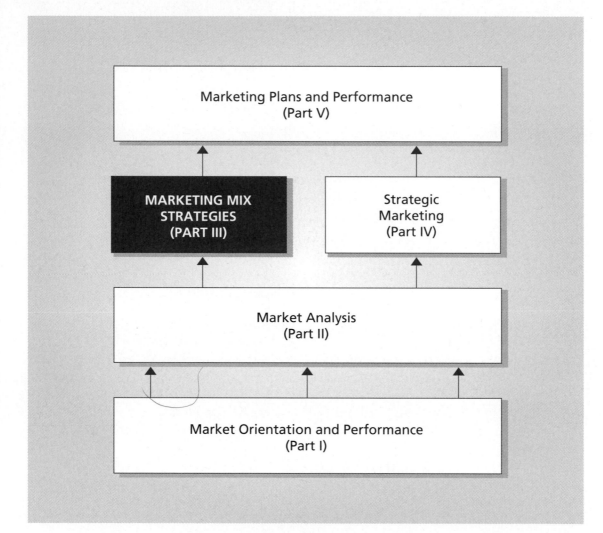

Marketing Mix Strategies

■ Your marketing mix means the combination of promotions, products, places (distribution channels), and prices you chose for your business. Including both short- and long-term strategies in the marketing mix can make for a more profitable business.*

Businesses lacking a market orientation are likely to price their products by simply checking the competition or by marking up costs to achieve a desired profit margin. Odds are good these businesses will hurt their customer value, market share, and profits. A market-based business, however, will set its prices based on customer needs and the strength of its product position relative to competitors.

Part III focuses on short-run tactical marketing strategies designed around the marketing mix for a particular target market. The market analysis concepts presented in Part II are a prerequisite for developing tactical marketing strategies. These strategies are based on market demand and the needs of a target segment, and they must be formulated within the context of a competitive environment.

Chapter 7 examines product positioning and differentiation, branding and brand management, and product line strategies. Chapter 8 presents alternative market-based pricing strategies.

In the previous chapter, we saw how the combination of product benefits and price creates a certain level of customer attraction for a business's product position. A business's share potential, however, cannot be fully realized unless the business also makes a strong marketing effort in terms of advertising, promotion, sales, and distribution. Chapter 9 considers the various marketing systems (channels and sales) that businesses use to reach target customers, and Chapter 10 focuses on the role of marketing communications in delivering a successful marketing mix strategy.

*Bobette Kyle, "7 Ways to Improve Profit Through Both Long- and Short-Term Strategies," *www.websitemarketingplan.com/ small_business/marketingmix.htm*.

Product Positioning, Branding, and Product Line Strategies

■ A strong umbrella brand creates a base from which flanker brands can achieve a faster market penetration at a lower cost.[1]

At an Intel conference, Paul Otellini, president and chief operating officer, began with a story about Wayne Gretzky and cited his famous quote: "*I skate to where the puck is going, not to where it is.*" Building on this theme, Mr. Otellini handed out a hockey puck to each Intel manager. On one side of the puck was written "Follow Me," and on the other side was the Intel logo and trademark slogan "Intel Inside," as pictured in Figure 7-1. Intel has built a flagship brand around this slogan for a product no customer ever sees, touches, or even understands how it really works. The Intel brand is one of the top 10 global brands with a brand equity valued at over $30 billion.[2] Under this flagship umbrella brand, Intel has been able to grow its sales with product line additions and sub-brand names.

Strong brand names such as Intel, Apple, Sony, Lexus, Victoria's Secret, and many others are more profitable than weaker brand names. The greater profitability is due to five fundamental benefits every strong brand possesses, as illustrated in Figure 7-1.

A *brand* is a name or symbol used to identify the source of a product. A strong brand adds significant value and profits as a result of the benefits derived from the name:

FIGURE 7-1 STRONG BRANDS HAVE BRAND EQUITY THAT YIELD HIGHER PROFITS

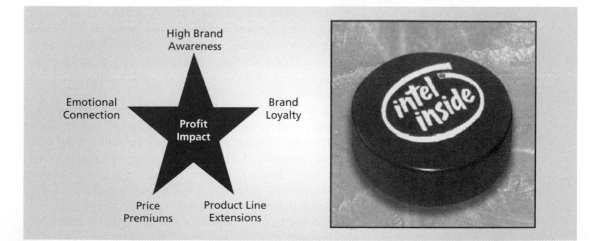

- **High Brand Awareness:** High-equity brands are well-known brands with well-defined brand images tightly linked to an important aspect of quality, performance, or price. Lexus is a high-awareness brand with a well-defined image that conveys quality and performance.
- **Emotional Connection:** Strong brands make an emotional connection with the brand's identity and reputation. For many Apple computer owners, the emotional connection is related to the product's spirit of innovation and creativity, which in turn leads them to promote the brand among friends, relatives, and associates.
- **Brand Loyalty:** Harley-Davidson customers are loyal, and they buy much more than motorcycles. High brand loyalty results in greater revenue per customer and high customer retention—and exceptional levels of customer profitability.

- **Price Premiums:** Strong brands like BMW and Mercedes carry a price premium. The value they create for customers goes beyond functional benefits to include psychological benefits for which customers will pay a premium.
- **Product Line Extensions:** Brand and product line extensions are more easily launched when tied to a strong brand. Sub-brands and line extensions benefit from the image of the core brand and are able to achieve higher levels of awareness at a lower cost. New Intel sub-brands carry the Intel brand equity and achieve faster market penetration after being launched.

Product positioning is at the core of every strong brand. A distinct and well-understood association exists between such a brand and its primary customer benefit. Before plunging into branding, brand equity, and branding strategies, let's first examine the topic of product positioning.

PRODUCT POSITIONING

The early Intel brand evolved from the Intel 286, 386, and 486 into the Intel Pentium processor by the early 1990s. By the mid 1990s, as illustrated in Figure 7-2, new opportunities emerged for more powerful processors at higher prices, which led Intel to design and introduce the Xeon processor. The Xeon was positioned at a higher price-performance point than the Pentium, offering more customer value at a higher price.

In the late 1990s, the lower-priced PC market emerged with the aid of Intel's competitor, Advanced Micro Devices. Intel could have responded by lowering the price on Pentium processors. Instead, to compete with Advanced Micro Devices in the lower-price segment of the PC market, Intel held the Pentium's price and launched the Celeron processor at a lower price-performance point. In the early 2000s, Intel also introduced the more powerful Itanium processor at a price point higher than Xeon's. This product line and brand management strategy has enabled Intel to remain competitive and to grow with market demand, maintaining a market share of over 80 percent.

The cordless drill market is partitioned into five needs-based segments, as shown in Figure 7-3.[3] At the low end are light-duty cordless drills, which are relatively low in power, torque, and endurance. At the other extreme are heavy-duty power cordless drills, which are high in power, torque, and endurance. Sears has elected to position products in each of the price-performance segments. Black & Decker, on the other hand, has positioned itself in four of the five cordless drill segments at much lower prices. DeWalt (a Black & Decker brand) is positioned higher than Sears in four of the five segments.

Although Sears' product-positioning strategy covers all five price-performance segments, its relative position is not the same in all five segments. At the low-price end of the

FIGURE 7-2 INTEL—PRODUCT POSITIONING, BRANDING, AND CUSTOMER VALUE

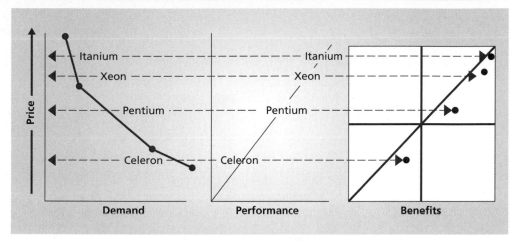

market (light duty), Sears is priced higher than Black & Decker for roughly the same performance. At the high-price end of the market (heavy-duty power), Sears is priced just below DeWalt. In the mid-price segments (medium duty, all purpose, and heavy duty), Sears faces both brands. In these segments, Sears is rated and priced slightly lower than DeWalt. Black & Decker is rated and priced significantly lower in the all-purpose and heavy-duty segments.

FIGURE 7-3 PRODUCT LINE POSITIONING—CORDLESS DRILLS

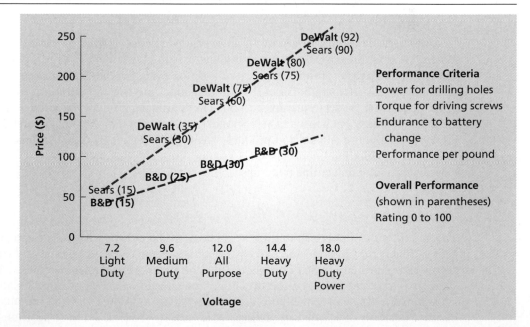

FIGURE 7-4 STARBUCKS' PRODUCT LINE AND TRADE-UP OPPORTUNITIES

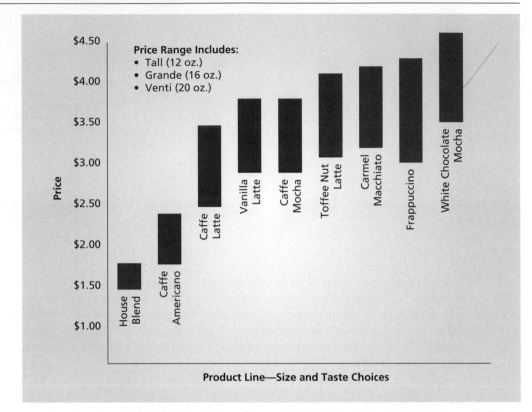

Although the primary purpose of an expanded product line is to attract more customers, product line variations can also allow existing customers to trade up to higher-quality, higher-priced products. In Figure 7-4, for example, the Starbucks product line offers three size alternatives for each of nine distinct product line offerings that vary in price from under $1.50 to just over $4.50. The Starbucks product line offers customers variety and choice, but it also enables Starbucks to grow margin per purchase because the higher-priced, more-specialized products have much higher margins. In this way, the Starbucks product line increases sales volume through customer attraction and raises margins through product line trade-ups.

Product Positioning and Market Share

The goal of a positioning strategy is to create a product-price position attractive to target customers and a good source of cash flow for the business. Achieving greater market share is a primary indicator of the success of a marketing strategy, and the extent of share growth is dependent on the strength of a business's product positioning and marketing effort. As shown in Figure 7-5, market share is represented as the business's product position multiplied by its marketing effort. A weak product position with a

FIGURE 7-5 PRODUCT-PRICE POSITION, MARKETING EFFORT, AND MARKET SHARE

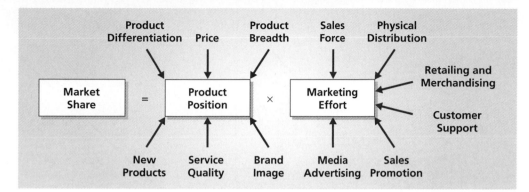

strong marketing effort will fail to deliver the desired level of market share. Likewise, an attractive product position with a weak marketing effort will also fail to achieve the desired share. To be successful, a business needs both an attractive product position and a strong marketing effort. Also shown in Figure 7-5 are the factors that contribute to a business's product position and marketing effort. Product differentiation, price, product breadth, new products, service quality, and brand image all strengthen a business's overall product position. As these influences on product positioning outperform those of competitors, the strength of a business's product position increases, becoming more attractive to target customers.

To illustrate how product positioning impacts marketing and profit performance, consider Samsung's successful repositioning of its consumer electronics products. Samsung had traditionally positioned its products at lower prices. Product quality and performance were generally lower than offered by competing products, and the products were sold through high-volume retailers like Wal-Mart. In 1997, sales were $22.6 billion and pre-tax profit was −$800 million, or −3.5 percent of sales.

Samsung senior management then put in place a strategy to reposition the business as a higher-quality, higher-priced brand. All aspects of product positioning and the marketing effort, shown in Figure 7-6, had to be changed to accomplish the repositioning objective. The effort entailed a massive investment in product development, with major expenses in research and development, but it paid off by 2001. Sales more than doubled to $46.4 billion and pre-tax profit increased to $3.8 billion, or 8.2 percent of sales. By 2006, the repositioning strategy produced sales of $85.4 billion and a pre-tax profit of $8 billion, or 9.4 percent of sales. The sales growth and pre-tax profit outperformed competitors and the industry by a wide margin.

Product Positioning Strategies

Creating an attractive product position and achieving a desired level of market share and profitability require several ongoing product management efforts. The first is the development of a positioning strategy based on target customers' needs. Two questions must be answered before formulating the positioning strategy: "Who is our target customer?"

FIGURE 7-6 SAMSUNG PRODUCT REPOSITIONING AND PERFORMANCE

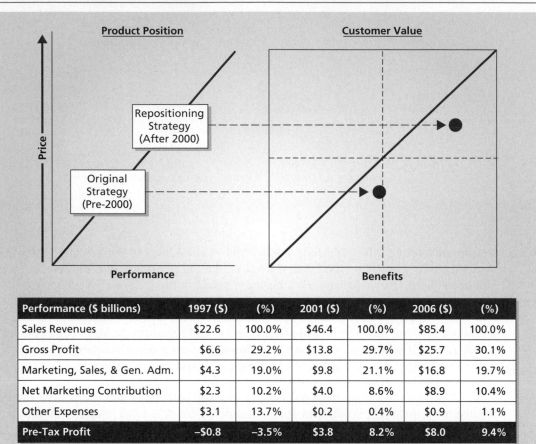

Performance ($ billions)	1997 ($)	(%)	2001 ($)	(%)	2006 ($)	(%)
Sales Revenues	$22.6	100.0%	$46.4	100.0%	$85.4	100.0%
Gross Profit	$6.6	29.2%	$13.8	29.7%	$25.7	30.1%
Marketing, Sales, & Gen. Adm.	$4.3	19.0%	$9.8	21.1%	$16.8	19.7%
Net Marketing Contribution	$2.3	10.2%	$4.0	8.6%	$8.9	10.4%
Other Expenses	$3.1	13.7%	$0.2	0.4%	$0.9	1.1%
Pre-Tax Profit	–$0.8	–3.5%	$3.8	8.2%	$8.0	9.4%

and "How do we offer superior value for target customers?" For a particular target price, a business needs to develop a position based on either a low price or some source of differentiation and product positioning that is meaningful to target customers. As we saw in the previous chapter and as we see again in Figure 7-7, a differential advantage can be based on some combination of cost, product, service, and brand.

A second important area of product management involves branding and brand management strategies. How broad should the product line be? How should brands be created to communicate a consistent image and desired target-market identity? How can a brand's assets and liabilities be managed to create higher levels of brand equity?

Finally, a third area of product management includes brand and product line strategies. To what degree should flanker brands be added as extensions of a strong umbrella brand? And when should a business bundle or unbundle products in order to attract and satisfy target customers? From a core product positioning strategy, these types of product line strategies need to be developed in order to fully leverage a business's capabilities and profit potential.

FIGURE 7-7 PRODUCT POSITIONING STRATEGIES

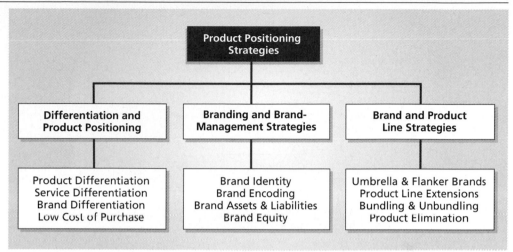

PRODUCT POSITIONING AND DIFFERENTIATION

On the basis of target customer needs, a business must develop a product position that is in some way differentially superior to competitors' product positions. In a price-sensitive market, product positioning generally requires a lower price because other sources of differentiation are not valued by target customers. For markets in which differentiation is possible and valued by target customers, a variety of strategies are possible. Product, service, and brand-image differences that are meaningful to target customers and differentially superior to those of competitors offer the potential to create a more attractive product position. Regardless of the product-positioning strategy pursued, the goal is to create customer value superior to that of competitors, as illustrated in Figure 7-8.

Product Differentiation

Many customers are willing to pay a higher price for products that deliver important customer benefits. Differences in product quality, reliability, and performance can attract customers who are seeking products that perform better than average. There are eight dimensions of product quality that can serve as a basis for product differentiation.[4] These dimensions can be arranged into four hierarchical categories of product quality, as shown in Figure 7-9. If a business fails to deliver acceptable or expected levels of reliability and conformance, an advantage in other dimensions of product quality will not matter. At the other extreme, quality aesthetics as a source of differentiation are of value only when all other aspects of quality are met with respect to customer quality expectations.

Product Quality Requirements

Customers expect reliability and conformance to specifications. Reliability and conformance are necessary if customers are even to consider purchase. Poor reliability and conformance are quality killers. Whether customers are buying a computer, an automobile, or a jet plane, they expect the product to conform to specifications. For example, Nescafé

FIGURE 7-8 DIFFERENTIATION AND CUSTOMER VALUE

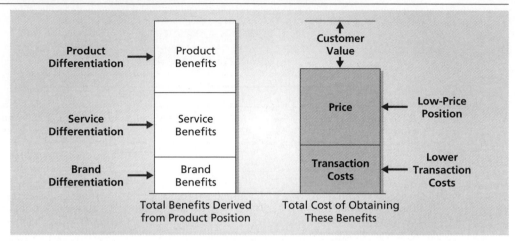

creates different blends of coffee to match customers' taste preferences in different international markets. This is conformance to expectations (i.e., specifications).

Customers also expect products to operate reliably. Companies such as General Electric (GE), Motorola, and Honeywell have engaged in *six-sigma programs*. Six sigma is a statistical term referring to the probability of product failure. At two sigma, a business with one million products would experience 40,000 failures. At six sigma, the

FIGURE 7-9 PRODUCT DIFFERENTIATION AND CUSTOMER VALUE

Quality Requirements

Reliability	Time to failure or malfunction for a given product
Conformance	Incidence of defects that should not have occurred

Quality Drivers

Performance	Operational characteristics that distinguish product performance
Durability	Product life and ability to endure demanding use conditions

Quality Enhancers

Features	Number and type of options that can be added
Serviceability	Ease, speed, and cost of maintenance and repair

Quality Aesthetics

Appearance	The fit, finish, and appearance of a product
Reputation	The image created by the brand name or company

failure rate drops to as close to failure-free as could be expected. GE has spent $1 billion to convert all its divisions to six-sigma principles. Higher conformance to specifications and fewer failures have enhanced GE's customer retention rate and improved the company's profitability.

Product Quality Drivers

Performance and durability are the workhorses of product quality. The automotive industry strives for continued improvements in performance, as seen in the advances in steering, braking, and fuel economy. BMW adds an extra coat of paint to its vehicles sold in Japan in order to meet the quality expectations of the Japanese luxury-car buyer. Manufacturers who cannot keep pace with performance improvements will lose market share over time. Those who can lead with improved product performance will see their positions improve due to product differentiation and a competitive advantage. Intel, for example, seeks to stay ahead of competitors by continuously improving its products. For over three decades, Intel has followed *Moore's Law:* Every 18 months the operating performance per unit of space should double. Its pursuit of ever-improving performance has enabled Intel to dominate its market with an 80 percent market share.

Durability is also a key component of product quality. Customers have expectations with respect to how long the product should last, or how well it should stand up under normal usage. A business that fails to meet customer expectations with respect to product durability will face difficulty both in attracting new customers and in retaining existing customers. Durability is a common source of advantage for industrial products used in demanding situations. ESCO Corporation, the specialty steel manufacturer that makes wear parts for front-end loaders and buckets for mining and earthmoving applications, offers customers greater product durability through proprietary steel chemistry and product designs. Durability—the low breakage rate and long life of the products—is a quality driver with strong appeal to ESCO's customers.

Product Quality Enhancers

A product that meets customer expectations with respect to conformance, reliability, performance, and durability can be differentiated with enhanced quality features. Additional options that can improve the ease of use, safety, or enjoyment of a product can be important sources of product differentiation. Air bags, automotive entertainment systems, cruise control, and navigation maps are examples of features that have been added to automobiles to enhance their quality. Features, as a source of differentiation, become more important as a business serves more affluent segments of the market. These customers often want more than the basic elements of product quality. They are seeking enhanced quality in the products they purchase.

Serviceability is another quality enhancer. Products that are easier to maintain and repair save time and money. The Saturn was engineered to make automotive repair easier and less time-consuming, resulting in lower repair costs. The Saturn design has also resulted in lower insurance premiums for owners due to lower than normal repair costs in the event of an accident. Both lower the total cost of ownership for a Saturn.

Product Quality Aesthetics

The appearance of a product and its reputation can also serve as sources of product differentiation. In Japan, the appearance of a product, or even of the package around the

FIGURE 7-10 SERVICE DIFFERENTIATION AND CUSTOMER VALUE

Quality Requirements

Service Reliability	Ability to deliver the promised service dependably and accurately
Service Assurance	Employee competency with respect to knowledge and courtesy

Quality Drivers

Performance	Able to outperform competitors and customer service expectations
Responsiveness	A service obsession to get it right when things go wrong

Quality Enhancers

Extended Services	Extra customer services that enhance the ease of purchase
Customer Empathy	Individualized attention to customer needs

Quality Asthetics

Appearance	The décor of facilities and appearance of employees
Reputation	The reputation you build at a service-oriented business

product, can have an enormous impact on the success of that product. A British stereo manufacturer, for example, introduced a high-quality system into the Japanese market but failed because the box the system was packaged in did not match the quality of the product inside.

Likewise, the image a brand projects or the reputation of the company can be important in some markets. The quality of products like Porsche, Rolex, and Chanel is judged not only on their functional characteristics, but also on their aesthetic characteristics, which are derived from the image they project. A watch comparable on all seven other aspects of quality listed in Figure 7-9, but not made by Rolex, would fail to attract customers who value the Rolex name and the image a Rolex watch projects.

Service Differentiation

Service can also be an important source of differentiation when it comes to positioning strategies. Nordstrom, FedEx, and Caterpillar are examples of businesses that have attained a superior position with a service differentiation. Because competitors can carry the same brand name products and can match the atmosphere found in Nordstrom stores, Nordstrom's superior service is a critical element in the company's positioning strategy. Service quality has dimensions similar to product quality, as shown in Figure 7-10.

Service Quality Requirements
One of the basic requirements of service quality is *service reliability*. Unreliable service is a quality killer.[5] Customers expect reliability first and foremost as a measure of service quality. For FedEx, the promise of *"when it absolutely, positively has to be there"* communicates the company's service position, a position based on reliability.

A second service-quality killer is poor *service assurance*. Service assurance includes the competence and courtesy of service personnel. Caterpillar has sought to strengthen its competitive position and customer benefits with a differential advantage in responsive service. Offering a 24-hour parts and repair service available anywhere in the world has helped Caterpillar differentiate itself from competitors, and it has created a valued service benefit for the company's customers. They can expect the same high-quality service from Caterpillar worldwide.

Service Quality Drivers

Nordstrom has always sought to achieve an unparalleled service quality advantage. This position of superior service differentiates it from competitors by offering customers higher levels of service *performance* and *responsiveness*. Nordstrom is legendary in delivering service at levels that go beyond customer expectations, always satisfying customer wants in a timely fashion. This may mean replacing a sweater that a customer shrank in the dryer despite a clearly labeled warning to line dry only. By going beyond customers' expectations of service, Nordstrom delivers greater customer value to target customers.

Service Quality Enhancers

Extended services and individualized customer attention (*customer empathy*) are other aspects of service quality through which a business can seek to build a differentiation advantage. For example, Marriott's customer relationship marketing program focuses on individual customer needs and preferences, even to the extent of prearranging tee times for golfers. Such highly customized attention creates a differential advantage based on service quality. Nordstrom offers customers the services of a "personal shopper" who will meet with them and get to know their tastes and preferences in design, color, and other characteristics.

Service Quality Aesthetics

The *appearance* and *reputation* of the service quality can also impact perceptions of service quality and differentiation. At Les Schwab Tires, a chain of stores in the Pacific Northwest, the nearest employee hurries to greet every customer who drives up and, in the service area, all personnel move quickly in performing their tasks. The quickness of the service personnel gives the appearance of exceptional service quality provided by energetic employees who care about getting customers promptly on their way. Les Schwab's service reputation leverages a small difference in employee behavior into a large differentiation advantage in its service quality and positioning.

Brand Differentiation

In many consumer and business-to-business purchases, customers are influenced by the status of a brand name or by the assurance of a well-known company. Brands like Lexus and Mercedes have strong associations with prestige or status. The importance of these brand benefits to many target customers enhances their positioning and differentiation advantage.[6]

Brand differentiation provides another way to position a business's products relative to competitors and to create incremental customer benefits and value, as illustrated in

Figure 7-8. For example, Marriott estimated that adding its name to Fairfield Inn increased Fairfield Inn's occupancy by 15 percent. Kellogg's found that in matched product tests, customer choice of corn flakes cereal increased from 47 percent when the brand was not known to 59 percent when the Kellogg's name was identified. And when Hitachi and a competitor jointly manufactured televisions in England, Hitachi sold its televisions at a $75 price premium and achieved a higher market share.[7] Each of these examples illustrates the importance of brand benefits to target customers and the brand equity these brand reputations create for the business.[8]

A strong brand enhances positive evaluations of a product's quality, maintains a high level of product awareness, and provides a consistent image or brand personality. A strong brand, such as Coca-Cola, extends each of these positive customer evaluations to brand extensions that include Coke Classic, Diet Coke, Caffeine-Free Coke, and Cherry Coke. Brand extensions are an effective source of differentiation, one that extends the positioning benefits of a core brand to many closely related flanker brands. However, there are limits to brand extensions.[9] At some point, it may be necessary to create new brand names and build another area of brand equity, as Coca-Cola did when entering the sports drink market with Powerade and the fruit-juice market with Fruitopia.

Low Cost of Purchase

So far, we have focused on differentiation and the benefits it provides. A business can also create a source of advantage with low costs, making it possible to offer a lower purchase price. Businesses with a low-cost advantage in markets in which price is an important determinant of customer value can utilize a low price as a basis for product positioning. In these market situations, however, a business cannot ignore product, service, or brand issues. A business must still meet customer expectations in these areas, even though the strength of its product position is built around a more attractive price.

Low-Price Position

Wal-Mart is an example of a retailer that uses low prices to create an attractive position relative to competing stores. With a low-price positioning strategy, Wal-Mart must achieve a lower cost of buying, inventorying, and retailing the products it sells. This positioning strategy requires Wal-Mart to continuously find ways to contain or lower costs in order for its prices to remain a source of competitive advantage, while still meeting target customer needs for product, service, and brand. With this positioning strategy, Wal-Mart creates customer value and obtains a competitive advantage.

While Wal-Mart uses large assortments of brand-name products and massive retail outlets, Trader Joe's is an upscale specialty food and wine chain with much smaller stores but prices that are still below average. With over 200 stores and growing at the rate of 20 stores every year, Trader Joe's carries 2,500 items, 80 percent of which are private-label products. The average grocery store carries 25,000 branded products and relatively few private-label goods, only about 16 percent. Wines at $3.99 are common at Trader Joe's, and the stores' promotion wine, Charles Shaw ("Two Buck Chuck"), sells for just $2.99. The Food Institute describes Trader Joe's as a "gourmet food outlet-discount warehouse." The main source of Trader Joe's advantage—low price—is not easily copied, being a combination of a low-cost structure and thousands of personally developed relationships with private-label producers all over the world.

Lower Transaction Costs

The total cost of purchase also includes a customer's transaction costs, as shown in Figure 7-8. Transaction costs are expenses, other than the purchase price, associated with the acquisition of a product. A business can build a low-cost advantage and customer value by lowering these non-price costs of purchase. For example, in Chapter 4 we saw that American Hospital Supply discovered that 50 cents of every dollar a hospital spent on equipment was for acquiring and inventorying the equipment. In response, American Hospital Supply devised a computerized ordering and inventory management system that would lower a hospital's cost of acquiring and inventorying equipment by 50 percent. In lowering these transaction costs, American Hospital Supply created a greater customer value and developed a source of advantage that enabled the company to become the market share leader in the hospital equipment market.

BRANDING AND BRAND MANAGEMENT STRATEGIES

To fully capture the total value of a product's positioning, it is important to brand a product in a way that communicates its intended positioning. A brand name gives an identity to a product or service, providing a way to quickly comprehend the brand's primary benefits, whether rational or emotional.

Brand Identity

The successful management of brands is built around sound marketing practices. A business with a strong market orientation that has segmented its target markets and tracks customer behavior by segment is in the best position to build a successful brand.[10] An internally focused business simply does not have the market intelligence needed to build a brand identity that would be meaningful to target customers. The first step in developing a brand identity is to define the desired product positioning and value proposition for a specific target market. Without these specifications, the branding identification process would quickly deteriorate into an internal process built around product features rather than customer benefits.

Brand Encoding

A great deal of strategy goes into the branding process and the creation of specific brand names.[11] Because of the great many possibilities for a brand name, a brand encoding system will help us understand how a product is positioned with a brand name for a specific market and desired image. The encoding system is presented as a hierarchy of possible naming components that starts with the company name, followed by a brand name and further enhanced or modified by sub-brand names, numbers, letters, product names, and benefits. A brand can be as broad as a company name like Dell, as narrow as a specific version of a product like Microsoft Windows ME, or as abstract as Altoids.

Company brand names such as Nike and General Electric create an image and umbrella brand under which important benefits can be communicated to many diverse product-markets. The Nike name carries an image of competitiveness and winning across product-markets that include track, golf, soccer, football, and basketball. General

Electric's image for reliability and good value reaches across lightbulbs, appliances, plastics, medical systems, power-generation systems, electric motors, transportation equipment, electrical distribution equipment, jet engines, credit, and other financial services. Companies such as Sony, Intel, and Ford have created specific brand names to supplement their company names and to enhance the identities and positions of their products.

Ford, for example, brands its cars with names such as Explorer, Taurus, and Mustang. Intel adds a product name to its company name and brand name to further distinguish its product positioning with Pentium processors, Celeron processors, and Xeon processors. Other companies use only a brand name, as Procter & Gamble does with Tide, Cheer, Bold, Bounce, Gain, and Ivory soap. Some combination of elements from the brand-encoding system allowed each of these companies to achieve their desired product positioning for each brand, while building a portfolio of brands that has both meaning and synergy.[12] A brand name may or may not use each of the elements in the code. Choosing the specific elements to include in a brand is a matter of determining which combination is most likely to exert the full power of a product position, as presented in the following brand-encoding strategies.

Company and Brand Name

Ford's branding strategy for its vehicles is similar to that of most other auto companies. As shown, Ford in many cases has enhanced its brand names with sub-brand names, letters, and numbers.

Company or Core Brand	Product or Sub-Brand	Letters or Numbers	Attribute or Benefit
Ford	Escape		
Ford	Explorer Sport Trac		
Ford	Lightning	SVTF-150	
Ford	Cobra	SVTF-150	
Ford	Land Rover Freelander		
Ford	Wagon	SE	

Brand and Sub-Brand Name

In 1846, Church & Dwight Co. began selling sodium bicarbonate as an ingredient for use in cooking under the brand name Arm & Hammer. For 120 years, food preparation was the only marketed use for Arm & Hammer baking soda. But then the company began extending Arm & Hammer's product application to deodorizers (for refrigerators, carpets, cat litter), personal care (toothpaste, antiperspirants, pharmaceuticals), household products (laundry detergents, air fresheners), industrial products (degreasing, cleaning, de-painting), and agricultural products (feed ingredients). In each case, the core brand Arm & Hammer was retained and its image leveraged with the addition of sub-brands, as illustrated here.

Company or Core Brand	Product or Sub-Brand	Letters or Numbers	Attribute or Benefit
Arm & Hammer	Baking Soda		
Arm & Hammer	Vacuum Free		
Arm & Hammer	Crystal Blend		
Arm & Hammer	Home Alone Pads		
Arm & Hammer	Super Scoop		
Arm & Hammer	Ultramax		

Company and Product Name

General Electric (GE) serves a diverse set of product-markets that include consumer goods, medical and industrial equipment, and financial services. The GE name and logo are key factors in communicating the company's long tradition of providing quality products and services at prices that deliver high customer value. However, General Electric has elected not to include the brands NBC and CNBC under the GE flagship brand. For strategic reasons, GE has preferred to minimize the association between the GE name and the NBC and CNBC names.

Company or Core Brand	Product or Sub-Brand	Letters or Numbers	Attribute or Benefit
GE	Aircraft Engines		
GE	Appliances		
GE	Capital		
GE	Industrial Systems		
GE	Lighting		
GE	Medical Systems		
GE	Plastics		
GE	Power Systems		
GE	Specialty Materials		
GE	Transportation Systems		
	NBC		
	CNBC		

Company, Brand, and Product Name

Intel encodes its brand names to include the company name, a unique brand name, and a product name. As shown in the list of Intel products, the encoding helps Intel communicate the positioning of four microprocessor families (Celeron, Pentium, Xeon, and Itanium). For its more complex products, Intel uses letters or a combination of letters and numbers to abbreviate the product name, using names such as the Intel IXP 1200 Network Processor, Intel PCA (Personal Client Architecture), and Intel IEA (Internet Exchange Architecture). The Intel company name doubles as an umbrella brand name that communicates Intel's reputation for quality and innovation. The individual product names enable Intel to position multiple products in the same markets and allows Intel to sell multiple products to the same customer without confusing the product application.

Company or Core Brand	Product or Sub-Brand	Letters or Numbers	Attribute or Benefit
Intel	Pentium	4	
Intel	Xeon		
Intel	Celeron		
Intel	Itanium		
Intel	Centrino		
Intel	Strata		Flash Memory
Intel		XP-1200	
Intel		PCA	
Intel		IEA	

Company Name, Brand Name, and Number

Microsoft uses a variation of the Intel strategy for leveraging its company name to brand individual products, using numbers and letters to identify versions of its software brands. Microsoft Outlook Express 6 allows buyers and users to quickly identify the Microsoft product and its newness relative to other versions of the product. This strategy allows the brand to date itself, as in the case of Microsoft Windows 95, 98, and 2000.

Company or Core Brand	Product or Sub-Brand	Letters or Numbers	Attribute or Benefit
Microsoft	Windows	NT	
Microsoft	Windows	EP	
Microsoft	Windows	ME	
Microsoft	Windows	XP	
Microsoft	Office	2003	
Microsoft	Outlook Express	6	
Microsoft	Vista		

Brand Name and Benefit

Braun has successfully branded the Oral-B toothbrush. Taking advantage of the well-known name and its image for quality, Braun extended the Oral-B brand name by including primary benefits that differentiate the brands. Oral-B Ultra Plaque Remover is clearly targeted at customers seeking the benefit of plaque removal, which customers can quickly tell is different from the intended benefit of the regular Oral-B toothbrush.

Company or Core Brand	Product or Sub-Brand	Letters or Numbers	Attribute or Benefit
Oral-B			Cross Action Power
Oral-B	Series	900	Advance Power
Oral-B			Advance Power Kids
Oral-B	Series	7000	Professional Care
Oral-B	OxyJet Center		Professional Care
Oral-B			Cross Action Vitalizer
Oral-B	Advantage		Control Group
Oral-B			Indicator
Oral-B	Satin Floss		
Oral-B	Super Floss		

Brand Name Only

Procter & Gamble (P&G) has long been known for its "brand name only" strategy. In markets served by multiple P&G brands, P&G brand teams work hard to maintain their unique

FIGURE 7-11 BRAND-NAME DEVELOPMENT

Founder and Owner Brands	Wal-Mart	HP	Hilton Hotels
No Attribute Association	Sam Walton	Hewlett & Packard	Conrad Hilton
Functional Brands	**DuraCell**	**FedEx**	**Microsoft**
Implied Functional Attribute	Long Lasting	Fast Delivery	Microcomputer Software
Invented Brands	**Kleenex**	**Google**	**Snapple**
Implied Association	Sanitary (Clean)	Mathematical (Solutions)	Healthy (Like an Apple)
Experiential Brands	**Big Bertha**	**Red Bull**	**Microsoft Explorer**
Implied Experience	Power (Longer Drives)	Power (Energy)	Discovery (Solutions)
Evocative Brands	**Apple Computer**	**Nike**	**Yahoo!**
Implied Attribute	Friendly (Easy to Use)	Greek Goddess (Victory)	Excitement (Discovery)

product positions. For example, the following are the P&G brands positioned in the laundry detergent market. Each brand has a unique focus and product-positioning strategy. Including the P&G name as a prominent component of the brand names could dilute the positioning of the individual product brands. Additionally, because the products are well understood and sold in specific retail locations, little if any value would be gained in adding a product name, letters, or sub-brand name. In the brand-name-only encoding strategy, the primary benefit is often embedded in the name for communicating the desired product position of the brand.

Company or Core Brand	Product or Sub-Brand	Letters or Numbers	Attribute or Benefit
Tide			
Downy			
Gain			
Cheer			
Bounce			
ERA			
Febreze			
Dreft			
Dryel			
Ivory Snow			
Bold			

Brand Name Development

Whether a new company, a new brand, or a new sub-brand, coming up with a name that has meaning with respect to positioning a product, as well as being short and easy to remember, can be a challenge. Summarized here and in Figure 7-11 are five ways for creating a new company, brand, and sub-brand name.[13]

1. **Founder and Owner Names:** Not surprisingly, many company names (core brands) are the names of company founders or owners, such as Dell Inc. (Michael Dell), Ford

Motor Company (Henry Ford), and Hilton Hotels (Conrad Hilton). Other names are derivations of a founders' names, like Wal-Mart (derived from Sam Walton). These brands had to build their brand equity without any association with a core customer benefit.

2. **Functional Names:** These names are derived from the basic benefit provided by the product. DuraCell (long lasting), Federal Express (fast delivery), and Microsoft (microcomputer software) each strived to build an association between the brand name and core function of the brand. Federal Express eventually shifted to a name morpheme (FedEx).

3. **Invented Names:** There are two kinds of invented names: those built from root words and morphemes, and those that are poetic constructions based on the rhythm or experience of saying them. Agilent and Alliant are invented company names from roots that mean "agile" and "ally." Poetically created brand names include Oreo, Kleenex, Snapple, and Google. Google was actually derived from the mathematical term *googol*.

4. **Experiential Names:** These are company or brand names associated with an experience, such as the experience of discovery, success, movement, or good health. The Internet portals Explorer, Magellan, Navigator, and Safari are names created to communicate the experience of surfing the Web. Big Bertha, Red Bull, Path Finder, and Silk Soy Milk are also brand names that convey meanings based on people's experience.

5. **Evocative Names:** Companies also create names that evoke a positive attribute or a feeling. Examples include Apple, Yahoo!, Virgin Airlines, and the low-cost airline Ted. The name Ted is intended to evoke a friendly image while retaining an association with Ted's parent company, Uni*ted* Airlines. Another good example of an evocative company name is Nike, the same name as the mythological Greek goddess of victory.

Creating a New Brand Name

Recognizing the various approaches to brand-name development, a business or management team ultimately needs to develop a specific name for a specific business situation. An example is the customer solution that Cisco Systems developed to streamline the complex processes of making a large information-processing purchase decision. This online software product helps customers sort out the many considerations, technical details, and suppliers but, more importantly, the product helps a customer determine the information-processing system that would be best for that customer's situation.

Cisco Systems then devised a process for determining a sub-brand name for its new customer solution. Figure 7-12 shows how Cisco's customer need, its product solution, and the resulting customer benefits could be distilled into several descriptive words and morphemes to serve as inputs for possible names. The goal was to create a name that related either to the experience of selecting from among many choices, or that evoked a positioning that was favorable to the product. Many possibilities were proposed, and from them Fast Track emerged as the most effective sub-brand name. The name conveys a quick and easy process, which gives customers confidence that they can use the product successfully. Cisco's value proposition for Fast Track is: *"Your shortcut through the IP communications decision-making process."*

FIGURE 7-12 CISCO SYSTEMS—DEVELOPING A BRAND-NAME EXTENSION

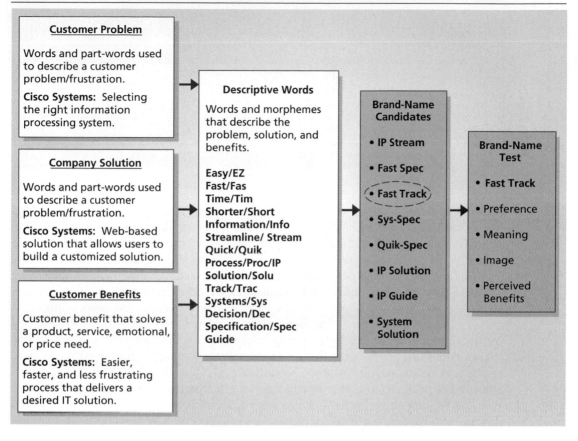

BRAND EQUITY

Brand names like Coca-Cola, Microsoft, and GE are worth billions of dollars. How did they achieve this level of value? What are their brand assets? Do they have any brand liabilities? Why are some brands able to leverage their brand assets while others incur brand liabilities that reduce their brand equity? To fully understand how a company or brand builds brand equity, let's first examine the concept of assets and liabilities as applied to a brand name.

Brand Assets

Like a business's financial assets, the brand name itself has different kinds of assets.[14] A brand like Coca-Cola creates brand assets based on its market leadership and high level of awareness. Brand assets that impact brand value are also derived from an exceptional reputation for quality, brand relevance, and high levels of customer loyalty. Although a variety of other influences could create brand assets,[15] the five brand assets in Figure 7-13 can be found to some degree in all top brand names.

■ **Brand Awareness:** Companies with high brand awareness can more easily introduce new products and enter new markets. Nike began with athletic shoes but now has a wide range of apparel products and accessories.

FIGURE 7-13 BRAND ASSETS SCORECARD

Brand Assets	Rel. Imp.	Very Low 0	Below Average 25	About Average 50	Above Average 75	Very High 100	Brand Assets Score
Brand Awareness	20%					X	20.0
Emotional Connectedness	10%			X			5.0
Brand Loyalty	20%				X		15.0
Product Line Extensions	30%			X			15.0
Price Premium	20%			X			10.0
Overall Brand Assets	**100%**						**65.0**

- **Emotional Connection:** A superior reputation for quality is a brand asset for companies such as Lexus. A brand name that relates to consumers on an emotional level can be a highly valuable brand asset. Over the past 20 years, Lexus has gained brand relevance among luxury-car buyers, while Cadillac has lost brand relevance as the lifestyle and demographics of this market have changed.
- **Brand Loyalty:** For brands like E*Trade, a high level of customer retention is a profitable brand asset that lowers marketing expenses and increases customer profitability.
- **Product Line Extensions:** The Honda name, once primarily identified with motorcycles, now appears on products ranging from SUVs to outboard motors. Many product line extensions carrying the brand name convey a company's confidence in its products and in turn inspire customers' confidence.
- **Price Premium:** Being able to command a price premium is a valuable asset for a brand. Market-share leaders such as Intel dominate the markets in which they compete, even with their higher prices.

One way to measure these brand assets is with the Brand Assets Scorecard shown in Figure 7-13. Using the scorecard, we can rate each brand asset based on the average among competitors in the same market. Individual brand asset scores can range from 0 to 20. With the five kinds of assets, the overall brand asset score ranges from 0 to 100. An average brand would attain an overall brand asset score of 50. Brands with large brand equity, such as Coca-Cola, Microsoft, and GE, should produce brand asset scores much greater than 50.

To understand how the scorecard would work, consider how we might have assessed each of the brand assets presented in Figure 7-13 for Cadillac and Lexus in 1990. Lexus was a relatively new brand, while Cadillac was the market leader with a 30 percent market share. Most luxury-car buyers in 1990 would have rated Cadillac higher than Lexus. For that year, the overall brand asset score for Cadillac would have been much higher than the score for Lexus. But if we had scored the two brand names every three or four years since 1990, we would have seen Lexus climb in brand assets and Cadillac slide, with its market share eroding to below 20 percent.[16] Recently, in an attempt to regain its brand reputation and relevance among luxury-car buyers, Cadillac has been fighting back with new models and a stepped-up advertising program.

Brand Liabilities

Brands can also incur brand liabilities due to product failure, lawsuits, or questionable business practices. A good example is Arthur Andersen, not long ago one of the world's top accounting firms. Before the Enron collapse, an assessment of Arthur Andersen's brand liabilities would have been highly favorable. But publicity about the firm's questionable practices at Enron led to substantial customer dissatisfaction. Arthur Andersen's brand liabilities escalated. Simultaneously, a loss of market share, an eroding reputation for quality, and declining brand loyalty caused brand assets to plummet. It was more than the firm could suffer. Among the many brand liabilities we could consider, the following five are particularly harmful.

1. **Customer Dissatisfaction:** High levels of customer complaint and customer dissatisfaction detract from brand equity. Customer complaints in the telecommunications industry have created brand liabilities for some telecom companies.
2. **Product or Service Failures:** Product failures, like the ones many customers experienced with Firestone several years ago, are a serious brand liability, one that can destroy even a powerful brand.
3. **Questionable Practices:** Business practices that lead to allegations, lawsuits, or prosecution also hurt brand liability. During the early 2000s, a flurry of prosecutions involving top executives of major corporations diminished the brand equity of those companies.
4. **Poor Record on Social Issues:** News reports that indicate a business may have a low level of social responsibility lessen its brand equity. Certain oil companies that became associated with poor environmental practices, and consumer goods companies whose "sweatshop" conditions at overseas assembly plants were publicized, saw declines in the equity of their brands.
5. **Negative Associations:** A brand that becomes identified in the public's mind with a disreputable individual, an unpopular venture, or an unpleasant event loses brand equity. A few year's ago, Wendy's saw a sudden but brief decline in its brand equity following media accounts, soon proven to be based on a false claim, that someone had found a finger tip in a bowl of Wendy's chili.

Brand liabilities can be assessed using the Brand Liabilities Scorecard presented in Figure 7-14. For most strong brands, brand assets will exceed brand liabilities. Using the Brand Liabilities Scorecard, we could assess Arthur Andersen's brand liabilities before and after the Enron debacle. We would find that our estimate of the brand liabilities increased after the Enron scandal. For Arthur Andersen, then, the Enron scandal resulted in a decrease in brand assets and an increase in brand liabilities, both contributing to a significant drop in brand equity.

Brand Equity

In a business, the owner's equity is the value of the owner's holdings in the company. It is determined by the difference between the company's assets and its liabilities. The larger

FIGURE 7-14 BRAND LIABILITIES SCORECARD

Brand Liabilities	Rel. Imp.	Very Low 0	Below Average 25	About Average 50	Above Average 75	Very High 100	Brand Liabilities Score
Customer Dissatisfaction	20%		X				4.0
Product or Service Failures	20%		X				4.0
Questionable Practices	20%			X			10.0
Poor Record on Social Issues	20%	X					0.0
Negative Associations	20%		X				4.0
Overall Brand Liabilities	**100%**						**22.0**

the ratio of assets to liabilities, the greater the owner's equity. As Figure 7-15 shows, brand equity can be assessed in the same way. To calculate brand equity, simply subtract the total brand liabilities score from the total brand assets score. Tracking changes in brand equity over time is an important part of the brand management process, because brand equity is not static.

For businesses such as Enron, Martha Stewart, and WorldCom, we can easily envision how brand equity quickly eroded as brand assets declined and brand liabilities grew. Likewise, it is easy for us to understand how the brand equity of companies such as Dell, Lexus, and Target has grown over the last 15 years as their brand assets grew without burdensome brand liabilities. In either situation, the brand equity model is a useful way to understand and manage a brand's equity.

FIGURE 7-15 BRAND BALANCE SHEET AND BRAND EQUITY

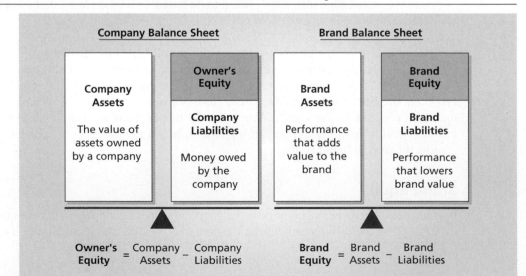

Building brand equity requires a significant effort, and some companies use alternative means of achieving the benefits of a strong brand. For example, brand equity can be borrowed by extending the brand name to a line of products in the same product category or even to other categories. In some cases, especially when there is a perceptual connection between the products, such extensions are successful. In other cases, the extensions are unsuccessful and can dilute the original brand equity.

BRAND AND PRODUCT LINE STRATEGIES

We have seen that the more products a business has to sell, the more ways it has to attract and satisfy customers. A broad line of products creates more selling opportunities for the sales force and channel partners. A business with a narrow line of products has to be more focused in order to be cost effective in its marketing efforts.

Because a broad product line gives a business more prospective customers and the potential to sell more to each customer, this type of marketing efficiency translates into more sales and higher levels of profitability. For example, in Figure 7-16, we can see that businesses with broad product lines are more profitable during the emerging and growing stages of the products' life cycles than are businesses with a narrow product line. It is particularly important, then, to expand a business's product line during these stages of a product life cycle. This is exactly what Microsoft did in the 1980s and 1990s in growing the computer market.

FIGURE 7-16 BREADTH OF PRODUCT LINE AND RETURN ON INVESTED ASSETS

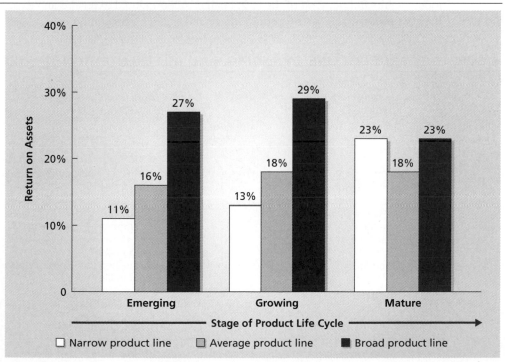

Product Line Development

When a business expands from one market segment into an adjacent segment in order to grow sales and profits, product line expansion requires considerable product differentiation and careful positioning. The business is now going to ask for a different price for a different combination of product, service, and brand benefits. In Chapter 6, we saw that Toyota sequentially expanded its product line from a low product-price segment in the 1960s to the point where the automaker today offers a full line of vehicles, each with a different product-price position and a unique brand-name identity, as illustrated in Figure 7-17.

In the beer market, we also saw in Chapter 6 that Anheuser-Busch's product line strategy uses separate brand names for each of the many positioning strategies it pursues, as also outlined in Figure 7-17. Each brand has a distinct product-price position that is attractive to different types of customers. Anheuser-Busch has expanded its product line to the microbrew segment with Michelob Hefeweizen, added Kirin to create an import brand position, and introduced Michelob Ultra to create a product position with a low-carbohydrate beer. In 2006, Anheuser-Busch added the regional brewery Rolling Rock to its product line portfolio. While this last addition may not seem significant, with Anheuser-Busch's marketing expertise and resources, a strong regional brand has every promise of growing into a strong national brand.

Umbrella and Flanker Brands

An *umbrella brand* is the core product of a business. For American Express, the core product is credit cards; for Whirlpool, it is washers and dryers; and for Johnson & Johnson, it is baby shampoo. From a consumer's point of view, the core product is the most visible embodiment of the brand name. Accumulated exposure and experience with the core product solidifies a certain image and quality expectation.

FIGURE 7-17 PRODUCT LINE, BRANDING, AND DIFFERENTIATION STRATEGY

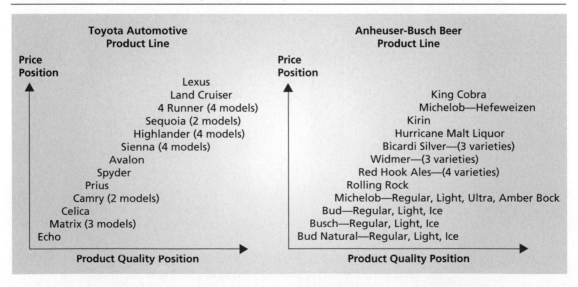

FIGURE 7-18 FRITO-LAY UMBRELLA AND FLANKER BRANDS

Frito's Corn Chips	Lay's Potato Chips	Ruffles Potato Chips	Cheetos Cheese Snacks	Tostitos Tortilla Chips	Doritos Tortilla Chips	Rold Gold Pretzels	Granola Bars	Cracker Jack
Frito's	Lay's		Cheetos		Doritos			
Twist	Bistro		Mystery		Extremes			
	Gourmet		Colorz		Tortilla			
	Chips		Snacks		Chips			
	Stax							

Umbrella branding involves the transfer of quality perceptions derived from a core product or brand to product line extensions that use the same brand name. The intent of umbrella branding is to enhance the effectiveness of marketing programs and to increase demand for product extensions by transferring brand awareness and perceptions of quality from the umbrella brand.[17] For example, the Frito-Lay core brands capture 59 percent of the U.S. snack-chip market. The sales growth of the Frito-Lay brands has been due largely to the introduction of new flanker brands under the core brands of Frito's corn chips, Lay's potato chips, Cheetos, and Doritos, as illustrated in Figure 7-18. These umbrella brands create a base from which to introduce flanker brands that enhance market penetration at a lower cost.[18]

Summarized here are four ways a flanker brand benefits from a strong umbrella brand, adding to a business's overall profitability:

1. **Brand Awareness:** The high level of market awareness attained by the core brand creates an umbrella under which related products can be introduced at a much lower cost of advertising.
2. **Known Quality:** The quality image of the core brand is transferred to product line extensions under the umbrella brand.
3. **Market Reach:** Retailers are more inclined to give precious shelf space to well-known brands. As a result, product line extensions under these umbrella brands gain easier access to retail outlets.
4. **Product Mix:** Product line extensions under the umbrella brand provide customers with more variety and the opportunity to buy variations of the core brand without having to switch to competing brands.

The purpose of line extensions under an umbrella brand is to leverage the awareness and image of the umbrella brand. But a company must take care that the new products will not dilute the reputation of the umbrella brand and adversely impact profits. Line extensions may not grow market demand and can even cannibalize the core brand or other extensions, while raising the total cost of marketing. Careful product line accounting is needed to ensure that product line extensions are profitable and, overall, that they incrementally improve the profitability of the entire product line.[19]

FIGURE 7-19 ARM & HAMMER—VERTICAL AND HORIZONTAL BRAND EXTENSIONS

Horizontal Product Line Extensions ⟶

Vertical Product Line Extensions ↓

Cooking	Deodorizers	Personal	Household	Industrial	Agricultural
Cooking Recipes (140)	Refrigerator Deodorizers	Dental Products	Laundry Detergents	Abrasive Products	Feed Ingredients
	Carpet Deodorizers	Deodorant Products	Swimming Pool Treatments	Cleaning Products	Feed Normalizers
	Cat Litter Deodorizer	Antiperspirant Products	Air Cleaning Products	Degreasing Products	
		Pharmaceutical Products	Cat Litter Disposal	Depainting Products	

Product Line Extensions

Vertical Brand Extensions

A successful brand can often be "franchised," meaning it can be extended to other versions of the product. This can be accomplished most easily with *vertical brand extensions* of the core brand. Arm & Hammer, as illustrated in Figure 7-19, offers an excellent example of how the company extended the company brand name vertically in markets ranging from cooking to agriculture. In market applications, the Arm & Hammer brand was vertically extended to multiple product applications. Gardenburger is another example as illustrated in Figure 7-20. Vertical brand names subsequently added to the basic Gardenburger brand name include Gardenburger Flame Grilled and Gardenburger Santa Fe. These vertical brand extensions provide variety for Gardenburger customers who may tire of the taste of one product. The brand extensions may also attract new customers

FIGURE 7-20 GARDENBURGER VERTICAL AND HORIZONTAL BRAND EXTENSIONS

Vertical Brand Extensions	Horizontal Brand Extensions 1	2	3	4	5
	Hamburgers	Chicken	Veggie	Meatless Meats	Dinners
1	Original	Chik'n Grill	Garden Vegan	Breakfast Sausage	Dinner Deluxe
2	Flame Grilled	BBQ Chik'n	Veggie Medley	Riblets	Crispy Pizza Nuggets
3	Santa Fe	Country Fried Chik'n	Savory Portabella	Meatballs	
4		Buffalo Chik'n Wings	Fire Roasted Vegetables	Meatloaf	
5				Sweet and Sour Pork	
6				Herb Crusted Cutlet	

FIGURE 7-21 HONDA'S PRODUCT LINE AND PRODUCT LINE EXTENSIONS

Product Line	Product Line Offerings
Automobiles	Accord, CMc Sedan, Civic Coupe, Civic Hybrid, Insight, Odyssey, Pilot, S-2000
Motorcycles	Standard, Touring, Sport Touring, Sport, Cruiser, Moto-Cross, Off-Road
Scooters	Silver Wing, Reflex, Elite 80, Metropolitan, Metropolitan II
Jet Skis	Aqua Trax F-12, Aqua Trax F-12X
All-Terrain Vehicles	Utility, Sport
Lawn and Garden	Lawn Mowers, Trimmers, Tillers
Snowblowers	Wheel-Drive, Track-Drive, Lightweight
Pumps	Construction, De-Watering, Multipurpose, Submersible
Generators	Handheld, Economy, Industrial, Super Quiet, Deluxe
Engines	GX Series, GC Series, Mini 4-Stroke

from other meat-substitute products, or even customers trying vegetarian meat-like products for the first time.

Horizontal Brand Extensions

Horizontal brand extensions within a product class are possible by adding complementary products. For Gardenburger, this meant adding a line that included meatless chicken, sausage, ribs, dinners, and veggie entrees. The horizontal brand extension in veggie entrees opened the door to additional vertical brand extensions. Each of these combinations leveraged the core Gardenburger brand while growing sales and profits.

New Product-Market Brand Extensions

Vertical and horizontal brand extensions provide excellent opportunities for growth within a given product-market. However, eventually a business will hit a point of diminishing returns and will need to examine the potential of its proven brand name in other product-market applications. Honda initially built a reputation in the motorcycle and automobile markets for reliable, high-quality products. The company's brand reputation allowed easy entry to other product-markets, often at a price premium. The Honda brand name is so strong that it has easily been transferred to such product-markets as lawn mowers, snowblowers, pumps, generators, and jet skis, as illustrated in Figure 7-21. Each product-market has a "related relevance" to the Honda core brand, and the benefits of the core brand—its reputation for quality and its other brand assets—has carried over to these new products.

Co-Branding

A business can also leverage a strong brand by entering another product-market with co-branding, rather than creating a brand extension. One example is Yoplait yogurt's co-branding with Trix, a children's cereal, to create Trix Yoplait yogurt for children.[20] High awareness and brand preference for Trix among children quickly led to a high volume of sales for Trix Yoplait yogurt, with no advertising. Another example is General Mills' co-branding of Reese's Peanut Butter Cups with a new cereal called Reese's Puffs. The cereal carries all the imagery of the Reese's Cups.

Co-branding takes advantage of the potential synergy of two brands that share a common market space. Healthy Choice has long had many brand extensions in the frozen dinner market. To enter the cereal market, co-branding with Kellogg's cereals saved considerable advertising money and provided easier access to cereal shelf space in retail stores. The composite product—"Healthy Choice from Kellogg's"—uses the Healthy Choice logo, colors, and packaging. Co-branding provided Healthy Choice with easy access to the already crowded cereal market, while it gave Kellogg's a credible product line extension that included a dimension of weight loss and health, a product concept that had previously failed without the Healthy Choice name.

Trix Yoplait and Healthy Choice from Kellogg's are examples of co-branding by combining two brands to name a single product. Co-branding can also include ingredient co-branding strategies. "Intel Inside" is a classic example of ingredient co-branding. The Intel microprocessor chip is an ingredient, a key component, of a personal computer. Intel's reputation for quality adds perceived quality to personal computers that carry the Intel logo. This co-branding strategy helped Dell grow its sales of personal computers and helped Intel grow its sales of microprocessors. Using the "Intel Inside" logo on all personal computers using Intel microprocessors is a low-cost way to keep the Intel name in front of personal computer users, with the realization that almost every user will sooner or later be a first-time or repeat customer.

Bundling and Unbundling Strategies

Products are often enhanced with additional features and services to provide customers with more complete solutions. Most personal computers are purchased with a variety of pre-installed software programs, such as word-processing, spreadsheet, an Internet browser, and other common programs. But some customers who may already have their own specialty software would seek to purchase a personal computer without the standard programs (i.e., unbundled) in order to lower the total cost of purchase. A computer company could use the bundling strategy to enhance the product's benefits or the unbundling strategy to lower the computer's cost, or the company could appeal to both customer types by making use of both strategies.

Product Bundling

Bundling products serves to create a complete customer solution that has the potential to create a superior customer value and attract customers. Products such as living room sets, entertainment packages, and software offered with the purchase of computers are product bundles that can create a superior value (economic and perceived) for target customers. There are two approaches to product bundling.

A *pure product bundling strategy* involves the sale of two or more products at an overall price lower than the total price that would be paid if the products were purchased separately. Even when the products are offered individually at a discounted price that makes the total cost equal to the bundled purchase price, customers rate the bundled offering higher in perceived value.

A *mixed bundling strategy* offers the customer the opportunity to purchase each of the items separately at a sale price or bundled with an additional level of savings. There is evidence that when both options are available, customer perceptions of value exceed those produced with a pure bundling strategy.[21] In addition, a mixed bundling strategy has been shown to be more profitable than pure bundling strategies.[22]

Product Unbundling

Unbundling a set of products that is normally sold as an integrated bundle or system can also be desirable in attracting and satisfying customers. For many complex industrial and commercial purchases, customers may want to purchase individual products or components and integrate them into a certain configuration that best serves their needs.[23] In some instances, value-added resellers (VARs) fill this role. For specialized applications in architecture, agriculture, or chemical processing, VARs will purchase unbundled products and integrate them in a customized bundle that best suits the target customers' application. HP may have an attractive product bundle, but it cannot meet the specific needs of all customers. By unbundling and selling individual products or component products to VARs and systems integrators, HP has been able to create value for its customers and sales growth opportunities for the business.

In the early evolution of a market, customer needs are generally less fragmented than in the later stages, and bundled product solutions are often very attractive. However, as markets grow and new customers enter, segments of the market emerge, and more customized product solutions are needed to satisfy different customers.[24] As a market matures, unbundling often becomes more important in attracting and satisfying customers.[25]

FIGURE 7-22 PRODUCT LINE SUBSTITUTION EFFECTS

Probability of Switching Between Brands

From - To	Core Brand	Multigrain	Reduced Fat
Core Brand	X	10%	25%
Multigrain	5%	X	20%
Reduced Fat	10%	5%	X

Area of Performance	Core Brand	Multi-grain	Reduced Fat	Product Line
Volume				
Primary Demand	50,000,000	10,000,000	20,000,000	80,000,000
Core Brand	32,500,000	5,000,000	12,500,000	
Multigrain	500,000	7,500,000	2,000,000	
Reduced Fat	2,000,000	1,000,000	17,000,000	
Net Volume	35,000,000	13,500,000	31,500,000	80,000,000
Wholesale Price per Unit	$1.95	$1.95	$1.95	$1.95
Sales	$68,250,000	$26,325,000	$61,425,000	$156,000,000
Variable Cost per Unit	$0.95	$1.00	$1.05	$1.00
Margin per Unit	$1.00	$0.95	$0.90	$0.95
Total Contribution	$35,000,000	$12,825,000	$28,350,000	$76,175,000

Product Line Substitution Effects

Product line additions can frequently have a substitution effect. This occurs when the flanker brand attracts new customers but also attracts customers away from the umbrella brand. Likewise, some flanker-brand customers may migrate to the umbrella brand or other brands in the product line as they become more familiar with the company's products.

For example, consider a well-known cracker with a retail price of $2.99 per box and a wholesale price of $1.95 per box. As shown in Figure 7-22, customers attracted to the product line by the core brand will switch 10 percent of the time to the multigrain product and 25 percent of the time to the reduced-fat version of the core brand. Similarly, there is switching to other product line offerings among customers attracted to the multigrain or reduced-fat cracker. After this level of switching is taken into account, we can see that the primary demand of 50 million boxes for the core brand is reduced to 35 million. Both the flanker brands result in higher volumes as customers switch from the core brand to the flanker brands. Despite some cannibalization of the core brand, the product line extensions add to the sales and profit of the product line. The margin per box is lower for the flanker brands, but the incremental demand created by the flanker brands creates a higher overall level of product line profit.

Product Line Scale Effects

Although not immediately obvious, there is also the potential for scale effects with respect to fixed manufacturing expenses when operating below capacity in production and leveraging fixed marketing expenses associated with sales and distribution. In our example, we have extended the product line profitability analysis to include these fixed expenses. First, assuming the business has excess production capacity, the flanker brands were added without expanding plant size or installing new equipment. As illustrated in Figure 7-23, the $40 million in fixed manufacturing overhead can now be spread over more units (80 million versus 50 million). This increases the gross profit of the core brand from $10 million ($50 million in total contribution minus $40 million in manufacturing overhead) to $36 million for the product line.

Also, some of the $10 million in marketing expenses can be shared with the flanker brands because no additional sales, customer service, or managerial personnel need to be hired to market the two flanker brands. The $10 million in fixed marketing expenses can now be allocated on a percentage of sales dollars to each of the brands. Each brand, however, still has some semi-variable marketing expenses that change with advertising and promotions. The net effect is a further increase in profitability from leveraging the use of excess production capacity and the fixed marketing expenses, which are incurred with or without the flanker brands.

These shared expenses are often overlooked, and when a brand appears to be producing a negative profit (net marketing contribution) a business may elect to remove that brand from the market. However, the total contribution may then drop (assuming it is positive), which contributes to fixed expenses in manufacturing and marketing. Decisions to eliminate products need to be made with care. Often the cost accounting used to produce product line profitability statements includes allocations of fixed manufacturing expenses to a line of products, which can distort the stated profitability of any single brand or product.

FIGURE 7-23 PRODUCT LINE SCALE EFFECTS

Area of Performance	Core Brand	Multigrain	Reduced Fat	Product Line
Volume				
Primary Demand	50,000,000	20,000,000	10,000,000	80,000,000
Core Brand	32,500,000	5,000,000	12,500,000	
Multigrain	500,000	7,500,000	2,000,000	
Reduced Fat	2,000,000	1,000,000	17,000,000	
Net Volume	35,000,000	13,500,000	31,500,000	80,000,000
Wholesale Price per Unit	$1.95	$1.95	$1.95	$1.95
Sales	$68,250,000	$26,325,000	$61,425,000	$156,000,000
Variable Cost per Unit	$0.95	$1.00	$1.05	$1.00
Margin per Unit	$1.00	$0.95	$0.90	$0.95
Total Contribution	$35,000,000	$12,825,000	$28,350,000	$76,175,000
Manufacturing Overhead	$17,500,000	$6,750,000	$15,750,000	$40,000,000
Gross Profit	$17,500,000	$6,075,000	$12,600,000	$36,175,000
Fixed Marketing Expenses	$4,375,000	$1,687,500	$3,937,500	$10,000,000
Variable Brand Expenses	$3,412,500	$789,750	$1,842,750	$6,045,000
Total Marketing Expenses	$7,787,500	$2,477,250	$5,780,250	$16,045,000
Net Marketing Contribution	$9,712,500	$3,597,750	$6,819,750	$20,130,000
Marketing ROS (%)	14.2	13.7	11.1	12.9
Marketing ROI (%)	124.72	145.23	117.98	125.46

■ Summary

For any specific target segment, a business needs to develop a tactical marketing strategy for positioning its product with respect to product features and price, and then marketing the product with respect to promotion and place. This chapter focused on product positioning, product line strategies, branding, and brand extensions. We saw that a successful marketing strategy requires an integrated mix of product, price, promotion, place, and service.

Product positioning and differentiation are key parts of a successful marketing strategy. How should a business position its products relative to customer needs and competitors? And what source of differentiation is needed to make this product position differentially superior to competitors' products?

Low-price differentiation is an important position to develop for any business serving a price-sensitive market. Lowering the customer's transaction costs can also be effective in achieving a cost advantage. For markets in which differentiation is possible, a business could build its differentiation around a product or packaging advantage, a service advantage, or an advantage in brand reputation. To be successful, the differentiation underlying the positioning strategy must be meaningful to target customers and sustainable (not easily duplicated by competitors).

A positioning strategy is enhanced by the brand name used to identify a product. Businesses with many products in many diverse markets need to take special care in encoding brand names to ensure both meaning and consistency across the product line. Commonly used brand-encoding systems include (1) company and brand name; (2) brand and sub-brand name; (3) company and product name; (4) company, brand, and product name; (5) company and brand name, followed by numbers or letters or a combination; (6) brand name and benefit; and (7) brand name only. Each of these brand-encoding systems has advantages and disadvantages with respect to distinctiveness, consistency, and communicating the product's positioning.

To grow, a business needs to leverage its product knowledge, production capabilities, marketing systems, and brand equity. Product line strategies provide an excellent opportunity to grow and leverage current assets and expenses. Related product line extensions, both horizontal and vertical, are important ways to achieve profitable growth. A business can leverage a high brand assets score for its core product into one or more flanker brands. Customer perceptions of the umbrella brand will carry over to the flanker products. But a business must be mindful of possible sales cannibalization as a result of substitution by customers along the product line, and of the diminishing returns of too many related products. A business must also be careful not to damage the image of the core brand with products that may prove a detriment to the business's customer satisfaction index. Product bundling and unbundling are also product strategies that can enhance customer attractiveness in certain markets.

Adding flanker brands offers the potential for scale effects when no investment in additional production, personnel, and marketing expenses is necessary. Leveraging excess production capacity and fixed marketing expenses helps ensure the profitability of each new product and improves the business's overall performance.

■ Market-Based Strategic Thinking

1 How did Intel's branding strategy help the company grow and maintain a dominant market share?

2 How would you evaluate the product line positioning of Black & Decker relative to Sears in terms of customer choice and customer value? See Figure 7-3.

3 How does Starbucks' product line positioning enhance both sales and profits?

4 How could a business with an attractive product position achieve a lower market share?

5 Why did Samsung's repositioning strategy yield higher sales and higher profits?

6 How would a business use the eight dimensions of quality differentiation in developing a product and package differentiation strategy?

7 How does a business such as McDonald's develop a positioning strategy around some aspect of service differentiation?

8 Why would a brand name such as Kodak, Disney, or Coca-Cola create customer value and provide a basis for product positioning and differentiation?

9 Why would the occupancy of a Fairfield Inn increase by 15 percent when the Marriott name is added to the building?

10 Why would an extension of a product line to include a small number of related products contribute to higher levels of profitability?

11 Why would a business use an experiential brand name versus an evocative brand name?

12 What are morphemes and how were they used in developing brand names such as InfoSeek, DuraFlame, and Compaq Computer?

13 What is the marketing logic that underlies Anheuser-Busch's product line and marketing strategy for the beer market?

14 What are the advantages of a product strategy involving a strong core brand with flanker brands? Under what conditions would this product line strategy fail?

15 Why are vertical brand extensions less expensive than horizontal brand extensions?

16 How does a well-known brand help in the marketing and profitability of a flanker brand?

17 Why did Healthy Choice co-brand with Kellogg's to introduce a new breakfast cereal? How did Kellogg's also benefit?

18 How might product line substitution effects have contributed to the sales of Intel Pentium microprocessors when the Xeon and Celeron brands were introduced?

19 Frito-Lay introduced Stax to compete with Pringles in 2003. Assuming the company had excess production capacity, how would the profits of other chip products be affected by the success of Stax?

20 Under what conditions would the elimination of a flanker brand with a negative operating income result in lower overall operating income if eliminated?

Marketing Performance Tools

The three **Marketing Performance Tools** described here may be accessed online at *www.rogerjbest.com*. These applied-learning exercises will add to your understanding of brand management and product line strategies.

7.1 Brand Equity
- Estimate the brand assets and brand liabilities for a brand you believe to be strong.
- Estimate the brand assets and brand liabilities for a brand you believe to be weak.
- Compute the brand equity for each and discuss how they may differ in profitability.

7.2 Product Line Substitution
- What would be the profit impact if each of the switching probabilities were doubled?
- What would be the profit impact if all the switching probabilities were equal to zero?

7.3 Product Line Scale
- How will the profits change if the Reduced-Fat product is discontinued?
- How will the profits change if only the Multigrain product is discontinued?
- What does the price of the Reduced-Fat product need to be in order to achieve the same overall profit that would result by eliminating this product from the product line?

Notes

1. Mary Jo Hatch and Majken Schultz, "Are the Strategic Stars Aligned for Your Corporate Brand?" *Harvard Business Review* (February 2001):128–134.
2. The Top 100 Brands," *Business Week* (August 5, 2002): 95–99.
3. "Drills for All Reasons," *Consumer Reports* (November, 1997): 24–28.
4. David Garvin, "Competing on Eight Dimensions of Quality," *Harvard Business Review* (November–December 1987): 101–105.
5. Valarie Zeithaml, A. Parasuramon, and Leonard Berry, *Delivering Quality Service* (New York: Free Press, 1990): Chapter 1.
6. Bradley Gale, "Creating Power Brands," in *Managing Customer Value* (New York: Free Press, 1994): 153–174.
7. Peter Farquhar, "Managing Brand Equity," *Marketing Research* (September 1989): 24–33.
8. David Aaker, *Managing Brand Equity: Capitalizing on the Value of a Brand Name* (New York: Free Press, 1991).
9. Daniel Sheinin and Bernd Schmitt, "Extending Brands with New Product Concepts: The Role of Category Attribute Congruity, Brand Affect, and Brand Breadth," *Journal of Business Research* 31 (1994): 1–10.
10. D. Aaker, *Building Strong Brands* (New York: Free Press, 1996): 356–357.
11. D. D'Alessandro, *Brand Warfare* (New York: McGraw-Hill, 2001).
12. S. Hill, C. Lederer, and K. Keller, *The Infinite Asset: Managing Brands to Build New Value* (Boston: Harvard Business School Press, 2001).
13. Igor International, www.igorinternational.com, "Name Development" (accessed 2004).
14. S. M. Davis, *Brand Asset Management* (San Francisco: Jossey-Bass, Inc., 2000).
15. K. Keller, "The Brand Report Card," *Harvard Business Review* (January–February 2000): 147–157.
16. C. Lederer and S. Hill, "See Your Brands Through Your Customers' Eyes," *Harvard Business Review* (June 2001): 125–133.
17. T. Erdem, "An Empirical Analysis of Umbrella Branding," *Journal of Marketing Research* (August 1998): 339–351; David Aaker, *Building Strong Brands* (New York: Free Press, 1995); P. Dacin and D. Smith, "The Effect of Brand Portfolio Characteristics on Consumer Evaluations of Brand Extensions," *Journal of Marketing Research* (May 1994): 229–242; and A. Rangaswamy, R. Burke, and T. Oliver, "Brand Equity and Extendibility of Brand Names," *International Journal of Research in Marketing* (March 1993): 61–75.
18. Mary Jo Hatch and Majken Schultz, "Are the Strategic Stars Aligned for Your Corporate Brand?" *Harvard Business Review* (February 2001): 128–134.
19. Bruce Hardle, "The Logic of Product-Line Extensions," *Harvard Business Review* (November–December 1994): 53–62.
20. D. Aaker, *Building Strong Brands* (New York: Free Press, 1996): 298–300.
21. Manjit Yadav and Kent Monroe, "How Buyers Perceive Savings in a Bundle Price: An Examination of a Bundle's Transaction Value," *Journal of Marketing Research* (August 1993): 350–358.
22. William Adams and Janet Yellen, "Commodity Bundling and the Burden of Monopoly," *Quarterly Journal of Economics* (August 1976): 475–498; and Richard Schmalensee, "Gaussian Demand and Commodity Bundling," *Journal of Business* 57 (1984): 211–230.
23. Lynn Wilson, Allen Weiss, and George John, "Unbundling of Industrial Systems," *Journal of Marketing Research* (May 1990): 123–138.
24. Roger Best and Reinhard Angelmar, "Strategies for Leveraging Technology Advantage," in *Handbook on Business Strategy* (Boston: Warren, Gorham, and Lamont, 1989): 2-1–2-10.
25. Barbara Jackson, *Winning and Keeping Industrial Customers* (Lanham, MD: Lexington Books, 1985); and Michael Porter, *Competitive Advantage* (New York: Free Press, 1985).

CHAPTER 8

Value-Based Pricing and Pricing Strategies

> ■ Price is only relevant in the context of the value of what it is you're offering.
> — *Joel Hoesktra*
> *CEO, General Mills*

C ost-based pricing is the most commonly used approach to pricing in business.[1] One study found that over 60 percent of the businesses surveyed used cost-based pricing as their primary basis for setting price.[2] This is consistent with another study of 50,000 managers from over 100 countries in which 64 percent used cost-based pricing to set price.[3]

As shown in Figure 8-1, the cost of making a product and the desired profit margin are the two determinants in setting a cost-based price. The price is then marked up by channel intermediaries to arrive at the purchase price that customers are asked to pay.

But something is missing from this approach to pricing. First, cost-based pricing ignores the fact that many customers need and will pay for a higher level of product performance. Secondly, this approach to pricing overlooks competitors' offerings relative to customer needs and price affordability.

Value-based pricing, in contrast, starts with the customer, the competition, and company positioning.[4] Based on customer needs, price sensitivity, and competing products, a company develops its price around a product's relative strengths to create greater value than competing products offer.

FIGURE 8-1 COST-BASED PRICING VERSUS VALUE-BASED PRICING

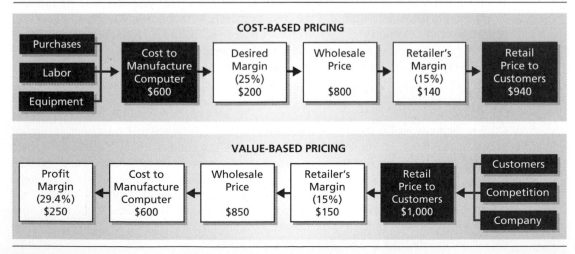

FIGURE 8-2 PRICE IS ONLY THE TIP OF THE ICEBERG IN VALUE-IN-USE PRICING

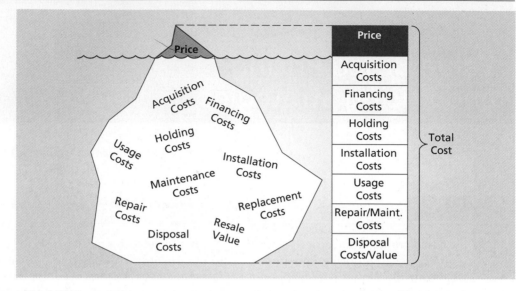

VALUE-BASED PRICING

Value-based pricing requires extensive customer and competitor intelligence.[5] Without high levels of both, this approach to pricing is simply not possible. Value-based pricing starts with a good understanding of customer needs and the benefits a product offers relative to competitors' products.[6] On the basis of customer benefits, price is set relative to competition to create a superior value. In this way, the price is determined in the market, not at the factory or in the financial department. This section discusses three kinds of value pricing:

■ **Value-in-Use Pricing:** Price is set based on providing customers an attractive savings after considering the life-cycle costs of acquiring, owning, using, maintaining, and disposing of a product.
■ **Perceived-Value Pricing:** Price is set based on the value provided customers when comparing price and benefits of the company's product relative to key competitors.
■ **Performance-Based Pricing:** Price is set based on customer preferences for different levels of price and performance and how the company and competitors are positioned with respect to delivering both price and performance.

Value-in-Use Pricing

Price is the most visible cost of any purchase, whether it be a new car, computer, insurance policy, vacation trip, or simple household cleanser. All customers are price sensitive to some degree. Some customers, however, are willing to pay more for extra benefits. These benefits often include reduced costs in other areas of product ownership. The other costs of owning a product are much less obvious than the purchase price. As shown in Figure 8-2, price is only the tip of the iceberg; the other costs of ownership are beneath the surface. Value-based pricing considers the total value of ownership benefits and all the ownership costs in determining the customer value of a product and its purchase price.[7]

FIGURE 8-3 PROFIT IMPACT OF COST-BASED VERSUS VALUE-BASED PRICING

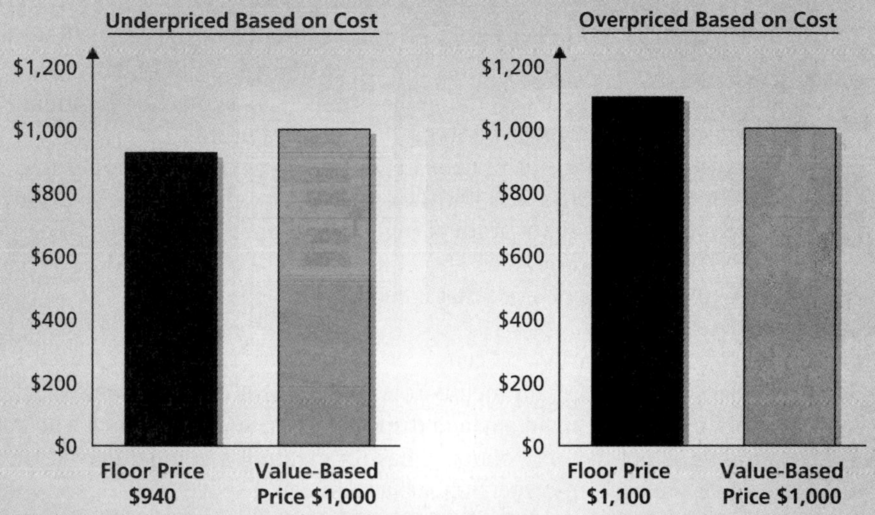

Underpricing Price Strategy	Volume	Price	Net Price	Unit Cost	Unit Margin	Gross Profit
Cost-Based	1,000,000	$940	$800	$600	$200	$200,000,000
Value-Based	1,000,000	$1,000	$850	$600	$250	$250,000,000
Lost Profit						$50,000,000

Overpricing Price Strategy	Volume	Price	Net Price	Unit Cost	Unit Margin	Gross Profit
Cost-Based	650,000	$1,060	$900	$600	$300	$195,000,000
Value-Based	1,000,000	$1,000	$850	$600	$250	$250,000,000
Lost Profit						$55,000,000

But this does not necessarily mean lowering prices. By considering the total cost of ownership incurred by target customers, a business can use value-based pricing to offer them an attractive savings (economic value) while maintaining a premium price. For example, in Figure 8-4, the price of a business's product is higher than the price of the competitor's product, but the customer's total cost of ownership is lower than with the competitor's product. Because of lower acquisition, use, and other costs over the life of the product, its value in use is higher than the competing product, and the customer saves money.

When using value-in-use pricing, the price is based on the attractive savings that customers realize over the life of the product, not just on the costs of manufacturing and marketing the product. Customers are interested in overall savings, or economic value, and the higher the savings, the more attractive the business's product. And the more attractive the product, the higher can be the purchase price, regardless of manufacturing and marketing costs. Chapter 4 discussed the various ways a business can lower the cost of ownership and thereby achieve higher price levels while still creating a superior value for target customers.

Value-based pricing results in higher profits. In the example in Figure 8-3, customers would pay $1,000 for a personal computer that is priced based on its benefits and the prices of competing computers (value-based pricing). Retailers would still want their traditional 15 percent margin, resulting in a net price of $850 to the manufacturer. At a cost of $600 per unit, the margin would be $250 per unit, which would be $50 higher than the margin obtained with cost-based pricing. Value-based pricing, then, would achieve a higher profit while delivering an attractive customer value. In this case, a cost-based price would have resulted in underpricing the product. As shown, underpricing relative to value would have cost the company $50 million in gross profits.

Overpricing relative to value is also possible when using cost-based pricing, and this also results in lost profits. Assume the cost-based pricing needed to achieve a desired margin is $1,060. While the margin is high at $300 per unit, at this price the company can expect its volume to drop to 650,000 units. The company would lose $55 million in gross profits with a cost-based price that is too high.

Understanding Life-Cycle Costs

A business tends to remain focused on price until it comes to understand how customers acquire, finance, use, maintain, and dispose of or resell its product. The business then realizes pricing is not the only option it has for creating a competitive advantage. By looking deeper into the costs of ownership, a business can discover new opportunities for customer savings and value creation. Let's begin with Figure 8-4, which is a life-cycle cost analysis of a material that a company hoped to sell in the automobile manufacturing market.

This market is highly price competitive, and customers simply do not pay price premiums. To do business in the market, the company was told it would need to set a price below the current $2 per pound. Had the company been a typical business, it would have then focused on ways to lower its price so its product would be attractive to the automotive industry. However, an analysis of the company's and competitors' life-cycle costs, as in Figure 8-4, reveals that a customer's total cost per pound for the competitor's product is $6. The $2 price is only one-third of the total cost of purchase; the other two-thirds are costs associated with acquiring and using the product.

The company's total cost of purchase (life-cycle cost) at a price equal to the competitor's price of $2 results in a $5.05 total cost of purchase. This would save customers 95 cents per pound compared to the competitor's product, as illustrated in Figure 8-4. The value-pricing question is: Can the company capture a price premium and still deliver a meaningful economic value to customers?

Price premiums can be difficult to explain when customers look only at the purchase price, but the company set its price at $2.20, a 10 percent price premium, in the belief customers in its market would readily see the substantial savings they would realize in a product that cut costs by 75 cents per pound.[8] If a customer used 10,000 pounds per month, the savings would be $7,500—or $90,000 annually. If volumes were 100,000 per month, the yearly savings would be $900,000. With savings at that level, any supplier business would strategize that a higher price can be justified based on the customer value provided. Even at a price of $2.30, which would save 65 cents per pound, a customer with monthly volumes of 100,000 would still save $780,000 annually.

Perceived-Value Pricing

Some customer benefits are more difficult to quantify in terms of economic value, yet they have an important perceived value.[9] These perceived customer benefits give us another approach to value-based pricing, known as *perceived-value pricing*.

FIGURE 8-4 VALUE-IN-USE PRICING

Life-Cycle Costs	Competitor	Company	Savings
Price	$2.00	$2.20	$0.20
Shipping Cost	$0.07	$0.05	–$0.02
Handling	$0.10	$0.13	$0.03
Inventory	$0.05	$0.01	–$0.04
Financing	$0.00	$0.00	$0.00
Usage	$3.50	$2.80	–$0.70
Quality Control	$0.03	$0.01	–$0.02
Waste	$0.10	$0.02	–$0.08
Waste Disposal	$0.15	$0.03	–$0.12
Life-Cycle Cost	$6.00	$5.25	–$0.75

Value-Pricing Strategy

In this example, the company felt it could price its product 10% higher, at $2.20 per pound, and still save the customer 75 cents. The savings represents a 13% lower total cost of purchase, despite the 10% higher purchase price.

Value-Pricing Strategy	VP1	VP2	VP3	VP4	VP5	VP6
Competing Price	$2.00	$2.10	$2.20	$2.30	$2.40	$2.50
Company Price	$2.00	$2.00	$2.00	$2.00	$2.00	$2.00
Price Premium	$0.00	$0.10	$0.20	$0.30	$0.40	$0.50
Customer Value	$0.95	$0.85	$0.75	$0.65	$0.55	$0.45
Percent Value Advantage	16%	14%	13%	11%	9%	8%

In Chapter 4, we learned to calculate and interpret the indexes for product benefits, service benefits, and brand benefits. For the business in Figure 8-5, the perceived benefits derived from its product (120), service (127), and brand (134) each outperforms the competition. In this case, each area of perceived benefits is a source of competitive advantage. When weighted by the relative importance of each source of benefits, as in Figure 8-6, the overall value index is 123, a 23 percent advantage over competitors with respect to all perceived benefits. The perceived-value-pricing question is: How much of a price premium can the business obtain and still deliver a meaningful level of customer value?

We can answer this question by first considering other costs of purchase that are important to the customer. Figure 8-6 lists service and maintenance costs and the depreciated value (how fast the equipment depreciates in value) as two other components, besides price, of the total cost of purchase (life-cycle cost). The business has some advantage in the area of service and maintenance costs and no advantage in depreciated value. If the business were to price its equipment at $5,000, it would have a cost advantage relative to its three competitors (60), resulting in a very high customer value index of 64. Even an index of 25 would be good. The business, then, should not sell at a lower price but set a price that results in a value index close to 25.

As shown in Figure 8-6, increasing the $5,000 purchase price by increments of $250 up to $5,750 changes the customer value index to 43. At a purchase price of $6,000, the

FIGURE 8-5 COMPETITIVE ADVANTAGE IS THE KEY TO VALUE PRICING

Product Benefits (Voice of the Customer)	Rel. Imp.	Our Bus.	Competitors A	Competitors B	Competitors C	Product Advantage
Reliable Performance	50	8.3	7.5	5.4	6.7	17
Ease of Use	30	5.6	5.1	7.7	4.9	−10
Product Life	20	7.6	5.2	5.2	6.1	13
	100					120

Service Benefits (Voice of the Customer)	Rel. Imp.	Our Bus.	Competitors A	Competitors B	Competitors C	Service Advantage
Parts Availability	60	7.2	6.3	4.3	6.7	20
Competent Service	20	6.5	6.8	6.6	5.5	0
Response to Problems	20	7.2	6.3	5.2	6.6	7
	100					127

Brand Benefits (Voice of the Customer)	Rel. Imp.	Our Bus.	Competitors A	Competitors B	Competitors C	Brand Advantage
Most Respected Brand	50	7.7	7.5	5.4	6.7	17
Known for Quality	50	7.5	6.7	6.6	3.5	17
	100					134

value index drops to 23, close to the target index of 25. The business elected to go with a price of $6,250, since it also produced a value index of 23. At this price, customers rated the price of equipment at 7.5. Competitor A, who offered a price of $6,000, was rated at 7.2. Competitor A's product was priced low but also had sub-par customer benefits, as shown in Figure 8-5. With a higher price than all three competitors, the business must make certain to communicate the value of its product's benefits so customers will know the higher price is more than offset by better value.

Performance-Based Pricing

If we were to ask a business's customers to name those things that most influence their purchase decisions, they will generally say everything. If we were to ask, "Is price important?" the answer would generally be "yes." So, what will a customer pay for? And, how do we determine if our offering has more value than our competitors' products at their prices?

Conjoint measurement is a method that marketing managers use to address these questions. The number of performance aspects that can be evaluated in one price-performance trade-off analysis is limited, but by using a simplified design, with two performance drivers across three levels of performance and three levels of price, we can determine the value customers place on different levels of performance and different levels of price.[10]

Figure 8-7 illustrates three levels of performance for two areas of product performance and three levels of price for fiber-cement construction siding. Customers can purchase the siding without the finish trim, with basic trim, or with full trim, and they can buy the siding unpainted, primed, or painted. The three price levels the customers are

FIGURE 8-6 PERCEIVED-VALUE PRICING (PERCEIVED BENEFITS MINUS COST)

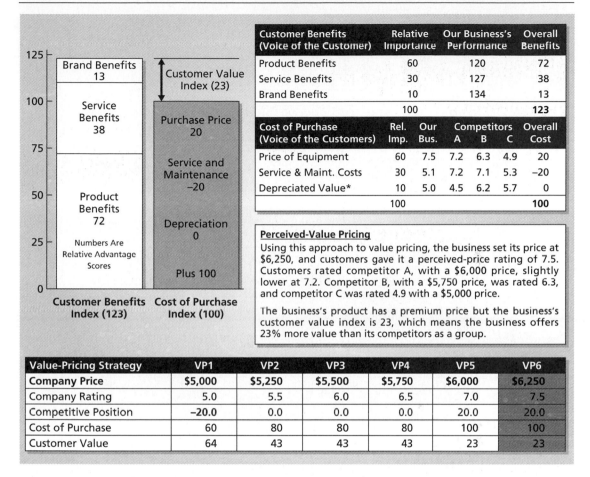

Customer Benefits (Voice of the Customer)	Relative Importance	Our Business's Performance	Overall Benefits
Product Benefits	60	120	72
Service Benefits	30	127	38
Brand Benefits	10	134	13
	100		123

Cost of Purchase (Voice of the Customers)	Rel. Imp.	Our Bus.	Competitors A	B	C	Overall Cost
Price of Equipment	60	7.5	7.2	6.3	4.9	20
Service & Maint. Costs	30	5.1	7.2	7.1	5.3	−20
Depreciated Value*	10	5.0	4.5	6.2	5.7	0
	100					100

Perceived-Value Pricing

Using this approach to value pricing, the business set its price at $6,250, and customers gave it a perceived-price rating of 7.5. Customers rated competitor A, with a $6,000 price, slightly lower at 7.2. Competitor B, with a $5,750 price, was rated 6.3, and competitor C was rated 4.9 with a $5,000 price.

The business's product has a premium price but the business's customer value index is 23, which means the business offers 23% more value than its competitors as a group.

Value-Pricing Strategy	VP1	VP2	VP3	VP4	VP5	VP6
Company Price	$5,000	$5,250	$5,500	$5,750	$6,000	$6,250
Company Rating	5.0	5.5	6.0	6.5	7.0	7.5
Competitive Position	−20.0	0.0	0.0	0.0	20.0	20.0
Cost of Purchase	60	80	80	80	100	100
Customer Value	64	43	43	43	23	23

asked to consider are $1, $2, and $3 per square foot. While there are 81 possible combinations, the table in Figure 8-7 fairly represents these combinations with nine alternatives. Note that no performance level or price is repeated in any column or row. Using this set of hypothetical choices, the business asks a sampling of target customers to rank the nine alternatives from most preferred to least preferred. Using the conjoint measurement process explained in Appendix 4.1, we can derive the performance curves presented in Figure 8-8.

In this example, customers place most value on trim (50%), second-most value on the siding's finish (43%), and least importance on price (7%). Using these results, the company can compare its competitive position to a key competitor. As shown, the business is positioned with full trim (1.0), a painted finish for the siding (0.9), and a price at $3 per square foot (0.4). The business's value score is 2.30. Its key competitor offers a product with basic trim (0.5), primed siding (0.6), and a price of $1.50 per square foot (0.55), resulting in a value score of 1.65. The difference (0.65) is the value advantage the business has over its competitor.

FIGURE 8-7 PERFORMANCE-BASED PRICING—CUSTOMER PREFERENCES

Performance and Price Levels

Finish Trim	Paint		
	Unpainted	Primed	Color
None	$1 sq. ft.	$2 sq. ft.	$3 sq. ft.
Basic	$3 sq. ft.	$1 sq. ft.	$2 sq. ft.
Full	$2 sq. ft.	$3 sq. ft.	$1 sq. ft.

Creating Customer Choice Alternatives

Choice A	Choice B	Choice C
· Finish Trim...None · Paint............Unpainted · Price.............$1 sq. ft.	· Finish Trim...None · Paint............Primed · Price.............$2 sq. ft.	· Finish Trim...None · Paint............Painted · Price.............$3 sq. ft.
Choice D	**Choice E**	**Choice F**
· Finish Trim...Basic · Paint............Unpainted · Price.............$3 sq. ft.	· Finish Trim...Basic · Paint............Primed · Price.............$1 sq. ft.	· Finish Trim...Basic · Paint............Painted · Price.............$2 sq. ft.
Choice G	**Choice H**	**Choice I**
· Finish Trim...Full · Paint............Unpainted · Price.............$2 sq. ft.	· Finish Trim...Full · Paint............Primed · Price.............$3 sq. ft.	· Finish Trim...Full · Paint............Painted · Price.............$1 sq. ft.

For customers in the performance-conscious segment of the siding market, a price 65 cents higher than a competitor's has more value based on their performance preferences and low level of price sensitivity. But in Figure 8-9, a different set of customer price-performance preferences yields a different set of performance curves for the market's price-sensitive segment. In this case, the customer is highly price sensitive (70%) and places less importance (30%) on performance. The company's value for these customers is only 1.20, while the competitor offers a value of 1.75. The company's value deficiency is largely due to the higher price, which customers find unattractive regardless of performance differences. The company could elect to create a more basic product at a more competitive price to improve its value deficiency, or it could simply decide not to compete in the market's price-sensitive segment.

Using more sophisticated conjoint analysis software programs, we can add more dimensions of performance, and we can include more levels of performance in any given dimension.[11] Conjoint analysis programs allow a business to test price-performance preferences and to evaluate its product's value based on the business's competitive position. For a business with a competitive price and a large value advantage, such an analysis would suggest the business could charge more for its product and still offer a good value.

FIGURE 8-8 PERFORMANCE-BASED PRICING—CREATING A VALUE ADVANTAGE

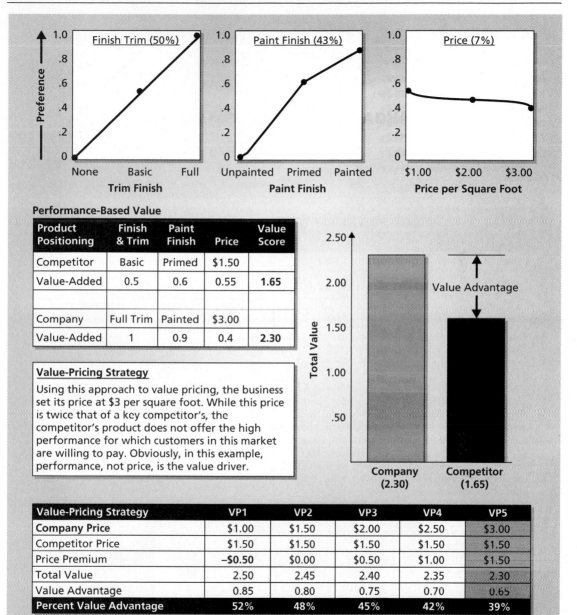

Performance-Based Value

Product Positioning	Finish & Trim	Paint Finish	Price	Value Score
Competitor	Basic	Primed	$1.50	
Value-Added	0.5	0.6	0.55	**1.65**
Company	Full Trim	Painted	$3.00	
Value-Added	1	0.9	0.4	**2.30**

Value-Pricing Strategy

Using this approach to value pricing, the business set its price at $3 per square foot. While this price is twice that of a key competitor's, the competitor's product does not offer the high performance for which customers in this market are willing to pay. Obviously, in this example, performance, not price, is the value driver.

Value-Pricing Strategy	VP1	VP2	VP3	VP4	VP5
Company Price	$1.00	$1.50	$2.00	$2.50	$3.00
Competitor Price	$1.50	$1.50	$1.50	$1.50	$1.50
Price Premium	−$0.50	$0.00	$0.50	$1.00	$1.50
Total Value	2.50	2.45	2.40	2.35	2.30
Value Advantage	0.85	0.80	0.75	0.70	0.65
Percent Value Advantage	52%	48%	45%	42%	39%

Likewise, a business with a competitive price and a large value deficiency would realize its price is high relative to value. In this case, a business has three options: (1) lower its price to create a comparable value based on positioning; (2) improve performance based on customer price-performance preferences to a level that creates meaningful customer value; or (3) do not compete in this segment of the market.

FIGURE 8-9 PERFORMANCE-BASED PRICING—SEEING A VALUE DEFICIENCY

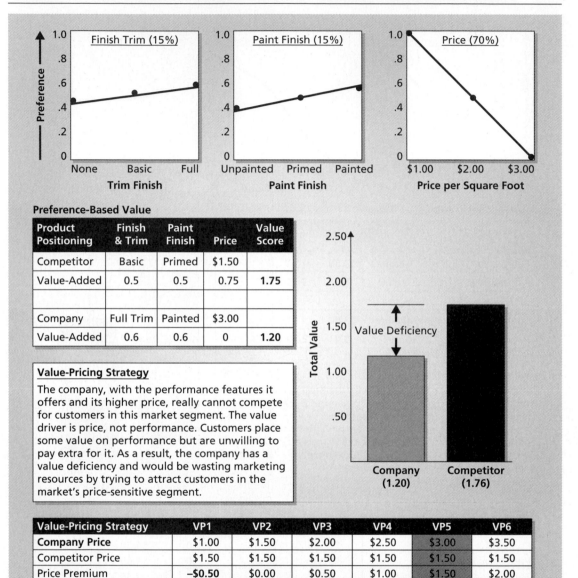

Preference-Based Value

Product Positioning	Finish & Trim	Paint Finish	Price	Value Score
Competitor	Basic	Primed	$1.50	
Value-Added	0.5	0.5	0.75	**1.75**
Company	Full Trim	Painted	$3.00	
Value-Added	0.6	0.6	0	**1.20**

Value-Pricing Strategy

The company, with the performance features it offers and its higher price, really cannot compete for customers in this market segment. The value driver is price, not performance. Customers place some value on performance but are unwilling to pay extra for it. As a result, the company has a value deficiency and would be wasting marketing resources by trying to attract customers in the market's price-sensitive segment.

Value-Pricing Strategy	VP1	VP2	VP3	VP4	VP5	VP6
Company Price	$1.00	$1.50	$2.00	$2.50	$3.00	$3.50
Competitor Price	$1.50	$1.50	$1.50	$1.50	$1.50	$1.50
Price Premium	−$0.50	$0.00	$0.50	$1.00	$1.50	$2.00
Total Value	2.20	1.95	1.70	1.45	1.20	2.25
Value Advantage	0.55	0.30	0.05	−0.20	−0.45	0.60
Percent Value Advantage	**33%**	**18%**	**3%**	**−12%**	**−27%**	**36%**

PRICE-MARGIN MANAGEMENT

The price paid by end users and the amount a business actually receives often vary greatly. This is especially so for businesses using indirect channels. Of course, when the cost of selling direct is greater than the margin given to intermediaries, the use of intermediaries is more profitable. But depending on channel strategies, price discounts, transaction costs, and

FIGURE 8-10 McKINSEY'S WATERFALL

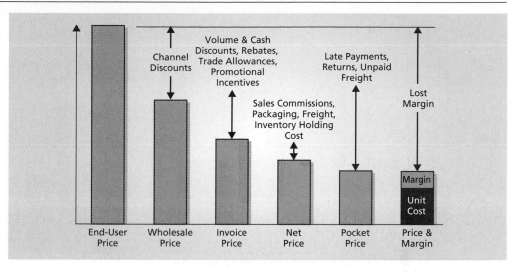

the reality of getting paid, a business can encounter an enormous gap between the price a customer pays for a product and the "pocket price"—the amount the business receives. Any pricing strategy, once implemented, has a series of costs known as McKinsey's waterfall. Figure 8-10 shows these costs as they "plunge" toward the pocket price.

The costs that contribute to the waterfall include the discounts a business gives its channel intermediaries, as well as customer discounts and the cost of other promotions. These lower the price to the invoice price. Deducting transaction costs then results in the net price. Late payments, unpaid freight, and returns can lower the net price still further to the pocket price. When the variable cost per unit sold is deducted from the pocket price, the result is the net margin per unit. Multiplying the margin per unit by the volume of units produces the total contribution from which all other expenses are deducted in arriving at the profit amount (operating income). Alternative marketing and distribution strategies, different pricing policies, and better management of payments and transaction costs offer many opportunities to reduce the lost margin inherent in a pricing strategy.

Pocket-Price Bandwidth

Plotting the pocket-price bandwidth is helpful for gaining insight into the profit impact of a pocket price. A business, however, will not have just one pocket price, but several. The volumes that pass through different channel intermediaries or are sold in different regions, for instance, can result in different pocket prices. A business can plot its pocket prices in relation to the volume sold for each pocket price, as illustrated in Figure 8-11. In this case, the dollar amount difference between the lowest pocket price ($3.80) and the highest ($5.80) is $2, which is a percentage difference of 53 percent (rounded). This is the pocket-price bandwidth. There can be, then, a lot of variance in the pocket price across a business's volume, with some portions of its volume performing well and other portions poorly. And while a pocket-price bandwidth of 53 percent may seem high, McKinsey Consulting Engagements has reported bandwidths of 65 percent for an electrical controls manufacturer, 80 percent

FIGURE 8-11 POCKET PRICE WITH 53 PERCENT BANDWIDTH

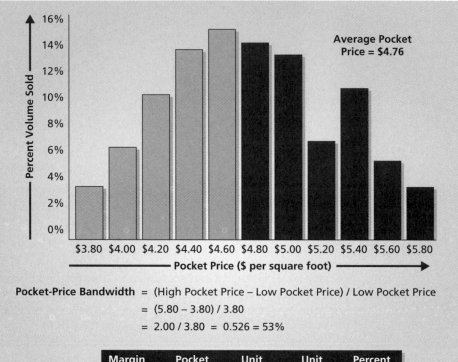

Pocket-Price Bandwidth = (High Pocket Price − Low Pocket Price) / Low Pocket Price
= (5.80 − 3.80) / 3.80
= 2.00 / 3.80 = 0.526 = 53%

Margin Range	Pocket Price	Unit Cost	Unit Margin	Percent Margin
Low	$3.80	$3.50	$0.30	7.9%
Average	$4.76	$3.50	$1.26	26.5%
High	$5.80	$3.50	$2.30	39.7%

for a medical equipment supplier, 170 percent for a specialty metals company, and 500 percent for a fastener supplier.[12]

Differences in pocket prices across a business's volume, of course, have margin and profit implications. As shown in Figure 8-11, the lowest pocket price has only a 7.9 percent profit margin when the unit cost is $3.50 per square foot. In contrast, the highest pocket price produces a margin of almost 40 percent. A manager looking at only the average pocket price would see a fairly acceptable 26.5 percent gross profit margin. But another manager looking at all the figures might be motivated to examine the causes for the below-average pocket prices, with the objective of identifying and addressing those areas where needless price leakage is occurring.

This manager might also take a close look at the above-average pocket prices. Is the reason for a higher pocket price related to customer buying behavior, channels, better price management, or some other factor? Just as knowing the causes for the lower pocket prices can be helpful in managing price and improving profits, so can an understanding of the reasons for the higher pocket prices.

FIGURE 8-12 PRODUCT LIFE-CYCLE PRICING STRATEGIES

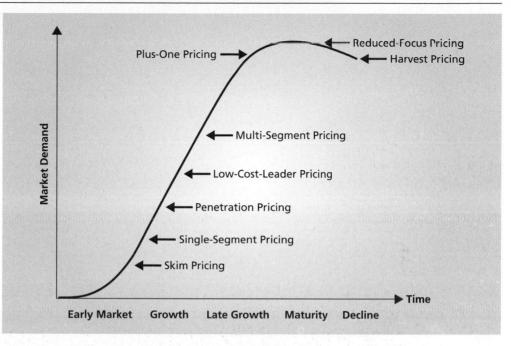

PRODUCT LIFE-CYCLE PRICING STRATEGIES

Pricing from a market point of view, using value-based pricing, is the primary pricing orientation of a market-based business. Different phases of the product life cycle, however,
call for different pricing strategies, including cost-based strategies. The same is true as a
company's positioning evolves or business conditions change.[13] Figure 8-12 shows eight
pricing strategies and the phases of the product life cycle when businesses are likely to
implement them. Each pricing strategy has its own positioning strategy and value proposition. And each pricing strategy impacts profits in a different way. This section examines
these pricing strategies—when and why to apply them, and how they impact profits.

Skim Pricing

Skim pricing is the strategy businesses often implement during the early stages of the
product life cycle, as illustrated in Figure 8-12. This is the phase when conditions can be
best for a skim-pricing strategy. As summarized in Figure 8-13, when a business has a
considerable and sustainable differentiation advantage in a quality-sensitive market with
few competitors, and entry to the market is difficult, skim pricing is a viable value-based
pricing strategy. When feasible, skim pricing allows a business to penetrate a market systematically as the business builds production capacity. When demand in the high-priced
segment becomes saturated, price can be gradually lowered to attract more customers,
eventually reaching a level affordable to most potential customers.

Often a business will have a proprietary-product advantage relative to competition
because it holds a patent for its product or because the product's capability cannot be

FIGURE 8-13 SKIM PRICING

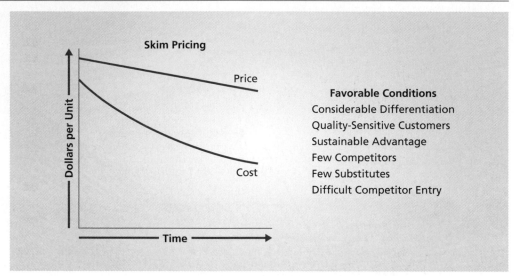

duplicated for other reasons. In such cases, a business usually pursues a skim-pricing strategy well into the market's growth stage. The skim-pricing strategy, which we can also call a premium-pricing strategy at this point, can be highly profitable as long as it delivers superior customer value. A business can stay with a premium-pricing strategy until such time that competitors may match the business's source of competitive advantage. Many prescription drugs, for example, are protected under patents, and the patent holders charge premium prices. During the patent period, the pharmaceutical company has a price umbrella. It is protected from price rivalry because any would-be competitors cannot match the business's relative advantage.

Single-Segment Pricing

As its product moves into the growth stage of its life cycle, a business will need to find a way to lower the cost to potential customers in order to attract their purchase volume. But this does not necessarily mean lowering prices. By considering the total cost of ownership incurred by target customers, a business can utilize *single-segment pricing*, which is a value-based pricing strategy, to produce an attractive savings (economic value) while maintaining a premium price. For example, in Figure 8-4, the price of the business's product is higher than the price of the competitor's product, but the customer's total cost of purchase, or cost of ownership, is lower than with the competitor's product. Because of lower acquisition, use, and other costs over the life of the product, its value in use is higher than the competing product, and the customer saves money.

When using single-segment pricing, the price is based on the attractive savings that customers realize over the life of the product, not just the costs of manufacturing and marketing the product. Customers are interested in overall savings, or economic value, and the higher the savings, the more attractive the business's product. And the more attractive the

FIGURE 8-14 PENETRATION PRICING

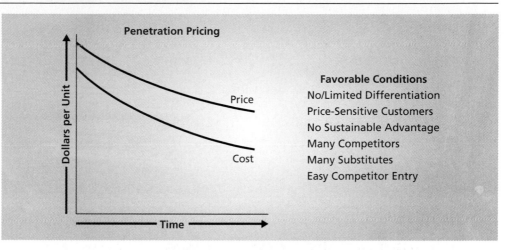

product, the higher can be the purchase price, regardless of manufacturing and marketing costs. In Chapter 4, we examined various ways a business can lower the cost of ownership and achieve higher price levels while still creating a superior value for target customers. We need to keep in mind, too, that focused-segment pricing, because it is based on value-in-use pricing, is only possible with a good understanding of customer needs and competitors' positions. Customer and competitor intelligence, along with a company's positioning, is where all value-based pricing starts, as illustrated earlier in Figure 8-1.

Penetration Pricing

Businesses focused on building volume may use a cost-based *penetration-pricing* strategy. As illustrated in Figure 8-12, this pricing strategy is most likely to be employed during the market's growth stage when volumes arc rapidly increasing in response to lower prices. The primary objective of penetration pricing is to build volume to drive down cost, as illustrated in Figure 8-14.

Cost-based penetration pricing is a mass-market strategy. It is most effective in the growth stage of the product life cycle because this is when product differentiation is minimal, customers are price sensitive, many competitors or substitutes exist, and competitor entry is easy. The volume leader can often gain a cost advantage and continue to lower prices, discouraging competitor entry while encouraging competitor exit. A volume leadership position, then, enables a business to use penetration pricing to build market share.

The price of dynamic random access memory (DRAM) chips is a good example of volume-sensitive pricing, as illustrated in Figure 8-15. In this product-market, prices decrease by 30 percent every time cumulative volume doubles.[14] A DRAM chip maker lowest on the cost curve because it has the highest volume can price lower than competitors and still maintain a desirable contribution margin. In any market where cost reduction is volume sensitive and product differentiation is minimal, a penetration pricing strategy can be a viable path to market leadership and profitable growth.

FIGURE 8-15 DRAM PRICE CURVE

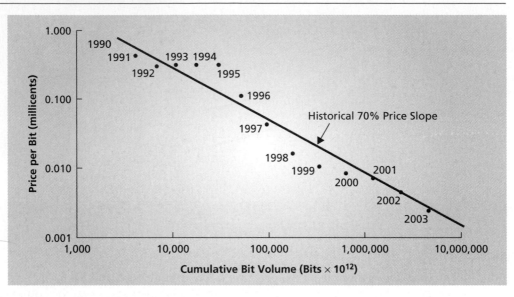

Low-Cost-Leader Pricing

The maker of BIC pens and lighters has always tried to keep its costs as low as possible and to offer a price no competitor can beat. Likewise, from its beginnings Wal-Mart sought to establish itself as the low-cost leader in retail by using a variety of management systems for reducing its cost for the goods it sells and for minimizing operating expenses. Both BIC and Wal-Mart have a volume advantage that contributes to their cost-reduction efforts, but a market's low-cost leader does not need to be the market's volume leader. Companies with smaller volumes can gain a cost advantage by having highly efficient operations, using superior technology, having highly motivated employees, and outsourcing parts of their operations. Even a low-share business can move into the low-cost-leader position.

Chi Mei, for example, is a low-cost producer of plastics and chemicals. The company operates with a minimal sales force and a small management staff, and it offers no technical services. All aspects of its business are designed to maintain a low-cost-leader position. Although Chi Mei is not its market's share or volume leader, it offers the market's lowest prices. Even in situations where customers pay more due to short supply, low-cost leaders base their prices on costs and slim margins. As illustrated in Figure 8-12, cost-based pricing by low-cost producers is most common in the growth stage of the product life cycle, a time when product differentiation is diminishing and price competition is increasing.

Multi-Segment Pricing

A primary goal of market segmentation is a form of value-based pricing known as *multi-segment pricing*. Customers in different segments of a product's market generally have different needs and different price sensitivities. A price-sensitive segment would be attracted by a low price regardless of additional product, service, or brand benefits, whereas customers in a quality-conscious segment would pay more for the additional benefits.

FIGURE 8-16 MULTI-SEGMENT PRICING

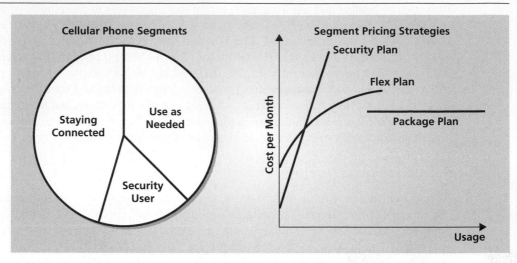

Let's consider the cellular phone market. This market consists of the three broad segments in Figure 8-16, although within each segment are many smaller segments. Customers in the *Staying Connected* segment are heavy users—people who use their phones many times a day. A package plan, with a relatively high monthly fee but a low per-minute rate, offers considerable economic value and cost certainty for customers in this segment. Customers in the *Use as Needed* segment are sporadic users, making fairly heavy use of their phones during some periods, perhaps while traveling, and light use of them during other times. Because their usage varies from month to month, their needs are best met with a flex plan that includes a set number of minutes at a moderate monthly fee, with additional minutes billed at a rate in line with the minutes covered by the monthly fee.

Finally, customers in the *Security User* segment use their phones only when essential or in emergencies. These customers like having a cellphone but, because they seldom use it, they are sensitive to its cost. For this segment, a security plan offers a low monthly fee but a high per-minute rate. All three value-based price programs are available to all customers, so customers in the different segments can choose the value-based pricing alternative that best fits their usage patterns and price sensitivities. A cellphone service provider can market to all segments at once but still serve the needs of the customers in the separate segments. As Figure 8-12 shows, multi-segment pricing is most likely to be used during the growth stage of the product life cycle.

Plus-One Pricing

As markets mature, competitors are able to emulate the best features of a business's product and, as a result, it becomes ever more difficult for the business's product to stand out as unique. To succeed in a mature market, a business needs some source of differentiation in order to maintain its product position. To do this, it can establish a plus-one product position[15] in order to justify a value-based price with a slight premium relative to competing products.

Plus-one pricing can be used when a business's product position equals competitors in every area of product and service quality, except that in one area of meaningful performance the business's product position is clearly superior. Volvo, in the luxury-car market, first strives to meet customer expectations in all aspects of performance. The company then uses safety as its plus-one product-differentiation strategy to set a value-based price relative to competing luxury cars. The safety features Volvo has designed into its cars are the business's source of differentiation and are central to Volvo's product-price positioning and value proposition. On the other hand, Lexus uses performance as its plus-one pricing strategy, and Mercedes uses its reputation. As Figure 8-12 illustrates, a plus-one pricing strategy is the value-based pricing strategy a business is most likely to use in the late stages of the product life cycle.

Reduced-Focus Pricing

As a market moves into its mature stage, prices and margins are often further eroded by intense competition. Because a business's product is still profitable in a mature market, it is not yet time for a harvest-pricing strategy. Instead, a *reduced-focus pricing* strategy can be applied to manage price and improve profits.[16]

A reduced-focus pricing strategy calls for price increases with the intent of reducing volumes and market share in exchange for higher margins. With the first price increase, many price-sensitive customers leave, and subsequent price increases further diminish their numbers. The goal is to raise prices incrementally to the point where the best combination of volume and margin is achieved.

For example, in Figure 8-17, a chemical company's paint division was in a mature market with low margins.[17] In this case, the average for the margins across the product line was 20.5 percent. As shown, just three of the products produced enough gross profit to cover their marketing and sales expenses. The reduced-focus pricing strategy resulted in the business's market share dropping from 11.7 to 8.6 percent. The share reduction corresponded with a drop in overall volume from 125 million to 92.1 million units. However, the average price for the product line increased from $1.46 to $1.85 per unit. More importantly, the average margin rose from 20.5 to 32.1 percent. This combination of volume and margin produced a gross profit of $54.6 million, $17.1 million higher than before the company implemented the reduced-focus pricing strategy. The company also curtailed the marketing expenses for three products, which further increased marketing profits. As shown in Figure 8-17, the overall net marketing contribution more than doubled, from $16 million to $36.1 million.

Harvest Pricing

During the late stages of a product's life cycle, margins are often low and volumes flat or declining. The net result is poor profits with little prospect for improvement. Many businesses in this situation are in the decline phase of the product life cycle, as illustrated in Figure 8-12. Based on cost and the need for higher margins, such a business will raise prices in anticipation of a reduction in volume. Subsequent cost-based price increases will result in higher margins as volume continues to fall. This sequence of price increases and volume reductions is normally continued until the business exits the market at a price customers simply will not pay.

Harvest pricing, however, has an interesting twist. In many instances a business will raise price to improve margins and expect to lose volume. This was true for an automobile

FIGURE 8-17 REDUCED-FOCUS PRICING STRATEGY AND PROFIT IMPACT

Area of Performance (millions)	Silicon Pigments	Primary Products	Special Products	Basic Colors	Color Enhancers	Overall Total
Market Demand	100	167	154	96	556	1,073
Market Share	10%	12%	13%	26%	9%	11.7%
Volume	10.0	20.0	20.0	25.0	50.0	125.0
Price per Unit	$4.50	$2.80	$1.60	$0.80	$0.60	$1.46
Sales Revenues	**$45.0**	**$56.0**	**$32.0**	**$20.0**	**$30.0**	**$183.0**
Cost per Unit	$3.50	$2.00	$1.30	$0.70	$0.54	$1.16
Percent Margin	22.2%	28.6%	18.8%	12.5%	10.0%	20.5%
Gross Profit	$10.0	$16.0	$6.0	$2.5	$3.0	$37.5
Marketing & Sales Expenses	$2.0	$7.0	$5.0	$3.0	$4.5	$21.5
Net Marketing Contribution	**$8.0**	**$9.0**	**$1.0**	**–$0.5**	**–$1.5**	**$16.0**

Area of Performance (millions)	Silicon Pigments	Primary Products	Special Products	Basic Colors	Color Enhancers	Overall Total
Market Demand	100	167	154	96	556	1,073
Market Share	8.6%	10.3%	10.7%	17.1%	6.0%	8.6%
Volume	8.6	17.2	16.5	16.4	33.4	92.1
Price per Unit	$4.95	$3.20	$1.90	$0.98	$0.75	$1.85
Sales Revenues	**$42.6**	**$55.0**	**$31.3**	**$16.1**	**$25.0**	**$170.0**
Cost per Unit	$3.50	$2.00	$1.30	$0.70	$0.54	$1.25
Percent Margin	29.3%	37.5%	31.6%	28.6%	28.0%	32.1%
Gross Profit	$12.5	$20.6	$9.9	$4.6	$7.0	$54.6
Marketing & Sales Expenses	$2.0	$7.0	$4.5	$2.0	$3.0	$18.5
Net Marketing Contribution	**$10.5**	**$13.6**	**$5.4**	**$2.6**	**$4.0**	**$36.1**

components manufacturer that raised prices 15 percent and lost the anticipated 30 percent of its business volume. A subsequent price increase of 10 percent, however, resulted in only a modest decrease in volume, and a third 10 percent price increase a year later resulted in no decrease in volume. At this combination of price and volume, the business had uncovered a

FIGURE 8-18 HARVEST PRICING AND PROFITABILITY

Market Situation	Price	Volume	Sales	Unit Cost	Margin per Unit	Gross Profit
Late in life cycle	$10.00	10 million	$100 million	$10.00	$0	$0
15% price increase	$11.50	7 million	$80.50	$10.00	$1.50	$10.5 million
10% price increase	$12.65	6 million	$75.90	$10.00	$2.65	$15.9 million
10% price increase	$13.92	6 million	$83.49	$10.00	$3.92	$23.5 million

FIGURE 8-19 PRICE-VOLUME SALES STRATEGY

Performance Factor	Metric	Current	Strategy
Market Demand	units	50,000	50,000
Market Share	%	20.0%	25.0%
Volume Sold	units	10,000	12,500
Average Selling Price	$/unit	$1,000	$900
Net Sales	$	$10,000,000	$11,250,000

profitable niche market and was able to manage price and volume to produce an attractive gross profit, as illustrated in Figure 8-18.

PRICING AND PROFITABILITY

Sales growth is an obsession in most businesses. Marketing and sales managers, as well as general managers and CEOs, generally believe that more is better: "If those in marketing can deliver more volume, more market share, and more sales revenues, then we can grow profits." This may be true in many cases, but managers need to be especially careful when using price to achieve this objective. Let's examine a fairly common business situation.

A business's senior management has challenged the marketing and sales team to grow sales revenues at a rate greater than 10 percent. The business's product-markets are price sensitive, and the marketing and sales team judges that a 10 percent price decrease would result in a volume gain of 25 percent, with sales revenues increasing from $10 million to $11.25 million, as shown in Figure 8-19.

The problem with this sales-oriented approach is that the strategy would lose money! As the analysis in Figure 8-20 illustrates, this lower-price strategy would indeed grow sales revenues, but it would not grow profit. It would, in fact, lead to a significant decline in profit. The 25 percent increase in volume would not offset a 30 percent reduction in margin. The goal of a pricing strategy should be to increase profit—not to increase sales or volumes. In this example, a pricing strategy to grow sales 11.5 percent would lower gross profit by almost 16.7 percent. Because all other fixed manufacturing, marketing, and operating expenses would not

FIGURE 8-20 PRICE-VOLUME STRATEGY AND PROFIT IMPACT

Performance Factor	Metric	Current	Strategy
Market Demand	units	50,000	50,000
Market Share	%	20.0%	25.0%
Volume Sold	units	10,000	12,500
Average Selling Price	$/unit	$1,000	$900
Net Sales	$	$10,000,000	$11,250,000
Unit Cost	$/unit	$700	$700
Percent Margin	%	30.0%	22.2%
Gross Profit	$	$3,000,000	$2,500,000

FIGURE 8-21 PRICE-VOLUME PROFITABILITY

Performance Factor	Metric	Current	Strategy
Market Demand	units	50,000	50,000
Market Share	%	20.0%	30.0%
Volume Sold	units	10,000	15,000
Average Selling Price	$/unit	$1,000	$900
Net Sales	$	$10,000,000	$13,500,000
Unit Cost	$/unit	$700	$700
Percent Margin	%	30.0%	22.2%
Gross Profit	$	$3,000,000	$3,000,000

change, the pricing strategy would lower overall profit. Marketing strategies that deliver superior sales growth but fail to contribute to profit will eventually bankrupt a company.[18]

To continue with our example, the first question the marketing and sales team should ask itself before lowering price, or before raising it, is: How much volume do we need to *maintain the current level of profitability?* As illustrated in the calculation that follows and in Figure 8-21, to maintain a gross profit of $3 million, a strategy that lowers price 10 percent would require a 50 percent share gain (from 20 to 30 percent), assuming no change in market demand. A 50 percent share gain would in turn produce a 50 percent volume gain. The required increases in share and volume are double those that the marketing and sales team had projected.

$$\text{Gross Profit} = \text{Market Demand} \times \text{Market Share} \times (\text{Unit Price} - \text{Unit Cost})$$

$$\textbf{Market Share Needed} = \frac{\text{Gross Profit Desired}}{(\text{Market Demand})(\text{Unit Price} - \text{Unit Cost})}$$

$$= \frac{3,000,000}{(50,000)(900-700)} = \frac{3,000,000}{(50,000)(200)} = \frac{3,000,000}{10,000,000} = .3 = \textbf{30\%}$$

While price elasticities are often hard to estimate, we can accurately determine the price elasticity needed to produce a profitable pricing strategy. In this case, the calculation that follows shows profits would be maintained with a price elasticity of −5, which means that for every 1 percent price decrease, volume increases 5 percent. A 10 percent price decrease, then, would produce a 50 percent volume increase. But this would just maintain current profits. To increase profits in this example, the price elasticity would need to be larger than −5. Price elasticities of this magnitude are rare, as would be a 10 point share gain with only a 10 percent price decrease. This pricing strategy, while it may grow sales, would almost certainly lower profits.

$$\textbf{Price Elasticity} = \frac{\text{Percentage Change in Volume}}{\text{Percentage Change in Price}}$$

$$= \frac{5,000/10,000}{(100/1000)(-1)} = \frac{0.5}{-0.1} = \textbf{-5}$$

FIGURE 8-22 TELECOMMUNICATIONS SERVICE PRICE ELASTICITY

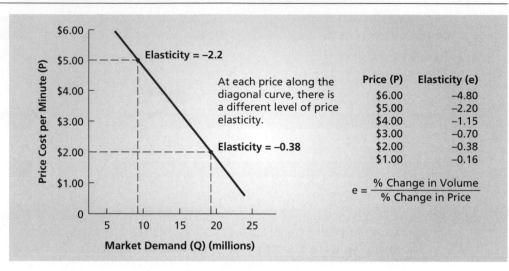

PRICE ELASTICITY AND PROFITABILITY

In most markets, market demand and market growth are dependent on price level. High prices deter customers from entering a market, as we saw in Chapter 3, and low prices attract customers. As prices for cellphone service, CD players, and computers have fallen, more customers have entered those markets. In one sense, price governs both the size of a market and how fast it will grow.

Figure 8-22 shows how market demand for voice messaging varies as a function of price. A telecommunications business that wants to limit initial demand for this service until it has the capacity to serve a large number of customers decides to price the service at $5 per minute. This price produces an estimated demand of 9,000 customers in a particular geographic market. At this price, the price elasticity is –2.2, which means that for each 1 percent reduction in price, demand will grow by approximately 2.2 percent. A 10 percent price reduction from $5.00 to $4.50 should then yield a 22 percent increase in customer demand (from 9,000 to 10,980).

A business might continue to lower price to grow demand, but when the price elasticity reaches –1, sales revenue will have reached its maximum potential. At this point, a price change either up or down would lower sales revenue. This price point would be ideal for a nonprofit organization that conducts fund-raising events, because the organization would be maximizing its revenues. A business, however, would price above or below this price point in an effort to maximize its profits.

Inelastic Price Management

As shown in Figure 8-23, when a price is inelastic, all aspects of performance are improved when prices are increased. Lowering price when it is inelastic will hurt sales, margins, and gross profit but increase unit volume.

For example, Yellow Pages advertising is known to be price inelastic, with an elasticity of approximately –0.7. What would be the consequence of a Yellow Pages business

FIGURE 8-23 PRICE ELASTICITY—VOLUME, SALES, AND PROFITABILITY

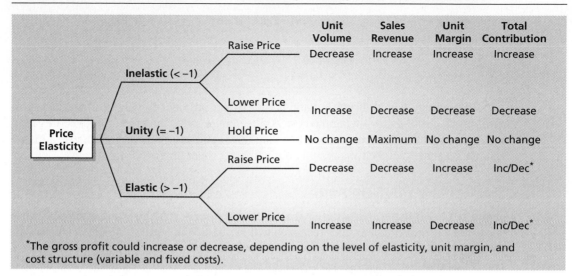

		Unit Volume	Sales Revenue	Unit Margin	Total Contribution
Inelastic (< –1)	Raise Price	Decrease	Increase	Increase	Increase
	Lower Price	Increase	Decrease	Decrease	Decrease
Unity (= –1)	Hold Price	No change	Maximum	No change	No change
Elastic (> –1)	Raise Price	Decrease	Decrease	Increase	Inc/Dec*
	Lower Price	Increase	Increase	Decrease	Inc/Dec*

*The gross profit could increase or decrease, depending on the level of elasticity, unit margin, and cost structure (variable and fixed costs).

lowering the price on its $100 ads by 10 percent? Assume that the business normally sells one million of those ads and that its variable cost is $50 per ad. The results are a unit margin of $50, sales revenues of $100 million, and a gross profit of $50 million.

Current Price Situation

Price per Ad = $100	Variable Cost per Ad = $50
Ad Volume = 1 million ads	Margin per Ad = $50
Sales Revenue = $100 million	Gross Profit = $50 million

A decision to lower prices by 10 percent when the price elasticity is equal to –0.7 would produce the following performance:

Lower-Price Strategy

Price per Ad = $90	Variable Cost per Ad = $50
Ad Volume = 1.07 million ads	Margin per Ad = $40
Sales Revenue = $96.3 million	Gross Profit = $42.8 million

The decision to lower price by 10 percent when prices were inelastic lowered margins by $10 per ad, lowered sales by $3.7 million, and lowered gross profit by $7.2 million, even though volume increased. This would have been a disastrous pricing decision. A business that does not know its price is inelastic could easily follow a strategy of lowering prices in response to competitor moves or customer concerns about price.

The correct strategy in this case would be to raise price, because the price is inelastic. A strategy to raise price by 10 percent when the price elasticity is –0.7 would produce the following estimate of performance:

Raise-Price Strategy

Price per Ad = $110	Variable Cost per Ad = $50
Ad Volume = 0.93 million ads	Margin per Ad = $60
Sales Revenue = $102.3 million	Gross Profit = $55.8 million

This strategy would increase margins by $10 per ad, sales by $2.3 million, and gross profit by $5.8 million. Knowing the correct direction to move the price improved this business's gross profit by 10 percent, while giving up 70,000 ads. Although there was a loss of unit market share (number of ads sold), dollar market share improved significantly.

Elastic Price Management

Figure 8-23 also shows that arriving at a successful pricing strategy is more difficult when prices are elastic. Although sales revenues will increase with a price cut and decrease with a price increase, the change in gross profit will depend on the level of price elasticity. Though a price may be elastic, it may not be elastic enough to produce the volume increase needed to more than offset the margin decrease created by a price cut.[19]

For example, let's assume that the price elasticity for the same Yellow Pages ad is –1.5. This is clearly an elastic price, and one that could lead many businesses to lower price to grow sales and volume. However, as the following shows, a strategy to lower price by 10 percent would lower the gross profit by $4 million.

Lower-Price Strategy

Price per Ad = $90	Variable Cost per Ad = $50
Ad Volume = 1.15 million ads	Margin per Ad = $40
Sales Revenue = $103.5 million	Gross Profit = $46 million

A strategy to raise prices by 10 percent when the price elasticity is –1.5 would result in less ad volume and sales revenue, but it would produce higher margins and a larger gross profit.

Raise-Price Strategy

Price per Ad = $110	Variable Cost per Ad = $50
Ad Volume = 0.85 million ads	Margin per Ad = $60
Sales Revenue = $93.5 million	Gross Profit = $51 million

The biggest challenge in using price elasticities is not the calculations; it is estimating a value for price elasticity. Every time a business changes its price, it has the opportunity to compute the actual price elasticity. It must do so, because market conditions change and those changes affect price elasticity. When the ease of switching suppliers is average, as in a buyer's market where supply exceeds demand, price elasticities can be high, as illustrated in Figures 8-24 and 8-25. Similarly, if the market shifted to a seller's market during a period of short supply, the price elasticities could drop to much lower levels for the same product.

FIGURE 8-24 FORCES THAT SHAPE PRICE ELASTICITY

Ease of Customer Switching	0	0.5	1	Score
Product Differentiation	Extensive	Some	None	0
Cost of Switching Suppliers	High	Modest	Low	0
Customer Loyalty	High	Modest	Low	.5
Ease of Switching Index				**.5**

Supply/Demand Conditions	0	0.5	1	Score
Supply Conditions	Short	Adequate	Excess	.5
Demand Conditions	Strong	Modest	Weak	0
Substitutes	None	Few	Many	.5
Supply/Demand Index				**1.0**

Customers' Switching Capacity

One dimension of price elasticity is the ease or difficulty of switching. The easier it is for customers to switch suppliers of a product or to substitute products, the higher the price elasticity. The level of product differentiation, cost of switching, and customer loyalty all impact the switching capacity of customers, as the following points make clear.

FIGURE 8-25 GUIDELINES FOR ESTIMATING PRICE ELASTICITY

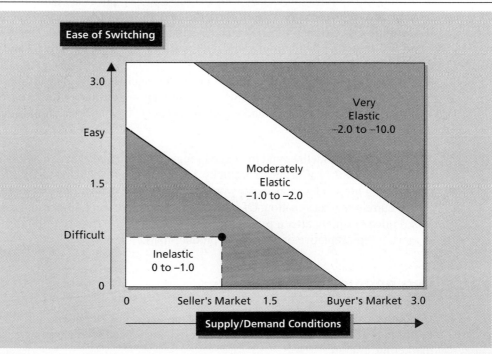

- **Product Differentiation:** The more unique a product is in its overall benefits, the more difficult it is for customers to replace the product with competitors' products or substitutes. In markets where product differentiation is strong, price elasticity is usually lower.
- **Cost of Switching:** The more expensive it is for customers to change suppliers, the harder it is for customers to switch to competitors when prices increase. Higher switching costs generally result in lower price elasticities.
- **Customer Loyalty:** The more loyal customers are to a brand or company, the less likely they will switch suppliers when prices go up. When customer loyalty is low, however, the ease of switching is much greater and prices are more elastic.

A manager can assess the ease of switching for a specific product-market by estimating levels of product differentiation, switching costs, and customer loyalty, and then calculating an ease of switching index, as in Figure 8-24. The index would roughly approximate one dimension of price elasticity for use in the guideline scale presented in Figure 8-25.

Supply-and-Demand Conditions

In markets where supply outpaces demand, price elasticity is usually high. In the family car market, for example, price elasticity is high because customers can easily buy a comparable product from many sources. But in markets where demand outpaces supply, as with Toyota's Prius, price elasticity is much lower. Supply conditions, demand conditions, and substitutes all have an impact on price elasticity, as described in these guidelines:

- **Supply Conditions:** In markets with an excess supply, prices are generally more elastic. In markets where supply is short, even in commodity markets, prices can be inelastic.
- **Demand Conditions:** When demand is strong and growing, prices tend to be less elastic. On the other hand, in markets with weak or flat demand, prices tend to be more price sensitive.
- **Substitutes:** In markets with many substitutes, such as in the soft drink market, price sensitivity is high because customers have numerous substitute products from which to choose. In pharmaceutical markets, many products have few substitutes, which lowers price elasticity.

Using these guidelines and the scale in Figure 8-25, a manager can assess market conditions and how they affect price elasticity. Using the supply/demand index, along with the ease of switching index, a manager would then calculate the elasticity of a product's price for the current market situation. Of course, assessing market conditions and calculating the actual price elasticity after a price change would enable a business to modify Figure 8-22 to make it representative of its specific product-market.

PRICE AND BREAK-EVEN ANALYSIS

Break-even analysis is generally viewed as an accounting concept, but it is extremely useful in evaluating the profit potential and risk associated with a pricing strategy or any marketing strategy.[20]

Price and Break-Even Volume

For a given pricing strategy and marketing effort, it is useful to determine the number of units that need to be sold in order to break even—that is, to produce an operating income equal to zero. Let's assume a business has a margin per unit of $2 and total fixed expenses (manufacturing, marketing, and operating expenses) of $50 million. We can see immediately that sales of 25 million units are required to break even: A margin of $2 per unit on 25 million units produces $50 million, the amount needed to equal the fixed expenses and give the business a zero operating income. The business's break-even volume, then, is 25 million units. It is the volume needed to cover fixed expenses, given the $2 margin per unit.

An actual business's fixed expenses and margin per unit are not likely to be round numbers that would make it easy to compute the break-even volume in our heads, so let's extrapolate a formula for figuring the break-even volume from the formula used for figuring operating income.

$$\text{Operating Income} = \text{Volume} \times \text{Margin per Unit} - \text{Fixed Expenses}$$

$$\textbf{Volume} = \frac{\text{Operating Income} + \text{Fixed Expenses}}{\text{Margin per Unit}}$$

$$= \frac{0 + 50 \text{ million}}{2}$$

$$= \textbf{25 million units}$$

In calculating the break-even volume, we want the operating income to equal zero in the equation. A zero used as an addend has no effect on the calculation for the break-even volume, so we can simplify the formula.

$$\text{Break-Even Volume} = \frac{\text{Fixed Expenses}}{\text{Margin per Unit}}$$

The lower the break-even volume is relative to manufacturing capacity or expected sales volume, the greater the profit potential.

Price and Break-Even Market Share

Because break-even volume is an unconstrained number, the reasonableness of the break-even volume requires additional considerations. Market share, in contrast, is constrained between 0 and 100 percent, and so break-even market share provides a better framework for judging profit potential and risk. Computing the break-even market share requires only that we divide the break-even volume by the size of the target market.

$$\text{Break-Even Market Share} = \frac{\text{Break-Even Volume}}{\text{Market Demand}}$$

With a break-even volume of 25 million units, if the market demand for the product were 200 million units per year, then the break-even market share would be 12.5 percent. The business has a 24 percent market share, which is 11.5 share points above break even, as shown in Figure 8-26. If the business had only a 15 percent share of its target market, the risk of a loss would be greater because the business's share would be closer to the break-even share.

FIGURE 8-26 BREAK-EVEN VOLUME AND BREAK-EVEN MARKET SHARE

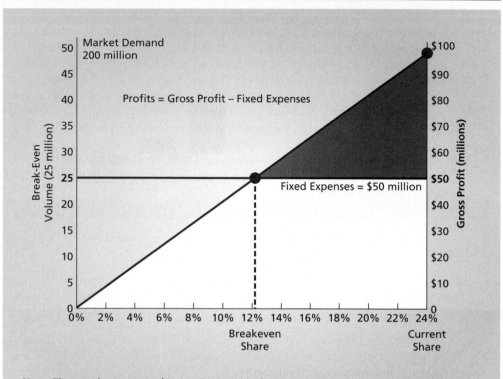

Note: The graph assumes a $2 margin per unit that remains constant as volume grows, although a significant rise in volume normally leads to a lower variable cost per unit, which improves margin. Ever-greater margins would result in more gross profit than shown.

PRODUCT LINE PRICING

As a business adds more products to its product line, it enhances sales growth but also increases the risk of cannibalizing existing product sales. It is necessary, then, to know both a product's price elasticity and the degree to which a cross elasticity exists with other products. Products that have a positive cross elasticity are substitutes; lowering the price of one product will decrease the demand for the other product. Products that have a negative cross elasticity are complementary products; lowering the price for one product will increase the demand for both products. Because the margins may be different for alternative products in a product line, a business needs to give careful consideration to any price change to ensure that the total profits for the entire product line will increase.

Pricing Substitute Products

In extending its product line, a business must recognize that some cannibalization will occur if customers can easily substitute one product in the line for another. Figure 8-27

FIGURE 8-27 PRICE AND CROSS-PRICE ELASTICITY OF COMPETING LAUNDRY DETERGENT BRANDS

Brand	Share (%)	Wisk	Tide	Surf	Era	Solo	Cheer	Bold-3	All	Fab
Wisk	22.7	−1.37	0.31	0.37	0.23	0.11	0.12	0.09	0.08	0.07
Tide	21.5	0.33	−1.39	0.37	0.23	0.11	0.13	0.09	0.08	0.07
Surf	19.5	0.48	0.46	−1.91	0.33	0.16	0.16	0.12	0.11	0.09
Era	13.5	0.36	0.33	0.39	−1.57	0.11	0.12	0.10	0.08	0.07
Solo	5.9	0.36	0.34	0.41	0.25	−1.78	0.13	0.11	0.10	0.07
Cheer	4.9	0.46	0.47	0.47	0.31	0.15	−2.20	0.12	0.13	0.09
Bold-3	4.4	0.49	0.44	0.49	0.34	0.18	0.16	−2.32	0.11	0.10
All	3.6	0.48	0.46	0.50	0.32	0.17	0.20	0.12	−2.36	0.10
Fab	3.6	0.50	0.50	0.49	0.33	0.16	0.17	0.14	0.12	−2.41

Elasticities: A 1% price change in the brand column creates the percent change in market share for each row of brands.

shows the price elasticities and market shares for nine laundry detergents, along with their cross elasticities.[21] The results of this empirical study illustrate the price elasticity of each brand of detergent, as well as the cross elasticity of substitutes. As shown, cross elasticity is much higher for the higher-share brands.

- **Tide Price Increase:** A 10 percent increase in Tide's price would lower Tide volume by 13.9 percent and increase the volume of Surf by 3.7 percent.
- **Surf Price Decrease:** A 10 percent decrease in Surf's price would increase Surf volume by 19.1 percent and lower Tide volume by 4.6 percent.

To fully understand the effects of product line substitutes, let's examine two coffees sold in the same coffee shop. Figure 8-28 shows the shop's regular coffee priced at $1.50 a cup and a specialty coffee priced at $2.50 a cup. The regular coffee is price elastic (elasticity equal to –2), while the specialty coffee is inelastic (–0.8). However, the regular coffee drinkers generally would be inclined to switch to the specialty coffee if the specialty coffee price is lowered, as the cross elasticity is 0.4. In contrast, the specialty coffee drinkers generally would not be inclined to switch to regular coffee if the price for the specialty coffee is raised, as the cross elasticity is 0.2. Although many pricing strategies could be tested, a 10 percent increase in the price of the specialty coffee should increase the coffee shop's monthly gross profit from $10,000 to $10,850, as shown in Figure 8-28.

Pricing Complementary Products

Of course, products that are complements will also be affected by a price change. Software, printers, and scanners are products that complement personal computers, and so the demand for these products varies with the price of personal computers. If the cross elasticity between PCs and spreadsheet programs were –0.6, then for each 1 percent change in the price of PCs, there would be a 0.6 percent change in the demand for

FIGURE 8-28 PRODUCT LINE PRICE IMPACT WITH SUBSTITUTE PRODUCTS

Price Elasticities	Regular	Specialty
Regular	-2.0	0.4
Specialty	0.2	-0.8

Current Situation

Coffee Product	Price	Volume	Sales	Cost	Margin	Profit
Regular	$1.50	10,000	$15,000	$1.00	33.3%	$5,000
Specialty	$2.50	5,000	$12,500	$1.50	40.0%	$5,000
Total	$1.83	15,000	$27,500	$1.17	36.4%	$10,000

Raise Price of Specialty Coffee 10%

Coffee Product	Price	Volume	Sales	Cost	Margin	Profit
Regular	$1.50	10,200	$15,300	$1.00	33.3%	$5,100
Specialty	$2.75	4,600	$12,650	$1.50	45.5%	$5,750
Total	$1.89	14,800	$27,950	$1.16	38.8%	$10,850

Lower Price of Regular Coffee 10%

Coffee Product	Price	Volume	Sales	Cost	Margin	Profit
Regular	$1.35	12,000	$16,200	$1.00	25.9%	$4,200
Specialty	$2.50	4,800	$12,000	$1.50	40.0%	$4,800
Total	$1.68	16,800	$28,200	$1.14	31.9%	$9,000

spreadsheet programs. If computer industry prices decrease by 10 percent, the demand for spreadsheet programs should go up by 6 percent. Conversely, if the price of personal computers were to increase by 10 percent, the demand for spreadsheet programs would go down by 6 percent.

For a better grasp of the effects of product line complements, let's examine how coffee and pastries are sold in the same coffee shop. The coffee is priced at $1.50 a cup and the pastries are $2.20 each, as shown in Figure 8-29. The coffee is a bit more price elastic (elasticity equal to -2) than the pastries (-1.5). However, customers who patronize the shop primarily for the coffee also often buy pastries, whereas the customers who come to the shop mainly for the pastries frequently do not also buy a cup of coffee. An increase in coffee sales, then, would also result in an increase in pastry sales, as the cross elasticity is -0.4. In contrast, additional pastry sales would not have much of an impact on coffee sales, because the cross elasticity is -0.1. As Figure 8-29 shows, a 10 percent decrease in the coffee price would increase the sales of both coffee and pastries, as we would assume. But this pricing strategy would be a mistake, as it would actually result in a slight decrease in the profit.

FIGURE 8-29 PRODUCT LINE PRICE IMPACT WITH COMPLEMENTARY PRODUCTS

Price Change	Coffee	Pastries
Coffee	−2.0	−0.4
Pastries	−0.1	−1.5

Current Situation

Coffee Product	Price	Volume	Sales	Cost	Margin	Profit
Coffee	$1.50	15,000	$22,500	$0.75	50.0%	$11,250
Pastries	$2.00	5,000	$10,000	$0.75	62.5%	$6,250
Total	$1.63	20,000	$32,500	$0.75	53.8%	$17,500

Raise Price of Pastries 10%

Coffee Product	Price	Volume	Sales	Cost	Margin	Profit
Coffee	$1.50	14,850	$22,275	$0.75	50.0%	$11,138
Pastries	$2.20	4,250	$9,350	$0.75	65.9%	$6,163
Total	$1.66	19,100	$31,625	$0.75	54.7%	$17,300

Lower Price of Regular Coffee 10%

Coffee Product	Price	Volume	Sales	Cost	Margin	Profit
Coffee	$1.35	18,000	$24,300	$0.75	44.4%	$10,800
Pastries	$2.00	5,200	$10,400	$0.75	62.5%	$6,500
Total	$1.50	23,200	34,700	$0.75	49.9%	$17,300

■ Summary

Customer value and business profitability depend on effective pricing strategies. High prices do wonders for margins but often result in low customer value, especially when a product's perceived benefits are less than its perceived price. In competitive markets where product differentiation is high, value-based pricing presents a pricing logic designed to deliver superior value for customers and high profitability for businesses.

Value-based pricing starts with customer needs, competitors' positions, and the business's product positioning, and then works backward to margin. In contrast, cost-based pricing starts with the cost of the product and a desired margin and then works forward to a market price. Cost-based pricing often leads to under- and overpricing in markets where significant product differentiation is possible. But in markets where differentiation is minimal and customers are price sensitive, cost-based pricing can be a viable approach to pricing. In this chapter we presented three value-based pricing methodologies:

■ **Value-in-Use Pricing:** Price is based on providing a customer an attractive savings after considering the life-cycle costs of acquiring, owning, using, maintaining, and disposing of a product.

■ **Perceived-Value Pricing:** Price is based on the value provided customers in terms of the price and benefits of the company's product compared to those of key competitors.

■ **Performance-Based Pricing:** Price is set based on customer preferences for different levels of price and performance and how the company and competitors are positioned with respect to delivering both price and performance.

Implementation of any pricing strategy results in a price waterfall. It starts with a "street price" offer to end-user customers and ends with a pocket price, the price the company receives after all channel discounts, promotional incentives, rebates, sales commissions, and inefficiencies. The pocket-price bandwidth is the percentage difference between the lowest and highest pocket price. Pocket-price bandwidths of 50 percent are common, and bandwidths over 100 percent are not rare. The pocket-price bandwidth needs to be understood and managed to ensure that margins are not being needlessly diminished.

Different value-based and cost-based pricing strategies are especially suitable for particular phases of the product life cycle. During the early stages of the life cycle, skim pricing, single-segment pricing, and penetration pricing are usually the appropriate strategies. As markets enter their growth phase, many companies focus on multi-segment value-added pricing, while low-cost leaders create value with a low price. As its product moves into the mature phase of the life cycle and becomes more commoditized, a business can use a plus-one strategy to differentiate the product based on a benefit meaningful to customers. Other businesses may pursue a reduced-focus strategy in an effort to shed price-sensitive customers to the point where a price-volume combination yields lower sales but higher profits. Finally, in the decline stage of the product life cycle a business may need to pursue a harvest-pricing strategy, raising prices systematically and reducing its marketing effort in anticipation of exiting the market. But some businesses, after implementing a harvest-pricing strategy, discover a profitable niche market that prompts a return to premium pricing.

Changes in price affect both volume and margin. A price decrease that grows volume and sales but results in a decrease in total contribution adversely impacts a business's profits. The goal of any pricing strategy should be to grow or at least maintain profits. A business always needs to determine how the gross profit will change with a price increase or decrease.

Because price affects margin, and because a certain level of fixed expenses is needed to achieve a certain level of market penetration, a business needs to assess the profit potential and risk of any pricing strategy it considers. A break-even volume analysis is helpful in assessing profit potential and risk, but not as helpful as a break-even market share analysis. Because a business's market share is always constrained between 0 and 100 percent, whereas volumes are unconstrained, the break-even market share is a better relative index by which profit potential and risk can be judged. Break-even market share enables a business to gauge the profit potential and risk of a pricing strategy by considering the target share in light of the difference between the business's current share and its break-even market share. For businesses operating below break even, a market share break-even analysis will also show the feasibility of achieving a break-even volume within a market context.

Price-volume relationships are made more complex by varying degrees of price elasticity. Price elasticity is a measure of price sensitivity. When prices are inelastic, price increases result in a decrease in volume but an increase in sales revenue and profits. A price decrease when prices are inelastic would result in higher volume but lower sales revenue and lower profits. When prices are elastic, a price decrease will result in higher volumes and higher sales revenue. Yet, profits may go down if margins are low. Price elasticities are not easy to estimate, and any change in customers' capacity to switch suppliers or a market's supply-and-demand conditions will cause price elasticities to vary. Understanding these forces and tracking price elasticities that result from price changes allows a business to build a set of guidelines for estimating price elasticity.

Product line pricing decisions are also complicated by cross elasticity. The price elasticity for a product may signal a particular pricing strategy, but when cross elasticity exists between products in the same line, a business needs a very careful analysis of the profit impact of a price change. The demand for products that are substitutes will change in the direction of the price change of the substitute. The demand for complementary products will change inversely to a price change in the product they complement.

■ Market-Based Strategic Thinking

1 How could cost-based pricing lead to a price lower than customers would have paid? How does this impact the profit of a business?

2 How could cost-based pricing lead to a price higher than target customers are willing to pay? How does this impact the profit of a business?

3 How does value-based pricing differ from cost-based pricing? What does a business do if the value-based price is not high enough to deliver desired levels of profitability?

4 How would an earthmoving equipment manufacturer go about determining its customer value using value-in-use pricing?

5 How would the earthmoving equipment manufacturer select a value price using value-in-use pricing?

6 How would Toyota use perceived-value pricing to set a price for the Prius? How would Toyota select a specific price that delivered a meaningful customer value?

7 At what price would the Prius not have any perceived customer value?

8 How could Toyota use performance-based pricing to determine a price that would create a good value for customers and a good price for Toyota?

9 What is the pocket price for a car like the Prius? How can the price waterfall help a company like Toyota improve its pocket price and profit margin?

10 How could the business illustrated in Figure 8-11 improve its profits by reducing its pocket-price bandwidth from 53 to 33 percent?

11 Why would Apple use a skim-pricing strategy for a new Apple product?

12 What kind of pricing is used for single-segment pricing? Why is single-segment pricing used early in the product life cycle?

13 Why would a business use a penetration-pricing strategy instead of a single-segment strategy? How does the penetration-pricing strategy create customer value?

14 How is a low-cost-leader-pricing strategy different than a penetration-pricing strategy?

15 Why would a business use multi-segment pricing in the early phase of the late-growth stage of the product life cycle?

16 What is plus-one pricing and why is it more likely to be used in the mature stage of the product life cycle?

17 What is reduced-focus pricing? How can a business possibility be more profitable with fewer customers and lower volumes?

18 Why would a business use harvest pricing? Why do many businesses using harvest pricing never exit the market?

19 How would a business estimate the price elasticity needed for a price decrease that would maintain the current level of profits?

20 Why would a business always raise price when it is inelastic?

21 When price elasticity is –1.5 to –2.0, why would a price reduction result in larger volumes, higher market share, and greater sales but lower profits?

22 Use the matrix presented in Figure 8-25, and the factors that determine a product's position in this matrix, to position (a) Apple iPod, (b) Toyota Prius, (c) Hamm's beer, and (d) Verizon Wireless.

23 Why is break-even market share more useful than break-even volume?

24 What happens to a substitute product when the price of another product in a business's product line is increased by 10 percent when the cross elasticity is –0.4? Why would a business intentionally shift sales volume from one product to another in its product line?

25 What happens to a complementary product when the price of another product in the product line is decreased by 10 percent when the cross elasticity is –0.4?

Marketing Performance Tools

The five **Marketing Performance Tools** described here may be accessed online at *www.rogerjbest.com*. These applied-learning exercises will add to your understanding of value-based pricing, pricing strategies, and price elasticity. The figure numbers that appear after the captions are related examples in Chapter 8, but the bulleted instructions pertain to the online examples.

8.1 Value-in-Use Pricing (Figure 8-4)
■ The life-cycle costs for a business's products that extend the life of machine fluids appear in the first example. Assess the economic value for several price points and select a price that creates a meaningful value for customers.
■ In this example, let's assume the usage cost for the business's product is futher reduced to $2.50 per pound. How would this impact customer value and the perception of the value price of $2.45?

8.2 Perceived-Value Pricing (Figures 8-5 and 8-6)
■ Assume the business can improve its ease of use from a 5.6 rating to a 7.5 rating. How would this change the overall benefits and customer value at the current price of $6,250?
■ With this higher ease-of-use rating, how would the customer value index change if the business raised its price to $6,500 and the business's rating on price of equipment increased from 7.5 to 8.0? Would you recommend this price increase?

8.3 Performance-Based Value Pricing (Figures 8-7 and 8-8)
■ Create three levels of car performance important to you for the performance factors and three levels of price. Modify the information presented to represent your performance factors, performance levels, and price level. Then print the choice matrix

and rank the nine alternatives from 1 (most preferred) to 9 (least preferred).

■ Input your preferences in ranked order and print the results. Interpret your performance-price curves and compute the total value for each of two cars, one of which you prefer and a competing car you do not prefer. How much more would you pay for your preferred car, and how would that change the value advantage?

8.4 Price-Volume Pricing (Figures 8-23 to 8-25)

■ The price elasticity for personal computers is estimated to be –2.0. For the PC manufacturer shown, evaluate the sales and profit impact of a 10 percent price increase and a 10 percent price decrease.

■ For each pricing strategy, determine the break-even market share and discuss the profit risk associated with each pricing strategy.

8.5 Product Line Pricing (Figures 8-28 and 8-29)

■ The elasticities and cross elasticities are shown for an umbrella brand and a flanker brand. Input a price increase of 10 percent for the flanker brand and evaluate its impact on sales and profit. Then input a price decrease of 10 percent and evaluate its impact. Which new price, if either, would you recommend for the flanker brand product line?

■ The elasticities and cross elasticities are shown for a leading brand of snack food sold in taverns. Input a price increase of 10 percent and evaluate its impact on sales and profit. Then input a price decrease of 10 percent and evaluate its impact. Which new price, if either, would you recommend for the product line?

Notes

1. P. Noble and T. Gruca, "Industrial Pricing: Theory and Managerial Practice," *Marketing Science,* 18, 3 (1999): 435–454.
2. G. Cressman, Jr., "Commentary on Industrial Pricing: Theory and Managerial Practice," *Marketing Science,* 18, 3 (1999): 455–457.
3. Roger J. Best, "Marketing Excellence Survey," www. MESurvey.com: (accessed September 2004).
4. A. Cleland and A. Bruno, *The Market Value Process* (San Francisco: Jossey-Bass, 1996): 106; and D. Kirkpatrick, "The Revolution at Compaq Computer," *Fortune* (December 14, 1992): 80–88.
5. Michael Morris and Gene Morris, *Market-Oriented Pricing* (Lincolnwood, IL: NTC Business Books, 1990): 93–100.
6. R. Dolan and H. Simon, *Power Pricing* (New York: Free Press, 1966): 82–83.
7. Thomas Nagle and John Hogan, *The Strategy and Tactics of Pricing* (Upper Saddle River, NJ: Prentice Hall, 2006): 27–44.
8. Gerald Smith and Thomas Nagle, "A Question of Value," *Marketing Management* (July–August 2005): 39–43.
9. Bradley Gale, *Managing Customer Value* (New York: Free Press, 1994).
10. John Morton and Hugh Devine, "How to Diagnose What Buyers Really Want," *Business Marketing* (October 1985): 70–83.
11. J. Axelrod and N. Frendberg, "Conjoint Analysis," *Marketing Research* (June 1990): 28–35; P. Green and V. Srinivasan, "Conjoint Analysis in Marketing Research," *Journal of Marketing* (October 1990): 3–19; D. Wittink and P. Cattin, "Commercial Use of Conjoint Analysis," *Journal of Marketing* (July 1989): 19–96; and A. Page and H. Rosenbaum, "Redesigning Product Lines with Conjoint Analysis," *Journal of Product Management* (1987): 120–137.
12. Michael V. Marn, Eric V. Roegner, and Craig C. Zawada, *The Price Advantage* (Hoboken, NJ: John Wiley & Sons, 2004): 24–37.
13. Thomas Nagle and John Hogan, *The Strategy and Tactics of Pricing* (Upper Saddle River, NJ: Prentice Hall, 2006): 265–274.
14. California Technology Stock Letter (February 4, 1999): 4.
15. Geoffrey Moore, *Inside the Tornado* (New York: HarperCollins, 1985).
16. Kathryn Rudie Harrigan, "Strategies for Declining Industries," *Journal of Business Strategy* (Fall 1980): 20–34.

17. George Seiler, "Colorful Chemicals Cuts Its Losses," *Planning Review* (January–February 1987): 16–22.

18. Gerald Smith and Thomas Nagle, "Financial Analysis for Profit-Driven Pricing," *Sloan Management Review* (Spring 1994): 71–84.

19. R. Dolan and H. Simon, *Power Pricing* (New York: Free Press, 1996): 222–241.

20. Thomas Nagle and John Hogan, *The Strategy and Tactics of Pricing* (Upper Saddle River, NJ: Prentice Hall, 2006): 175–204.

21. Gerard Tellis, "The Price Elasticity of Selective Demand: A Meta-Analysis of Econometric Models of Sales," *Journal of Marketing Research* (November 1988): 331–341.

CHAPTER 9

Marketing Channels and Channel Mapping

■ Marketing channels are the conduits that create customer access to a company's products.

No matter how great the benefits of a product may be, how attractive its price, and how alluring the communication of the value proposition, without marketing channels there can be no sales. Marketing channels make it possible for target customers to buy the business's product at their desired points of purchase. For some customers, the preferred point of purchase may be a retail store, while others prefer to buy online, through a catalog, or from the business's sales representative.

Marketing channels connect businesses with their target customers. As shown in Figure 9-1 an electronics manufacturer utilizes a combination of direct and indirect marketing channels to reach three different target market segments. The purpose of this chapter is to understand how channel partners impact marketing channel performance, and to examine the ways that marketing channels can be configured to reach customers with different needs.

In this chapter, we will also discover the ways that marketing channels can serve as a source of competitive advantage. Finally, we will examine the impact that alternative channel systems have on a business's overall financial performance.

FIGURE 9-1 CHANNEL MAP FOR AN ELECTRONIC COMPONENTS COMPANY

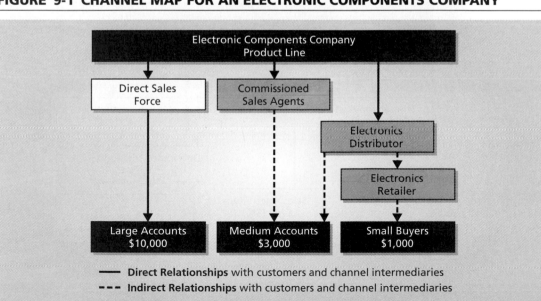

CHANNEL MAPPING

A diagram of the types of purchase points a business uses is called a *channel map*. Figure 9-1 shows the channel map for a large electronic components manufacturer. The business uses a direct sales force to reach and serve the needs of its large accounts, those customers who make major purchases. In the diagram, the average purchase amount of large-account customers is $10,000. The company employs the sales force and pays all expenses related to direct sales. Independent sales agents call on the medium accounts. The average purchase amount of customers in this category is $3,000. The sales agents for the medium accounts represent the company but not as employees. They receive commissions on their sales. Once a sale is final, the products are shipped by a distributor, which is more efficient than shipping from the company. In the small-buyers market, the average purchase amount is $1,000, and these customers typically buy a limited portion of the company's product line. To reach these customers, the company uses distributors that supply electronic components retailers.

Each channel to the market produces a different level of sales revenue and has its own set of costs. The channel costs may include discounts to intermediaries, transaction costs, and commissions. No discounts for intermediaries figure into the costs for the large-accounts direct channel, but there is a 5 percent transaction cost for order processing, handling and shipping, invoicing, and bookkeeping. With an average of $10,000 per purchase, then, the average pocket price is $9,500. For the medium accounts, the sales reps receive a 5 percent commission, which equates to an average commission of $150 per purchase, and the distributors that ship the products receive a 15 percent discount, an average of $450 per shipment. After taking into account a 2 percent transaction cost, the average pocket price for this channel is $2,793.

FIGURE 9-2 MAPPING CHANNEL PRICING AND POCKET PRICE

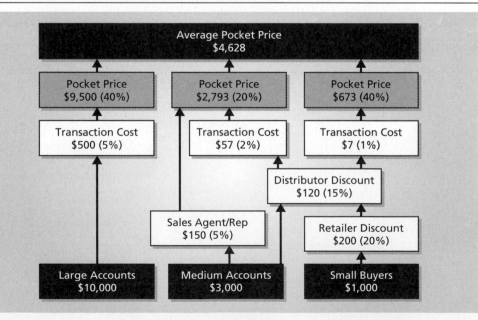

For the small-buyer market, retailers receive a 20 percent discount (an average of $200 per purchase), and the distributors that ship to retailers take 15 percent of the wholesale price to retailers (an average $120 per shipment). After deducting a 1 percent transaction cost, the channel pocket price on a $1,000 purchase would be $673. In Figure 9-2, the percentage figure after the pocket price for each channel is the percent of sales the company obtains in that channel. The average pocket price for the company, across all channels, is the average of the three pocket prices weighted by percent of sales. In this case, the overall average pocket price is $4,628.

Knowing the pocket price of each channel allows a business to determine the profitability of each channel based on cost of goods sold and the marketing and sales expenses allocated to each channel for marketing communications, sales, service, and technical support. Figure 9-3 shows the costs and marketing profits of each channel.

After deducting the cost of goods sold from the pocket price for each channel, we see that the margin was highest in the medium-accounts channel (a margin of 46.3%) and lowest in the small-buyer channel (a margin of 25.7%). The overall margin was 34.3 percent. One way, then, to improve the overall profit margin would be to shift sales away from the small-buyer channel to the medium-accounts channel. For example, a sales mix of 40 percent direct sales, 30 percent agent-distributor, and 30 percent distributor-retailer would increase the pocket price from $4,628 to $4,840 and increase margin from 33.3 to 36.3 percent.

FIGURE 9-3 MAPPING CHANNEL AND CHANNEL PROFITABILITY

Area of Performance	Direct	Mixed	Indirect	Average
Channel Strategy	Direct Sales	Agent & Dealer	Wholesaler & Dealer	
Target Customer	Large Accounts	Medium Accounts	Small Buyers	**Served Market**
Percent of Sales	40%	20%	40%	100%
Revenue per Purchase	$10,000	$3,000	$1,000	$5,000
Retailer Discount			20%	
Wholesale Price		$3,000	$800	
Distributor Discount		15%	15%	
Sales Agent Commission		5%		
Net Price	$10,000	$2,400	$680	$4,752
Company Sales Commission	0%	0%	0%	
Transaction Cost	5%	2%	1%	
Pocket Price	$9,500	$2,352	$673	$4,540
Cost of Goods Sold	$6,000	$1,500	$500	$2,900
Percent Margin	36.8%	36.2%	25.7%	36.1%
Marketing & Sales Expense (%)	15.0%	8.0%	5.0%	9.6%
Marketing & Sales Expense ($)	$1,425	$188	$34	$436
Net Marketing Contribution	$2,075	$664	$140	$1,204
Marketing ROS	21.8%	28.2%	20.7%	26.5%
Marketing ROI	146%	353%	415%	276%

But the profit margin is only one aspect of channel profitability. To fully understand channel profits, we need to know for each channel the marketing and sales expenses required for a certain level of market share. The direct-sales strategy for the large accounts is the most expensive in dollars, costing 15 percent of channel sales ($1,425 of the pocket price of $9,500). The channel has the highest net marketing contribution ($2,075) but the lowest marketing ROI (146%).

The agent-distributor channel is half as profitable as the direct sales channel in net marketing contribution but the most efficient with a marketing ROS of 38.3 percent and marketing ROI of 479 percent. Shifting sales to the agent-distributor channel would increase the overall net marketing contribution to $1,072 per sale, increase marketing ROS to 26.4 percent, and increase marketing ROI to 267 percent. As a way to improve pocket price, margins, and profits, this change in channel strategy would be worth additional consideration.

In the personal computer market, many marketing channels have emerged in an effort to reach and serve many types of customers. As shown in Figure 9-4, Hewlett-Packard has built its business by using a combination of direct and indirect marketing channels. In contrast, market leader Dell grew to its number-one position by directly serving all segments of the market. In 2007, however, Dell made the move to sell its computers through Wal-Mart, the world's largest retailer. Wal-Mart gives Dell more customer reach, manages inventory, and handles customers' purchase transactions. However, for these advantages Dell is relinquishing some profit margin in the form of the compensation Wal-Mart receives for its role in reaching and selling to customers.

FIGURE 9-4 MARKETING CHANNELS—DELL'S AND HEWLETT-PACKARD'S

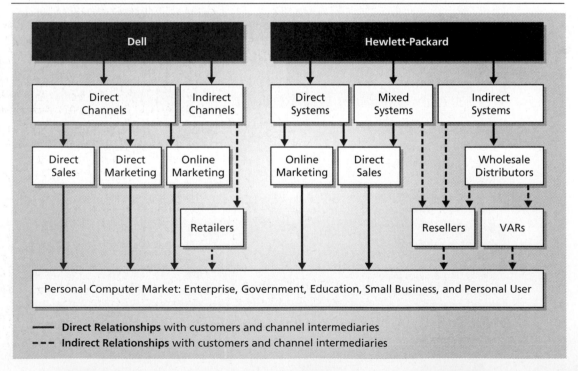

FIGURE 9-5 CHANNEL PERFORMANCE

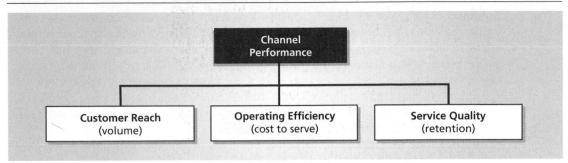

MARKETING CHANNEL PERFORMANCE

Marketing channel performance is based on the three areas shown in Figure 9-5: customer reach, operating efficiency, and service quality. To achieve the desired levels of sales and profits, a channel must do well in all three areas.[1]

Consider the relationship between sales and the number of dealerships owned by a large car dealer, as represented in Figure 9-6. The multiple dealerships strategy has allowed this particular car dealer to become the eighth largest in the United States. For the automobile companies whose vehicles this channel intermediary carries, the strategy has produced significant sales. The goal of the channel intermediary is $11 billion in sales by 2014, which it hopes to achieve by adding more dealerships across the United States.[2]

The productivity of its channels is all-important to a business. If a channel's operations are inefficient, the cost of serving customers will be too high for the channel to be profitable, regardless of how many customers it attracts and its quality of service. And if customer service is inferior, customer satisfaction will suffer and retention will decline, negating any initial benefits the business derived from the channel's good customer reach and high operating efficiency. Poor performance in any one of the three areas causes the channel to perform poorly overall.

FIGURE 9-6 SALES AND CHANNEL CUSTOMER REACH

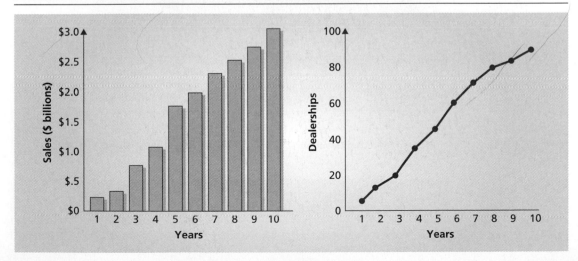

Customer Reach

A primary objective of a marketing channel is to reach target customers. With direct marketing channels, a business engages in contact with its customers by directly marketing and selling to them. Traveling sales representatives, direct mail, media advertising, trade shows, telemarketing, and e-marketing are some examples of direct channels. With indirect marketing channels, a business uses wholesalers, distributors, retailers, original equipment manufacturers, value-added resellers, and other intermediaries to reach customers and sell to them. The nature of a business, its stage of development, and its target customer profile are the factors that most influence a channel strategy.

To illustrate the impact of marketing channels on customer reach and sales, let's examine how Dow Chemical modified its channel strategy for epoxies. The worldwide business-to-business (B2B) market demand for epoxy is approximately $5 billion. This market consists of about 2,000 customers, with 20 percent of them accounting for 80 percent of the purchases. For these 400 customers, the average revenue per customer is $10 million annually. As Figure 9-7 shows, Dow Chemical serves this group of customers with a direct marketing channel. This channel is profitable for the major customers, but it would not be a cost-effective channel for reaching the other 1,600 epoxy customers around the world who buy considerably less. The cost of directly selling to a small customer, especially one in a distant location, would make the direct marketing effort unprofitable.

A few years ago, with the intent of reaching a significant number of these 1,600 small customers in a cost-effective way, Dow Chemical invested $2 million in an e-marketing channel it named *e-epoxy.com*. The Web site attracted 1,400 new visitors and 700 repeat visitors during its first 7 weeks. Two-thirds of the orders generated by the channel came from customers who had never done business with Dow Chemical.[3] The end results were increased sales, a market gain, and many new customers the company could now manage for retention.

FIGURE 9-7 REACHING NEW CUSTOMERS WITH AN E-MARKETING CHANNEL

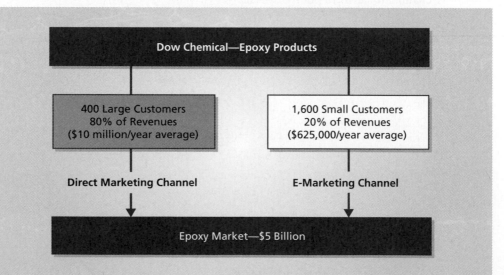

The marketing channel with the most potential to expand customer reach is the e-marketing channel. The ability to reach a world of prospective customers at an insignificant marketing cost has led most every business, large and small, to invest in e-marketing. The e-marketing channel that General Electric launched to supplement its traditional marketing channels saw immediate results. The channel generated $7 billion in first-year sales for GE, and this figure doubled the next year. A large portion of the e-marketing channel sales for those years was attributed to new customers.[4]

The e-marketing channel is also reaching new consumer retail customers. As shown in Figure 9-8, in 2004 online sales were $10 billion and 3.5 percent of all retail sales.[5] By 2006, online retail sales grew to $16 billion and 5.2 percent of all retail sales. This trend is projected to continue, with a slowdown after 2010. In 2011, online sales are projected to be $28 billion and 7 percent of all retail sales.

Also shown in Figure 9-8 are the product categories most engaged in e-marketing. Roughly two of every five purchases of computers and software programs are made online and about one of every four computer peripherals is bought online. The level of online buying for computers and related products illustrates how important the e-marketing channel is to companies serving this market and how equally important it is for them to improve the customer experience in these purchases. Traditional retailers have responded to this competing channel by upgrading the interiors of their stores and improving customer services in an effort to make the in-store experience uniquely satisfying and enjoyable for customers.

Operating Efficiency

Just as different marketing channels vary in customer reach, they also vary in cost structure. A direct marketing channel produces higher margins, but the business must bear the cost of channel management and all marketing expenses. An indirect marketing channel produces lower margins, but the costs of channel management and marketing are lower.

FIGURE 9-8 ONLINE SALES AS A PERCENTAGE OF ALL RETAIL SALES

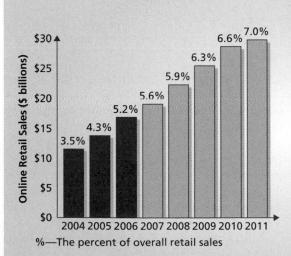

Category	Sales Made Online (%)
Computer (Hardware/Software)	41%
Travel	29%
Computer Peripherals	24%
Books	21%
Music and Video	17%
Toys and Video Games	16%
Baby Products	15%
Gift Cards/Certificates	15%
Event Tickets	15%
Consumer Electronics	14%
Office Supplies	11%

%—The percent of overall retail sales

In the following example, the net marketing contribution of each channel is the same but the revenue and cost structures differ. Each channel produced sales of 100,000 units. The direct marketing channel had a higher margin per unit ($5) but incurred higher marketing expenses ($250,000). The indirect marketing channel had a lower margin per unit ($3), but marketing expenses ($50,000) were not as high. As a result, both channels produced the same marketing profitability.

$$\text{NMC} = \text{Volume} \times \left[\frac{\text{End-User}}{\text{Price}} \times (1 - \% \text{ Channel Cost}) - \frac{\text{Cost of}}{\text{Goods}} \right] - \frac{\text{Marketing}}{\text{Expenses}}$$

$$
\begin{aligned}
\textbf{Direct Channel} &= 100,000 \times [\$10 \times (1 - 0) - \$5] - \$250,000 \\
&= 100,000 \times (\$10 \times 1 - \$5) - \$250,000 \\
&= \$500,000 - \$250,000 \\
&= \mathbf{\$250,000}
\end{aligned}
$$

$$
\begin{aligned}
\textbf{Indirect Channel} &= 100,000 \times [\$10 \times (1 - .2) - \$5] - \$50,000 \\
&= 100,000 \times (\$10 \times .8 - \$5) - \$50,000 \\
&= \$300,000 - \$50,000 \\
&= \mathbf{\$250,000}
\end{aligned}
$$

E-marketing channels have improved the operating efficiency of many businesses. A well-designed and implemented e-marketing channel can lower variable costs and marketing expenses, as well as reduce other operating expenses. GE's cost to serve customers, as one example, was reduced by $1 billion with the implementation of e-marketing channels. For many businesses, e-marketing channels have provided a low-cost way to market to smaller, hard-to-reach customers.

Online buying also saved GE $1 billion on the purchase of goods and services in its second year of implementation. Improved operating efficiency was also achieved by Hewlett-Packard when it introduced e-sourcing with *b2eMarkets.com* for conducting electronic requests for proposals, price quotes, and other information. The e-marketing channel has reduced HP's costs and time in its procurement of products and services.

Service Quality

Every channel also has different levels of service quality. With direct marketing channels, businesses control service quality because they, not channel intermediaries, interface with the customer at this and at all other customer contact points. This advantage allows for service enhancements, streamlining, and quick responses to customer problems.

Indirect marketing channels remove a business from the end-user customer. As a result, the business is dependent on channel partners to deliver the desired levels of customer service. Channel intermediaries usually represent many different lines of products and have a good knowledge of them, but they may not fully understand the customer value that a specific product offers in meeting customer needs.

E-marketing channels that improve the ordering process and track deliveries without multiple phone calls have lower costs and improve customer satisfaction. Many businesses have enhanced their e-marketing channels with a customer relationship management (CRM) system, a feature that facilitates one-on-one customer relationships with target customers. The CRM system identifies problems, resolves them, and dialogues with customers about how the company can improve its service quality.

ALTERNATIVE MARKETING CHANNELS

A business first decides whether to use a direct, indirect, or mixed channel system.[6] All things being equal, most businesses would prefer to sell and distribute directly to target customers. A direct channel system gives businesses full control when interfacing with customers, and it offers the greatest potential for value-added sales and services. On the other hand, a business lacking the expertise and resources needed to implement and fund a direct channel system might elect to reach target customers through an indirect channel system. Or a business may choose to use a mixed channel system—a combination of both direct and indirect channels—in order to reach different target markets cost effectively or to deliver the service level expected by target customers. These three channel systems are shown in Figure 9-9.

FIGURE 9-9 ALTERNATIVE CHANNEL SYSTEMS

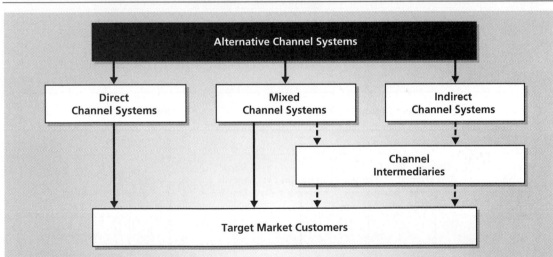

- ——— **Direct Relationships** with customers and channel intermediaries
- - - - **Indirect Relationships** with customers and channel intermediaries

- **Direct Channel Systems** use one or more direct channels to reach customers, with the business interfacing with customers at all contact points and retaining ownership (title) of the product until delivery.
- **Indirect Channel Systems** use one or more indirect channels, with the channel intermediaries taking ownership of the product and interfacing with customers at all customer contact points.
- **Mixed Channel Systems** use a combination of direct and indirect channels. A business reaches, sells to, and services some customers directly but has channel intermediaries perform these functions for other customers, or a business and its intermediaries separately interface with the same customers at different contact points.

Direct Channels

As Figure 9-10 illustrates, a direct approach in business-to-consumer (B2C) markets can include a direct sales force, direct marketing, telemarketing, online marketing, and manufacturer's representatives. In each case, the business retains ownership of the products and the responsibility for distribution, service, and collection of payment for products sold. Although a direct sales force offers the best opportunity for sales communication and customer interaction, the cost of direct customer sales contact is high and increasing. Reaching target customers in this way is too expensive for many businesses. The fully loaded cost (salary, benefits, and expenses) of a direct salesperson in many business-to-business markets can range from $100,000 to over $300,000 per year. One way to reduce these costs is to use manufacturers' representatives, sales agents, and brokers who assume the selling responsibility for the business and are paid a commission when a sale occurs. Direct marketing, which includes direct mail and catalog sales, offers a less expensive alternative, but the opportunity for sales communication is more limited.

Telemarketing provides a better opportunity for a sales communication but is more labor intensive and usually more expensive than direct marketing. E-marketing channels, when implemented well, can greatly enhance customer reach, customer interactivity, information searches, purchasing, and after-sale customer service. Online marketing

FIGURE 9-10 ALTERNATIVE B2C MARKETING CHANNELS

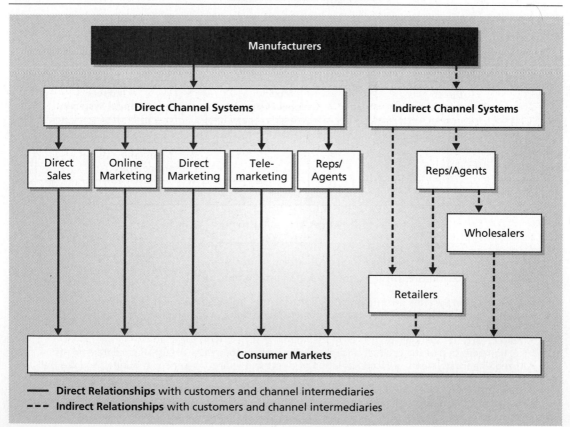

channels can be efficient and offer good opportunities for customer interaction in home shopping and Internet computer-based purchasing.[7]

Indirect Channels

Because using a direct channel system is often expensive, it limits the number of customers a business can profitably reach. Customers who make small purchases usually cannot be profitably served with a direct channel system. In these situations, a business has to at least consider an indirect channel system. An indirect channel system is inherently more complex because it involves at least one intermediary who takes over both ownership of the product and most, if not all, of the control in both sales and distribution. As shown in Figures 9-10 and 9-12, an indirect channel system could include retailers, manufacturers' representatives or agents, dealers, and wholesalers.

Retailers take over the sales and point-of-purchase distribution in consumer markets, and distributors or dealers assume this responsibility in business-to-business markets. Compensation for their services is usually in the form of discounts, which typically range from 10 to 50 percent, but sometimes more, of the customer's purchase price.

Wholesalers offer an intermediate point of sales and physical distribution between a business and retailers or dealers. There are full-function wholesalers who offer a complete range of products and services (inventory, delivery, credit, and stocking) and limited-function wholesalers who offer a narrow range of products and services. One kind of limited-function wholesaler is cash-and-carry wholesalers who do not deliver products or offer credit. Because wholesalers offer fewer services than retailers and dealers, the discount a business offers wholesalers is less than that for retailers and dealers.

Mixed Channels

In some instances, a combination of direct and indirect channel systems provides the best way to reach and serve target customers.[8] Many industrial and business-to-business firms employ a sales force or manufacturers' representatives to perform the sales contact, but use localized dealers or distributors to provide product availability information, arrange payment terms with the customer, make deliveries, and provide after-sale service.

Mixed channel systems are particularly important for specialized and technological products for which customers need localized availability or service. Microsoft and Hewlett-Packard, for example, have direct sales forces that call on large corporate accounts, often referred to as enterprise customers. While the technical sales team works with the customer to create the desired customer solution, the local reseller of the companies' products handles the actual sale, delivery, and after-sale service.

B2C Channels

Businesses in different kinds of consumer markets need different channel systems—direct, indirect, or mixed—and different kinds of channels within those systems to reach customers, meet their needs, and produce acceptable levels of profitability. Figure 9-10 outlines the various B2C, or business-to-consumer, channel systems that businesses use.

Traditionally, businesses in consumer markets have used indirect channels, mainly wholesalers and retailers, to reach target customers effectively and cost efficiently. However, advances in computer software beginning in the 1970s have opened new and attractive direct channels. Direct marketing through consumer catalogs, mailings, telemarketing, and e-marketing has grown as the result of advances in computers and software programs, and future technological improvements will add to the effectiveness and use of these direct channels. Cost-efficient printing and database technology enable companies like Esprit, Eddie Bauer, and L.L.Bean to use catalogs in marketing directly to the huge consumer apparel market. But some businesses in large consumer markets have long-relied on another direct marketing channel. Mary Kay Cosmetics, Electrolux, and Amway are examples of businesses that, since early in their development, have reached their target consumers through direct sales distributors. Although independent, the distributors are in effect the sales forces for these businesses.

The emergence of online retailing has opened up a new type of indirect B2C channel. Just as with in-store retailing, online retailers buy their products from manufacturers or wholesalers and resell them to consumers over the Internet. Easy price comparisons and "anytime shopping" make online stores very convenient for consumers. This indirect channel works particularly well for standard products, such as books or CDs, that customers do not need to inspect before they buy.

B2B Channels

Most businesses, as noted earlier, would prefer to sell and distribute with a direct channel system. Direct channels provide a greater degree of control and specialized knowledge that can be customized for the end-user customer. But for manufacturers of industrial products, as illustrated in Figure 9-11, only 25 percent of sales are generated by direct channel systems.[9] This relatively low percentage is partly the result of the cost of a business-to-business direct

FIGURE 9-11 CHANNEL MAP FOR A WELDING ROD MANUFACTURER

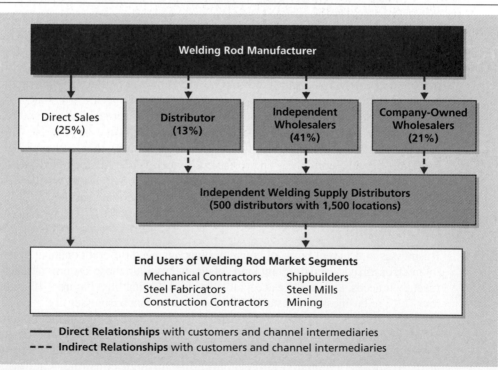

sales call, which ranges from $100 to over $300. In industrial markets, about 50 percent of all sales are derived from the combination of manufacturers' reps or sales agents and industrial distributors. For many inexpensive industrial and commercial products, wholesalers are used. In some instances, as in hospital supply products, a large hospital supply wholesaler may sell directly to hospitals and other medical institutions.

Unique to the business-to-business market, as included in Figure 9-12, are value-added resellers (VARs) and original equipment manufacturers (OEMs). VARs purchase a variety of components from several manufacturers and package them as a system. A VAR often provides the total system, as well as specialized services, to help the customer learn, use, maintain, and upgrade the system. For example, a VAR in the agricultural market may purchase computers, printers, modems, and telecommunications equipment from several manufacturers, along with specialized software, to produce an information and management system for use in farming, a system that would encompass planting, fertilizing, irrigation, and rotation requirements for a wide variety of crops. The agricultural customers could buy all these products separately, but they prefer to purchase a complete (bundled) system that is customized to their specific needs.

An OEM is similar but actually creates a new product manufactured from components it buys. Ford, IBM, and Caterpillar are examples of OEMs that buy parts from other manufacturers and assemble them to make their products. Ford purchases many kinds of components, from body parts to tires, for manufacturing its vehicles. The tires come from Firestone and other tire makers, which also operate company-owned retail stores, but the automobile industry is an all-important indirect channel sales opportunity for the tire companies. IBM buys disk drives from Seagate and computer chips from Intel, but it also makes its own.

FIGURE 9-12 ALTERNATIVE B2B MARKETING CHANNELS

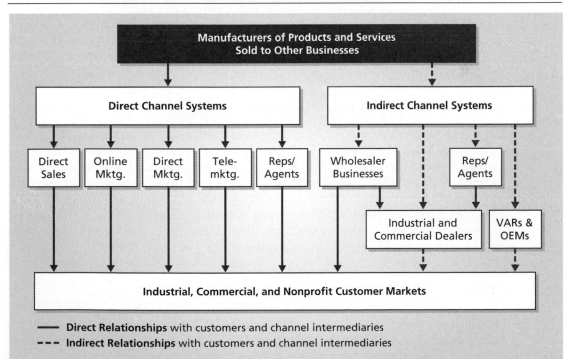

FIGURE 9-13 MARKETING CHANNELS USED TO REACH B2B AND B2C CUSTOMERS

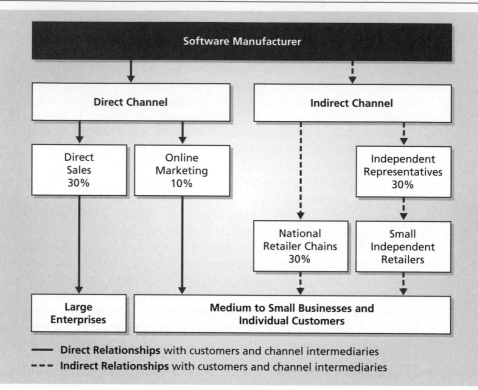

Virtually all B2B businesses have some e-marketing capability. Many aspects of an e-marketing channel are informational, while others facilitate order placement and solicit delivery preferences.

B2B and B2C Marketing Channels

Software manufacturers like Adobe and Microsoft serve both business and consumer customers. As illustrated in Figure 9-13, software manufacturers use a direct marketing channel to reach and serve large enterprises, such as *Fortune* 500 companies. To reach medium-sized and small businesses and individual consumers, software companies use online marketing as part of their direct channel systems, but, to a greater degree, they also use indirect channels. They sell direct to large national chains, but they use independent, commissioned representatives to reach smaller independent retailers. Each of the channels has different levels of cost, control, sales contact, and ownership.

MARKETING CHANNELS THAT IMPROVE CUSTOMER VALUE

A business's channel system can consist of one or many channels, and a system with multiple channels can have all direct, all indirect, or any combination of direct and indirect channels. To be successful, however, a channel system must enhance customer value by

FIGURE 9-14 HOW MARKETING CHANNELS CONTRIBUTE TO CUSTOMER VALUE

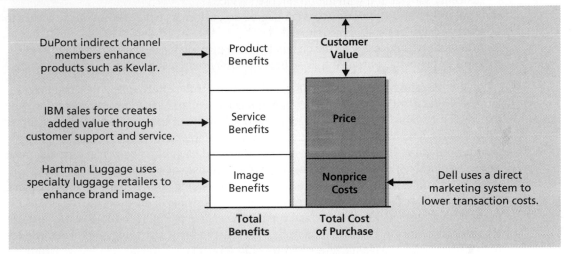

increasing customer benefits, lowering customer cost of purchase, or both, as shown in Figure 9-14.

Product Benefits

If a business's product is perishable or can be easily damaged, it is important to use channels that can deliver the product to target customers in the condition that meets or exceeds customer expectations. In selecting a particular channel system, a business needs to consider how that channel system either enhances or detracts from the following product benefits:

- **Product Quality:** Can the channel system deliver the product with the quality level required and expected by target customers?
- **Product Assortment:** Can the channel system provide the range of products required in order to achieve a desired level of customer appeal?
- **Product Form:** Can the channel system provide the product, in the form needed, to both intermediaries and final customers?

A channel system is not a viable alternative unless it meets every one of these product benefits, as sought by target customers.[10] Customers will not buy products that do not meet their buying needs. Almost always customers can find competing alternatives.

Service Benefits

Every channel has advantages and limitations with respect to service. The need for delivery, installation, training, technical support, repair, terms of payment, credit, and easy return are all service benefits that a business must consider in selecting a particular channel system. To determine whether a channel system is viable, a business has to evaluate the following points with respect to a customer's service needs and expectations.

- **After-Sale Services:** What are the after-sale services that are critical to achieving total customer satisfaction with the product or service?
- **Availability and Delivery:** To what degree do customers benefit from quick access to goods or services and immediate delivery?
- **Transaction Services:** Can the channel system provide for the customer's credit needs, terms of payment, warranty, free on board (FOB) pricing, and return of faulty products?

All three of these service benefits are important for the effectiveness of a channel system. A business with a better product may not achieve market success if it fails to provide the service benefits required by target customers. To be successful in meeting customer expectations, a business has to make the product available at the target customer's desired point of purchase. In addition, it must meet or exceed each of its customer's product and service requirements, whether the customer is an end user or a channel intermediary.

Let's consider again the fiber-cement construction siding discussed in previous chapters, this time in view of the way marketing channels can add value to the product. The product is made from a combination of paper and cement. As shown in Figure 9-15, these raw materials are needed at a low cost on a reliable basis in order to serve a growing market demand for fiber-cement siding. Manufacturers add roughly 45 cents per square foot by transforming these raw materials into a semi-finished product. However, in this form, at the point of production, the product has no value to home owners. A marketing channel is needed to reach the end-user customer. Producers sell to wholesalers who have in place a system of distribution that reaches the many construction retailers around the United States. Wholesalers add 10 cents per square foot to the price of the product in exchange for their logistics and distribution services. Construction retailers add 30 cents per square foot in performing their role in offering localized inventory, desired purchase quantities, and customer service by offering information on the product and directing purchasers to contractors who can install the product. Contractors add trim and paint the product to achieve the desired performance and appearance. The net result is a cost to home owners of roughly $1.50 per square foot of siding, a superior customer value in light of the product's benefits—resistance to fire, bug infestation, and rot, and a 50-year warranty—plus the value added by the channel intermediaries.

FIGURE 9-15 HOW MARKETING CHANNELS ADD VALUE TO A FIBER-CEMENT SIDING PRODUCT

Raw Material Producers	Siding Producer	Wholesale Distributor	Building Material Retailers	Building Contractors	Home Owners
($.05/sq. ft.)	($.50/sq. ft.)	($.60/sq. ft.)	($.90/sq. ft.)	($1.50/sq. ft.)	
Basic Inputs	Product Creation	Supply Chain Logistics	Retail Services	Installation and Finish	Customer Value
Low Cost and Reliable Supply	Value-Added Product Benefits	Availability and Reliable Delivery	Availability and Order Quantity	Performance and Appearance	Durability Low Maint.

Brand Image

Another important consideration is how a channel system will affect the image of a product or manufacturer. Hartman Luggage, for example, manufactures a high-quality line of luggage and has built an image among quality-conscious customers. Hartman is selective in choosing retailers who will support or enhance this brand image.

Likewise, Perfume de Paris manufactures and markets perfume at about one-third the price of Chanel and other high-priced perfumes. It is important for Perfume de Paris to have its product sold through mass merchandisers who emphasize price, because mass merchandising is consistent with its target customer profile and its product- and price-positioning strategy.

Company Benefits

With relationship marketing, overall benefits can be enhanced, adding to customer value.[11] As we have seen, direct channel systems offer the greatest opportunity for presenting product information and controlling interaction with customers during the sale. This opportunity to enhance the total benefits through personal relationships developed with customers can be important. Strong relationships between a business and its customers produce high degrees of commitment by both parties, and high commitment has the potential to enhance customer value.

When a business cannot directly interact with target customers, it must take care to select a channel system conducive to building effective customer relationships.[12] For a given product and customer profile, the inclusion of the right channels in the channel system requires a certain level of product knowledge, sales and negotiation skill, call frequency, and after-sale service. In the end, any channel system that does not provide effective sales interaction with target customers will be of little value.

With an e-marketing channel, a business with 10,000 customers should look at customers not as a segment of 10,000 customers but as 10,000 segments, each with one customer. Today, e-marketing channels can be extended with customer relationship marketing and the development of one-on-one marketing relationships. Whether a consumer business with thousands of customers or an industrial business with hundreds, the use of customer relationship marketing and e-marketing enables businesses to interact with customers, make customized offerings, and build customer loyalty.

Dow Corning has been the market leader in silicon technology applications for many decades. Its products have a multitude of industrial uses, as well as many applications in the electronics, health care, and construction markets. As would be expected, though, many of Dow Corning's products become less competitive as they reach the mature stage of the product life cycle. The company's traditional full-service consultative engineering approach does not work well for these products. In response, Dow Corning has augmented its overall marketing strategy with a new and radically different marketing channel.[13]

In developing this new marketing channel, Dow Corning researched the silicon-based product market and found that two segments could still be served profitably with the company's traditional marketing approach. As Figure 9-16 shows, the company would serve the innovation technology segment directly and use intermediaries for the service quality segment. A direct channel was appropriate for new applications, as was an indirect channel for high-growth applications. But a new marketing channel was needed that could accommodate highly competitive prices through reduced sales and service expenses. The

FIGURE 9-16 MARKETING CHANNELS THAT ENHANCE VALUE PROPOSITIONS (VPs)

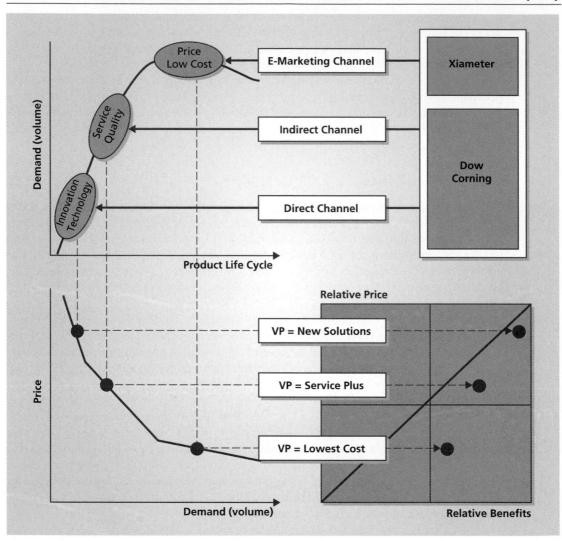

company responded by developing an e-marketing channel for the price-sensitive segment. Because it was a major departure from the company's core product positioning, Dow Corning decided the 400 silicon-based products targeted for the e-marketing channel strategy would be sold under a new brand name, Xiameter.

The Xiameter e-marketing channel lets customers compare Xiameter's prices with competitors' prices, a feature any price-sensitive customer would find appealing. Customers order online, with each order having a guaranteed shipping date. Xiameter's success is directly linked to its cost-efficient e-marketing channel applications in the mature stage of their product life cycles, when prices generally fall.

For long-established businesses like Dow Corning, General Electric, and Charles Schwab, e-marketing complements their other marketing channels. E-marketing gives these companies one more way to attract new customers while serving present ones. The businesses find e-marking is cost efficient because it leverages existing brand equity, supply chain capabilities, and operating expenses already in place. But many businesses that have started up since the advent of the Internet have chosen to rely almost exclusively on e-marketing, using it as their primary means for building brand equity, interfacing with customers, and delivering products. Businesses like Amazon.com, E*Trade, and eBay were founded on the premise that e-marketing could be their primary marketing channel and a core component of their business model. The customer value these businesses create and the sales and profits they generate are directly related to their successful management of e-marketing.

Improving Cost Efficiency

By making its product readily available, a business can lower customers' transaction costs. Customers have preferred points of purchase. If a business does not make products readily available at those points of purchase, it inherently raises the cost of the transaction. For undifferentiated products, customers' transaction costs are high when availability is limited because customers must make an extra effort to find the products. Many customers will instead purchase a conveniently available competing product. On the other hand, the more differentiated a product and the greater its perceived value, the more willing customers are to incur a higher transaction cost.

   Another way to increase customer value (total benefits less total costs) is to lower the cost of reaching customers. The more cost efficient a channel system is, the greater is the opportunity to lower customer costs or to increase business profitability. An important responsibility for a business's marketing managers is to identify and develop a channel system that is cost efficient while still delivering the benefits sought by customers.

FIGURE 9-17 INDUSTRY-WIDE TRANSACTION COST WITHOUT WHOLESALERS

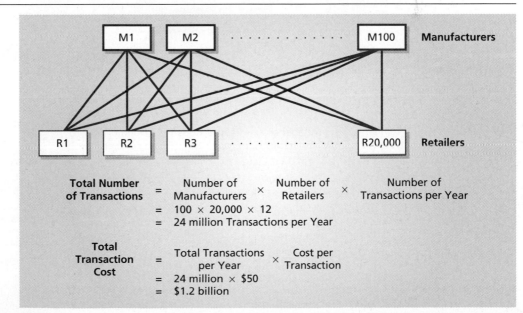

It is often assumed that the more intermediaries a channel system has, the higher the total cost of purchase. In general, this assumption is not true. Consider, for example, the channel system presented in Figure 9-17, in which 100 manufacturers in a certain industry each contact 20,000 retailers once a month. With this channel system, each manufacturer incurs a monthly $50 transaction cost per retailer for order placement, handling, delivery, and billing. The net result is an industry that has an overall channel system transaction cost of approximately $1.2 billion, as shown.

When an extra layer—wholesalers—is added to the channel system, each of the 100 manufacturers can now sell to the wholesalers at a cost of $25,000 per month, as illustrated in Figure 9-18. For the manufacturers, the cost per transaction is much higher than the cost per transaction of selling to retailers because much more merchandise is handled and delivered to the wholesalers each month. But the number of transactions is far less. In this channel system, the wholesalers then distribute to the 20,000 retailers each month. The wholesalers' cost is $750 per transaction, which is also much higher than the manufacturer-to-retailer cost in Figure 9-17 because wholesalers, who represent a large number of retailers, ship many more products at a time. But the number of wholesaler-to-retailer transactions in Figure 9-18 is only 10 percent of the manufacturer-to-retailer transactions in Figure 9-17. Adding wholesalers to the channel system reduces the total annual transaction costs for the industry by 82.5 percent, to only $210 million, or almost $1 billion less than the channel system without a wholesaler function.

FIGURE 9-18 INDUSTRY-WIDE TRANSACTION COST WITH WHOLESALERS

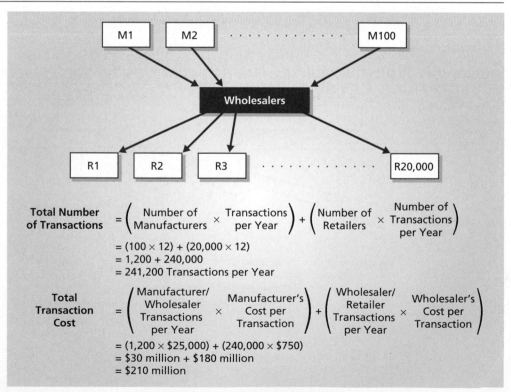

Although a business generally builds customer value through a combination of product, service, and image benefits, along with the cost of acquiring these benefits (price and transaction costs), any given channel system can enhance or detract from the delivered customer value. Selecting a channel system, then, requires both careful consideration of the benefits sought by customers and the costs the business would incur by the various channel systems that could deliver those benefits.

MARKETING CHANNELS AND COMPETITIVE ADVANTAGE

For any sale to occur, customer contact is essential. This contact can take many forms, whether direct or indirect. With direct channel systems, a business must have a sufficient number of salespeople to establish and maintain an effective level of customer contact. With indirect channel systems, a business must have enough outlets to reach a high percentage of its target customers, whether retail or wholesale. Either a direct or an indirect channel system can be a source of competitive advantage when implemented in a manner that creates value for customers and a relative advantage over competitors.

Sales Force Advantage

When a business selects a direct channel system as the best way to reach and effectively serve target customers, it is essential that the business have a sufficient number of salespeople. Assume that a business has 1,000 target customers and the required rate of customer contact for sales effectiveness and customer satisfaction is two customer visits per month. This translates into 24,000 customer contacts per year. Further assume that a salesperson in this particular industry can make three customer visits per day and has 4 days per week to make customer calls. This translates into a need for 38 salespeople.

If competitors have an average of only 20 salespeople, they cannot accomplish the same level of sales coverage. These competitors will either contact fewer customers or contact the same number of customers less frequently. In either case, the business with 38 salespeople is better able to reach more customers and better serve customers' needs, and both are sources of competitive advantage.

The quality of a business's sales force can also be a source of competitive advantage. A sales force with exceptional product knowledge and a strong market orientation is in a good position to serve target customer needs. Of course, the behavior and attitudes of the sales force are in part influenced by the market orientation of the business.[14] As a result, a business with a strong market orientation is in a better position to build customer relationships that enhance customer satisfaction and retention. The sales force is, in fact, creating a source of competitive advantage when this level of sales effort is valued by customers and cannot be matched by competitors.[15]

Sales Productivity

Businesses that have a high level of sales productivity can also develop a source of competitive advantage. A business with a more efficient sales force, in terms of sales per salesperson, will have a lower cost per sale than a less productive business with the same sales revenue. An efficient sales force translates into higher levels of profitability per sales dollar and a source of competitive advantage.

FIGURE 9-19 DISTRIBUTION OUTLET SHARE VERSUS MARKET SHARE

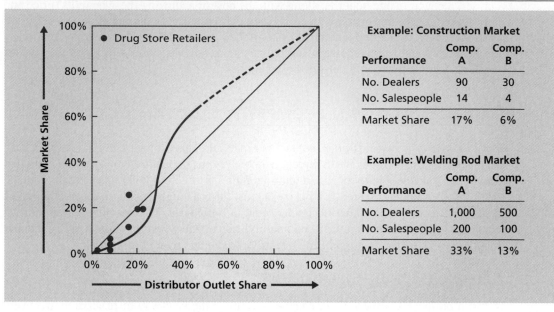

But how does a business develop high levels of sales productivity? Businesses with high-quality products, broad lines of related products, and efficient sales administrative systems produce high levels of sales per salesperson. High-quality products are easier to sell than low-quality products, and they can often be sold at price premiums. A broad product line provides more sales opportunities per sales call—and the use of computer networks and other telecommunications systems has been shown to improve sales administrative efficiency and to allow for more time with customers.

Distribution Advantage

For markets in which indirect channel systems are the dominant channel system used to reach target customers, share of distributor outlets can be directly linked to market share. As shown in Figure 9-19, generally the higher a drug store chain's outlet share, the higher its market share. Empirical studies have shown that the relationship between outlet share and market share is nonlinear and generally S-shaped, as in Figure 9-19. A small distributor share produces proportionately smaller market shares. However, as outlet share grows, market share grows at a faster rate until it exceeds outlet share. Then, as outlet share continues to increase, the rate of market share growth decreases.

There are only a few cases in which extremely high outlet and market shares have been observed. The lower part of the curve, below a 50 percent outlet share, is well documented.[16] However, because market share must equal 100 percent when outlet share equals 100 percent, the upper half of the curve in Figure 9-19 can be extrapolated with some confidence. Recognizing this relationship, for markets in which indirect retail or dealer channel systems are required to reach and serve target customers, businesses with dominant distribution shares have a source of competitive advantage. Why? Because in

FIGURE 9-20 CHANNEL MARGIN VERSUS CHANNEL MARKETING EXPENSES

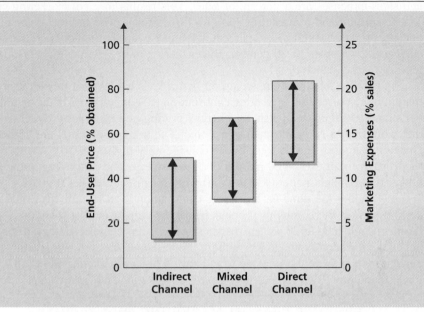

any given market, there is a finite number of distributors, and fewer good ones. Because the number of available distributors or retailers is limited, the business that dominates this industry-wide channel system can control market access by blocking market entry.

PROFIT IMPACT OF ALTERNATIVE MARKETING CHANNELS

In determining the profitability of any channel strategy, several aspects of profitability come into play. The reach of a marketing channel will impact the volume it produces, and net prices and marketing expenses also vary by type of marketing channel. As shown in Figure 9-20, direct marketing channels are able to capture most, if not all, of the end-user price, but the cost of most direct marketing channels is generally higher because the business is responsible for selling, distribution, and payment. E-marketing is an exception. Once the online selling infrastructure is in place, direct online sales can yield very high margins.

Mixed channel systems, with their combination of direct sales and intermediary distribution channels, lower the cost of marketing (as a percent of sales), but revenues derived from mixed marketing channels are lower because intermediaries take a portion of the purchase price for their services. As shown in Figure 9-20, indirect marketing channels result in the lowest out-of-pocket marketing expenses. However, the net price derived from the use of indirect marketing channels is much less than from direct channels because multiple intermediaries capture percentages of the end-user price.

Consider, for example, a manufacturer that sells 200,000 units annually to a market in which it has a 20 percent share. These sales are currently achieved with an indirect marketing channel, as shown in Figure 9-21. After discounting the end-user price of $1,000 per unit to $800 (20 percent discount) and accounting for a 2 percent transaction cost, a pocket price of $784 is obtained. With a unit cost of $650, the margin is 17.1 percent. Marketing and sales expenses are 5 percent of sales. This results in a net marketing contribution of $18.96 million and a marketing ROS of 12.1 percent. The indirect channel strategy produced a marketing ROI of 242 percent and break-even share of 5.9 percent, well below the current market share of 20 percent. But is there a more profitable channel strategy at this level of market penetration?

To address this question, we might first ask: What level of market share is needed to maintain the current net marketing contribution ($18.96 million) using an alternative channel strategy? Figure 9-21 lists the channel pricing and costs for a direct channel strategy that would use a company-paid sales force. The transaction costs are higher but, with no channel discounts, the pocket price is considerably higher ($950). At the same unit cost, this results in an estimated margin of 31.6 percent. The marketing and sales expenses, however, are much higher ($30 million) with this direct channel strategy.

To produce the same net marketing contribution ($18.96 million) would require a 16.3 percent market share, roughly 4 points below the current market share of 20 percent. If the business could hold its 20 percent market share with this channel strategy, it could increase the net marketing contribution to $36 million, almost double the current marketing profits. At a 20 percent market share this strategy would have a higher marketing ROS (18.4 percent) but a lower marketing ROI (120 percent), since the marketing and sales budget is so much greater

FIGURE 9-21 ALTERNATIVE CHANNEL MARKETING PROFITABILITY

Area of Performance	Current	Same Profit	Same Share
Channel Strategy	Indirect Retailer	Direct Sales Force	Direct Sales Force
Market Demand	1,000,000	1,000,000	1,000,000
Market Share	20.0%	16.3%	20.0%
Volume	200,000	163,000	200,000
End-User Price	$1,000	$1,000	$1,000
Retailer Discount	20%		
Wholesale Price	$800	$1,000	$1,000
Distributor Discount			
Sales Agent Commission			
Net Price	$800	$1,000	$1,000
Company Sales Commission	0%	0%	0%
Transaction Costs	2%	5%	2%
Pocket Price	$784	$950	$980
Sales Reveunes	$156,800,000	$154,850,000	$196,000,000
Unit Cost	$650	$650	$650
Percent Margin	17.1%	31.6%	33.7%
Marketing & Sales Expenses (%)	5.0%	19.4%	15.3%
Marketing & Sales Expenses ($)	$7,840,000	$30,000,000	$30,000,000
Net Marketing Contribution	$18,960,000	$18,900,000	$36,000,000
Marketing ROS	12.1%	12.2%	18.4%
Marketing ROI	242%	63%	120%
Break-Even Market Share	5.9%	10.0%	9.1%
Market Share – Break-Even Share	14.1%	6.3%	10.9%

than that required for the indirect channel strategy. Given this level of profit potential, a business may feel the investment is worthwhile. A business unwilling to make the investment in marketing and sales would essentially give up $18 million in profits. We will discuss in Chapter 16 how this decision would limit earnings-per-share growth and shareholder value.

The break-even analysis for each marketing channel strategy, also shown in Figure 9-21, provides a way to assess the profitability risk of each channel. The break-even market share is lower for the indirect channel, whether at a projected market share of 16.3 or 20 percent. Even though margins are lower in the indirect channel, the marketing expenses are much lower and, as a result, the break-even market share is lower. Still, the break-even share of 9.1 percent for the strategy that maintains current share is less than half of the 20 percent current share. The risk is slight when weighed against the profit potential.

■ Summary

Regardless of how attractive a business's products or services may be, if the business cannot reach target customers with a desired level of services, it has little chance of marketing success. Customers have product and service requirements, along with preferred points of purchase. Likewise, a business has image requirements and the need for sales effectiveness and cost efficiency. To be successful, a channel system must meet both customer and business requirements.

The biggest decision is whether to use a direct, indirect, or mixed channel system. In a direct system, the business is responsible for many of the selling, delivery, warehousing, and transaction activities. Direct channel systems include direct selling, direct marketing, telemarketing, and the use of manufacturers' reps and sales agents. An indirect system uses intermediaries who have varying degrees of responsibility for selling, warehousing, delivery, and transaction activities. Indirect systems include different combinations of wholesalers and retailers in the consumer market. In the business-to-business market, indirect systems can also include different combinations of wholesalers and dealers, value-added resellers (VARs), and original equipment manufacturers (OEMs). A mixed channel system uses a combination of direct and indirect channels.

The proliferation of e-marketing channels since the 1990s represents a major change in the way businesses market directly to customers. For virtually all long-established businesses, e-marketing has leveraged their ability to reach customers and capitalize on existing brand awareness, order-entry systems, and operating expenses. For dot-com businesses like eBay, e-marketing is the primary marketing channel and a core element of their approach to serving customers. Many other dot-com businesses, however, failed within a few years of their inception because of ineffective e-marketing channels. Managed successfully, e-marketing channels have proven to be an important marketing channel in both B2C and B2B markets.

In many instances, multi-tiered channel systems are more cost efficient than direct systems, as well as more effective in reaching customers. The belief that having more intermediaries in a channel system drives up the cost and, therefore, the price of a product is not true. If a more efficient system were available, marketers would find it. However, rarely is one channel sufficient for reaching all target customers—and the greater a business's market coverage, with either a direct, indirect, or mixed channel system, the greater its market share. An important part of a profitable marketing strategy, then, is a well-thought-out and well-managed marketing channel strategy.

■ Market-Based Strategic Thinking

1 Why is it advantageous for a business to use more than one marketing channel?
2 Why is the purchase amount likely to be different in different marketing channels?
3 Why is the pocket price lower in one market channel than another even when the end-user price is the same?
4 Why would a business pay higher channel costs and receive a lower pocket price? Wouldn't it always be better to use a direct marketing channel?
5 How can a marketing channel with a lower marketing ROI be more profitable?
6 Why would Dell add an indirect marketing channel using Wal-Mart?
7 Why are online retail sales likely to top out at 10 percent of all retail sales? What could cause the rate of online retail sales to rise to 20 percent of all retail sales?
8 What is the difference between a direct and an indirect marketing channel? Why might a business use both?
9 What is a mixed marketing channel? Why would Microsoft Office be marketed with a mixed channel system to large business customers?
10 Are there examples of a direct sales marketing channel in consumer markets? How do they differ from the business-to-business market?
11 What role do online marketing channels play in the way we buy airline tickets and stocks?
12 How does e-marketing help businesses reach customers, lower costs, and improve customer service?
13 What role do VARs play in business-to-business markets? How do they enhance customer value?
14 How does the use of multiple channels affect the growth of a business?
15 How does the use of a channel system either enhance or detract from customer value?
16 What specific factors need to be considered in selecting one channel system over another?
17 Why can a channel system be a source of competitive advantage?
18 What are some of the ways a channel system can be a source of advantage and contribute to a higher market share?
19 How can improved sales force quality and sales force productivity be a source of competitive advantage?
20 How would you go about determining the profit impact of an alternative channel system?

Marketing Performance Tools

The three **Marketing Performance Tools** described here may be accessed online at *www.rogerjbest.com*. These applied-learning exercises will give you an in-depth understanding of marketing channels and how they affect a business's profitability.

9.1 Channel Mapping and Pocket Price (Figures 9-1 and 9-2)

■ How does the overall average pocket price change if the business modifies its sales mix to 30 percent direct sales, 40 percent agent-distributor, and 30 percent distributor-retailer?

■ How does the average pocket price change if the business replaces the direct sales channel with an agent-distributor channel, with a sales mix of 60 percent agent-distributor and 40 percent distributor-retailer?

9.2 Marketing Channel Profitability (Figure 9-3)

■ How does the overall average pocket price change if the business modifies its sales mix to 30 percent direct sales, 40 percent agent-distributor, and 30 percent distributor-retailer?

■ How does the average pocket price change if the business replaces the direct sales channel with the agent-distributor channel, with a sales mix of 60 percent agent-distributor and 40 percent distributor-retailer?

9.3 Alternative Channel Profitability (Figure 9-21)

■ How much do the marketing and sales expenses need to be increased for a 20 percent share using the alternative channel, maintaining the same level of net marketing contribution?

■ How much do channel costs in the indirect channel need to be reduced to produce the same net marketing contribution as the alternative channel at a 20 percent market share?

Notes

1. O. Brooks, "Art of the Deal," *Oregon Business* (April 2006): 18–22.
2. Martin Lindstrom and Tim Frank Andersen, *Brand Building on the Internet* (Dover, NH: Kogan Page Limited, 2000).
3. K. Schnepf, "Customers of Epoxy Resin and Related Products Find E-epoxy.com a Powerful Procurement Channel," www.news/dow.com/prodbus/2001: (accessed December 2001).
4. M. Richtel and B. Tedeschi, "As Some Grow Weary of Web, Online Sales Lose Momentum," *New York Times* (June 17, 2007): 1.
5. Jack Welch, *Jack: Straight from the Gut* (New York: Warner Books, 2001): 341–351.
6. Kasturi Rangan, Melvyn Menezes, and E. P. Maier, "Channel Selection for New Industrial Products: A Framework, Method and Application," *Journal of Marketing* (July 1992): 69–82.
7. R. Oliva, "Painting with Business Marketers' Web Palette," *Marketing Management* (Summer 1998): 50–53.
8. F. Cespedes and R. Corey, "Managing Multiple Channels," *Business Horizons* (July–August 1990): 72.
9. Robert Haas, *Industrial Marketing Management: Text and Cases*, 4th ed. (Northridge, CA: Kent, 1989): 239; and Michael Morris, *Industrial and Organizational Marketing* (Old Tappan, NJ: Macmillan, 1988): 489–523.
10. Niraj Dawar and Philip Parker, "Marketing Universals: Consumers' Use of Brand Name, Price, Physical Appearance, and Retailer Reputation as Signals of Product Quality," *Journal of Marketing* (April 1994): 81–95.
11. James Anderson and James Narus, "A Model of Distributor Firm and Manufacturer Firm Working Partnerships," *Journal of Marketing* (January 1990): 42–58.
12. David Morris, "What's Old Is New in Relationship Marketing," *Marketing News* (February 1994): 4, 8; and Robert Robicheaux and James Coleman, "The Structure of Marketing Channel Relationships," *Academy of Marketing Science* (Winter 1994): 38–51.
13. J. Nicholas DeBonis, Eric Balinski, and Phil Allen, *Value-Based Marketing for Bottom-Line Success*, (New York: McGraw-Hill, 2003).
14. Judy Siguaw, G. Brown, and Robert E. Widing, "The Influence of Market Orientation of the Firm on Sales Force Behavior and Attitudes," *Journal of Marketing Research* (February 1994): 106–116.
15. Robert Ping, "Does Satisfaction Moderate the Association Between Alternative Attractiveness and Exit Intention in a Marketing Channel?" *Academy of Marketing Science* (Fall 1994): 364–371.
16. Gary Lilien, Philip Kotler, and K. Moorthy, *Marketing Models* (Upper Saddle River, NJ: Prentice Hall, 1992): 434–438; P. Hartung and J. Fisher, "Brand Switching and Mathematical Programming in Market Expansion," *Management Science* (August 1965): 231–243; and Gary Lilien and Ambar Rao, "A Model for Allocating Retail Outlet Building Resources Across Market Areas," *Operations Research* (January–February): 1–14.

FIGURE 10-2 COMMUNICATION OBJECTIVE AND CUSTOMER RESPONSE

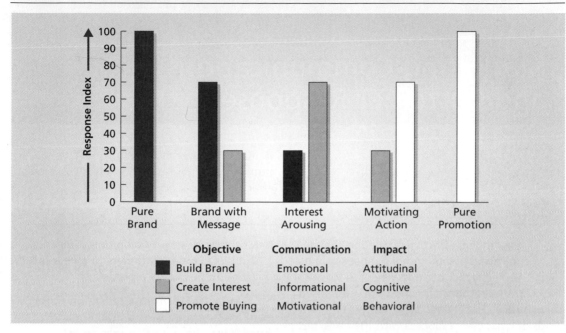

Figure 10-2 is an adaptation of the Brand Interaction Model developed by Richard Rosen.[1] In this model, the intent of a "pure brand" communication is entirely emotional in nature. The message, as with the image from the television ad in Figure 10-1, seeks only to instill in the minds of target customers an impression with respect to the brand. Its one purpose is to make

FIGURE 10-3 DESIRED CUSTOMER RESPONSE—INTEREST-AROUSING

CHAPTER 10

Marketing Communications and Customer Response

■ Marketing communications need a measurable customer-response objective to be effective.

Creating an effective marketing communication begins with a clear sense of its objective. A business needs to identify the customer response the message is supposed to produce. Businesses seek many different kinds of customer responses with their ads, but the objectives of most marketing communications fall into three general categories:

■ **Brand-Building Communications** seek to establish an emotional connection between the brand and the target customer.
■ **Interest-Arousing Communications** seek to motivate target customers to retain and acquire more information.

■ **Motivating-Action Communications** seek to stimulate target customers to take a specific action to buy or try a product.

Figure 10-1 is from a television advertisement that ran purely as a brand-building communication. Its objective was to establish an emotional connection among target customers with the Lance Armstrong Foundation, HP, and AMD. Sales of Lance Armstrong signature brand laptops helped raise money for the foundation's support of cancer research. This communication, as is true with many brand-building ads, needed little message content to achieve its objective.

FIGURE 10-1 DESIRED CUSTOMER RESPONSE—EMOTIONAL CONNECTION

a significant percentage of target customers aware of the business and its products or services. This kind of marketing communication is a pure brand-building communication, or an "awareness-building" communication.

The print ad in Figure 10-3 is a more complete presentation of the product, listing its benefits and price. It is an interest-arousing communication designed to provide information needed to form a favorable evaluation of the brand. The success of this marketing communication would be judged on the level and accuracy of retained information and the degree to which a favorable impression was formed.

The marketing communication in Figure 10-4 is "pure promotion." Its one intent is to stimulate

FIGURE 10-4 DESIRED CUSTOMER RESPONSE—MOTIVATING ACTION

FIGURE 10-5 DESIRED CUSTOMER RESPONSE—CREATE INTEREST

Who Leads In Marketing Excellence?

Join over 30,000 managers who have found the answers with MES.
Benchmark your business against world-class Fortune 500 companies operating in a variety of industries that span 100 countries.

The Marketing Excellence Survey Has The Answers
To learn more about who leads your company, go to www.mesurvey.com

target customers to purchase by offering an array of incentives, many more than in the smaller ad reproduced in Figure 10-3. These two marketing communications have different objectives, and the effectiveness of each is measured with a different customer response metric.

Between the two extremes shown in Figure 10-2 are three kinds of marketing communications that to varying degrees seek a dialogue or exchange of information between a target customer and the business. While brand building is a secondary objective, the primary goal of brand-interaction communications is to create contact between the business and the customer without any emphasis on purchase.

Figure 10-5 is a print advertisement for a firm that measures the level of marketing knowledge and marketing attitudes of managers within a business and then benchmarks the results with the levels of marketing knowledge and marketing attitudes of other managers in the firm's database and with other major businesses. The ad is an example of an interest-arousing marketing communication that will

lead to a dialogue. The intent is to raise the interest of target customers, to make them curious enough to visit the firm's Web site for more information. A print ad alone cannot always tell the whole story. In this case, the goal of the print ad is to provide only enough information to prompt customers to visit the firm's Web site.

The Web site's home page, reproduced in Figure 10-6, outlines the information the site contains and has a link to "Frequently Asked Questions." The site encourages target customers to contact the firm by clicking a link at the upper right of the home page, which allows them to submit information about themselves and their businesses. A target customer's decision to purchase is the net result of the information exchange prompted by the interest-arousing print ad, and the person-to-person contact prompted by the online brand interaction. Over 30 percent of those who contact the firm for additional information eventually buy the marketing benchmarking service, and 80 percent of those who become customers say they would recommend the service.

FIGURE 10-6 DESIRED CUSTOMER RESPONSE—INFORMATION ACQUISITION

BUILDING ADVERTISING AWARENESS

For a marketing communication to have any chance of achieving its customer-response objective, it must have some level of message frequency. To better understand how message frequency impacts the effectiveness of a marketing communications campaign, let's examine the results of a customer-response study conducted by a large nationwide department store. The target market was well defined, the selected media covered 75 percent of the target market, and the campaign featured merchandise known to have appeal in this target market. Full-page advertisements ran for 5 consecutive days in two daily newspapers, and radio spots aired the same 5 days on two stations that ran the ads two times in each of four time slots—early morning, midday, early evening, and late night.

Each evening during the 5-day advertising campaign, target customers were surveyed to determine their level of response. Figure 10-7 shows the level of advertising awareness for each of the 5 days. Although the ad awareness grew to 68 percent by day 5, most of the ad awareness, over 60 percent, was attained by the third day. But of the 68 percent who were aware of the marketing communication, only 43 percent could accurately describe the

FIGURE 10-7 ADVERTISING AWARENESS AND MESSAGE FREQUENCY

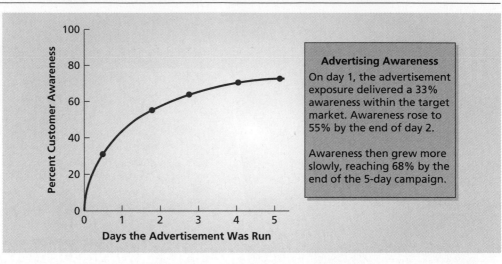

FIGURE 10-8 ADVERTISING EFFECTIVENESS AND CUSTOMER RESPONSE

ad content and store name, as shown in Figure 10-8. Of these respondents, a third stated an intention to act on the marketing communications, and 61 percent of those intending to buy the advertised merchandise actually made the purchase. The net result was that 4.3 percent of the target market took the intended action by purchasing the advertised merchandise.

When buyers were asked how they learned of the advertised merchandise, 46 percent mentioned newspaper A, 23 percent mentioned newspaper B, 18 percent said they heard about it from someone else, and 13 percent mentioned the radio ads. Perhaps a more significant finding was that the average purchase amount was $60, of which the advertised merchandise accounted for only about half. The marketing communications drew 4.3 percent of the target market to the store to buy the advertised merchandise, but these customers bought an almost equal amount of non-advertised merchandise. The net result was a meaningful gain in net marketing contribution.

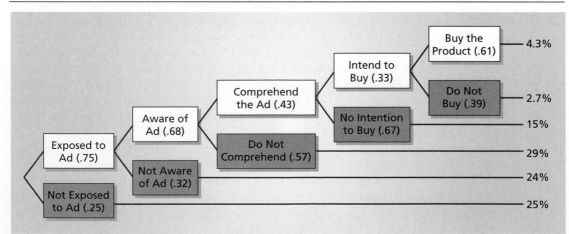

Customer Response Index

An effective marketing communications effort begins with building awareness and understanding of the message among target customers. A successful effort then creates an intent to purchase among a significant number of target customers, with a good portion of these customers actually making a purchase.

Figure 10-9 illustrates a hierarchical set of customer-response effects. Awareness, comprehension, intentions, and action are major steps upward in the hierarchy of customer response. If a marketing communication fails to reach target customers (exposure, the first stage in the hierarchy), none of the customer-response effects that follow are possible. In this example, the marketing communication did not reach 37 percent of the target market, and so these target customers did not have a chance to become aware, comprehend, form intentions, or take action. Of the 63 percent who were exposed to the ad, 54 percent recalled seeing it. This means another 29 percent of target customers (the 46 percent who were not aware of the ad out of the 63 percent who were exposed to it) had no possibility of further customer response due to having no awareness of the ad. The combination of target customers lost due to lack of exposure (37 percent) and awareness (29 percent) is 66 percent.

Of those target customers who were exposed to the ad and had an awareness of it, 77 percent adequately understood it, while 23 percent did not fully comprehend the content and its intended message. This created an additional lost-customer response of about 8 percent. Of those who understood the ad, 68 percent intended to take a desired action. Thirty-two percent of those who understood the ad were not motivated to take action, which resulted in another 8 percent loss in customer response. Target customers who intended to take action but did not created an additional loss of potential customer response

FIGURE 10-9 MARKETING COMMUNICATIONS AND CUSTOMER RESPONSE INDEX

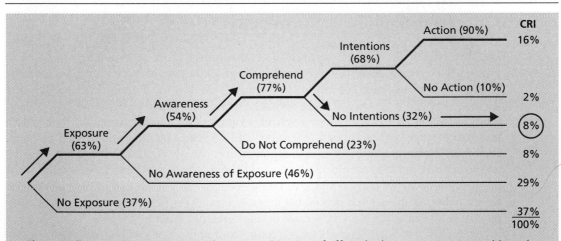

The overall customer response index for any combination of effects in the customer-response hierarchy is the product of the proportions of individual effects that make up that combination. For example, the customer response index for customers who were exposed to the communication (63%), are aware of it (54%), comprehend its content (77%), but are *not* interested in the product or service (32%) is as follows:

CRI = % Exposed × % Aware × % Comprehend × % Not Interested
= 0.63 × 0.54 × 0.77 × 0.32
= **0.08, or 8%**

FIGURE 10-10 CAUSES OF LOW LEVELS OF CUSTOMER RESPONSE

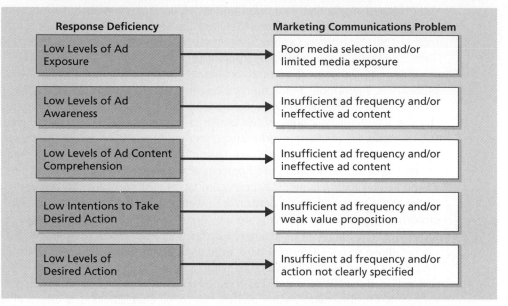

of 2 percent. Finally, target customers who were exposed, were aware, comprehended, intended to take action, and took the desired action produced an overall customer response index (CRI) of 16 percent. In order to achieve a higher CRI, a business would need to assess the weaker stages in the customer response hierarchy with an eye toward strengthening them.

STRATEGIES TO INCREASE CUSTOMER RESPONSE

Possible causes of poor performance in the customer-response hierarchy are listed in Figure 10-10. A low level of target market reach (exposure) usually occurs because the wrong media were chosen or media coverage was too narrow. If appropriate media were used and exposure was broad, then deficiencies in the marketing communication itself are probably at fault for any low levels of awareness and comprehension. Insufficient message frequency (not enough repetition) and poor ad copy both contribute to target customers' lack of awareness and comprehension. A low percentage rate for the customers who intend to act could also be the result of ineffective ad copy, or of a weak value proposition. Poor ad copy could also be the reason for a disappointing response with regard to taking the desired action, but other factors might be responsible, such as competitor actions or unsatisfactory service during order placement.

Identifying the deficiencies in a marketing communication enables a business to correct them. For example, assume for the situation in Figure 10-9 that the business used media that reached more target customers and the ad was run more often, increasing awareness from 63 to 75 percent. This increase would translate into a potential increase in the overall CRI from 16 to 19 percent.

$$\textbf{CRI} \ (\text{current}) = 0.63 \times 0.54 \times 0.77 \times 0.68 \times 0.90 = \textbf{0.16}$$
$$\textbf{CRI} \ (\text{improved}) = 0.75 \times 0.54 \times 0.77 \times 0.68 \times 0.90 = \textbf{0.19}$$

Assume also, because of improved ad copy, that target customers' comprehension of the marketing communication increased from 54 to 67 percent. The combined effects of increased awareness and comprehension would result in a 50 percent increase in the CRI, from 16 to 24 percent.

$$\textbf{CRI}\ (\text{improved}) = 0.75 \times 0.67 \times 0.77 \times 0.68 \times 0.90 = \textbf{0.24}$$

Even a well-positioned product with an attractive customer value (perceived benefits that are greater than perceived costs) and a strong marketing channel system will not achieve full marketing success without a good marketing communications program. If target customers are largely unaware of the product and its benefits, cost, and value, sales cannot be anything but slow.

For example, Johnson Controls is a *Fortune* 500 business that serves a variety of markets, one of which is the commercial building services market. Johnson Controls has built an excellent reputation among its current customers. However, a market research study revealed a low awareness level of the business among potential customers in the commercial building services market; potential customers mentioned Johnson Controls with a disappointing low frequency when asked to identify suppliers of commercial building services.[2]

In response to this information, Johnson Controls developed the "Classic Buildings" marketing communication reproduced in Figure 10-11. This print ad was run in *Forbes*, *Fortune*, *Business Week*, and *The Wall Street Journal*, each of which reaches building and facilities managers—the target customers—in *Fortune* 1000 businesses. Nine months after the campaign, measurements were made. Unaided recall of Johnson Controls had

FIGURE 10-11 JOHNSON CONTROLS' "CLASSIC BUILDINGS" PRINT AD

STRUCTURALLY SOUND *with*

GOOD *fire* RESISTANCE

although LAWNCARE & GENERAL

GROUNDSKEEPING

COULD BE *upgraded.*

When we look at a building, we see it as being more than simply steel, glass or brick. We see it as a total building environment.

That means comfortable indoor temperatures. Great lighting and truly balanced acoustics.

It also means the outside of the building. The landscaping, the groundskeeping. It means painting and cleaning. In fact, it can include security, and even food service.

We are, in short, committed to creating the ideal building environment.

One of the most economical and practical ways to achieve this is through outsourcing. Whereby you contract an outside company to perform everyday services that are quite separate from your core business.

With over 40 years of experience in integrated facility management, we have the skills to provide a complete range of services. From mail services to heating, ventilation and air conditioning to structural maintenance.

The savings are often quite dramatic. And, ultimately, outsourcing

lets you spend more of your valuable time doing what you do best.

As the experienced leader, we realize that any building, given the right kind of attention, can become more comfortable and productive. There is absolutely no reason why your business can't be as well.

Which is precisely why we have always been interested in improving life in the great indoors. Not to mention outdoors.

[El Castillo, Chichen Itza, Mexico]

increased by 30 percent. The marketing communications effort had increased awareness of the company and helped pre-sell its services. Both effects contributed to an increase in sales.

The importance of customer awareness and response is highlighted in Figure 10-12. For any level of awareness, the levels of comprehension, intention, and purchase are successively lower. Perhaps more important is the fact that the level of customer loyalty is lower still. Sustained profitability depends on customer retention, and each step in the hierarchy of customer response is a step toward profitability. In this example, we can see that 30 percent awareness results in a low level of customer loyalty. When awareness is raised to 80 percent, the subsequent customer responses and customer loyalty are higher. Awareness is the first step in new-customer acquisition. The higher the awareness for a product, the higher is the customer response and the higher the potential for customer retention. A 5 percent increase in retention produces a 25 percent increase in the average lifetime value of a customer. Raising awareness, then, is a first step in building profits based on brand and customer loyalty.

FIGURE 10-12 ADVERTISING EFFECTIVENESS AND CUSTOMER RESPONSE

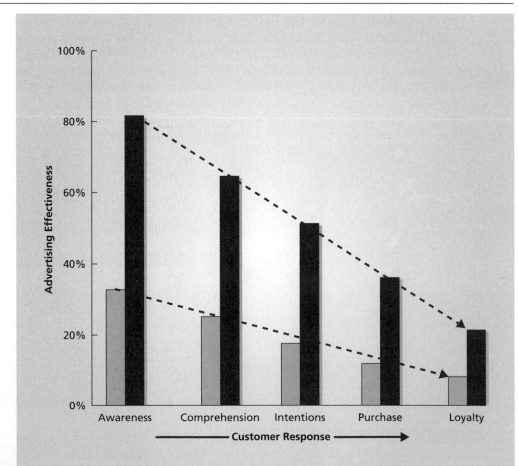

BUILDING CUSTOMER AWARENESS AND COMPREHENSION

Creating awareness among a large number of people is not the objective of most marketing communications. The objective is to create awareness among and communicate effectively to *target customers*. Even a memorable advertisement that is well known among the general population is a failure if it does not achieve a high level of awareness and comprehension among target customers.

Media Selection and Customer Awareness

As we saw in Figure 10-10, target-customer awareness and comprehension are affected by media selection, message frequency, and ad copy. To reach target customers effectively, a business has to have a good understanding of the media habits of its target customers. Do they watch television, and, if they do, which programs? Do they listen to the radio, and, if so, which stations and at what times? Which newspapers and which sections of the newspaper do they read? Which magazines do they subscribe to? With respect to exposure to outdoor signage, which streets and highways are they likely to drive? Do they use the *Yellow Pages*? Are they Internet users or cable TV shoppers? Do they respond to direct mail advertising? A business must consider all these questions in order to select the right combination of media outlets for cost effectively reaching its target customers.

A key measure of effective media selection is target market reach. Target market reach is the percentage of target customers who will be exposed to the business's message given a certain combination of media. A golf ball manufacturer, for example, would want to reach golfers. The manufacturer might advertise in print media such as *Golf Digest*, *Golf Magazine*, *The Wall Street Journal*, and *Business Week* and on television during broadcasts of golf tournaments. With this combination of media, let's assume the manufacturer reaches 63 percent of its target customers. To obtain a target market reach greater than 63 percent would require the manufacturer to add media that reach target customers not exposed to the ads by the current combination of media. If the cost of the incremental reach were more than the incremental economic benefit derived from it, then the business would not want to go beyond its current level of target market reach.[3]

Message Frequency and Customer Awareness

Once a business has found the right combination of media for effectively reaching target customers, the business then needs to determine how often to expose target customers to its message in order to achieve a high level of awareness. With infrequent exposure, most target customers will not become fully conscious of the message, resulting in low levels of awareness and comprehension. On the other hand, too many exposures could irritate target customers and produce an adverse effect on retained information, as well as on perceptions of the ad, product, or company.

A few years ago, AFLAC insurance had a name recognition rating of only 13 percent in the United States. The company decided to undertake a marketing communications campaign to cut through the clutter of mundane insurance ads and raise brand awareness. The TV commercials it would use had to be unique and memorable. The company found what it was looking for and initially spent $35 million on its commercials. The now-famous AFLAC duck produced more sales leads in the first 2 weeks that the commercials aired than in the

FIGURE 10-13 ADVERTISING FREQUENCY AND AWARENESS IN A BUSINESS-TO-BUSINESS MARKET

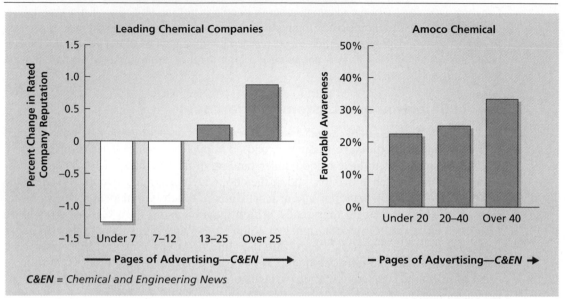

previous 2 years, resulting in record revenues. AFLAC's recognition rating skyrocketed to over 90 percent, and revenues grew 30 percent annually over the duration of this advertising campaign. But after several years of hearing the duck screaming "AFLAC!" in various situations, people grew tired of the ads and even found them irritating. At some point, the positive impact of repetition begins to regress into negative perceptions.

Figure 10-13 shows how the frequency of print advertising by leading chemical companies affects the year-to-year change in ratings of company reputation. Leading chemical companies that advertise fewer than 12 times annually in *Chemical and Engineering News (C&EN)* adversely affect their reputations, whereas those at higher levels of frequency positively affect their reputations.[4] For Amoco Chemical, the level of favorable awareness steadily increased with the level of message frequency in *C&EN*. If Amoco Chemical were to stop its marketing communications, over a relatively short time its level of awareness among target customers would diminish.

Shown in Figure 10-14 are the results of a classic study on message frequency and awareness.[5] In a "concentrated frequency" strategy, 13 consecutive messages were directed to target customers over 13 weeks. As shown, the message awareness steadily increased each week until it reached its highest level in week 13. However, after week 13, no more messages were directed to target customers for the remainder of the year and, as shown, the message awareness decayed to almost zero. This marketing communications strategy would be appropriate for building awareness and comprehension for seasonal products, political candidates, and special events.

The same message was also sent to a different group of target customers once every 4 weeks throughout the year in a "distributed frequency" strategy. These target customers, like the other group, also received 13 message exposures, but the exposures were spread out over the entire year. During the 4-week period following each exposure, recall of the message decreased, but at the end of each 4-week period, recall was still above the level it had been just prior to the most recent exposure, as Figure 10-14 illustrates. Each additional

FIGURE 10-14 MESSAGE FREQUENCY AND MESSAGE AWARENESS

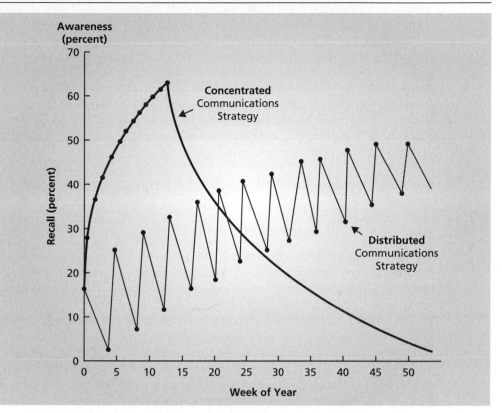

exposure, then, built from a higher base position—and although this pattern of exposure frequency produced a longer-lasting effect, it never reached the highest level of awareness produced by the concentrated frequency effort. The distributed frequency strategy would be appropriate in building and maintaining target customer awareness and comprehension.

Figure 10-14 assumes that all target customers were exposed to every one of the 13 messages. Typically, however, any one target customer is exposed to only a fraction of the total number of messages in an advertising campaign. So, for most marketing communications, there are more messages sent than received, as illustrated in the following:

Number of Ads Recalled	Proportion Recalling	Weighted Average
0	0.10	0.00
1	0.10	0.10
2	0.10	0.20
3	0.10	0.30
4	0.15	0.60
5	0.20	1.00
6	0.15	0.90
7	0.05	0.35
8	0.05	0.40
Total	**1.00**	**3.85**

In this example, eight marketing communications were directed to target customers. Ten percent did not recall seeing any of the ads, while 5 percent recalled seeing all eight. A weighted average of this recall yields an average message frequency of approximately 4. This means the average target customer was exposed to only about four of the eight marketing communications that the business directed to its target customers during the exposure period. In television advertising, the combined impact of message frequency and reach produces an index called *gross rating points* (GRPs). A business with a 60 percent reach and a frequency of 4 produces an impact of 240 GRPs. Because GRPs measure the extent to which an ad reached the target market and how often the ad was seen, they are a far better measure of advertising effectiveness than the dollars spent on advertising.

$$\textbf{Gross Rating Points} = \text{Reach} \times \text{Frequency} = 60 \times 4 = \textbf{240}$$

Ad Copy and Customer Response

Because ad copy plays such a key role in creating awareness, comprehension, and intentions, it is important that a business be sure its message is received and accurately interpreted by target customers. For Gardenburger, the stakes were extremely high when it ran an advertisement during the final episode of *Seinfeld*, at a cost of $1.5 million. The cost of this one ad increased the company's advertising expenses by 500 percent. That Gardenburger should first test the ad had seemed appropriate, and the company did in fact run a storyboard of its ad past various focus groups to test the ad's concept before producing it. Once tested and refined, Gardenburger proceeded with the 30-second ad. The results were sensational! The ad reached 76 million people, and store sales improved by 328 percent over the same week of the previous year. Even though expensive, this marketing communication produced an increase in both sales and profits.

But a highly memorable marketing communication that does not communicate the product and its benefits will fail to raise interest in the product and will lower the overall level of customer response. Ad copy can best attract customers when it is based on customer needs and situations familiar to customers. It must integrate customer needs and situations with the product's benefits and business name.[6] If an ad is attractive but fails to create product interest, the ad copy is of limited value to the customer and to the business.

Loctite, for example, once introduced a product under the brand name RC-601.[7] The ad copy, aimed at production managers, was highly technical, which seemed appropriate. But the ad failed to generate any demand for RC-601. Follow-up customer research revealed that the true target customers for the ad should have been machine maintenance and repair workers, a group generally not accustomed to reading highly technical language. Based on a revised profile of its target customer, Loctite renamed the product Quick Metal and reintroduced it along with new ad copy aimed at machine maintenance and repair workers. This ad copy, with photographs showing the product's applications, served for both a direct mail piece and a trade-press advertisement. The results were remarkable. Quick Metal achieved first-year sales at a level higher than any other new product in the company's history.

MESSAGE REINFORCEMENT

Although building the awareness, comprehension, and intentions of target customers is critical to achieving a high level of customer response, this level will diminish if the message is not continually reinforced. We saw that Johnson Controls' marketing communications program improved awareness of the company, but to hold or grow awareness, the company needed to keep its message in front of target customers.

Message Reinforcement and Pulsing

Maintaining a high level of awareness is expensive and requires new ad copy as the old copy wears out. One cost-effective approach to message reinforcement that maintains awareness and reduces copy wear-out is called *pulsing*.[8] Pulsing involves the use of alternating exposure periods. An example of pulsing is a television advertisement that achieves 150 GRPs over a 4-week exposure period and is run in alternating 4-week periods. As shown in Figure 10-15, a certain level of awareness is built up during a 4-week

FIGURE 10-15 MESSAGE REINFORCEMENT STRATEGIES

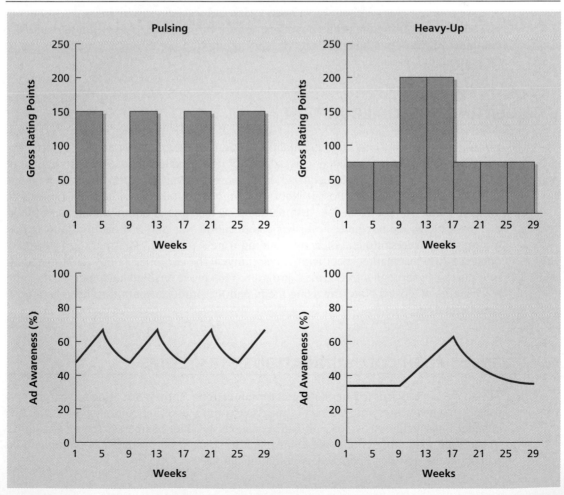

exposure period; it then diminishes during the following 4-week period of no message exposure, and then awareness is built up again in the next 4-week exposure period.

If a business can maintain a desired level of awareness with pulsing, it can reduce the cost of advertising because no advertising costs are incurred in the alternating 4-week periods of no exposure. A secondary benefit of pulsing is that it reduces copy wear-out due to overexposure to the same message. Because the marketing message is not seen on a continual basis, the ad copy's novelty and appeal wear out at a slower rate. Pulsing also reduces the potential for overexposure, which can cause customer irritation and reduce ad effectiveness.

Heavy-Up Message Frequency

Because certain products are purchased more frequently at some times of the year than at others, a business may use a heavy-up exposure pattern to build higher levels of awareness, comprehension, and, it is hoped, interest in the advertised product or service. Figure 10-15 illustrates a heavy-up marketing communications program for a well-known brand with a high level of consumption during the summer. Many other exposure patterns are possible but, in this example, the business elects to maintain a certain level of base awareness throughout most of the year and to heavy-up its message frequency just before and during the prime buying period for this product. The business could also combine a heavy-up strategy for its primary promotion period with a pulsing strategy throughout the rest of the year.

STIMULATING CUSTOMER ACTION

Informing target customers and maintaining awareness are often not enough to stimulate customer action. More is needed, particularly for new products whose benefits cannot be fully realized until they have been tried. For example, advertising copy that attempted to explain the benefits of the Post-it Note was simply not taken seriously by target customers.[9] After 18 months in four test markets, 3M's efforts to communicate the benefits of Post-it Notes led nowhere. A further complication was that 3M had a policy against giving away free samples when introducing a new product. The marketing director opened a fifth test market specifically to circumvent the corporate policy and to generate trial purchases through a free-sample program. This move enabled customers to discover the benefits of Post-it Notes by using them, and the product went on to become a great commercial success.

PULL VERSUS PUSH COMMUNICATIONS STRATEGIES

So far we have discussed marketing communications as they are aimed at target customers, but businesses with indirect channels also aim marketing communications at their channel intermediaries. Among all U.S. consumer product businesses, about two-thirds of the total marketing communications expense is spent on customer communications and about one-third on intermediary communications.

FIGURE 10-16 PUSH-PULL COMMUNICATIONS AND CUSTOMER RESPONSE

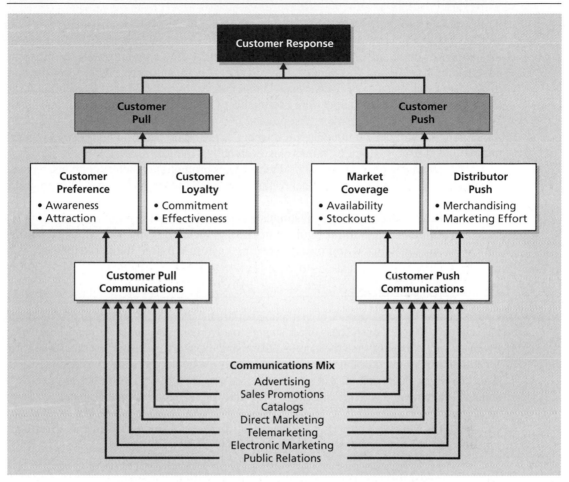

Customer-directed marketing communications are *pull* communications. The objectives of a pull marketing communication, as shown in Figure 10-16, are to build awareness, attraction, and loyalty and to reduce search costs. When a pull marketing communication is successful, customers will seek out the product and, in effect, by the interest they create, pull the product through the channel. A pull strategy must ensure that channel intermediaries carry the product in sufficient quantities.

Push communications are directed at channel intermediaries. The objective in this case is to motivate channel intermediaries to carry a particular product or brand and, in this way, make it more available to customers. When successful, push communications result in wider availability, fewer stockouts, more-visible merchandising (shelf space), and a more efficient use of marketing dollars.

It is important, however, to understand that it is the combination of both pull and push marketing communications that creates the greatest impact on customer response and, therefore, market share gains.[10]

PULL COMMUNICATIONS AND CUSTOMER RESPONSE

As also shown in Figure 10-16, a wide range of alternative marketing communications can be used to fashion a communications mix designed to create customer pull.[11] To illustrate the power of media advertising, consider the fate of L&M cigarettes. Before cigarette advertising on television was banned, L&M had a 17 percent market share. After the ban, the decision was made to stop advertising altogether, because L&M management believed that other forms of advertising were ineffective. The managers were wrong, and today L&M is no longer on the market. The product had good brand recognition and good customer pull, but without continued reinforcement of the brand name and its positioning, the product faded from customers' minds and, eventually, from the marketplace.

There are many forms of customer-directed sales promotions, such as coupons, rebates, sweepstakes, gifts, and rewards. When United Airlines initiated its Mileage Plus program, it changed how customers selected airlines and flights. Catalogs like those published by L.L.Bean, Eddie Bauer, and Spiegel stimulate customer pull every month with mailings to targeted customers. Other forms of direct marketing, including e-marketing, take a similar but even more customized approach to creating customer pull in the marketplace.

Advertising Elasticity

Understanding the sales impact of marketing communications is important in market-based management. The responsiveness of consumers to advertising expenditures can be measured as *advertising elasticity*. One measure of advertising elasticity is the percent change in sales or volume per 1 percent change in advertising effort. Although there are considerable variations among products and market situations, short-run advertising elasticities are relatively small when compared with price elasticities. A study of 128 advertising elasticities produced an average advertising elasticity of 0.22, with very few advertising elasticities greater than 0.5. An advertising elasticity of 0.22 means that for every 1 percent change in advertising expenditures, the volume sold will change by 0.22 percent.[12]

One way to estimate advertising elasticity for a change in marketing expenditures is to estimate the advertising elasticity needed to maintain current marketing profits (net marketing contribution). For example, in Figure 10-17 the business has an advertising budget of $1 million, sales of $20 million, and a net marketing contribution of $3 million. The marketing team feels a 25 percent increase in advertising would achieve a 21.5 percent market share. To hold the current level of net marketing contribution ($3 million), the business needs a 20.8 percent share, which produces a 4 percent increase in sales. As shown in Figure 10-17, this requires a 0.16 advertising elasticity. If the advertising elasticity were smaller than 0.16, the strategy to increase advertising expenditures would lower profits. If the advertising elasticity were greater than 0.16, the strategy would increase profits. For the strategy to achieve the target share of 21.5 percent, the advertising elasticity would have to be 0.30.

For the Gardenburger advertisement that aired once during the *Seinfeld* finale, the advertising elasticity was 0.66. Gardenburger sales increased 328 percent with a 500 percent increase in advertising budget.

$$\textbf{Advertising Elasticity} = \frac{\text{Percent Change in Sales (weekly)}}{\text{Percent Change in Advertising Expense (weekly)}} = \frac{328\%}{500\%} = \textbf{0.66}$$

FIGURE 10-17 ESTIMATING ADVERTISING ELASTICITY

Performance Factor	Current	Hold Profit	Goal
Market Demand	100,000	100,000	100,000
Market Share	20.0%	20.8%	21.5%
Volume Sold	20,000	20,800	21,500
Price	$1,000	$1,000	$1,000
Net Sales	$20,000,000	$20,800,000	$21,500,000
Percent Margin	30.0%	30.0%	30.0%
Gross Profit	$6,000,000	$6,240,000	$6,450,000
Advertising Expense	$1,000,000	$1,250,000	$1,250,000
Other Marketing & Sales Exp.	$2,000,000	$2,000,000	$2,000,000
Total Marketing & Sales Budget	$3,000,000	$3,250,000	$3,250,000
Net Marketing Contribution	$3,000,000	$2,990,000	$3,200,000
Percent Change in Sales		4.0%	7.5%
Percent Change in Advertising		25.0%	25.0%
Advertising Elasticity		0.16	0.30

It is important to keep in mind that there are limits to what advertising can accomplish with respect to sales response at different stages of the product life cycle. During the introductory stage, a business builds awareness, comprehension, and interest, but the market demand might be small. Even when advertisements have good reach, high awareness, and excellent ad copy, a new product may at first achieve only a limited sales response.

The growth stage of the product life cycle offers the greatest opportunity for sales gains using advertising. A business that does not invest in advertising during this phase is missing its best opportunity to grow sales, because advertising elasticities will be greatest during this period. However, as a market matures, less new volume comes into the market, and the effects of advertising on sales response begin to diminish. Finally, in declining markets, a business needs to cut back on advertising because dollars spent on advertising produce little, if any, sales response.

Advertising Carryover Effects

In addition to a short-run advertising impact on sales response, advertising also has been shown to have a long-run carryover effect—that is, the advertising effort made in a given period will produce some additional sales response in subsequent sales periods. Advertising carryover coefficients range from 0 to less than 1, with the average carryover coefficient equal to approximately 0.5.[13] This means that in the period immediately following the ad effort, a 0.5 sales effect from the previous period will carry over. In the second period, the carryover effect of 0.5 is squared, and 0.25 of the sales response produced two periods earlier occurs, and so on, as shown in Figure 10-18.

For the *Seinfeld* Gardenburger ad, assume that the carryover effect was 0.5. Recall that the Gardenburger advertising elasticity was 0.66. This produced first-week incremental sales

FIGURE 10-18 MEDIA ADVERTISING AND SALES CARRYOVER

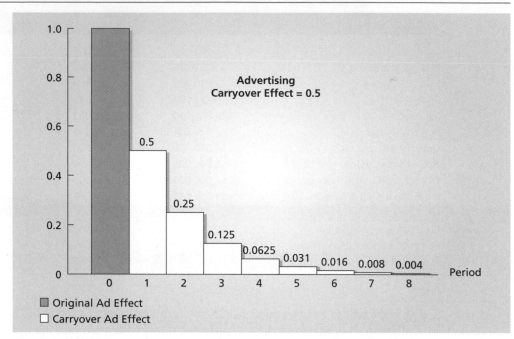

(sales above the norm) of approximately $1.5 million. With a 0.5 advertising carryover effect, the total impact of this ad expenditure effect would be approximately $3 million.

$$\textbf{Total Sales Effect} = \frac{\text{Incremental Sales}}{1 - \text{Carryover Effect}} = \frac{\$1.5 \text{ million}}{1 - .5} = \textbf{\$3 million}$$

The overall sales response to the advertising effort would be double the short-run effect shown in Figure 10-18.

Although there are statistical methods that can be used to estimate the carryover effect of a marketing communication, Figure 10-19 presents a simple method for estimating the

FIGURE 10-19 ESTIMATING ADVERTISING CARRYOVER SALES EFFECT

Advertising Period:	0	1	2
Advertising Expense	$10,000	$15,000	$10,000
Sales Performance—			
Without Ad Spending Increase	$195,000	$200,000	$205,000
With Ad Spending Increase		$220,000	$210,000
Incremental Sales		$ 20,000	$5,000
Estimated Carryover Effect	0.25		
Total Incremental Sales	$26,667		
Carryover Sales (after period 1)	$6,667		

next period's carryover sales. In this example, sales were growing at 2.5 percent monthly with the business's customary amount of advertising. With a 1-month 50 percent increase in the advertising effort ($10,000 to $15,000), sales during that month increased by 10 percent, resulting in an advertising elasticity of 0.2. However, in the month following the increased advertising effort, sales were $5,000 above what would have been expected. This 25 percent increase over normal sales represents an estimate of the carryover effect. A 0.25 carryover effect results in total incremental sales of $26,667. The marketing communications campaign, then, produced an increase in sales of $20,000 during the month of increased advertising, and additional sales of $6,667 over the next several months.

$$\textbf{Total Sales Effect} = \frac{\text{Incremental Sales}}{1 - \text{Carryover Effect}} = \frac{\$20,000}{1 - .25} = \textbf{\$26,667}$$

Direct Marketing Promotions

Database marketing makes customized direct mail programs a viable means for efficiently reaching target customers and giving them an incentive to take action. Consider a new sparkling wine for which the producer direct mailed 100,000 known champagne consumers a $5 coupon. As shown in Figure 10-20, only 5 percent of the target customers responded by using the coupon. Of these 5,000 customers, 2,000 tried the new sparkling wine but did not repurchase; 1,000 used the coupon and became occasional buyers at the rate of one bottle per year; and 2,000 used the coupon and became regular purchasers at the rate of four bottles per year. Among the 95 percent who did not respond, 30 percent never opened the mailer, and 65 percent opened it and were favorably impressed. Of these 65,000 customers, 5,000 purchased the product without the coupon at a later date. In total, 16,000 bottles of the new sparkling wine were purchased as a result of the direct mail program, even though there was only a 5 percent initial response.[14]

FIGURE 10-20 CUSTOMER RESPONSE TO A DIRECT MARKETING PROMOTION

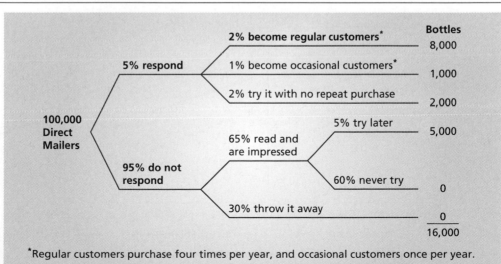

*Regular customers purchase four times per year, and occasional customers once per year.

Promotional Price Elasticity

The average price elasticity for consumer nondurable products is −1.76, according to a study of 367 brands.[15] For the three product categories shown in Figure 10-21, however, the price elasticities are considerably higher.[16] Assume the market demand for sparkling wine is 10 million bottles per month and that a particular brand has a 4 percent market share, which results in a unit volume of 400,000 bottles. Without advertising, this brand should experience a promotional price elasticity of −10. A 5 percent price promotion should then yield a 50 percent increase in unit volume, from 400,000 to 600,000 per month.

$$\textbf{Unit Volume} = (10 \text{ million} \times .04) \times [1 + (-10 \times -.05)]$$
$$= 400,000 \times 1.5$$
$$= \textbf{600,000 bottles}$$

By combining a price promotion with advertising, the promotional price elasticity can be further increased, as shown in Figure 10-22. For example, the promotion price elasticity of sparkling wine increases to approximately −14 with the support of an advertising campaign. This would produce additional unit sales of 80,000 with a 5 percent price promotion.

$$\textbf{Unit Volume} = (10 \text{ million} \times .04) \times [1 + (-14 \times -.05)]$$
$$= 400,000 \times 1.7$$
$$= \textbf{680,000 bottles}$$

In all three cases shown in Figure 10-21, the promotional price elasticity increased significantly with the use of advertising. For cat litter, this effect was very dramatic, doubling promotional elasticities. It is also important to note that the promotional elasticities decreased with the increase in market share.

FIGURE 10-21 PROMOTIONAL PRICE ELASTICITY WITH AND WITHOUT ADVERTISING

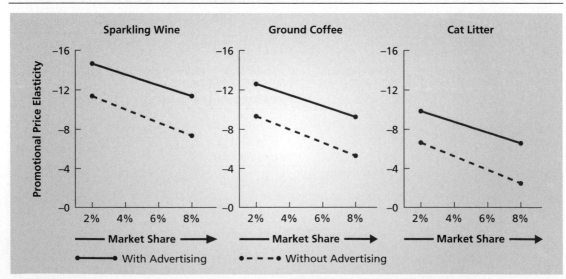

Recognizing the high level of price sensitivity to promotions and the tremendous short-run revenue gain they can achieve, we can understand why many businesses have increased their use of them. But a marketing strategy that seeks profitable growth must also produce a higher net marketing contribution. In a market-based business, managers will then also assess the profit impact of a marketing communications effort.

PUSH COMMUNICATIONS AND CUSTOMER RESPONSE

As we saw earlier, marketing communications directed at channel intermediaries are designed as push communications; they stimulate intermediaries to engage in aggressive customer promotion efforts. Figure 10-16 shows that the objective of push communications is to build greater product availability and marketing effort. Businesses that are aggressive in rewarding and supporting channel intermediaries are able to obtain more market coverage (number of desired distributors) than are nonaggressive businesses. This support provides several mechanisms to deliver effective in-store merchandising and marketing efforts of a business's products.

Trade Promotions and Customer Response

Trade promotions designed to stimulate purchase are common among businesses that sell their products through intermediaries. Quite often, trade promotions involve price reductions to distributors or retailers. The idea is that the price incentive will motivate intermediaries to push the product.

Let's assume that a normal can of orange juice concentrate costs $1.49 and the manufacturer offers a 20 cent discount to encourage the retail trade to push the sale of the manufacturer's brand of frozen concentrate. Assume also that the normal sales level is 1 million cans per month, the retailer margin is normally 19 cents per can, the manufacturer's sales and distribution costs are 15 cents per can, and each unit costs 50 cents to produce. In nonpromotion months, the manufacturer would expect to make $650,000 in gross profit, as shown here:

$$\begin{aligned} \underset{\text{(current)}}{\overset{\textbf{Gross}}{\textbf{Profit}}} &= \frac{\text{Current}}{\text{Volume}} \times \left(\frac{\text{Retail}}{\text{Price}} - \frac{\text{Retailer}}{\text{Margin}} - \frac{\text{Sales and}}{\text{Distribution Cost}} - \frac{\text{Unit}}{\text{Cost}} \right) \\ &= 1{,}000{,}000 \times (\$1.49 - \$0.19 - \$0.15 - \$0.50) \\ &= 1{,}000{,}000 \times \$0.65 \\ &= \mathbf{\$650{,}000} \end{aligned}$$

An important question for the manufacturer should be how much volume a trade promotion would have to produce to make a promotional period as profitable as a typical non-promotional period. With the discount, the manufacturer's net promotional margin per unit drops to 45 cents per can. As shown, the business would have to increase sales by 44 percent to 1.44 million cans in order to produce the same level of profitability.

$650,000 = Promotion Volume $\times$ ($1.49 - $0.19 - $0.15 - $0.50 - $0.20 discount)
$650,000 = Promotion Volume $\times$ $0.45
Promotion Volume = **1.44 million units**

Market Infrastructure and Push Communications

Figure 10-22 illustrates the non-market sources that influence a communications market infrastructure consisting of both end-user customers and intermediaries.[17] For example, marketing communications targeted at industry gurus, consultants, and financial analysts create secondary marketing communications that then influence the trade press, the business press, and the general press. These non-market sources of influence in turn provide information to channel intermediaries and customers.

The solid lines in Figure 10-22 represent normal marketing communications targeted at customers or intermediaries. Dashed lines are indirect communications—the type of communications targeted at individuals and institutions that influence customers and

FIGURE 10-22 MARKET INFRASTRUCTURE AND PUSH MARKETING COMMUNICATIONS

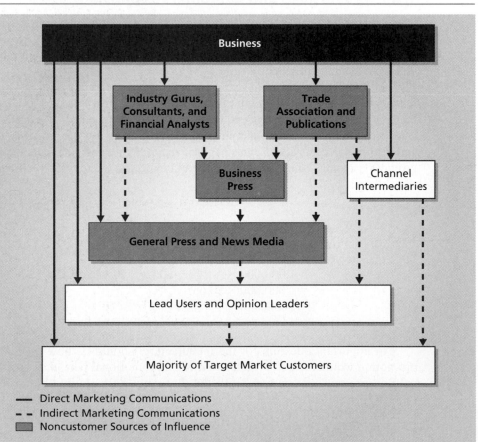

channel intermediaries. Some of these indirect communications are primary communications (from the company to the source of the influence), and others are secondary communications (from one source of influence to another). Of course, one of the most important sources of secondary marketing communications is from lead users and opinion leaders who communicate by word of mouth to the larger market of target customers.

■ Summary

Without an effective marketing communications program, a marketing strategy will fail. Target customers must be made aware of the product and its benefits, be continually reminded of these benefits, and be stimulated to take action. Building awareness, message comprehension, and interest are essential phases in achieving a high level of customer response. The customer response index is a diagnostic tool that enables a management team to determine the sources of weakness in its marketing communications program.

To be effective and cost efficient, a business's marketing communications must reach target customers and have an adequate level of message frequency to maintain desired levels of awareness, comprehension, and interest. Pulsing enables a business to use alternate exposure periods to more economically maintain customer awareness and interest, while reducing the problem of ad copy wear-out. Heavy-up efforts enable a business to build awareness and interest to higher levels during seasonal buying periods.

To build market share, a business needs both pull and push marketing communications. Pull marketing communications are targeted at customers with the intent of creating enough awareness and interest to motivate them to demand the business's product. This customer demand creates market pull on intermediaries who, in turn, want the business's products on hand to satisfy this customer demand. Push marketing communications are directed at intermediaries, with the intent of pushing the product through the channel. The objectives of push communications are to create greater availability of, interest in, and access to the business's products.

Although the sales response to a marketing communication is difficult to know in advance, the customer response index, advertising elasticity, advertising carryover effects, and promotional price elasticity provide systematic methods for estimating this response. But sales response should not be the primary objective of a marketing communication. For marketing communications designed to increase sales, it is more important to estimate the profit impact of that promotion. Many sales promotions are not profitable, but businesses are forced into them to minimize losses.

Most markets contain a marketing communications infrastructure that includes customers, intermediaries, and non-market sources of influence. Some push marketing communications are public relations–type communications directed at non-market sources that can influence channel intermediaries and customers.

■ Market-Based Strategic Thinking

1 What type of marketing communication is Lexus most likely to create? How could the company measure the effectiveness of its communications effort?

2 What type of marketing communication would be most effective in motivating individuals to donate to a social cause?

3 How would a company such as Apple uses a combination of the communication strategies shown in Figure 10-2?

4 Why would an interest-arousing communication be more effective for a brand with low awareness?

5 What role does message exposure play in the success of a marketing communication?

6 Why are customer awareness and message comprehension critical to the success of a marketing strategy?

7 How can interest in ad copy affect interest in a product and subsequently influence customer response?

8 When a business has an excellent marketing communications program and high intention by customers to purchase, but a very low customer response, what kind of a marketing problem does it face?

9 When should a business use a combination of pulsing and heavy-up marketing communications?

10 Why is the message frequency for a marketing communication considerably lower than the number of messages sent?

11 Why will a business's market share be lower if it is not effective with both pull and push marketing communications?

12 At what stage of a product's life cycle is advertising elasticity likely to be highest?

13 How should the carryover sales effect of an advertising effort be used in evaluating the profit impact of the advertising effort?

14 What are the various behaviors that need to be tracked in order to evaluate the profit impact of a trade promotion?

15 How does the promotional price elasticity for a product change with advertising support? What effect does market share have on promotional price elasticity?

16 Why are the marketing communications infrastructure and public relations–type marketing communications important to the overall success of a marketing communications effort?

17 If advertising elasticity is so much smaller than promotional price elasticity, why should a business advertise?

18 How should a business use the advertising carryover effect in evaluating the sales response and profitability of a marketing communication?

19 Why are indirect sales promotions rarely profitable? Why do manufacturers continue to offer indirect sales promotions despite their unprofitability?

20 How does retailer forward buying affect trade promotion profitability?

Marketing Performance Tools

The three **Marketing Performance Tools** described here may be accessed online at *www.rogerjbest.com*. These applied-learningexercises will add to your understanding ofcustomer response to marketing communications, advertising elasticity, and the advertising carryover effect. The instructions refer to the online examples, not the related Chapter 10 figures cited.

10.1 Marketing Communications and Customer Response (Figure 10-9)

- Using the data provided, how do the results of this marketing communication change when advertising exposure is only 50 percent?
- Using the results provided, evaluate the impact of improving ad awareness from 54 to 68 percent.
- For future advertisements, would it be more effective to work on increasing comprehension by 5 points (from 77% to 82%) or to work on improving intentions to purchase by 5 points (from 68% to 73%)?

10.2 Estimating Advertising Elasticity (Figure 10-17)

- Using the data provided, how does the advertising elasticity change when the increase in sales after advertising is 10 percent instead of 4 percent?
- What would be the profit impact if the advertising budget were increased as proposed but sales do not change?

10.3 Estimating the Advertising Carryover Effect (Figure 10-18)

- Using the data provided, how does the carryover effect change when the incremental sales revenue after advertising is $10,000 rather than $5,000?
- How does the new carryover effect (estimated in the previous question) impact the overall incremental sales of the marketing communications effort?

Notes

1. Richard G. Rosen, "A New Model for Successful Marketing in the Age of Accountability," Institute for Direct Marketing: www.theidm.com/index.cfm?fuse Action=contentDisplay.&chn=3&tpc=214&stp=0%pg e=24099: (accessed November 2007).
2. Betty Arndt, "Johnson Controls' 'Classic Buildings' Marketing Campaign—A Pre- and Post-Campaign Evaluation," in *Drive Marketing Excellence* (New York: Institute for International Research, 1994).
3. Peter Danaher and Roland Rust, "Determining the Optimal Level of Media Spending," *Journal of Advertising Research* (January–February 1994): 28–34.
4. David Bender, Peter Farquhar, and Sanford Schulert, "Growing from the Top," *Marketing Management* (Winter/Spring 1996): 10–19.
5. H. Zielske, "The Remembering and Forgetting of Advertising," *Journal of Marketing* (January 1959): 140; and J. Simon, "What Do Zielske's Real Data Really Show About Pulsing," *Journal of Marketing Research* (August 1979): 415–420.
6. Brian Wansink and Michael Ray, "Advertising Strategies to Increase Usage Frequency," *Journal of Marketing* (January 1996): 31–46.
7. Bill Abrams, "Consumer-Product Techniques Help Loctite Sell to Industry," *The Wall Street Journal* (April 2, 1981): 29.
8. Vijay Mahajan, Eitan Muller, John E. Little, and Hugh Zielske, "Advertising Pulsing Policies for Generating Awareness of New Products," *Marketing Science* (Spring 1986): 86–106.
9. Cliff Havener and Margaret Thorpe, "Customers Can Tell You What They Want," *Management Review* (December 1994): 42–45.
10. David Reibstein, "Making the Most of Your Marketing Dollars," *Drive Marketing Excellence* (New York: Institute for International Research, 1994).
11. Gary Lilien, Philip Kotler, and K. Moorthy, *Marketing Models* (Upper Saddle River, NJ: Prentice Hall, 1992): 329–356.
12. Gert Assmus, John Farley, and Donald Lehmann, "How Advertising Affects Sales: Meta Analysis of Econometric Results," *Journal of Marketing Research* (February 1984): 65–74.
13. Ron Schultz and Martin Block, "Empirical Estimates of Advertising Response Factors," *Journal of Media Planning* (Fall 1986): 17–24.
14. Stan Rapp and Tom Collins, *Maximarketing* (New York: McGraw-Hill, 1987).
15. Robert Blattberg and Scott Neslin, *Sales Promotion Concepts, Methods and Strategies* (Upper Saddle River, NJ: Prentice Hall, 1990): 356.
16. Albert Bemmaor and Dominique Mouchoux, "Measuring the Short-Term Effect of In-Store Promotion and Retail Advertising on Brand Sales," *Journal of Marketing Research* (May 1991): 202–214.
17. Regis McKenna, *The Regis Touch: New Marketing Strategies for Uncertain Times* (Reading, MA: Addison-Wesley, 1985).

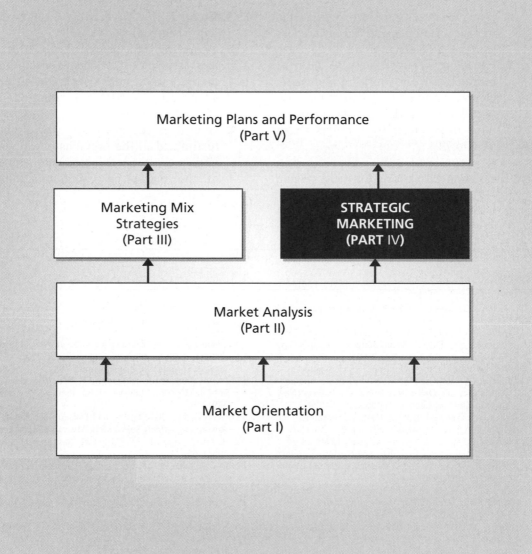

PART IV

Strategic Marketing

■ If you come to a fork in the road, take it.
—*Yogi Berra*
Major League Baseball Hall-of-Famer

Just going left or right when encountering a fork in the road is one way for a business to set strategic direction. A better way, one far more likely to lead to its performance objectives, would be for the business to first consider the probable outcomes of its options.

Strategic market planning sets the long-run direction for a business and has a major role in realizing the business's objectives of sales growth, profit performance, and share position over time. Marketing mix strategies, covered in Part III, are more tactical but essential to establishing desired target market positions and generating short-run growth and profits. These target market position strategies take a business incrementally toward its long-run goals. Both short-run marketing mix strategies and long-run strategic market plans promote growth, profitability, and share position.

In undertaking a strategic market planning process, a business assesses each product-market of interest with respect to market attractiveness and the business's competitive position. Using these two dimensions of strategic opportunity and position, Chapter 11 presents a method for building a strategic market planning portfolio that covers a business's existing and potential product-markets.

The strategic market plans generated by the portfolio analysis can be either offensive or defensive. Offensive strategic market plans, presented in Chapter 12, are growth-oriented plans to spur share penetration or market growth, or to prepare for entry into new, emerging, or growing markets. Offensive strategic market plans are critical to a business's future growth, market position, and profitability.

The purpose of defensive strategic market plans, presented in Chapter 13, is to protect market positions and profitability. Defensive plans can be based on limiting market focus to improve profitability, or on harvesting and divestment strategies that terminate in market exit. When properly executed, defensive strategic market plans improve current share, sales, and profit performance.

CHAPTER 11

Portfolio Analysis and Strategic Market Planning

■ Strategic market planning provides a sales and profit roadmap for the next 3 to 5 years.

Portfolio analysis and strategic market planning focus on gaining an understanding of a business's current and future positions with respect to sales and profit. In Figure 11-1, the business with Portfolio A is in an excellent current position for profits. But its product portfolio is *unbalanced*. The business has not invested in new products and, as the products in its portfolio move through their product life cycles, sales and profits will at some point decline.

Portfolio B has been managed more effectively and is a *balanced* portfolio. It has a high percentage of sales (size of circle) at the late-growth and mature stages of the product life cycle, resulting in good profitability (dashed line in graph).

More importantly, Portfolio B has a great future. Roughly a third of its sales are in the early or growth stages of the product-market life cycle. As product A goes into its decline stage, each of the other products will progress at its market growth rate to the next stage of its product-market life cycle.

While Portfolio A has good short-run profitability, mismanagement will eventually leave this business with declining sales and profits. Portfolio B, while perhaps not quite as profitable in the short run, is the better-managed portfolio. It will continue to deliver growth in both sales and profits over time, for as long as the business maintains a balanced portfolio of products that offer good customer value.

FIGURE 11-1 PRODUCT LIFE CYCLES OF TWO PRODUCT PORTFOLIOS

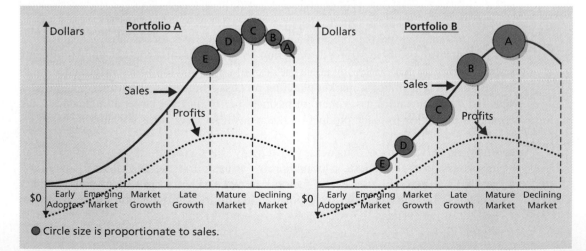

● Circle size is proportionate to sales.

FIGURE 11-2 PORTFOLIO ANALYSIS AND STRATEGIC MARKET PLANNING

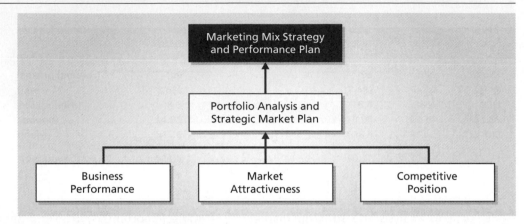

STRATEGIC MARKET PLANNING

Successful companies like General Electric, Procter & Gamble, and Toyota achieve success year after year with a great deal of strategic market planning.[1] The executives and managers of these companies are committed to serving shareholders by continuously reviewing current performance, tracking the results of funding and investment decisions aimed at promoting a balance of short- and long-run performance, and seeking new opportunities. An important part of this process is investing for the future and maintaining portfolio diversification to reduce large swings in overall performance.

Each product-market in a business's portfolio in some way affects both the short- and long-run performance of the business, as illustrated in Figure 11-1. The business may want to increase its investment in some product-markets, depending on their current and potential share positions and their performance levels, in order to grow or defend important strategic market positions. In other product-markets, the business may want to reduce its focus in order to achieve a stronger competitive position and profit contribution with available resources. For yet other product-markets, the business may decide to withdraw its resources and divest. Because resources in any business are limited, a strategic market plan is needed to carefully map a business's future share position, sales growth, and profit performance. A strategic market plan sets the direction and provides guidelines for resource allocation.[2]

In order to specify a strategic direction for each product-market and to allocate resources in a way that will bring about the desired short- and long-run performance, businesses engage in a strategic market planning process.[3] Figure 11-2 outlines this process. The first step is a careful assessment of business performance, market attractiveness, and competitive position for each product-market a business serves or is considering serving.

- **Business Performance:** Businesses have many ways to assess their performance, but any assessment will include sales and profits as basic considerations.
- **Market Attractiveness:** Several factors can make one market attractive and another less attractive. Product life-cycle position and market growth rate are measures of market attractiveness that we know correspond to sales and profits, as we saw in Figure 11-1.

FIGURE 11-3 PRODUCT LIFE CYCLE VERSUS COMPETITIVE POSITION PORTFOLIO

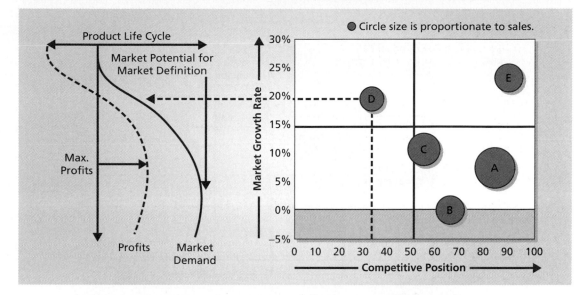

■ **Competitive Position:** Several measures of competitive position help a business discern a strong competitive position from a weak one. One measure that corresponds to sales and profit performance is *relative market share*. The stronger a business's or a product's relative market share, the more profitable it is.[4] Another measure we can use is the share development index, which also relates share growth to sales and profit.

In creating the matrix for a portfolio based on the life cycles of a business's products, we begin by building the market attractiveness dimension of the portfolio. Figure 11-3 illustrates how the product's sales and profits vary over the product life cycle. The different levels of performance at different stages of the product life cycle require that a business implement different strategies and allocate different levels of marketing resources as a product moves through its life cycle.

Examining the sales and profits of product D in Figure 11-3 helps us understand the relationship between the stages of the product life cycle and market attractiveness. Assume the market demand for product D, now in the early growth stage of its product life cycle, is 1 million units annually and the product captures 10 percent of this demand with a price of $100 per unit. The result is $10 million in sales.

$$\textbf{Sales (Current)} = \text{Market Demand} \times \text{Market Share} \times \text{Price}$$
$$= 1{,}000{,}000 \text{ units} \times 10\% \times \$100 \text{ per unit}$$
$$= \textbf{\$10 million}$$

With the market growing at 20 percent annually and the business maintaining its 10 percent market share, sales should increase by $2 million.

$$\textbf{Sales (Year 1)} = \text{Market Demand} \times \text{Market Share} \times \text{Price}$$
$$= 1{,}200{,}000 \text{ units} \times 10\% \times \$100 \text{ per unit}$$
$$= \textbf{\$12 million}$$

FIGURE 11-4 MARKET SHARE AND COMPETITIVE POSITION

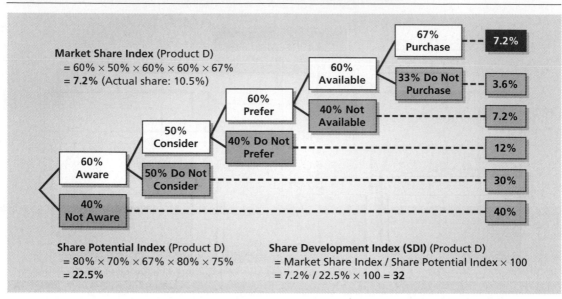

Although this example is an oversimplification, because the price would undoubtedly decrease somewhat, it demonstrates the attractiveness of a market in terms of sales when the product is in the growth stage of its life cycle. If the price were to decrease 3 percent, from $100 to $97, sales would still be $11.64 million.

But what about profits? By including in the equation the unit cost and the marketing and sales expenses, we can estimate the marketing profits produced with a hold share strategy for product D. The current-year net marketing contribution with a 10 percent market share, 40 percent margin, and marketing and sales expenses at 15 percent of sales is $2.5 million.

$$\begin{aligned} \text{NMC} \atop \text{(Current)} &= \frac{\text{Market}}{\text{Demand}} \times \frac{\text{Market}}{\text{Share}} \times \left(\frac{\text{Unit}}{\text{Price}} - \frac{\text{Unit}}{\text{Cost}} \right) - \frac{\text{Marketing}}{\text{Expenses}} \\ &= 1{,}000{,}000 \text{ units} \times 10\% \times (\$100 - \$60) - \$1.5 \text{ million} \\ &= \$4 \text{ million} - \$1.5 \text{ million} \\ &= \mathbf{\$2.5 \text{ million}} \end{aligned}$$

The marketing return on sales is 25 percent. With marketing and sales expenses kept at 15 percent of sales, a hold share strategy would produce a $3 million marketing profit in year 1.

$$\begin{aligned} \text{NMC} \atop \text{(Year 1)} &= \frac{\text{Market}}{\text{Demand}} \times \frac{\text{Market}}{\text{Share}} \times \left(\frac{\text{Unit}}{\text{Price}} - \frac{\text{Unit}}{\text{Cost}} \right) - \frac{\text{Marketing}}{\text{Expenses}} \\ &= 1{,}200{,}000 \text{ units} \times 10\% \times (\$100 - \$60) - \$1.8 \text{ million} \\ &= \$4.8 \text{ million} - \$1.8 \text{ million} \\ &= \mathbf{\$3 \text{ million}} \end{aligned}$$

FIGURE 11-5 SHARE PERFORMANCE METRICS AND SHARE DEVELOPMENT INDEX

Products' Share Indexes		Gate 1 Awareness	Gate 2 Interest	Gate 3 Price	Gate 4 Availability	Gate 5 Purchase	Share Index	Share Development Index
A	Current	90%	67%	60%	85%	60%	18.5%	84
	Potential	90%	70%	60%	90%	65%	22.1%	
B	Current	85%	67%	50%	80%	67%	15.3%	67
	Potential	90%	70%	60%	90%	67%	22.8%	
C	Current	70%	70%	50%	60%	75%	11.0%	54
	Potential	75%	70%	60%	80%	80%	20.2%	
D	Current	60%	50%	60%	60%	67%	7.2%	32
	Potential	80%	70%	67%	80%	75%	22.5%	
E	Current	70%	88%	80%	60%	73%	21.6%	90
	Potential	80%	70%	67%	80%	80%	24.0%	

We can see, then, that the product life cycle serves as a good indication of market attractiveness not only in terms of share growth and sales, but also with regard to profit.

But what about measuring competitive position? While we can measure a business's competitive position in different ways, the one single measure that provides a reliable assessment of competitive position is the level of market share. Market share is highly representative of a business's competitive position in the market place, and it can be managed over the product life cycle for positive impacts on sales and profit. But, again, a word of caution: A business must manage market share gains to improve profit, not just sales and market share. For this reason, we have selected the share development index (SDI) as the strategic measure of competitive position for the portfolio based on product life cycles in Figures 11-3 and 11-6. The SDI also indicates the level of opportunity that a business has for improving a product's competitive position: Product D's relatively low SDI of 32 as shown in the two charts means its potential for greater sales and profit is very high.

Recall that in calculating a product's SDI, we first estimate its market share and share potential indexes. Using the share development path presented in Chapter 3, we can estimate that product D has a market share index of 7.2 percent, as shown in Figure 11-4. The share potential index is the share index that product D would achieve if it could reach all of the potential performance targets in Figure 11-5. In this case, the share potential index is estimated at 22.5 percent. The ratio of current to potential share multiplied by 100 produces the share development index of 32.

The market share index for each product listed in Figure 11-5 is the function of five sequential share performance metrics. Many other share performance models are possible based on a business's particular product-market and how market share is achieved. In some product-markets, for example, a trial is an important step in the share performance hierarchy and would be included in the share development path. It is also possible and even likely that different products in the same market would have different share performance structures. However, for simplicity, in Figure 11-5 we used the same share performance structure for all five portfolio products.

Remember that the market share index is not intended to represent a business's actual market share. Many factors besides the ones in the share development path shape actual market share. However, the market share index is a summary index of the more important share performance metrics—in this case, the five metrics we chose. A business can expect gains in actual market share to the extent that it improves its market share index.

The following example illustrates how an improved market share index can lead to sales and profit growth. A business with sales of $10 million increased its marketing resources to improve its market share index from 7.2 percent to 10 percent during year 1 of its strategic market plan, resulting in a 1 percent increase in actual market share—from 10 to 11 percent.

$$\textbf{Sales (Year 1)} = \text{Market Demand} \times \text{Market Share} \times \text{Price}$$
$$= 1{,}200{,}000 \text{ units} \times 11\% \times \$100 \text{ per unit}$$
$$= \textbf{\$13.2 million}$$

The increase in market share resulted in $3.2 million in additional sales revenue. But what about profits? Is this market share strategy profitable? To calculate the net marketing contribution, we take into account that the marketing budget was increased from $1.8 to $2 million to support the improvement in the market share performance metrics.

$$\begin{aligned}\textbf{NMC} \atop \textbf{(Year 1)} &= \frac{\text{Market}}{\text{Demand}} \times \frac{\text{Market}}{\text{Share}} \times \left(\frac{\text{Unit}}{\text{Price}} - \frac{\text{Unit}}{\text{Cost}}\right) - \frac{\text{Marketing}}{\text{Expenses}} \\ &= 1{,}200{,}000 \text{ units} \times 11\% \times (\$100 - \$60) - \$2 \text{ million} \\ &= \$5.28 \text{ million} - \$2 \text{ million} \\ &= \textbf{\$3.28 million}\end{aligned}$$

Had the business pursued a hold share strategy with no increase in the marketing budget, the net marketing contribution would have been $3 million. A grow share strategy in a market growing 20 percent per year resulted in a marketing profit 9.3 percent higher than a hold share strategy would have produced.

But it is equally important to examine a situation where market share gains result in higher sales and higher market share but a lower marketing profit. Product A in Figures 11-3 and 11-6 is a good example. It is approaching the mature stage of its product life cycle and has achieved 84 percent of its share potential. Given a 5 percent rate of market growth and little price erosion, sales of product A can be expected to increase from $100 million to $105 million with a 20 percent market share.

$$\textbf{Sales (Current Year)} = \text{Market Demand} \times \text{Market Share} \times \text{Price}$$
$$= 10{,}000{,}000 \text{ units} \times 20\% \times \$50 \text{ per unit}$$
$$= \textbf{\$100 million}$$

$$\textbf{Sales (Year 1)} = \text{Market Demand} \times \text{Market Share} \times \text{Price}$$
$$= 10{,}500{,}000 \text{ units} \times 20\% \times \$50 \text{ per unit}$$
$$= \textbf{\$105 million}$$

FIGURE 11-6 PRODUCT LIFE CYCLE/SHARE DEVELOPMENT PORTFOLIO

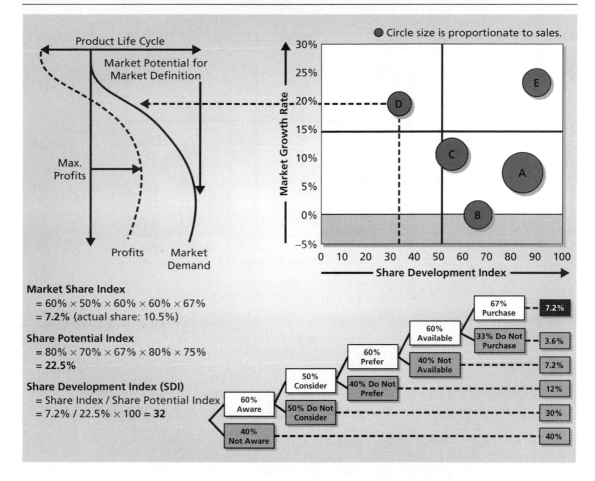

With sales of $100 million for the current year, the marketing profit is $10 million based on a 20 percent margin and marketing and sales expenses of 10 percent of sales.

$$\begin{aligned} \frac{\text{NMC}}{\text{(Current Year)}} &= \frac{\text{Market}}{\text{Demand}} \times \frac{\text{Market}}{\text{Share}} \times \left(\frac{\text{Unit}}{\text{Price}} - \frac{\text{Unit}}{\text{Cost}}\right) - \frac{\text{Marketing}}{\text{Expenses}} \\ &= 10{,}000{,}000 \text{ units} \times 20\% \times (\$50 - \$40) - \$10 \text{ million} \\ &= \$20 \text{ million} - \$10 \text{ million} \\ &= \textbf{\$10 million} \end{aligned}$$

For year 1, a grow share strategy for product A calls for a price reduction of 5 percent. The product's price elasticity is −2.0, and a 5 percent price decrease would lead to a 10 percent increase in volume sold. The expected outcome would be a 2 percent increase in the business's share of a market that is growing at 5 percent annually, resulting in a significant increase of $9.7 million in sales over the current year.

$$\begin{aligned} \textbf{Sales (Year 1)} &= 10{,}500{,}000 \text{ units} \times (20\% \times 1.1) \times \$47.5 \\ &= \textbf{\$109.7 million} \end{aligned}$$

FIGURE 11-7 PRODUCT PORTFOLIO PLAN

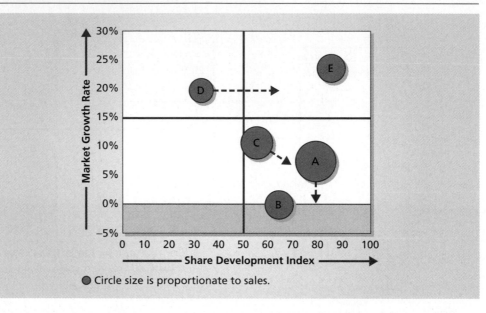

● Circle size is proportionate to sales.

But would this grow share strategy be more profitable even when marketing and sales expenses are held at the current-year level of $10 million?

$$\frac{\text{NMC}}{\text{(Year 1)}} = \frac{\text{Market}}{\text{Demand}} \times \frac{\text{Market}}{\text{Share}} \times \left(\frac{\text{Unit}}{\text{Price}} - \frac{\text{Unit}}{\text{Cost}}\right) - \frac{\text{Marketing}}{\text{Expenses}}$$

$$= 10{,}500{,}000 \text{ units} \times 22\% \times (\$47.5 - \$40) - \$10 \text{ million}$$

$$= \$17.3 \text{ million} - \$10 \text{ million}$$

$$= \mathbf{\$7.3 \text{ million}}$$

Despite the gains in market share and sales, the grow share strategy would reduce profits in year 1 by $2.7 million even with the 5 percent growth in market demand and no increase in the marketing budget. The grow share strategy in this case is a good example of how a blind pursuit of greater market share and sales can lead to lower profits.

Product Life Cycle/Market Share Portfolio

The product portfolio plan in Figure 11-7 incorporates all three elements a business uses in the market planning process: business performance, market attractiveness, and competitive position. Performance is represented by the size of each product's circle, which is proportionate to the current-year sales revenue the product generates. The vertical axis represents the market growth rate, a major factor in determining market attractiveness. The market growth rate corresponds to the stages of the product life cycle presented in Figure 11-1. And the horizontal axis is a scale for the share development index, our measure of competitive position. With this portfolio we can assess the five products with an eye toward selecting the kind of strategic market plan that would be most effective for each one, given the attractiveness of its market, its competitive position, and its present sales performance and potential for improved performance.

- **Product A**—The portfolio position of product A in Figure 11-6 is in the mature stage of its product life cycle. Market demand, however, is still growing at 5 percent annually, and the product's share development index of 84 indicates a strong competitive position. The combination of these factors suggests the product is well worth protecting. This is the time to carefully manage the profit that the product produces, with the knowledge that any large investment in marketing and sales expenses would only draw down marketing profits. Product A is a key source of profitability for the business, and it supports the business's other products and the development of new ones.

- **Product B**—Like product A, product B is also in the mature stage of its product life cycle, but market demand is no longer growing. The business sees some room to grow the product's market share, but a grow share strategy with price cuts would result in about the same level of profit. Product B's future is limited, yet it is still an important part of the business's overall profitability. Eventually margins and marketing profits will fall below performance benchmarks, and then a harvest strategy will be the best approach to take for product B. But the business, as it incrementally raises prices while harvesting, should be on the lookout for the possible formation of a profitable niche market for this product.

- **Product C**—As product C approaches the late-growth phase of the product life cycle, it needs an investment in marketing expenses that will enable it to maintain market share in a growing market. An even larger marketing budget would be required for a strategy to grow share at this stage of the product life cycle. From both strategic and long-run profit perspectives, it is important to grow share before the product enters the mature stage of its life cycle. Product C will be a major contributor to the portfolio's sales and profits as it moves into late market growth (maximum profits) and eventually the mature stage of the product life cycle.

- **Product D**—Now in the early growth stage of its product life cycle, product D needs marketing resources to take advantage of the rapid growth in demand. Its low share development index of 32 also suggests the business needs an effective strategy for achieving more of the product's share potential at this stage of its product life cycle. Strategically, because it is just entering the growth phase of its life cycle, product D will be in a rapidly growing market for some time. Gaining market share now is critical and would make product D a valuable source of profits until market demand reaches its full potential, which is a long ways off.

- **Product E**—As product E moves from the emerging market stage of the product life cycle to early growth stage, it is in a very strong competitive position with a share development index of 90. Product E requires continued investment to hold its excellent share position in a market that's growing 25 percent annually. An inadequate marketing budget at this point would result in share slippage and greatly reduced future profits.

GE/McKinsey Portfolio Analysis

Market attractiveness and competitive position cannot always be fairly represented by a single factor. Many factors can contribute to market attractiveness. The product life cycle, the market's growth rate, and the market development index are certainly important considerations, but so are the size of the market its competitive environment, and the ease or difficulty of accessing the market.

FIGURE 11-8 GE/McKINSEY PORTFOLIO

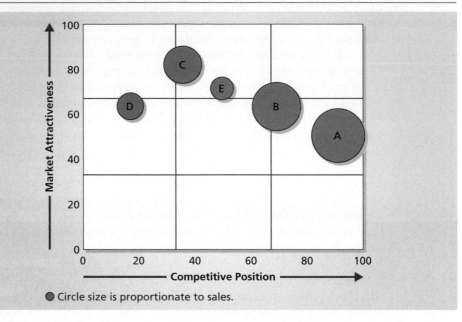

● Circle size is proportionate to sales.

Likewise, competitive position could include more than a business's relative market share or its share development index. A strong brand, high product performance, outstanding service quality, high awareness, and high net promoter index are also important in shaping competitive position.

For these reasons, General Electric and McKinsey Consulting have developed a portfolio matrix that uses multiple factors to index market attractiveness and competitive position. The multi-factor indexes create a scale that varies from 0 to 100, and a portfolio divided into nine strategic positions, as shown in Figure 11-8. Based on these assessments, the overall portfolio position of product A is average in market attractiveness but very strong in competitive position. A business would likely consider a strategic market plan to protect this product position. But before we go further into portfolio analysis and strategic market planning, let's take a close look at how these market attractiveness and competitive position indexes are constructed.

MARKET ATTRACTIVENESS

The long-run direction that a business's managers want their strategic market plan to reflect serves as the basis for developing performance objectives and a tactical marketing mix strategy. This important step in the strategic market planning process requires an in-depth examination of *market attractiveness*. In comparing the relative attractiveness of different product-markets, a business uses a common set of attractiveness criteria for each one. To facilitate this step in the strategic market planning process, we need a systematic way to assess market attractiveness.

In assessing and indexing the attractiveness of a product-market, a business must ask itself, *"What factors make a market attractive or unattractive?"* Factors that typically shape market attractiveness are market size, market growth, competition, margin potential, market access, and a "good fit" with the company's core capabilities. These factors can be meaningfully grouped into three dimensions of market attractiveness: market forces, competitive environment, and market access, as shown in Figure 11-9.

To create a measure of market attractiveness, each of these three dimensions can be weighted to reflect its importance in relation to the others. In the example presented in Figure 11-10, market forces and market access are both weighted at 30 percent of the total importance, whereas competitive environment is weighted a little more heavily at 40 percent. Each dimension is further broken down into several factors that contribute to that particular dimension of market attractiveness, and each of these factors is also weighted to represent its relative importance within its respective dimension of market attractiveness.

By rating the attractiveness of each factor within each dimension, we can calculate an index for overall market attractiveness, as illustrated in Figure 11-10. The industry forces that influence market attractiveness differ from one industry to another, so for a particular business the factors appropriate for analysis in each dimension may be different than the ones listed in Figure 11-10. Special care should be taken to ensure that all factors that shape a particular market's attractiveness are represented, on the basis of market and profit performance.[5]

For the product-market in Figure 11-10, each individual market attractiveness factor is rated from "very unattractive" (0) to "very attractive" (100). This rating is multiplied by the relative importance of that factor to obtain a weighted individual factor attractiveness score. For each dimension, its individual factor scores are totaled and multiplied by the importance given that dimension.

For example, market size is given a rating of 80 for attractiveness and is assigned a relative importance of 40 percent within the market forces dimension. This method of indexing market attractiveness results in a score of 32 (80 × 0.4) for the market size factor. This score is added to the scores of the other factors in this dimension to arrive at a total factor-weighted score of 62. This score is then multiplied by 0.3, the relative importance weight assigned to the market forces dimension, to produce a weighted score of 18.6 for market forces. When this process is completed for all the market attractiveness factors and dimensions, the result is an overall market attractiveness index of 70 (rounded).

FIGURE 11-9 FACTORS THAT SHAPE MARKET ATTRACTIVENESS

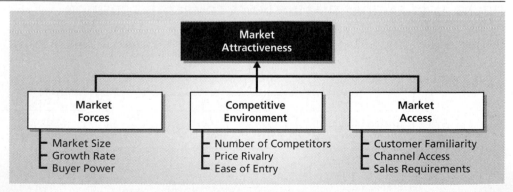

FIGURE 11-10 MARKET ATTRACTIVENESS INDEX

←		Market Attractiveness			→
Very Unattractive	Unattractive	Somewhat Unattractive	Somewhat Attractive	Attractive	Very Attractive
0	20	40	60	80	100

Market Forces Factor Importance: 30%	Relative Importance	Attractiveness Rating	Attractiveness Score
Market Size	40%	80	32
Growth Rate	30%	60	18
Buyer Power	30%	40	12
	100%		62

Competitive Environment Factor Importance: 40%	Relative Importance	Attractiveness Rating	Attractiveness Score
Price Rivalry	50%	40	20
Ease of Competitor Entry	30%	40	12
Number of Competitors	20%	60	12
	100%		44

Market Access Factor Importance: 30%	Relative Importance	Attractiveness Rating	Attractiveness Score
Customer Familiarity	40%	80	32
Channel Access	40%	100	40
Sales/Service Requirements	20%	60	12
	100%		84

$$\text{Market Attractiveness Index} = 30\% \times 62 + 40\% \times 44 + 30\% \times 84$$
$$= 18.6 + 17.6 + 25.2$$
$$= 61$$

COMPETITIVE POSITION

The process of developing a competitive position index is similar to computing the market attractiveness index. The first question is, *"What makes one business strong, with respect to competitive position, and another weak?"* In answering this question, many businesses will arrive at a list of factors that determine competitive position. These factors, as we saw

FIGURE 11-11 FACTORS THAT INFLUENCE COMPETITIVE POSITION

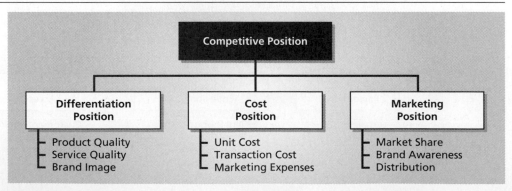

FIGURE 11-12 COMPETITIVE POSITION INDEX

◄─────────────── Competitive Position ───────────────►					
Considerably Behind	Clearly Behind	Somewhat Behind	Somewhat Ahead	Clearly Ahead	Considerably Ahead
0	2	40	60	80	100

Differentiation Advantage Factor Importance: 40%	Relative Importance	Attractiveness Rating	Attractiveness Score
Product Quality	40%	80	32
Service Quality	30%	60	18
Brand Image/Reputation	30%	80	24
	100%		74

Cost Advantage Factor Importance: 40%	Relative Importance	Attractiveness Rating	Attractiveness Score
Cost of Goods Sold	70%	40	28
Marketing and Sales Expenses	20%	60	12
Overhead Expenses	10%	60	6
	100%		46

Marketing Advantage Factor Importance: 20%	Relative Importance	Attractiveness Rating	Attractiveness Score
Market Share	40%	40	16
Brand Awareness	30%	40	12
Distribution	30%	20	6
	100%		34

Competitive Position Index $= 40\% \times 74 + 40\% \times 46 + 20\% \times 34$
$= 29.6 + 18.4 + 6.8$
$= 55$

in Chapter 6, can be categorized into three dimensions of competitive position: a differentiation position, a cost position, and a marketing position. All three drivers of competitive position also have underlying forces that shape the business's competitive position,[6] as shown in Figure 11-11.

Each of the three dimensions of competitive position is assigned a relative weight, just as we did in determining the market attractiveness index, and the relative importance for each of the underlying factors within the three dimensions is also rated, as illustrated in Figure 11-12. Each factor is assessed with respect to the competitive position of the business in its existing market or its potential position in new markets under consideration. When the score for each of the three dimensions of competitive position is weighted by its relative importance, and the three weighted scores are then added, the result is a competitive position index of 55 (rounded).

As shown in Figure 11-12, the competitive forces that shape a differentiation position for this business are relatively strong and make up more than half of the competitive position index. The business's weighted competitive position score with respect to a marketing advantage is a weak 6.8 (20% times 34) due to a lower dimension weighting and generally lower attractiveness ratings for the factors in that dimension. The business's index of 55 places its competitive position in the midrange.

FIGURE 11-13 PORTFOLIO STRATEGIES AND STRATEGIC MARKET PLANS

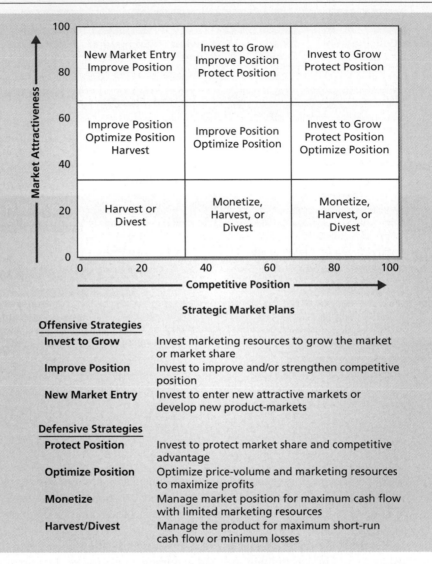

PORTFOLIO ANALYSIS AND STRATEGIC MARKET PLANS

A *portfolio analysis* is an evaluation of a business, product, or market with respect to market attractiveness and competitive position as an aid in identifying the kind of strategic plan that would be most appropriate. Figure 11-13 shows how this analysis uses the market attractiveness index and the competitive position index in combination with a portfolio of the different types of strategic plans. Product-markets with high indexes for both market attractiveness and competitive position have the strongest portfolio position and the best opportunities for profit performance.[7] Having a product-market in this position usually leads to a strategic market plan to invest to protect the product-market's attractive position. At any point where the two indexes may intersect, there is at least one strategic market plan to be considered.[8] The different kinds of strategic plans can be named based on their objectives:

- **Invest to Grow**—An offensive strategic market plan to invest marketing resources to grow the market or a product's position in a market. Dell, because of a strong portfolio position, has invested heavily over the past 20 years to grow both the personal computer market and its share of the market.
- **Invest to Improve Position**—An offensive strategic market plan that seeks to improve a business's competitive position in an attractive segment of the market. Toyota invested early to strengthen its competitive position in the hybrid segment of the automotive market. When Toyota first entered this segment, it was growing in market attractiveness, but many competing car companies were not entering it and afterward were slow to enter. As a result, Toyota built an early lead in an attractive market.
- **New Market Entry**—An offensive strategy to enter new attractive markets. Again, we can cite Toyota's entry into the hybrid market as an example of this strategy. The company now plans to strengthen its competitive position in this market by expanding its line of hybrid cars and stepping up production. New market strategies focus on developing the market and are required for most new product-markets, as was the case for flat-screen televisions, cellular phones, and DVD players. New market development strategies require a large investment in marketing resources and will operate at a loss until market volumes reach break-even levels.
- **Protect Position**—A defensive strategy to invest to protect an attractive market position in which the business dominates with respect to competitive position. Gatorade in the sports drink market and Red Bull in the energy drink market both have market shares of over 80 percent. Although these markets are attractive and growing, these products will come under increasing attack as new competitors enter the market.
- **Optimize Position**—Many businesses implement a defensive strategy in the late-growth stage or the mature stage of the product life cycle. When growth potential is limited and competitive position is set, businesses need to optimize the marketing mix to produce maximum marketing profits. This is the time in the product life cycle when volumes are nearly at full potential and margins are still somewhat attractive. Additions to marketing resources can be made at a slower rate because the product-market is mature or nearing maturity. A business using this defensive strategy undertakes a conscious effort to reduce its customer base in order to reach a more profitable level of business. Many banks, for example, have redefined their customer base by charging fees for small accounts that cannot be profitably served. As higher fees cause many customers to leave, these banks are able to grow profits with a smaller, more focused customer base. When managed correctly, optimizing position at the later stages of the product life cycle should allow the product to produce its maximum profits.
- **Monetize Strategy**—A defensive strategy used in less attractive markets in which a business has some level of competitive position. A monetize strategy manages prices and marketing resources in a way that maximizes cash flow without exiting the market. Businesses in the cash flow mode often place limits on payment terms, do not pay for shipping, and offer few customer services. Although price competitive, these businesses minimize investment in their products and strive for maximum cash flow from their market position.
- **Harvest Strategy**—A defensive strategy for maximizing profits and cash flow as a business slowly exits a product-market. Prices are increased to improve margins as

volumes decline. In the short run, the strategy produces a higher gross profit. Reductions in marketing expenses lower the cost of marketing. The business exits the market when no prospect for a short-run profit remains.

■ **Divest Strategy**—A defensive strategy for exiting a market by selling or closing down the business or eliminating the product. Exiting a product-market is simply a way to cut losses quickly and reallocate marketing resources to more productive endeavors.

As shown in Figure 11-13, attractive product-markets usually warrant an offensive strategic market plan. The various kinds of offensive strategic market plans all take advantage, but in different ways, of favorable market conditions and a business's ability to profit in that market. The plan may map out a strategy for growing the market or growing the business's share, or it may present ways for improving competitive position. An offensive strategic market plan could also address entry into another existing market, or developing an entirely new product-market.

On the basis of a portfolio analysis and performance objectives, a business selects either an offensive or defensive strategic market plan. First, with respect to performance objectives, offensive strategic market plans are geared to deliver above-average performance in the areas of sales growth, share position, and long-run profit performance. Defensive strategic market plans, in contrast, are for protecting important share positions and producing short-run profit performance, while also contributing to long-run profit. Strategic market planning for a business with multiple product-markets often requires a careful balance of offensive and defensive strategic market plans. In this way, the business can meet short-run profit objectives and investor expectations, while investing to protect attractive strategic positions and simultaneously developing share positions in existing or new markets.

Offensive Portfolio Strategy

Because offensive strategic market plans are more growth oriented than defensive plans, they are more likely to be used in attractive markets.[9] Consider a consumer electronics manufacturer whose sales in the base year of its strategic market plan were $19.38 billion. The business's base-year market share was 10.2 percent of a market that was growing at 5 to 6 percent annually. Although industry margins were declining, this business, as the market's leader, maintained above-average margins and produced $3.88 billion in gross profit in the base year. With an efficient marketing strategy, the business produced a net marketing contribution of $2.23 billion in the base year. The results were a marketing ROS of 11.5 percent and a marketing ROI of 135 percent.

Actual Base-Year Performance

$$\text{Sales Revenues} = \text{Market Demand} \times \text{Market Share}$$
$$= \$190 \text{ billion} \times 10.2\%$$
$$= \textbf{\$19.38 billion}$$

$$\text{Gross Profit} = \text{Sales Revenue} \times \text{Percent Margin}$$
$$= \$19.38 \text{ billion} \times 20\%$$
$$= \textbf{\$3.88 billion}$$

$$\text{Net Marketing Contribution} = \text{Gross Profit} - \text{Marketing \& Sales Expenses}$$
$$= \$3.88 \text{ billion} - \$1.65 \text{ billion}$$
$$= \textbf{\$2.23 billion}$$

Figure 11-14 shows actual performance of this consumer electronics company, the estimated results of the company's offensive strategy, the estimated results of a possible defensive strategy, and the actual outcome for year 3 of the performance plan. The offensive strategy to continue growing share, from 10.2 to 15 percent, in an expanding market presented the greater strategic challenge. This strategic market plan would require the company to increase its marketing resources from $1.6 billion in the base year to $3.6 billion in year 3 of the plan. Based on market growth and market share assumptions, sales were projected to grow to $39 billion.

The business expected its margins would decrease as it incrementally lowered prices to attract more customers in an effort to grow market share. The year-3 margin was projected at 17.5 percent, resulting in a gross profit of $6.8 billion. The offensive plan to grow share to 15 percent would produce an increase in net marketing contribution of $1.1 billion. However, decreasing margins and increasing marketing and sales expenses would lead to declines in the year-3 marketing ROS (8.5 percent) and marketing ROI (94 percent).

Year 3: Offensive Strategy to Grow Share

$$\text{Sales Revenues} = \text{Market Demand} \times \text{Market Share}$$
$$= \$260 \text{ billion} \times 15\%$$
$$= \textbf{\$39 billion}$$

$$\text{Gross Profit} = \text{Sales Revenue} \times \text{Percent Margin}$$
$$= \$39 \text{ billion} \times 17.5\%$$
$$= \textbf{\$6.83 billion}$$

$$\text{Net Marketing Contribution} = \text{Gross Profit} - \text{Marketing \& Sales Expenses}$$
$$= \$6.83 \text{ billion} - \$3.51 \text{ billion}$$
$$= \textbf{\$3.32 billion}$$

Although the business's efficiency in producing marketing profits is projected to diminish, the investment to grow market share will increase marketing profits by approximately $1.1 billion. This investment in market share will also have future benefits as this market approaches maturity and market share gains will be more difficult.

FIGURE 11-14 OFFENSIVE VERSUS DEFENSIVE PORTFOLIO STRATEGIES

3-Year Strategic Market Plan Consumer Electronics Business	Actual Base Year	Offensive Plan Grow Share	Defensive Plan Hold Share	Year-3 Actual
Market Demand ($ millions)	$190,000	$260,000	$260,000	$280,000
Market Share	10.2%	15.0%	10.0%	14.5%
Sales Revenues ($ millions)	$19,380	$39,000	$26,000	$40,600
Percent Margin	20.0%	17.5%	19.0%	17.5%
Gross Profit ($ millions)	$3,876	$6,825	$4,940	$7,105
Marketing & Sales Expenses (%)	8.5%	9.0%	8.0%	8.8%
Marketing & Sales Expenses ($ millions)	$1,647	$3,510	$2,080	$3,573
Net Marketing Contribution ($ millions)	$2,229	$3,315	$2,860	$3,532
Marketing ROS	11.5%	8.5%	11.0%	8.7%
Marketing ROI	135%	94%	138%	99%

Defensive Portfolio Strategy

The purpose of defensive strategic market plans is to protect important strategic market positions and to add significantly to short-run cash flow and profit performance. As shown in Figure 11-13, defensive strategic market plans are most commonly implemented in attractive markets by businesses with a strong competitive position or in unattractive markets by businesses with a low competitive position index.

In Figure 11-13, one kind of defensive strategic market plan is for protecting market position within an existing market.[10] Defensive strategic market plans can also involve monetizing for maximum cash flow, harvesting market share positions in existing markets, or divesting.[11] Monetizing and harvesting plans are not likely to generate significant sales revenue growth, and divesting disposes of a losing product-market, but defensive plans to protect (hold) share can greatly improve sales in a fast-growing market. All four types of defensive strategic market plans aim to improve short-run cash flow and profit performance, and, in many ways, they define the business's current level of share, sales, and profit performance.

Let's return to Figure 11-14 and look at an estimate for this company's 3-year performance using a defensive strategic market plan to protect market share in the growing market. Using the same assumptions already made for market growth, margin erosion, and marketing and sales expenses, the business's 3-year performance projections under a defensive strategic market plan are far less impressive than under the offensive plan.

Year 3: Defensive Strategy to Hold Share

$$\textbf{Sales Revenues} = \text{Market Demand} \times \text{Market Share}$$
$$= \$260 \text{ billion} \times 10\%$$
$$= \textbf{\$26 billion}$$

$$\textbf{Gross Profit} = \text{Sales Revenue} \times \text{Percent Margin}$$
$$= \$26 \text{ billion} \times 19\%$$
$$= \textbf{\$4.94 billion}$$

$$\textbf{Net Marketing Contribution} = \text{Gross Profit} - \text{Marketing \& Sales Expenses}$$
$$= \$4.94 \text{ billion} - \$2.08 \text{ billion}$$
$$= \textbf{\$2.86 billion}$$

A defensive strategic market plan to protect market share, then, might have yielded a $6.6 billion increase in sales revenue and a $630 million increase net marketing contribution. Although many factors could have kept these goals from being met, this strategy, if successfully implemented, would have protected share position, grown sales revenue, and produced a slightly higher net marketing contribution. But the projections for share, sales, gross profit, and net marketing contribution are well below these same projections under the offensive strategic market plan. The business naturally chose to pursue the offensive plan as the better option for profitable growth. The business's actual performance in year 3, it turns out, was better than the projected performance levels because of higher than expected growth in market demand. The net marketing contribution exceeded the year-3 projection by $200 million. With the market now entering the late-growth stage of its product life cycle, the business may need to reconsider a defensive strategy to protect its market leadership position and remain profitable.

FIGURE 11-15 OFFENSIVE AND DEFENSIVE STRATEGIC MARKET PLANS

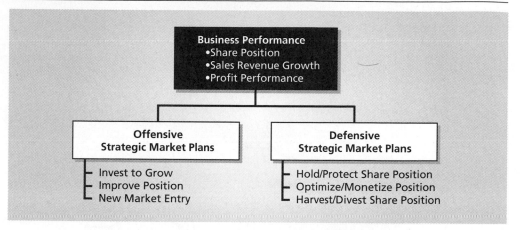

Figure 11-15 outlines the kinds of offensive and defensive strategic market plans we have been discussing. As we have seen, a portfolio analysis is a valuable aid in selecting the plan best suited for a particular product-market.

PORTFOLIO DIVERSIFICATION

Diversification across product-markets adds two important advantages to the overall performance of a business. First, it reduces dependence on a single product-market. Second, by diversifying, a business increases the likelihood of consistency in overall performance because adverse conditions in one product-market can be offset by favorable conditions in another.

For example, Figure 11-16 illustrates the overall sales of a business that is diversified across different product-markets. In product-market A, the business's core market, sales are growing at an average rate of 1.5 percent annually, but this growth varies from year to year due to economic conditions and competitive forces. Because the business is also positioned in two other product-markets, it is able to take advantage of offsetting product life cycles and competitive forces. Product-market B is growing at 4 percent annually and product-market C at almost 15 percent. Although sales in each of these two markets are much less than in the business's core market, each contributes to overall sales growth and performance stability.

The unexplained sales variance over the time period shown for product-market A is 42 percent, and for product-markets B and C, 17 and 57 percent, respectively. When the sales performances of all three product-markets are combined, the offsetting effects created by different competitive conditions and product life cycles produce more consistent growth, with only a 6 percent unexplained variance in sales.

Two Levels of Diversification

Product diversification is one of two levels of diversification. Obviously, the less dependent a business is on a single product, the less vulnerable it is to a major change in performance. Coca-Cola, for instance, has a broad line of beverage products that serves virtually all world

FIGURE 11-16 PORTFOLIO DIVERSIFICATION AND SALES PERFORMANCE

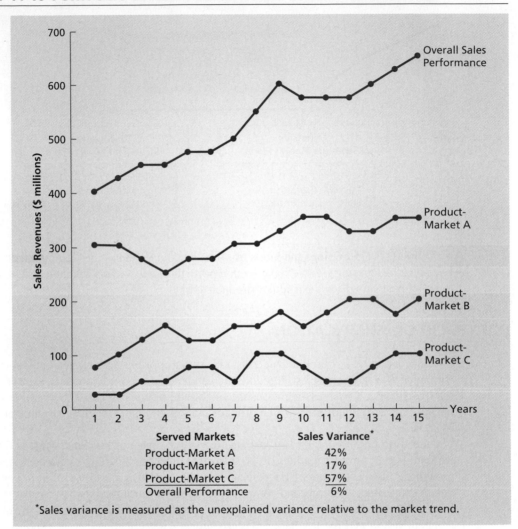

Served Markets	Sales Variance*
Product-Market A	42%
Product-Market B	17%
Product-Market C	57%
Overall Performance	6%

*Sales variance is measured as the unexplained variance relative to the market trend.

markets. For Procter & Gamble, product diversification goes further, because it has developed product positions in widely diversified consumer household product-markets.

Market diversification provides another way to achieve growth and reduce risk. DuPont, for example, has diversified across many markets that range from carpets to swimsuits to cookware, using materials such as Nylon, Dacron, Teflon, Lycra, and Kevlar. By serving multiple markets and not being dependent on any one product or market, DuPont has grown to a $50 billion company. In the early 1990s, US West split its company in two to better serve diverse markets. US West Communications remained in charge of the more mature core telecommunications businesses, while MediaOne Group was created to grow in high-technology markets. In the late 1990s, Hewlett-Packard pursued the same strategy when it split itself into two companies: an $8 billion test and measurement business named Agilent Technologies, and a $39 billion computer and imaging business that kept the company's original name. This split enabled Hewlett-Packard to move faster in the emerging computer and imaging markets without abandoning its core product-markets in test and measurement.

Every product-market will experience performance swings, but it is unlikely all product-markets of a diversified business will experience the same conditions at the same time. This is why participation in several diversified product-markets contributes to performance stability. Product-markets that perform well offset those that do not, whether the poor performance is caused by product life-cycle influences, competitor moves, economic conditions, or some other factor.

MARKETING MIX STRATEGY AND PERFORMANCE PLAN

But to make a strategic market plan actionable, a business must develop a marketing mix strategy in accordance with the strategic market plan and the allocated resources. As the strategic market plan and a corresponding marketing mix strategy are rolled out over a planning horizon of 3 to 5 years, a performance plan outlines the targeted short- and long-run share position, sales growth, and profitability.[12] By examining certain aspects of the strategic market planning process, we will discover sound approaches to making short- and long-run projections for each area of business performance.

As we have seen, a strategic market plan is a long-term strategy with a 3- to 5-year time horizon and specific performance objectives. A marketing mix strategy is a short-term marketing strategy with a 1-year time horizon. A marketing mix strategy needs to be reviewed each year with respect to changing market conditions and adjusted accordingly to achieve the long-run performance objectives of a strategic market plan. In some instances, market conditions may change so dramatically or suddenly that the strategic market plan will need to be reassessed to determine its continued suitability as the best long-run plan to achieve the business's performance objectives in a particular product-market.

Marketing Mix Strategy

For any strategic market plan, a detailed tactical marketing strategy—or *marketing mix strategy*—needs to be developed with respect to product positioning, price, promotion, and place. The degree to which the performance objectives of a strategic market plan are achieved depends on the effectiveness of the tactical marketing strategy that supports this strategic market plan.

For example, Intel's strategic market plan to enter the low-end personal computer market required a different tactical marketing strategy than the one required by the company's strategic market plan to defend its high-share position in microprocessors. Each plan required different product positioning, pricing approaches, promotions, and sales outlets to achieve a position that would be attractive to target customers relative to competitors' product-price positions.

The strategic market plan sets the strategic direction and provides broad guidelines for resource allocation. However, the marketing mix strategy is the workhorse that has to succeed in order for the strategic market plan to achieve both its short- and long-run performance objectives. The right strategic market plan with the wrong marketing mix strategy normally will not produce the desired levels of performance.

FIGURE 11-17 ZI-TECH'S BASE-YEAR PORTFOLIO PERFORMANCE

Base-Year Portfolio Performance	Market M1	Market M2	Market M3	Market M4	Company Total
Market Growth Rate	3.0%	0.0%	15.0%	–5.0%	5.1%
Market Demand	$400	$400	$500	$200	$1,500
Market Share	20.0%	25.0%	10.0%	10.0%	14.5%
Sales Revenues	$80	$100	$50	$20	$250
Percent Margin	40.0%	30.0%	40.0%	10.0%	33.6%
Gross Profit	$32	$30	$20	$2	$84
Marketing & Sales Expenses (%)	10.0%	10.0%	10.0%	10.0%	10.0%
Marketing & Sales Expenses ($)	$8	$10	$5	$2	$25
Net Marketing Contribution	$24	$20	$15	$0	$59
Marketing ROS	30.0%	20.0%	30.0%	0.0%	23.6%
Marketing ROI	300%	200%	300%	0%	236%

Dollar figures are millions.

Performance Plan

We saw earlier that the performance objectives and conditions under which a business would use either an offensive or a defensive strategic market plan are very different. Offensive strategic market plans are geared to deliver above-average performance in the areas of sales growth, improved share position, and improved long-run profit. Defensive strategic market plans are important in producing short-run profit performance and protecting important share positions, while also contributing to long-run profit performance and strategic position.

Offensive strategic market plans require investment for growth, which limits short-run profit performance while building sales revenue and improving share position. In the long run, a growth-oriented market strategy will shift from an offensive strategic market plan to a defensive strategic market plan. Defensive strategic market plans promote short-run profit performance but are not that effective in growing sales revenue or improving the long-run share position.

Consider Zi-Tech Acoustics, a $250 million business that engineers, manufactures, and markets a variety of acoustic products. Figure 11-17 specifies the market share, sales revenues, and net marketing contribution for Zi-Tech in each of the four product-markets it serves. A portfolio analysis based on market attractiveness and competitive position produced the product-market portfolio illustrated in Figure 11-18. Here is a summary of the strategic market plans for each of the company's product-markets:

■ **Market 1—Invest to Protect Market Share:** Market 1 is a mature market from which Zi-Tech derives a considerable 30 percent of its sales and an even more considerable 40 percent of the business's overall net marketing contribution. The intent of the strategic market plan is to protect share and profits. Everything will be done to hold margins while investment in marketing and sales expenses increases as sales increase and at the same rate. While growth is nominal (3%), this strategy should produce a modest increase in sales and marketing profits.

FIGURE 11-18 ZI-TECH'S PORTFOLIO ANALYSIS AND STRATEGIC MARKET PLAN

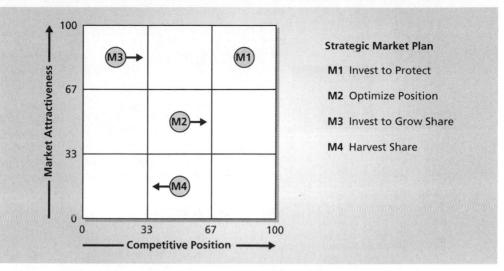

Strategic Market Plan

M1 Invest to Protect

M2 Optimize Position

M3 Invest to Grow Share

M4 Harvest Share

■ **Market 2—Optimize Position:** Market 2 is a mature market with no opportunity for growth. Management believes now is the time to optimize market share to achieve greater profits. Market 2 is 40 percent of overall sales and 34 percent of overall marketing profits. The strategic intent is to increase prices and decrease marketing and sales expenses as a percent of sales, which will probably erode market share. But the goal is to find a more profitable combination of margin and market share, one that yields greater marketing profits.

FIGURE 11-19 ZI-TECH'S YEAR-3 PERFORMANCE PLAN

Portfolio Strategy: Market:	Hold/Protect Share M1	Optimize Position M2	Invest to Grow M3	Harvest Share M4	Company Total
Market Growth Rate	3.0%	0.0%	15.0%	−5.0%	6.7%
Market Demand	$437	$400	$760	$171	$1,769
Market Share	20.0%	20.0%	15.0%	5.0%	14.5%
Sales Revenues	$87	$80	$114	$9	$290
Percent Margin	40.0%	37.0%	37.0%	35.0%	37.8%
Gross Profit	$35	$30	$42	$3	$110
Marketing & Sales Expenses (%)	10.0%	8.0%	12.5%	3.0%	10.2%
Marketing & Sales Expenses ($)	$9	$6	$14	$0	$30
Net Marketing Contribution	$26	$23	$28	$3	$80
Marketing ROS	30.0%	29.0%	24.5%	32.0%	27.6%
Marketing ROI	300%	363%	196%	1011%	270%

Dollar figures are millions.

FIGURE 11-20 PERFORMANCE PLAN FOR ZI-TECH'S FOUR PRODUCT-MARKETS

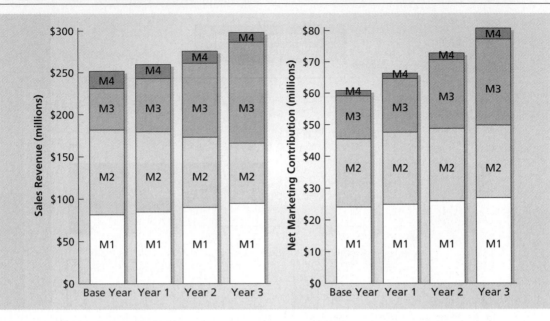

- **Market 3—Invest to Grow Market Share:** Market 3 is an attractive and growing market. The strategic intent is to invest to grow market share during the growth stage of the product life cycle. Market 3 is 25 percent of overall sales and 25 percent of overall marketing profits. Implementation of this strategic market plan is likely to result in lower prices and margins, along with increases in marketing and sales expenses, but market share should grow from 10 to 15 percent in a market that is growing 15 percent annually.
- **Market 4—Harvest Share Position:** Market 4 is an unattractive market in decline with an average competitive position. This market is less than 10 percent of overall sales and produces a zero marketing profit. A harvest strategy is recommended, which would maximize short-run marketing profits over the next 3 years. The strategy would involve price increases to improve margins, along with reductions in marketing and sales expenses. Market share and sales are expected to decrease significantly, but profits should increase over the next 3 years.

Given this set of strategic market plans, Zi-Tech hopes to grow sales from $250 million in the base year to $290 million in 3 years. As shown in Figure 11-19, Market 3 will then be more important to overall portfolio performance in both sales and net marketing contribution. More importantly, the combination of strategic market plans promises to increase the net marketing contribution from $59 million in the base year to $80 million in year 3. This set of strategic market plans will also improve Zi-Tech's marketing ROS from 23.6 to 27.6 percent and marketing ROI from 236 percent to 270 percent.

Figure 11-20 illustrates Zi-Tech's 3-year path for profitable growth. Market 1 will grow modestly in sales and profits. Market 2 is projected to decline in sales but increase modestly in marketing profits. Market 3 is projected to increase in both sales and marketing profits. And market 4 is projected to decrease in sales but improve from zero marketing profits to about $3 million. If this set of strategic market plans is successful, Zi-Tech will have improved its strategic position in served markets while growing sales and profits over a 3-year period. In Chapter 16, we will look more closely at how strategic market plans translate into shareholder value. For now, we can safely assume a 16 percent increase in sales revenues and a 34 percent increase in net marketing contribution contribute positively to net profit and shareholder value.

■ Summary

Strategic market planning is a process. It involves assessing business performance with respect to market attractiveness and competitive position. The assessment is made for each of the business's product-markets and any new ones the business may be considering. The product life cycle serves as the basis for an important portfolio analysis whereby a business can display its product line over the product life cycle with respect to sales, sales growth, and profitability. A balanced product life-cycle portfolio will include a mix of early, growth, and mature markets.

Several measures of competitive position can be used in a portfolio analysis. One measure that corresponds to sales and profit performance is *relative market share*, which is the ratio of a business's market share to the total share of its three largest competitors. Another measure of competitive position, one that also considers sales and profit, is the *share development index.*

The GE/McKinsey portfolio model includes an index of several market attractiveness factors and an index of several competitive position factors. Separate ratings of importance and performance shape the overall performance of these two dimensions. Market attractiveness is indexed with respect to market forces (market size, growth, buyer power), competitive environment (price rivalry, ease of market entry, number of competitors), and market access (customer familiarity, channel access, sales requirements). Competitive position is indexed with respect to cost advantage (unit cost, transaction costs, marketing expenses), differentiation advantage (product quality, service quality, brand image), and marketing advantage (market share, brand awareness, distribution). The portfolio analysis identifies one or more possible strategic market plans for each product-market the business serves or may enter in the future, based on the product-market's position in the portfolio.

A strategic market plan is a long-run, 3- to 5-year strategic market objective that involves share position but has corresponding implications for short- and long-run sales revenue growth, and profit performance. Strategic market plans can be offensive or defensive. Offensive strategic market plans involve market penetration strategies to grow share position, sales, and long-run profitability. Offensive strategies include investing to grow, investing to improve position, entering another market, and developing a new market. Defensive strategies include protecting or optimizing position for maximum profits, monetizing for maximum cash flow, harvesting, and divesting. A combination of strategic market plans (one for each product-market) results in an overall view of how the business will grow with respect to share, sales, and profits.

Portfolio diversification in both products and markets is also an important aspect of strategic market planning. A portfolio too concentrated in one line of products or in one market is subject to more variance in sales and profits. Diversification into unrelated product-markets protects a business's overall performance against downward swings if one product-market should encounter unfavorable conditions. Diversification adds stability to a business's overall performance.

Although the strategic market plan for a given product-market sets short-run and long-run goals with respect to market share, sales revenues, and profits, it does not specify how this performance will be achieved. Each strategic market plan, then, has a corresponding tactical marketing plan. The tactical marketing plan is a marketing mix strategy (product, price, place, promotion, and service) and resource allocation (marketing budget) that specifies the tactical details of how the objectives of a given strategic market plan will be achieved. A performance plan is developed based on these marketing tactics, the marketing budget, and a 3- to 5-year forecast of market share, sales revenues, and net marketing contribution.

■ Market-Based Strategic Thinking

1 Why is the product life cycle used in evaluating the current and future sales and profits of a business's portfolio of products?

2 What could be done with regard to Portfolio A in Figure 11-1 to make it a more balanced portfolio over the next 3 to 5 years? How would this impact short- and long-run sales and profits?

3 What is meant by the "strategic market planning process"?

4 What is the difference between market attractiveness and competitive position? Why are both used in many portfolio models?

5 Why is relative market share a better measure of competitive position than market share?

6 Why would a business elect to use the GE/McKinsey portfolio model over other portfolio models?

7 How is a strategic market plan different from a strategic market planning process?

8 How would you assess the attractiveness of a new consumer product-market for Procter & Gamble? Be specific as to those factors you would include in building an index of market attractiveness for a Procter & Gamble consumer market.

9 How would you assess the competitive position Procter & Gamble would have in a new consumer product-market? Be specific as to those factors you would include in building an index of competitive position for a Procter & Gamble consumer market.

10 Using the following information, create a portfolio analysis and specify a strategic market plan for a business that serves the three product-markets.

Product-Market	Share (%)	Sales ($ millions)	Market Attractiveness	Competitive Position
A	10	$20	20	40
B	33	$50	75	80
C	5	$10	85	15

11 Using the information presented in item 10 and the additional information that follows, create a 3-year performance plan with respect to market share and sales revenues for each product-market, given the strategic market plan specified. Also create a projection of overall sales for each year of the 3-year planning horizon.

Product-Market	Strategic Market Plan	Share Objective (%)	Market Demand ($ millions)	Market Growth (%)
A	Optimize Position	5	$200	5
B	Protect Share	33	$150	7
C	Grow Share	10	$200	20

12 Under what conditions would a business specify an offensive strategic market plan?

13 Under what conditions would a business specify a defensive strategic market plan?

14 What role do offensive and defensive strategic market plans play in the short- and long-run performance of a business?

15 How does the level of product-market diversification affect sales growth and performance consistency?

16 Why would the overall variation in sales revenues over a 10-year period be different when comparing General Electric and Dell?

17 How would the sales and profit performance over a 3-year period differ between a business with only defensive strategic market plans and a business with only offensive strategic market plans? Why is it important to have a balance of offensive and defensive plans?

18 Why is a tactical marketing plan for each strategic market plan an important part of the strategic market planning process?

19 How does a manager develop a tactical marketing plan and a marketing budget to achieve a specific strategic market plan?

20 How would the tactical marketing plan and marketing budget for a strategic market plan to grow market share (offensive) differ from those of an optimize position strategic market plan to reduce share?

21 How does a business create a forecast of its future performance based on the strategic market plans for each product-market it intends to serve over a given planning horizon?

Marketing Performance Tools

The three **Marketing Performance Tools** outlined here may be accessed online at *www.rogerjbest.com*. These applied-learning exercises will improve your ability to use portfolio analysis in selecting an appropriate strategic market plan. The instructions refer to the online examples, not the related Chapter 11 figures cited.

11.1 Product Life Cycle Portfolio (Figure 11-1)
- Using the data provided, adjust the proposed product life cycle portfolio to the recommended percentage of sales and product life-cycle position. How will the revised portfolio perform in the future with respect to sales and profit?

11.2 Market Development–Share Development Portfolio (Figure 11-6)
- Using the data provided, adjust the portfolio position based on market redefinition and efforts to improve share performance metrics. What is the potential impact for future sales and profits?

11.3 GE/McKinsey Portfolio (Figure 11-8)
- Using the data provided, alter the market attractiveness and competitive position ratings to create a revised portfolio. How will the revised portfolio perform with respect to sales and profits?

Notes

1. Michael Treacy and Fred Wiersama, *The Discipline of Market Leaders* (Reading, MA: Addison-Wesley, 1995).
2. Some analysts believe the guidelines of the market plan may lead to a strategic advantage. See David A. Garvin, "Leveraging Processes for Strategic Advantage," *Harvard Business Review* (September–October 1995): 77.
3. Roger A. Kerin, Vijay Mahajan, and P. Rajan Varadarajan, *Strategic Market Planning* (Boston: Allyn and Bacon, 1990).
4. Robert Buzzell and Bradley Gale, *The PIMS Principles: Linking Strategy to Performance* (New York: Free Press, 1987).
5. Kasturi Rangan, Melvyn Menezes, and E. P. Maier, "Channel Selection for New Industrial Products: A Framework, Method and Application," *Journal of Marketing* (July 1992): 69–82.
6. L. W. Phillips, D. R. Chang, and R. D. Bussell, "Product Quality, Cost Position, and Business Performance: A Test of Some Key Hypotheses," *Journal of Marketing* 47 (January 1983): 26–43.
7. Michael E. Porter, *Competitive Advantage* (New York: Free Press, 1986).
8. David Aaker, "Formal Planning System," in *Strategic Market Management* (New York: Wiley, 1995): 341–353.
9. Thomas Powell, "Strategic Planning as Competitive Advantage," *Strategic Management Journal* 13 (1992): 551–558; Scott Armstrong, "The Value of Formal Planning for Strategic Decisions: Reply," *Strategic Management Journal* 7 (1986): 183–185; and Deepak Sinha, "The Contribution of Formal Planning to Decisions," *Strategic Management Journal* (October 1990): 479–492.
10. William K. Hall, "Survival Strategies in a Hostile Environment," *Harvard Business Review* (September–October 1980): 75–85.
11. Kathryn Rudie Harrigan, *Strategies for Declining Businesses* (Lexington, MA: Lexington Books, 1980); and Kathryn Rudie Harrigan and Michael E. Porter, "End-Game Strategies for Declining Industries," *Harvard Business Review* (July–August 1983): 111–120. Also see Kathryn Rudie Harrigan, *Managing Maturing Businesses* (Lexington, MA: Lexington Books, 1988).
12. Frances V. McCrory and Peter G. Gerstberger, "The New Math of Performance Measurements," *Journal of Business Strategy* (March–April 1992): 33–38.

CHAPTER 12

Offensive Strategies

■ You miss 100 percent of the shots you don't take.
—Wayne Gretsky
Former National Hockey League All-Star

S tarbucks is a great example of a company that's not passing up any shots. It is on the offensive with a wide range of growth strategies, as presented in Figure 12-1. This company's managers have never waited for the game to come to them; they have always been on the attack, and we have to wonder at this stage whether they have any real competition left. Starbucks continues to grow market share, opening about 1,000 new

FIGURE 12-1 STARBUCKS' OFFENSIVE GROWTH STRATEGIES

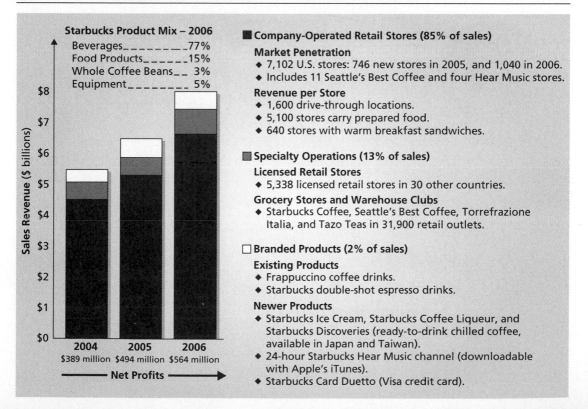

Starbucks Product Mix – 2006
Beverages_____77%
Food Products_____15%
Whole Coffee Beans__ 3%
Equipment_____ 5%

Sales Revenue ($ billions)

	2004	2005	2006
Net Profits	$389 million	$494 million	$564 million

■ **Company-Operated Retail Stores (85% of sales)**
Market Penetration
◆ 7,102 U.S. stores: 746 new stores in 2005, and 1,040 in 2006.
◆ Includes 11 Seattle's Best Coffee and four Hear Music stores.
Revenue per Store
◆ 1,600 drive-through locations.
◆ 5,100 stores carry prepared food.
◆ 640 stores with warm breakfast sandwiches.

■ **Specialty Operations (13% of sales)**
Licensed Retail Stores
◆ 5,338 licensed retail stores in 30 other countries.
Grocery Stores and Warehouse Clubs
◆ Starbucks Coffee, Seattle's Best Coffee, Torrefrazione Italia, and Tazo Teas in 31,900 retail outlets.

☐ **Branded Products (2% of sales)**
Existing Products
◆ Frappuccino coffee drinks.
◆ Starbucks double-shot espresso drinks.
Newer Products
◆ Starbucks Ice Cream, Starbucks Coffee Liqueur, and Starbucks Discoveries (ready-to-drink chilled coffee, available in Japan and Taiwan).
◆ 24-hour Starbucks Hear Music channel (downloadable with Apple's iTunes).
◆ Starbucks Card Duetto (Visa credit card).

stores a year, including many drive-through locations. Additionally, revenue per store is growing, not only because the company continues to attract new customers, but also because of increased sales of food products and music CDs. Specialty operations include licensed stores for international market penetration and packaged Starbucks products sold in 31,900 retail grocery stores. Brand products, while only 21 percent of sales, take the Starbucks name into a diversified line of new products.

STRATEGIC MARKET PLANS

Many businesses experienced considerable growth during the 1990s and early 2000s. Starbucks, Apple, Toyota, Microsoft, and Wal-Mart are but a few examples. The rapid growth of these five businesses was the result of a variety of strategic market plans, from market-share penetration to the development of completely new products for new markets. In all five cases, the strategic market plans addressed three basic performance objectives:

■ **Share Position:** How will the strategic market plan contribute to the business's share position in served markets?
■ **Sales Growth:** To what degree will the strategic market plan contribute to sales growth?
■ **Profit Performance:** How will the strategic market plan impact short- and long-run profit performance?

FIGURE 12-2 MARKET GROWTH AND OFFENSIVE AND DEFENSIVE STRATEGIES

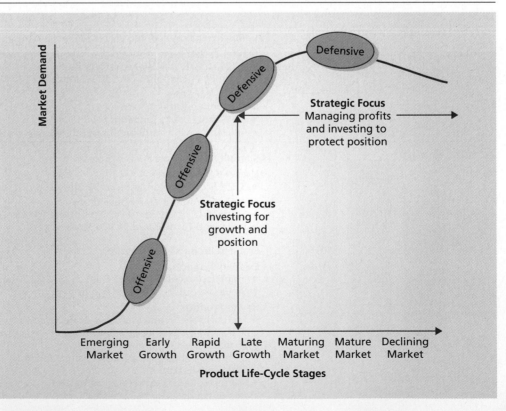

FIGURE 12-3 PORTFOLIO POSITIONS AND STRATEGIC MARKET PLANS

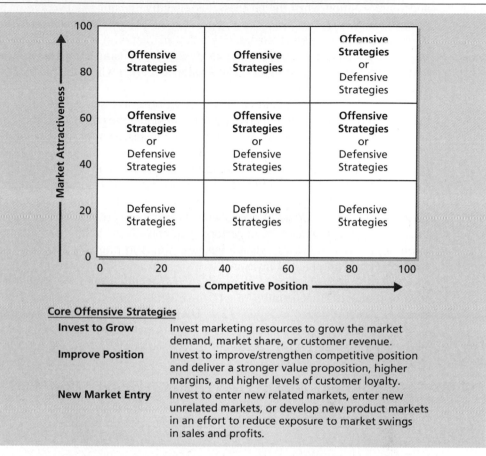

Core Offensive Strategies

Invest to Grow	Invest marketing resources to grow the market demand, market share, or customer revenue.
Improve Position	Invest to improve/strengthen competitive position and deliver a stronger value proposition, higher margins, and higher levels of customer loyalty.
New Market Entry	Invest to enter new related markets, enter new unrelated markets, or develop new product markets in an effort to reduce exposure to market swings in sales and profits.

To make the best use of limited resources, a business needs a strategic market plan that carefully maps out the business's future growth and profit performance.[1] Every strategic market plan a business develops will in some way affect both its short- and long-run performance in each of the three areas identified. Depending on the situation, some strategic market plans will be offensive plans and some will be defensive.

As we saw in Chapter 11, offensive strategic market plans are usually growth oriented and are more appropriate for the growth stage of a product-market life cycle,[2] as shown in Figure 12-2. Their objective is to produce sales growth and improve share position and future profit performance. Defensive strategic market plans, on the other hand, are generally more suitable for the later stages of a product-market life cycle and are often designed to protect important share positions and be major contributors to short-run sales revenues and profits. This chapter examines the different kinds of offensive strategic market plans, and Chapter 13 looks at defensive strategic market plans.

OFFENSIVE STRATEGIC MARKET PLANS

The combination of market attractiveness and competitive position creates a portfolio position for any given product-market.[3] As shown in Figure 12-3, attractive markets are most likely to warrant an offensive strategic market plan to improve competitive position and share position when the business's competitive position is average or below. These offensive strategies can range from improving the competitive position and market share in existing product-markets to entering a new market with no established share position. In addition, a business could explore the possibility of using an offensive strategic market plan to cultivate an emerging or underdeveloped market where the business would have a strong position of advantage.

Of the six portfolio positions in which an offensive strategic market plan could be used, the three with average market attractiveness and the one with highest market attractiveness and highest competitive position could instead, under some conditions, be more suitable for a defensive strategic market plan. For these portfolio positions, we would need more information before we could decide whether an offensive or defensive strategic market plan would be more effective. For example, an offensive strategic market plan may be warranted, depending on a business's sources of relative advantage. On the other hand, a defensive strategic market plan to protect the current position may be the better alternative for achieving desired performance objectives. A defensive plan could also be appropriate, in some cases, when a business wants to improve profits by optimizing its market focus with minimal investment.

Offensive strategic market plans are fundamentally geared for growth and inherently involve strategies for penetrating or growing existing markets or entering or developing new markets, as summarized in Figure 12-4. The range of potential offensive strategic market plans is wide.[4] A logical place to start is within *existing* markets. A business that already has a good working knowledge of customers and competitors, and has the resources in

FIGURE 12-4 STRATEGIC MARKET PLANS AND OFFENSIVE STRATEGIES

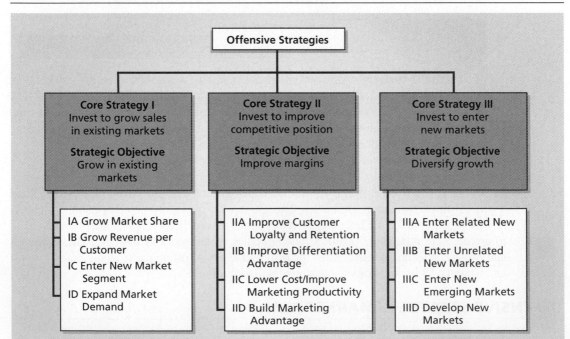

place to serve existing markets, should seek to leverage its existing market position with an offensive strategic market plan to further penetrate and develop its product-markets.

Coca-Cola has been described as the "perfect growth company," even though it already commands a 50 percent market share of the worldwide carbonated soft drink market. From the company's point of view, Coca-Cola represents only a 2 percent *share of stomachs* on a worldwide basis. The point was driven home in a Coca-Cola annual report that pictured 47 empty Coke bottles and one full bottle. Looking at its market in this way has helped Coca-Cola grow its volume at the rate of 7 to 8 percent, while PepsiCo, its chief rival, is growing unit volume at the rate of only 1 percent. Clearly, Coca-Cola is challenging its marketing managers to think offensively in finding ways to grow Coca-Cola's share of the non-alcoholic beverage market.

OFFENSIVE CORE STRATEGY I: INVEST TO GROW SALES

Figure 12-4 shows the three offensive core strategies used in strategic market planning. For each core strategy, one or more of four fundamental offensive strategic market plans can be developed to support the objective of the core strategy. For example, the objective of the first core strategy is to grow the business in its existing market. The specific strategic market plans for achieving the objective range from share penetration to growing market demand.[5] A business could grow its market share, increase its revenue per customer, enter new market segments, or it could expand market demand and thereby create a bigger pie, with its slice proportionately bigger. The offensive core strategies are numbered I, II, and III, and each of their four specific offensive strategies are designated A, B, C, and D. This system of numbering and lettering implies no order of importance; it just helps us keep track of the different types of offensive core strategies and their specific marketing strategies.

Offensive Strategy IA: Grow Market Share

One of the more obvious market strategies is to grow market share. But many factors can affect a business's ability to grow share and profitability.[6] Its share potential is one consideration. To what degree has the business achieved its share potential? What factors driving share development need to be managed to grow share in a given product-market? Finally, will share growth actually contribute to profitability? Each is an important consideration in developing an offensive strategic market plan to grow share.

In Chapter 3, we calculated the share development index (SDI) as the ratio of actual market share to share potential. The share potential of a business is the market share that a business believes it can achieve with a successful tactical marketing strategy, given the strength of its competitive position and its marketing effectiveness in a given product-market. In the following share development path, a business estimates it should perform at a 90 percent level in product awareness, 50 percent in product preference, 80 percent in intentions to purchase, 80 percent in product availability, and 70 percent in rate of purchase. Performing at these levels results in a market share potential of just over 20 percent.

$$\begin{array}{l}\textbf{Market Share}\\ \textbf{Potential}\end{array} = \begin{array}{c}\text{Product}\\ \text{Awareness}\end{array} \times \begin{array}{c}\text{Product}\\ \text{Preference}\end{array} \times \begin{array}{c}\text{Purchase}\\ \text{Intentions}\end{array} \times \begin{array}{c}\text{Product}\\ \text{Availability}\end{array} \times \begin{array}{c}\text{Purchase}\\ \text{Rate}\end{array}$$

$$= 0.90 \times 0.50 \times 0.80 \times 0.80 \times 0.70$$

$$= \textbf{20.2\%}$$

If a business's actual market share was 8 percent, the business would be underperforming and would have an SDI of 40.

$$\text{Share Development Index} = \frac{\text{Current Market Share}}{\text{Market Share Potential}} = \frac{8\%}{20\%} \times 100 = \textbf{40}$$

This would mean the business has achieved only 40 percent of its potential market share. It would have a good opportunity to grow market share with a market-penetration strategy.

To grow share, a business has to examine each area of performance along the share development path with respect to its expected versus its actual market performance. For instance, the business in the example expects to achieve 90 percent product awareness in its target market. If its actual target market awareness were only 67 percent, this performance gap would prevent the business from reaching its full market share potential. To grow share, this business would need to examine the key performance gaps in its market share response.

There is also the possibility a business has reached its share potential but feels it can still grow its share with a new strategic market plan. Product improvements that would increase product preference from 50 to 70 percent would raise the market share potential from 20.2 to 28.2 percent. Of course, to achieve this level of share penetration, the business would have to adequately communicate and deliver these product improvements to the full satisfaction of target customers.

The most important consideration in developing strategies to grow share is to make sure the planned share growth will be profitable. Some methods of growing share can actually result in a lower net marketing contribution, as illustrated by the Santa Fe Sportswear example in Chapter 2. Market share is a key competitive metric, but market-based businesses need to resist emphasizing it to the point of ignoring other market-based metrics. It is easy to become caught up in a share battle to the point of forgetting about the unprofitable possibility of winning the battle for share but losing the war with respect to profits.

Offensive Strategy IB: Grow Revenue per Customer

Harley-Davidson derives 77 percent of its $4.1 billion in sales from the sale of motorcycles. The other 23 percent comes from purchases of clothing, parts, and accessories. In clothing alone, Harley-Davidson introduces 1,200 new items annually (excluding riding boots, baby clothes, and clothing for pets). The retail clothes are so important to communicating the brand that every dealership now has fitting rooms. Sales of clothing, parts, and accessories represent 23 percent of Harley-Davidson's annual per-customer revenue of $13,630. Even better for Harley-Davidson, the incremental sales of related products have much higher margins and build customer loyalty. The apparel sales also enhance brand awareness and brand equity, with the wearers of Harley-Davidson clothing helping to communicate the brand name.

As a business approaches 100 percent of its share development index, additional growth based on market share gains becomes increasingly difficult. Up to this point, a business's overall performance could be improved with share gains achieved by correcting ineffective tactical marketing strategies, improving competitive position, or increasing a business's marketing effort. Now, with its share potential almost fully realized, overall performance improvement relies more on growing sales with existing customers, which increases the amount of revenue per customer.

As another example, McDonald's in its early years sold a limited product line of hamburgers, French fries, and drinks. With product line extensions that now include chicken and fish sandwiches, salads, desserts, and a breakfast menu, McDonald's has been able to grow the average amount spent by its existing customers. Of course, these line extensions have also attracted new customers, both those who did not previously buy at fast-food restaurants and those who had been competitors' customers.

For businesses with well-known brand names, such as Kodak, Nike, Honda, IBM, and Disney, it is easy to introduce line extensions by leveraging the high awareness and positive image of the companies' brand names.[7] When Honda entered the lawn mower market in the early 1990s, sales of its mowers were driven by the company's name. Customers immediately perceived them as reliable, high-quality products. This perception had been created by Honda's reputation in automobiles, motorcycles, and other motorized products. The high level of name awareness helped the company to quickly penetrate the lawn mower market. When Honda saw that many of its lawn mower customers owned other Honda products, the company then developed a growth strategy based on increasing volumes along its entire product line by marketing to existing customers.

Honda's strategy to target existing customers for its other products is aptly expressed in the company's marketing objective: "*Our goal is to have five Hondas in every garage*." This motto reflects an offensive strategic market plan to capture the purchases by owners of Honda cars of lawn mowers, recreational vehicles (motorcycles, snowmobiles, jet skis, all-terrain vehicles, outboard motors), portable motors, and generators. For Honda, the strategy has been instrumental in growing the company. For any business with a solid brand reputation, the existing customer base offers a considerable opportunity for growing per-customer revenue through sales of other products.

Revenue per customer can also be increased through price premiums. Businesses that enhance their products with value-added services or have built a superior reputation for quality can charge higher prices than competing businesses and still maintain a superior customer value. General Electric's turbine engines, for example, command a price premium because they are of high quality, installation services are first rate, and the company has a global reputation for innovative engineering and technical know-how. The price premium enables GE to attain more revenue per customer than many competing turbine manufacturers.

Offensive Strategy IC: Enter New Market Segments

Another offensive growth strategy within existing markets is to enter a new customer segment within an existing market.[8] As the personal computer market grew, the under-$1,000 segment emerged. Intel, which did not have a product for this segment, saw Advanced Micro Devices and other competitors take the lead in this segment. With demand in the segment growing faster than in any other, Intel responded with a new product designed for price-sensitive customers. As shown in Figure 12-5, the Celeron chip provided PC manufacturers a low-cost Intel microprocessor for this market segment. Intel's offensive strategic market plan for entering a new market segment gave the company a new source of sales revenue and profitability.

FIGURE 12-5 INTEL NEW SEGMENT ENTRY STRATEGY

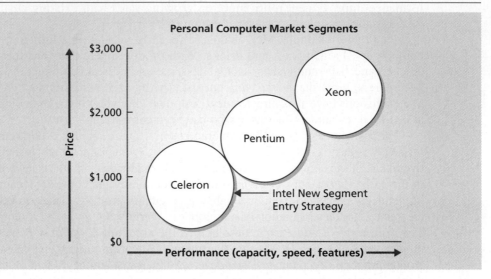

Another illustration of a company successfully entering new segments took place in the vodka market. This market is divided into four segments based on price and differences in taste, brand image, and packaging, as illustrated in Figure 12-6. Absolut Spirits had been successful in the premium vodka market segment and was number two in overall market share behind market leader Smirnoff. Although Absolut held a strong position in the $15 to $25 premium segment, it lacked market positions in the super-premium segment (over $25) and the traditional segment ($10 to $15). Grey Goose, a competitor's product in the super-premium segment, had seen its U.S. sales increase from 100,000 cases to 1.4 million cases in 2003. Because the market attractiveness of this segment was clearly improving, Absolut saw a good opportunity for growth. It introduced Level in the super-premium segment to compete with Grey Goose, Belvedere, and Ketel One. The company also positioned Danzka with unique packaging (in a metal container for faster chilling, shaped like a cocktail shaker) in the traditional segment at a suggested price of $13 to $14 per bottle.

Offensive Strategy ID: Expand Market Demand

Because at any point in time the number of customers in any given market is finite, strategies to enlarge a business's customer base include a focus on winning over competitors' customers, but they can also focus on growing market demand by drawing new customers into a market. For example, the market for flat-screen TVs was 4 million per year in 2003. Although Sony and Samsung battle each other for market share, their common offensive strategy is to grow market demand. They estimate that this market increased from 14 million units per year in 2005 to 30 million in 2007. Clearly the worldwide market potential is much greater. This type of offensive growth strategy is likely to benefit both companies in the years ahead.

In Chapter 3, we learned to calculate the market development index (MDI). The MDI is simply the ratio of current market demand to maximum market demand (the maximum

FIGURE 12-6 NEW SEGMENT OFFENSIVE GROWTH STRATEGY IN THE VODKA MARKET

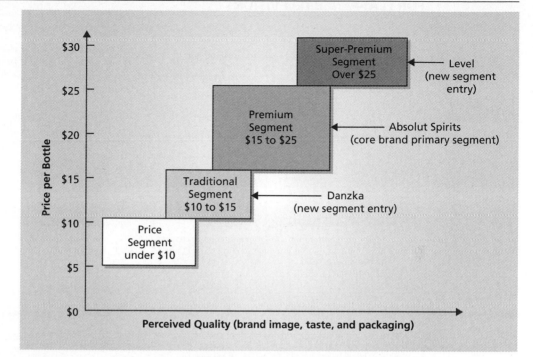

number of customers possible for a particular geographic market scope). For example, the market development index for the flat-panel TV for the worldwide market is estimated at approximately 30.

$$\text{Market Development Index} = \frac{\text{Market Demand for Flat-Panel TVs (2007)}}{\text{Market Potential for Flat-Panel TVs}} \times 100$$

$$= \frac{30 \text{ million (2007)}}{100 \text{ million (worldwide)}} \times 100$$

$$= 30$$

This means the market has many potential customers who for various reasons have not entered it. As shown in Figure 12-7, five basic forces need to be addressed for the market to reach its full potential. A strategic market plan to grow either the entire market or a specific segment within the market would carefully consider each of these forces.

Of the five major forces that limit market demand, the three most restrictive are price, availability, and compatibility. Until prices decrease dramatically, many potential customers will not be able to enter the market.

Availability can be addressed with wider distribution networks, recognizing that a flat-panel TV manufacturer may find it economically infeasible to serve customers in some parts of the world. Unless availability is improved, many potential customers will remain outside the market regardless of lower prices.

FIGURE 12-7 FACTORS TO BE ADDRESSED IN GROWING THE MARKET DEMAND FOR FLAT-PANEL TELEVISIONS

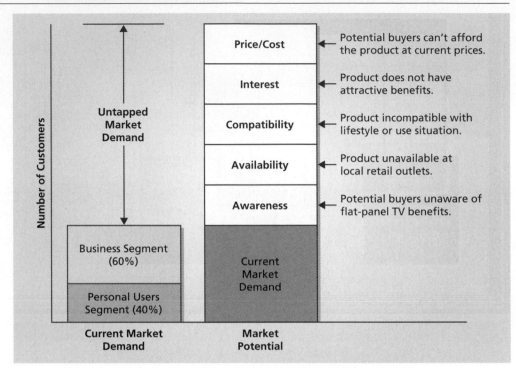

For the flat-panel TV market, compatibility at first glance does not seem to be a problem. But living environments in many parts of the world are too small for easy viewing of a flat-panel TV. No or poor electricity service in some areas also limits product application (compatibility) and slows market development.

Finally, awareness and attraction to benefits best occur from actually seeing a flat-panel TV in operation, but in many worldwide markets, opportunities to view flat-panel TVs are limited by high prices or unavailability. The market for the product will move toward its full potential only when the forces that limit market development diminish.

OFFENSIVE CORE STRATEGY II: IMPROVE COMPETITIVE POSITION

In situations where a business is in an attractive market but has a weak or average competitive position, an investment to improve competitive position may be the best strategy to pursue. The better a business's competitive position, the better are its chances of achieving price premiums and a high level of customer retention, which in turn will improve the business's margins and net marketing contribution. This section discusses the four offensive strategies for improving competitive position, as shown in Figure 12-4.

Offensive Strategy IIA: Improve Customer Loyalty and Retention

Businesses spend money to attract new customers in growing markets, but if they do not retain these customers, they will experience higher marketing expenses and lower marketing profits. As we saw in Chapter 1, it costs much more to acquire a new customer than to keep one—from 5 to 10 times more. Further, a 2 percent increase in loyal customers has been shown to lower marketing costs by 10 percent. An offensive strategy to increase customer retention and customer loyalty will have an immediate impact on marketing profits (net marketing contribution).

For example, in Figure 12-8 we can see that AT&T has an 89.2 percent customer retention rate. With 65.7 million customers, this means AT&T lost 7.1 million customers in 2007. To hold its customer base at 65.7 million, AT&T had to acquire 7.1 million new customers. Not only is this 5 to 10 times more expensive with respect to marketing expenses, but new customers often use less service, resulting in a lower average monthly margin per customer. If AT&T could improve its customer retention rate from 89.2 to 94.2 percent, the company would increase the lifetime value of its customers by 25 percent. For any business, retaining a higher percentage of customers and improving their loyalty is an offensive strategic investment that not only impacts short-term profits but also greatly enhances long-run performance.

Offensive Strategy IIB: Improve Differentiation Advantage

One of the major customer complaints in the wireless communications market is reliability. To address this problem and turn it into a differentiation advantage, Verizon Wireless created a team of 50 "road warriors" who each drove 100,000 miles annually (a total of 5 million miles) in specially equipped cars to test the reliability of Verizon's network against several competitors' phones. An onboard computer system made synchronized inbound and outbound calls of 2 1/2 minutes each to the home office, with 15 seconds between calls. Besides connection quality, sound quality was checked by playing recordings of 20 phrases representing all sounds in the English language. Verizon's computer system logged each call and used a global positioning system to note the precise locations where problems occurred. Gridlock produced the most severe test and was the best indicator of how well the system was working. Verizon's efforts to improve reliability resulted in an increase in customer retention from 90 to 92.8 percent over a 3-year period.

To enhance the differentiation advantage achieved through the actual improvement in reliability, Verizon launched an advertising campaign using its "road warrior" testing process as the theme. The often-repeated question in the ads, "Can you hear me *now*?" became a signature

FIGURE 12-8 CELLULAR PHONE SERVICE CUSTOMER RETENTION

Major Cellular Phone Service Providers (2007)	Customers (millions)	Customer Retention (%)	Lost Customers (millions)
AT&T (AT&T Mobility Ltd.)	65.7	89.2	7.1
Verizon Wireless	61.1	92.8	4.4
Sprint Nextel	53.7	89.2	5.8
T-Mobile USA	28.2	86.8	3.7

line for the company, familiar to almost everyone. The ads' refrain emphasized the importance customers place on reliability when making a vendor choice. Verizon depends heavily on its source of differentiation because the company is not a low-cost service provider.

Offensive Strategy IIC: Lower Costs/Improve Marketing Productivity

Sony found its profit margins were shrinking in consumer electronics as prices eroded faster than manufacturing costs could be lowered. Even with higher volumes, gross profits were in decline as margins dropped. To address this problem and restore margins to more acceptable levels, Sony examined its cost structure closely and identified several areas where costs could be cut. To promote standardization, the number of components used in Sony consumer electronics was pared from 840,000 to just 100,000. To reduce material costs further, the number of suppliers was slashed from 4,700 to just 1,000. Sony also moved more production from Japan to China, where labor costs are much lower, and added more technology to its manufacturing processes. By lowering its costs, Sony improved its profitability and remained a leader in a highly competitive market.

As another example, a 3M business found many of its distributors who made below-average purchases were frequently late in paying. These distributors were moved to an online purchasing system where they had to provide a credit card number to initiate a purchase. This change left them somewhat dissatisfied, but they were told what they would have to do in order to improve their buying status. In the end, few distributors were lost and the 3M business greatly reduced its marketing expenses and improved its cash flow. Both of these factors contributed to a higher net marketing contribution and to a higher marketing productivity (net marketing contribution per dollar of marketing expense).

Offensive Strategy IID: Build Marketing Advantage

Nautilus was a pioneer brand in the $5 billion home-fitness equipment market. The company's direct marketing approach was successful, but Nautilus had not responded to market trends that included more emphasis on cardiovascular equipment and a shift toward in-store purchases. Although Nautilus could retool to produce new products, the shift from direct marketing channels, including the company's heavy reliance on infomercials, to selling through retail stores would be much harder. But because 80 percent of the $5 billion in sales in this market occurred in retail stores, this change was essential. To close this gap and build a marketing advantage, Nautilus not only began selling through specialty sports equipment retailers, but also developed partnerships with Amazon.com, Costco, and The Sports Authority. These indirect channel partnerships improved Nautilus's competitive position by giving the company a marketing advantage over its competitors.

Starbucks serves coffee around the world to millions of customers every week, who spend an average of about $4 per visit. As we saw earlier, the company has become the coffee shop market leader by holding a marketing advantage created mainly by a large number of stores, a worldwide presence, a strong brand reputation, and great perceived quality. Starbucks has been growing its number of retail coffee outlets by about 30 percent annually, expanding from 3,000 stores in 2000 to 12,440 in 2007. These stores include 1,600 drive-through outlets in the United States and almost 5,338 coffee outlets in 30 international markets, most of which are even more profitable than the U.S. outlets. Starbucks' dominant advantage in store numbers, along with the global scope of its operations, has been the engine propelling the company's remarkable growth despite industry downturns.

OFFENSIVE CORE STRATEGY III: ENTER NEW MARKETS

At some point, every business will need to examine growth opportunities outside its existing markets.[9] Any of three fundamental reasons could lead a business to enter a new market: (1) a limited number of attractive market opportunities within existing markets; (2) attractive opportunities, in terms of meeting the business's overall performance objectives, outside existing markets; and (3) a desire to diversify sources of profitability to reduce variation in performance.[10]

The four basic offensive strategic market plans for entering new markets, as in Figure 12-4, are (1) entry into established related markets, (2) entry into established markets unrelated to markets served by the business, (3) entry into new emerging markets, and (4) entry into markets with considerable undeveloped market potential. Entry into established markets (related or unrelated) means competing with established competitors for existing market demand, while entry into emerging markets requires significant investment to develop market demand, but often in the absence of competition.

Offensive Strategy IIIA: Enter Related New Markets

Not content to rest on its laurels with a 50 percent market share of the worldwide carbonated soft drink market, Coca-Cola has entered the $1 billion energy drinks market, illustrated in Figure 12-9. This is a related new market entry strategy that allows Coca-Cola to develop new sources of sales growth by leveraging its core competencies and competitive advantages.

FIGURE 12-9 NEW MARKET ENTRY OPPORTUNITIES FOR COCA-COLA

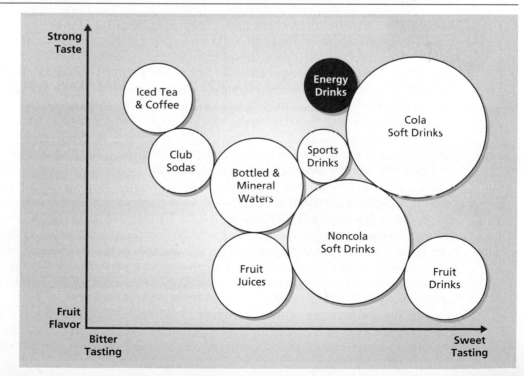

K2 is best known as a ski manufacturer. Over a 10-year period beginning in the mid-1980s, K2 steadily increased its share of the American ski market until in the mid-1990s it became the market share leader. But the American ski market was by then mature, and opportunities to grow sales through either market growth or increased market share were limited. This situation led K2 to a related new market entry strategy for the snowboard and inline skate markets. K2 planned to achieve significant sales revenue growth during the subsequent 10 years as a result of this strategy, and in fact the company grew sales dramatically to $1.4 billion by 2006. The strategy also enabled K2 to leverage its brand-name awareness, reputation for quality, manufacturing and design expertise, and, in some instances, its existing marketing channel and sales systems. These factors resulted in a variety of cost and marketing efficiencies, and K2 achieved an impressive average gross profit margin of 35.4 percent. In 2006, K2's sales were derived from marine and outdoor products (29.2 percent), action sports (30.2 percent), team sports (27.5 percent), and apparel and footwear (13.1 percent).

Sometimes a business discovers that entry into a new market is blocked by the cost of entry, technology requirements, or a lack of market access. To overcome the entry barriers, a business can join forces with two or more partner companies with complementary market expertise and leverage. By blending the strengths of businesses from related markets, the new entities are better equipped for developing and marketing products that more completely serve and fulfill customer needs. In the telecommunications industry, barriers to new market entry led to many mergers, joint ventures, and strategic alliances among telecommunications, computer, and cable TV companies.

Offensive Strategy IIIB: Enter Unrelated New Markets

Westinghouse acquired CBS in the mid-1990s. A week earlier, Disney had acquired ABC. The Disney acquisition was a *related* new market entry strategy in which Disney could leverage its name, reputation for quality, and creative and production expertise. In contrast, the Westinghouse acquisition was an *unrelated* new market entry strategy that moved Westinghouse into the increasingly attractive communications market. Disney was leveraging its strength in the communications industry, whereas Westinghouse was redefining itself by acquiring CBS in the hope of adapting its competitive advantage to a new, highly inviting market. The two businesses, however, had one thing in common: Both were pursuing new sources of market share, sales growth, and profit performance.

One of the primary advantages of an unrelated new market entry strategy is reduced market dependency. Because most markets go through periods of expansion and contraction, investments in unrelated businesses will have a smoothing effect on the revenues and profits of the combined portfolio of product-markets. For example, the residential construction market is a slow-growth market that fluctuates with economic conditions. A manufacturer of earthmoving equipment for this market could reduce the magnitude of swings in performance by entering the mining or agriculture markets or another market unrelated to the residential construction market. In this way, variations in overall business performance could be minimized.

An additional advantage of market diversification is reduced vulnerability. If a business derives the bulk of its performance from one type of market, a permanent downward change in that market would threaten the company's performance and, potentially, its survival. In the mid-1970s, the National Cash Register Corporation (NCR) was focused primarily on the cash register market and had over an 80 percent share of this market. When competitors entered with a new cash register technology, NCR's market share declined rapidly. In less than 6 years, its share shrank to less than 25 percent, and the company's survival was at stake.

A business, then, might pursue an unrelated new market entry strategy for three reasons:

1. **New Source of Growth:** New market diversification offers the potential of adding to the business's sales growth and profit performance.
2. **Smoother Performance:** New market diversification offers customer diversification, which can reduce the magnitude of swings in sales and profit performance.
3. **Reduced Vulnerability:** New market diversification reduces market dependence and vulnerability, which helps protect the business's performance and, in some instances, its survival.

Although these are important benefits, many businesses have failed to perform effectively in diversified markets and have retreated to their core markets. Mobil's acquisition of Montgomery Ward, Coca-Cola's acquisition of Columbia Pictures, and General Motors' acquisition of Data Information Services were each an unsuccessful diversified new market entry strategy. The new market ventures were too far removed from the marketing and business expertise of the acquiring company. On the other hand, Phillip Morris's acquisition of the Miller Brewing Company, Pepsi's acquisition of Kentucky Fried Chicken, and Motorola's move into wireless communication products provided the advantages previously identified. These companies, in their new markets, successfully leveraged their marketing and business expertise.

Offensive Strategy IIIC: Enter New Emerging Markets

A business can also grow by entering new emerging markets where the number of current customers is small but market potential is great. Although considerably riskier with respect to profit performance, this strategy can enable a business to establish an early leadership position in the market. From this position, a business can influence product positioning and market growth.

High-technology markets have rapidly emerging market demand and relatively short product and market life cycles. Businesses in these markets need to move quickly to capitalize on emerging new market opportunities or they will completely miss this opportunity for growth.[11] The pioneer in these emerging new markets has the potential to achieve a competitive advantage if it can sustain its advantage in these early stages of market development.[12] When pioneers can establish a *dominant design*, a standard emerges that other businesses entering the market must follow in order to compete.[13] A good example of establishing a dominant design was the way VHS prevailed over Beta as the design standard in the early evolution of the VCR market.

As an emerging market begins to grow, *early followers* enter the market. Early followers emulate the dominant design and enter the market after letting the pioneer invest in developing the technology, establishing the design standard, and initiating market development. Many Japanese companies use an early follower strategy. Comcast and EarthLink both entered the broadband Internet market as early followers. CompuServe,

Prodigy, and America Online established dominant positions in the dial-up Internet service market, but as the technology developed and the broadband market emerged, EarthLink and Comcast came into the market, capitalizing on emerging new market demand for high-speed Internet.

When many customers are attracted to the market, with customer use and experience quickly increasing, the market is in its rapid-growth phase. It is during this phase of market development, as customer needs become more salient and numerous, that segments begin to form. The rapid growth attracts more competitors, many of them focusing on niche markets made up of subsets of customers with unique needs.[14] This is a critical point for a market leader, which must respond by developing multi-segment solutions. A market leader that remains narrowly focused will see its market share erode as new competitors deliver more attractive value propositions for specific segments. A market pioneer that can sustain its market leadership position through this phase of a market's development is in the best position to achieve high levels of performance.[15]

Offensive Strategy IIID: Develop New Markets

Apple Computer's initial entry into the personal computer market was a market-growth strategy that focused on the enormous untapped potential of the personal computer market. Apple's philosophy was to bring computing power to the masses. The company's original positioning strategy for Macintosh was: "Only a few have the expertise to operate computers. . . . Introducing Macintosh, for the rest of the world." In the beginning, Apple had few competitors because it focused on a market ignored by the major computer manufacturers. Only after Apple's early success revealed the potential of this new market did competitors begin to flow into it.

China, India, and Africa make up over half the world's population, yet many of the products manufactured for the United States, Western Europe, and the more affluent Asian countries have not been formulated for these markets. Constraints due to price, use compatibility, and availability create a large, untapped new market potential for many products.

For example, products that operate with electricity have no market in rural areas of underdeveloped countries where no electrical service is available. General Electric, with its expertise in turbines for jet engines, adapted its technology to enable businesses in areas with no electrical power to produce their own electricity and sell their excess to local utilities. By enabling businesses to "co-generate" electricity on a small scale, GE has created markets for many of its electrical products in remote parts of the world.

A growth strategy to develop an untapped new market potential involves high risk but offers the potential for high return.[16] The cost of developing a market can be significant even with a good customer solution. On the other hand, with few competitors, if any, a business has the opportunity to pioneer a market that has so far been largely ignored. With a "first-mover" advantage, there is the potential to own the market until other competitors venture entry. A notable example is a company called Under Armour, which was launched in 1995 with $40,000 by a college student who maxed out five credit cards developing the market for specialty undergarments for athletes. By 2002, Under Armour had sales of $50 million, and sales have continued to increase by a remarkable 72 percent annually to $430 million, despite market entry by Nike, Adidas, and other large sports apparel companies when they became aware of this attractive emerging market.

FIGURE 12-10 ALTERNATIVE OFFENSIVE STRATEGIC MARKET PLANS

Area of Performance	Share Penetration Strategy		Market Development Strategy	
	First Year	In 5 Years	First Year	In 5 Years
Market Demand	600,000	600,000	20,000	200,000
Market Share (%)	15	20	80	50
Market Growth Rate (%)	3	3	158	158
Target Volume	90,000	120,000	16,000	100,000
Revenue per Customer	$450	$450	$950	$450
Total Revenue (millions)	$40.5	$54.0	$15.2	$45.0
Variable Cost per Customer	$250	$250	$650	$200
Total Variable Cost (millions)	$22.5	$30.0	$10.4	$20.0
Margin per Customer	$200	$200	$300	$250
Total Contribution (millions)	$18.0	$24.0	$4.8	$25.0
Marketing Expenses (millions)	$7.0	$10.0	$6.0	$12.0
Net Marketing Contribution (millions)	$11.0	$14.0	–$1.2	$13.0

CHOOSING OFFENSIVE STRATEGIC MARKET PLANS

Businesses, especially highly ambitious and aggressive businesses, often pursue multiple offensive strategies. Starbucks Coffee, for example, has an objective of becoming the world's most recognized and respected brand. To accomplish this, the company has implemented a wide variety of offensive strategic market plans that have led to rapid growth, as we saw in Figure 12-1.

A market-based business will often find it has more market opportunities than it has resources to fund. In that case, the business will have to prioritize strategic market opportunities on the basis of its performance objectives. A business with a short-run need for better profit performance would be inclined to select the share penetration strategy shown in Figure 12-10, rather than a long-run market development strategy. The share penetration strategy for the business in this example is expected to produce $14 million in net marketing contribution in 5 years. It offers immediate profit performance and a reasonable level of sales revenue and profit growth.

On the other hand, a business with a good cash position but facing stagnant growth in maturing markets might pursue the market development strategy shown in Figure 12-10. This offensive strategy would produce a $1.2 million negative net marketing contribution in the first year of a new market development strategy. However, in 5 years, the strategy would be expected to produce $13 million in net marketing contribution. Although riskier, this new market development strategy could provide this business with needed growth and diversification into an attractive market. The selection of one offensive strategic market plan over another depends on the business's short-run profit needs, strategic position and resources, and opportunities for growth.

■ Summary

Businesses have a short-term obligation to investors to meet growth and performance expectations. At the same time, businesses have an obligation to investors, as well as employees, to carve out a set of market strategies that will improve the position of the business in the long run. The purpose of strategic market planning is to examine the attractiveness of each market served by a business and to determine the business's competitive position in each market. On the basis of its assessment, a business develops a strategic market objective and allocates resources accordingly. To accomplish its performance objective, a business generally needs a combination of offensive and defensive strategic market plans.

Offensive strategies are more growth oriented and are generally most effective during the growth phase of the product life cycle, while defensive strategies are more suitable for maturing, mature, and declining markets. Offensive strategies can be broken down into three core offensive strategies: sales growth, margin improvement, and diversified growth. Each of these core offensive strategies has four specific strategies.

Offensive strategies for pursuing sales growth are focused on existing markets. Sales growth offensive strategies include (1) increasing market share, (2) growing customer purchases, (3) expanding into new market segments, and (4) expanding market demand by growing market potential. Offensive strategies to improve competitive position with the objective of margin improvement are focused on existing markets and strategies that can improve profit margins. Offensive strategies to improve margin include (1) increasing customer loyalty, (2) improving a differentiation advantage, (3) lowering costs and improving marketing productivity, and (4) building a stronger marketing advantage. Offensive strategies with the goal of diversified growth are focused on new markets and strategies that can achieve sales growth outside the current market domain. Diversified sales growth offensive strategies include (1) entering new related markets, (2) entering new unrelated markets, (3) entering new emerging markets, and (4) developing new markets. A business selects a good mix of offensive strategic market plans by considering the expected impact of each strategy on short- and long-run growth in revenues and profitability.

■ Market-Based Strategic Thinking

1　What is the difference between offensive strategic market plans and defensive strategic market plans?

2　Explain why a business might shift from an offensive strategy to a defensive strategy over the life cycle of a particular product.

3　How can a business meet short-run growth and profit performance targets and still invest in strategic market plans that are focused on long-run objectives with respect to share position, sales growth, and profit performance?

4　How has Harley-Davidson's offensive strategy to grow revenue per customer impacted its sales and profits?

5　How would a Nike offensive strategy to grow market penetration differ from a strategy to grow customer purchases (revenue per customer) in the under-18 female athlete market?

6　Why would Google use an offensive sales growth strategy to expand the Internet search market versus going for more market share of this market?

7 Why would margin improvement be an offensive strategy?

8 Why would AT&T's efforts to improve customer retention be an offensive strategy to improve margins?

9 Absolut Vodka entered two new market segments as part of an offensive strategy to grow sales. Explain the logic of this offensive strategy and why the company elected to create new brand names for each segment shown in Figure 12-6.

10 Microsoft has developed a product called Meeting Pro to help facilitate the running of small business meetings. Although this is a value-added software product, Microsoft offers the product at no cost to Windows users. Explain how this is an offensive market share strategy.

11 Why are offensive strategies crucial for the long-run success of a business? What kind of offensive strategies could McDonald's use to ensure future growth in sales and profits?

12 Microsoft has embarked on a joint venture with Sony to develop an online alternative to the telephone. What type of offensive market strategy best describes this joint venture, and what would be the expected short- and long-run performance objectives?

13 How does a market penetration strategy to grow market share differ from a strategy to enter a new segment in the same market?

14 Why is a market strategy to grow customer purchases (revenue per customer) potentially more profitable than many other offensive market strategies?

15 Why would a business first pursue offensive market strategies to increase market share or grow revenue per customer rather than other offensive market strategies?

16 What forces limit new customer growth within existing markets? How could a business grow market demand by addressing these forces?

17 What are the important differences between a related new market entry strategy and an unrelated new market entry strategy?

18 When would a business pursue an unrelated new market entry strategy?

19 What is the advantage of growing market demand in a new emerging market?

Marketing Performance Tools

The three **Marketing Performance Tools** described here may be accessed online at *www.rogerjbest.com*. These applied-learning tools allow you to evaluate the four relevant market strategies for each of the three offensive core strategies.

12.1 Offensive Strategies—Core Strategy I: Grow in Existing Markets (Figure 12-4)
- Using the data provided, evaluate the four market strategies for growing sales within existing markets.

12.2 Offensive Strategies—Core Strategy II: Improve Margins (Figure 12-4)
- Using the data provided, evaluate the four market strategies for improving margins with sales in existing markets.

12.3 Offensive Strategies—Core Strategy III: Diversified Growth (Figure 12-4)
- Using the data provided, evaluate the four market strategies for growing sales with diversified growth.

Notes

1. David Aaker, "Portfolio Analysis," *Strategic Market Management* (New York: Wiley, 1995): 155–169.
2. Bernard Catry and Michel Chevalier, "Market Share Strategy and the Product Life Cycle," *Journal of Marketing* (October 1974): 29–34.
3. Philippe Haspeslagh, "Portfolio Planning: Uses and Limits," *Harvard Business Review* (January–February 1982): 58–73; and S. Robinson, R. Hichens, and D. Wade, "The Directional Policy Matrix Tool for Strategic Planning," *Long-Range Planning* (June 1978): 8–15.
4. David Aaker, "Growth Strategies," *Strategic Market Management* (New York: Wiley, 1995): 238–259.
5. Charles Lillis, James Cook, Roger Best, and Del Hawkins, "Marketing Strategies to Achieve Market Share Goals," in *Strategic Marketing Management*, H. Thomas and D. Gardner, eds. (New York: Wiley, 1985).
6. David Szymanski, Sundar Bharadwaj, and Rajan Varadarajan, "An Analysis of the Market Share-Profitability Relationship," *Journal of Marketing* (July 1993): 1–18; and C. Davis Fogg, "Planning Gains in Market Share," *Journal of Marketing* (July 1994): 30–38.
7. Daniel Sheinen and Bernd Schmitt, "Extending Brands with New Product Concepts: The Role of Category Attribute Congruity, Brand Affect and Brand Breadth," *Journal of Business Research* (September 1994): 1–10.
8. Gary Hamel and C. K. Prahalad, "Seeing the Future First," *Fortune* (September 5, 1994): 64–70.
9. Edward Roberts and Charles Berry, "Entering New Business: Selecting Strategies for Success," *Sloan Management Review* (Spring 1985): 3–17.
10. Richard Rumelt, "Diversification, Strategy and Profitability," *Strategic Management Journal* 3 (1982): 359–369.
11. G. Stalk Jr., "Time: The Next Source of Competitive Advantage," *Harvard Business Review* (July–August 1988): 41–51; and Thomas Robertson, "How to Reduce Market Penetration Cycle Times," *Sloan Management Review* (Fall 1993): 87–96.
12. William Robinson and Claes Fornell, "Sources of Market Pioneer Advantage in Consumer Goods Industries," *Journal of Marketing Research* (August 1985): 305–317; and William Robinson, "Sources of Market Pioneer Advantages: The Case for Industrial Goods Industries," *Journal of Marketing Research* 25 (1988): 87–94.
13. Roger Best and Reinhard Angelmar, "Strategies for Leveraging Technology Advantage," in *Handbook on Business Strategy* (New York: Warren, Gorham and Lamont, 1989): 2.1–2.10.
14. Vijay Mahajan, Subhash Sharma, and Robert Buzzell, "Assessing the Impact of Competitive Entry on Market Expansion and Incumbent Sales," *Journal of Marketing* (July 1993): 39–52.
15. Glen Urban, T. Carter, S. Gaskin, and Z. Mucha, "Marketing Share Rewards to Pioneering Brands: An Empirical Analysis and Strategic Implications," *Management Science* 32 (1986): 635–659.
16. Igal Ayal and Jehiel Zif, "Market Expansion Strategies in Multinational Markets," *Journal of Marketing* (Spring 1979): 84–94.

CHAPTER 13

Defensive Strategies

■ The goal of defensive strategies is profit maximization, not growth.

Figure 13-1 summarizes the performance of a division within a well-established chemical company.[1] All products the division sells are in very mature markets where market growth is minimal and price rivalry fierce. As the table shows, the division is barely making a profit, with an overall net marketing contribution of just 3.5 million against sales of $183.1 million. Two products, basic colors and color enhancers, are not covering their marketing and sales expenses, with losses of $1.5 and $2.0 million, respectively. The results are an overall marketing ROS of 5.4 percent and an overall marketing ROI of 68 percent, both well below corporate averages.

The company recently tried to sell the division but could not find a buyer. With nothing to lose, the company's managers then decided to pursue a defensive strategy to reduce share but improve margins with price increases. To further improve cash flow, the managers cut the division's marketing expenses. The managers expected to lose market share but were not sure how much. With a smaller share of the

FIGURE 13-1 PRODUCT LINE PERFORMANCE FOR ONE DIVISION OF A MAJOR CHEMICAL COMPANY

Area of Performance (millions)	Silicon Pigments	Primary Products	Specialty Products	Basic Colors	Color Enhancers	Overall Total
Market Demand (pounds)	100	167	154	96	556	1,073
Market Share	10.0%	12.0%	13.0%	26.0%	9.0%	11.7%
Volume Sold (pounds)	10	20.0	20.0	25.0	50.0	125.1
Price (per pound)	$4.50	$2.80	$1.60	$0.80	$0.60	$1.46
Sales Revenues	$45.0	$56.1	$32.0	$20.0	$30.0	$183.1
Unit Cost (per pound)	$3.90	$2.40	$1.40	$0.80	$0.60	$1.25
Percent Margin	13.3%	14.3%	12.5%	0.0%	0.0%	13.3%
Gross Profit	$6.0	$8.0	$4.0	$0.0	$0.0	$18.0
Marketing & Sales Expenses	$3.0	$5.0	$3.0	$1.5	$2.0	$14.5
% Marketing & Sales Exp.	6.7%	8.9%	9.4%	7.5%	6.7%	7.9%
Net Marketing Contribution	$3.0	$3.0	$1.0	–$1.5	–$2.0	$3.5
Marketing ROS	6.7%	5.4%	3.1%	–7.5%	–6.7%	5.4%
Marketing ROI	100%	60%	33%	–100%	–100%	68%

FIGURE 13-2 RESULTS OF A DEFENSIVE STRATEGY TO MANAGE THE DIVISION FOR CASH FLOW

Area of Performance (millions)	Silicon Pigments	Primary Products	Specialty Products	Basic Colors	Color Enhancers	Overall Total
Market Demand (pounds)	100	167	154	96	556	1,073
Market Share	8.6%	10.3%	10.7%	17.1%	6.0%	8.6%
Volume Sold (pounds)	8.6	17.2	16.5	16.4	33.4	92.1
Price (per pound)	$4.95	$3.20	$1.90	$0.98	$0.75	$1.85
Sales Revenues	$42.6	$55.0	$31.3	$16.1	$25.0	$170.0
Unit Cost (per pound)	$4.05	$2.55	$1.50	$0.77	$0.67	$1.71
Percent Margin	18.2%	20.3%	21.1%	21.4%	10.7%	18.2%
Gross Profit	$7.7	$11.2	$6.6	$3.4	$2.7	$31.6
Marketing & Sales Expenses	$ 2.5	$4.5	$3.5	$1.0	$1.5	$13.0
% Marketing & Sales Exp.	5.9%	8.2%	11.2%	6.2%	6.0%	7.6%
Net Marketing Contribution	$5.2	$6.7	$3.1	$2.4	$1.2	$18.6
Marketing ROS	12.3%	12.1%	9.9%	15.2%	4.7%	11.0%
Marketing ROI	210%	148%	88%	245%	78%	143%

market and lower volumes, they also expected the unit cost per pound to go up. With fewer units being sold, each unit would need to absorb more of the manufacturing overhead. The company's managers were somewhat concerned that their defensive strategy could possibly lower the division's already low profits.

But as Figure 13-2 shows, the strategy dramatically improved profits despite significant decreases in market share, lower volumes, and generally higher per-unit costs. The combination of higher prices and lower volumes produced sales of $170 million. This total was $13 million lower than previous sales, but the overall margin was much higher, increasing from 13.3 to 18.2 percent. The higher margin resulted in a 76 percent increase in gross profit, from $18 million to $31.6 million. A higher gross profit and lower marketing and sales expenses allowed the overall net marketing contribution to increase from $3.5 million (5.4 percent of sales) to $18.6 million (11 percent of sales). The marketing ROIs for all products improved, resulting in an increase in the overall marketing ROI from 68 to 143 percent. We can see, then, that the managers' defensive strategy to reduce volume with higher prices and lower marketing investment yielded a significant gain in profits.

DEFENSIVE STRATEGIC MARKET PLANS

Historical share leaders such as General Motors, AT&T, and IBM have been under attack in their core markets for some time. For each, a loss of just one share point is considerable in terms of sales revenues, net profits, and cash flow. Relatively new share leaders such as Intel, Cisco Systems, and Microsoft face the same challenge. These businesses, like other share defenders, are engaged in a battle to protect their share positions in the markets they serve.[2]

Businesses in less attractive markets or businesses with fewer resources are often forced to reduce share in an effort to find a more profitable combination of market share

FIGURE 13-3 STRATEGIC MARKET PLANS AND PERFORMANCE

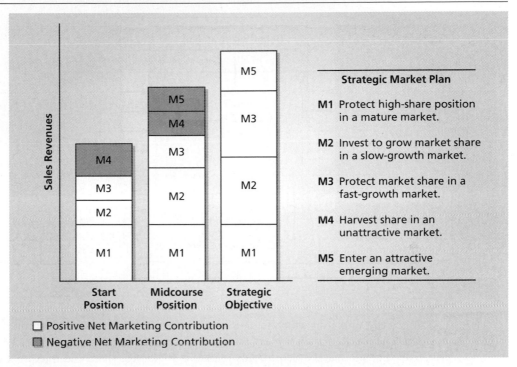

and profitability. Others may be forced to exit markets slowly with a harvest strategy or quickly with a divestment strategy. All defensive strategies are intended to maximize or protect short-run profits or to minimize short-run losses.

A key part of Intel's long-run performance has been its ability to successfully implement a protect share strategy in the microprocessor market. Any degree of share erosion would lower unit volume, sales revenues, and net marketing contribution. However, a defensive strategy to protect share should not be misinterpreted to mean a hold resources constant strategy. To protect share in a market growing at 15 to 20 percent a year, Intel will have to continue its rollout of new products and add to its marketing budget. Not doing either would almost guarantee erosion of the company's share position in the microprocessor market.

In general, businesses in high-share positions in growing or mature markets will use defensive strategic market plans to maintain a level of cash flow that supports short-run profit performance and shareholder value. Without these defensive strategic market plans and their profitability, the businesses would face a difficult short-run situation in terms of profit performance and would lack the resources to invest in growth-oriented offensive market opportunities.

For example, consider the business situation presented in Figure 13-3. The business is in four markets, one of which is losing money. The first market (M1) is a maturing market in which the business holds a high-share position. The business's strategic market plan for this market is to protect the high-share position. The second market (M2) is a slow-growth market in which this business's strategic market plan is to grow share. The third market (M3) is

FIGURE 13-4 STRATEGIC MARKET PLANS AND DEFENSIVE STRATEGIES

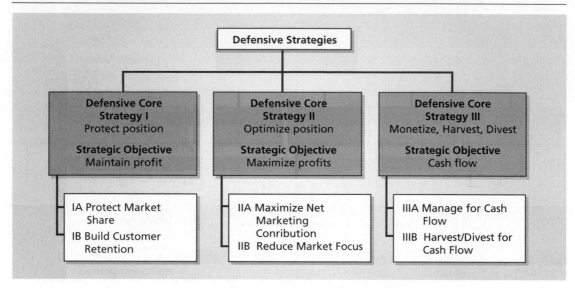

a high-growth market in which the business's strategic market plan is to protect its share position. The fourth market (M4) is losing money and has been determined to be unattractive. The strategic market plan for this market is to harvest share and maximize short-run profits as the business systematically exits the market. A fifth strategic market plan is to enter an attractive emerging market (M5) in which the business will lose money initially but which will be a good source of future growth and long-run cash flow.

With these five market-based management strategies, this business hopes to grow revenue and profits through a series of strategic moves to protect, grow, or harvest market share.[3] Each strategic market plan plays an important role in the business's short- and long-run sales and profitability. For two of these markets, defensive strategic market plans are needed to protect the company's share position in different ways. One other market calls for a defensive strategy to harvest whatever profitability can be squeezed out of that market.

The primary goal of a defensive strategy is to protect profitability and key strategic share positions that are worth the investment. A secondary goal of a defensive market strategy is to manage the profitability of businesses that are moving beyond the potential for high growth or profitability. With these goals in mind, Figure 13-4 outlines defensive strategic market plans that may be appropriate in different situations.

As shown in Figure 13-5, certain portfolio positions, based on market attractiveness and competitive advantage, can lead to more than one possible defensive strategy. For example, a business with a strong competitive advantage in a fairly attractive market may find that protecting the share position might be appropriate, or it may choose to defend the market by optimizing or monetizing it. In all cases, defensive market strategies are focused on maximizing short-run profits and protecting or improving the overall strategic position of a business.

FIGURE 13-5 PORTFOLIO POSITIONS AND DEFENSIVE STRATEGIC MARKET PLANS

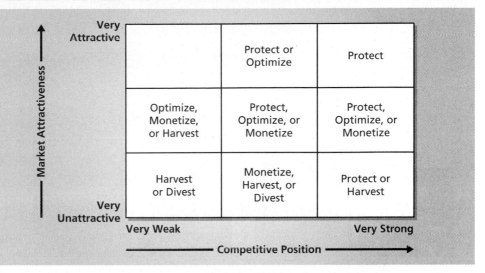

DEFENSIVE CORE STRATEGY I: PROTECT POSITION

In many competitive environments, whether sports or business, the best defense is a good offense. Quite often businesses with a dominant share and a strong competitive position are lulled into the delusion that they are undefeatable, eventually awakening too late to the stark reality that they are about to be overtaken by more aggressive challengers. To hold a high-share position in an attractive, growing market, a business must continue investing in a determined effort to sustain its competitive position.

Defensive Strategy IA: Protect Market Share

Share leaders in many industries have market shares in excess of 50 percent. However, the conditions under which they have to defend their share positions can be drastically different. Campbell's Soup, for example, has a 60 percent share position in the mature American soup market; Gillette has a 70 percent share and is the share leader in the razor and blade market, which is also mature; and Kodak has more than a 60 percent share of the declining American film market. Their defensive strategies in slow-growing mature markets will be different from those of businesses with high shares in fast-growth markets. Intel, with an 85 percent share of the fast-growing computer market, and Microsoft, with a 95 percent share of the rapidly developing desktop operating-system market, will each have to exert greater marketing efforts to protect their high-share positions while their markets are still experiencing rapid growth. However, each has the same fundamental objective: invest to protect market share. Depending on the nature of the market situation, a defensive strategy to protect market share might take different forms.

FIGURE 13-6 MARKET GROWTH RATE AND SHARE EROSION

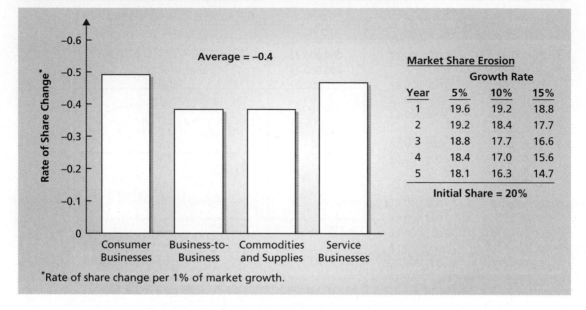

*Rate of share change per 1% of market growth.

Investing to Protect Position in Growth Markets

Protecting a share leadership position in a growth market requires a much greater marketing effort and more investment in new products than would be required in a mature market. The faster a market is growing, the greater must be the marketing resources to protect share in the face of an ever-increasing number of competitors, as well as moves by existing competitors. If a business does not invest to protect share in a growth market, its market share is almost certain to decline. Because growing markets are inherently prone toward inducing share loss, the resources needed to offset the effects of growth, using a defensive strategic market plan to protect share, must be much greater.

In the Profit Impact of Marketing Strategies (PIMS) database, the average business will experience approximately a –0.4 percent annual rate of market share change per 1 percent of market growth rate. Thus a business in a market growing at 10 percent annually would encounter a 4 percent rate of share erosion if the effects of market growth are not offset by a defensive strategic market plan. Using this average, a business with a 20 percent market share in a market growing 10 percent annually would have an estimated share loss of almost four points in 5 years if it did nothing to offset the negative impact of market growth. Of course, if the market were growing at 15 percent annually, the business would experience a much faster rate of share erosion, as shown in Figure 13-6.

The effects of market growth on market share change are different from industry to industry but still fairly uniform. Figure 13-6 shows the impact of market growth on market share erosion for four categories of businesses.

Investing to Protect a High-Share Position

Market share leaders such as Eastman Kodak, Campbell's Soup, and Cisco Systems have strong share positions that generate considerable sales revenues and profits that directly affect their financial performance. Defensive strategies to protect their high-share positions

FIGURE 13-7 MARKET SHARE EROSION AND CURRENT SHARE POSITION

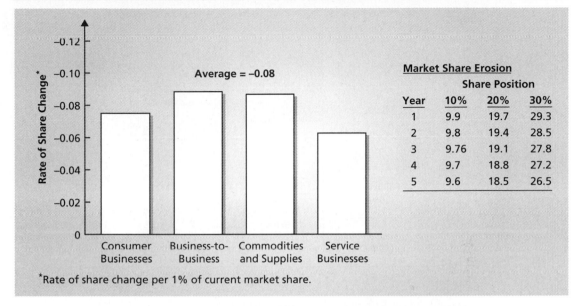

*Rate of share change per 1% of current market share.

are critical to short-run profit performance and provide a major source of cash for investment in offensive market strategies for future growth and profit performance.

It is hard to imagine how having a large market share could be a handicap with respect to protecting market share. However, in the PIMS database we consistently find an inverse relationship between size of market share and change in market share. As shown in Figure 13-7, the average PIMS business would experience an approximate rate of change in market share of –0.08 percent for every 1 percent of current market share. Thus a business with a 30 percent market share would experience a –2.4 percent annual rate of share loss, which would lead to a 26.5 percent share loss in 5 years. A business with a 10 percent market share would never really feel this effect, because the size of its market share is much smaller, and its share would erode only to an estimated 9.6 percent in 5 years.

High-share businesses, then, have to invest considerably more to protect share independent of other share-eroding market forces, such as market growth, competitor entry, or competitor strategies. As we come to fully understand the impact that high share and high-market growth rate have on eroding market share, we can better understand the losses in market share experienced by Eastman Kodak, IBM, AT&T, General Motors, and other high-share businesses. And, as it is on market growth, the impact of market share on the rate of market share change is fairly consistent among diverse areas of business in the PIMS database, as illustrated in Figure 13-7.

To successfully defend high-share positions, businesses need to continuously improve their competitive advantage and marketing effort. Share leaders that make temporary cuts in marketing to improve short-run profit only hurt next year's profits with a reduced market share. Share leaders must remain committed to (1) new product development, (2) efforts to improve product and service quality at a rate faster than the competition, and (3) fully supporting the marketing budgets needed to protect a high-share position.[4]

FIGURE 13-8 MARKET STRUCTURE AND SHARE POSITION

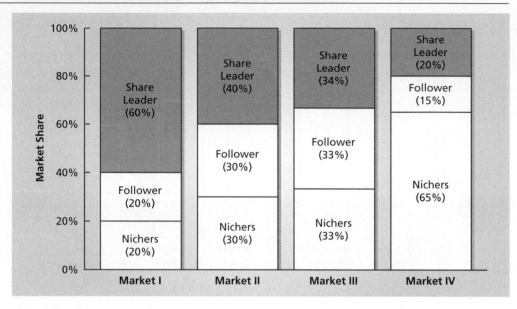

Investing to Protect a Follower Share Position

Not every business can be a share leader in its market. Illustrated in Figure 13-8 are four market structures, each presenting followers with different share positions. A business that is second in market share, but is a close follower (Market II), has an interesting strategic market decision to consider. Does this follower challenge the leader with an offensive share penetration strategy? Or does it protect its share position and maximize the profits that can be extracted from that share position? Depending on the strength of the share leader, the share leader's commitment to defending its share position, and the follower business's resources and short-run profit needs, either strategic market plan could be pursued. But what does a successful defensive follower strategy look like?[5]

Figure 13-9 profiles the average follower business in the PIMS database that has above-average profitability (number-two share position), and the average follower business with below-average profit performance. With respect to competitive advantage, share followers with above-average profits have higher relative product quality, which helps support higher levels of customer value, price, and unit margin. However, they also invest more aggressively in marketing as a percentage of sales, as well as on a relative basis, when compared with competitors. These effects produce a slightly higher share, which contributes to a higher level of capacity utilization.

These businesses also invest more in research and development (R&D) as a percentage of sales. This investment translates into a higher level of technological advantage that most likely results in a higher relative product quality. The more profitable followers, then, protect their number-two share positions with investments in both R&D and marketing. As pointed out earlier, without these types of investments, a business could not protect a share position, even in relatively slow-growth markets.

FIGURE 13-9 SUCCESSFUL VERSUS UNSUCCESSFUL SHARE FOLLOWER STRATEGIES

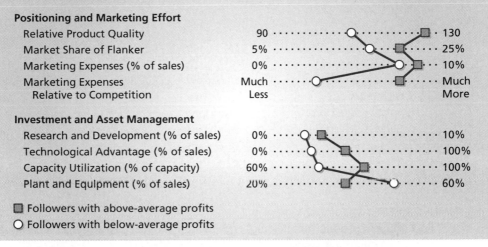

Area of Performance

Positioning and Marketing Effort
Relative Product Quality	90	130
Market Share of Flanker	5%	25%
Marketing Expenses (% of sales)	0%	10%
Marketing Expenses Relative to Competition	Much Less	Much More

Investment and Asset Management
Research and Development (% of sales)	0%	10%
Technological Advantage (% of sales)	0%	100%
Capacity Utilization (% of capacity)	60%	100%
Plant and Equipment (% of sales)	20%	60%

■ Followers with above-average profits
○ Followers with below-average profits

Investing to Protect a Niche Share Position

The strategic decision on whether to engage in a long-run offensive or defensive strategic market plan must also be made by businesses in niche segments of their markets. For example, the niche share businesses in Figure 13-8 may elect to pursue offensive strategic market plans to challenge share leaders in the larger market. But the market situation could instead lead a niche business to pursue a defensive strategy to protect its profitable niche market. In many ways, a niche business is simply the share leader in a more narrowly defined market. Share leaders, followers, and niche businesses, then, can all pursue defensive strategies to protect their market share positions.

A niche business could be a small business with limited resources or a large business that pursues a reduced-focus strategy in a larger market while still achieving high levels of profitability.[6] For whatever reason, a niche business could attain a dominant position in a niche market but have only a small share of the overall market when compared to the share held by the market leader. Within its market niche, however, the business is the share leader and has the same need to defend its share position as the share leader in the overall market.

Shown in Figure 13-10 are average profiles for profitable high-share and profitable low-share niche businesses. A close examination of the two profiles reveals only two areas of commonality: relative product quality and relative sales force expense. Having above-average product quality and above-average customer contact and market coverage are key success factors for both profitable high-share businesses and profitable low-share niche businesses.

But to achieve above-average levels of profitability, low-share niche businesses need to focus in order to keep expenses low.[7] Their niche focus is most evident in their narrow product line, limited new product development, and limited advertising effort relative to competitors. In addition, a low-share niche business's prices are slightly below the average relative price index of 100. With an average relative price near 96,

FIGURE 13-10 MARKET STRATEGIES FOR PROFITABLE SHARE LEADERS AND PROFITABLE LOW-SHARE NICHE BUSINESSES

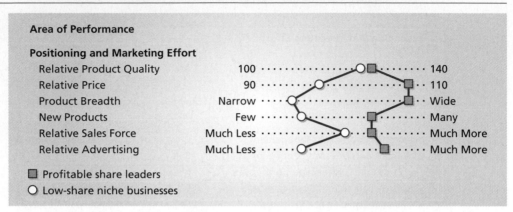

Area of Performance

Positioning and Marketing Effort

Relative Product Quality	100	140
Relative Price	90	110
Product Breadth	Narrow	Wide
New Products	Few	Many
Relative Sales Force	Much Less	Much More
Relative Advertising	Much Less	Much More

▇ Profitable share leaders
○ Low-share niche businesses

and relative product quality close to 123, these successful niche businesses create an attractive customer value:

$$\textbf{Customer Value} = \text{Relative Benefits} - \text{Relative Price}$$
$$27 = 123 - 96$$

As shown in Figure 13-11, low-share niche businesses with above-average customer value are more profitable. As a matter of fact, a low-share business with above-average customer value is more profitable than a high-share business with below-average customer

FIGURE 13-11 CUSTOMER VALUE, MARKET SHARE, AND PROFITABILITY

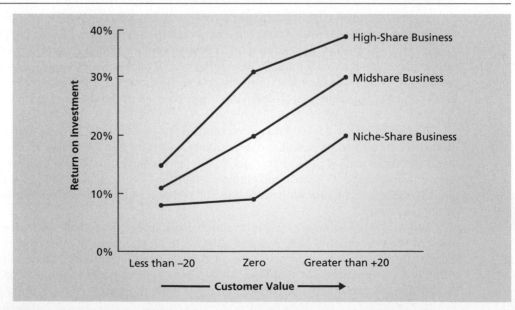

FIGURE 13-12 PROFIT IMPACT OF CUSTOMER RETENTION STRATEGY

	75% Customer Retention*				80% Customer Retention*		
Year	Net Cash	Discount Factor	Value	Year	Net Cash	Discount Factor	Present Value
0	−$500	$1.000	−$500	0	−$500	1.000	−$500
1	+$300	0.870	+$261	1	+$300	0.870	+$261
2	+$325	0.756	+$246	2	+$325	0.756	+$246
3	+$350	0.658	+$230	3	+$350	0.658	+$230
4	+$379	0.572	+$215	4	+$375	0.572	+$215
5	0	0.497	0	5	+$400	0.497	+$199
	Net Present Value at 15% = +$452				Net Present Value at 15% = +$651		

*Customer Life = 1/(1 − Customer Retention)

value. We can see that an important component of success for niche-share businesses is above-average customer value and sales coverage with a careful product focus.

Defensive Strategy IB: Build Customer Retention

Protecting a valued share position is certainly a defensive strategy at the core of many successful businesses. The profit impact of holding a 30 percent market share, however, can be quite different for high and low levels of customer retention.

For example, assume two businesses each produce $400 of margin per customer the first year and that the margin grows by $25 each year the customer is retained. Further assume that each business spends $500 to acquire a new customer and $100 per year to retain a customer. As shown in Figure 13-12, the business with 75 percent customer retention will retain customers an average of 4 years, whereas an 80 percent customer retention rate will keep customers for an average of 5 years. That's an extra $199 in discounted net cash flow. The analysis demonstrates how a business that can build a higher level of customer retention can be more profitable than a business that maintains the same customer retention rate, even when both have the same market share. Whether a high-share market leader, a share follower, or a low-share niche business, a business can build profits with a defensive strategy to protect share while building customer retention.

DEFENSIVE CORE STRATEGY II: OPTIMIZE POSITION

Product-markets in late-growth and mature stages of their product life cycles need to be managed to optimize marketing profits. It is during the late stages of market growth that maximum marketing profits are obtained, as shown in Figure 13-13. As volume produced by market demand nears its maximum potential and margins are yet to be fully squeezed, a business is able to extract its highest level of gross profit. Because sales are slowing, investments in marketing expenses should also slow. Managed properly, this combination of volume, margin, and reduced marketing expenses should yield maximum marketing profits over the product life cycle, as shown in Figure 13-14. Businesses that mismanage price and margin or overinvest in marketing at this point are likely to miss their best opportunity for profits.

FIGURE 13-13 PRODUCT LIFE CYCLE AND MARKETING PROFITABILITY

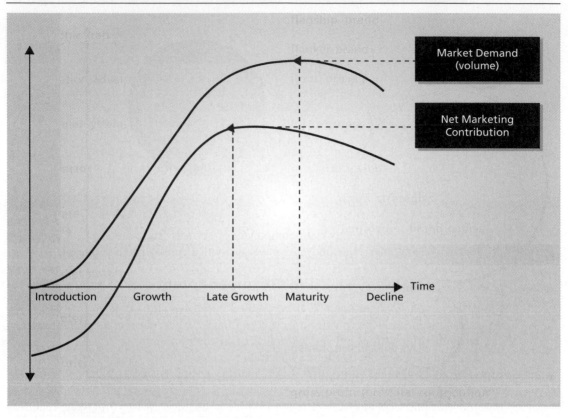

Defensive Strategy IIA: Maximize Net Marketing Contribution

A strategy to maximize a business's net marketing contribution requires careful margin management and efficient use of marketing resources. In later stages of the product life cycle, a business can no longer afford to make pricing errors or over-allocations of marketing expenses. Increases in volume are unlikely to overcome these mistakes, as might be the case in the earlier stages of the product life cycle. The first step in optimizing net marketing contribution, then, is to focus on optimal management of margin-volume rather than price-volume.

Price-volume strategies in the growth phase of the product life cycle are rewarded with higher volumes, sales, and marketing profits. However, in the late-growth and mature stages of the product life cycle, lower prices—which mean lower margins—are not likely to produce higher volumes; market growth is limited and competitive reaction to losses in volume are likely to be substantial. The strategic market planning challenge is to find the right combination of margin and volume, the combination that yields the highest gross profit:

$$\text{Gross Profit} = \text{Volume (units)} \times \text{Margin per Unit}$$

$$= \text{Market Demand} \times \text{Market Share} \times (\text{Price} - \text{Variable Cost})$$

FIGURE 13-14 PROFIT LIFE CYCLE AND COMPONENTS OF MARKETING PROFITABILITY

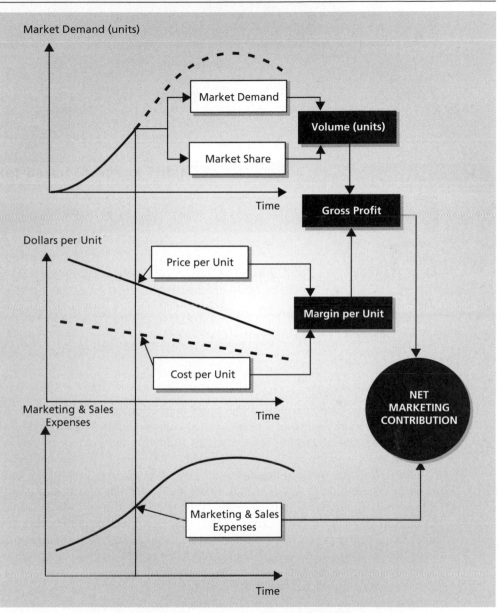

Proper margin management is the first step in achieving an optimized position. In the personal computer market, the price elasticity is close to –2 for most PCs. Margins for PCs are usually 20 percent or lower. As the market for PCs matures, a business may need to rethink its pricing in order to optimize profits as market growth slows.

Figure 13-15 shows (1) the profit impact of a 10 percent price decrease to grow volume and sales, and (2) an optimizing strategy for a PC priced at $2,000 with a 20 percent margin in a market with a price elasticity of –2. As shown, the price decrease will produce

FIGURE 13-15 PROFIT IMPACTS OF PC PRICE DECREASE AND INCREASE

10% Price Decrease Area of Performance	Current	Proposed	Change
Market Demand	2,000,000	2,000,000	0
Volume	100,000	120,000	20,000
Market Share (%)	5.0	6.0	1.0
Price	$2,000	$1,800	−$200
Sales Revenues	$200,000,000	$216,000,000	$16,000,000
Variable Cost per Unit	$1,600	$1,600	$0
Margin per Unit	$400	$200	−$200
Gross profit	$40,000,000	$24,000,000	−$16,000,000

10% Price Increase Area of Performance	Current	Proposed	Change
Market Demand	2,000,000	2,000,000	0
Volume	100,000	80,000	−20,000
Market Share (%)	5.0	4.0	−1.0
Price	$2,000	$2,200	$200
Sales Revenues	$200,000,000	$176,000,000	−$24,000,000
Variable Cost per Unit	$1,600	$1,600	$0
Margin per Unit	$400	$600	$200
Gross Profit	$40,000,000	$48,000,000	$8,000,000

a 20 percent volume increase, a one-point market share increase, and a $16 million increase in sales revenues. In a sales-oriented culture, this strategy would be viewed as a great success, but because of lower margins following the price decrease, this business would actually lose $16 million in gross profit.

An optimizing strategy to raise prices by 10 percent in a maturing market would result in lower volumes, lower market share, and lower sales, as shown in Figure 13-15. Although these are not promising results, this defensive strategy would actually yield an $8 million *increase* in gross profit. If the strategic objective is to optimize position in order to maximize profits, then a price increase is the best strategic market plan to implement. Reduced spending on marketing and sales at this stage of the product life cycle could also improve marketing profits, as shown here:

$$\text{Net Marketing Contribution} = \text{Gross Profit} - \text{Marketing Expenses}$$
$$= \text{Gross Profit} - (\text{Acquisition Costs} + \text{Retention Costs})$$

Because market demand is slowing, investments in marketing to acquire new customers should be reduced, and a greater proportion of the marketing budget should focus on customer retention. Recall that acquiring a new customer costs 5 to 10 times more than retaining an existing customer and, as a market reaches its full potential, fewer customers are entering the market. At this point, the business should be able to maintain its market share with a lower level of marketing expenses, assuming customer retention is at a good level of performance.

Low customer retention at this stage of the product life cycle would make it impossible to achieve maximum marketing profits because the business would need to spend heavily on new customer acquisition just to replace lost customers and preserve market share.

Defensive Strategy IIB: Reduce Market Focus

As shown earlier in Figure 13-5, a business may find itself in a portfolio position that can lead to more than one defensive strategic market plan. Would it be best for the business to invest in strengthening its competitive position, to allocate resources to protect its share position, or to reduce its focus position within the market to maximize profitability? All can be viable strategic market plans, depending upon different market and business conditions.

A decision to pursue a reduced-focus defensive strategy would be most appropriate when a business does not have sufficient resources to invest to protect the current share position or when greater levels of profitability can be derived from a narrower, more selective choice of target customers. A reduced-market focus, then, prescribes a defensive strategic market plan that involves narrowing market focus and trimming market share in an effort to improve profit performance. This approach may produce a reduction in revenue and entail cuts in the marketing budget, but it will likely lead to higher levels of profitability as a percentage of sales.[8]

The main purpose of a reduced-focus strategy is to become more efficient. In Figure 13-16, we see that a mass-market approach is less efficient than a reduced-market focus in terms of marketing productivity. Although sales and profits diminish, a reduced-focus strategy is able to improve marketing productivity from a net marketing contribution of $2 to $3 per budgeted marketing dollar. This business had to shrink to become more efficient in producing profits.

FIGURE 13-16 SELECTIVE MARKET FOCUS, MARKETING RESOURCES, AND MARKETING PRODUCTIVITY

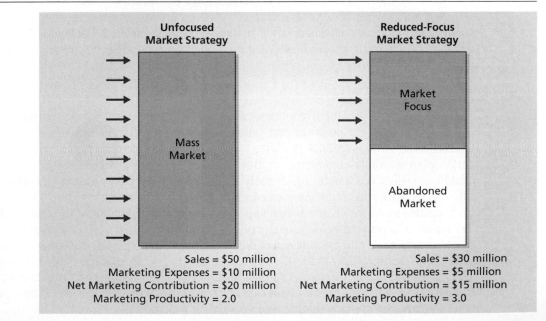

DEFENSIVE CORE STRATEGY III: MONETIZE, HARVEST, OR DIVEST

At some point in every product-market life cycle, markets will be less attractive and will need to be managed for short-run profits regardless of competitive position. In some mature or declining markets, an attractive cash flow can be managed for some time with a monetize defensive strategy. In other situations, the best defensive strategy may be a slow market exit (harvest strategy) or a rapid market exit (divest strategy). In either case, the intent of the defensive strategy would be to maximize immediate cash flow.

Defensive Strategy IIIA: Manage for Cash Flow

In many mature markets, market demand can be expected to remain strong for many years. When an optimize position strategy is not viable, a business may elect to remain in the market with a monetize cash flow strategy. This defensive strategy operates with minimal marketing resources and usually with low pricing levels. Many mature commodity products can be managed with competitive prices and sold with no sales or service. These products are not typically advertised and are often sold on a cash basis. The goal of a monetize strategy is to extract the maximum short-run cash flow from the market. At the point when this can no longer be accomplished at a desired level of cash flow, a business may elect to pursue a harvest or divest strategy.

Defensive Strategy IIIB: Harvest or Divest for Cash Flow

Portfolio positions that warrant a defensive strategy to exit from a market can lead to a harvest market strategy (slow exit) or to a divest strategic market plan (fast exit), as illustrated in the portfolio model in Figure 13-5. When additional profits can be made with a slow exit, a harvest strategy can be a good source of short-run profits. But if a business is losing money in its market, management might be more inclined to pursue a fast market exit strategy and divest the business's share position as quickly as possible. In this case, a divest strategy also improves short-run profits by eliminating a source of negative cash flow.

Harvest Price Strategy

The combination of unattractive markets and weak competitive advantage translates into both a weak strategic position and potentially weak profit performance.[9] When a reduced-focus strategy cannot produce desired levels of performance, an exit strategic market plan warrants consideration. But rather than divest a share position and exit quickly, a business can often significantly improve short-run performance by systematically raising prices and reducing marketing expenses, as illustrated in Figure 13-17.[10]

Consider again the chemical business discussed at the beginning of the chapter. In a very mature market with below-average profits, the business used a harvest price strategy to reduce volume. While price increases did result in lost market share and lower volumes, overall sales declined only modestly with the higher prices. More importantly, the higher prices produced higher margins. The combination of lower volumes and higher margins resulted in a higher gross profit. In this case, the company's managers devised a more profitable combination of price, margin, and volume.

A harvest price strategy would continue to raise prices with expected decreases in volumes until the business has slowly exited the market. In many instances, however, a harvest strategy leads to a core of customers who would have paid more all along but, given the lower price, they gladly took it. Price increases in these situations rid a business of price buyers, making the remaining customer base less price sensitive. Often at this point, price is not a major issue for the remaining customers, and a business finds that even additional price increases do not seriously reduce demand. Even in commodity markets, some customers value on-time delivery, a reliable supply, and trusted relationships more than a competitive price. When a business sees that it still has a good group of core customers despite the higher prices, it can abandon its harvest-and-exit strategy and focus on maintaining high profits with much smaller volumes. In one large chemical company, this situation occurred, with the company's least profitable product becoming the company's most profitable product.

Harvest Marketing Resources Strategy

In many instances, a business may not be able to raise prices as a strategy to harvest share while maximizing short-run profits. A soft drink manufacturer's prices, for instance, are difficult to alter in the end market. In such a case, a business can reduce the marketing resources it devotes to that product and its market share position. Slice is a low-share soft drink with minimal marketing support. Its market share is less than 5 percent of the lemon-lime soft drink segment and well behind Sprite, which has a 56 percent segment share. Although Pepsi has examined different ways to either revitalize the brand or reposition it, its market share remains relatively stagnant. By not supporting Slice, the company is maximizing what profits it can take as Slice slowly exits the market.

In heavily advertised consumer goods markets, major reductions in the advertising budget can lead to rather dramatic share erosion. The PIMS database tells us the rate of share change is affected by the rate of change in advertising budget. The calculation that follows gives us the rate of share loss for a consumer product that experienced a 25 percent

FIGURE 13-17 HARVEST PRICE STRATEGY

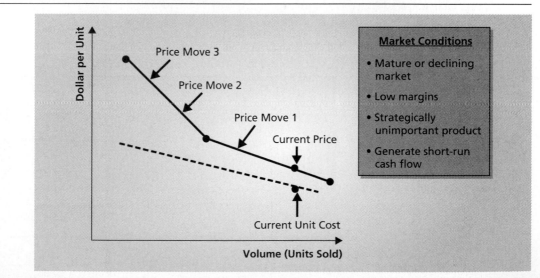

reduction in its advertising budget for each of 3 consecutive years. In this case, a 10 percent market share eroded to 9.6 percent in 3 years.

$$\textbf{Market Share} \text{ (3 years)} = \text{Market Share } [1.00 + (0.05 \times \text{Change in Advertising Budget})]^3$$
$$= 10\% \times [1.00 + (0.05 \times -0.25)]^3$$
$$= 10\% \times (1.00 - 0.0125)^3$$
$$= 10\% \times .96$$
$$= \textbf{9.6\%}$$

When advertising budgets are large, reductions of 25 percent for three successive years result in substantial savings. As long as the product has an adequate profit margin, a business could improve short-run profits as it reduces marketing expenses and slowly loses market share. The profits taken in the short run from the harvested product would normally be reallocated to a more attractive product-market in which the business hopes to build a stronger share position and achieve its desired level of profit.

Divest Market Strategy

One of the most difficult decisions any business faces is whether it should quickly sell off (divest) an unattractive product. In some instances, the product is one that the company was built on, and it is difficult to let it go. In other cases, the product represents a major investment, and a business resists abandoning it because of the money already spent to make it a successful venture. As a result, businesses often hang on to unattractive market positions for far too long despite a weak or average competitive position.

Figure 13-18 shows the portfolio of General Electric's clock and timer products as it existed in the late 1970s. Many of the products were in unattractive markets, had a weak

FIGURE 13-18 GENERAL ELECTRIC'S DIVESTMENT STRATEGY FOR UNATTRACTIVE PRODUCT-MARKETS

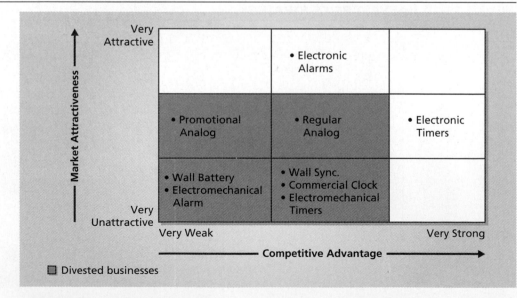

FIGURE 13-19 SELECTING BETWEEN TWO MARKET STRATEGIES

Area of Performance	Estimated Performance in 3 Years	
	Protect Share Strategy	Reduced-Focus Strategy
Market Demand (millions)	2,000	2,000
Market Share (%)	30	20
Unit Volume (millions)	600	400
Unit Price	$400	$450
Sales Revenues (millions)	$240	$180
Unit Variable Cost	$300	$300
Unit Margin	$100	$150
Gross Profit (millions)	$60	$60
Marketing & Sales Expenses (millions)	$30	$20
Net Marketing Contribution (millions)	$30	$40

competitive position, or both. GE divested the businesses shown and invested in the two that were in more attractive markets. Eventually, these product-markets were also divested because they did not match the overall performance objectives of the company.

To divest a share position, a business can either find a buyer for the business or simply close down the operation and sell its assets. In most cases, the desired choice is to find a buyer. Selling usually yields a greater return and preserves the employment of those working in the business.

A divest strategy, although desired, may sometimes not be feasible. For example, a business that has a 25-year commitment to produce a critical component for a government missile cannot easily exit the product-market; it has a responsibility to supply that product for the duration of the contract. Likewise, producers of pharmaceuticals or other life-supporting products may have a difficult time divesting a share position for either legal or ethical reasons.

SELECTING A DEFENSIVE STRATEGY

Consider a business that is making $25 million in net marketing contribution with an average competitive position in a market with below-average attractiveness. The business is performing reasonably well, but an average competitive position in an unattractive market does not warrant an offensive strategic market plan to grow share. The share position is profitable enough to keep, so a harvest defensive strategy may not be appropriate either. The choices left for this business are a protect share strategy and a reduced-focus strategy.

As shown in Figure 13-19, if the business were to pursue a protect share strategy, it would need to invest in marketing and other activities, such as R&D, to maintain its 30 percent share. By doing so, the business estimates it could produce sales revenues of $240 million over the next 3 years. A strategy of investing to protect share would produce $30 million in net marketing contribution. With marketing expenses also equal to $30 million, a protect share strategy would yield a marketing productivity equal to 1.

The alternative defensive market plan would be to reduce focus. This strategy would intentionally reduce market share from 30 to 20 percent. But the selective focus of the strategy would yield a higher average price and unit margin and would require less in marketing expenses. The result would be a $60 million reduction in sales revenue but an increase in net marketing contribution from $30 million to $40 million. With marketing expenses of $20 million, this strategy would result in a marketing productivity of 2, twice that of the protect share strategy.

A business will encounter many market situations and must maintain a well-defined set of objectives. Some performance objectives are short run, others are long run. Recognizing its objectives and its positioning in each of its markets, the business needs to develop a set of strategic market plans that will meet its objectives. Businesses generally need a combination of offensive and defensive strategic market plans. The offensive plans are geared for growth and improving share position, and the defensive plans are important sources of short-run profits and essential in defending strategic share positions. Both kinds of market plans play key roles in meeting a business's performance objectives.

■ Summary

Businesses have a short-term obligation to investors to fulfill promises of growth and profit performance. At the same time, they have an obligation to investors and employees to carve out a set of strategic market plans that will improve the position of the business in the long run. The primary purpose of a defensive strategic market plan is to protect a key strategic share position while managing the business's competitive position to produce the short-run growth and profit that meet the business's performance objectives.

Defensive strategic market plans are critical to the short-run profit performance of a business and in protecting key strategic share positions that will support future profit performance. Strategically, important share positions require a defensive strategic market plan to protect share position. A protect market position defensive strategy can include improved customer retention which, while maintaining a share position, can have a dramatic impact on profits with little or no change in sales revenue. A business may also use a reduced-focus market strategy to more narrowly allocate its resources in an effort to better defend a desired share position and improve the profits derived from this market.

Protecting market share requires much more than a business-as-usual marketing effort. Market forces such as market growth rate, market share size, and competitor entry all create share-eroding forces that can cause share to decrease if not offset by improved competitive position or increased marketing effort. Declines in relative competitive position in the areas of new product sales, product quality, and service quality can also contribute to market share erosion—and decreases in marketing effort in the areas of sales force and marketing communications will adversely affect defensive strategic market plans designed to protect an important share position.

In less attractive markets that are maturing, or in mature markets where growth is limited and margins are at low levels, a business may shift from an invest-to-protect defensive strategy to an optimize defensive strategy. A maximize profits strategy could involve price increases to improve profits while sacrificing volume, share, and sales revenues, as well as reductions in marketing expenses to a level focused primarily on customer retention. A reduced-focus strategy goes one step further in raising prices to drastically reduce market volume by focusing on certain customers in order to optimize profits.

If a business either is in an unattractive market or has a weak competitive position, it may elect to use an exit strategic market plan. If the business is profitable and capable of producing good short-run profits, a harvest strategy would be used. A harvest strategy could involve raising prices or reducing marketing resources, or both. This type of defensive strategic market plan enables a business to exit a market slowly while maximizing short-run profits.

On the other hand, if a business is losing money or would like to free up resources at a faster rate, a divest strategy would be more appropriate. A divest strategy would normally seek to sell the business in order to maximize the value derived from its assets and goodwill. If there are no buyers, a business may have to use an accelerated harvest strategy. In some instances, a business may be prevented from exiting a share position because of legal or ethical considerations.

Finally, companies tend to keep businesses that should be divested too long. Holding on to these businesses ties up resources that the company could redirect to offensive market strategies designed to improve the performance of another of its businesses.

■ Market-Based Strategic Thinking

1 How do defensive market strategies contribute to a business's performance objectives (sales growth, share position, and profit performance)?

2 What are the differences between defensive market strategies and offensive market strategies?

3 Why is it more difficult to protect market share in a high-growth market than in a slow- or no-growth market?

4 Why do share leaders have to work harder than share followers to protect share?

5 What are some of the key aspects of performance that would enable a share follower to achieve the same level of profit as a share leader?

6 What aspects of positioning and marketing effort can be managed to achieve a high profit with a reduced-focus niche-market strategy?

7 Why should a reduced-focus niche strategy with above-average customer value deliver above-average profit?

8 How do defensive market strategies contribute to the long-run share position and profit performance of a business?

9 Compare defensive market strategies to protect a share position with strategies to exit a product-market in terms of their contributions to short-run profit performance and the overall share position of the business.

10 Why would a business pursue a reduced-focus strategic market plan?

11 What is the primary objective of a monetize strategic market plan?

12 Under what conditions would a business select an exit market strategy over a protect share position strategy?

13 When should a business pursue a harvest market strategy, and how could that strategy affect short-run profit performance?

14 When should a business pursue a divest market strategy, and how could that strategy affect short-run profit performance?

15 Why might companies continue to support businesses in harvest- or divest-share portfolio positions rather than harvest or divest the businesses?

Marketing Performance Tools

The three **Marketing Performance Tools** described here may be accessed online at *www.rogerjbest.com*. These applied-learning tools allow you to evaluate the two relevant market strategies for each of the three defensive core strategies.

13.1 Defensive Strategies—Core Strategy I: Protect Position (Figure 13-4)
  ■ Using the data provided, evaluate the two strategies for protecting profits.

13.2 Defensive Strategies—Core Strategy II: Optimize Position (Figure 13-4)
  ■ Using the data provided, evaluate the two strategies for maximizing profits without exiting markets.

13.3 Defensive Strategies—Core Strategy III: Monetize, Harvest, or Divest (Figure 13-4)
  ■ Using the data provided, evaluate the two strategies for maximizing short-run cash flow.

Notes

1. George Seiler, "Colorful Chemicals Cuts Its Losses," *Planning Review* (January–February 1987): 16–22.
2. Donald Potter, "Strategy to Succeed in Hostile Markets," *California Management Review* (Fall 1994): 65–82.
3. Sidney Schoeffer, "Market Position: Build, Hold or Harvest," PIMS Letter No. 3 (1978): 1–10.
4. Philip Kotler and Paul Bloom, "Strategies for High-Market Share Companies," *Harvard Business Review* (November–December 1975): 63–72.
5. Donald Clifford and Richard Cavanagh, *The Winning Performance: How America's High and Mid-Size Growth Companies Succeed* (New York: Bantam Books, 1985).
6. Carolyn Woo and Arnold Cooper, "The Surprising Case for Low Market Share," *Harvard Business Review* (November–December 1982): 106–113.
7. Robert Linneman and John Stanton Jr., "Mining for Niches," *Business Horizons* (May–June 1992): 43–51.
8. Robert Hamermesh and Steven Silk, "How to Compete in Stagnant Industries," *Harvard Business Review* (September–October 1979): 161–168.
9. V. Cook and R. Rothberg, "The Harvesting of USAUTO?" *Journal of Product Innovation Management* (1980): 310–322.
10. Kathryn Rudie Harrigan, "Strategies for Declining Businesses," *Journal of Business Strategy* (Fall 1980): 27.

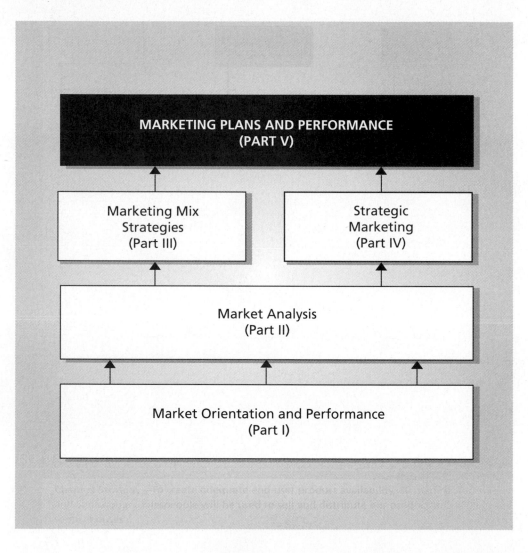

PART V

Marketing Plans and Performance

■ It is better to be prepared for an opportunity and not have one than to have an opportunity and not be prepared.
—*Whitney Young Jr.*
   1960s Civil Rights Leader, Executive Director of the Urban League, Dean of School of Social Work, Atlanta University

Given a specific strategic market plan and performance objectives, a marketing mix strategy and marketing plan must be developed and successfully implemented in order to move a business toward its planned performance objectives.

Chapter 14 presents a process and structure for developing a marketing plan. Chapter 15 addresses implementation of a marketing plan and the various forces that affect the success or failure of a marketing plan. Ownership, commitment, performance measurement, adaptation, and resource allocation are important aspects of market-based management and successful implementation. Process marketing metrics such as customer awareness, customer perceptions of performance, trial usage, and customer satisfaction are key market-based performance metrics that are tracked, along with end-result metrics that generally measure profit performance.

Finally, it is important that those in responsible marketing positions understand how marketing strategies individually and collectively affect net profit, cash flow, investment, and, ultimately, shareholder value. Chapter 16 carefully illustrates how each aspect of a marketing strategy ripples through the organizational maze of financial accounting to affect each aspect of profitability and, ultimately, shareholder value. Regardless of a business's assets, technology, and financial leverage, there is only one source of positive cash flow, and that is the customer; everything else is expense.

Building a Marketing Plan

■ Chance favors the prepared mind.
—*Louis Pasteur*

tericycle Inc. is in the business of recycling medical waste. It offers health care providers a safe, cost-effective, and environmentally effective disposal method. As shown in Figure 14-1, the company's sales were $22 million in 1995 and reached $790 million by 2006.[1] In the first edition of *Market-Based Management* (MBM), we made a 3-year forecast of sales and marketing profits for Stericycle. The forecast for 1998 was $59 million, and actual sales were $64 million. Actual marketing profits were also slightly higher than our 1995 projection.

FIGURE 14-1 MARKET-BASED PLAN: 3-YEAR PLAN VERSUS ACTUAL

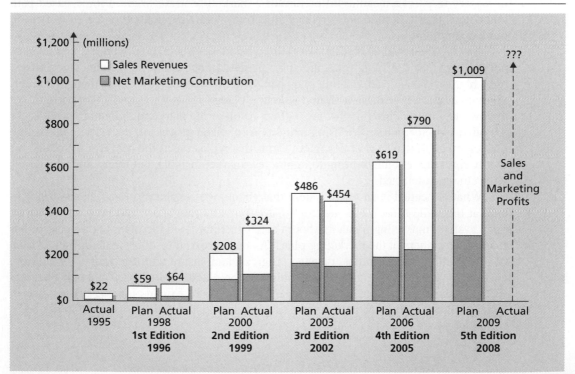

In the second edition of MBM, our 3-year forecast for 2000 was for $208 million in sales, and actual sales were $324 million. In the third edition, our forecast for 2003 was for $486 million, and actual sales were $454 million. In the fourth edition, the projected 3-year forecast for 2006 was $619 million, and actual sales were $790 million. In this fifth edition, our 3-year market plan projects sales to reach $1.1 billion. The purpose of this chapter is to present the process of building a strategic market plan, using as an example our 2007–2009 Stericycle Sample Marketing Plan.

CREATIVITY VERSUS STRUCTURE

The process of building a proactive marketing plan takes a delicate balance of creativity and structure. It is a process where the opportunity to think creatively—to explore marketing issues outside the realm of day-to-day business—is a prerequisite. Yet, as shown in Figure 14-2 a marketing plan must be structured to ensure accuracy and comprehensiveness, with marketing strategies, resources, and performance objectives credibly linked to the market situation.

Developing a strategic market plan is similar to creating a painting. The imaginative use of light and color can make a painting interesting and appealing, but without some degree of form to add meaning to the composition the painting may be intriguing but confusing. On the other hand, all form and no creative expression yields a sterile picture. The same is true for a marketing plan: Both creative insight and analytical structure are necessary to paint a meaningful picture of a marketing strategy and a logic-based path that connects it to desired performance objectives within the context of a well-portrayed market situation.

A well-developed marketing plan helps a business systematically understand its market and provides a strategy for achieving a predetermined set of performance objectives, but a highly formalized marketing plan, paradoxically, can be little better than no marketing plan at all.[2] A business with no marketing plan obviously forgoes the opportunity to uncover key market insights that are a direct result of the marketing planning process. At the other extreme, a business using a highly formalized process to develop its marketing plan can regress to a level of filling out forms that will serve as the basis for the plan.[3] An overly rigid process might bring to light a few market insights, but many important ones will remain undetected.

What is needed is an open system that encourages exploration and creative insight and, at the same time, has a structure that ensures thoroughness and accuracy. With an open system, marketing planners should act as facilitators in the planning process rather than as developers of the marketing plan.[4] As facilitators, they coordinate the acquisition of information, set schedules, manage progress, and ensure that the business's mission, customers, and goals remain as focal points in the planning process. Although there are recognizable organizational hurdles, businesses that use a formal planning process are, in general, more likely to achieve improved performance than businesses that do not use a formal process.[5]

FIGURE 14-2 BUILDING A MARKETING PLAN—CREATIVITY VERSUS STRUCTURE

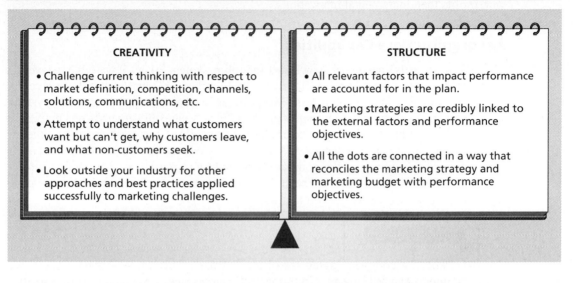

BENEFITS OF BUILDING A MARKETING PLAN

A good marketing plan is indispensable to a proactive market orientation. Businesses with a strong market orientation are in continuous pursuit of customer, competitor, and market intelligence and work cross-functionally to create value-added customer solutions. Although these activities are ongoing, important benefits result from the process of developing a marketing plan.

Identifying Opportunities

It is not the *plan* itself, but the *process*, that helps a business uncover new opportunities and recognize important threats. A systematic evaluation of the market and internal capabilities provides an opportunity to step back from day-to-day tactical marketing decision making and take a broader, more comprehensive view of the market and business situation.[6] K2, for example, has become the market share leader in the U.S. market for snow skis. K2's systematic evaluation of the U.S. ski market revealed that it was a mature market, which made additional share penetration difficult. However, while performing this situation analysis, K2 was able to more fully recognize the emerging markets in snowboards and inline skates. This discovery, in turn, led to new-market-entry strategies that have provided significant growth, a more diversified strategic position, and new sources of profit.

New opportunities also include all new product markets with distinctly different value propositions. Toyota introduced the Prius hybrid as the first environmentally friendly car. For target customers, the Prius made all other cars irrelevant. The authors of

Blue Ocean Strategies[7] report that true innovations such as Toyota's lead to better sales and profits than incremental innovations.

Leveraging Core Capabilities

As K2 aggressively entered the snowboard and inline skate markets, it was able to leverage its brand name and awareness in closely related markets. K2 was also able to leverage existing manufacturing and engineering expertise, as well as sales and distribution systems that served the ski market. One important benefit to a carefully thought-out marketing plan, then, is the greater utilization of production capabilities and business and marketing systems already in place. Likewise, Clif Bar Inc. introduced the Luna nutritional energy bar for women, leveraging the company's product and marketing knowledge into an unserved segment of the market. The same is true for Bayer as it expanded the use of its aspirin product for preventing heart attacks.[8]

Focused Market Strategy

Most markets are complex aggregates of many smaller markets and market segments. These segments can be broken down further into market niches. Without a good marketing plan, a business could find itself vaguely positioned in a variety of market segments—a situation that could lead it in all directions in the search for customers without really being able to fully satisfy any of them.

A good marketing plan will profile target customers to the extent that the positioning strategy can be customized around the needs of the target segment and the marketing effort can be directed at these target customers. The process for developing the marketing plan in this way brings target customers into sharp focus, separating them from everyone else. The quote in earlier chapters by Charles M. Lillis, CEO of MediaOne Group, is relevant here also: "I will know when our businesses have done a good job of market segmentation and planning when they can tell me to whom we should *not* sell."

Resource Allocation

A well-defined target market focus is also cost efficient. If managers do not accurately identify the business's target customers, they will spend much time and money marketing to people who are not likely to buy. Or, if non-target customers do buy, they will be difficult to retain because the value proposition will not deliver the customer satisfaction they desire. A well-focused marketing plan is more productive, with fewer dollars needed for accomplishing performance objectives because resources are not misspent on non-target customers.

Building a Performance Roadmap

A marketing plan also serves as a roadmap for both marketing strategy and expected performance. An effective plan includes projections for market share, sales revenue, and profits over a specified planning horizon. Mapping the future in this way may seem a fairly easy task, but the complexity of the business world is such that many circumstances influence a given market, a business's strategy, and the resources needed.

Constantly changing conditions within a business's market include those related to customer needs, competitors' moves, and the economy. In addition, market information is often incomplete or inaccurate or both.

The environment *within* a business can also contribute to difficulties in the marketing planning process. Marketing strategies are often driven internally by short-run profit objectives rather than by market-based performance objectives. Further, resources are not always allocated on the basis of strategy needs and performance objectives but are dictated by organizational needs, political motives, or a desire to improve short-run profits. These factors and others make meaningful marketing plans challenging to develop and impede their successful implementation.

BUILDING A MARKETING PLAN

An effective marketing plan is the result of a systematic, creative, and yet structured process that uncovers market opportunities and threats a business can then address in order to achieve its performance objectives. As illustrated in Figure 14-3, the development of a marketing plan is a *process*, and each step in the process has a *structure* that enables the marketing plan to evolve from abstract ideas and a compilation of information into a comprehensive document that is easy to understand and logical in its conclusions, and which demonstrates the high probability of the success of its proposed strategies. This section is devoted to an in-depth discussion of each step in this process.

PART I: SITUATION ANALYSIS—WHERE ARE WE NOW?

The strategic marketing planning process outlined in Figure 14-3 starts with a detailed *situation analysis* of the market and business with respect to current market forces, the business's competitive position, and its current performance. The primary purpose of a situation analysis is to uncover key performance issues that usually go unnoticed in day-to-day business operations. First, we need to go deeper into the market and the business's operations to fully understand customer needs, competition, and channel systems, as well as business positioning, margins, and profitability.

A thorough situation analysis is required for a business to understand current performance and market conditions and to uncover the key issues that affect performance. As shown in Figure 14-4, the output of the situation analysis is the marketing strategy. The marketing strategy must reconcile current performance and market conditions with desired performance objectives. The combination of the situation analysis and marketing strategy drives the objectives of the marketing plan with respect to market share, sales, margins, and marketing profitability.

To better understand this process, let's see how it is applied. As in the previous four editions of *Market-Based Management*, we will use a 3-year market plan for Stericycle, the company whose sales revenues and marketing profits are profiled in Figure 14-1. The 3-year plan is only an example—not the company's actual plan—for the purpose of illustrating the building of a market-based, performance-driven market plan. The sample plan uses publicly available data, but it also uses some data improvised by the author to illustrate certain points. The sample plan should not be construed as a plan created by or for Stericycle.

FIGURE 14-3 BUILDING A MARKETING PLAN—PROCESS

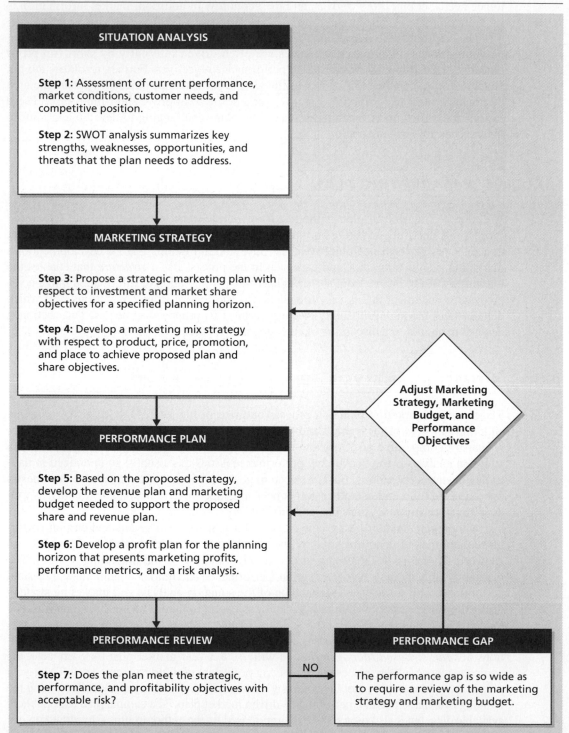

SITUATION ANALYSIS

Step 1: Assessment of current performance, market conditions, customer needs, and competitive position.

Step 2: SWOT analysis summarizes key strengths, weaknesses, opportunities, and threats that the plan needs to address.

MARKETING STRATEGY

Step 3: Propose a strategic marketing plan with respect to investment and market share objectives for a specified planning horizon.

Step 4: Develop a marketing mix strategy with respect to product, price, promotion, and place to achieve proposed plan and share objectives.

PERFORMANCE PLAN

Step 5: Based on the proposed strategy, develop the revenue plan and marketing budget needed to support the proposed share and revenue plan.

Step 6: Develop a profit plan for the planning horizon that presents marketing profits, performance metrics, and a risk analysis.

Adjust Marketing Strategy, Marketing Budget, and Performance Objectives

PERFORMANCE REVIEW

Step 7: Does the plan meet the strategic, performance, and profitability objectives with acceptable risk?

NO

PERFORMANCE GAP

The performance gap is so wide as to require a review of the marketing strategy and marketing budget.

FIGURE 14-4 BUILDING A MARKETING PLAN—CORE BUILDING BLOCKS

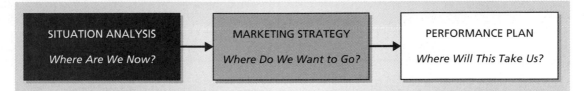

In Figure 14-6, the first page of the Stericycle Sample Marketing Plan shown summarizes the company's market position and the purpose of this sample marketing plan. The next page of the sample plan is an introduction to the situation analysis section (Part I of the plan).

We will explore the process of building a market-based marketing plan by following the steps in Figure 14-3, and we will begin with the two components of the situation analysis: (1) an assessment of a business's current situation and (2) a SWOT analysis. Later, we will apply the situation analysis in creating a marketing strategy (Part II of the sample plan) and a performance plan (Part III).

Step 1: Current Situation

A fact-based analysis of the current situation is the first requirement in building a successful marketing plan. But acquiring accurate information on "where we are now" with respect to performance, market conditions, and competitive position is often the most challenging aspect of building a market-based performance plan. When specific information is not readily available, managers can be tempted to work around it, as though it were information not relevant to appraising their business's current situation. Unfortunately, this is not an acceptable approach. In some cases, the information may truly be unavailable, and then managers will have to make estimates based on their experience and market knowledge. Where estimates are vulnerable to error, they should be noted and reconsidered as the plan evolves. The marketing plan is not an event; it is the product of an ongoing process to improve a business's understanding of its market and its position and performance in that market.

For managers new to the process of building a market-based performance plan, conducting an analysis of the current situation is particularly challenging. Seeing it applied as we move through the Stericycle Sample Marketing Plan will help. But when applying it to your own marketing plan, the realities of achieving performance objectives within a specific timeline will hit you right between the eyes. For managers experienced with performance-driven situation analyses, the Stericycle Sample Marketing Plan will likely offer new information and add to their confidence. The sample plan focuses on an accurate assessment of the company's current situation in building an effective marketing strategy and performance plan. So let's get started with the hard part.

Figure 14-5 summarizes the data needed for fully capturing the essence of the current situation. As mentioned, estimates or assumptions may often have to replace actual data, especially when marketing managers are new to the process of developing a market-based analysis of a business's current situation. Over time, however, any estimates or assumptions will be replaced with market data. Managers may feel a bit uneasy in making estimates or

FIGURE 14-5 COMPONENTS OF CURRENT SITUATION

assumptions, but almost every marketing manager needs to make them when developing a business's initial assessment of its current situation. The assessment, however, will force on a business's marketing managers a better knowledge of their market, leading to the discovery of new data sources. The real enemy is a completely blank piece of paper. Even using a guess is better than using nothing. Estimates and assumptions at least can be modified as the actual data emerge, but a blank piece of paper provides no guidelines at all for thinking about and arriving at an understanding of a business's current situation.

The remaining portion of this section discusses each aspect of the current situation presented in Figure 14-5. To help us understand the assessment process, we will apply each aspect in developing a situation analysis for the Stericycle Sample Marketing Plan.

Current Performance

The best place to begin work on an analysis of the current situation is with an accurate appraisal of the business's performance. The appraisal might include only the most recent year of sales, margins, and profits, or it could include the same information for the previous two, three, or more years. In our Stericycle Sample Marketing Plan, we present on page 1.1 the sales and marketing profits at 3-year intervals from 1995 to 2006, as well as a summary of current performance for 2006. If the information is available, a separate page of a business's marketing plan could present the results of various marketing performance metrics, such as those for customer satisfaction, customer retention, customer profitability, and customer loyalty, with the last finding including the net promoter score. Chapter 1 discusses the information needed for calculating these metrics.

Market Demand

An important element of a situation analysis is an appraisal of the market with respect to demand. What is the market's present size, and where is the market heading in terms of its growth rate and price trends? What is the upper limit on market demand, the point at which the market will reach its full potential? Each of these considerations has strategy implications. A market in early development, far from its market potential and growing rapidly, will require a strategy different than one for a fully developed and very slow-growing market.

For Stericycle, the market demand in 2006 was $3.5 billion and growing at a rate of 8 percent annually. As indicated on page 1.2 of the sample plan, market demand in 2009 is projected at $4.2 billion. Also of significance is the fact that the market is divided into two distinct segments—small-quantity customers and large-quantity generators. Each segment has different needs, demographics, and behaviors with respect to medical waste. The small-quantity customers include physicians, dentists, veterinarians, small clinics, and small labs that produce relatively little medical waste. The large-quantity generators include hospitals, blood banks, research labs, and pharmaceutical companies that produce large amounts.

As page 1.2 of the sample plan shows, the small-quantity segment is larger and growing at a faster rate than the large-quantity generator segment. Again, the overall market growth rate, the sizes of the two market segments, and the growth rate of each segment all have implications for marketing strategy development and future performance.

Competition and Industry Attractiveness

One page of the situation analysis section presents a summary of the competitive and industry forces that influence profit performance, either favorably or unfavorably. As with any page in the marketing plan, the layout and design will reflect the talents and creativity of the individual or team building the marketing plan. The goal is to make each page highly readable, informative, easily understood, and consistent in appearance and writing style with the other pages.

With respect to competitors, the medical waste industry consists of many, mostly small businesses. As page 1.3 shows, the top four competitors account for only 31.3 percent of sales. Stericycle, with a 22.6 percent market share, is far and away the market leader. The two next largest competitors have market shares of about 4 percent. With many competitors having a market share of less than 1 percent, we can expect the industry to continue to consolidate. Consolidation within the industry should favor market share growth for Stericycle.

The industry forces for both market segments are favorable. For the small-quantity customers, an overall industry attractiveness index of 70 suggests that this segment has the potential for profits well above average. The industry attractiveness index for the large-quantity generators is 52, which suggests industry forces also favor, to a lesser degree, above-average performance in this segment. Chapter 6 covers industry forces and the industry attractiveness index.

Share Performance Metrics

To help us understand Stericycle's opportunities to grow its market share and achieve its share potential, page 1.4 of the sample plan presents the company's share performance metrics. The page includes a share development path, which, as we saw in Chapter 3, is a sequence of share performance metrics that shape market share. At each step of the share development path, share performance is measured by a particular performance metric. By multiplying Stericycle's positive share metrics, we arrive at a market share index of 22.7.

Stericycle's market share index, then, is nearly the same as its actual market share of 22.6 percent. Such a parallel is not an expectation; many businesses have a market share index somewhat different than their actual market share. But the market share index should approximate actual market share if all the input data for the performance metrics are accurate.

The share potential index is an estimate of the share performance index if the business were to achieve maximum levels of performance for each share metric. For Stericycle, when we divide the current share index of 22.7 by the share potential index of

41 and multiply by 100, we obtain a share development index of 55. This means that Stericycle has attained 55 percent of its share potential. These concepts are explained in Chapter 3.

Addressing the largest areas of share leakage in the Stericycle marketing strategy should allow the company to continue building market share. As page 1.4 shows, most of the share potential is lost due to "Served Market" (40 percent) and "Awareness" (15 percent). To improve the served market performance metric, Stericycle must expand its market reach. A greater reach will likely require acquisitions and more transfer centers. To improve awareness, Stericycle needs more effective marketing communications, particularly in the small-quantity segment, which is highly fragmented with over 1 million customers. Addressing these issues, particularly in a market where the competition is relatively weak, should allow Stericycle to grow market share over the next 3 years.

Customer Needs and Market Segmentation

Since the medical waste market is segmented and customers within both segments differ with regard to needs and demographics, the marketing plan includes a separate page for each segment. Page 1.5 presents the customer needs, demographics, and Stericycle's competitive position for the small-quantity customer segment.

In the small-quantity segment are over a million physicians, dentists, veterinarians, and small clinics and laboratories. The medical waste they each produce is not nearly as great as the amount that large health care facilities generate, but it must still be stored and disposed of in a safe and efficient manner. Stericycle performs extremely well in this segment, owing to its product, service, and sales and distribution efforts. The company's performance in product, service, and brand outperforms competitors in all cases. Chapter 4 explains how the relative advantage scores for these areas are determined, and how the scores are used in calculating an overall benefits index. Stericycle's overall benefits index for the small-quantity segment is 149, meaning that it has a 49 percent advantage in customer benefits over its top three competitors.

Stericycle is priced above its competitors in this segment, so the company's small-quantity customers have a higher cost of purchase. But the company's highly efficient and safe storage system lowers customers' costs. The net result is an overall cost of purchase index of 126, meaning that Stericycle's 49 percent greater customer benefits are only 26 percent more expensive than the average price charged by competitors. Thus Stericycle offers its small-quantity customers superior value, as indicated by its high customer value index of 23 (149 minus 126). The cost of purchase and customer value indexes are also explained in Chapter 4.

Page 1.6 presents the customer needs, demographics, and competitive position for the large-quantity generator segment. These customers include hospitals, blood banks, research labs, and pharmaceutical companies. They have large amounts of medical waste and are much more price sensitive than the customers in the small-quantity segment. Many have their own incinerators for burning medical waste. In this segment, Stericycle has an overall advantage in customer benefits, with a benefits index of 127, while the company's overall cost of purchase index is 100. Again, Stericycle offers superior customer value, having a customer value index of 27 (127 minus 100). But in the large-quantity segment price rivalry is fierce, with many of the small competitors willing to offer a price well below average in return for the business of a large-quantity generator.

FIGURE 14-6 STERICYCLE SAMPLE MARKETING PLAN: SITUATION ANALYSIS

SAMPLE MARKETING PLAN: 2007–2009

STERICYCLE

> Stericycle is the market leader in the growing medical waste disposal market. The purpose of this marketing plan is to review the current situation and propose a marketing strategy that will achieve profitable growth over the next 3 years.
>
> The marketing plan is organized into the following three sections:
>
> - Situation Analysis: *Where We Are Now.* . . . . .Pages 1.0–1.8
> - Marketing Strategy: *Where We Want to Go.* . . . . .Pages 2.0–2.6
> - Performance Plan: *What We Expect to Achieve.* . . . Pages 3.0–3.6

*The purpose of this marketing plan is purely instructional. All information has been taken from published reports or created by the author for educational purposes. All assumptions, estimates, and strategies are those of the author and not those of **Stericycle Inc**.*

Roger J. Best, 2007
Market-Based Management

SAMPLE MARKETING PLAN: 2007–2009   [STERICYCLE]

**PART I
SITUATION ANALYSIS**

The situation analysis is the bedrock of a performance-driven marketing plan. It provides a meaningful summary of sales, share, and profit performance. As important is a careful assessment of customer needs, competitive position, and customer value, and a SWOT analysis that summarizes key strengths, weaknesses, opportunities, and threats.

Page 1.0

PAST PERFORMANCE   [STERICYCLE]

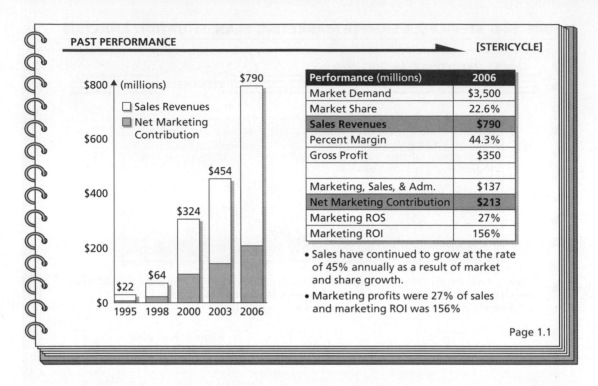

Performance (millions)	2006
Market Demand	$3,500
Market Share	22.6%
Sales Revenues	$790
Percent Margin	44.3%
Gross Profit	$350
Marketing, Sales, & Adm.	$137
Net Marketing Contribution	$213
Marketing ROS	27%
Marketing ROI	156%

- Sales have continued to grow at the rate of 45% annually as a result of market and share growth.
- Marketing profits were 27% of sales and marketing ROI was 156%

Page 1.1

MARKET DEMAND   [STERICYCLE]

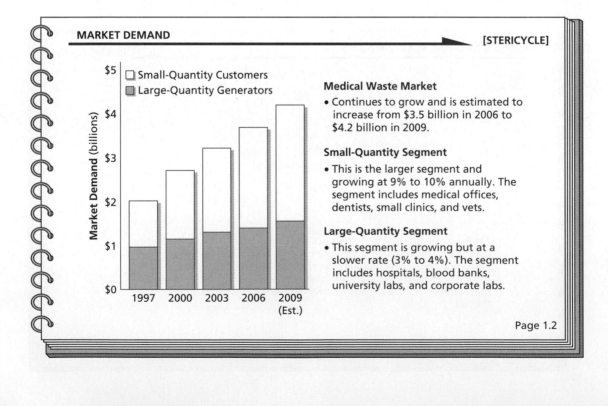

Medical Waste Market
- Continues to grow and is estimated to increase from $3.5 billion in 2006 to $4.2 billion in 2009.

Small-Quantity Segment
- This is the larger segment and growing at 9% to 10% annually. The segment includes medical offices, dentists, small clinics, and vets.

Large-Quantity Segment
- This segment is growing but at a slower rate (3% to 4%). The segment includes hospitals, blood banks, university labs, and corporate labs.

Page 1.2

INDUSTRY AND COMPETITION   [STERICYCLE]

- Stericycle is the dominant market leader with a 22.6% market share. The next two largest competitors have less than one-fifth the share. Yet 68.7% of the market is still served by small companies and on-site incinerators.

Industry Forces	Rel. Imp.	SQ Seg.	LQ Seg.
Competitor Entry	20%	60	75
Competitor Exit	10%	90	65
Substitutes	20%	80	50
Buyer Power	25%	65	40
Seller Power	5%	90	90
Price Rivalry	20%	60	30
	100%	70	52

- The small-quantity (SQ) segment has the potential for higher profits based on industry forces. However, the large-quantity (LQ) segment also offers good profit potential.

Competition	Sales (millions)	Market Share	Relative Share*
Stericycle	$789.9	22.6%	260
America Ecology Corp.	$145.6	4.2%	15
Microtek Medical Holdings	$145.1	4.1%	15
Waste Management Inc.	$13.2	0.4%	1
All Others (100+)	$2,406	68.7%	<1

*Competitor's share divided by top three competitors.

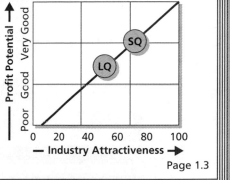

Page 1.3

SHARE PERFORMANCE METRICS   [STERICYCLE]

Share Metrics	Performance	Potential
Served Market	60.0%	75.0%
Awareness	75.0%	90.0%
Consideration	70.0%	75.0%
Preference	80.0%	90.0%
Purchase	90.0%	90.0%
Market Share Index (MSI)	22.7%	41.0%
Share Development Index (SDI)*		55

*SDI = Market Share Index / Share Potential Index × 100

Year	2006
Market Share	22.6%

- The MSI of 22.7% is close to the actual market share of 22.6%. Stericycle's share potential index is 41%, which produces an SDI of 55.

- To grow market share, Stericycle needs to address served market and awareness metrics.

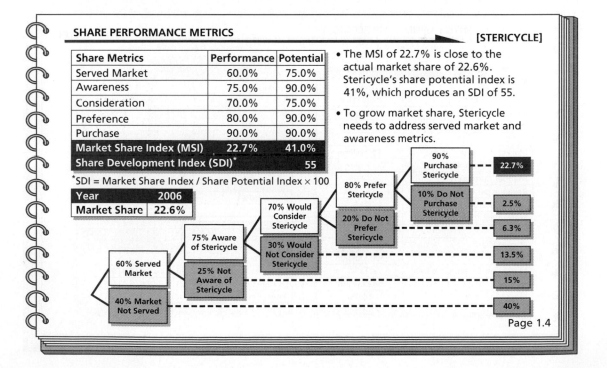

Page 1.4

SMALL-QUANTITY CUSTOMER SEGMENT   [STERICYCLE]

Small-Quantity Customers: Physicians, dentists, vets, small clinics, small labs

Segment Profile	Segment Metric
Value Driver	Service
Primary Benefit	Easy & Safe Disposal
Price Sensitivity	Low
Waste Management Expertise	Low
Market Demand—2006	$2.3 billion
Market Growth Rate	8.0%
Number Customers	343,800
Revenue per Customer	$1,425
Percent Margin	54.9%
Margin per Customer	$782
Market Share	21.3%
Sales Revenues	$490 million
Marketing & Sales Expenses	20%
Net Marketing Contribution	$171 million
Marketing ROS	34.9%
Marketing ROI	**175%**

Customer Needs & Positioning

Small Quantity Customer Needs	Rel. Imp.	STR	A	B	C	Net Pos.
Product (60%)						
Reliability	60	7.2	6.5	5.8	4.2	20
Safety	20	7.2	6.1	4.1	5.2	14
Ease of Use	20	6.5	6.1	3.8	4.2	14
	100					148
Service (30%)						
Reliable Pick-Up	60	7.5	6.7	5.0	6.5	20
Safety Training	40	8.5	6.7	5.0	4.5	27
	100					147
Brand (10%)						
Well Known	60	8.5	6.5	4.5	4.5	60
Environmental Record	40	5.6	6.5	4.2	5.5	0
	100					160
Overall Benefits Index						149
Cost of Purchase						
Cost of Service	60	7.5	6.5	5.1	4.8	40
Storage Cost	20	4.5	5.0	6.4	7.2	−7
Safety Cost	20	3.5	5.0	5.7	6.5	−7
Cost of Purchase Index	100					126

Page 1.5

LARGE-QUANTITY GENERATOR SEGMENT   [STERICYCLE]

Large-Quantity Customers: Hospitals, blood banks, research labs, pharmaceutical companies

Segment Profile	Segment Metric
Value Driver	Low Cost
Primary Benefit	Low Price
Price Sensitivity	High
Waste Management Expertise	High
Market Demand—2006	$1.2 billion
Market Growth Rate	3.5%
Number Customers	8,600
Revenue per Customer	$34,844
Percent Margin	27%
Margin per Customer	$9,408
Market Share	25.0%
Sales Revenues	$300 million
Marketing & Sales Expenses	13%
Net Marketing Contribution	$42 million
Marketing ROS	14.0%
Marketing ROI	**108%**

Customer Needs & Positioning

Small Quantity Customer Needs	Rel. Imp.	STR	A	B	C	Net Pos.
Product (70%)						
Reliability	75	7.2	6.5	5.8	4.2	25
Safety	15	7.2	6.1	4.1	5.2	10
Ease of Use	10	6.5	6.1	5.0	6.0	0
	100					135
Service (20%)						
Reliable Pick-Up	80	7.5	6.7	6.0	6.5	0
Safety Training	20	8.5	6.7	6.0	4.5	7
	100					107
Brand (10%)						
Well Known	60	8.5	6.5	6.0	4.5	20
Environmental Record	40	5.0	7.0	4.2	5.5	−13
	100					107
Overall Benefits Index						127
Cost of Purchase						
Cost of Service	90	7.0	6.5	6.0	6.0	0
Storage Cost	10	4.5	5.0	6.4	6.0	0
Safety Cost	0	3.5	5.0	5.7	6.5	0
Cost of Purchase Index	100					100

Page 1.6

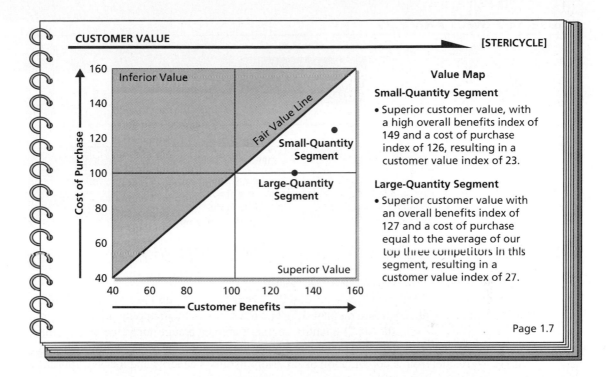

CUSTOMER VALUE   [STERICYCLE]

Value Map

Small-Quantity Segment

- Superior customer value, with a high overall benefits index of 149 and a cost of purchase index of 126, resulting in a customer value index of 23.

Large-Quantity Segment

- Superior customer value with an overall benefits index of 127 and a cost of purchase equal to the average of our top three competitors in this segment, resulting in a customer value index of 27.

Page 1.7

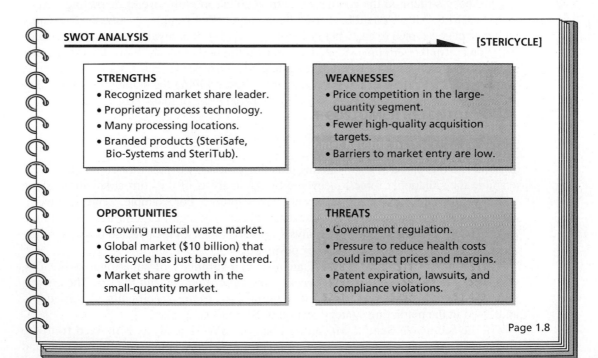

SWOT ANALYSIS   [STERICYCLE]

STRENGTHS

- Recognized market share leader.
- Proprietary process technology.
- Many processing locations.
- Branded products (SteriSafe, Bio-Systems and SteriTub).

WEAKNESSES

- Price competition in the large-quantity segment.
- Fewer high-quality acquisition targets.
- Barriers to market entry are low.

OPPORTUNITIES

- Growing medical waste market.
- Global market ($10 billion) that Stericycle has just barely entered.
- Market share growth in the small-quantity market.

THREATS

- Government regulation.
- Pressure to reduce health costs could impact prices and margins.
- Patent expiration, lawsuits, and compliance violations.

Page 1.8

FIGURE 14-7 SWOT ANALYSIS

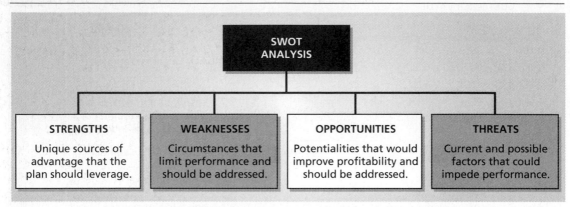

Competitive Position and Customer Value

By plotting the overall benefits index and the overall cost of purchase index we can create a value map, as illustrated on page 1.7. The details of value mapping are explained in Chapter 4. As shown, the small-quantity segment creates a superior value as a result of outstanding customer benefits. In the large-quantity segment, customer value is about the same but results from a combination of superior customer benefits and a cost of purchase equal to Stericycle's top three competitors in that segment.

We have structured the company's current situation with several marketing performance metrics, but we could have used many more. For example, businesses frequently include a page devoted to customer satisfaction and customer loyalty. Others may include pages on customers' lifetime value, the competition, marketing channels, the product life cycle, and perhaps additional details regarding customer needs. The order of presentation is subject to the preferences of the manager or team building the situation analysis. The organization of the analysis in the sample plan is only one of many possibilities.

Step 2: SWOT Analysis

To complete this phase of the marketing planning process, we must now comprehensively examine the situational forces uncovered by the analysis of the current situation, along with other forces that the analysis may not have captured. For example, trends in government regulation, health costs, and waste disposal could be significant influences on future performance. The role of a SWOT analysis is to document all present and possible future influences on performance, negative or positive.

As Figure 14-7 shows, a SWOT analysis is a summary of situational influences, which are categorized as *strengths, weaknesses, opportunities,* and *threats*. Then, using this organizational structure, the most important issues are specifically identified and addressed in the marketing strategy section of the marketing plan.

In the Stericycle Sample Marketing Plan, the SWOT analysis is derived from the analysis of the medical waste recycling market and Stericycle's current position and performance in it. Page 1.8 shows several strengths, weaknesses, opportunities, and threats Stericycle needs to address in building its marketing plan. By examining the factors identified in the SWOT analysis, the business will come to understand the degree to which each of these key issues affects the results of its performance metrics.

Because the key issues serve as the primary guideline in developing the marketing strategy, they must be carefully specified and articulated. This step in the planning process will have a major part in determining the marketing strategy and its impact on future performance.

PART II: MARKETING STRATEGY—WHERE DO WE WANT TO GO?

As they prepare to develop a marketing strategy, a business's managers must carry forward into their strategic thinking each issue identified in the situation analysis, including those articulated in the SWOT analysis. The first box in Figure 14-8 lists the components of the situation analysis, and it is around these components that the issues are organized. They affect the strategy the managers will develop for taking the business to the desired level of performance. Developing a marketing strategy for a marketing plan encompasses two steps in the overall process of building a marketing plan, as presented earlier in Figure 14-4. The Stericycle Sample Marketing Plan includes both steps.

Step 3: Strategic Market Plan

On the basis of the insights brought to light by the situation analysis, a business's managers develop a strategic market plan that will guide the development of a specific marketing mix strategy. The primary purpose of a strategic market plan is to give a business a *strategic direction*, with a set of performance objectives, and to guide the development of a marketing mix strategy.[9] To facilitate this process, a strategic market planning portfolio is used. The portfolio could be based on any of the models presented in Chapter 11.

FIGURE 14-8 BASING THE MARKETING STRATEGY ON THE SITUATION ANALYSIS

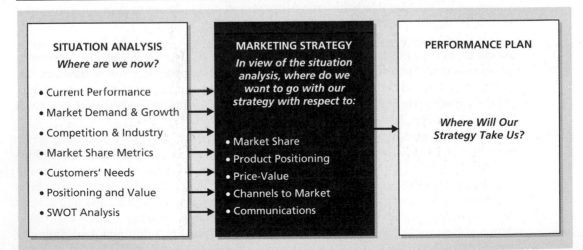

FIGURE 14-9 COMPONENTS OF A MARKETING STRATEGY

In most cases, the vertical axis of the portfolio represents the attractiveness of a market. Product life cycle position, market growth rate, market development opportunity, or an index of several forces is commonly used to represent market attractiveness. The horizontal axis is typically a measure or multi-factor index of the business's or product's competitive position. Market share, relative market share, market share index, customer value, or a multi-factor competitive position index is commonly used to represent competitive position.

Based on the product's or market's portfolio position and the influences uncovered in the situation analysis, a strategic market plan is specified for each product or market in the portfolio.[10] These strategic market plans provide the direction for achieving share objectives, future positioning, and investment, as illustrated under the box for "Strategic Market Plan" in Figure 14-9. Recall from earlier chapters that strategic market plans may be offensive or defensive. Examples of offensive strategic market plans are presented in Chapter 12. These include investment strategies to grow market share, improve competitive position, keep pace with fast-growing markets, and invest selectively in attractive customers within a market. A variety of defensive strategic market plans are presented in Chapter 13. These include hold strategies to protect an important strategic position, optimizing strategies, and harvest and divestment strategies.

For our Stericycle Sample Marketing Plan, the multi-factor GE/McKinsey Portfolio model is used, as presented on page 2.1 of Figure 14-10. The small-quantity segment is positioned in a highly attractive market, with a strong competitive position. Based on this portfolio position and the opportunities to grow share in this segment, an invest-to-grow-market-share strategy is recommended. This establishes the strategic direction for this segment's market plan.

The large-quantity segment is positioned in the portfolio as slightly below average in overall market attractiveness and slightly above average in competitive position. This market segment has profitable growth potential but, due to strong competitive forces in the segment, profits are a bit more difficult to obtain. A selective investment strategy is recommended. This strategy would invest in customers deemed to be good investments because of their high lifetime customer value. The strategic roadmap for this segment is different than for the small-quantity segment and will require a different marketing mix strategy to achieve the segment's performance objectives.

Market Share Objectives

For each strategic market plan, we need to have very specific market share objectives and share performance metrics for the planning horizon. We could simply state how share is expected to play out over the planning period, but a more comprehensive approach would be to specify objectives for share development during the plan's time horizon, along with the changes necessary in the share performance metrics to realize these objectives. In the Stericycle Sample Marketing Plan, we elected to use a separate page for share objectives.

On page 2.2 of Figure 14-10, we chose to treat both segments of Stericycle's market with one share development path. If market share and share forces of one segment were different from the other, we would be better served by including a separate set of share objectives and share metrics for each segment. In this case, the share objective is to grow Stericycle's market share in the overall market from 22.6 percent in 2006 to 24 percent by 2009. Also shown are the projected results of the share performance metrics for each year of the marketing plan. Performance gains in served market, awareness, and consideration each are critical to growing Stericycle's market share index from 22.7 percent in 2006 to 24.7 percent in 2009. While the projected improvement in the market share index may at first seem insignificant, it represents an increase of almost 9 percent. Collectively, the improvements in the three areas identified will have the potential to significantly impact Stericycle's share growth over the next 3 years. Without these improvements, it would be difficult to defend as realistic the share objectives as stated in the marketing plan.

Step 4: Marketing Mix Strategy

The next step in the marketing planning process is the development of a *marketing mix strategy* to put the strategic market plan into effect. Although an overall marketing strategy to protect, grow, reduce focus, harvest, enter, or exit a market position is set by the strategic market plan, more specific marketing mix strategies are needed for each of the key performance issues. Each element of a marketing mix strategy is a specific response to a key performance issue identified by the assessment of the current situation. The marketing mix strategies a business develops will be only as good as the key performance issues uncovered as an output of the situation analysis.

Figure 14-9 includes the major elements of a marketing mix strategy: a product positioning strategy, a pricing strategy, a channel strategy, and a communications strategy. Stated in another way, the marketing mix strategy covers the four Ps: "product (including service), pricing, place, and promotion." The rest of this section discusses them in the context of the Stericycle Sample Marketing Plan.

Product Positioning Strategy

The purpose of the positioning strategy page is to make explicit the current and proposed product positioning with respect to product, service, and brand benefits. What specifically is going to change with respect to benefits as a result of this marketing strategy? How are prices going to be managed given changes in delivered benefits? How are the non-price costs of purchase expected to change with the proposed positioning strategy? Finally, what will be the impact on customer value and how will these changes impact the proposed value proposition? All these considerations must be clearly addressed to achieve the desired impact with respect to product positioning.

In the Stericycle Sample Marketing Plan, we elected to create two separate positioning strategies since the product-price positioning in each of the company's two market segments is different due to different customer needs and competitive pressures. As shown on page 2.3, the positioning strategy for the small-quantity segment is to increase product and service benefits around safety, while modestly increasing prices. The goal of the strategy is to maintain a superior level of customer value while increasing prices and margins. Customer value is measured as the difference between overall benefits and overall cost of purchase. The value proposition for the small-quantity segment will be built around safety and reliability.

The positioning strategy recommended for the large-quantity segment appears on page 2.4. The sanitized return tubs will be improved with respect to both product and service benefits. The improvements will allow overall benefits to increase as shown, but prices and the total cost of purchase will remain at competitive levels. The net result will be an increase in customer value and a stronger value proposition. This improved value and the stronger value proposition should enhance Stericycle's efforts to selectively grow its customer base in the large-quantity segment. Chapter 4 explains how customer value is computed and how a superior value contributes to above-average profits.

Channel Strategy

A business's channel strategy is a roadmap the business follows in selling and delivering its products and services to target customers. For each channel that links the business with customers, the business benefits by knowing the average revenues, margins, and marketing and sales expenses. Managers can then compute the marketing ROI for each channel and take into account the profitability of their various channels when making distribution decisions. Channel mapping and channel strategies are presented in Chapter 9.

FIGURE 14-10 STERICYCLE SAMPLE PLAN: MARKETING STRATEGY

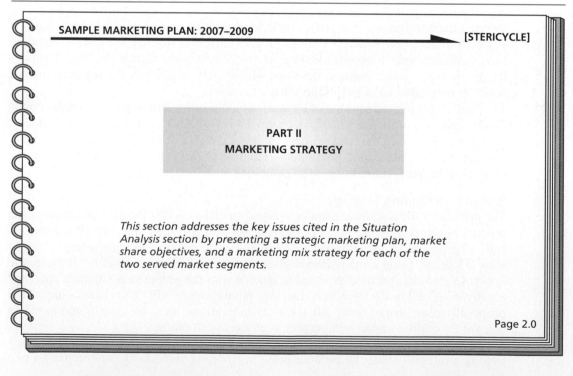

SAMPLE MARKETING PLAN: 2007–2009 [STERICYCLE]

PART II
MARKETING STRATEGY

This section addresses the key issues cited in the Situation Analysis section by presenting a strategic marketing plan, market share objectives, and a marketing mix strategy for each of the two served market segments.

Page 2.0

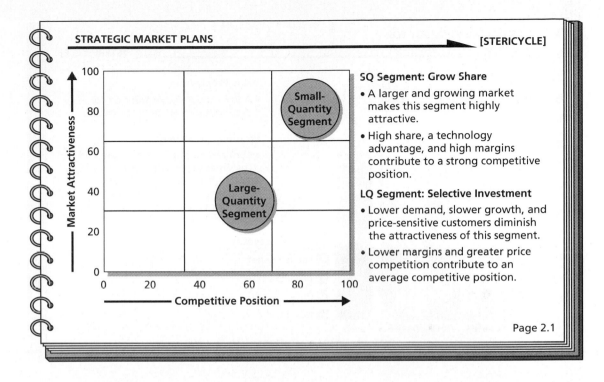

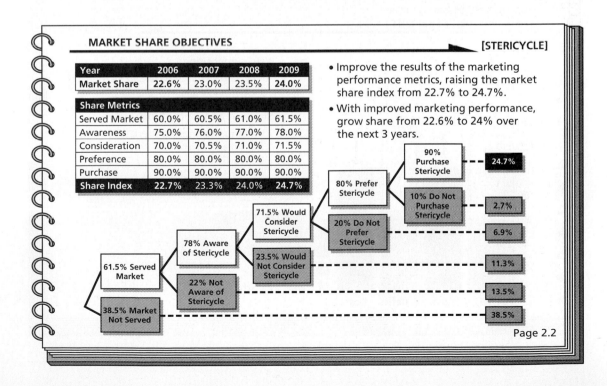

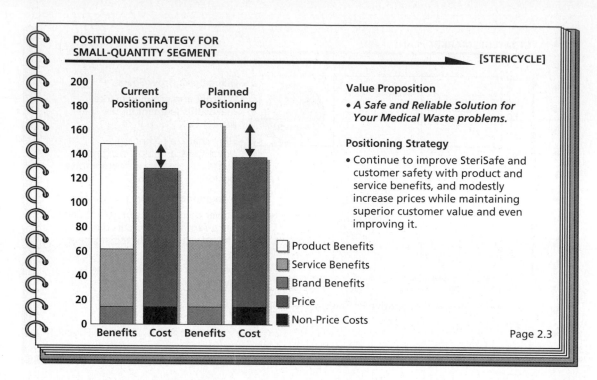

POSITIONING STRATEGY FOR SMALL-QUANTITY SEGMENT

[STERICYCLE]

Value Proposition

• *A Safe and Reliable Solution for Your Medical Waste problems.*

Positioning Strategy

• Continue to improve SteriSafe and customer safety with product and service benefits, and modestly increase prices while maintaining superior customer value and even improving it.

Legend: Product Benefits, Service Benefits, Brand Benefits, Price, Non-Price Costs

Page 2.3

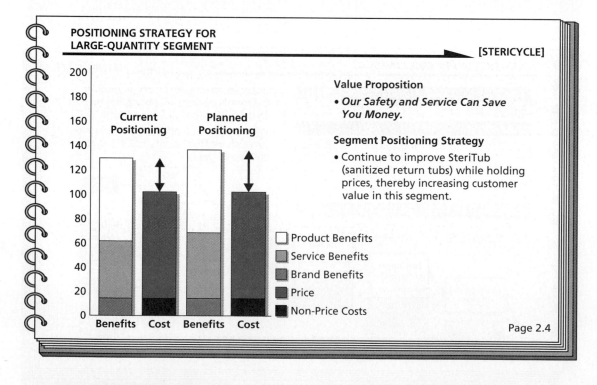

POSITIONING STRATEGY FOR LARGE-QUANTITY SEGMENT

[STERICYCLE]

Value Proposition

• *Our Safety and Service Can Save You Money.*

Segment Positioning Strategy

• Continue to improve SteriTub (sanitized return tubs) while holding prices, thereby increasing customer value in this segment.

Legend: Product Benefits, Service Benefits, Brand Benefits, Price, Non-Price Costs

Page 2.4

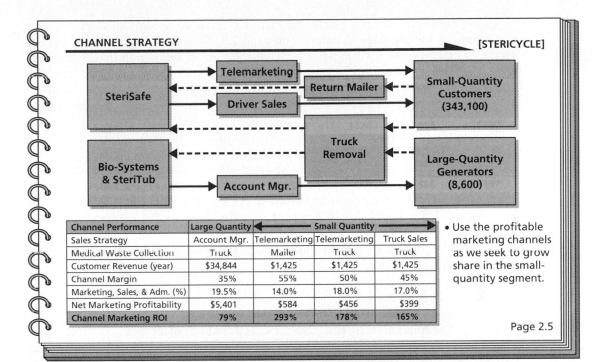

CHANNEL STRATEGY   [STERICYCLE]

Channel Performance	Large Quantity	Small Quantity		
Sales Strategy	Account Mgr.	Telemarketing	Telemarketing	Truck Sales
Medical Waste Collection	Truck	Mailer	Truck	Truck
Customer Revenue (year)	$34,844	$1,425	$1,425	$1,425
Channel Margin	35%	55%	50%	45%
Marketing, Sales, & Adm. (%)	19.5%	14.0%	18.0%	17.0%
Net Marketing Profitability	$5,401	$584	$456	$399
Channel Marketing ROI	79%	293%	178%	165%

• Use the profitable marketing channels as we seek to grow share in the small-quantity segment.

Page 2.5

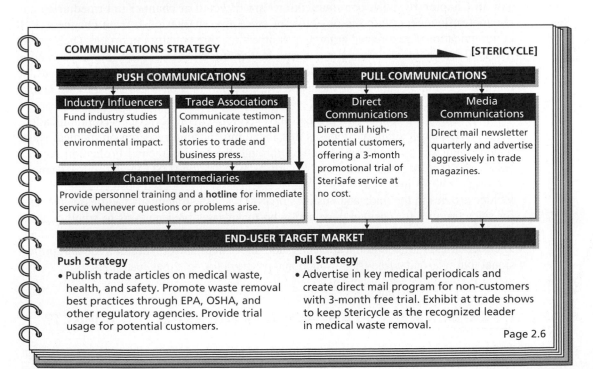

COMMUNICATIONS STRATEGY   [STERICYCLE]

PUSH COMMUNICATIONS

Industry Influencers
Fund industry studies on medical waste and environmental impact.

Trade Associations
Communicate testimonials and environmental stories to trade and business press.

Channel Intermediaries
Provide personnel training and a **hotline** for immediate service whenever questions or problems arise.

PULL COMMUNICATIONS

Direct Communications
Direct mail high-potential customers, offering a 3-month promotional trial of SteriSafe service at no cost.

Media Communications
Direct mail newsletter quarterly and advertise aggressively in trade magazines.

END-USER TARGET MARKET

Push Strategy
• Publish trade articles on medical waste, health, and safety. Promote waste removal best practices through EPA, OSHA, and other regulatory agencies. Provide trial usage for potential customers.

Pull Strategy
• Advertise in key medical periodicals and create direct mail program for non-customers with 3-month free trial. Exhibit at trade shows to keep Stericycle as the recognized leader in medical waste removal.

Page 2.6

In the Stericycle Sample Marketing Plan, we chose to present channel maps for both segments on one page. As shown on page 2.5, SteriSafe is the primary service offered to small-quantity customers, with the sales effort relying on driver presentations. The collection of medical waste from the 343,100 customers in this segment is by truck pickup and waste-return mailers. In some geographical markets, the trucks move waste to transfer centers that in turn move it to Stericycle waste treatment sites. All three marketing channels offer very good marketing ROIs. The channel that uses a combination of telemarketing for sales and return mailers for removal has the highest marketing ROI (293%).

Sales in the large-quantity generator segment are the function of customer account managers. The process promotes good service, problem solving, and the discovery of opportunities to improve products and services. All removal is by truck. While revenue per customer in this segment is high, percent margins are lower and percent marketing and sales expenses higher. The net result is a lower channel marketing ROI (79%) but a very high marketing profit per customer due to the large quantity of medical waste removed from most customer sites.

Communications Strategy

The marketing mix strategy section of a marketing plan should also include a page on "Marketing Communications." This page presents a concise but all-inclusive presentation of the kinds of communications needed to impact customer awareness, consideration, trial, and preference. The material includes both push and pull communications. As we saw in Chapter 10, push communications are directed at channel intermediaries and channel influencers, with the objective of creating a market push from channels. Pull communications are directed at target customers and are equally important. Their objective is to create interest among customers, motivating them to acquire more information or to evaluate products. The page does not include the cost and other details about the marketing communications, as these specifics are part of a business's marketing budget and media plan.

Page 2.6 of the sample plan presents the overall intent of Stericycle's communications strategy. The push strategy proposes that the company fund research on medical waste management and promote best practices through the Environmental Protection Agency (EPA), the Occupational Safety and Health Administration (OSHA), and other agencies and organizations involved in waste management issues. Proposed push communications include articles in the trade and business press. The push strategy also addresses the need for sales training for channel personnel who make sales presentations to small-quantity customers, and it calls for improved two-way communications between the business and intermediaries. Pull communications include direct mail, advertising in trade and professional journals, and a free-trial promotional program for potential customers.

PART III: PERFORMANCE PLAN—WHAT IS THE EXPECTED IMPACT?

The market plan's section on marketing mix strategy leads us to the performance plan, covered in the third and last section of a marketing plan. Earlier, in the plan's first section, the situation analysis helped us understand where the business is now and to identify the

FIGURE 14-11 DEVELOPING A PERFORMANCE PLAN

key issues that were then addressed in the marketing strategy. The marketing strategy in turn will give the business an overall strategic direction. It serves as a general guideline in developing the marketing mix strategy for carrying out the marketing strategy. As shown in Figure 14-11, each element of the marketing strategy, including the tactical marketing mix components, will impact the performance plan, as will certain elements of the situation analysis. For example, let's assume that in the situation analysis section the market was projected to grow at 8 percent annually. With an objective of growing share from 22.6 percent to 24 percent, we know sales projections will also need to be increased. Similarly, if we had found that the overall market was going to grow at 10 percent annually, this also would affect sales projections and the marketing budget needed to keep pace with faster-than-expected sales growth.

Recognizing the effects that the marketing strategy and situation analysis have on it, the purpose of the performance plan is to address each of the areas of performance shown in Figure 14-12. We will discuss each of these areas, using the performance plan in the Stericycle Sample Marketing Plan for illustration. Figure 14-14 presents the sample plan pages for these aspects of the performance plan.

Step 5: Develop a Revenue Plan and Marketing Budget

Revenue Plan

In developing a performance plan, a business first translates the objectives of the market share strategy into a *revenue plan*. One important part of a revenue plan is information on the market demand page in the situation analysis section (page 1.2). Based on current demand and estimated market growth rates, the page offers an estimate for future demand. Sales are a function of this demand and the market share objectives.

FIGURE 14-12 COMPONENTS OF A PERFORMANCE PLAN

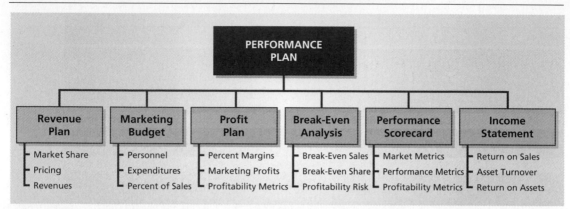

For example, in the Stericycle Sample Marketing Plan, market demand is projected to grow from $3.5 billion in 2006 to $4.2 billion in 2009. With Stericycle's objective to grow market share from 22.6 percent in 2006 to 24 percent in 2009, sales revenues should grow from $790 million in 2006 to slightly over $1 billion in 2009. This information appears on page 3.1 of the performance plan in Figure 14-14. Also presented is a revenue plan for each market segment. Separate plans are needed because each segment has different pricing, percent margins, and marketing and sales expenses, and subsequently each has different levels of marketing profitability and different marketing ROIs.

Marketing Budget

Market share gains are not free. Even a strategy to hold market share in a growing market needs an increased marketing budget. A business needs to allocate resources in the form of a *marketing budget* based on the strategic market plan and the marketing mix strategy. Without adequate resources the marketing mix strategies cannot succeed, and performance objectives will not be achieved.

Determining the marketing budget is one of the more difficult parts of the marketing planning process. Specifying the budget does not need to be a precise process, but allocations must represent a logical connection with the strategy and performance objectives. Businesses use one of three ways to build a marketing budget that is based on a specific strategic market plan and the marketing mix strategy designed to achieve the target level of performance. Stericycle, for example, could elect to use any of the three kinds of budgets described in the following paragraphs.

Percent-of-Sales Marketing Budget.   For a percent-of-sales marketing budget, the percent of sales used is often based on previous experience but could vary from past experience, depending on the nature of the strategic market plan that will be implemented. An aggressive growth strategy might require more than the normal percent of sales to achieve share and sales objectives. On the other hand, a harvest strategy may slowly reduce marketing and sales expenses as a percent of sales while market share is being harvested over time.

A typical hold strategy may keep marketing and sales expenses as a percent of sales at the same level. But the marketing budget's dollar amount will still change as a constant percent of increasing sales. The Stericycle Sample Marketing Plan uses the percent-of-sales budget methodology. As illustrated on page 3.2 of the plan, the marketing budget as a percent of sales will increase from $137 million in 2006 (17.3 percent of sales) to $178 million in 2009 (17.6 percent of sales). The figures for percent of sales modestly increase each year because the strategy calls for growing share in a growing market.

Customer-Mix Marketing Budget.   For a customer-mix marketing budget, the cost of customer acquisition and retention and the combination of new and retained customers are used to establish the budget. Because the rate of new-customer acquisition can change the marketing budget required, the customer-mix approach to funding the marketing budget is seen by many market-based businesses as the best approach to take.

Assuming the acquisition cost per customer is about five times the retention cost per customer, and assuming the acquisition cost of a new customer is $1,000 and the cost to retain an existing customer is $175, we can determine the marketing budget for 2006 as follows:

$$
\begin{array}{c}
\textbf{Marketing} \\ \textbf{Budget} \\ \textbf{(2006)}
\end{array}
=
\begin{array}{c}
\text{Marketing} \\ \text{Administration} + \\ \text{Cost}
\end{array}
\begin{array}{c}
\text{Acquisition} \\ \text{Cost} \quad \times \\ \text{per Customer}
\end{array}
\begin{array}{c}
\text{Number} \\ \text{of New} + \\ \text{Customers}
\end{array}
\begin{array}{c}
\text{Retention} \\ \text{Cost} \quad \times \\ \text{per Customer}
\end{array}
\begin{array}{c}
\text{Number of} \\ \text{Retained} \\ \text{Customers}
\end{array}
$$

$$= \$18 \text{ million} + \$1,000 \times 70,480 + \$175 \times 281,920$$

$$= \$18 \text{ million} + \$70.5 \text{ million} + \$49.3 \text{ million}$$

$$= \textbf{\$137.8 million}$$

In this example, we estimated the fixed marketing administrative expense at $18 million. The estimate is for illustration purposes only and should not be interpreted as Stericycle's actual administrative expense. We also assumed Stericycle had a 90 percent customer retention rate and was growing its overall customer base at 10 percent annually. In 2006, this would mean attracting 70,480 new customers at the per-customer acquisition cost of $1,000. The 90 percent of customers who were retained (281,920) cost $235 per customer. As shown, the acquisition cost is much higher than the retention cost. As Stericycle approaches its achievable market share, the total cost of acquisition will go down because more customers will be retained and the pool of prospective customers will be smaller. The challenge in this approach to estimating marketing expenses is determining how much of the nonmarketing administrative expenses should be designated for customer acquisition and how much for customer retention.

Bottom-Up Marketing Budget.   A bottom-up approach to developing a marketing budget requires specifying each marketing task and the amount needed to accomplish it, given a particular strategic market plan and marketing mix strategy. For example, Figure 14-13 is a hypothetical representation of the marketing budget needed for Stericycle to produce sales of $790 million in 2006. The sample budget is for the purpose of illustration only. The figures for the various allocations are the author's, based on estimates of the amounts a business of this type would spend on the different aspects of its marketing and sales effort.

In using a bottom-up approach to developing a marketing budget, it is helpful to classify expenses as personnel and non-personnel. For marketing management, personnel costs include all salaries and benefits. Non-personnel expenses typically include travel and living expenses, as well as commissioned studies and consultants' fees. Overall, personnel expenses make up 53.7 percent of the marketing and sales budget needed to produce sales of $790 million in 2006. This is 9.4 percent of sales.

FIGURE 14-13 SAMPLE BOTTOM-UP MARKETING BUDGET

Marketing Budget Expense	Personnel	Non-Personnel	Total
Marketing Management	$5,000,000	$1,000,000	$6,000,000
Marketing Administration	$5,000,000		$5,000,000
Sales Management	$5,000,000	$2,000,000	$7,000,000
Planning & Market Development	$2,000,000	$1,000,000	$3,000,000
Account Managers	$8,000,000	$2,000,000	$10,000,000
Telemarketing	$35,000,000		$35,000,000
Technical Support	$7,000,000	$2,000,000	$9,000,000
Customer Safety Training	$5,000,000	$2,000,000	$7,000,000
Sales Training	$1,000,000		$1,000,000
Marketing Communications	$1,000,000	$5,000,000	$6,000,000
Sales Literature		$10,000,000	$10,000,000
Safety Manuals		$5,000,000	$5,000,000
Sales Promotions		$5,000,000	$5,000,000
Trade Shows		$1,000,000	$1,000,000
Advertising		$25,000,000	$25,000,000
Other Miscellaneous		$2,700,000	$2,700,000
Total Marketing Budget	**$74,000,000**	**$63,700,000**	**$137,700,000**
Percent of Total	**53.7%**	**46.3%**	**100.0%**
Percent of Sales	**9.4%**	**8.1%**	**17.4%**

In the sample budget, the non-personnel marketing budget expenses were 46.3 percent of the overall marketing budget of $137 million in 2006, or 8.1 percent of sales. Using this information, a business could extend the analysis by specifying for each cost item the percent of sales spent on acquiring customers, retaining customers, and marketing overhead. Knowing the cost of acquiring a customer and the cost of retaining one could lead a business to adopt the customer-mix approach to developing a marketing budget, an approach that would allow for more effective adjustments in marketing expenses as the business approaches its market share potential. At full market share penetration, the marketing budget may be reduced because the effort to acquire new customers would be mostly limited to replacing lost customers for the purpose of holding market share at full share potential.

Step 6: Develop a Profit Plan

In the profit plan, all elements of a marketing plan merge into a forecast of percent margins and marketing profitability. Sales revenues are brought forward from the revenue plan, and the budget allocations needed to support these sales forecasts are also brought into the profit plan. When combined, as shown on page 3.3 of the sample plan, we can estimate the net marketing contribution for each year of the planning horizon. In this case, the marketing profits are projected to grow from $213 million in 2006 to almost $300 million at the end of 2009. Both marketing ROS and marketing ROI are also projected to improve over the 3-year plan.

Because market segment profitability has such a major role in the overall profit plan, we created separate profit plans for the two market segments. As shown on page 3.3, the small-quantity segment is the more critical to the overall profit plan. It is this segment

FIGURE 14-14 STERICYCLE SAMPLE MARKETING PLAN: PERFORMANCE PLAN

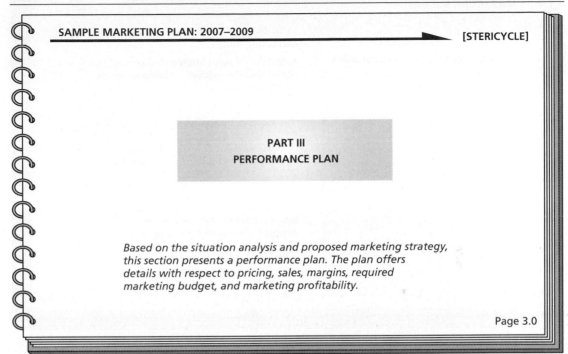

SAMPLE MARKETING PLAN: 2007–2009 ▸ [STERICYCLE]

PART III
PERFORMANCE PLAN

Based on the situation analysis and proposed marketing strategy, this section presents a performance plan. The plan offers details with respect to pricing, sales, margins, required marketing budget, and marketing profitability.

Page 3.0

REVENUE PLAN ▸ [STERICYCLE]

Stericycle Inc.

• Annual sales revenues continue to grow and are projected to increase from $790 million in 2006 to over $1 billion in 2009.

Stericycle Inc.	2006	2007	2008	2009
Market Demand	$3,500	$3,720	$3,956	$4,209
Market Share	22.6%	23.0%	23.4%	24.0%
Sales Revenues	$790	$855	$927	$1,009

Small-Quantity Segment

• This is the larger segment and is growing at 9% to 10% annually. Sales revenues are projected to increase from $490 million in 2006 to $681 million in 2009.

Small-Quantity Seg.	2006	2007	2008	2009
Market Demand	$2,300	$2,484	$2,683	$2,897
Market Share	21.3%	22.0%	22.7%	23.5%
Sales Revenues	$490	$546	$609	$681
Revenue/Customer	$1,425	$1,450	$1,475	$1,500
Customers (000)	343.8	376.9	412.9	453.9

Large-Quantity Segment

• This segment is growing but at a slower rate (3% to 4%). Sales revenues are projected to increase from $300 million in 2006 to $328 million in 2009.

Large-Quantity Seg.	2006	2007	2008	2009
Market Demand	$1,200	$1,236	$1,273	$1,311
Market Share	25.0%	25.0%	25.0%	25.0%
Sales Revenues	$300	$309	$318	$328
Reveune/Customer	$34,844	$34,719	$34,945	$34,894
Customers (000)	8.6	8.9	9.1	9.4

Page 3.1

MARKETING BUDGET

[STERICYCLE]

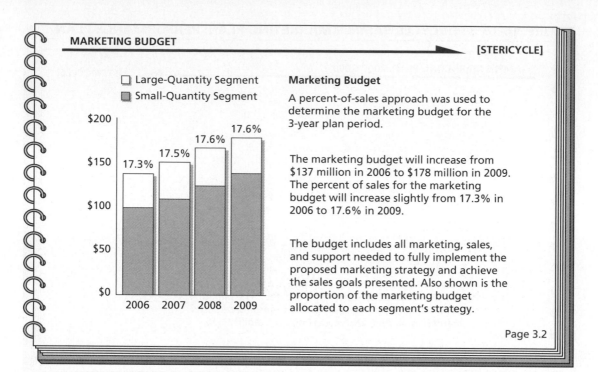

☐ Large-Quantity Segment
■ Small-Quantity Segment

Marketing Budget

A percent-of-sales approach was used to determine the marketing budget for the 3-year plan period.

The marketing budget will increase from $137 million in 2006 to $178 million in 2009. The percent of sales for the marketing budget will increase slightly from 17.3% in 2006 to 17.6% in 2009.

The budget includes all marketing, sales, and support needed to fully implement the proposed marketing strategy and achieve the sales goals presented. Also shown is the proportion of the marketing budget allocated to each segment's strategy.

Page 3.2

PROFIT PLAN

[STERICYCLE]

Overall marketing profits are expected to grow from $213 million to $300 million.

While each segment has different profitability characteristics, overall the marketing investment will increase the marketing ROI from 156% in 2006 to 169% in 2009.

Small-Quantity Seg.	2006	2007	2008	2009
Sales Revenues	$490	$546	$609	$681
Percent Margin	54.9%	55.8%	56.5%	57.3%
Gross Profit	$269	$305	$344	$390
Mktg., Sales, & Adm. (%)	20%	20%	20%	20%
Mktg., Sales, & Adm. ($)	$98	$109	$122	$136
Net Marketing Cont.	$171	$196	$222	$254
Marketing ROS	34.9%	35.9%	36.5%	37.3%
Marketing ROI	175%	180%	182%	187%

Stericycle Inc.	2006	2007	2008	2009
Sales Revenues	$790	$855	$927	$1,009
Percent Margin	44.3%	45.4%	46.4%	47.4%
Gross Profit	$350	$388	$430	$478
Mktg., Sales, & Adm. (%)	17.4%	17.5%	17.6%	17.6%
Mktg., Sales, & Adm. ($)	$137	$149	$163	$178
Net Marketing Cont.	$213	$239	$267	$300
Marketing ROS	27.0%	28.0%	28.8%	29.7%
Marketing ROI	155%	160%	164%	169%

Large-Quantity Seg.	2006	2007	2008	2009
Sales Revenues	$300	$309	$318	$328
Percent Margin	27.0%	27.0%	27.0%	27.0%
Gross Profit	$81	$83	$86	$89
Mktg., Sales, & Adm. (%)	13%	13%	13%	13%
Mktg., Sales, & Adm. ($)	$39	$40	$41	$43
Net Marketing Cont.	$42	$43	$45	$46
Marketing ROS	14.0%	13.9%	14.2%	14.0%
Marketing ROI	108%	108%	110%	107%

Page 3.3

BREAK-EVEN ANALYSIS   [STERICYCLE]

2009 Break-Even Market Share
- The graph illustrates the break-even market share will occur at 9% market share in 2009. The break-even market share in 2006 was 8.8%.

Share-Risk Premium
- The share-risk premium in 2006 was 13.7% (market share minus break-even share). In 2009, the share-risk premium is projected to be 15%.

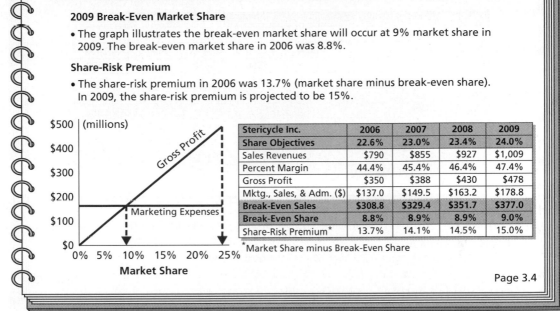

Stericycle Inc.	2006	2007	2008	2009
Share Objectives	22.6%	23.0%	23.4%	24.0%
Sales Revenues	$790	$855	$927	$1,009
Percent Margin	44.4%	45.4%	46.4%	47.4%
Gross Profit	$350	$388	$430	$478
Mktg., Sales, & Adm. ($)	$137.0	$149.5	$163.2	$178.8
Break-Even Sales	$308.8	$329.4	$351.7	$377.0
Break-Even Share	8.8%	8.9%	8.9%	9.0%
Share-Risk Premium*	13.7%	14.1%	14.5%	15.0%

*Market Share minus Break-Even Share

Page 3.4

PERFORMANCE SCORECARD   [STERICYCLE]

Many of the performance scorecard metrics are *process* metrics that are leading indicators of *result* financial metrics.

The share performance metrics are good indicators of how share will change. If we are unable to hit these performance targets, it is unlikely we will achieve our target share.

Margin and marketing ROI metrics are also important to ensure we are on track to obtain target profits.

Performance Metrics	2006	2007	2008	2009
Market Share	22.6%	23.0%	23.4%	24.0%
Market Share Index	22.7	23.3	24.0	24.7
Market Served	60.0%	60.5%	61.0%	61.5%
Awareness	75.0%	76.0%	77.0%	78.0%
Considerartion	70.0%	70.5%	71.0%	71.5%
Preference	80.0%	80.0%	80.0%	80.0%
Purchase	90.0%	90.0%	90.0%	90.0%
Sales Growth Rate	29.7%	8.3%	8.4%	8.8%
Percent Margin	44.3%	45.4%	46.4%	47.4%
Mktg., Sales, & Adm. (%)	17.3%	17.5%	17.6%	17.7%
Marketing ROS	26.9%	27.9%	28.8%	29.7%
Marketing ROI	156%	160%	164%	168%

Page 3.5

INCOME STATEMENT   [STERICYCLE]

Stericycle Inc.	2005	2006	2007	2008	2009
Sales Revenues	$609	$790	$855	$927	$1,009
Percent Margin	44.0%	44.3%	45.4%	46.4%	47.4%
Gross Profit	$268	$350	$388	$430	$478
Mktg., Sales, & Adm. ($)	$93	$137	$149	$163	$178
Net Marketing Contribution	$175	$213	$239	$267	$300
Marketing ROS	28.7%	27.0%	28.0%	28.8%	29.7%
Other Expenses (1.4%)	$8.5	$10.8	$12.0	$13.0	$14.1
Operating Income	$166.5	$201.7	$226.8	$254.0	$285.4
Pre-Tax Return on Sales	27.3%	25.5%	26.5%	27.4%	28.3%
Pre-Tax Return on Assets	15.9%	15.2%	15.9%	16.4%	17.0%
Sales-to-Asset Ratio	0.58	0.59	0.60	0.60	0.60

Pre-Tax Income
• Projected to grow from $201.7 million (25.5% of Sales) to $285.4 million (28.3% of sales).

Pre-Tax Return on Assets
• Projected to grow from 15.2% to 17% over the next 3 years.

Page 3.6

that will produce the greater part of the profitable growth. The large-quantity segment, while profitable, is affected by market conditions that make profitable growth more difficult. But both segments are important in achieving the planned overall performance and must be managed to achieve their respective performance objectives.

Break-Even Analysis

Understanding the concept of break-even sales helps us evaluate the effort needed to recover a business's investment in a marketing budget. In 2006, Stericycle invested $137.7 million in marketing and sales. Break-even sales in 2006 were $309 million, as shown on page 3.4. Once a business goes beyond the break-even level of sales, it starts making a profit.

However, as we saw in Chapter 8, a more desirable measure is break-even market share, because it provides a better framework for judging profit potential and risk. Recognizing that market share can only vary between zero and 100 percent, the question is: How much market share is needed to break even? For Stericycle, break-even market share was 8.8 percent in 2006. By 2009, the break-even share will grow slightly to 9 percent, but actual market share is projected to grow from 22.6 percent in 2006 to 24 percent in 2009. In implementing a strategy to grow share, we know from Chapter 8 that a business with an actual market share close to break-even market share faces a greater risk of loss than a business with a large difference between the actual and break-even market share. For Stericycle, the share-risk premium improves from 13.7 percent in 2006 to 15 percent in 2009.

Performance Scorecard

A performance scorecard typically gives us the results of important market metrics, customer metrics, and profitability metrics. These performance measurements help us understand the reasons behind a business's performance with regard to sales, margins, marketing and sales expenses, and marketing profits. Many of the marketing performance metrics included in a performance scorecard are the process and result metrics discussed in Chapter 2. Measures of customer satisfaction, customer retention, customer loyalty, and the net promoter index allow us to track performance over time. If these performance metrics are not meeting their performance benchmarks, then it is less likely the business will achieve its objectives.

In the Stericycle Sample Marketing Plan, page 3.5 presents a set of market, customer, and profitability metrics. With more information with respect to customer metrics, this performance scorecard could be expanded considerably. If Stericycle were to develop separate marketing plans for each segment, then each segment would have its own performance scorecard.

Income Statement

While not a necessity for a performance plan, this section of a business's marketing plan could include an income statement. Preparing the statement requires a good knowledge of the nonmarketing overhead expenses and some method of projecting the changes the expenses will undergo with changes in sales. Using a percent-of-sales approach can be a safe way to estimate these expenses. On the income statement in the Stericycle Sample Marketing Plan, the overhead expenses, or "other expenses," are 1.4 percent of sales, as shown on page 3.6. The income statement uses this same percentage to estimate the overhead expenses for future years. We can then estimate the pre-tax income and pre-tax return on sales. As shown in the sample plan, pre-tax return on sales is projected to increase from 25.5 percent in 2006 to 28.3 percent in 2009.

The income statement in the sample plan also has the sales-to-asset ratio for 2005, which was 0.58. For every $1,000 of sales, the business has $580 in assets. The sample plan projects this ratio to improve modestly to 0.60.

Multiplying the pre-tax return on sales by the sales-to-asset ratio gives us the pre-tax return of assets.

$$\textbf{Pre-Tax ROA (2006)} = \text{Pre-Tax ROS} \times \text{Sales-to-Asset Ratio}$$
$$= 27.3\% \times 0.58$$
$$= \textbf{15.9\%}$$

Using this methodology, we can project the pre-tax return on assets for each year of the marketing plan. The income statement in the sample plan estimates that the pre-tax return on assets will grow to 17 percent by the end of 2009.

Step 7: Performance Review

Step 7, the *performance review*, involves the ongoing monitoring of marketing and profit performance in light of the marketing plan's timeline. If the business fails to meet the desired performance objectives stated in the strategic marketing plan, then the marketing plan must be reevaluated with respect to all inputs used in the marketing planning process, as shown in Figure 14-3. These performance gaps require the business to consider several options. One is to reexamine its pricing, customer and channel discounts, unit costs, and the marketing budget to determine if, in fact, there are opportunities to improve performance.

A second alternative is to reexamine the entire marketing plan. The situation analysis and the key performance issues would be reviewed to see if other tactical marketing mix strategies would more effectively achieve the desired performance objectives. Whichever the case, a credible marketing mix strategy must be linked to the market situation, key performance issues, and available resources, and then linked to the projections of external marketing metrics and internal profit metrics.

The Stericycle Sample Marketing Plan represents a map for strategically navigating the business toward greater profitability over a 3-year period. As shown in Figure 14-3, after the marketing plan is implemented, performance gaps are likely to emerge because of changing market conditions and the effectiveness of the proposed marketing tactics. Addressing these performance gaps as they occur is a critical part of the marketing planning process. Modifying, adapting, or even abandoning a strategy is part of the process of building and implementing a marketing plan. We will learn more about successfully implementing a marketing plan in the next chapter.

■ Summary

A marketing plan serves as a roadmap. It carefully outlines where a business is currently, the desired destination (objectives), and the conditions the business will face on the way to its destination. Assessing the market situation reveals a set of key issues that will need to be addressed in order to reach the destination. A situation analysis and an identification of key performance issues are the major inputs to any marketing plan and essential for accomplishing the business's performance objectives.

The strategies presented in a marketing plan will not succeed just because they have been laid out. Resources in the form of people and money need to be allocated to implement the strategies. If adequate resources are not available, attainment of a business's objectives may not be possible, and marketing strategies will have to be revised or abandoned.

The benefits of a good marketing plan are many. The planning process leads a business to discover new market opportunities, to make better use of assets and capabilities, to clearly define its market focus, to improve marketing productivity, and to establish an effective process for evaluating progress toward goals. There is a planning paradox, however. It goes without saying that businesses with no marketing plans severely restrict themselves, but it is also true that those with highly formalized marketing plans are not in a much better position. The business with no marketing plan will not see the market around it, and it will therefore be largely unaware of the opportunities and threats that need to be addressed while pursuing its objectives. But businesses that develop highly formalized plans can in the process regress to merely filling out forms and miss the subtler aspects of the market that a structured approach balanced with creativity would reveal.

Developing a marketing plan involves both structure and creativity. The process begins with a broad view of market opportunities, a view that encourages consideration of all market opportunities. For each market opportunity, a strategic market objective is set, based on market attractiveness and competitive position attained or attainable in the market. For each market the business pursues, a separate situation analysis and marketing plan are required. The situation analysis enables the business to uncover factors that may limit performance. These key performance issues are the basic materials from which marketing strategies are built. Each aspect of the strategy must be scrutinized with respect to the market situation, key issues, and the resources needed to achieve specific performance objectives. With the marketing strategy and budget set, an estimate of marketing and financial performance metrics must be projected over a specified time frame. If the marketing plan fails to produce desired levels of performance, the marketing strategy needs to be reexamined.

■ Market-Based Strategic Thinking

1 How would the process of developing a marketing plan help Stericycle achieve a higher level of sales growth and profitability?

2 Why would a business with a strong market orientation do a better job of preparing a situation analysis than a business with a poor market orientation?

3 How could businesses engaged in no marketing planning or in highly formalized marketing planning both miss meaningful market insights?

4 How would a business with a sound marketing planning process differ from a business with no marketing plan in the following?

Discovering opportunities

Leveraging existing systems, assets, and core capabilities

Implementing a market-focused strategy

Allocating resources

Planning performance

5 Why does the first step in the marketing planning process involve a situation analysis?

6 What is the role of a SWOT analysis in the marketing planning process? What is the role of key issues in the SWOT analysis?

7 For each product-market opportunity, how is a strategic marketing plan determined?

8 How does the strategic marketing plan for a given product-market influence the marketing mix strategy for that product-market?

9 How are key performance issues identified in the SWOT analysis used in selecting a strategic marketing plan and building a marketing mix strategy?

10 Why is the development of a marketing budget so important to the success of the marketing plan?

11 What are the various ways one could develop a marketing budget for a given strategic marketing plan and the supporting marketing mix strategy?

12 How should the resources needed to support a marketing plan be logically linked to the key issues, marketing strategies, and expected performance?

13 What is the purpose of the performance plan? What role should it play in the successful implementation of a marketing plan?

Marketing Performance Tools

The three **Marketing Performance Tools** described here may be accessed online at *www. rogerjbest.com*. These applied-learning exercises will add to your understanding of effective marketing planning and its positive impact on profits.

14.1 Small-Quantity Customer Segment
- Evaluate how segment profits and overall company profits would change if the market growth rate were 10 percent instead of 8 percent.
- Estimate the same profit impact if the market growth rate were 6 percent.

14.2 Large-Quantity Generator Segment
- Evaluate how segment profits and overall company profits would change if the market growth rate were 5 percent instead of 3 percent.
- Estimate the same profit impact if the market growth rate were 1 percent.

14.3 Market Share Strategies
- What would be the profit impact on each of Stericycle's two market segments of a strategy to grow market share in each segment to 26 percent?
- What would be the impact on the company's overall profits?

Notes

1. Stericycle Inc., *2006 Annual Report*, Selected Consolidated Financial Data: 20.
2. David Aaker, "Formal Planning System," *Strategic Market Management* (New York: Wiley, 1995): 341–353.
3. Arie Rijvnis and Graham Sharman, "New Life for Formal Planning Systems," *Journal of Business Strategy* (Spring 1982): 103.
4. Henry Mintzberg, "The Fall and Rise of Strategic Planning," *Harvard Business Review* (January–February 1994): 107–114; and Benjamin Tregoe and Peter Tobia, "Strategy Versus Planning: Bridging the Gap," *Journal of Business Strategy* (December 1991): 14–19.
5. Thomas Powell, "Strategic Planning as Competitive Advantage," *Strategic Management Journal* 13 (1992): 551–558; Scott Armstrong, "The Value of Formal Planning for Strategic Decisions: Reply," *Strategic Management Journal* 7 (1986): 183–185; and Deepak Sinha, "The Contribution of Formal Planning to Decisions," *Strategic Management Journal* (October 1990): 479–492.
6. Philip Kotler, *Marketing Management: Analysis, Planning, Implementation and Control*, 7th ed. (Upper Saddle River, NJ: Prentice Hall, 1991): 62–72.
7. W. Chan Kim and Renee Mauborgne, *Blue Ocean Strategy: How to Compete in Uncontested Market Space and Make Competition Irrelevant*, (Boston: Harvard Business School Press, 2005).
8. David Aaker, "Think Big," *The Wall Street Journal* (September 15–16, 2007): R10.
9. Gary Hamel and C. K. Prahalad, "Strategic Intent," *Harvard Business Review* (May–June 1989): 63–75; and Michael Treacy and Frederic Wiersema, "Customer Intimacy and Other Value Disciplines," *Harvard Business Review* (January–February 1993): 84–93.
10. Rajan Varadarajan, "Product Portfolio Analysis and Market Share Objectives: An Exposition of Certain Underlying Assumptions," *Journal of the Academy of Marketing Science* (Winter 1990): 17–29.

CHAPTER 15

Performance Metrics and Strategy Implementation

■ If you can't measure it, you can't manage it.
—*from* The Balanced Scorecard *by*
  Robert Kaplan and David Norton
  Harvard Business School Press, 1996

Businesses are obsessed with **financial results** because they tell *what has happened*. But rarely do businesses fully understand the reasons behind their financial results. **Marketing performance metrics** measure the factors that are *actually driving profits* in the market.

In Chapter 2, we saw that several marketing performance metrics lead financial performance. A business, for example, sees that its sales and profits are staying steady, but it also sees that its net promoter and customer satisfaction indexes are falling. The declines signal a problem that if not addressed will show up

FIGURE 15-1 MARKETING PERFORMANCE SCORECARD

THE EFFECTS
Financial Results
• Financial Metrics
• Profitability Metrics
• Productivity Metrics
• Cost Metrics

↑

THE CAUSES
Marketing Performance
• Market Metrics
• Customer Metrics
• Competitiveness Metrics
• Marketing Profitability Metrics

MARKETING PERFORMANCE SCORECARD						
Performance Metrics		Performance Impact*				
Market Metrics	Index	1	2	3	4	5
Product Life Cycle	80				4	
Industry Attractiveness	25			3		
Relative Market Share	40			3		
Customer Metrics						
Customer Satisfaction	60	1				
Customer Retention	67		2			
Net Promoter Index	10		2			
Competitiveness Metrics						
Relative Performance	110			3		
Cost of Purchase	120	1				
Customer Value	−10		2			
Marketing Profitability Metrics						
Percent Gross Margin	25%			3		
Marketing ROS	12%		2			
Marketing ROI	105%		2			

*Performance impact varies from 1 (very poor) to 5 (outstanding).

FIGURE 15-2 MARKETING PERFORMANCE METRICS

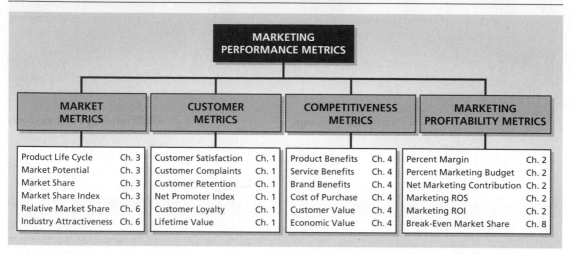

sometime in the future with fewer new customers coming on board and many existing ones leaving for more preferred alternatives.

Figure 15-1 presents a *marketing performance scorecard* that includes four categories of marketing performance metrics. We know from earlier chapters that *market metrics*, listed as the first category, measure market conditions and a business's performance in that market, with the measurements expressed as indexes or scores. A high index or score in one market, however, may be a poor one in another. Because the standards for the different levels of performance vary across industries, a business normally sets its own performance benchmark for each market metric.

The three other categories of marketing performance metrics are *customer metrics*, *competitiveness metrics,* and *marketing profitability metrics*. The metrics listed under each category in the scorecard are only a few of the marketing performance metrics discussed in earlier chapters. These and most other performance metrics covered in this edition of *Market-Based Management* are also listed in Figure 15-2, with a reference to the chapter

that covers each metric. Other metrics we discussed that are not listed include the percent awareness metric and the preference metric, both important customer metrics. Another metric not listed, but one that is also important in many markets, is the relative price metric, which is a business's price for its product relative to the average price charged by competitors. In many markets, the relative price metric is a key measurement, one that can be correlated with profitability.

Chapter 2 opened with comments on the importance of supporting marketing strategies with credible performance metrics. The accompanying Figure 2.1 reported on a survey of CEOs in which 51 percent said a lack of credible performance metrics was their biggest concern with regard to marketing effectiveness.[1] The marketing performance scorecard in Figure 15-1 helps address this concern by communicating marketing's contribution to a business's performance and profitability. In the sections that follow, we will review the role that marketing performance metrics have in tracking performance and how marketing strategies contribute to a business's overall financial performance.

FIGURE 15-3 MARKETING PERFORMANCE METRICS AND SHAREHOLDER VALUE

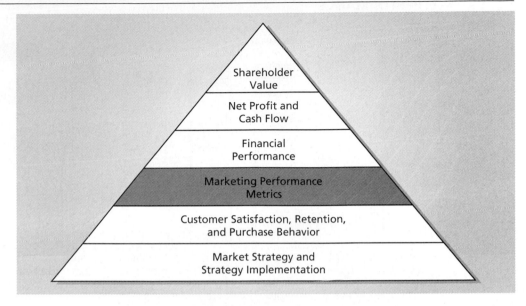

MARKETING PERFORMANCE METRICS

No matter how efficient a business's production operations, how expert its R&D, or how wise its financial management, if customers do not buy a business's products or services and make repurchases, the business's marketing strategy will fail. As shown in Figure 15-3, market-based marketing strategies are designed to deliver customer satisfaction and improve customer retention. As we saw in Chapter 2, the degree to which a marketing strategy is successful will be detected first by marketing metrics that track customer satisfaction, retention, and perceptions of value. Only subsequently will success or failure in financial performance be seen in the form of gains in revenue, total contribution, net profit, and cash flow. And, as also shown in Figure 15-3, ultimately the results of a marketing strategy will affect shareholders in the form of earnings growth and expectations of continued growth.

The best the investment community can do is to report financial performance and expectations based on a business's performance projections. A business managed by a market-based management system, however, can detect and report future success by tracking marketing metrics, especially those that forecast changes in financial performance.

For example, an increase in the percentage of dissatisfied customers may not result in an immediate decrease in sales or net profits, for two reasons. First, dissatisfied customers often give a business a chance to correct the source of their dissatisfaction. Remedying problems quickly and meaningfully often translates into improved customer loyalty. Second, it often takes time for customers to make a change in product or supplier, which creates a time lag between customer dissatisfaction (a marketing performance metric) and sales decline (a financial performance metric).

To illustrate the profit impact of the results of marketing metrics, consider the example in Figure 15-4. In period I, the business had no customer dissatisfaction and a net

FIGURE 15-4 CUSTOMER BEHAVIOR, MARKETING METRICS, AND PROFIT PERFORMANCE

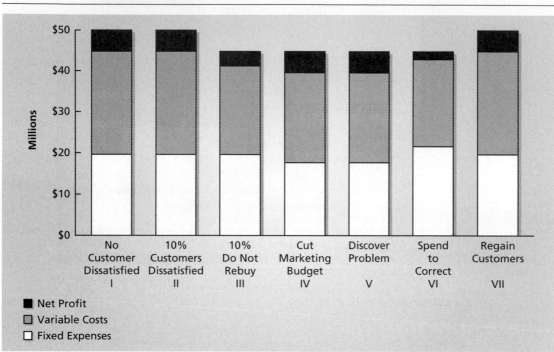

profit of $5 million on sales of $50 million. The total variable cost was $25 million and fixed expenses were $20 million. In period II, 10 percent of the business's customers became dissatisfied. In this example, however, the business did not have a market-based metric that tracked customer dissatisfaction. As a result, the business had no reason for concern because sales and profits were at the normal and expected level.

In period III, dissatisfied customers began to leave the business, and sales slowly declined. During this period, all fixed expenses remained the same, but margins declined and, hence, both sales and profits were down. The business took action in period IV by cutting marketing expenses in proportion to lost net income with the goal of returning net profits to their previous level. However, sales were still down and, in period V, the business created a task force to investigate the problem. The task force found that the customers who had been lost had left because of one particular source of dissatisfaction.

In period VI, the business restored the marketing budget and added funds to correct the problem and to replace the lost customers. No immediate sales gain resulted, and net profit decreased because of the increased expenses. However, in period VII, the business finally was back to where it had been in period I: no customer dissatisfaction, sales of $50 million, and a net profit of $5 million.

That sequence of events could have easily occurred over a period of 3 to 5 years, but a market-based business would have detected the problem in period II and would have immediately made corrections to restore customer satisfaction and retain its customer base. If the problem had been detected and corrected in period II, net profits over the seven periods would have totaled $35 million. The total in Figure 15-4 is $25 million. In

other words, the business had $10 million less in profits to reinvest and contribute to earnings, and stockholder value was diminished.

The purpose of this example is twofold. First, it points out the importance of marketing metrics that track the patterns of customers who, let's remember, are the only source of a business's positive cash flow. Second, it demonstrates that many marketing metrics are indicators of future financial performance and are important market-based management tools that contribute to better financial performance.

PROCESS VERSUS RESULT METRICS

Chapter 2 introduced us to the two broad categories of marketing performance metrics: *process metrics* and *result metrics* (see Figure 2-7). Primarily, marketing metrics are ongoing measures of marketing performance. Because many marketing performance metrics precede financial performance, using them is critical to strategy implementation and financial performance. However, not all marketing performance metrics are indicators of future financial performance. Some are *process* marketing performance metrics and others are *result* marketing metrics.[2] Both are important, but process marketing metrics are particularly important because they are the indicators of future financial performance.[3] Result marketing metrics correspond more closely to internal financial metrics that measure past performance.

Process Marketing Performance Metrics

Customer awareness, customer interest, product trial, and customer satisfaction, along with perceptions of relative product quality, service quality, and customer value, all are process marketing performance metrics. Changes in each, positive or negative, precede actual changes in customer behavior. As a result, these in-process measures of customer thinking and attitudes are important indicators of a business's future performance.

For example, perhaps customers are satisfied, but their perceptions of the value they derive from the product, relative to competing alternatives, are steadily diminishing. A business may have done nothing wrong to dissatisfy its customers; competitors may have

FIGURE 15-5 CUSTOMER SATISFACTION—A KEY PROCESS MARKETING METRIC

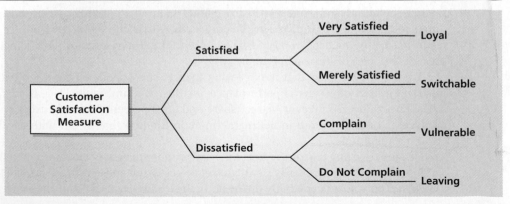

simply improved their delivery of customer value based on a combination of total bene-fits and total cost. However, the net effect is that customer perceptions of the value cre-ated by the business's product have diminished. This change, in turn, opens the door to competitors' products that the business's customers may be inclined to try or purchase.

The whole purpose of process marketing metrics is to track customer perceptions and attitudes that precede changes in customer behavior and a business's financial perfor-mance. For example, customer satisfaction is an important metric with many alternative measures.[4] Figure 15-5 shows how the customer satisfaction metric is broken into its dif-ferent classifications. Very satisfied customers are loyal and buy in relatively large amounts.[5] Merely satisfied customers are less loyal and usually switch back and forth with competitors' products. Dissatisfied customers, of course, are likely to leave, although those who complain can be retained but will be vulnerable to competitors until the source of their dissatisfaction is addressed. However, as pointed out in Chapter 1, less than 10 percent of dissatisfied customers ever complain,[6] and of the over 90 percent who do not complain, most stop buying from the business. Because the vast majority of dis-satisfied customers never complain, a business may not know it has a problem. Eventually these customers leave, and to maintain sales and profits the business has to attract new customers. Businesses that use measures of customer satisfaction effectively have a process metric that enables them to take corrective action in time to avoid a nega-tive impact on financial performance.

A market-based business with several process marketing metrics, then, will detect at once any changes in customer attitudes and perceptions. With an early warning signal, a market-based business can take corrective action before customers alter their purchase behavior. Without process marketing metrics, a customer-satisfaction problem would likely go undetected and unresolved until after declines in financial performance, as Figure 15-4 illustrates.

Result Marketing Performance Metrics

Result marketing metrics include the metrics that measure market share, customer reten-tion, and revenue per customer. These metrics occur simultaneously with financial per-formance metrics, but they provide a different set of diagnostic insights into a business's performance. For example, let's assume sales revenues are increasing and ahead of fore-cast, and financial performance is also better than expected. Most businesses would feel pretty good about this improving performance. However, if result marketing performance metrics show that the business is losing market share in a growing market, and poor cus-tomer retention is masked by new customer growth, there should be concern. Without result marketing metrics, a business has only internal measures of performance, which present only part of the total picture.

Even for a business that is not losing market share, poor customer retention has a powerful impact on financial performance, as illustrated in Figure 15-6. In this example, a business with a 20 percent market share and a 90 percent level of customer retention produces 24 percent more in net marketing contribution than it did with an 80 percent customer retention.

Because existing customers generally spend more than new customers and the cost of serving an existing customer is less than that of acquiring and serving a new customer, the margin per customer is generally different. In this example, an existing customer produces

FIGURE 15-6 CUSTOMER RETENTION—A KEY RESULT MARKETING METRIC

Area of Performance	80% Retention	90% Retention	Performance Gain
Customer Demand	1,000,000	1,000,000	None
Market Share (%)	20	20	None
Customer Volume	200,000	200,000	None
Revenue per Customer	$460	$480	+$20
Total Revenue (million)	$92	$96	+$4
Retained Customers	160,000	180,000	+20,000
Revenue per Customer	$500	$500	None
Cost per Customer	$200	$200	None
Margin per Customer	$300	$300	None
Gross Profit (million)	$48	$54	+$6
New Customers	40,000	20,000	−20,000
Revenue per Customer	$300	$300	None
Cost per Customer	$400	$400	None
Margin per Customer	−$100	−$100	None
Gross Profit (million)	−$4	−$2	+$2
Overall Gross Profit (million)	$44	$52	+$8
Marketing Expenses (million)	$15	$16	−$1
Net Marketing Contribution (million)	$29	$36	+$7

$300 of margin per year, whereas a new customer results in a net loss of $100 per year. Retaining a larger percentage of existing customers improves gross profit and net marketing contribution even when an additional $1 million is added to marketing expenses for a customer retention program. Overall, the assets increase a little because higher revenues result in proportionately higher accounts receivable. However, return on assets still increases from 18 to over 30 percent.

We can see, then, that the combination of market share, customer retention, and revenue per customer provides a totally different picture of performance than do the financial performance metrics. Both kinds of metrics—marketing metrics and financial metrics—are important, with each marketing metric and each financial metric providing insight into a business's performance. Together, marketing metrics and financial metrics give a business a comprehensive picture of its present performance and a forecast of future performance, and they indicate the extent to which a business's strategic marketing plan is being successfully implemented.

SUCCESSFUL STRATEGY IMPLEMENTATION

Nike is famous for innovation and its *Just Do It* marketing campaign—but the company's marketing success did not happen by accident. Nike has a company culture that motivates management behaviors conducive to the successful implementation of strategies. Nike's Eleven Maxims foster an awareness and understanding of the company's approach to marketing among all managers and other employees:

1. It Is Our Nature to Innovate.
2. Nike Is a Company.
3. Nike Is a Brand.
4. Simplify and Go.
5. The Consumer Decides.
6. Be a Sponge.
7. Evolve Immediately.
8. Do the Right Thing.
9. Master the Fundamentals.
10. We Are on the Offense. Always.
11. Remember the Man (Bill Bowerman).

Nike's Eleven Maxims set a tone and style that favors successful implementations. Success often requires high levels of persistence and adaptability, as actual market conditions are likely to be different than those carefully articulated in a marketing plan.

We have seen that a strategic marketing plan provides a business with the roadmap it needs to pursue a set of performance objectives. However, it does not guarantee that the objectives will be reached, any more than having a roadmap guarantees a traveler will arrive at the desired destination. A marketing plan must also be successfully implemented. Successful implementation is directly related to the structure of a business's marketing effort.

For example, a manufacturer of electric utility equipment engaged in an extensive market segmentation project in an effort to revitalize its sales and profitability. The effort revealed several new market segments, all reachable and judged as attractive. The manufacturer then developed a multi-segment strategy with a separate strategy for each market segment. But the sales force was structured into three geographical regions and had not participated in the segmentation study and strategy development. The marketing manager knew that without the support of the sales reps, the marketing strategy would lack their commitment and fail.

To implement this strategy successfully, the marketing manager had to sell it to the three regional vice presidents for sales. Two VPs agreed to implement the strategy, but the third chose not to participate. The results, shown in Figure 15-7, illustrate the importance of effective strategy implementation. In the two regions where the marketing strategy was implemented, sales increased by 18 and 12 percent, even though these were markets where total demand declined by 15 percent. By contrast, the region that did not implement the marketing strategy had only a 3 percent sales gain.[7]

To achieve marketing success and its performance objectives, a business needs both a good marketing plan and a well-executed implementation of the plan. A good marketing plan without a dedicated implementation effort will fail. The next two sections cover the forces that affect the implementation of a strategic marketing plan and the mechanics of a marketing plan variance analysis.

MANAGING SUCCESSFUL STRATEGY IMPLEMENTATION

Even a flawless marketing plan provides no guarantee that its strategy will achieve its performance objectives. The marketing plan must still be successfully implemented. It is next to impossible to implement a poor plan and obtain good results, but implementing a

FIGURE 15-7 SALES IMPACT OF A SUCCESSFUL STRATEGY IMPLEMENTATION

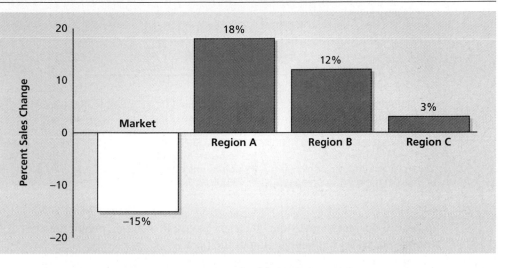

superb plan can also fail to deliver the desired performance. Figure 15-8 shows three major forces that contribute to success or failure in implementing a strategic marketing plan. Each of these forces is influenced by underlying factors that can cause the force to have a positive or negative impact on successful implementation. Collectively, these factors will shape the behavior and organizational structure in a way that either facilitates or impedes successful implementation.[8]

Owning the Marketing Plan

Perhaps the most common reason a marketing plan fails is a lack of ownership. If a business's senior managers, its marketing and sales managers, and other key employees do not have an ownership stake in the plan, with a responsibility for its success, it will be business as usual for all but a frustrated few. As shown in Figure 15-8, the ownership of a marketing plan can be enhanced with detailed action plans, a champion and ownership team, compensation based on performance metrics, and top management involvement.

Detailed Action Plans

In determining the success of a marketing plan, the single most effective practice that management of a market-based business can employ is the development and use of detailed action plans. Each aspect of the marketing strategy is supported with a plan that specifies the actions that need to occur for the marketing plan to be implemented. Figure 15-9 outlines how a particular tactical marketing strategy within a marketing plan would be implemented. In this case, the strategy is broken into five important action items, each of which must occur for that aspect of the marketing plan to succeed. As shown, for each of the five action items, an individual is assigned a responsibility, a measure or goal is delineated, and a time frame within which the action item should be completed is agreed upon.

Any number of action items could be added to this action plan, but the important point is that significant elements of this strategy have specific ownership. In this way, individuals take personal responsibility and become accountable for implementing a portion of the marketing plan. With individuals taking ownership of particular aspects of the

FIGURE 15-8 SUCCESSFUL IMPLEMENTATION OF A MARKETING PLAN

process, a business breaks the "business as usual" routine, creating an environment that fosters successful implementation of the plan.

Champion and Ownership Team

Assigning individual responsibilities with detailed action plans involves a wide range of people in implementation, but every successful marketing strategy has a champion or an ownership team—one person or a group of persons who are highly devoted to and lead the successful implementation of the strategic marketing plan. Although there is nothing wrong with having a single owner or champion, the creation of an ownership team can leverage the unique talents of multiple people and exert more organizational leverage than a single individual.[9] With an ownership team, the implementation process can stay on track even when some members of the team are gone for extended periods of time because of business trips, training programs, illness, or vacations.

Compensation

Most people respond to financial rewards. Tying the compensation of those principally responsible for implementing the marketing plan to performance metrics increases their incentive for success. Compensation can be tied to both external marketing metrics and

FIGURE 15-9 DETAILED ACTION PLAN FOR A CHANNEL STRATEGY

Channel Strategy—To create adequate end-user product availability, 80 manufactures' reps and 5 missionary salespeople will be used to sell and distribute our product to 5,000 industrial supply houses.

No.	Action Item	Responsibility	Measure	Time Frame*
1.	Identify target supply houses and establish contracts.	P. Elliot	5,000 Dealers	12 months
2.	Contact manufacturers' reps.	T. Garcia	80 Reps	6 months
3.	Hire missionary sales force.	P. Wilson	5 People	3 months
4.	Develop rep training program.	S. Bradley	Program Pilot	6 months
5.	Develop dealer training program.	R. Otto	Program Pilot	6 months

*From time of implementation

internal financial metrics. Marketing metrics are most important in the early stages of implementing a marketing plan. Measurements of end-customer awareness and interest, product availability, and trial can occur well before the results of such financial metrics as sales revenue and net profit are reported. The purpose of tying compensation to the results of marketing metrics is to immediately create motivation and responsibility.

Management Involvement

Senior managers must stay committed to their involvement with the marketing planning process and to their review of its progress. When top managers lessen the time they spend reviewing the development of the marketing plan and its performance after implementation, they implicitly signal a lack of interest and support. This signal weakens the motivation of the ownership team and the chances for successful implementation.

Supporting the Marketing Plan

Many factors affect the degree to which a business is committed to a marketing plan, but the most important ones are time to succeed, resource allocation, communication, and skills to succeed.[10]

Time to Succeed

In many instances, commitment to a marketing plan weakens when financial performance is not on track. If meaningful marketing metrics are not employed, a business may pull support for a marketing plan without knowing why the plan is not working. It may be that the marketing strategy and plan are good, but implementation has been poor. It may also be that the marketing metrics are on target but the financial metrics need more time to achieve the desired or targeted levels of performance.

The length of time it will take to succeed depends in part on the marketing strategy and the nature of the market opportunity. A share-penetration strategy in an existing market should take less time to succeed than a strategy to enter a new, undeveloped market. In either case, the time to succeed, along with marketing metrics that measure progress, is an important aspect of the marketing plan and its successful implementation.

Resource Allocation

If the process and structure of strategic marketing planning are followed as described in Chapter 14, the marketing plan will have sufficient resources with respect to personnel and funding. If less than the required resources are reserved for implementing the plan, the chances for success are greatly reduced. Of course, if the resources needed are not systematically determined in the strategic marketing planning process, it is even more likely that the plan will be under-resourced. (It is rare that marketing plans are over-resourced.) An important step in the successful implementation of a plan is to ensure that the necessary resources are being committed.

Communication

It is difficult to obtain support either internally, within the company, or externally, from the market, if the marketing plan and its strategic intent are not aggressively communicated. Although senior management and the marketing management team are likely to fully understand the logic and tactics of the marketing plan, others in sales, customer support, manufacturing, and finance may not be entirely aware of the objectives and strategy. As a result, these employees, who may have key roles in successful implementation, will continue in a business-as-usual mode of operation. To facilitate communication and understanding, some businesses create videos that describe their marketing strategy and objectives, showing the videos to all appropriate employees.

Internal communication of a marketing plan, including the specific role individuals within the business play with respect to implementation, is critical. To the degree possible, these job functions should be integrated into the detailed action plans. Key individuals will then understand their roles and responsibilities in the successful implementation of the plan.

External communication of the marketing plan is also critical. Each of the following groups must be made aware of different aspects of the plan:

- **Target Customers**—Must be made aware of the benefits of the product, the value proposition, and where the product can be acquired.
- **Channel Intermediaries**—Must understand who the target customers are, their profit potential, and inventory, sales, and service requirements.
- **The Trade Press**—Must be informed as to product benefits and the availability of the product.
- **Market Influencers**—Must be informed of product benefits, the value proposition, and availability (includes consultants, financial analysts, or others who influence customers and channel intermediaries).
- **The General and Business Press**—Must receive news releases that further communicate the marketing plan to target customers, distributors, and investors.

Of course, the extent to which external marketing communications are engaged depends on the nature of the marketing strategy and product. A new product made to more effectively treat metal-working fluids in small machine shops would not interest most individuals, the general press, or even the business press. However, trade press publishers, consultants, the Environmental Protection Agency, and others may be interested in promoting awareness of a new product that greatly reduces the problems of disposal of hazardous waste, lowers the cost of disposal, and improves working conditions.

Skills to Succeed

Do those implementing the strategic marketing plan have the skills to effectively implement the plan?[11] For example, a bank wanting to improve customer satisfaction and retention may have to do some training to communicate new policies and customer-oriented employee attitudes. Two of the five action items detailed in Figure 15-9 involve training. For that marketing strategy to succeed, it is essential to train manufacturers' reps and distributors with respect to product knowledge, service requirements, how to sell the product, and how to explain the value derived from this product. Without a training effort, this strategy would likely not succeed.

In many instances, even members of the management team may need additional training to successfully implement the marketing plan. A business implementing a program to increase sales by introducing a product that offers new customer benefits may need to provide some management training on the benefits. Without the necessary skills, the management team might produce a meaningful objective but have no way of accomplishing it.

Adapting the Marketing Plan

The strategic marketing planning process does not stop when implementation begins; it continues during the plan's time horizon. As do all systems, a marketing plan needs to be adapted to survive unanticipated changing conditions. To survive, as well as to succeed, the marketing plan needs built-in adaptability. Four factors that contribute to the adaptive nature of a marketing plan are continuous improvement, feedback measurements, persistence, and an incremental, adaptive rollout of the plan.

Continuous Improvement

A strategic marketing plan that does not adapt to changing market conditions will fail. Because market conditions are complex and almost always in flux, a business must modify its marketing plan in response to the changing conditions. In many instances, the modifications will be minor, made in order to finely tune the business's marketing strategy and value proposition. However, in some cases, a major shift in strategy may be required.

The term *adaptive persistence* has been used to describe the success of many Japanese marketing strategies. One of Japanese management's greatest assets is the ability to adapt when a marketing plan is not working and to stick with the plan—*to persist*. The whole concept of continuous improvement is implicit in Japanese marketing plan implementation. Although the marketing plan sets the direction and provides the roadmap, once it is in place, the flexibility to adapt is an important aspect of continuous improvement.

Feedback Measurements

An essential element of any adaptive system, whether mechanical, electrical, or human, is feedback. Mechanical, electrical, and human systems have internal sensors and feedback mechanisms. Management systems also require measurements to provide a mechanism for feedback. The results of process-oriented marketing metrics are the internal sensors for a marketing plan feedback system. These measurements signal the status of the marketing plan with respect to its progress toward achieving its performance objectives in such areas as sales, market share, net profit, and net marketing contribution.

Key process marketing metrics that provide leading signals as to the success of the marketing plan include:

■ Customer awareness, interest, intentions to buy, trial, and repeat purchase;
■ Channel intermediary market coverage, interest, support, and motivation; and
■ Business responsiveness to customer inquiries and problems.

Each of these marketing metrics has to reach an effective level of performance before the financial metrics will show improved results. The marketing metrics provide an early indication of the progress of the marketing plan. If the results of the marketing metrics are behind the target performance levels specified in the marketing plan, then improved performance as measured by financial metrics will materialize more slowly than projected. The marketing metrics also signal which aspects of the marketing plan may be failing. Is it the channel system, the communications strategy, or the product-price positioning strategy that is the cause of the plan's slow progress toward its objectives? Knowing the source of the problem enables a business to devise effective new strategies for improving the plan in light of market conditions.

Persistence

Again we can turn to Japanese companies for insight. They are often cited as exemplars of successful marketing, but rarely have Japanese marketing strategies worked initially. As mentioned, one of the great traits of Japanese managers is their inherent ability to adapt and persist throughout the implementation of their marketing plans. Japanese marketing managers remain committed to the strategic marketing objective and persist by adapting their marketing plans. It is their determination to make their marketing plans work that underlies the secret of their marketing success.

On the other hand, American managers are often quick to drop a marketing plan when it meets the first bit of resistance. Perhaps expectations of performance have been overstated, or time to succeed underestimated. Because strategic marketing plans developed in a corporate office can lack the realism of the marketplace, they may need to be adapted during implementation. Without a high degree of management persistence, there is little chance of successful implementation, particularly when aspects of the marketing plan need to be modified.

Adaptive Rollout

An adaptive rollout is an incremental implementation of a marketing strategy that allows for feedback and corrective adjustments early in the implementation process. The rollout starts in one region of a broader market—the southwestern states, for example. After the regional rollout, the strategy is refined and then rolled out in another region. This process of fine-tuning the strategy continues until all regions of the market are served.

A region-by-region rollout has many benefits as opposed to a nationwide launch, and it signals a business's marketing strategy to competitors just as effectively. First, fewer resources are required in a small-scale regional launch of a marketing plan than in a nationwide launch. Second, problems with distributors, marketing communications, and product positioning can more readily be addressed and corrected on a small scale. Third, if the marketing plan is more effective than planned, additions can be made to production capacity without the potential of stockout and the loss of opportunities to capture customers when they want to buy. Fourth, even for a marketing plan that is tracking as planned on a regional basis, additional marketing insights will result that can be advantageously integrated into the plan as full implementation is pursued. Fifth, the financial metrics generated from a successful regional rollout signal long-run profit potential and can be used to help fund the full introduction. Because of these benefits, many foreign competitors have used regional rollouts when entering the U.S. market.

Many U.S. businesses nevertheless are reluctant to take the time to engage in an adaptive rollout of a marketing plan. But rarely does a marketing plan succeed exactly as conceived on paper. A market-wide launch risks all customers and distributors if the business's value proposition is ineffectively presented. In addition, the cost of a full-market introduction when things go wrong is enormous, even when customers and distributors are retained through the repositioning period.

Assessing the Implementation of a Marketing Plan

Figure 15-10 lists the main ingredients of success in implementing a strategic marketing plan and shows a profile of a business that worked to improve its plan implementation. No single factor presented in Figure 15-10 will make or break the successful implementation of a marketing plan. However, when the whole of these factors is adequately addressed, the chances for successful implementation are greatly improved. Although this business did not perform well for every factor, its overall performance was much better than in the past. This level of implementation effort, along with a good marketing strategy and plan, will enable the business to achieve its desired level of marketing success within the time frame allotted.

At the heart of the successful implementation of a marketing plan is a business's market orientation. The greater the degree to which the business has created a market orientation, the better are its chances for implementing its plan successfully.[12] A market-based business with a strong customer focus and competitor orientation across job functions has a greater level of market sensitivity and urgency from which to both develop and implement a strategic marketing plan.

VARIANCE ANALYSIS

After implementing a marketing plan, comparing the planned results with the actual results at the end of each year in the plan's time horizon will reveal which variables are contributing to the plan's performance. If a business achieves the first-year net marketing contribution (NMC) performance objective projected in its marketing plan, it might well be due to all strategic variables having performed as planned. On the other hand, the same result could be due to an underperformance in some variables of the NMC equation shown here, combined with an over-performance in others. Variance analysis allows a

FIGURE 15-10 ASSESSING THE IMPLEMENTATION OF A MARKETING PLAN

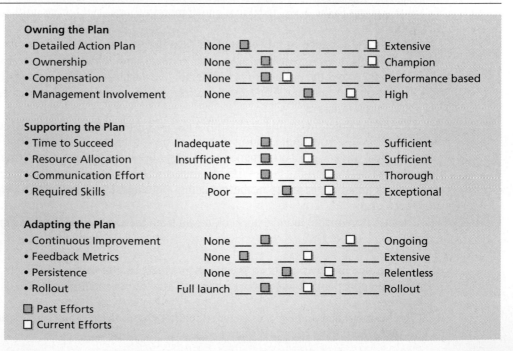

business to isolate the components of marketing performance to understand better how each component is contributing to the NMC.

$$NMC = \text{Volume} \times \text{Margin per Unit} - \text{Marketing Expenses}$$
$$= (\text{Demand} \times \text{Share}) \times (\text{Price} - \text{Variable Unit Cost}) - \text{Marketing Expenses}$$

Consider the business in Figure 15-11, which has a marketing plan that projected $420,000 for the net marketing contribution for year 1 of the plan. The actual NMC at the end of year 1 was $86,800 less than estimated in the plan, as calculated in the first tier of the diagram. What was the primary cause of this shortfall in performance?

The second tier in the diagram shows the calculation of the variances between actual and planned volume (V_a minus V_p), actual and planned marketing expenses (ME_a minus ME_p), and actual and planned margin per unit (M_a minus M_p). The volume sold was higher than planned, the unit margin was lower, and marketing expenses were higher. The $10,000 negative variance in the NMC attributable to marketing expenses is easily determined by the difference between actual and planned marketing expenses. However, performance variances in volume and margin can be broken down further.

As illustrated in Figure 15-11, a variance in volume reflects any difference in actual versus planned market demand, plus any difference in actual versus planned market share. In this example, a positive variance in market demand was responsible for an increase in the NMC of $75,000, and a negative variance in market share was responsible for a decrease by $46,000. Taken together, the greater-than-planned market demand and the smaller-than-planned market share were responsible for the positive variance of $29,000 in volume ($75,000 minus $46,000). The volume variance in turn contributed the same amount to the NMC ($10 in planned margin times 2,900 more units sold equals $29,000).

The margin variance in this example is also derived from more than one source of performance. Actual prices were lower than planned and actual costs were higher than planned. In this case, the price variance and unit cost variance each had a negative impact of $52,900 on the net marketing contribution, for a combined negative variance of $105,800 in total margin.

The fundamental marketing profitability metric for planning purposes is the net marketing contribution equation. Examining the sources of the net marketing contribution in terms of their underlying performance variances allows us to see which aspects of the plan worked and which did not. With this information, a marketing manager is better equipped to make adjustments in the marketing plan and to project future performance more accurately.

The insights a marketing manager could gain from the variance analysis in Figure 15-11 include:

- If market demand had not been greater than expected, the performance gap in the net marketing contribution would have been much wider. In other words, a little luck was involved.
- If the business had achieved its planned market share, the net marketing contribution shortfall would have been less than it was.

FIGURE 15-11 VARIANCE ANALYSIS—PLAN VERSUS ACTUAL PERFORMANCE

Area of Performance	Plan	Actual	Variance
Market Demand (units)	200,000	230,000	30,000
Market Share (%)	25.0	23.0	−2.0
Volume	50,000	52,900	2,900
Price per Unit	$16.00	$15.00	−$1.00
Sales Revenues	$800,000	$793,500	−$6,500
Variable Cost per Customer	$6.00	$7.00	$1.00
Margin per Unit	$10.00	$8.00	−$2.00
Gross Profit	$500,000	$423,200	−$76,800
Marketing Expenses (% sales)	10.0	11.3	1.3
Marketing Expenses	$80,000	$90,000	$10,000
Net Marketing Contribution	$420,000	$333,200	−$86,800

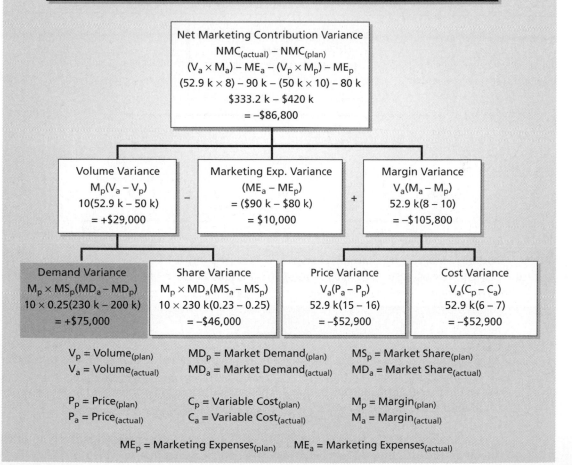

Net Marketing Contribution Variance
$NMC_{(actual)} - NMC_{(plan)}$
$(V_a \times M_a) - ME_a - (V_p \times M_p) - ME_p$
$(52.9 \text{ k} \times 8) - 90 \text{ k} - (50 \text{ k} \times 10) - 80 \text{ k}$
$333.2 \text{ k} - 420 \text{ k}$
$= -86,800$

Volume Variance
$M_p(V_a - V_p)$
$10(52.9 \text{ k} - 50 \text{ k})$
$= +29,000$

Marketing Exp. Variance
$(ME_a - ME_p)$
$= (90 \text{ k} - 80 \text{ k})$
$= 10,000$

Margin Variance
$V_a(M_a - M_p)$
$52.9 \text{ k}(8 - 10)$
$= -105,800$

Demand Variance
$M_p \times MS_p(MD_a - MD_p)$
$10 \times 0.25(230 \text{ k} - 200 \text{ k})$
$= +75,000$

Share Variance
$M_p \times MD_a(MS_a - MS_p)$
$10 \times 230 \text{ k}(0.23 - 0.25)$
$= -46,000$

Price Variance
$V_a(P_a - P_p)$
$52.9 \text{ k}(15 - 16)$
$= -52,900$

Cost Variance
$V_a(C_p - C_a)$
$52.9 \text{ k}(6 - 7)$
$= -52,900$

$V_p = \text{Volume}_{(plan)}$ $MD_p = \text{Market Demand}_{(plan)}$ $MS_p = \text{Market Share}_{(plan)}$
$V_a = \text{Volume}_{(actual)}$ $MD_a = \text{Market Demand}_{(actual)}$ $MD_a = \text{Market Share}_{(actual)}$

$P_p = \text{Price}_{(plan)}$ $C_p = \text{Variable Cost}_{(plan)}$ $M_p = \text{Margin}_{(plan)}$
$P_a = \text{Price}_{(actual)}$ $C_a = \text{Variable Cost}_{(actual)}$ $M_a = \text{Margin}_{(actual)}$

$ME_p = \text{Marketing Expenses}_{(plan)}$ $ME_a = \text{Marketing Expenses}_{(actual)}$

FIGURE 15-12 VARIANCE ANALYSIS SHOWING "HIDDEN" CONCERNS

Area of Performance	Plan	Actual	Variance
Market Demand (units)	1,000,000	1,250,000	250,000
Market Share (%)	25.0	20.0	–5.0
Volume	250,000	250,000	0
Price per Unit	$450.00	$460.00	$10.00
Sales Revenues	$112,500,000	$115,000,000	$2,500,000
Variable Cost per Unit	$200.00	$210.00	$10.00
Margin per Customer	$250.00	$250.00	$0.00
Gross Profit	$62,500,000	$62,500,000	$0
Marketing Expenses (% sales)	13.3	13.0	–0.3
Marketing Expenses	$15,000,000	$15,000,000	$0
Net Marketing Contribution	$47,500,000	$47,500,000	$0

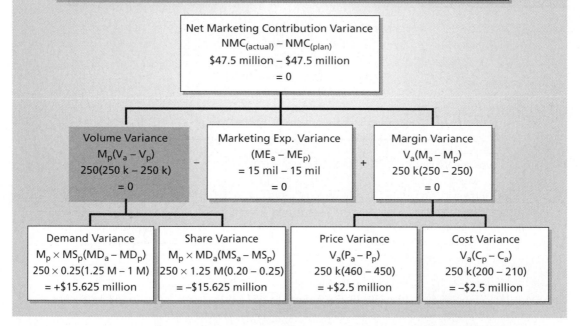

Net Marketing Contribution Variance
$NMC_{(actual)} - NMC_{(plan)}$
$47.5 million – $47.5 million
= 0

Volume Variance
$M_p(V_a - V_p)$
250(250 k – 250 k)
= 0

Marketing Exp. Variance
$(ME_a - ME_p)$
= 15 mil – 15 mil
= 0

Margin Variance
$V_a(M_a - M_p)$
250 k(250 – 250)
= 0

Demand Variance
$M_p \times MS_p(MD_a - MD_p)$
250 × 0.25(1.25 M – 1 M)
= +$15.625 million

Share Variance
$M_p \times MD_a(MS_a - MS_p)$
250 × 1.25 M(0.20 – 0.25)
= –$15.625 million

Price Variance
$V_a(P_a - P_p)$
250 k(460 – 450)
= +$2.5 million

Cost Variance
$V_a(C_p - C_a)$
250 k(200 – 210)
= –$2.5 million

■ A higher cost per unit and lower unit prices than planned both contributed to a lower net marketing contribution.

■ The higher-than-planned marketing expenses will have to be addressed in future profit planning.

A situation in which actual marketing profits are less than planned is likely to draw the attention of senior management. But what about a situation in which no differences occur between actual and planned net marketing contribution, actual and planned volume sold, and actual and planned marketing expenses, as illustrated in Figure 15-12? Why worry? The strategic marketing plan is obviously on track. A finance-oriented business would note that price per unit is $10 higher but would also investigate the higher variable cost per unit. A finance-oriented business, however, would rarely look beyond volume and would probably fail to recognize performance variances in market demand and market share.

A business that does not track market share, market demand, and other marketing performance metrics will usually discover too late that its strategic marketing plan is not working. In contrast, a market-based business that tracks performance metrics and conducts an annual variance analysis over the life of the plan will know whether its actual marketing performance is on track with the planned performance, and where any shortcomings in the plan are.

The variance analysis in Figure 15-12, for instance, shows the independent effects of variances in market demand and market share on the net marketing contribution. This information would alert the business to a disturbing performance gap in market share. It may be, with the market growing faster than expected, that the business under-resourced its marketing expenses, which is causing the business to fall short of its intended share goal. With this variance analysis, a market-based business would recognize the higher-than-expected market demand and would be able to take steps to achieve the target market share of 25 percent. Although the analysis shows that performance variances in price and variable cost had a smaller impact on the net marketing contribution for that particular year, the price and variable-cost variances are nevertheless important in modifying the marketing plan or in developing an effective future plan.

With the examples presented in Figures 15-11 and 15-12, we can clearly see why the implementation of a marketing plan is more likely to succeed when a business's managers track performance metrics and conduct an annual variance analysis to determine how well the plan is performing over its time frame.

■ Summary

Developing a sound strategic marketing plan is only one-half of marketing success. The plan must also be effectively implemented. Without ownership, support, and adaptation, the plan will fail. Detailed action plans, a marketing plan champion or ownership team, performance-based compensation, and the involvement of top management and other appropriate personnel contribute to ownership of the marketing plan and improve its chances of successful implementation.

Successful implementation also requires time to succeed, sufficient resources, a comprehensive communications effort, and skills on the part of those involved. Also required is a readiness to respond to any unanticipated obstacles, such as swings in market conditions, that will likely arise during implementation. The probability of unexpected impediments requires that marketing plans be adaptive. Continuous efforts to improve the plan, based on feedback measures, are an important part of successful implementation. Businesses that are persistent in adapting their marketing plans have a greater chance for success. A regional rollout provides a less expensive venue than a full-scale rollout, and one that entails fewer risks, for adapting the marketing plan.

Performance metrics play a key role in implementing a strategic marketing plan. There are marketing performance metrics and financial performance metrics. Marketing metrics are external measures of marketing performance, such as awareness, customer satisfaction, and market share. Financial performance metrics are internal measures of performance, such as unit margin, net profit, and return on investment. Marketing performance metrics consist of both process metrics and result metrics. Customer awareness, customer satisfaction, and perceived product performance are examples of process marketing performance metrics that occur ahead of result marketing performance metrics, such as those for market share, revenue per customer, and customer retention. Process marketing metrics can forecast the success or failure of a marketing plan and its implementation effort, and they are also indicators of future financial performance.

Finally, an important part of assessing the implementation of a marketing plan is determining which parts of the plan are performing as expected and which are not. Variance analysis is an annual systematic assessment of each area of performance. While holding the effects of all other variables constant, a single variance between planned and actual performance can be assessed with respect to its impact on profits. The analysis allows a manager to fully understand the reasons behind a marketing plan's performance for any year of the plan's time horizon and to take corrective action. In some situations, managers may discover large negative variances hidden behind many smaller positive variances. After a marketing plan ends its final year of implementation, a variance analysis is used to assess the plan's success during the entire course of its time frame, giving managers the information they need to develop ever-more effective marketing plans in the future.

■ Market-Based Strategic Thinking

1 Why is implementation as important as marketing plan development in achieving marketing success?
2 How do detailed action plans contribute to individual ownership of a strategic marketing plan?
3 Why does a marketing plan need a champion or an ownership team?
4 How should a business tie compensation to successful implementation of a marketing plan?
5 Why is "time to succeed" an important part of implementing a marketing plan?
6 What signal is senior management sending when it does not take the time to review the strategic marketing planning process and the performance of the plan after implementation?
7 What is meant by *persistence* in terms of commitment? What is meant by the term *adaptive persistence* as it is often used to describe the Japanese style of marketing plan implementation?
8 Why are continuous improvement and feedback measures important aspects of successfully implementing a strategic marketing plan?
9 What are the advantages and disadvantages of a regional rollout of a marketing plan?
10 What role do resources, organizational communications, and training play in the successful implementation of a strategic marketing plan?
11 Why are performance metrics important to the implementation process?

12 What is the difference between a marketing performance metric and a financial performance metric?

13 Why are process metrics an important part of the implementation process? What is the relationship between process metrics and result metrics?

Marketing Performance Tools

The three **Marketing Performance Tools** described here may be accessed online at *www.rogerjbest.com*. These applied-learning exercises will add to your understanding of using a variance analysis to assess the performance of a strategic marketing plan.

15.1 Variance Analysis—Market Demand and Market Share

■ Change the actual market demand to 1,250,000 and the actual market share to 23 percent, separately, to first evelute the impact of each change on sales and profits. Then change both actual values to evalute the combined effect on both variances on sales and profits. When finished, return both values to the plan values.

15.2 Variance Analysis—Revenue and Cost per Customer

■ Change the actual price to $460 and the variable cost per unit to $210, separately, to evaluate the impact of each change on sales and profits. Then change both actual values to evaluate the combined effect of both variances on sales and profits. When finished, return both values to the plan values.

15.3 Variance Analysis—Marketing Expenses

■ Change the actual marketing expenses as a percent of sales to 14 percent to evalute the impact on profits.

Notes

1. P. Hyde, E. Landry, and A. Tipping, "Making the Perfect Marketer," *Strategy + Business* (Winter 2004).
2. Dennis Gensch, "Targeting the Switchable Industrial Customer," *Marketing Science* (Winter 1984): 41–54.
3. George Cressman, "Choosing the Right Metric," *Drive Marketing Excellence* (November 1994), New York: Institute for International Research.
4. Robert Kaplan and David Norton, "The Balanced Scorecard—Measures That Drive Performance," *Harvard Business Review* (January–February 1982): 71–79.
5. Robert Peterson and William Wilson, "Measuring Customer Satisfaction: Fact or Artifact," *Journal of the Academy of Marketing Science* 20 (1992): 61–71.
6. Thomas Jones and Earl Sasser Jr., "Why Satisfied Customers Defect," *Harvard Business Review* (November–December 1995): 88–99; Frederick F. Reichheld and W. Earl Sasser Jr., "Zero Defections: Quality Comes to Services," *Harvard Business Review* (September–October 1990): 106–111; and Frederick F. Reichheld, "Loyalty-Based Management," *Harvard Business Review* (March–April 1993): 64–73.
7. Patrick Byrne, "Global Logistics: Only 10 Percent of Companies Satisfy Customers," *Transportation and Distribution* (December 1993); and Tom Eck, "Are Customers Happy? Don't Assume," *Positive Impact* (July 1992): 3.

8. Nigel Piercy and Neil Morgan, "The Marketing Planning Process: Behavioral Problems Compared to Analytical Techniques in Explaining Marketing Plan Credibility," *Journal of Business Research* 29 (1994): 167–178; and Nigel Piercy, *Marketing Organization: An Analysis of Information Processing, Power and Politics* (Chicago: George Allen & Urwin, 1985).

9. Robert Ruekert and Orville Walker Jr., "Marketing's Interaction with Other Functional Units: A Conceptual Framework and Empirical Evidence," *Journal of Marketing* (January 1987): 1–19.

10. William Egelhoff, "Great Strategies or Great Strategy Implementation—Two Ways of Competing in Global Markets," *Sloan Management Review* (Winter 1993): 37–50.

11. Thomas Bonoma, *The Marketing Edge: Making Strategies Work* (New York: Free Press, 1985).

12. George Day, "Building a Market-Driven Organization," *Market-Driven Strategy* (New York: Free Press, 1990): 356–376.

CHAPTER 16

Market-Based Management and Financial Performance

■ Customers are the only source of cash flow. Everything else is expense.

—*Peter Drucker*

In Chapter 14 we reviewed a sample marketing plan for Stericycle Inc., the market leader in medical waste recycling. The company's sales of $790 million in 2006 were the result of a 22.6 percent market share, five times greater than the closest competitor. Stericycle's pricing and product positioning enabled it to obtain a 44.3 percent gross margin, resulting in a gross profit of $350 million. This level of sales and gross profit was not free, however. It required an investment of $137 million in marketing and sales, but the investment resulted in a marketing profit of $213 million.

As Figure 16-1 shows, the company's marketing profitability yielded a marketing ROS of 27 percent and a marketing ROI of 156 percent.

FIGURE 16-1 HOW MARKETING PROFITS CONTRIBUTE TO FINANCIAL PERFORMANCE

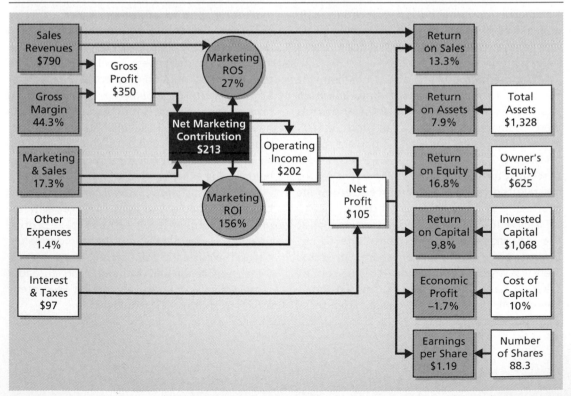

FIGURE 16-2 HOW MARKETING PROFITS IMPACT NET PROFIT AND EARNINGS PER SHARE

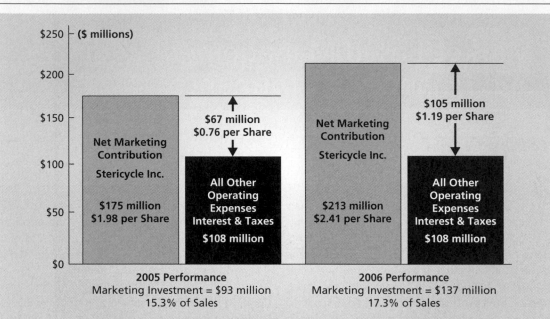

Net marketing contribution, marketing ROS, and marketing ROI are the marketing profitability metrics that drive the financial metrics shown in the chart.

The marketing profit of $213 million was the only source of positive cash flow, and from it all other expenses and interest and taxes were deducted to produce a net profit of $105 million. The results were a 13.3 percent return on sales, a 7.9 percent return on assets, a 16.8 percent return on equity, a 9.8 percent return on invested capital, a −1.7 percent economic profit, and $1.19 in earnings per share.

Figure 16-2 illustrates another way to look at the way marketing profits contribute to net income and earnings per share. In 2005, Stericycle invested $93 million—15.3 percent of sales—in marketing and sales and had a net marketing contribution of $175 million. From these

marketing profits all other expenses were deducted to arrive at a net income of $67 million and earnings per share of 76 cents. The marketing profits per share were $1.98. In 2006 the net marketing contribution grew to $213 million, or $2.41 per share. Other expenses and interest and taxes stayed the same ($108 million), producing a net income of $105 million and earnings per share of $1.19. In 2006, then, each additional dollar in marketing profits went directly to shareholder value as increased earnings per share.

In this last chapter, we will consider market-based management in light of its capacity for producing higher levels of marketing profits, financial performance, and shareholder value, making explicit the relationship between customer satisfaction and profitability. In a broader sense, we will see how every marketing strategy affects profits and shareholder value.

FIGURE 16-3 HOW TO OVERWHELM CUSTOMERS AND SHAREHOLDERS

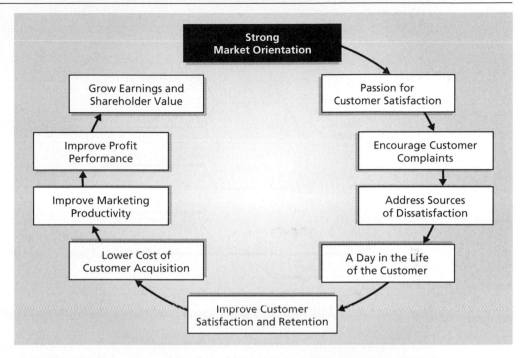

HOW TO OVERWHELM CUSTOMERS AND SHAREHOLDERS

The process starts with a strong market orientation and a passion for customer satisfaction, as illustrated in Figure 16-3. Businesses can find many ways to better serve customers in an effort to improve customer satisfaction, but a business with a passion for customer satisfaction will start with its dissatisfied customers by encouraging them to complain.

Encouraging customer complaints is easier said than done. Most customers do not complain, for a variety of reasons. A market-based business, however, develops proactive customer-satisfaction programs and systems to encourage customer complaint, and it measures its success by the rate at which dissatisfied customers complain. Capturing customer complaints gives the business a highly efficient means for discovering and addressing sources of dissatisfaction. The most effective and lowest-cost customer research any business will ever engage in is listening to its dissatisfied customers.

A business with a passion for customer satisfaction uses customer complaints to develop an understanding of customer needs and frustrations, and to discover opportunities for creating customer solutions that build higher levels of customer satisfaction. A day in the life of a customer, as described in Chapter 4, is one way to find new ways of building customer satisfaction. A day in the life of a customer is a *process*-focused, not a *product*-focused, effort to understand how customers acquire, use, and replace products, and to observe the sources of frustration that occur in these processes. The outputs of this

FIGURE 16-4 CUSTOMER SATISFACTION AND 80 PERCENT CUSTOMER RETENTION

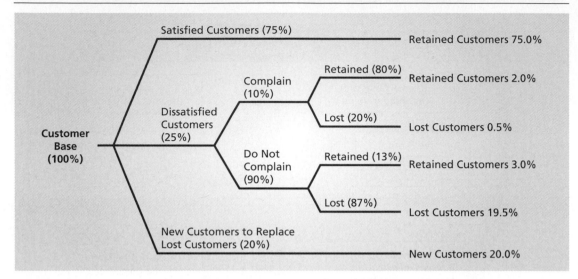

effort are customer solutions designed to enhance customer satisfaction and improve customer retention, as shown in Figure 16-3.

With higher customer retention, a business lowers its cost of customer acquisition and improves its marketing productivity. Recall the rule of thumb that it is five times more expensive to replace a customer than to retain one. A higher customer retention rate, then, means fewer dollars of the marketing budget are needed to maintain the business's market share. These gains drop to the bottom line, which contributes directly to an improved net profit and greater shareholder value.

CUSTOMER SATISFACTION AND PROFITABILITY

The American Customer Satisfaction Index (ACSI) was developed by Claus Fornell at the University of Michigan Business School to measure customer satisfaction with respect to goods and services available to household consumers in the United States. Research using this measure of customer satisfaction revealed that businesses scoring in the top 50 percent in customer satisfaction produced an average shareholder value 2.4 times greater than businesses in the bottom 50 percent. Fornell explains the importance of the relationship between customer satisfaction and shareholder value as follows:

> With few exceptions cash flows accrued from two sources: current customers and new customers. For most companies, the flow is much greater from the current customers. It is as simple as that. The satisfaction of current customers has a great deal of impact on shareholder value.[1]

A business that examines its levels of customer satisfaction, dissatisfaction, complaint recovery, and customer retention, as well as its cost of customer acquisition, gains a keen understanding of the impact satisfied customers have on profits. Figure 16-4 presents a breakdown of a business's customer base by satisfaction and retention, where the overall retention rate is 80 percent. In this example, the business has a 75 percent level of customer

FIGURE 16-5 PROFITABILITY AT 80 PERCENT CUSTOMER RETENTION

Area of Performance	80% Customer Retention			
	Retained Customers	Lost Customers	New Customers	Total Customers
Number of Customers	280,000	70,000	70,000	350,000
Revenue per Customer	$2,265	$1,100	$1,100	$2,251
Sales (millions)	$634	$77	$77	$788
Percent Margin	46.1%	29.2%	29.2%	42.8%
Gross Profit (millions)	$292	$22.5	$22.5	$337
Marketing Expenses (millions)	$70	$18	$100	$188
Marketing Expenses per Customer	$250	$257	$1,429	$537
Net Marketing Cont. (millions)	$222	$5	–$78	$149
Other Operating Expenses (millions)				$12
Operating Income (millions)				$137
Interest and Taxes (46.5%) (millions)				$64
Net Profit (millions)				$73
Return on Sales				9.3%

satisfaction and retains essentially all satisfied customers. The other 5 percent of retained customers come from the ranks of the dissatisfied customers. At the levels of customer satisfaction and retention shown, 20 percent of the business's customer base needs to be replaced every year with new customers just to maintain the same level of sales.

The diagram reveals other interesting facts. While only 10 percent of the dissatisfied customers complain, the business retains 80 percent of them. In contrast, of the 90 percent who do not complain, the business retains only 13 percent. The business loses 87 percent of the dissatisfied customers it *does not* hear from.

Figure 16-5 shows the business's sales and profits at the 80 percent level of customer retention. The business produces $788 million in sales and a net marketing contribution

FIGURE 16-6 PROFITABILITY AT 90 PERCENT CUSTOMER RETENTION

Area of Performance	90% Customer Retention			
	Retained Customers	Lost Customers	New Customers	Total Customers
Number of Customers	315,000	35,000	35,000	350,000
Revenue per Customer	$2,265	$1,100	$1,100	$2,257
Sales (millions)	$713	$38.5	$38.5	$790
Percent Margin	46%	28.6%	28.6%	44.3%
Gross Profit (millions)	$328	$11	$11	$350
Marketing Expenses (millions)	$79	$9	$50	$138
Marketing Expenses per Customer	$251	$257	$1,429	$394
Net Marketing Cont. (millions)	$249	$2	–$39	$212
Other Operating Expenses (millions)				$12
Operating Income (millions)				$200
Interest and Taxes (46.5%) (millions)				$93
Net Profit (millions)				$107
Return on Sales				13.5%

of $149 million. After other operating expenses and interest and taxes are paid, the business has a net profit of $73 million, or 9.3 percent of sales. Nearly all marketing profits come from the retained customers ($222 million). The cost of acquiring new customers is expensive, and new customers purchase less than retained customers. As a result, new customers have a sizeable negative impact on the NMC of $78 million.

Figure 16-6 shows that improving customer retention to 90 percent with better customer satisfaction management would increase marketing profits by $63 million. Retained-customer marketing profitability improves by $27 million, while the lost marketing profits as a result of lost customers and attracting new customers to replace them is almost cut in half, from $73 million to $37 million. The overall net marketing contribution increases to $212 million, resulting in an improvement in net profit of $34 million. The return on sales, despite only a 0.25 percent increase in sales revenues, improves from 9.3 to 13.5 percent. Better market-based management of customer satisfaction and retention is the one reason for the greatly improved performance.

In Figure 16-7, we see that at 80 percent customer retention the business's marketing profits equate to $1.69 per share. When other expenses and interest and taxes are deducted, the result is 83 cents in earnings per share. At 90 percent customer retention, marketing profits equate to $2.40 per share. While other expenses and interest and taxes go up, the $34 million increase in net profit results in an earnings per share of $1.21, a 46 percent increase. This impressive gain occurs with essentially no change in sales, market share, or pricing and margins—just more efficient market-based management of customer satisfaction and retention.

HOW MARKETING STRATEGIES AFFECT PROFITABILITY

Businesses with a strong market orientation see current and prospective customers as the primary source of profitability, cash flow, and earnings. Customers, products, and assets are all important parts of business and success in business, and each needs to be managed on a day-to-day basis for a business to be efficient and profitable. But the one source of revenue is customers. In those businesses that lack a market orientation, financial reports and product line statements tend to dominate the thinking of managers. A market-based business, however, never forgets that its only enduring asset is the customer. Keeping in mind that the customer is the one source of positive cash flow, it is the responsibility of those in marketing to understand how customers affect a business and its profitability.[2] This section attempts to bring into focus the important role customers have in making a business profitable.

Customer Volume

Recognizing the customer as a primary source of profit, a market-based business will expand its focus beyond products and units sold to include customers and markets.[3] The expanded scope is an important strategic step because the number of potential customers is finite, but a wide range of products and services can be sold to each. The number of customers a business serves in its market is the business's customer volume. It is the business's share of the market in terms of customers, not volume of units sold.

Customer Volume = Market Demand (customers) × Market Share Percentage (customers)

FIGURE 16-7 HOW CUSTOMER RETENTION IMPACTS NET PROFIT AND EARNINGS PER SHARE

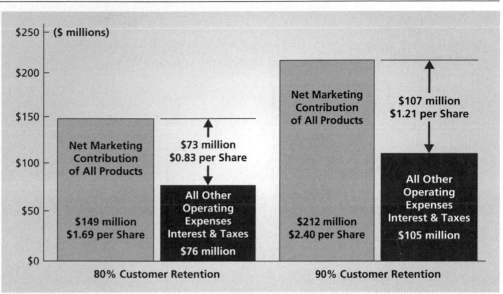

The flow chart in Figure 16-8 shows how the market-based net profit is derived. Customer volume is the result of a market's customer demand and a business's share of that demand. Marketing strategies that affect customer volume include those that:

■ Attract new customers to grow market share,
■ Grow the market demand by bringing more customers into a market, and
■ Enter new markets to create new sources of customer volume.

Each of these customer-focused marketing strategies affects net profit, invested assets, cash flow, and, as we will see, shareholder value. A key component of profitability and financial performance is the level of customer purchases, or the collective customer volume produced. Without customer purchases, a business obviously has no positive cash flow or potential for a net profit or shareholder value.

Margin per Customer

When customers decide to purchase an assortment of products and services from a business, the result is a certain revenue per customer. Of course, a corresponding set of variable costs associated with each sales transaction must be taken into account to determine margin per customer, as shown in Figure 16-8.

Margin per Customer = Revenue per Customer − Variable Cost per Customer

This measure of customer profitability could be computed on a transaction basis, monthly or annually. The bottom line is that a business has to make a positive margin per

FIGURE 16-8 MARKET-BASED MANAGEMENT MODEL OF PROFIT BEFORE TAXES

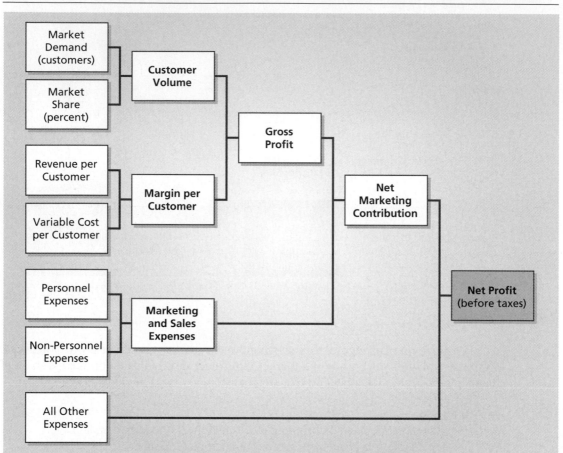

customer or it will produce no profit and, therefore, no shareholder value. In many businesses, the customer margin for a new customer is a small or even a negative one. Over time, we would expect a business to adopt marketing strategies that would increase the customer margins for these customers. If those strategies fail, the business might consider no longer serving low-margin customers as part of a new marketing strategy. Marketing strategies designed to improve margin per customer include strategies that:

- Grow revenue per customer by product line extensions;
- Grow revenue per customer by adding services that enhance customer value;
- Offer improved products and services for which the customer is willing to pay a premium price;
- Develop more cost-efficient marketing systems that lower variable sales and transaction costs; and
- Eliminate customers who, despite the business's marketing efforts, fail to produce an acceptable customer margin.

Because the customer is the primary unit of focus of market-based management, the marketing strategies that a market-based business develops will systematically build customer volume and customer margin.

Gross Profit

Ultimately, whether tracking product revenues and variable product costs or tracking customer volume and margin per customer, the end result will be the gross profit produced by the implemented marketing strategies. Once again, both approaches are needed in managing different aspects of a business. However, those in marketing should be more concerned with a customer perspective and how to develop marketing strategies that affect both customers and gross profit.

$$\text{Gross Profit} = \text{Customer Volume} \times \text{Customer Margin}$$

The gross profit produced by a marketing strategy is an important component in the profitability equation because from this point forward only expenses are introduced. With this in mind, developing market-based strategies that increase the gross profit becomes a priority in improving bottom-line financial performance.

Net Marketing Contribution

Every marketing strategy requires some level of marketing effort to achieve its market share objective. Implementing a strategy designed to obtain the targeted customer volume entails expenses associated with the sales effort, marketing communications, customer service, and marketing management. Figure 16-8 represents these costs as marketing and sales expenses. We know from earlier chapters that the marketing and sales expenses are deducted from the gross profit to produce the net marketing contribution.

$$\text{Net Marketing Contribution} = \text{Gross Profit} - \text{Marketing and Sales Expenses}$$

In effect, the net marketing contribution represents the marketing function's contribution to the business's profit. If the marketing team develops a strategy that fails and therefore lowers the net marketing contribution, then that strategy has in effect lowered the net profit of the business.

Marketing strategies are generally designed to improve gross profit, whether by increasing market demand, market share, or revenue per customer, or by decreasing variable cost per customer. The net marketing contribution equation should make it clear that such strategies are profitable only if the increase in gross profit exceeds the increase in marketing expenses required to produce the gross profit increase. Said in another way, for a strategy to improve profits, it has to improve the net marketing contribution.

Net Profit (Before Taxes)

Although marketing strategies contribute to a business's net profit (before taxes) through the net marketing contribution, the net profit is generally beyond the control of the marketing function or the marketing management team. Marketing strategies produce a certain level of net marketing contribution from which all other business expenses must be deducted before a net profit is realized, as illustrated in Figure 16-8. These operating expenses include fixed expenses, such as human resources management, research and development, and administrative expenses, as well as utilities, rent, and fees. In most instances, a business would also have allocated corporate overhead, which includes legal fees, corporate advertising, and executive salaries.

Net Profit (before taxes) = Net Marketing Contribution − Operating Expenses

Sometimes a marketing strategy will require an increase in operating expenses. For example, a strategy to upgrade a product to attract more customers and build market share could call for research and development expenses for product improvement.

HOW MARKETING STRATEGIES AFFECT ASSETS

Most businesses do not realize the impact marketing strategies have on a business's investment in assets. As we will see, the assets of a business are indirectly affected by marketing strategies. We will limit our discussion to accounts receivable, inventory, and fixed assets, as they are the assets normally accounting for most of a business's investment in assets.

Investment in Accounts Receivable

Marketing managers seldom think about the effect a marketing strategy has on accounts receivable. Receivables are the money owed a business, and the amount varies in proportion to sales revenues and customer payment behavior. As sales revenues increase or decrease, a corresponding change in accounts receivable occurs. Likewise, customer payment behavior affects the total owed. If customers take an average of 45 days to pay their bills, for approximately 12.5 percent of the year (45 divided by 365) customers are holding the business's money. If annual sales were $100 million, the accounts receivable would be approximately $12.5 million at any point in time.

Accounts Receivable = Sales Revenues × Percent Days Outstanding

= $100 million × 0.125 (12.5%)

= **$12.5 million**

To put this in marketing terms, accounts receivable is a function of customer volume, revenue per customer, and customer payment behavior.

$$\frac{\textbf{Accounts}}{\textbf{Receivable}} = \frac{\text{Customer}}{\text{Volume}} \times \frac{\text{Revenue}}{\text{per Customer}} \times \frac{\text{Percent Days}}{\text{Outstanding}}$$

= 20,000 × $5,000 × 0.125 (12.5%)

= **$12.5 million**

We can readily see how strategies that affect customer volume, revenue per customer, and customer payment behavior affect accounts receivable. Of these three factors, a business might find that it can most readily address the last one. The business could, for example, hone its selection of target customers to include their bill-paying behavior. By avoiding slow-paying customers, the business would lower the amount invested in accounts receivable. Among residential phone customers, for instance, about 3 percent are "movers and shakers." They run up big telephone bills and then move on and shake loose before paying. A business that identifies and avoids customers with poor payment histories will have a relatively low accounts receivable figure.

A business's service quality also affects customers' payment behavior. Consider the following:

■ Eight out of 10 *Fortune* 500 companies report that the level of customer service they receive affects their decision to pay a bill on time.
■ More than half of *Fortune* 500 companies withhold payment from suppliers when they are dissatisfied with the level of service they have received.[4]

It seems likely, then, that a business with a strong market orientation and a commitment to service quality and customer satisfaction will be paid faster than a business that delivers a lower level of service quality or customer satisfaction. This is one way a marketing strategy—by including a focus on service quality and improving customer satisfaction—can lower a business's investment in accounts receivable.

Investment in Inventory

Many businesses must carry large inventories to serve their customers. Other businesses may have long production runs that lead to a large number of finished products on hand for several months. Businesses also from time to time encounter a diminished market demand that results in a large inventory of goods. There are also work-in-process inventories (partially finished goods) and raw materials inventories. All inventories are assets with market values. As with accounts receivable, the size and value of inventories vary with sales revenues and customer purchase behavior. At any point in time, a business's inventory is roughly equal to the total cost of goods sold times a percentage of days of inventory on hand. The need to have inventory on hand to cover an average of 30 days of sales would equate to 8.2 percent days of inventory (30 days divided by 365). If the manufactured cost of goods sold for a year is $40 million, the average investment in inventory would be $3.28 million.

$$\textbf{Inventory Investment} = \text{Total Cost of Inventory} \times \text{Percent Days of Inventory}$$
$$= \$40 \text{ million} \times 0.082 \ (8.2\%)$$
$$= \textbf{\$3.28 million}$$

In terms of a market strategy, the investment in inventory is expressed as:

$$\frac{\textbf{Inventory}}{\textbf{Investment}} = \frac{\text{Customer}}{\text{Volume}} \times \frac{\text{Unit Cost}}{\text{per Customer}} \times \frac{\text{Percent Days}}{\text{of Inventory}}$$
$$= 200,000 \times \$200 \times 0.082 \ (8.2\%)$$
$$= \textbf{\$3.28 million}$$

Marketing strategies that affect market demand, market share, and the unit manufacturing cost will affect investment in inventory. Channel marketing strategies will also affect investment in inventory. A change from a direct sales distribution system to a distributor channel system could lead to lower inventories as a business shifts its inventory requirements to distributors, which would lower the business's investment in inventory and, in turn, its investment in overall assets.

Investment in Fixed Assets

Fixed assets include investments in land, buildings, equipment, and furnishings. Most of these assets are annually depreciated as business expenses and, at least from a financial accounting perspective, lose value over time. The value of fixed assets at any point in time, however, is relative to sales volume. A market strategy to grow sales substantially in a growing market would typically require additional fixed assets to accommodate the increase in volume.

Fixed assets, then, are a function of sales volume, which in turn is a function of marketing strategies to grow customer volume or volume per customer, or both. Most businesses have excess manufacturing capacity, which is a large component of fixed assets. A marketing strategy to grow volume, by growing customer demand or increasing customer market share, will increase capacity utilization. If the larger volume increases the net profit, this strategy leads to an overall improvement in the business's return on assets because no addition to assets was necessary. Naturally, in situations where fixed assets have to be added to accommodate growth, the investment in assets will be greater. A business that derives profits from an increase in volume has to have profits sufficiently large to produce a higher return on assets.

Every marketing decision affects one or more of the return-on-assets components. For example, consider a scanner manufacturer's marketing strategy to capture a significant share of the retail scanner market. The business's managers knew that a major customer was price sensitive and that competitors would price aggressively to obtain this customer's volume. Recognizing the importance of price, the scanner manufacturer offered a price lower than competing prices but required full payment within 10 days, with no cash discount. Unit margins were lower, but the large volume captured produced a good net profit and, with a minimal investment in accounts receivable, the business produced a much higher return on assets.

RETURN MEASURES OF PROFITABILITY

Accounting and financial measures of profitability include net profit, return on sales (ROS), return on assets (ROA), and return on equity (ROE). As the following formula shows, the net marketing contribution is a key driver of net profit. To grow net profit in any given year, a business has two fundamental options: lower operating expenses or grow the net marketing contribution.

$$\frac{\text{Net Profit}}{\text{After Taxes}} = \frac{\text{Market}}{\text{Demand}} \times \frac{\text{Market}}{\text{Share}} \times \frac{\text{Percent}}{\text{Market}} - \frac{\text{Marketing}}{\text{Expenses}} - \frac{\text{Other}}{\text{Expenses}} - \frac{\text{Interest}}{\text{\& Taxes}}$$

FIGURE 16-9 STERICYCLE'S MARKETING PROFITS AND FINANCIAL PERFORMANCE

Area of Performance	1997 Actual	2000 Actual	2003 Actual	2006 Actual	2009 Plan*
Market Demand	$1,000	$1,500	$2,000	$3,500	$4,209
Market Share	4.6%	21.6%	22.7%	22.6%	24%
Sales	$46	$324	$453	$790	$1,009
Revenue per Customer	$1,075	$1,336	$1,510	$2,242	$ 2,178
Percent Margin	26.4%	39.3%	43.4%	44.3%	47.4%
Gross Profit	$12	$127	$197	$350	$478
Marketing Expenses	$11	$60	$66	$137	$178
Marketing Expenses (% sales)	23.9%	18.5%	14.6%	17.3%	17.6%
Net Marketing Contribution	$1	$67	$131	$213	$300
Marketing ROS	2.2%	20.7%	28.9%	27.0%	29.7%
Marketing ROI	9%	112%	198%	156%	169%
Other Expenses	$0	$46	$5	$11	$14
Income	$1	$21	$126	$202	$286
Interest & Taxes	$0	$8	$61	$97	$120
Net Profit	$1	$13	$65	$105	$166
Assets & Liabilities					
Total Assets	$61	$598	$707	$1,328	$1,678
Total Liabilities	$16	$453	$300	$703	$803
Equity & Capital					
Owner's Equity	$45	$145	$408	$625	$875
Invested Capital	$45	$480	$570	$1,068	$1,264
Financial Performance Metrics					
Return on Sales	2.2%	4.0%	14.3%	13.3%	16.5%
Return on Assets	1.6%	2.2%	9.2%	7.9%	9.9%
Return on Equity	2.2%	9.0%	15.9%	16.8%	19.0%
Return on Capital	2.2%	2.7%	11.4%	9.8%	13.1%
Economic Profit**	−350.0%	−269.2%	12.3%	−1.7%	23.9%
Sales-to-Asset Ratio	0.75	0.54	0.64	0.59	0.60

Dollar amounts rounded to millions.

*Based on the Sample Marketing Plan in Chapter 14.

**Assumes a 10% cost of capital.

The three fundamental measures of profit performance—ROS, ROA, and ROE—are based on the net profit produced in any given period:

$$\text{Return on Sales (ROS)} = \frac{\text{Net Profit (after taxes)}}{\text{Sales}}$$

$$\text{Return on Assets (ROA)} = \frac{\text{Net Profit (after taxes)}}{\text{Assets}}$$

$$\text{Return on Equity (ROE)} = \frac{\text{Net Profit (after taxes)}}{\text{Equity}}$$

For example, as shown in Figure 16-9, Stericycle's sales in 1997 were $46 million and net profit was $1 million, resulting in a return on sales of 2.2 percent. In 1997, Stericycle had assets of $61 million that resulted in a return on assets of 1.6 percent. With owner's equity of $45 million, the return on equity was 2.2 percent.

The growth plan introduced in 1997 produced tremendous gains in sales and profits by 2000, and the gains continued to 2003, as shown. The net marketing contribution grew from $1 million in 1997 to $131 million in 2003, which played a significant part in the growth of net income. While financial performance metrics improved fairly well from 1997 to 2000, the company achieved much greater improvements by 2003. The improvements corresponded with much higher levels of marketing ROS (28.9 percent) and marketing ROI (198 percent).

In line with its aggressive growth strategy, Stericycle grew sales to $790 million by 2006. With an investment of $137 million in marketing and sales, the strategy produced a net marketing contribution of $213 million. After deductions of other operating expenses and interest and taxes, the net profit was $105 million, a 13.3 percent return on sales. The return on assets declined from 9.2 percent in 2003 to 7.9 percent in 2006, while the return on equity increased from 15.9 to 16.8 percent.

MEASURES OF SHAREHOLDER VALUE

Recognizing the importance of the customer satisfaction management and generally all aspects of market-based management with respect to net profit, assets, and return measures of profit performance, we can now broaden our discussion of the ways that market-based management affects shareholder value.[5]

In looking at the impact that market-based management has on shareholder value, we will keep in mind that return measures of performance, such as ROS, ROA, and ROE, are valid indicators of a business's financial well-being. They are excellent measures of financial performance. Shareholder value metrics, however, are especially important because they measure earnings per share, economic profit,[6] and the price-earnings ratio. All of these metrics start with market demand and the efficiency of a business's effort to capture market share. As Figure 16-10 shows, the shareholder value metrics in the boxes at the lower right are driven by Stericycle's market-based management and its operational excellence in managing the collection and disposal of medical waste. We can define these metrics as follows:

- **Earnings per Share (EPS)**—Net profit (after taxes) divided by the number of shares equals earnings per share. For Stericycle, a net profit (after taxes) of $105 million and 88.3 million shares translates to $1.19 per share, as Figure 16-10 shows.
- **Economic Profit (EP)**—Net profit (after taxes) minus the business's capital investment first multiplied by the cost of capital yields a measure of how much value the business created by that level of net profit (earnings). For Stericycle, its after-tax net profit ($105 million) minus its capital investment ($1.068 billion) first multiplied by the cost of capital (10 percent) yields an EP of −$1.8 million, or −1.7 percent of the net income of $105 million.
- **Price-Earnings Ratio (PE Ratio)**—The PE ratio is a ratio of a business's stock price to earnings per share. The higher the PE ratio, the greater is the risk to investment. For Stericycle, the PE ratio is close to 40. At $1.19 per share of earnings in 2006, this translates to a value of about $48 per share of stock.

FIGURE 16-10 MARKET-BASED MANAGEMENT MODEL OF FINANCIAL PERFORMANCE

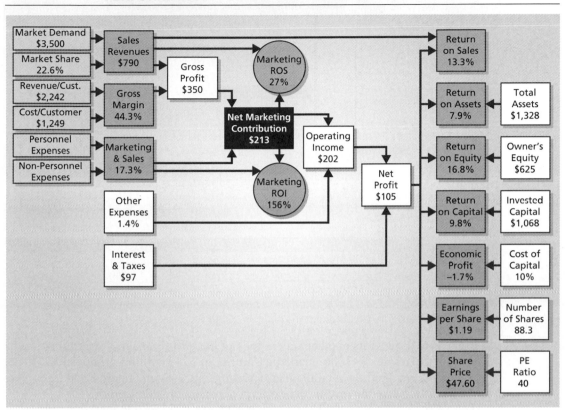

Based on the sample marketing plan developed for Stericycle in Chapter 14, we can present a forecast of financial performance in terms of shareholder value. As shown in Figure 16-11, the market is projected to grow from $3.5 billion in 2006 to $4.2 billion in 2009. The market growth alone would contribute to growth in earnings per share. However, a strategy to grow market share from 22.6 percent in 2006 to 24 percent in 2009 will further promote profitable growth. We can project sales growing from $790 million in 2006 to $1.009 billion in 2009.

But, as we have seen, sales growth is not free. The Stericycle marketing budget is projected to increase from $137 million in 2006 to $178 million in 2009.

The projection for percent margin is an increase from 44.3 to 47.4 percent with up-selling of Stericycle's value-added branded products, resulting in an increase in marketing profits from $213 million in 2006 to $300 million in 2009. In each year, the marketing profits will pay for other expenses and interest and taxes, and the amount left will be the business's net profit for that year. As shown, the projected growth in net profit is from $105 million in 2006 to $166 million in 2009. Based on the number of shares outstanding in 2006, the growth in net profit will see earnings per share increase from $1.19 in 2006 to $1.88 in 2009. Stericycle in 2006 had a PE ratio of 40 and a stock price close to $48. The same PE ratio in 2009, if Stericycle achieves its 3-year performance objectives, would have the company's stock priced at over $75 per share.

FIGURE 16-11 STERICYCLE'S PROJECTED PROFITS AND SHAREHOLDER VALUE

Area of Performance	2006 Actual	2007 Plan*	2008 Plan*	2009 Plan*
Market Demand	$3,500	$3,720	$3,956	$4,209
Market Share	22.6%	23.0%	23.4%	24.0%
Sales	$790	$855	$927	$1,009
Percent Margin	44.3%	45.4%	46.4%	47.4%
Gross Profit	$350	$388	$430	$478
Marketing Expenses	$137	$149	$163	$178
Marketing Expenses (% sales)	17.3%	17.5%	17.6%	17.6%
Net Marketing Contribution	$213	$239	$267	$300
Other Expenses	$11	$12	$13	$14
Operating Income	$202	$227	$254	$286
Interest & Taxes	$97	$101	$109	$120
Net Profit	$105	$126	$145	$166

Shareholder Value	2006	2007	2008	2009
Earnings per Share	$1.19	$1.43	$1.64	$1.88
Price-Earnings Ratio	40	40	40	40
Stock Price	$47.60	$57.17	$65.69	$75.20

*Based on the Sample Marketing Plan in Chapter 14. Dollar amounts rounded to millions.

Figure 16-12 presents another way to look at the profit impact of marketing profits on earnings per share. In 2006, marketing profits of $213 million produced $2.41 per share in marketing profits. After all other operating expenses and interest and taxes were paid from these marketing profits, the earnings per share in 2006 were $1.19.

The Stericycle Sample Marketing Plan in Chapter 14 projected marketing profits of $300 million in 2009. Those marketing profits would equate to $3.40 per share, assuming the same number of shares as in 2006. While other operating expenses and interest and taxes are projected to increase, the projected net profit of $166 million would produce $1.88 in earnings per share.

The extent to which Stericycle would achieve the projected net profit and earnings per share depends on the degree to which it could successfully execute the proposed sample marketing plan. Assuming the PE ratio would not change drastically, we could expect this marketing plan would reward shareholders with a much higher stock price.

MARKET-BASED MANAGEMENT

To be profitable, a business needs to achieve above-average marketing and operational performance.[7] In fact, marketing and operational performance are interrelated, as illustrated in Figure 16-3. A business with a low level of customer satisfaction can expect sales to decline and the time that customers take in paying their invoices to become longer. These businesses have to spend more marketing dollars in an effort to keep sales at their present level. The combination of falling sales among current customers, higher

FIGURE 16-12 HOW MARKETING PROFITS CONTRIBUTE TO EARNINGS PER SHARE

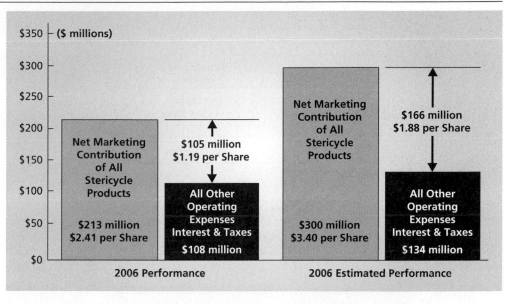

accounts receivable, and more money spent on marketing influence the results of all marketing and financial metrics used to measure a business's performance.

The central theme of this and the previous editions of *Market-Based Management* has been that businesses with strong market orientations empower themselves to develop marketing strategies that:

■ Deliver high levels of customer satisfaction and superior customer value;
■ Improve market position, sales, and profitability; and
■ Improve earnings and shareholder value.

Market-based management, as shown in Figure 16-13, is at the base of a business with a strong market orientation. A strong market orientation translates into a strong customer and competitor focus and a team approach that cuts across organizational functions. The result is a market-based business that is in a very favorable position to develop and deliver market-based strategies designed to attract, satisfy, and retain customers. Implemented successfully across a wide range of market situations, a market-based approach will deliver higher levels of profitability, cash flow, and shareholder value than will a cost-based approach.

We need always remember that the only source of positive cash flow is the customer. Technology, assets, and management are of little value without customers. The job of a market-based business is to understand customers, the competition, and the market environment within the context of the business's technology, assets, and management capabilities, and to render a market-based strategy that delivers superior levels of customer satisfaction, profitability, and shareholder value.

FIGURE 16-13 MARKET-BASED MANAGEMENT AND SHAREHOLDER VALUE

■ Summary

Marketing strategies directly affect customers and sales revenues. They also affect margins, net profit, and marketing expenses. These factors in turn lead to a net marketing contribution. Because operating and overhead expenses are beyond the control of marketing managers, the net marketing contribution plays an important role in evaluating the profit impact of marketing strategies. Throughout this book we have sought to determine the profit impact of a marketing strategy based on the net marketing contribution it produces.

Marketing strategies also directly impact assets. Changes in sales produce corresponding changes in accounts receivable and inventory. Likewise, a major increase in volume based on a particular marketing strategy may require additional operating expenses and investment in fixed assets. Marketing strategies impact both the numerator and denominator of the ROA equation. This awareness gives us a much broader view of the impact a marketing strategy has on a business's profitability.

The net marketing contribution for each marketing strategy contributes to both profit performance and shareholder value. Return measures of profit performance (ROS, ROA, and ROE) are driven by marketing performance and the net marketing contribution. Shareholder measures of performance (earnings per share, economic profit, and the price-earnings ratio) are directly influenced by marketing performance and profitability.

Finally, at the heart of market-based management is a strong market orientation that enables a business to develop effective marketing strategies for attracting, satisfying, and retaining target customers. A market-based managed business should at the same time be evaluating alternative marketing strategies that contribute to the business's growth, short- and long-run profit performance, and strategic position. Market-driven businesses with well-developed and implemented strategies deliver high levels of customer satisfaction, profitability, and shareholder value.

■ Market-Based Strategic Thinking

1 Why is it important for marketing managers to understand the profit impact of marketing strategies?

2 What should be the role of the net marketing contribution in the development of a marketing strategy?

3 Why is net profit often a misleading indicator of the profit impact of a marketing strategy?

4 How does a marketing strategy affect the assets of a business? Why should the accounts receivable and inventory change with a change in marketing strategy? When will the fixed assets change?

5 How does the net marketing contribution of a marketing strategy affect return on assets (ROA)?

6 How do investments in customer retention contribute to higher levels of profit performance?

7 Explain how the net marketing contribution of a marketing strategy affects return measures of profit performance.

8 How do changes in customer retention affect shareholder measures of performance, such as earnings per share?

9 Explain how Stericycle's market share gain affected its net marketing contribution, net profit, and return measures of performance.

10 Why should shareholders and Wall Street analysts be interested in a business's customer retention?

11 Why would two businesses with the same sales have different shareholder value if one had a 60 percent level of customer retention and the other an 80 percent level?

12 How would you use the net marketing contribution for each product-market to forecast earnings and earnings per share?

13 What role does net marketing contribution play in understanding the earnings level of a business?

14 How does the market orientation of a business affect customers, business performance, and shareholders?

15 Why should a market-oriented business with a passion for customer satisfaction produce higher levels of earnings per share and, therefore, have greater shareholder value than a business that is not market oriented?

Marketing Performance Tools

The three **Marketing Performance Tools** described here may be accessed online at *www.rogerjbest.com*. These applied-learning exercises will add to your understanding of the positive impact market-based management has on financial performance.

16.1 Market Demand and Market Share
- Change the market demand from $4,000 to $3,800 and market share from 25 to 22.6 percent and evaluate how sales, profits, and financial performance change.

16.2 Percent Margin and Marketing Expenses
- Lower the revenue per customer to $1,480 and reduce market share to 24.67 percent. Then return revenue per customer to $1,500 and increase marketing expenses from 17 to 18 percent. Which change has made the greatest impact on performance?

16.3 Asset Management and Invested Capital
- Increase assets from $1,500 to $1,550 to lower the assets-to-sales ratio from 0.67 to 0.65 and evaluate the impact on financial performance. Then return assets to $1,500 and decrease the long-term debt from $500 to $400 and evaluate the effects of this change on financial performance.

Notes

1. "Customer Satisfaction: The Fundamental Basis for Business Survival," *Siebel Magazine* (vol. 50, no. 1): 19–25.
2. Robert Kaplan and David Norton, "The Balanced Scorecard—Measures that Drive Performance," *Harvard Business Review* (January–February 1992): 71–79.
3. Eric Hardy, "The *Forbes* 500's Annual Directory," *Forbes* (April 22, 1996): 232–278.
4. "Customer Service Impacts Cash Flow," *Positive Impact* (August 1993): 5–6.
5. Sidney Schoeffler, "Impacts of Business Strategy on Stock Prices," PIMS Letter No. 20 (1980): 1–9.
6. "Valuing Companies," *The Economist* (August 2, 1997): 53–55; Eric Olsen and Thomas Rawley, "Stock Prices Performance: Corporate Agenda for the 1980s," *Journal of Accounting and Corporate Finance* (Spring 1987): 3–15; Bill Birchard, "Mastering the New Metrics," *CFO: The Magazine for Senior Financial Executives* (October 1994); Bill Barmhardt, "Chicago's Top 100 Companies," *Chicago Tribune* (May 15, 1995); Thomas Rawley and L. Edwards, "How Holt Methods Work for Good Decisions, Determine Business Value More Accurately," *Corporate Cashflow Magazine* (September 1993); and Bernard Reimann, "Stock Price and Business Success: What Is the Relationship?" *Journal of Business Strategy* (Summer 1987): 38–50.
7. Robert Hayes, "Strategic Planning: Forward in Reverse," *Harvard Business Review* (November–December 1985): 111–119.

CREDITS

Chapter 4

Page 105, Figure 4-5: Ad courtesy of the Weyerhaeuser Corporation. Used with permission. Page 115, Figure 4-13: Ad courtesy of Sealed Air Corporation. Page 116, Figure 4-14: Ad courtesy of Rohm and Haas Company.

Chapter 5

Page 156, Figure 5-15: Advertising and photo courtesy of DuPont.

Chapter 10

Page 307, Figure 10-1: Ad courtesy of E. I. du Pont de Nemours and Company. Used with permission. Page 308, Figure 10-3: Ad courtesy of Hewlett-Packard Development Company, L.P. Page 309, Figure 10-4 Ad courtesy of Hewlett-Packard Development Company, L.P. Page 310, Figure 10-5: Ad courtesy of The Marketing Excellence Survey. Page 311, Figure 10-6: Ad courtesy of The Marketing Excellence Survey. Page 315, Figure 10-11: Ad courtesy of Johnson Controls, Inc.

GLOSSARY

acquisition cost The marketing expense to acquire one new customer.

adjacent segment strategy Segment strategies targeted at customers with slightly different needs than current customers.

advertising carryover effects Sales occurring after the period in which an advertisement was run.

advertising elasticity The percent change in volume per 1 percent change in advertising expenditures.

advocates Customers classified as "top performers" who buy nearly everything a company has to sell.

agents, brokers, and reps Salespeople who work for a business on a commission basis.

articulated market demand Current market demand based on articulated customer needs.

assets Cash, accounts receivable, inventory, plant and equipment, and other assets.

big spenders Customers classified as "high potentials" who buy a lot from a company but are not loyal to the company.

bottom-up marketing budget A budget based on the cost of each specific marketing task needed to implement a marketing mix strategy.

brand assets Assets a brand can attain based on market leadership, awareness, brand relevance, reputation for quality, and brand loyalty.

brand encoding The process of branding products within a business based on a combination of company name, name, sub-brand name, number, letter, product name, or key benefit.

brand equity The attractiveness of a brand based entirely on its name and image.

brand image The perceived image of what a brand stands for in the mind of a target customer.

brand interaction (information exchange) A communications strategy designed to create a customer dialogue and information exchange.

brand liabilities Liabilities a brand can incur as the result of customer dissatisfaction, environmental problems, product failures/recall, lawsuits/consumer boycotts, and questionable business practices.

brand management The process of naming products, managing brands, and brand-line extensions to attain maximum brand equity and a brand's full profit potential.

brand personality The personality a brand takes on based on human personality characteristics.

break-even market share The market share needed to reach break-even volume.

break-even volume The unit volume at which total sales equal total cost.

build brand (pure brand) A communications strategy designed to create an emotional customer response in an attempt to build an emotional connection between the target customer and the product.

capital Owner's equity plus long-term debt add up to the capital a business has invested in its business.

channel mapping The process of mapping all relevant channels from a pocket price to target customer prices, or from target customer prices to company pocket price.

channel margin Margin required by a channel intermediary.

channel marketing expenses Marketing and sales expenses associated with a marketing channel.

channel partners Companies within a business's marketing channels that distribute, resell, or add value to a business's products and participate in the process of connecting businesses with endusers.

channel system A particular combination of distribution and sales channels.

co-branding Combining two brand names to create a new brand.

company benefits The level of perceived benefit a customer attaches to a company or brand name.

competitive advantage A relative advantage one business has over another that is sustainable and translates into a benefit that is important to target customers.

competitive benchmarking Benchmarking a company outside an industry on a certain business practice in which the benchmark company is known for excellence.

competitive bid pricing Pricing a bid based on the historical success of past price-to-cost bid ratios and the competitive bid situation.

competitive performance metrics Marketing metrics that gauge the competitive position of a product or business.

competitive position A business's position relative to a benchmark competitor's position with regard to price, product quality, delivery, new product sales, and so on.

competitor analysis Benchmarking a key competitor with respect to important areas of performance.

competitor orientation The degree to which a business tracks competitors' strategies and benchmarks its performance relative to competitors.

competitor response price elasticity The percentage change in a competitor's price per 1 percent change in the price of a business's product.

complementary products Products customers buy for use with another product they have purchased.

conjoint analysis (measurement) A statistical method for deriving the customer preferences for different levels of price and product performance.

cost advantage A sustainable lower cost relative to competition.

cost of capital The percentage paid (like interest) for capital (money obtained from investors and lenders).

cost-based pricing Pricing that is determined by a business's cost and margin requirements.

cost-plus pricing Price that is set based on the cost of the product plus a desired profit margin.

cross price elasticity The percent change in volume in one product when the price is changed 1 percent in another product.

cost of purchase index A measurement of a product's relative advantage against competing products with regard to customer cost considerations.

customer focus The degree to which a business seeks to understand customer needs and use situations, and tracks customer satisfaction.

customer life The number of purchase periods a customer is retained by a business.

customer's lifetime value The net present value of cash flows produced over a customer's life.

customer loyalty Allegiance on the part of customers to a particular business or product.

customer loyalty index A measurement of a business's level of customer satisfaction, customer retention, and customer recommendation.

customer metrics Marketing performance metrics that track customer satisfaction, customer retention, customer loyalty, and customer value.

customer mix marketing budget A marketing budget based on the cost of new customer acquisition and retention.

customer profitability Gross margin per customer minus the marketing expenses needed to serve a customer.

customer relationship management A process devoted to developing and managing one-on-one relationships with target customers.

customer relationship marketing Marketing programs designed to personalize or customize a business's offerings to selected customers.

customer retention rate The percentage of customers retained from one purchase period to another.

customer satisfaction The degree to which customers are satisfied or dissatisfied with a business, product, or specific aspect of a product or service provided by a business.

customer satisfaction index An overall index of a business's customer satisfaction.

customer surveys Marketing surveys that track customer purchases, intentions to purchase, and performance perceptions.

customer terrorists Dissatisfied customers who seek to tell others of their dissatisfaction with a product, brand, or company.

customer touch points The opportunities that a business has to interact with customers and thereby improve the customer's experience.

customer value Total benefits minus the cost of acquiring those benefits.

database marketing A database of customer purchases, preferences, needs, and demographics used in customized marketing communications, product offerings, and extra services.

day in the life of a customer A market-research approach that involves observing the process a customer goes through in acquiring, using, and disposing of a product.

defensive strategy (defensive strategic market plan) A long-run plan to protect or exit a market position.

demographic trap Segmenting customers on the basis of demographics alone without considering customer needs.

differentiation advantage A sustainable product or service advantage that translates into a benefit important to target customers.

direct channel system A channel system that retains ownership of the product and requires management of its sales, distribution, and customer service.

discount factor The net present value of $1 when discounted from a particular point in time and at a particular discount rate.

discount rate A business's cost of capital.

distributors Intermediaries who take title (ownership) of a product and are responsible for its sale and distribution and for customer service.

divest market strategy A defensive strategic market plan to exit a market by selling or closing down a business.

early adopters Customers who follow innovators and account for the second 13.5 percent of customers to adopt a new product or technology.

early majority The customers (34 percent) who follow innovators and early adopters in adopting a new product or technology.

earnings per share Net profits (after taxes) divided by the number of shares held by shareholders.

economic profit Net income after taxes minus capital times the cost of capital.

economic value The value created based on the total cost of purchase of two competing products.

e-marketing Electronic marketing using the Internet as a marketing channel.

empathic design process An observational approach to discovering customer problems, frustrations, and inconveniences in using a company's product.

evocative brand names Brand names designed to evoke a feeling or perception.

exit market strategies Defensive strategic market plans that specify a market exit strategy that can range from immediate exit with a divestment strategy to a slow exit with harvesting strategy.

experiential brand names Brand names that communicate the experience a customer will have, such as the experience of discovery conveyed by the brand name Navigator.

external performance metrics Marketing performance metrics that track external performance with respect to market penetration, competitive position, and customer satisfaction.

flagship brand The highest priced and quality brand in a business's product line.

flanker brand A product extension of a business's core brand.

floor pricing A price that is set on a financial requirement such as gross margin or return on investment.

focus groups A discovery method in which target customers answer questions about a product or customer use situation.

forward buying The practice of buying a greater volume of a product when it is on sale.

frontal attack strategies Competitive strategies that directly attack a competitor's market share.

founder and owner brand names Brand names derived from the founder or owner of a business.

functional brand names Brand names derived from the basic function of a product.

GE/McKinsey Portfolio A portfolio matrix that uses multiple factors to index market attractiveness (vertical axis) and competitive position (horizontal axis).

generic product life cycle The product life cycle for a product category, or "generic product-market," such as cereal or cars.

gross profit (or "total contribution") Total sales minus total variable costs.

grow market share strategy A long-run offensive strategic market plan to grow market share.

harvest market strategy A defensive strategic market plan to slowly exit a market while maximizing profits.

harvest pricing Raising price in a series of steps in an effort to improve margins and maximize gross profit until the product exits the market.

heavy-up message frequency A period in which a business increases its advertising effort.

high potentials Profitable customers who are not yet loyal to a product or business.

horizontal brand-line extension Extending the brand to a line of related products.

horizontal market opportunity A market with closely related substitute products.

indirect channel systems Channels in which intermediaries take ownership of a business's product and the responsibility for its sale and distribution and for customer service.

industry analysis A structural analysis of a competitive environment based on competitor entry/exit, buyer/supplier power, substitutes, and competitive rivalry.

ingredient co-branding Adding a brand name to another product's brand like "Intel inside" on Dell and Compaq computers.

interest-arousing Marketing communications designed to create interest in a brand or product.

internal performance metrics Performance metrics that are internal measures of a business's operations.

in-the-box strategy Internal strategies that lack both customer and competitor intelligence.

innovators The very first 2.5 percent of customers to adopt a new product or technology.

invented brand names Brand names created from root words or partial words, or names that are poetic constructions based on rhythm or the experience of saying the name.

inventory turnover The number of times an inventory is sold per year.

knowledge advantage An advantage in both customer and competitor intelligence that a business has over its competitors.

large-segment strategy A segment strategy that is focused on the largest market segment in a market.

laggards The last 16 percent of customers to adopt a new product or technology.

late majority The 34 percent of customers who adopt a new product or technology after 50 percent of the market has already adopted it.

lead-user analysis An examination of the ways that innovators and highly involved early adopters use a new product, which can offer insights into how a product can be improved or a new product developed.

life-cycle cost analysis A method for discovering the total cost of a product to a customer over the usage life of the product.

low-cost leader pricing The low-cost producer sets price based on cost in an effort to have the lowest market prices.

loyalists Customers under the broader classification of "top performers" who are very loyal to a business's products or services.

margin per unit The selling price of a product minus all the variable costs associated with producing, distributing, and selling the product.

market adoption forces Market forces that affect the rate of new-product adoption.

market analysis An external analysis of market demand, customer needs, competition, distributors, and environmental forces that influence market demand and customer behavior.

market attractiveness The relative attractiveness of a market based on market forces, competitive environment, and market access.

market-based business A business organized around markets with market units as profit centers.

market-based management The commitment of a strong market orientation and management of markets that strives to deliver superior customer value and profitability.

market-based pricing Pricing based on target customer need, competitors' product position, and the strength of a business's product, service, or brand advantage.

market definition A specification of market scope that makes clear current and potential customers.

market development index The ratio of current market demand to market potential (maximum market demand).

market focus A business orientation that is focused on customers and competitors.

market infrastructure Channel intermediaries and channel influencers that shape opinions and communicate information about a business and its products.

market orientation The degree to which a business has a strong customer-focus and competitor orientation and works as a team across functions to develop and deliver a market-based strategy.

market penetration strategies Offensive strategic market plans designed to further penetrate existing markets or enter new markets.

market performance metrics Marketing metrics that track the attractiveness of a market.

market potential The maximum market demand that should occur when all potential customers have entered a market.

market segmentation Grouping customers into segments on the basis of similar needs and differentiating demographic characteristics.

market share The percentage of current market demand obtained by a business.

market share index A hierarchy of market share factors (such as awareness, availability, interest, intention to buy, and purchase) that results in an estimate of market share.

market vision A broad view of the market based on a fundamental customer need that goes beyond existing product solutions.

marketing advantage A sustainable advantage over competitors in either channels of distribution, sales force, or marketing communications.

marketing EPS The net marketing contribution of a business or product divided by the number shares, which provides a metric on the extent to which the marketing effort contributes to earnings per share (EPS).

marketing expenses All fixed expenses associated with selling, marketing, and managing of a marketing strategy targeted at a particular market.

marketing mix A combination of the 4 Ps (product, price, promotion, and place) and service designed for a specific target market.

marketing mix strategy The year to year marketing mix plan that will guide an overall strategic market pan to a desired marketing and profitability objective.

marketing performance metrics Metrics that track how a product or business is performing with respect to market performance, customer performance, competitive performance, and marketing profitability.

marketing planning process A process that starts with a situation analysis, which leads to a specific strategic market plan, tactical marketing strategy, and marketing budget, and results in a performance plan.

marketing productivity Dollars of net marketing contributions produced by a strategy per dollar of fixed marketing expenses.

marketing profitability The net marketing contribution for a product, business, or company.

marketing profitability metrics Net marketing contribution, marketing ROS, and marketing ROI.

marketing profitability portfolio A portfolio matrix that shows the positions of products or markets relative to marketing ROS on one axis and marketing ROI on the other.

marketing ROI The net marketing contribution divided by marketing expenses for a product, business, or company.

marketing ROS The net marketing contribution divided by sales for a product, business, or company.

mass collaboration A Web-based methodology designed to allow customers, professionals, suppliers, and employees to share their ideas with respect to improving existing products or developing new ones.

mass customization An individualized marketing mix in which products, prices, promotion, place, and service are customized to the individual needs of a niche market or individual customers.

mass market A market that is not segmented and all customers and potential customers are treated as one.

mass personalization Individualized marketing communications that recognize individual customers by name, purchase behavior, needs and demographics.

message awareness The average number of times that target customers recall seeing an advertisement in a given period of time.

misfits Customers classified as "non-profits" who will not remain customers due to a poor fit with the business's product, and as a result the business will never recover the cost of acquiring these customers.

mixed channel system A combination of direct and indirect channels whereby a business reaches, sells to, and serves some customers but intermediaries reach, sell to, and serve others, or a business and intermediaries interact with the same customers at different customer touch points.

monetizing strategies Strategies that minimize marketing investment and seek to maximize cash flow.

morphemes Parts of words that are used to create brand names.

motivating-action Marketing communications designed to motivate action, often the purchase of a product.

multi-segment strategy Two or more separate and distinct marketing mix strategies (4 Ps plus service) that are created for different needs-based market segments.

multi-tiered marketing channel A channel and sales system that involves two or more intermediaries.

needs-based segmentation Market segmentation based on customer needs and/or the benefits they seek in satisfying a particular problem or buying situation.

net marketing contribution Gross profit (sales times percent margin) minus the marketing expenses incurred to produce it.

net present value The value in today's dollars of a cash flow that occurs over time and is evaluated with a particular discount rate.

net profit Sales revenues minus all expenses including taxes and interest.

net promoter score The percentage of customers who would highly recommend a product or service to others (promoters) minus the percentage of detractors (those who would recommend that others not buy a particular product or service).

new market entry strategies Offensive strategic market plans designed to enter new markets.

new opportunities A business's first-time customers ("new potentials") or returning customers ("win-back customers") who are not yet profitable but, when well managed, will become loyal and profitable.

new potentials New customers under the broader classification of "new opportunities" who fit the business's profile for target customers and can become loyal and profitable when well managed.

niche market (segment) A small segment of a market that is often overlooked or ignored by large competitors.

nonprofits Customers who are not profitable and not loyal to a product or business.

oblique strategies Indirect, non-combative competitive strategies that lead competitors to follow a competitive move.

offensive strategies (offensive strategic market plans) Long-run plans (3 to 5 years) to penetrate markets or enter new markets.

one-on-one marketing Building one-on-one relationships with key customers a business wants to retain.

operating expenses Overhead expenses that are not the direct result of marketing activities.

operating income Sales minus all expenses before taxes and interest.

optimizing strategies Strategies that seek to optimize the marketing mix and marketing investment needed to maximize profits.

original equipment manufacturers (OEMs) Businesses that manufacture new products from component products they buy from other manufacturers and suppliers.

penetration pricing A low price strategy to achieve a high market share/high volume position.

perceived value pricing Pricing to create a greater customer value based on customer perceptions of product, service, company benefits, and the perceived cost of acquiring those benefits.

perceptual mapping A display of competing products based on their relative substitutability and customer ideal products based on their strength of preference for each competing product.

performance-based value pricing Selecting a price that when combined with other performance features yields a total score (value) greater than competing total scores derived from a conjoint analysis.

performance plan A summary of strategic thinking, given a particular market situation, that results in a sales plan, marketing budget, and marketing profit plan.

performance scorecard A summary of a business's marketing performance using selected marketing performance metrics.

performance timeline A 3- to 5-year forecast of market and profit performance metrics.

plus-one pricing Adding at least one differentiating feature that allows a product to price slightly above competing products that lack this product or service feature.

pocket price The actual price paid to a company for a product after all discounts, sales commissions, shipping charges, and other transaction costs are deducted.

pocket-price bandwidth A business's different channels or regional markets produce different pocket prices for the same product, and the percentage difference between the lowest pocket price and the highest is the pocket-price bandwidth.

portfolio analysis An evaluation of a product, market, or business with respect to market attractiveness and competitive advantage.

price-earnings ratio The price of a share of stock in a business divided by the business's earnings per share.

price elasticity The percentage change in unit volume for a product per 1 percent change in price.

price per unit The selling price of a product or service.

price premium The dollar amount, or percentage, by which the price of a product exceeds competing products.

prisoner's dilemma A price situation in which businesses are forced to follow downward price moves by competitors to remain competitive.

process performance metrics Performance metrics that occur during a reporting period and precede result performance metrics.

product adoption forces Product forces that impact the rate of new-product adoption.

product benefits The overall benefit a customer derives from the product performance and features.

product bundling Combining for sale two or more products at a total price that would be lower than the price paid if each product were purchased separately.

product differentiation The degree to which a business's product is meaningfully different and superior when compared by customers to competing products.

product-focused business A business that is focused internally on product development and utilizes marketing primarily as an advertising and sales function.

product line advantage Broader product lines offer customers more choices which creates a competitive advantage that contributes to a higher level of profits.

product life cycle The life of a product as it progresses from introduction through growth, maturity, and decline.

product life-cycle portfolio A product portfolio positioned along the product life cycle based on percentage of total sales.

product life-cycle/share development portfolio A strategic market-planning portfolio that uses the product life cycle on the vertical axis and the share development index on the horizontal axis to depict a combination of profitability and growth.

product positioning The manner in which customers perceive a business's product features and price in comparison to competitors' product features and prices.

product unbundling Offering for sale an individual product that is normally sold as part of a product bundle.

product line extensions Products that are added to a product line under an umbrella brand that is well known and has an established reputation for quality.

product line positioning A planned sequence of alternative product offerings that differ in product performance and price.

product line scale The effect product line extensions or deletions have on the cost of producing and marketing a line of products.

product line substitution The degree to which the sales of products are cannibalized with the addition of substitute products to the product line.

product-market A term referring to the market served by a product.

product-market diversification The degree to which a business has different products across different markets.

promotional price elasticity The percent volume increase per 1 percent price decrease during a price promotion.

protect strategies A defensive strategic market plan in which a business develops a marketing strategy to protect its competitive position and market share.

pull communications Marketing communications directed at end-user customers in an attempt to motivate target customers to seek a business's

products (i.e., pull the products through the channel).

pure promotion (stimulate action) A communications strategy designed to stimulate action, often to motivate purchase.

push communications Marketing communications directed at intermediaries in an attempt to motivate them to push a business's product through the channel in an effort to reach target customers.

quality aesthetics Product and service attributes that impact the perceived quality of a product.

quality drivers The critical product and service attributes that drive customer perceptions of performance.

quality enhancers Extra product and service attributes that enhance customer satisfaction.

quality killers Product and service attributes that do not perform at the levels customers expect.

reactive strategies Strategies based on either customer intelligence or competitor intelligence.

reduced focus strategy A defensive market strategy that uses a planned reduction in market share (by reducing focus to a smaller number of customers) to improve profitability.

relative cost A business's cost per unit relative to a competitor's cost per unit.

relative market share A business's market share divided by the share of the market share leader competitor or next largest share competitor.

relative price A business's price divided by the price of a competitor or the average price of several competitors.

relative product quality An overall relative index based on customer perceptions when comparing a business's product against a competitor's product on each aspect of product quality.

relative service quality An overall relative index based on customer perceptions when comparing a business's service against a competitor's service on each aspect of service quality.

result performance metrics Performance metrics that occur at the end of a normal accounting period.

retention cost The cost of retaining one customer over a given period of time.

return on assets The net profit produced by a business divided by its total assets.

return on capital The net income after taxes produced by a business divided by its investment in capital.

return on equity The net profit produced by a business divided by its owner's equity.

return on sales The net profit produced by a business divided by its total sales.

reverse innovation—invent to order A process that starts by listening to lead users articulate "what they want, but cannot get" from present products, followed by an effort to create value with a new product that addresses these unfulfilled needs.

sales revenue The price times the volume sold for each of the products sold by a company.

segment attractiveness The attractiveness of a segment based on market forces, competitive intensity, and marketing access to the segment.

segment identification The demographic characteristics that distinguish a needs-based segment from other needs-based segments.

segment marketing mix strategy A marketing mix developed specifically for a target market segment.

segment marketing profitability The net marketing contribution a business derives from a particular market segment.

segment positioning The product-price position and value proposition developed specifically for customers in a given market segment.

segment pricing Pricing based on segment price sensitivity and customer need for additional product features and/or services.

segment strategy acid test A test of the segment product positioning strategy and value proposition that involves the proposed strategy and two competing alternatives.

served market demand The size of the target market to be served by the business.

service benefits The overall benefit a customer derives from the various components of service a business provides.

service differentiation The degree to which a business's service is meaningfully different and superior when compared by customers to competing products.

share development index The percentage of a business's potential market share which the business has already achieved.

share follower A business that is not the share leader in its market but does have a relatively significant share of the market.

share performance metrics Marketing performance metrics related to a product's market share, such as metrics for customer awareness, product availability, customer preference and interest, intent to buy, purchasing, and service quality, which work in a hierarchy to collectively produce a market share index.

situation analysis An external analysis of market forces and internal analysis of business performance that are used to identify key performance issues and guide strategic market planning and development of tactical marketing strategies.

skim pricing A high price position that attracts a limited number of customers but is sustainable because competitors cannot match the business's competitive advantage and value proposition.

spinners Customers under the broader classification of "nonprofits" who buy only when a promotion is offered and as a result are not profitable and not loyal.

strategic market definition A broad definition of market demand that includes the business's served market and relevant substitute product-markets.

strategic market planning The specification of a long-run (3- to 5-year) strategic market plan that will result in specific performance objectives with respect to market share, sales revenues, and profitability over the planning horizon.

strategy implementation The actions taken to implement, track, and adapt a tactical marketing plan derived from a specific strategic market plan.

subsegment strategy A further delineation of customers within a segment based on demographics or product usage.

substitute products Products that can be substituted for one another.

supply chain management Involves the management of the flow of physical materials, information, and money to and from a business and its suppliers and channel partners.

SWOT analysis A summary of strengths, weaknesses, opportunities, and threats that were uncovered in a situation analysis.

tactical marketing strategy A 1-year marketing mix strategy (the 4 Ps plus service) for a particular target market and specific strategic market plan.

target market A collection of customers that the business has decided to focus on in building a marketing mix strategy.

team approach The degree to which a business works across functions as a team in creating and delivering market-based customer solutions and implementation strategies.

test market A test of a product in an isolated market in which sales can be tracked and evaluated to determine the impact of a new product or variation in the marketing mix.

tipping point The inflection point in the product life cycle curve where market demand shifts from slow growth to an exponential rate of market growth.

top performers Customers who are profitable and loyal to a product, business, or company.

top-down marketing budget A marketing budget based on a certain percentage of sales.

total customer experience The satisfactions and challenges that customers encounter during all aspects of acquiring, owning, using, and replacing a product or service.

trade-off analysis Customer preferences for different combinations of price, product, service, and company benefits.

transaction value The economic value a channel partner can obtain from transactions with a company based on margin per square foot inventory (square feet), inventory turnover, and marketing expenses.

umbrella brand A core brand that is well known and under which brand extensions can be easily introduced.

unarticulated market demand Market demand that has not occurred because customers have not recognized a need for a product or product feature.

underachievers Customers under the broader classification of "high potentials" who are loyal (they buy often) but are not profitable or are minimally profitable (they buy in small amounts).

untapped market opportunities The gap between current market demand and market potential, also called the "untapped market potential."

value in-use pricing (value pricing) Pricing to create a savings for a customer based on a lower total life-cycle cost when compared to a competitor's total life-cycle cost.

value map A graph of relative performance and relative price.

value proposition A short statement that communicates how a product or business creates value for target customers.

value-added resellers (VARs) Businesses that buy a variety of components from several manufacturers and package them as a system for certain market applications.

variable cost per unit All of the variable costs associated with one unit sold.

variance analysis A breakdown of net marketing contribution based on actual and planned performance to better understand how a marketing plan achieved its results.

vertical brand-line extensions Variations in the brand that add more variety and options for customers.

vertical market opportunities Forward or backward integration along the supply chain that starts with raw materials and moves vertically through different stages of production, distribution, sales, and service.

volume The number of units sold for a particular product in a given period of time.

win-back customers Customers under the broader classification of "new opportunities" whom a business previously lost to a competitor but who are buying again from the business and, if well managed, can become loyal and profitable customers.

INDEX

A

ABC, 199
Absolut Spirits, 372
Acid test, 154, 155–156
Adaptive persistence, 459
Adaptive rollout, 460
Adidas, 380
Adjacent-segment strategy, 158–159
Adrenaline Rush, 72
Advanced Micro Devices, 210, 371
Advertising
  awareness, building, 311–314
  carryover effects of, 325–327
  elasticity, 324–325
  strategy, 55
  see also Marketing communications
Advocates, 22
AFLAC, 317–318
Agilent Technologies, 226, 357
AirCap, 114–115
Alliant, 226
Amazon.com, 297, 376
AMD, 307
America Online, 380
American Customer Satisfaction Index
  (ACSI), 472
American Express, 166, 195, 232
American Hospital Supply, 113–114, 221
Amoco Chemical, 318
Anheuser-Busch, 186, 232
Anixter, 199
Apple Computer, 20, 78, 209, 210, 226,
  266, 380
Arm & Hammer, 222

Arthur Andersen, 229
The Art of War (Sun Tzu), 187
Assets
  accounts receivable investments and,
    478–479
  brand equity and, 227–228
  fixed assets investments and, 480
  inventory investments and, 479–480
AT&T, 25, 195, 375, 386
Availability, market demand and, 78
Average selling price, 48

B

Bain & Company, 20, 101
Barbie dolls, 167
Bayer, 414
Belvedere, 372
Benchmarking marketing profitability,
  56–61
  managing marketing performance
    and, 60–61
  marketing return on investment and, 58
  marketing return on sales and, 57–58
  profit impact of, 59–60
Betty Crocker, 127
BIC pens, 258
Big Bertha, 226
Big spenders, 23
BioTronics, 36–39, 59–60, 62

Black & Decker, 210, 211
Blue Ocean Strategies (Kim and
        Mauborgne), 414
BMW, 110, 189, 217
Boeing, 111
Bottom-up marketing budget, 437–438
Brand(s)
  defined, 209
  equity, 227–231
    brand assets and, 227–228
    brand balance sheet and, 230
    brand liabilities and, 229–230
  name, benefits derived
        from, 209–210, 224
  see also Brand management strategies;
        Product line(s); Product
        positioning
Brand Assets Scorecard, 228
Brand benefits index, 122
Brand encoding, 221–225
  brand and sub-brand name, 222
  brand name and benefit, 224
  brand name only, 224–225
  company and brand name, 222
  company and product name, 223
  company, brand, and product
        name, 223
  company name, brand name, and
        number, 224
Brand Interaction Model, 308
Brand Liabilities Scorecard, 229, 230
Brand management strategies, 221–227
Brand-building communications, 307
Braun, 224
Breadman toaster, 119
Break-even analysis, 441, 442
Buick, 189
Bundling strategy, 236–237
Business Week, 155, 315, 317
Business-to-business (B2B) marketing
        channels, 290–292
Business-to-consumer (B2C) marketing
        channels, 288, 289–290, 292
Buying decision, 82

C
Cadillac, 228
Campbell's Soup, 180, 184, 389, 390
Caterpillar, 157, 218, 291
CBS, 199, 378
Celeron microprocessor, 210, 223, 371
Chanel, 183, 218
Channels. *See* Marketing channel(s)
Charles Schwab, 296
*Chemical and Engineering News
        (C&EN),* 318
Chevrolet, 126, 158
Chi Mei, 258
Chicago Bulls, 127
Church & Dwight Co., 222
Cisco Systems, 226, 386, 390
Citicorp, 195
"Classic Buildings" marketing
        communication, 315
Clif Bar Inc., 414
CNBC, 223
CNN, 199
Co-branding, 235–236
Coca-Cola, 70–71, 157, 220, 227, 228,
        355–356, 369, 377
ColorPlus, 140–141, 162
Columbia Pictures, 379
Comcast, 379, 380
Communications strategy, 433, 434
Company benefits index, 122
Competitive advantage
  customer value and, 175–176
  profitability and, 176
  sources of, 175–177
    cost advantage, 177–181
    differentiation advantage, 181–183
    knowledge, 187
    marketing advantage, 183–187
  sustainable, 199–200
Competitive position, 348–349
  offensive core strategy II and, 374–376
  portfolio, 339
Competitive position index, 349
Competitiveness metrics, 40, 448

Competitor intelligence, 189–195
  analysis of, 191
    sample, 193–194
  benchmarking, 189–191, 194–195
  obtaining, 191–192
Competitive position
  measuring, 339, 341
Complete solutions, 80
CompuServe, 379–380
Conjoint analysis, 130, 248–249
Consumer awareness, 78
Consumer Reports, 117–118
Cost advantage, 177–181
  marketing and, 180
  operating and, 180–181
  profitability and, 178
  variable, 178–180
Cost of purchase, 220–221
  lower transaction costs and, 221
  low-price position and, 220
Cost of purchase index, 123–124
Cost reduction strategy, 54–55
Cost-based pricing, 243, 245
Costco, 20, 199, 376
Cost-focused sustainers, 146
Customer adoption forces, 82–83
Customer awareness and comprehension,
    317–320
  ad copy and, 320
  media selection and, 317
  message frequency and, 317–320
Customer dissatisfaction, 11–14
  complaint behavior/customer retention
    and, 11–12
  profit impact of, 13–14
Customer empathy, 219
Customer experience, 102–108
  current *vs.* desired, 103–104
  customer touch points and, managing,
    107–108
  empathic design and, 102–103
  of lead users, 104–106
  reverse innovation and, 106–107
  see also Mass collaboration

Customer focus, 26–29
  behaviors and practices, customer-
    focused, 27
  defined, 26
  marketing knowledge and, 26–27
  marketing performance and, 28
  marketing performance tools and, 31–32
  profitability and, 6–14, 28–29
    managing, 49–51
  see also Customer satisfaction
Customer loyalty, 21–26
  communicating strategic market
    plan to, 458
  customer relationship marketing
    and, 22–26
  high potentials, 23–24
  managing, 22
  marketing performance tools and, 31–32
  measuring, 21–22
  new opportunities, 24
  nonprofits, 24–26
  offensive core strategy IIA and, 375
  promotions, 24
  target/nontarget customers and, 24
  top performers, 22–23
Customer loyalty score (CLS), 21–22
Customer metrics, 40, 448
Customer position, strategic market
    planning and, 425, 426
Customer relationship management
    (CRM), 163, 165, 167–169
Customer relationship marketing, 163–169
  customer loyalty and, managing, 22–26
  customer relationship management and,
    167–169
  customer value *vs.* company value and,
    164–165
  database marketing and, 165–166
  mass customization and, 166–167
  mass personalization and, 166
Customer response index (CRI), 313–314
Customer retention, 14–20
  customer life expectancy and, 16–17
  customer satisfaction and, 15–16

Customer retention (*Continued*)
  defensive core strategy IB and, 395
  dissatisfied customers who don't
      complain and, 11–12
  estimating, 16
  lifetime value of a customer and, 17–19
  net promoter score and, 19–20
  online customers and, net present value
      of, 19
  profit impact of, 13–15
Customer revenue strategy, 54
Customer satisfaction, 7–12
  customer focus and, 7
  marketing performance metrics and, 8–9
  overwhelming customers/shareholders
      and, 471–472
  profitability and
    customer retention and, 472–474
    de-averaging, 10–12
  underwhelming customers/shareholders
      and, 6–7
  wide-angle view of, 9–10
Customer satisfaction index (CSI), 8–9
Customer value
  vs. company value, 164–165
  product differentiation and, 216
  service differentiation and, 218–219
  strategic market planning and, 425, 426
Customer value index (CVI), 124–126,
      132–133
Customer-mix marketing budget, 437

D
Danzka, 372
Data Information Services, 379
Database marketing, 165–166
Defensive core strategies
  I: protect position, 389–395
    IA: protect market share, 389–395

investing to protect a follower share
    position, 392–393
investing to protect a high-share
    position, 390–391
investing to protect a niche share
    position, 393–395
investing to protect position in
    growth markets, 390
  IB: build customer retention, 395
  II: optimize position, 395–399
    IIA: maximize net marketing
        contribution, 396–399
    IIB: reduce market focus, 399
  III: monetize, harvest, or divest, 400–403
    IIIA: manage for cash flow, 400
    IIIB: harvest or divest for cash flow,
        400–403
      divest marketing strategy, 402–403
      harvest marketing resource strategy,
          401–402
      harvest price strategy, 400–401
Defensive portfolio strategy, 353, 354–355
Dell Inc., 5, 167, 199, 225, 230, 236,
      282, 351
Dell, Michael, 225
Demographics
  firm, 146
  influences, 144
  trap, 147–148
DeWalt, 210, 211
Differential advantage, 177, 181–183, 219
  Differentiation, 181–183
  brand, 219–220
  low cost of purchase and, 220–221
  offensive core strategy IIB and, 375–376
  product advantage and, 181–182,
      215–218
  reputation advantage and, 183
  service, 182–183, 218–219
Direct marketing channels, 288–289
Disney, 371, 378
Disposal costs, 116–117
Distributed frequency strategy, 318–320
Divest strategy, 352, 400–403

Dominant design, 379
Domino's Pizza, 12
Dow Chemical, 106–107, 284
Dow Corning, 295–296
DuPont, 113, 156–157
DuraCell, 226
Dynamic random access memory (DRAM)
    chips, 257

ESCO Corporation, 181–182, 217
ESPN, 199
Esprit, 290
E*Trade, 228, 297
Experience curve coefficient,
    estimating, 204
Explorer Internet portal, 226
Extended services, 219

E
Early adopters, 80, 81
Early followers, 379
Early majority, 81
Early market, 80
Earnings per share (EPS), 482
EarthLink, 379, 380
eBay, 297
Economic profit (EP), 482
Economic value
    analysis, 114
    communicating, 115
    lower disposal cost as a source of,
        116–117
    see also Life-cycle cost(s)
Eddie Bauer, 290, 324
Elastic price management, 266–268
Electrolux, 290
Eli Lilly, 110
E-marketing channels, 295–296
Emotional benefits, value creation
    and, 126–128
    brand personality and, 127–128
    psychological value and, 126
Empathic design, 102–103
Employees, mass collaboration, 111
Engineered solutions segment, 151
Enron, 229, 230
Enterprise Rent-A-Car, 5, 20
Environmental Protection Agency (EPA),
    434, 458

F
Fairfield Inn, 220
Fast Track, 226
Federal Express (FedEx), 20, 73, 182,
    218, 226
Feedback measurements, 459
Fifth market (M5), 388
Financial performance
    competitive advantage and, 199, 200
    competitor analysis and, 193
    marketing managers and, 60
    vs. marketing performance, 36–37
    marketing performance metrics and, 36,
        37, 39–42
    marketing profitability metrics
        and, 60–61
    marketing ROS and, 58
Firestone, 229, 291
First market (M1), 387
Flanker brand, 232–233
Follow-Me-Home, 103
Food Institute, 220
Forbes, 315
Ford, Henry, 226
Ford Motor Company, 116, 222,
    225–226, 291
Fornell, Claus, 472
Fortune magazine, 315
Fortune 500 companies, 35, 292, 315, 479
Fourth market (M4), 388

FP International (FPI), 116
Franchised brands, 234
Free on board (FOB) pricing, 294
Frito-Lay, 233
Fruitopia, 220
Full Throttle, 72

G
Gardenburger, 234, 235, 320, 324,
    325–327
Gates, Bill, 73
Gatorade, 72
General Electric (GE), 129, 216, 217,
    221–222, 223, 227, 228, 285, 286,
    296, 338, 346, 371, 380, 402–403,
    428
  GE Capital, 113, 115
General Mills, 195, 235
General Motors, 5, 199, 379, 386
  Cadillac Division of, 17–18
Gillette, 389
Gladwell, Malcolm, 69
Golf Digest, 317
Golf Magazine, 317
Google, 199, 226
GPS navigation, 110
Gretzky, Wayne, 6, 209
Grey Goose, 372
Gross rating points (GRPs), 320
Growth-oriented entrepreneurs, 146

H
Hardiplank, 140
HardiTrim, 140–141, 162
Harley-Davidson, 210, 370
Hartman Luggage, 295

Harvest pricing, 260–262
Harvest strategy
  defensive core strategy III and, 400–403
  market 4 and, 360
  portfolio analysis and, 351–352
Head, 57–59, 193
Healthy Choice, 235–236
Heavy-up message frequency, 322
Hewlett-Packard (HP), 8–9, 22, 122, 127,
    177, 237, 286, 289, 307, 357
High potential customers, 23–24
  big spenders, 23
  underachievers, 23
Hilton, Conrad, 226
Hilton Hotels, 226
Hitachi, 220
Home Depot, 128, 129
Honda, 102, 108, 116–117, 179, 189, 228,
    235, 371
Honeywell, 216
Horizontal brand, 234, 235

I
IBM, 110, 291, 371, 386
Improvement, continuous, 459
Income statement, 442, 443
Indirect marketing channels, 289
Industry analysis, 196–199
  competitive rivalry and, 198
  customer buying power and, 197
  entry barriers and, 196–197
  exit barriers and, 197
  product substitutes and, 197–198
  supplier selling power and, 197
  the prisoner's dilemma and, 199
Industry attractiveness, 419, 423
Inelastic price management, 264–266
Innovators, 80, 81
Inside-the-box strategy, 188
Intel, 85–86, 209, 210, 217, 222, 223, 236,
    357, 371, 386, 387, 389

Interest-arousing communications, 307, 310
Intuit, 103, 108
IPod, 110

J

James Hardie, 140, 141
Johnson & Johnson, 232
Johnson Controls, 315–316, 321
Jordan, Michael, 127

K

Kathon MWX, 113, 116
Kellogg, 220, 236
Kentucky Fried Chicken, 379
Ketel One, 372
Kirin, 186
Kleenex, 226
KMX, 72
Knight, Phil, 73
Knowledge advantage, 187–188
Kodak, 5, 157, 184, 371, 389, 390
Kool-Aid, 128
K2, 57–59, 141, 193, 378, 413

L

Lafley, A. G., 108
Laggards, 81
Lance Armstrong Foundation, 307
Large-segment strategy, 157–158
Late majority, 81
Lead customers, 80

Lead users, 104–106
Learning effects, 179–180
LEGO, 110
Les Schwab Tires, 219
Lexus, 101, 102, 106, 122, 127, 167, 209,
        210, 219, 228, 230
Life-cycle cost(s), 111–117, 246
    acquisition costs and, 113
    defined, 111
    disposal costs and, 116–117
    economic value and, 111–113, 117
    maintenance costs and, 115–116
    ownership costs and, 115
    price paid and, 113
    usage costs and, 114–115
Lillis, Charles, 25, 151, 414
Lincoln, 189
L.L.Bean, 195, 290, 324
L&M cigarettes, 324
Loctite, 113, 116, 320
Los Angeles Performing Arts Center, 160
Low-cost-leader pricing, 258
Loyalists, 22

M

Macintosh, 380
Magellan Internet portal, 226
Mainstream market, 80–81
Mapping
    marketing channel and, 279–282
    value creation, 119–120
Market attractiveness, 346–348
Market attractiveness index, 348
Market definition, 70–73
Market demand, 47
    market potential and, 74
    strategic market planning and,
        418–419, 422
Market development index (MDI), 77, 87,
        96–97, 372–373
Market growth, 80–84

Market growth (*Continued*)
   accelerating, 81–82
   customer adoption forces and, 82–83
   forces affecting, fundamental, 79–80
   product adoption forces and, 83–84
Market growth strategy, 52–53
Market metrics, 40, 448
Market penetration, 79
Market potential, 73–77, 79
   estimating, 75
   limiting factors and, 77–79
   market demand and, 74
   market growth and, forces affecting, 77–79
Market segmentation
   customer needs and, 143–145
      business culture and, 146
      business market needs and, forces that
         shape, 144
      demographic influences and, 144
      differences in, forces that
         shape, 143, 145
      firm demographics and, 146
      lifestyle influences and, 144
      usage behaviors and, 144, 145, 146
      (see also Needs-based market
         segmentation)
   of health insurance market, 152
   market-based management and, 146
   mass-market strategy *vs.* segment
      strategy and, 140
   of small-business market, 147
   strategies, 157–163
      adjacent-segment, 158–159
      large-segment, 157–158
      mass-market, 157
      multi-segment, 159–161
      niche-segment, 161
      small-segment, 161
      sub-segment, 161–163
Market share, 47
   advantage, 184–185
   competitive position and, 340
   defensive core strategy I and, 389–395
   objectives, strategic market planning
      and, 429, 431
   offensive core strategy I and, 369–370
   potential, 94–95
   product positioning and, 212–213
Market share index, 94
Market share performance metrics, 91–94
   price acceptable and, 93–94
   product attractiveness and, 93
   product availability and, 94
   product awareness and, 92–93
   service experience and, 94
   share development index and, 96–97,
      341–342
   share potential/management and, 94–95
Market share portfolio, 344–346
Market vision, broad, 72–73
Market-based business
   competitor analysis and, 191
   customer value/focus and, 107–108
   market definition and, key benefits
      of, 73
   marketing performance metrics and, 8
   practices of, 59
   process marketing metrics and, 41–42
   value-based pricing and, 255
Market-based management, 3
   customer focus and, 26–29
   customer retention rates and, 16–17
   customer satisfaction and, 11, 12
   financial performance and, 484–486
   market segmentation and, 146
   market share advantage and, 185
   marketing analysis and, 67, 199–200
   marketing performance metrics and,
      39, 42
   mass collaboration and, 134
Market-Based Management (MBM),
      411–412, 415, 448, 485
Market-based strategy, 38–39
   see also Strategic market plan
Marketing advantage, 183–187
   channel advantage and, 186–187
   market share advantage and, 184–185
   offensive core strategy IID and, 376
   product line advantage and, 185–186
Marketing attitudes, 26, 27

Marketing budget, developing,
    436–438, 440
    bottom-up marketing budget, 437–438
    customer-mix marketing budget, 437
    percent-of-sales marketing budget,
        436–437
Marketing channel(s)
    advantage, 186–187
    alternative, 287–292
        B2B, 290–292
        B2C, 288, 289–290, 292
        direct, 288–289
        indirect, 289
        mixed, 289
        profit impact of, 301–303
    competitive advantages of, 299–301
        distribution and, 300–301
        sales force and, 299
        sales productivity and, 299–300
    customer value and, 292–299
        brand image and, 295
        company benefits and, 295–297
        cost efficiency and, improving,
            297–299
        product benefits and, 293
        service benefits and, 293–294
    discount, 48
    mapping, 279–282
    performance, 283–287
        customer reach and, 283–285
        operating efficiency and, 285–286
        service quality and, 286–287
    strategy, 55–56, 430, 433, 434, 458
Marketing communications, 307–331
    advertising awareness and, building,
        311–314
    brand building communications, 307
    customer action, stimulating, 322
    customer awareness and comprehension,
        317–320
    customer response and
        customer response index and, 313–314
        desired, 307–311
        increasing, strategies for, 314–316
        pull communications and, 324–329
    pull vs. push communications
        strategies, 322–323
    push communications and, 329–331
    interest-arousing communications, 307
    message reinforcement, 321–322
        heavy-up message frequency, 322
        pulsing and, 321–322
    motivating-actions communications, 307
    objectives, 307
Marketing cost scope effect, 180
Marketing education, 26–27, 30
Marketing expenses, 48
Marketing influencers, 458
Marketing knowledge, customer focus and,
    26–27
Marketing mix, 91
Marketing mix strategy, 357–358
    channel strategy, 430, 433, 434
    communications strategy, 433, 434
    developing, 429–434
    product positioning strategy,
        429–430, 432
Marketing performance
    vs. financial performance, 36–37
    market-based strategy, 38–39
    measuring and tracking, 37–39
    profit impact of (see Marketing
        profitability metrics)
Marketing performance metrics, 37–42,
    448–453
    classes of, 40
    customer behavior/profit performance
        and, 450
    customer focus and, 28
    customer satisfaction and, 8–9
    vs. financial performance, 36–37, 39–42
    internal vs. external, 40
    market-based business and, 8
    market-based management and, 39, 42
    measuring and tracking, 37–39
    need for, 35
    process vs. result marketing metrics and,
        41–42, 450, 451
        process marketing performance
            metrics, 451–452

Marketing performance metrics (*Continued*)
  result marketing performance metrics, 452–453
  see also Marketing profitability metrics
Marketing performance scorecard, 447
Marketing performance tools
  brand management/product line strategies, 241
  competitor analysis/competitive advantage, 202
  customer focus, 31–32
  economic value, customer value, transaction value, 136
  financial performance, impact of market-based management on, 487–488
  market strategies for defensive core strategies, 406
  market strategies for offensive core strategies, 383
  marketing channels, 304–305
  marketing communications/customer response, 332–333
  marketing planning and impact on profits, 446
  marketing profitability, managing/profit impact of, 63
  portfolio analysis/strategic market planning, 363–364
  product life cycle, 99
  segmentation strategies, 171–172
  value-based pricing, pricing strategies, price elasticity, 276
  variance analysis, using to assess strategic market plan performance, 467
Marketing profitability metrics, 42–51, 448
  financial performance and, 60–61
  managing
    customer focus, 28–29, 49–50
    product focus, 47–49
  need for, 35
  performance metrics and, 44–46
  product life cycle and, 89–91
  product lines and, 46–47

profits and, 42–44
  see also Marketing strategies, profit impact of
Marketing return on investment, 29, 44–46, 58–59
Marketing return on sales, 29, 44–46, 57–59
Marketing strategies, profit impact of, 51–56
  advertising strategy and, 55
  channel strategy and, 55–56
  cost reduction strategy and, 54–55
  customer revenue strategy and, 54
  market growth strategy and, 52–53
Marlboro, 157
Marriott, 169, 219, 220
Martha Stewart brand, 230
Mary Kay Cosmetics, 290
Mass collaboration, 108–111
  employees and, 111
  market-based management and, 134
  partnerships and, 110
  prosumers and, 110
  suppliers and, 110–111
Mass customization, 166–167
Mass personalization, 166
Mass-market strategy, 157
MBNA America, 13
McDonald's, 181, 371
McKinsey Consulting, 253–254, 346, 428
McKinsey's waterfall, 253
MediaOne Group, 25, 151, 356, 414
Mercedes, 126, 161, 189, 210, 219
Merix Corporation, 192–193
Michelob, 186, 232
Microsoft, 5, 73, 78, 221, 224, 226, 227, 228, 231, 366, 386, 389
Miller Brewing Company, 379
Misfits, 24–25
Mixed bundling strategy, 236
Monetize strategy, 351, 400–403
Moore's Law, 217
Motivating-action communications, 307
Motorola, 216, 379

Multi-segment pricing, 258–259
Multi-segment strategy, 159–161
Multnomah County Library, 192

N

NASCAR, 195
National Cash Register Corporation
    (NCR), 379
National Public Radio, 109
Nautilus, 376
Navigator Internet portal, 226
NBC, 199, 223
Needs-based market segmentation, 139,
    140–143, 146–157
  customer preferences for features *vs.*
      price, 142
  demographic trap, 147–148
  features *vs.* price, 141
  market segments, 148–149
  segment attractiveness, 150–151
  segment identification, 149–150
  segment marketing mix strategy,
      156–157
  segment positioning, 154–155
  segment profitability, 151–154
  segment strategy acid test, 154, 155–156
  segmentation process, 148
Nescafé, 215–216
Net economic gain, 111
Net marketing contribution (NMC)
  advertising strategy and, 55
  channel strategy and, 55–56
  cost reduction strategy and, 54–55
  customer retention and, 14, 15
  customer revenue strategy and, 54
  defensive core strategy IIA and,
      396–399
  market share strategy and, 53
  marketing profitability and, 44–47

  marketing strategy and, 47–49, 51–52
  product life-cycle demand and profits
      and, 86
  variance analysis and, 461–462
Net promoter score, 19–20
New market entry
  complete solutions and, 81
  market development and, 79–80
  offensive core strategy III and, 377–380
  strategic market plans and, 351
New opportunity customers, 24
New potential customers, 24
New product-market brand, 235
The New York Times, 17
Niche-segment strategy, 161
Nike, 73, 127, 177, 184–185, 221, 226,
    227, 371, 380, 453–454
Nikon, 183
Nonprofit customers, 24–26
  misfits, 24–25
  spinners, 25
Nordstrom, 122, 177, 218, 219

O

Occupational Safety and Health
    Administration (OSHA), 434
Offensive core strategies
  I: invest to grow sales, 369–374
    IA: grow market share, 369–370
    IB: grow revenue per customer,
        370–371
    IC: enter new market segments,
        371–372
    ID: expand market demand, 372–374
  II: improve competitive position,
      374–376
    IIA: improve customer loyalty, 375
    IIB: improve differentiation
        advantage, 375–376

Offensive core strategies (*Continued*)
  IIC: lower costs/improve marketing
      productivity, 376
  IID: build marketing advantage, 376
  III: enter new markets, 377–380
  IIIA: enter related new markets,
      377–378
  IIIB: enter unrelated new markets,
      378–379
  IIIC: enter new emerging markets,
      379–380
  IIID: develop new markets, 380
Offensive portfolio strategy, 352–353, 355
Oreo, 226
Original equipment manufacturers
      (OEMs), 291
Otellini, Paul, 209
Overall benefits index, 123

P
Partnerships, 110
Path Finder, 226
PearlParadise.com, 24
Penetration pricing, 257–258
Pentium microprocessor, 210, 223
Pepsi, 379
Perceived benefits, value creation and,
      120–126
  company or brand benefits, 122
  company or brand benefits index, 122
  cost of purchase index, 123–124
  customer value and profit impact, 126
  customer value and value map, 125
  customer value index, 124–126
  overall benefits index, 123
  overall customer benefits, 123
  product benefits, 120–121
  product benefits index, 120
  service benefits index, 121
Perceived-value pricing, 246–248, 249
Percent experience curve, estimating, 204

Percent margin, 48
Percent-of-sales marketing budget, 436–437
Performance plan, 358–361, 418, 422
  review, 443–444
Performance scorecard, 441, 442–443
Performance-based pricing, 248–252
Perfume de Paris, 295
Perrier, 122, 183
Persistence, management, 460
Phillip Morris, 379
Phillips, 157
Plus-one pricing, 259–260
Pocket price, 253–254
Pocket-price bandwidth, 253–254
Porsche, 218
Portfolio analysis
  defined, 350
  diversification, 355–357
  GE/McKinsey, 345–346
  product-life cycles and, 337
      vs. competitive position portfolio, 339
      market share portfolio, 344–346
  strategic market plans and, 350–355
      defensive portfolio strategy, 353,
          354–355
      kinds of, 351–352
      offensive portfolio strategy,
          352–353, 355
Post-it Notes, 322
PowerAde, 220
Present value table, 33
Press, communicating through, 458
Price elasticity, 263–268
  customers' switching capacity and,
      267–268
  estimating, guidelines for, 267
  forces that shape, 267
  inelastic price management and, 264–266
  management of, 266–268
  supply-and-demand conditions, 268
Price performance, value creation and,
      117–120
  customer value and, 118, 119
  relative performance and, 117–118
  relative price and, 118–119
  value mapping and, 119–120

Price segment, 154
Price-earnings ratio (PE ratio), 482–484
Price-margin management, 252–255
  pocket-price bandwidth and, 253–254
Pricing
  break-even analysis and, 268–270
  price-volume profitability and, 263
  price-volume strategy/profit
        impact and, 262
  product line, 270–273
    of complimentary products, 271–273
    of substitute products, 270–271, 272
  profitability and, 262–263
  value-based, 244–252
    vs. cost-based, 243, 245
    perceived-value pricing and,
        246–248, 249
    performance-based pricing and,
        248–252
    value-in-use pricing and,
        244–246, 247
  see also Price elasticity
Pricing strategies, 255–262
  harvest, 260–262
  low-cost-leader, 258
  multi-segment, 258–259
  penetration, 257–258
  plus-one, 259–260
  reduced-focus, 260, 261
  single-segment, 256–257
  skim, 255–256
The prisoner's dilemma, 199
Process marketing metrics, 41–42, 60
Procter & Gamble, 108–109, 111, 180,
        184, 222, 224–225, 338, 356
Prodigy, 380
Product(s)
  adoption forces, 83–84
  advantage, 181–182
  affordability of, 79
  attractiveness, 93
  availability, 78, 83, 94
  awareness, 78, 92–93
  benefits, 79, 120–121
  branding (see Brand management
        strategies)

ease of use, 78, 83
performance, 83
price acceptable, 93–94
service experience, 94
substitutes
    industry analysis of, 197–198
    pricing of, 270–271, 272
Product benefits index, 120
Product differentiation, 215–218
  aesthetics, 217–218
  drivers, 217
  enhancers, 217
  requirements, 215–217
Product line(s)
  advantage, 185–186
  extensions, 234–236
    co-branding, 235–236
    horizontal brand, 234, 235
    new product-market brand, 235
    vertical brand, 234–235
  marketing profitability metrics and, 46–47
  pricing, 270–273
    of complimentary products, 271–273
    of substitute products, 270–271, 272
  strategies, brands and, 231–239
    bundling and unbundling, 236–237
    product line development, 232
    product line extensions, 228, 234–236
    product line scale effects, 238–239
    substitution effects, 238
    umbrella and flanker brands, 232–233
Product positioning, 210–215
  market share and, 212–213
  strategies, 213–215, 429–430, 432
Product-life cycle(s), 84–97
  demand/profits and, 85–86
  vs. generic product-market life cycle,
        84–85
  margins/marketing expenses and, 88
  market demand/prices and, 86–87
  market share index and, 94
  market share potential and, 94–95
  marketing profitability and, 89–91
  of product portfolios, 337
  see also Market share performance
        metrics; Pricing strategies

Profit Impact of Marketing Strategies (PIMS), 390–391, 392
Profit plan, developing, 438, 440, 442–443
  break-even analysis, 441, 442
  income statement, 442, 443
  performance scorecard, 441, 442–443
Profitability
  competitive advantage and, 176
  cost advantage and, 178
  customer focus and, 6–14, 28–29, 49–51
  customer satisfaction and, 10–12, 472–474
  customer volume and, 474–475
  financial performance and, 60–61
  gross profit and, 477
  margin per customer and, 475–477
  market segmentation and, 151–154
  net marketing contribution and, 477
  net profit (before taxes) and, 477–478
  pricing and, 262–263
  return measures of, 480–482
  see also Benchmarking marketing profitability; Marketing profitability metrics
Prosumers, 110
Pull communications
  advertising carryover effects, 325–327
  advertising elasticity and, 324–325
  customer response and, 324–329
  direct marketing promotions, 327
  promotional price elasticity, 328–329
  vs. push, 322–323
Pulsing, 321–322
Pure product bundling strategy, 236–237
Pure promotion, 309–310
Push communications
  customer response and, 329–331
  market infrastructure and, 330–331
  vs. pull, 322–323
  trade promotions and customer response, 329–330

Q
Quick Metal, 116, 320
QuickBooks, 103, 108
Quicken, 103, 108

R
Reactive strategies, 188
Red Bull, 71–72, 226, 351
Reduced-focus pricing, 260, 261
Reichheld, Fred, 20
Relative market share, 339
Relative price, 118–119
Reputation advantage, 183
Research and development (R&D), 392
Result marketing metrics, 41–42
Return on equity (ROE), 480–481, 482
Return on investment (ROI), 29, 44–46, 58–59, 480–482
Return on sales (ROS), 29, 44–46, 57–59, 480–482
Revenue plan, developing, 435–436, 439
Reverse innovation, 106–107
Rohm-Haas, 113, 116
Rolex, 183, 218
Rosen, Richard, 308
Rossignol, 57–59, 193

S
Safari Internet portal, 226
Sales, general, and administrative (SG&A) expenses, 59
Salomon, 57–59, 193
Samsung, 213, 372

Santa Fe Sportswear, 43–52, 53, 54, 370
Saturn, 217
Scale effect, 179–180
Scope effect, 179–180
Sealed Air, 114–115
Sears, 5, 199, 210–211
Second market (M2), 387
Seinfeld, 320, 324, 325
Service assurance, 219
Service benefits
   customer value and, 293–294
   value creation and, 121–122
Service benefits index, 121
Service differentiation
   aesthetics, 219
   drivers, 219
   enhancers, 219
   requirements, 218–219
Service reliability, 218
Service solutions segment, 153
Share development index (SDI), 96–97,
   341–342, 344–346, 369–370
Share development path, 91–92
Share performance metrics, 419–420, 423
Shareholder value
   customer satisfaction and, 471–472
   market-based management and, 486
   measures of, 482–484
Silent Floor, 129–130, 131
Silk Soy Milk, 226
Single-segment pricing, 256–257
Six-sigma programs, 216–217
Skim pricing, 255–256
Small-segment strategy, 161
Smith, Fred, 73
Snapple, 226
Sony, 157, 209, 222, 372, 376
South Beach, 72
Southwest Airlines, 20
Space value, 128–129
Spiegel, 324
Spinners, 25
The Sports Authority, 376

Standard Industrial Classification
   (SIC), 146
Starbucks Coffee, 212, 365–366,
   376, 381
Stericycle Inc. (Stericycle Sample Market
   Plan), 411–412, 415, 417–444,
   469, 481–484
Strategic market plan, 338–346
   assets and, affect on, 478–480
   business performance and, 338
   competitive position and, measuring,
      339, 341
   defensive, 386–389
      choosing, 403–404
      market-based management strategies,
         387–388
      (*see also* Defensive core strategies)
   market attractiveness, product life cycle
      and, 338, 339, 341
   offensive, 367–369
      choosing, 381
      (*see also* Offensive core strategies)
   performance plan and, 358–361
   profitability and, affect on, 474–478
   see also Marketing mix strategy;
      Portfolio analysis; Strategic
      market plan implementation
Strategic market plan, building, 411–446
   benefits of, 413–415
   creativity *vs.* structure and, 412–413
   Part I: situation analysis, 415–427
      step 1: current situation, 418–426
         competition and industry
            attractiveness, 419, 423
         customer needs and market
            segmentation, 420, 424
         customer position and customer
            value, 425, 426
         market demand, 418–419, 422
         performance, 418, 422
         share performance metrics,
            419–420, 423
      step 2: SWOT analysis, 425, 426

Strategic market plan, building (*Continued*)
  Part II: market strategy, 427–434
    step 3: strategic market plan, 427–429,
      430–431
      market share objectives, 429, 431
    step 4: marketing mix strategy,
      developing, 429–434
      channel strategy, 430, 433, 434
      communications strategy, 433, 434
      product positioning strategy,
        429–430, 432
  Part III: performance plan, 411–412,
    434–444, 439
    step 5: revenue plan and marketing
      budget, developing, 435–438,
      439–440
    step 6: profit plan, develop, 438, 440,
      442–443
      break-even analysis, 441, 442
      income statement, 442, 443
      performance scorecard, 441, 442–443
    step 7: performance review, 443–444
  3-year plan *vs.* actual, 411–412
Strategic market plan implementation,
  454–461
  adapting the plan, 459–460
    adaptive rollout, 460
    feedback measurements, 459
    improvement, continuous, 459
    persistence, 460
  assessing, 460–461
  ownership and, 455–457
    action plans, detailed, 455–456
    champion and ownership team, 456
    compensation, 456–457
    management involvement, 457
  sales impact of, 455
  support and, 457–458
    communication, 457–458
    resource allocation, 457
    skills to succeed, 458
    time to succeed, 457
  variance analysis and, 461–465
Sub-segment strategy, 161–163

Sub-Zero refrigerators, 161
Sun Microsystems, 167
Sun Tzu, 187
Sunbeam, 118–119
Suppliers, 110–111
Supply chain, 129–130
Sustainable advantage, 199–200
SWOT analysis, 425–427

T
Tapscott, B. D., 108
Target, 199, 230
Target customers
  customer loyalty and, 24
  customer response index and, 313–314
  niche-segment strategies and, 161
  product attractiveness and, 93
Technology trap, 165
Ted Airlines, 226
Third market (M3), 387–388
3M, 106, 108, 322, 376
Timberland, 127
Tipping Point (Gladwell), 69
Top performing customers, 22–23
  advocates, 22
  loyalists, 22
Touch points, 107–108, 169
Toyota, 157, 158–159, 186, 268, 338, 351,
  366, 413–414
Trade-off analysis computations, 138
Trader Joe's, 220
Transaction cost, value creation
  and, 128–130
  space value and, 128–129
  transaction value and, 129
  value creation across the supply chain
    and, 129–130
Transaction value, 129
Trialability, 83

U

UCLA, 127
Umbrella brand, 232–233
Unbundling strategy, 236–237
Under Armour, 380
Underachievers, 23
United Airlines, 166, 226, 324
University of Michigan Business School, 472
US West Communications, 356

V

Value creation
  emotional benefits and, 126–128
  perceived benefits and, 120–126
  price performance and, 117–120
  product benefits and, 120–121
  transaction cost and, 128–130
Value drivers, identifying, 130–133
  customer preferences and, 131–132
  customer value and, 132–133
Value mapping, 119–120, 125
Value proposition, 154–155
Value-added resellers (VARs), 237, 291
Value-in-use pricing, 244–246, 247
Variance analysis, 461–465
Verizon, 375–376
Vertical brand, 234–235
Vertical brand extensions, 234–235
Victoria's Secret, 209
Virgin Airlines, 226
Volvo, 157, 189, 260

W

The Wall Street Journal, 6, 155, 315, 317
Wal-Mart, 5, 128, 177, 179, 181, 199, 213,
    220, 226, 258, 282, 366

Walton, Sam, 226
Wells Fargo, 163
Wendy's, 229
Westinghouse, 378
Weyerhaeuser Corporation, 103–104, 108,
    112, 114
Whirlpool, 232
*Wikinomics: How Mass Collaboration
    Changes Everything* (Tapscott and
    Williams), 108
Wikipedia, 108, 110
Williams, A. D., 108
Win-back customers, 24
Wooden, John, 127
WorldCom, 230

X

Xeon microprocessor, 210, 223
Xerox, 115, 195
Xiameter, 296
XLA, 107

Y

Yahoo!, 226
Yellow Pages, 264–266, 317
Yoplait yogurt, 235, 236

Z

Zero Spenders, 166
Zi-Tech Acoustics, 358–361